Meanings and Other Things

Meanings and Other Things

Themes from the Work of Stephen Schiffer

EDITED BY
Gary Ostertag

UNIVERSITY PRESS

OXFORD
UNIVERSITY PRESS

Great Clarendon Street, Oxford, OX2 6DP,
United Kingdom

Oxford University Press is a department of the University of Oxford.
It furthers the University's objective of excellence in research, scholarship,
and education by publishing worldwide. Oxford is a registered trade mark of
Oxford University Press in the UK and in certain other countries

© the several contributors 2016

The moral rights of the authors have been asserted

First Edition published in 2016

Impression: 1

All rights reserved. No part of this publication may be reproduced, stored in
a retrieval system, or transmitted, in any form or by any means, without the
prior permission in writing of Oxford University Press, or as expressly permitted
by law, by licence or under terms agreed with the appropriate reprographics
rights organization. Enquiries concerning reproduction outside the scope of the
above should be sent to the Rights Department, Oxford University Press, at the
address above

You must not circulate this work in any other form
and you must impose this same condition on any acquirer

Published in the United States of America by Oxford University Press
198 Madison Avenue, New York, NY 10016, United States of America

British Library Cataloguing in Publication Data
Data available

Library of Congress Control Number: 2016940202

ISBN 978-0-19-968493-9

Printed in Great Britain by
Clays Ltd, St Ives plc

Links to third party websites are provided by Oxford in good faith and
for information only. Oxford disclaims any responsibility for the materials
contained in any third party website referenced in this work.

Contents

Acknowledgements	vii
List of Contributors	ix
Introduction	1

Part I

1. Easy Ontology and its Consequences Amie L. Thomasson	34
2. From *Remnants* to *Things*, and Back Again Thomas Hofweber	54
3. Objects of Thought Ian Rumfitt	73
4. Schiffer's Unhappy-Face Solution to a Puzzle about Moral Judgement Michael Smith	95

Part II

5. Propositional Platitudes Gary Ostertag	111
6. Schiffer's Puzzle: A Kind of Fregean Response Ray Buchanan	128
7. Constraint with Restraint Nathan Salmon	149

Part III

8. Schiffer on Indeterminacy, Vagueness, and Conditionals Dorothy Edgington	156
9. Vagueness, Partial Belief, and Logic Hartry Field	172
10. On the Characterization of Borderline Cases Crispin Wright	190
11. The Nature of Paradox Paul Horwich	211

vi CONTENTS

Part IV

12. Silent Reference — 229
    Stephen Neale

13. Abiding Intentions — 343
    Anita Avramides

14. Schiffer on Russell's Theory and Referential Uses — 364
    Kent Bach

Part V. Replies to the Essays
Stephen Schiffer

Acknowledgements — 385

15. Pleonastic Entities: Responses to Amie Thomasson, Thomas Hofweber, Ian Rumfitt, and Michael Smith — 387

16. *De Re* Belief Reports: Response to Gary Ostertag — 426

17. The Relativity Feature: Response to Ray Buchanan — 441

18. *De Re* Subtleties: Response to Nathan Salmon — 449

19. Vagueness and Indeterminacy: Responses to Dorothy Edgington, Hartry Field, and Crispin Wright — 458

20. A Source of Paradox: Response to Paul Horwich — 482

21. Gricean Semantics and Reference: Responses to Anita Avramides, Stephen Neale, and Kent Bach — 493

Bibliography of Stephen Schiffer's Writings — 529
Index — 533

Acknowledgements

This volume rests on the work of its contributors. I am grateful for the thoughtful essays we are able to present to Stephen—a testament both to the skill and dedication of the contributors and to the depth and lasting influence of Stephen's work. I am grateful, also, for the support and encouragement given to me along the way. It does take a village, even if, in this case, the village is a close but geographically dispersed network of family, friends, and colleagues. Particular thanks go to Ray Buchanan—who helped out at every stage—Ronald Ostertag, Romina Padró, Consuelo Preti, Frank Pupa, Rosemary Twomey, Scott Walden, and Monique Whitaker. Thanks, also, to my friends and colleagues at Nassau Community College—Consuelo Arias, Evelyn Deluty, Amanda Favia, Mark Halfon, and Frank and Scott—for providing such a congenial and warm working environment, and to my colleagues at the Graduate Center, especially Michael Devitt, Saul Kripke, and Iakovos Vasiliou. I'm grateful to Peter Momtchiloff for his interest in the project and his continuing support.

Let me add a word of thanks to Susana Nuccetelli for advice and encouragement, to Jennifer Ware for her expert help in preparing the final version, to Oliver Marshall for crucial last-minute assistance, and to Hayley Buckley and Lydia Shinoj for their painstaking work in turning the manuscript into a book.

My gratitude to Eileen O'Neill should go without saying. But it's fun to say it anyway.

I first encountered Stephen in a seminar on Mental and Linguistic Representation he taught in the spring of 1985, when he was visiting The Graduate Center, CUNY, and I was a first-year student. All through that spring we worked through the manuscript of *Remnants of Meaning* as it emerged from his word processor. I'll never forget the excitement of that period—of being exposed, week after week, to yet another cutting-edge work, cast in its definitive form, only to see it unravel under Stephen's relentless, merciless scrutiny. He came to The Graduate Center as a permanent faculty member a few years later, whereupon I had the experience of having my own work subjected to the same exacting standards. (He has of course long since resettled at NYU.) I'm forever grateful to Stephen for the example he set, and for the writing, teaching, and mentorship that has been an inspiration, not just for me, but (at this point) generations of students.

Chapter 7 originally appeared as "The Resilience of Illogical Belief," *Noûs* 40(2) (2006): 369–75, and is reprinted here by permission of Blackwell Publishing.

List of Contributors

ANITA AVRAMIDES is Reader in Philosophy of Mind at Oxford University. She is the author of the volumes *Meaning and Mind* and *Other Minds*, and of a number of essays in the philosophy of mind and philosophy of language.

KENT BACH is Emeritus Professor of Philosophy at San Francisco State University. He is the author of the volumes *Thought and Reference* and (with Robert Harnish) *Linguistic Communication and Speech Acts*, and of numerous papers in the philosophy of language, philosophy of mind, pragmatics, and related areas.

RAY BUCHANAN is Associate Professor of Philosophy at University of Texas at Austin. He is the author of a number of articles in pragmatics and the philosophy of language.

DOROTHY EDGINGTON was formerly Waynflete Professor of Metaphysics at Oxford and is now Senior Research Fellow at Birkbeck College, University of London. She is the editor of *Conditionals* and has written numerous papers in philosophy of logic and language.

HARTRY FIELD is University Professor and Silver Professor of Philosophy at New York University. He is the author of the volumes *Science without Numbers*; *Mathematics, Meaning and Modality*; *Truth and the Absence of Fact*; and, most recently, *Saving Truth from Paradox*. He has published widely in philosophy of language, philosophy of mind, metaphysics, philosophy of mathematics, and philosophical logic.

THOMAS HOFWEBER is Professor of Philosophy at the University of North Carolina at Chapel Hill. He is the author of *Ontology and the Ambitions of Metaphysics* and numerous papers in metaphysics, philosophy of language, philosophical logic, and related areas.

PAUL HORWICH is Professor of Philosophy at New York University. He is the author of *Probability and Evidence*; *Asymmetries in Time*; *Truth*; *Meaning*; *From a Deflationary Point of View*; and *Truth—Meaning—Reality*. He has published widely in philosophy of science, philosophy of language, philosophy of mind, and related areas.

STEPHEN NEALE holds the John H. Kornblith Family Chair in the Philosophy of Science and Values at the Graduate Center, CUNY. He is the author of *Descriptions*, *Facing Facts*, and numerous papers—book-length and otherwise—in philosophy of language, semantics, pragmatics, philosophical logic, and philosophy of law.

GARY OSTERTAG is Associate Professor of Philosophy at Nassau Community College and Affiliated Associate Professor of Philosophy at the Graduate Center, CUNY. He is the editor of *Definite Descriptions: A Reader* and the author of articles in the philosophy of language, the history of analytic philosophy, and musical ontology.

IAN RUMFITT is Senior Research Fellow, All Souls' College, Oxford. He is the author of *The Boundary Stones of Thought* and articles in the philosophy of language, philosophy of mathematics, and philosophical logic.

NATHAN SALMON is Professor of Philosophy at the University of California, Santa Barbara. He is the author of *Reference and Essence, Frege's Puzzle*, and numerous papers in philosophy of language, metaphysics, and philosophical logic, many of which are collected in his *Metaphysics, Mathematics, and Meaning: Philosophical Papers I*, and *Content, Cognition, and Communication: Philosophical Papers II*.

MICHAEL SMITH is McCosh Professor of Philosophy at Princeton University. He is the author of *The Moral Problem*, the collections *Ethics and the A Priori: Selected Essays on Moral Psychology and Meta-Ethics* and (with Frank Jackson and Philip Pettit) *Mind, Morality, and Explanation: Selected Collaborations*, and of numerous articles in ethics, philosophy of mind, and philosophy of action.

AMIE L. THOMASSON is Professor of Philosophy at the University of Miami. She is the author of the volumes *Fiction and Metaphysics, Ordinary Objects*, and *Ontology Made Easy*. She has published widely in metaphysics, philosophy of art, philosophy of mind, and phenomenology.

CRISPIN WRIGHT is Distinguished Professor of Philosophy at New York University. He is the author of the volumes *Wittgenstein on the Foundations of Mathematics; Frege's Conception of Numbers as Objects; Truth and Objectivity; Realism, Meaning, and Truth; The Reason's Proper Study* (with Bob Hale); *Rails to Infinity*; and *Saving the Differences*. He is also the author of numerous papers in philosophy of language, metaphysics, epistemology, philosophy of mathematics, and philosophical logic.

Introduction

In his first book, *Meaning* (1972), Stephen Schiffer attempted a reduction of linguistic meaning to the propositional attitudes of speakers—of linguistic representation to mental representation (to use the then-fashionable terminology).[1] His second book, *Remnants of Meaning* (1987), launched a full-blown attack on the first book, and then some: not only was the proposed reduction challenged, *Remnants* also took aim at a key element of the original analysis—the notion of a proposition—and in addition cast doubt on the possibility of a physicalistically acceptable account of the attitudes. The goal of "naturalizing meaning" was thwarted.

In time, a rapprochement would occur, reconciling the two conflicting time-slices. In *Remnants*, Schiffer despaired of the possibility of a theory of mental and linguistic representation—the idea that there could be such a theory, Schiffer now argued, rested on false presuppositions. But *The Things We Mean* (2003) introduced a framework that allowed for theoretical (albeit deflationary) accounts of meaning and representation, even while granting the pessimistic lessons of the earlier book.

The current collection of critical essays focuses on Schiffer's contributions to the philosophy of language, metaphysics, and ethics. The emphasis here will be primarily, though not exclusively, on topics he addresses in *Things* and subsequent work, omitting coverage of other areas (including epistemology and the philosophy of mind) to which Schiffer has made signal contributions.

I will begin, in section I.1, by providing a thumbnail sketch of the development of Schiffer's views on meaning. Section I.2 fills in some details, describing the early, reductionist program and Schiffer's *Remnants*-era rejection of that program's goals and presuppositions. Section I.3 briefly shows how some of these themes are taken up in recent work. The final section provides synopses of the individual contributions, situating them in their dialectical environment and relating them to concerns in Schiffer's *oeuvre*.

I.1 Schiffer on Meaning: A Brief History

It is not an overstatement to say that *Meaning* is one of the most intellectually demanding books in the philosophy of language canon. At a mere 170 pages, with a slender list of references and a minimum of formalism, the book attempts to construct a theory of speaker meaning and then to use the notion of speaker meaning to articulate a theory of public-language meaning.[2] The former theory addresses the question: 'What are the facts in virtue of which Ada means what she does in uttering the sentence "Serena won the match"?' The latter theory addresses the question: 'What are the facts in virtue of which the sentence "Serena won the match" means, among English speakers, that Serena won the match, and not either something else or nothing at all?'

Some of our actions are communicative actions. For example, in nodding in my direction the bank teller communicates to me that I can approach the window. This is a case of *speaker meaning*: in producing her "utterance" (i.e., nodding in a certain way) the teller intends, among other things, for me to form a particular belief—namely, that I'm to come to the window—and to act accordingly. The general outlines of a now highly influential account of this concept of speaker meaning were first put forward in H. P. Grice's 1957 paper, "Meaning." Grice's paper defined speaker meaning in terms of complex audience-directed intentions on the part of the speaker. (For details, see section I.2.1, below.)

Grice's classic paper seemed an exercise in Moorean analysis: its concern was simply to come to an understanding of the concept of speaker meaning and thereby to explain why we classify certain utterances or inscriptions as meaningful. (Grice also provided a rough indication of how one might extend the analysis of speaker meaning to accommodate public-language meaning—the meaning that a linguistic expression, simple or complex, has among a community of speakers.) One might read Schiffer's *Meaning* as driven by the same concerns. Indeed, on the first page of that book, he takes it as his objective to gain "an understanding of the *concept* of meaning" (emphasis added)—the sense, he adds, "especially relevant to an understanding of language and communication."

But the air of conceptual analysis that seems to permeate *Meaning* had dispersed by the time of Schiffer's next excursion into the theory of meaning, his 1982 essay "Intention-Based Semantics." This essay focuses more explicitly on the *metaphysics* of meaning. Whereas *Meaning* could be viewed as furthering the analytic program—i.e., providing analyses of 'meaning' and its cognates—subsequent work, starting with the aforementioned paper, is more clearly focused on meaning *properties*. The shift can be seen as reflecting a prioritizing of the metaphysics of meaning over the analysis of 'meaning'. This metaphysical orientation towards problems of meaning and content was not entirely new: what Hartry Field labeled "Brentano's Problem" in his 1978 paper, "Mental Representation," concerned the question of how a physical state or process can have representational properties. There is no talk in Field's paper of analysis. Indeed, the crucial term here—'representation'—is itself a term of art.[3]

The metaphysical orientation—with respect to the semantic properties of expression-types—is clearly spelled out on the first page of "Intention-Based Semantics":

The subject matter of the philosophy of language, if it has one, is the nature of the semantical properties of linguistic items. But no complete account of those properties will leave unanswered these two questions:

(1) How is the semantic related to the psychological?
(2) How are the semantic and the psychological related to the physical?

I believe, for familiar reasons, later briefly to be touched on, that (2) is the urgent question, in this sense: that we should not be prepared to maintain that there *are* semantic or psychological facts unless we are prepared to maintain that such facts are completely determined by, are nothing over and above, physical facts. (1982: 199; emphasis in text)

If our concern is with explaining meaning facts, then we can be satisfied with the reduction of such facts to the psychological facts *only if* the psychological itself is reducible. "Certainly I felt the project of defining the semantic in terms of the psychological was fairly pointless," Schiffer wrote retrospectively in 1987, "if one was going to then view propositional attitudes as primitive and inexplicable" (xiv). On his view, the very attempt cannot avoid the question of a further reduction of the attitudes.[4] Still, while subsequent writings claim that even in the earlier book the motivation behind the reduction of expression meaning—the meaning of expressions in a public language such as English—to propositional attitudes was merely as a first step in a larger project, one might easily come away with the impression that Schiffer was initially attempting to provide an *analysis* of the concept of speaker meaning in order to provide a further analysis of the idea of public-language meaning.

This would be a mistake. The idea of arriving at metaphysical truths independently of philosophical analysis only came to be recognized as an available option with Kripke's *Naming and Necessity*, itself published the very year *Meaning* appeared (1972). Indeed, prior to Kripke no sharp demarcation between conceptual analysis and metaphysics existed. It is thus somewhat anachronistic to read *Meaning* as a mere exercise in analysis. The shift between *Meaning* and subsequent work is best seen as not one of subject matter—*concepts of meaning* as opposed to *meaning facts*—but one of methodology. Whereas *Meaning* attempts to understand the nature of meaning in terms of the tools of conceptual analysis, the 1982 paper and what follows it are no longer constrained by this methodology.[5]

The project drew increased interest in the 1980s, when questions about the reduction of the attitudes to a physicalistically acceptable idiom took center stage.[6] Although they were interested primarily in the reduction of the attitudes to states of the brain or central nervous system, many philosophers welcomed the possibility of a reduction of speaker meaning to propositional attitudes (and a further analysis of expression meaning in terms of speaker meaning), since this would place meaning within "the natural order."[7] As Fodor wrote in his review of *Remnants*:

> If the Gricean program and the Naturalization program can be carried through, then IBS [Intention-Based Semantics] will have solved one of the Great Metaphysical Problems: it will have found a place for meaning in the natural order. It would certainly be nice to solve a Great Metaphysical Problem; philosophy could do with a success or two. (1989: 177)

While Fodor and others were on board for the positive program, *Remnants* delivered a profoundly negative message: IBS could not be sustained; the Great Metaphysical Problem would remain unsolved and was, possibly, unsolvable.[8] The reasons are numerous, but here's a partial list: the "naturalization" program Fodor championed was doomed, as the property of being a belief that, say, snow is white could not be made sense of according to the most promising theories of the attitudes consistent with physicalism; the crucial notion of a proposition could not play its supporting role as the object of the attitudes; and the reduction of public-language meaning to speaker's meaning would meet insuperable challenges.[9]

Although *Things* is an attempt to salvage some of what was lost in *Remnants*, the concerns of the later book are not precisely those of the earlier. *Remnants* argues that there are no non-pleonastic meaning properties—no meaning properties other than the superficial ones, such as *the property of meaning that snow is white*, that fall out of our property-constructing discourse. It sounded a pessimistic note about the prospects of the theory of meaning. Rather than challenge this wisdom, *Things* embraced it, and provided accounts of belief reports, meaning ascription, psychological explanation, vagueness, and moral realism within the general constraints imposed by *Remnants*.[10]

Let me discuss, in order, the program of "naturalizing meaning" and of Schiffer's *Remnants*-era response to it, before returning to *Things*.

I.2 Meaning-Reduction: A Sketch of the Logical Geography

I.2.1 Speaker meaning

As we have seen, one goal of *Meaning* was to provide an account of expression meaning by appealing to an analysis of speaker meaning along lines initially suggested by Grice. As is well known, Grice sought to analyze speaker meaning in terms of complex mental states—namely, certain of the audience-directed intentions of speakers. He took 'S means something by x' as being "(roughly) equivalent" to: S intends "the utterance of x to produce some effect in an audience by means of the recognition of this intention" (1957: 385). This led to an analysis of 'S means p' which, fully dressed, can be stated as follows:

S means that p in uttering u $=_{def}$ For some audience A and property Φ, S intends:
  (a) A to recognize that u has Φ;
  (b) A to think, at least partly on the basis of thinking that u has Φ, that (*) S uttered u intending A to think that p;
  (c) A to think—at least partly on the basis of thinking that (*)—that p. (Schiffer 1987: 243)

On the proposed analysis, for S to mean, in gesturing towards the clock, that she wants to leave soon is for her to intend to produce a certain set of interrelated responses in her audience, A—for A to recognize that gesturing towards the clock has the property of being a "particularly efficacious way" (in Schiffer's phrase) of conveying that the "speaker" wants to leave soon; for A to infer from this fact that S gestured as she did with the intention that the audience, A, think that S wants to leave soon; and, finally, for A to think that S wants to leave soon partly on the basis of the latter inference.

(The above, I hasten to add, is a mere "toy analysis." While it suffices to show the power and richness of the approach developed in *Meaning*, it neglects details that are necessary for a full evaluation.)[11]

Schiffer's *Meaning* invokes meaning intentions, thus defined, in developing an account of expression meaning.[12] This analysis would play a role in the reductionist project: Stage 1 involves explicating public-language semantic properties in terms of propositional attitudes; Stage 2 involves making sense of the propositional attitudes in a manner acceptable to the physicalist. Before turning to Stage 2, I will say a little bit more about what Jonathan Bennett (1976) subsequently called the "meaning-nominalist strategy"—the strategy of reducing public-language semantic properties to the propositional attitudes of speakers.

I.2.2 Public-language meaning

The account of public-language meaning proceeds as follows. First, we develop a notion of non-composite utterance-type meaning. This concerns the meaning, in a community of speakers, of simple signals—signals without constituent structure—that express propositions. Crucial ingredients of the account to be discussed are the conception of a language as a set of sentence-meaning pairs—what Schiffer (forthcoming a) calls a "Lewis-language"—and the idea of mutual knowledge. I then proceed to a general account of utterance-type meaning. The crucial element here, which I go on to describe, is the actual-language relation—the relation a community of speakers bears to a language L just when L is the language of that community.

I.2.2.1 THE INVISIBLE HAND AT WORK: SIMPLE PROPOSITIONAL SIGNAL TYPES

That French is a language spoken by almost the entire population of France is a contingent truth. There are, after all, possible worlds where the population of France speaks some other language.[13] And while it is a necessary truth that a given sentence means what it does *in* French—that, say, 'L'enfer est d'autres personnes' means that hell is other people—it is merely a contingent truth that it means this *among the French-speaking population of France*. They might have spoken a distinct but related language, or, perhaps, an entirely unrelated language—one in which this sequence of characters (or the corresponding sequence of phonemes) means something quite different, if anything at all.

The French language is thus naturally understood as an abstract entity, spoken in some worlds, not in others, but with intrinsic properties that hold of it in every world, whether spoken there or not. For current purposes, it will be convenient to adopt the convention, due to David Lewis, of identifying French with a particular set of sentence-proposition pairs $<\sigma, p>$ (equivalently, a function mapping each French sentence σ to its meaning, p) (Lewis 1975). There will of course be a French lexicon and a French syntax, with a set S containing precisely the acceptable sequences generated by the syntax. But how S gets generated is not something that needs to be addressed at the moment. For now, it suffices to think of French—and languages more generally—as an infinite set of sentence-proposition pairs.

The idea of a language as an abstract pairing of sentences and propositions, although artificial, captures all that we need of that notion for Schiffer to formulate an answer to the questions that this section seeks to address: 'In virtue of what does a sentence like "L'enfer est d'autres personnes" mean what it does among the French?' Or, more generally: 'In virtue of what does a given sentence σ mean that p among a community of speakers, G?' This, however, requires that we address a more basic question, one that focuses on simple propositional signals—that is, utterance-types that express propositions but which have no grammatical structure (the "non-composite whole-utterance types" mentioned above). (Examples of these might be raising one's hand to indicate that one has a question or turning on a blinker to signal a turn. These both are signals—types of utterance, in an extended sense of that term—but cannot themselves be analyzed into more basic components.) Our question thus is:

Q-1. In virtue of what does a simple propositional signal mean that p among a population, G?

Before proceeding, however, a word needs to be said about mutual knowledge, another key ingredient in Schiffer's analysis.

If S utters x intending to produce a certain response in A in virtue of some perceptible feature Φ of x, then the success of S's project turns on whether or not Φ, and thus S's intention, is "out in the open" (1982: 121). The idea of *mutual knowledge* was originally conceived as a way of making this "openness" more precise. On Schiffer's original formulation, S and A mutually know that p just in case: (*a*) both S and A know that p; (*b*) both S and A know that (*a*); (*c*) both S and A know that (*b*); and so on (1972: 30–1).[14] But in subsequent work, Schiffer expressed doubts about the psychological reality of mutual knowledge thus described (1982: 121). He consequently understood the notion "as a dummy for whatever condition secures that, in the needed sense, S intends his meaning-constitutive intentions to be out in the open" (1987: 249). Thus, by the time of *Remnants*, mutual knowledge was no longer prior to the idea of openness, but to be understood in terms of it. Thus, we now take the idea of openness as basic.

Schiffer's answer to the above question, (Q-1), flows naturally from his account of speaker meaning. Indeed, in recent work he speaks of an "*invisible hand* that guides [the theorist] from the intentions that define speaker-meaning to an account of expression-meaning in terms of those intentions" (forthcoming *a*: 13; emphasis in text). Consider an utterance of 'grrr,' produced to express the speaker's anger, in a context where there is no shared language between speaker and hearer. Schiffer maintains that communication is possible in such a case. All we need to assume is that the speaker intends for the hearer to recognize that 'grrr' is the sound animals make when angry and, on the basis of this, infer that the speaker is angry.

There is of course no guarantee, with respect to an unprecedented human growling, that the speaker's intentions will be divined. But once a precedent has been established—once successful communication has been achieved—we have crossed a line: an utterance of 'grrr' now becomes a good indication of the speaker's intention. This is because 'grrr' is at this point preferable to any alternative means (for which there is no precedent) of communicating one's anger. (There is, recall, no shared language between speaker and hearer.) At this point, we should "expect, *ceteris paribus*, a member of G to be able to mean that he is angry by uttering 'grrr' in virtually any circumstance in which it is not already precluded that he should mean that he is angry..." (1987: 250). If 'grrr' has the property alluded to, then the fact that u is an utterance of 'grrr' "constitutes very good evidence that the utterer means by u that he is angry." And *this* fact will likely make 'grrr' the utterance-type of choice for a G member who wants to communicate that he is angry. But then, the thought continues, 'grrr' will "be mutually known to have a new feature—of being what members of G utter whenever they mean that they are angry—that makes it *an even more reliable device in G for meaning that one is angry*" (250; emphasis added). This, as Schiffer tells us, gives us a "neat, self-perpetuating regularity"—a convention. More specifically, it gives us *a conventional device for meaning that one is angry among G*.[15]

We are now in a position to answer (Q-1):

A-1. A simple propositional signal σ means p among G if, and only if, (*i*) it is mutual knowledge in G that there is a practice in G of meaning p by uttering σ and (*ii*) this practice provides the feature of σ that G members exploit in using σ to mean *p*. (Adapted from 1993: 241)

But this takes us only so far. (A-1) tells us when an utterance-type means something among a community of speakers. But it fails to illuminate how a community of speakers can communicate using a shared language like that of French—a language that has an infinite number of sentences. (A-1), after all, only applies to simple propositional signals—utterance types whose meanings are not compositionally determined—and so is limited to finite languages.

We thus need an answer to the more general question, (Q-2):

Q-2. In virtue of what does a sentence σ mean that *p* among a group of speakers, G?

Answering (Q-2) requires that we give an account of the actual-language relation.[16] The actual-language relation is a relation that holds between a community of speakers G and a language L just when L is used by G—i.e., just when L is the *language of G*. Accordingly, the form that an answer to (Q-2) should take is:

A-2. σ means *p* among G just when, for some language L, (*i*) L is used by G and (*ii*) σ means *p* in L.[17]

All that remains is to say precisely when L is used by G—when L is the actual language of G. The use of 'means' in (*ii*) is, it should be noted, in no need of analysis. We have stipulated that L is a set of ordered pairs. To say that σ means *p* in L is just to say that <σ, *p*> is "in" L. There is no further question that needs to be addressed.

I.2.2.2 THE ACTUAL-LANGUAGE RELATION

Before we get to the answer, let us adopt the following stipulation. Let's say that there is *a practice in G of meaning in L* just in case, for all *p*, a situation in which a member of G means *p* is (typically) one in which she utters an L sentence that means *p*. (I use the qualifier 'typically' to allow for the fact that a member of G may occasionally mean *p* through other means—for example, by speaking non-literally or through a particularly efficacious gesture.)

With this accomplished, we are now ready to state the IBS account of the actual language relation:

A-3. L is used by G just in case (1) it is mutual knowledge in G that there is a practice in G of meaning in L; and (2) when a member of G, S, utters an L-sentence σ and thereby means what it means in L, S intends it to be mutual knowledge between her and her audience both that (1) *and* that she intends this mutual knowledge to be the basis, in part, of their mutual knowledge that S in uttering σ meant that *p*. (Adapted from Schiffer 1987: 252–3 and 1993: 241)

Thus, the claim that the French language is used by the Québécois is made true by the following sort of fact: first, that the Québécois know (and know each other to know, etc.) that there is a practice among them of meaning in French and, second, that when a Yvette, a Québécois, utters the French sentence 'L'enfer est d'autres personnes' and thereby means that hell is other people, she does so fully intending both that the existence of the aforementioned practice be mutual knowledge between her and her audience, Jean, and that based in part on this mutual knowledge Jean comes to know that in uttering what she did Yvette meant that hell is other people.

On this picture, when S wants to communicate q to fellow G-speaker A, she finds an L-sentence σ that means q and utters it, confident that it is mutually known between her and A that σ means q in L *and* that there is a practice in G of meaning in L. "It is by virtue of this mutual knowledge," Schiffer writes, "that she can mean q, and be recognized as meaning q, in uttering σ" (1993: 241).

1.2.2.3 THE ACTUAL-LANGUAGE RELATION POST-IBS

This is but the barest outline of how IBS tackles the problem of public-language meaning; things don't end here. In fact, Schiffer (1993) holds that (A-3) is implausibly intellectualist—requiring speakers to have beliefs about their language that they don't generally appear to have—and, what is more, that it fails to provide a necessary condition for L's being the language of G. He argues that any creature remotely like us would (so to speak) assign a given sentence σ its L-correlated proposition p—the proposition it means in L—via an internally represented grammar. But then it is not too much of stretch to suppose that this very grammar would also play a crucial role in the transition from the hearer's perception of the utterance of σ to her belief that the speaker meant p—the L-correlated proposition—in uttering σ. If so, Schiffer claims, then a plausible alternative to (A-3) is available.

Addressing these concerns, the following definition of the actual-language relation invokes what Schiffer calls an "L-determining translator"—a "language-processing mechanism" that maps each L sentence σ to a synonymous sentence in the speaker's system of representation—her language of thought. This signals a departure from IBS, as it no longer requires that speakers interpret utterances via "IBS-required propositional attitudes" (1993: 242).

The definition reads as follows:

> A-4. L is used by G just in case (1) there is a practice in G of meaning in L; and (2) the processing of L utterances proceeds via an L-determining translator. (1993: 246)

As Schiffer notes, the system in which an utterance of σ is processed—the language of thought—is a language and is thus itself (according to our stipulation) a mapping of sentence-sized sequences to propositions. But then the actual-language relation arises with respect to *it*. We can ask: "What relation must hold between a language L and a person x in order to make it the case that L is x's actual language of thought—that is, in order to make it the case that x thinks in L?" (1993: 247).

The question is pressing. To keep things simple, consider the claim that Ada thinks in (what I'll call) Neural English (*NE*). A natural suggestion is that Ada thinks in *NE* just in case it is necessary and sufficient for her to believe p that, for some sentence σ, σ means p in *NE*—formally, *NE* (σ) = p—and σ is tokened in Ada's "belief box."[18] Since Ada can only token a finite number of *NE* sentences in her belief box, we can ask what makes it the case that Ada thinks in *NE* and not a warped Sartrean variant—one that assigns to each sentence containing more than sixty words the proposition that hell is other people. If we are to go by the natural suggestion just floated, we can equally say that Ada thinks in the Sartrean variant of *NE*. What, then, singles out unmodified *NE* as Ada's actual language of thought? This is an instance of a problem—the *meaning-without-use problem*—Schiffer posed to David Lewis in response to his account of the actual-language relation for public languages in *Convention*.[19]

The challenge is to "nail down the unused part" of Ada's language. To this end, Schiffer appeals to the idea of a compositional supervenience theory.[20] A *compositional supervenience theory* (CST) for *NE* is a theory that (via a set of "base clauses") assigns to each word and basic structure in *NE* a physical property and in virtue of these assignments assigns each *NE* sentence σ a physical property Φ meeting the following conditions:

- The claim that σ has Φ is "logically equivalent" to the claim that Φ's components and structure have the properties assigned them in the base clauses;
- A metaphysically sufficient condition for x to believe the proposition $NE(\sigma)$ is for σ to possess Φ and for σ to be tokened in x's belief box.[21]

The basic idea is as follows. Since we think in *NE*, the words and basic syntactic structures of the *NE* sentences will be exemplified by the token representations in our individual belief boxes. But the constituent-level and structural features that fix the meaning-determining properties of these tokened sentences can be extrapolated to untokened sentences. For the *un*tokened sentences to have the meaning-determining properties they have is just for them to have the (CST-assigned) constituent-level and structural properties *they* have—properties, it should be emphasized, that are already exemplified in the tokened sentences.

In short, a CST "nails down" the unused portion of *NE* by assigning each unused sentence a meaning-determining property, a property it has in virtue of the properties its constituents and its structure already exemplify in actually tokened beliefs.

With the concept of a CST firmly in hand, the final definition is straightforward:

A-5. x thinks in L just in case "there is a true compositional supervenience theory for L with respect to x." (1994: 297; see also *Things*, 167)

(A-4) and (A-5) represent Schiffer's thinking post-IBS. We now return to IBS and the propositional attitude facts that are implicated in the IBS reduction. (Readers wishing a more detailed account of CSTs and how they differ from compositional meaning theories should consult Schiffer (1994: 289–97) and *Things*, 160–8.)

I.2.3 Physicalism and the propositional attitudes

IBS is a reductionist project: it aims to reduce meaning properties to propositional attitude properties (Stage 1), and then in turn to reduce propositional attitude properties to properties expressible in physicalist or topic-neutral terms (Stage 2). We have seen a sketch of the meaning-reduction portion of the project; let's now look briefly at the second half of the reduction.

Consider, then, a sample propositional attitude property—for example, being a belief that snow is white. This property, call it B', is a property of "states of the central nervous system, tokens of neural state types."

Suppose, then, that s is my present belief that snow is white. Then the question arises: What makes s a belief that snow is white? Which is to ask: In what does its having the property B' consist? (1982: 131)

It is already here assumed that dualism is false and that my belief that snow is white just *is* a physical state s of my central nervous system. As Schiffer writes, the fact that s is a belief and, in particular, a belief that snow is white, "cannot be a brute, primitive, irreducible fact but must *somehow* be one that is explicable in terms of more basic facts, facts that are statable in a nonmentalistic and nonintentional idiom but determine all the psychological facts there are" (1987: 7; emphasis in text).[22] It is also assumed that there is no first-order property of state-types Φ, such that s's being Φ explains why s is a belief that snow is white—in the way that some pre-Kripkeans might have thought that a state's being a token of a specific first-order state-type Ω, discovered or not yet discovered by neuroscience, explains why that state is a pain. In what, then, does s's having the property B' consist? One answer—an answer that seems consistent with the idea that beliefs are relations to propositions—involves the concept of a *functional role*, that is, a property that a first-order state-*type* will possess if its tokens share certain causal or counterfactual relations to perceptual "input", to behavioral or verbal "output", and to other states of one's nervous system. Again, its tokens need not be—and in general will not be—tokens of a single first-order state-type. Functionalism thus allows for the possibility of *multiple realization*.

The core idea of a functionalist theory of belief properties is the following:

(FR) For each proposition p there is some functional role F such that being a belief that p = being a token of a state-type that has F. (1987: 23)

The idea here is straightforward: every belief property—every property that can be expressed as an instance of 'being a belief that p'—is equivalent to the property of being a token of a given state-type. For example, the property of being a belief that someone is at the door is just the property of being a token of a state-type that is caused (among other things) by the doorbell's ringing and that itself causes other beliefs and desires to be tokened—perhaps, the belief that the UPS person has arrived, the desire to run downstairs and sign for the delivery, etc.—and for certain bodily motions to ensue.

Now, a functional theory is an empirical theory about the internal organization of an input–output system. If we reverse-engineer a device such as a pocket calculator we will, in time and with sufficient ingenuity, come up with a functional theory of that device: describing not only the algorithms it implements, but the state transitions involved in their execution. The doctrine Schiffer is considering here is not a functional theory *per se*—he is not endorsing a particular theory of a given human's functional organization—but "a philosophical theory about the nature of the attitudes" (1987: 26). The claim of this philosophical theory is that there exists some further theory that correctly defines attitudes such as belief and desire. The further theory would identify the functional role that a state-type must possess for it to count as being the belief that p, for each proposition p (*mutatis mutandis* for desire and the other attitudes).

In the brief heyday of IBS, Schiffer endorsed the functionalist reduction of belief properties. However, by the time of *Remnants*, he came to reject it. Unfortunately, in a brief introduction it is impossible to do justice to the depth and complexity of the challenges he pressed against the functionalist approach. My purpose here is to give a sense of how the functionalist approach fits into the overall reductionist program, not to provide a detailed account of the position and Schiffer's criticisms of it. Readers who want the details are advised to turn to Chapter 2 of *Remnants* (also *Things*, pp. 341–7).[23]

The functionalist approach fits nicely within the IBS program: we are able to make sense of propositional attitudes—essential to the IBS analysis of speaker meaning and thus expression meaning—in a manner consistent with physicalism. But the failure of functionalism as an account of belief properties doesn't necessarily spell the end of the IBS theorist's reductionist ambitions. An alternative tack takes belief to involve a relation, not to meanings or propositions, but to things that *have* meanings—public language sentences or sentences in a language of thought. Since the former approach—*sententialism*—takes belief to involve a relation to a public-language sentence, it ultimately leads us in a circle. Stage 1 of the reduction involves explicating public-language meaning facts in terms of facts about the propositional attitudes of speakers. It would hardly be satisfying if Stage 2 helped itself to precisely the facts that Stage 1 sought to reduce. On the latter approach, to believe *p* is to have a neural sentence that "means" *p* in one's belief box (with meaning *p* explicated independently of any public-language semantic properties).[24] I won't discuss Schiffer's argument against this approach here, both for reasons of space and also because his main focus, since *Remnants*, has been on theories that take belief to be a relation to things that are meanings—propositions—as opposed to things that *have* meanings—whether public language sentences or formulae in a language of thought.

I.3 Meaning Reconceived: Schiffer's Later Work

I.3.1 *Meanings and meaning ascriptions*

In 1982's "Intention-Based Semantics," Schiffer proposed an ambitious reduction of meaning to the attitudes and, in turn, of a functionalist reduction of the attitudes. Five years later, in *Remnants*, Schiffer gave this program definitive expression—albeit as he was in the process of dismantling it. The landscape at book's end is dreary—all we are left with is a "no-theory theory of meaning" and a "no-theory theory of mental representation" (1987: 265–71). Schiffer, that is to say, acknowledged defeat: we cannot say what it is about Tanya's belief that Gustav is a dog that makes it a belief with precisely that content. Similarly for public-language semantic facts or properties: although we cannot deny that (1) is true, we also cannot say what fact makes it the case:

1. 'Snow is white' means that snow is white.

For one thing, Schiffer rejected the approach to public-language meaning discussed in sections I.2.2.1 and I.2.2.2.[25] And this was by far the most promising account of what makes meaning ascriptions such as (1) true. For another, he denied (in Chapter 3 of *Remnants*) that there is anything that could function as the referent of the that-clause in (1). Thus, the surface structure of such ascriptions is itself misleading: appearances to the contrary, (1) cannot assert a relation between a sentence type and an entity to which its that-clause refers. But then it is utterly unclear what sort of truth condition it could have. We are left with the unsatisfying conclusion that "there are true but irreducible meaning ascribing sentences; there are no 'non-pleonastic' semantic facts or properties" (1987: 269).

In *Things*, Schiffer softened on this idea—to an extent. Chapter 1 of that book endorses what he calls "the face-value theory of belief reports". On the face-value theory, the logical form of 'Lois believes that Superman flies' recapitulates its surface form: *believes* is represented as a relation, $Bel(x, y)$, between a believer and a proposition. This would seem to bait the 1987 time-slice of Schiffer: 'There can be no such entities as propositions,' we can hear the ghost of Schiffer past asking, 'so how the hell can they figure in the truth-clauses of a theory of belief reports?' But Chapter 2 of *Things* provides a novel theory of both the existence and individuation of propositions, one that attempts to put such skeptical worries to rest. In particular, twenty-first-century Schiffer comes to the realization that, although the sentence quoted above is true—"there are no 'non-pleonastic' semantic facts or properties"—this is not the end of the theory of meaning, but a new starting point.

On Schiffer's new view, propositions are shallow entities, ones whose very existence depends on our belief-reporting practices. They are derived from pleonastic restatements of ontologically neutral discourse. These restatements are sanctioned by "something-from-nothing principles" intrinsic to our belief reporting practices. Consider (SN):

SN. Lassie is a dog just in case that Lassie is a dog is true.

Here we move from (comparatively) non-committal 'Lassie is a dog' to ontologically loaded 'that Lassie is a dog is true.' The former is neutral on the question of the existence of propositions; the latter is not.

The pleonastic theory of propositions provides the face-value theory with the ontology it requires. Meaning ascriptions such as (1), however, resist a face-value analysis of the sort enjoyed by belief reports. While the things we *believe* are propositions, the things we *mean* in uttering sentences cannot be propositions, contrary to what the IBS theorist would have us believe. It follows that the standing meaning of a sentence σ—what a competent speaker knows when she knows what σ means—cannot be identified with a proposition template, a sort of "meaning blueprint" that contextual parameters enter into and complete.

An example makes this clear. Consider the command:

2. Finish your coffee!

If we identify the meaning of this sentence type with the template, ⌜the proposition that *i* finishes her coffee⌝ (where *i* is assigned the addressee relative to the context of utterance), then we fail to distinguish its meaning from that of either (3) or (4):

3. Are you finishing your coffee?
4. You're finishing your coffee.

At the same time, we also fail to distinguish what Ada means in a literal utterance of (2) from what she would have meant had she uttered either (3) or had she uttered (4).

So the theory fails to tell us what we know when we know what (2) means and, because of this, fails to tell us what we know when we know what *Ada* means in uttering (2).

The standard view identifies a sentence meaning with a proposition template of the above sort, something that we can construe, following David Kaplan, as a *character*—a function from a context to a complete proposition. But the above discussion shows that this view cannot be right, as it would identify what Ada means in uttering (2) with the propositional content of her utterance. To know what Ada means, we equally need to know the kind of speech act she intends to perform in uttering the sentence; knowledge of its propositional content is not enough. In response to this, Schiffer generalizes Kaplan's notion of a character to represent the enriched conception of meaning. The meaning of (2) is best captured not by the aforementioned template but by its *character**, something he represents as a structured entity: <*commanding*, the proposition that *i* finishes her coffee at *t*> (where *t* is an implicitly referred-to time). Similarly for (3) (here we get <*asking-whether*, the proposition that *i* finishes her coffee at *t*>) and (4) (<*asserting*, the proposition that *i* finishes her coffee at *t*>).

This enrichment of the standard view requires a revision in our conception of knowledge of meaning. On Schiffer's view, to understand what linguistic meaning is—say, the meaning of a sentence σ—we look to what a speaker knows when she knows the meaning of σ. In a slogan: meaning is what knowledge of meaning is knowledge *of*. Schiffer's suggestion is that this "thing meant" is a character*. What Ada knows when she knows what Gloria means in uttering (2) is something that tells her not only the *content* of Gloria's utterance—that Ada finishes her coffee—but also the fact that Gloria is issuing a command. This information is precisely what (2)'s character*—(2)'s meaning—encapsulates.

However attractive, the view has an awkward consequence. On the one hand, a character* captures what we know when we know the meaning of a sentence. At the same time, the claim that (2) *means* <*commanding*, the proposition that *i* finishes her coffee at time *t*> is not something that our "common sense conception of meaning...would enable us to *discover*" (113). A character*, that is, is not readily recognizable to a speaker *as* a meaning and so not well suited to be the thing knowledge of which her knowledge of meaning consists in. It seems, indeed, preposterous to claim that Ada's knowledge of what Gloria means in uttering (2) is underwritten by Ada's knowledge that (2) bears a *meaning* (or *character**) relation to <*commanding*, the proposition that *i* finishes her coffee>.

In response, Schiffer claims that, while (2) has a character* and is meaningful in virtue of this fact, for Ada to *know* what this sentence means is not for her to know that it bears a meaning (or character*) to a character*. Rather, it is for this character* to be invoked at the appropriate point in Ada's unconscious processing of (2) (*Things*, 115–18). The state that plays the "knowledge of meaning role" is understood functionally—as whatever state it is that "links" the perception of a sentence to its character*. For the role to be the knowledge of meaning role, the linkage must be such that Ada, in perceiving *S*'s utterance, knows that *S* is performing a speech act of kind *A* with content of kind *p* (116).[26] Thus, the challenge that Ada would not recognize (2) as meaning a given character*—a speech-act-type–proposition pair—is diffused: knowing what (2) means is not (or need not be) knowing a proposition relating Ada to either (2)'s meaning, or a way of grasping (2)'s meaning.

The next section provides individual synopses of the contributions, relating them to the main thread of the argument in *Things* or to topics taken up elsewhere in Schiffer's work, both early and late. The idea of a pleonastic proposition—of an entity that exists in virtue of our linguistic practices—figures centrally in many of these essays. While pleonastic propositions are not "the things we mean" of the title—if anything answers to that phrase, it is the entities that are invoked in sentence processing—they are fundamental to a proper understanding of both sentence meaning and utterance meaning. Moreover, getting clear on their nature—to the extent they have any—enables us to address a number of central issues in the philosophy of language: among other things, the semantics of belief reports, the phenomena of vagueness, the semantics and pragmatics of conditionals, and the nature of evaluative discourse. In addition, it provides an occasion to investigate the scope of so-called "easy ontology." These topics, among others, will be discussed in the following section.

I.4 Synopses of the Contributions

I.4.1 Amie Thomasson, "Easy Ontology and its Consequences"

For Thomasson, *serious ontology* is the view that existence questions are substantive and not to be resolved by invoking definitions or stipulations. Thus, whether or not (say) chairs exist is a substantive matter that cannot be settled by conceptual analysis. *Easy ontology*, on the other hand, takes the existence of chairs to be a conceptual question, in the following sense: If the world meets certain conditions—if particles are, conveniently, arranged "chair-wise"—then chairs exist; if not, they do not. (True, there is a factual component here. But all parties to the debate agree that particles are, on occasion, arranged chair-wise. This does not settle the question as to the existence of chairs to everyone's satisfaction.)

It is often thought that the easy approach to such questions entails a deflationary take on their answers. If ontological questions are easy to answer, the answers themselves must be correspondingly cheap. Or so the thought goes. Schiffer himself shares this view, as can be seen from a passage in *Things* discussing the ontology of *Remnants*:

> The doctrine of pleonastic propositions and properties is merely, so to speak, a hypostatization of what I used to say when I denied that there were such things as properties and propositions—except 'pleonastically speaking' as I said even then. (91)

The transition from the nominalism of *Remnants* to the realism of *Things* marks a shift in ontology, but not, one might say, in seriousness. Indeed, Schiffer's epiphany seems to have been that one can do ontology without taking it seriously (in the technical sense in question).

Thomasson is a well-known proponent of easy ontology. While she accepts Schiffer's pleonastic theory, she also argues that his policy of comparatively easy entry into the realm of what there is should not be limited to the items considered in

Things—fictional entities, properties, and propositions—but should be extended to include, among other things, everyday objects.

The suggestion is a natural one to make. Both Schiffer and Thomasson derive existence claims from an uncontroversial claim coupled with a conceptual truth. For Schiffer, such a derivation might run as follows:

Conceptual Truth	If S, then that S is true.
Uncontroversial Claim	Snow is white.
Derived Claim	That snow is white is true.

Although, as we have seen, Thomasson focuses on *concreta*—tables, chairs, and the like—her procedure is similar:

Conceptual Truth	If there are particles arranged tablewise, then there is a table.
Uncontroversial Claim	There are particles arranged tablewise.
Derived Claim	There is a table.

Thomasson's paper is a sustained argument in favor of a more inclusive "easiness." She also takes issue with Schiffer's claim that the derived claims displayed above "are in some sense 'cheap' or 'lightweight,' or that the existence claims should be taken as somehow deflated" (p. 35). On her view, these derivations should be seen as committing us to a genuine realism about the entities in question. Although the path to the existence claim is indeed an easy one, this has no bearing on the nature of the claim itself. To exist pleonastically is to exist in precisely the same way that "underived" entities exist.

I.4.2 *Thomas Hofweber, "From* Remnants *to* Things, *and Back Again"*

Hofweber's contribution looks at *Things* through the lens of Schiffer's previous work, in particular *Remnants*. One key feature of the earlier book is what Hofweber calls its "no-reference theory" of that-clauses. In *Remnants*, Schiffer claimed that English has a compositional semantics only if that-clause reference is compositionally determined. Since, he maintained, that-clauses do not refer—due, he argued, to the fact that there are no things that can function as their referents—English does not enjoy a compositional semantics.

An advocate of the no-reference theory needs to explain the appearance of quantification over propositions as in, e.g., 'Ada doubts everything Gloria said.' In *Remnants*, Schiffer espoused a substitutional treatment of propositional quantification. Rather than saying that (E) 'something is F' is true just in case some object in the domain satisfies 'F', the substitutional theory claims that the quantification is true just in case there exists a substitution instance that makes (E) true. But then 'some proposition is inexpressible in English' cannot be true, since 'that S is inexpressible in English' will be false for every English sentence S.

Schiffer dismissed this problem in *Remnants*. Why, he asked, "should we suppose that the use of quantificational idioms in ordinary language is exactly captured by some precisely defined technical notion?" (1987: 289, note 6). But, as Hofweber remarks, "this just raises the question more vividly how such quantifiers are supposed to be understood" (p. 58).

Things faces a parallel problem. Pleonastic propositions, being mere shadows of 'that'-clauses, "do not form a language-independent domain of entities" (p. 58). But there is still the phenomenon of apparent quantification over such propositions. How is the Schiffer of *Things* to make sense of this phenomenon? Extrapolating from Schiffer's treatment of an analogous problem involving inexpressible properties (*Things*, 71), Hofweber offers the following response on his behalf: we understand quantification over propositions in terms of an "enrichment of our own language," one which contains the relevant 'that'-clauses. Of course, we are within our rights to ask precisely what the notion of an enrichment of a language amounts to. As Hofweber observes, an enrichment of L in the intended sense cannot merely be a language that has "more words"—even more words not synonymous with words in L—since these might be synonymous with composite expressions already in L. Rather, an enrichment of L must be one that *extends L's* expressive capacity. But it is hard to make sense of this idea without taking it to mean: *expresses more propositions than are expressible in L*. And, as Hofweber points out, it is far from clear that this construal is compatible with the theory of pleonastic propositions. (On the face of it, it presupposes a realm of language-independent propositions.) As he writes: "The problem of inexpressible propositions is much more serious than Schiffer's brief discussion makes it out to be" (p. 63).

Hofweber develops an "inferential role" treatment of quantifiers which, he shows, handles the contexts that are troublesome for Schiffer, all within the framework of a no-reference theory of 'that'-clauses. (This treatment of quantification is meant to supplement, not replace, standard objectual quantification.) Hofweber thus resolves an open question in the *Remnants*-era approach and, as his title suggests, this puts him more in line with the ontology of the earlier book than that of *Things*.

I.4.3 Ian Rumfitt, "Objects of Thought"

Like Hofweber, Rumfitt is concerned with Schiffer's theory of propositions. He focuses on an important contrast that Schiffer emphasizes, one exemplified by the following pair:

1. Henri admires Braque.
2. Ralph believes that George Eliot was a woman.

We determine (1)'s truth-value by identifying the referents of the respective names and then determining whether they satisfy the relation *admires*. It would be "laughable," says Schiffer, to suggest that we first ascertain the sentence's truth condition and only then determine to whom the respective names refer (*Things*, 73). But this is precisely what happens in (2). We do not first determine what the that-clause denotes and then see whether Ralph bears the believing relation to it. Rather, we ascertain what is required for the entire sentence to be true. Only then do we establish the that-clause's reference.

While Rumfitt agrees that "any acceptable account must respect this difference between belief reports and (for example) attributions of admiration" (p. 78) he notes that the pleonastic theory, which is in part motivated by the above-displayed asymmetry, raises a question whose solution is unclear. For Schiffer, the identity conditions of the proposition referred to by (2)'s that-clause are established by features of the context of utterance. This, however, tells us precious little about precisely when two utterances express the same proposition or two that-clause tokens co-refer.

In responding to this, Schiffer makes much of an analogy with Fregean accounts of statements of number. On such views, reference is determined only after truth conditions have been established. While Rumfitt acknowledges that the analogy helps us understand more clearly how (2) is supposed to be relational in the face of the contrast with (1), he adds: "Closer examination... reveals a large hole in Schiffer's defense of the face-value theory" (p. 78).

His worry is the following. In the case of cardinal numbers, we have a criterion for identity: cardinal numbers X and Y are the same just in case their constituent concepts are equinumerous. That is, the number of As = the number of Bs just in case the As are equinumerous with the Bs. Moreover, as Rumfitt points out, what allows us to treat the cardinal numbers as identical is the fact that equinumerosity is an equivalence relation between concepts.

One might suppose that the "hole" in Schiffer's defense could be filled if we were to find a parallel strategy with respect to the contents of our attitudes—if, that is, we could find "an equivalence relation among beliefs which ensures that the laws of identity will not be violated if we treat contents as objects" (p. 79). However, as Rumfitt is quick to note, our practices of belief reporting do not, on their own, "yield up such a relation." In light of this, our criteria for determining the truth and falsity of belief reports "will need to be refined and tightened if they are to yield an equivalence relation that can serve as the basis for an abstraction" (p. 80). This is potentially bad news for the pleonastic theory of propositions, which individuates propositions on the basis of the very criteria emanating from our practices of belief reporting. Moreover, refining and tightening these practices can be done in a variety of ways, each yielding a different equivalence relation.

Rumfitt does describe a particular equivalence relation over assertions (or "sayings")—that of equipollence. Two assertions are equipollent just in case a competent speaker cannot "'grasp' both... without being in a position to know that they share a truth-value" (p. 81). But the domain of assertions he considers is restricted to those of interest to the logician and focuses on the logical content of these assertions. This, as he notes, is of little use to Schiffer, whose concern is not limited to assertions made in logical deductions.

The problem does not, as Rumfitt notes, "refute Schiffer," but it does show us where more work needs to be done in defending a theory, such as Schiffer's, which respects the contrast exemplified in (1) and (2) while also adhering to Fregean intuitions about content-identity.

I.4.4 Michael Smith, "Schiffer's Unhappy-Face Solution to a Puzzle about Moral Judgement"

The theory of pleonastic propositions is the lynchpin to *Things*. As mentioned (Section I.3, above), they are derived from pleonastic restatements of ontologically neutral discourse. These "something-from-nothing transformations" would seem to afford an easy route to cognitivism. Our practices, after all, do not differentiate between the aforementioned transformation and the one from 'Kicking Lassie is permissible' to 'that Kicking Lassie is permissible is true.'

Smith's contribution challenges what he calls "Schiffer's Conclusion"—that cognitivism is a direct consequence of the theory of pleonastic propositions. The discussion centers on a variant of the "Argument from Internalism"—an argument against cognitivism that Schiffer discusses in *Things*:

(*a*) Necessarily, one who states—we are to assume sincerely—that she morally ought not to X wants to refrain from X-ing.
(*b*) If there were moral propositions, then a person who *states* that she morally ought not to X would be expressing her *belief* that the proposition that she morally ought not to X is true.
(*c*) There are no propositions *p* and *q* such that, when someone believes that *p*, she wants that *q*.
Therefore, (*d*) there are no moral propositions.

The variant, according to Smith, shows clearly—more clearly than Schiffer's original—why the theory of pleonastic propositions, far from entailing that cognitivism is true, is neutral on this question. As he argues, (*e*)—a fundamental claim of the pleonastic theory and, in fact, the face-value theory it is a completion of—is inconsistent with the premises of the revised argument.

(*e*) The things we state or assert are the very same things that we believe.

While Schiffer himself rejects the argument, denying premise (*c*), this rejection does not flow from the pleonastic theory. According to Smith, a pleonastic theorist could equally embrace (*c*) as stating one of the *a priori* truths that "are constitutive of the concept of a proposition" (95).

I.4.5 Gary Ostertag, "Propositional Platitudes"

According to the face-value theory, 'believes' as it occurs in '*A* believes that *S*' stands for a binary relation between a thinker and a proposition. The analysis, Schiffer argues in *Things*, has a default status among competing approaches. But, as he notes, it is only a template, and needs to be supplemented by a completing theory of propositions. One such theory is Russell's theory of structured propositions. However, the face-value theory, combined with a Russellian approach to propositions, results in the theory of direct reference, and Schiffer rejects this approach (see section I.4.7, below).

On the view Schiffer defends, propositions are entities whose very existence depends on our belief-reporting practices. As we have seen, they are derived from pleonastic restatements of ontologically neutral discourse—from neutral 'Lassie is a dog' to ontologically committing 'that Lassie is a dog is true.' In addition, the entities thus introduced have no nature beyond the role they play as the referents of token 'that'-clauses. Thus, there is nothing more to the proposition referred to by my utterance of 'Ralph believes that George Eliot was a man' than its having whatever properties we must suppose it to have in order for the utterance's truth conditions to be what the context establishes them to be.

Ostertag's essay questions some of the motivations behind the theory—in particular, why it is to be preferred over an alternative that Schiffer considered and rejected in earlier work—the hidden-indexical theory of belief reports. In this earlier work (for example, "Belief Ascription"), Schiffer argued that this alternative theory makes implausible predictions about the ordinary speaker's meaning intentions in uttering belief reports ("the meaning-intention problem") and makes independently unmotivated claims about the logical form of belief reports ("the logical form problem").

Ostertag argues that the meaning-intention problem—if it is indeed a problem—is equally a problem for the pleonastic theory. He also suggests that a contextualist construal of the hidden-indexical theory—wherein modes of presentation are not referred to or quantified over, but are provided by a process of free enrichment—might enable the theorist to avoid the logical form problem.

Finally, Ostertag raises questions about the positive proposal. After a discussion of the theory's treatment of *de re* attitude reports, he argues that the pleonastic theory fails to account for disagreement between belief reporters.

I.4.6 Ray Buchanan, "Schiffer's Puzzle: A Kind of Fregean Response"

In a 2005 paper, "What Reference Has to Tell Us about Meaning," Schiffer discusses a feature of certain propositions that he calls *the relativity feature*. Suppose José says to Ada, 'I'm thirsty.' Although he clearly intends for Ada to come to believe that he, José, is thirsty, he just as clearly doesn't intend for her to think of him, in grasping his intention, in the way that he thinks of himself. First, that would seem impossible; second, it would not produce the desired effect (say, for Ada to hand José a bottle of water) even if it were.

According to Schiffer, a proposition has the relativity feature "provided it's an x-dependent proposition the entertainment of which requires different people, or the same person at different times or places, to think of x in different ways" (2005b: 129). It would be nice if Fregean propositions had the relativity feature, since they then could be the propositions I share with my interlocutor and which at the same time present me in that special way in which only I can be presented to myself. But no Fregean proposition can have this feature.

While Fregeans agree that no proposition can be both self-presenting and communicable to one's audience, they deny that this is an insurmountable problem. Here's a suggestion floated by John McDowell:

> There is no reason that [Frege] could not have held...that in linguistic exchanges of the appropriate kind, mutual knowledge—which is what successful communication achieves—requires not shared thoughts but different thoughts that are mutually known to stand in a suitable relation of correspondence. (McDowell 1984: 105)

McDowell's proposal is that *the proposition my utterance expresses* and *the proposition that my interlocutor entertains on the basis of my utterance* need not be identical; it suffices for them to be mutually related, so that, while I don't intend for my hearer to entertain *my* thought, I do intend for her to entertain one that is, although not necessarily graspable by me, suitably positioned (so to speak) with respect to mine.

The price that the Fregean has to pay is that José's utterance of 'I'm thirsty' ends up having no determinate propositional content. Thus *the no-content theory*: One can't report what José said in uttering what he did, since he didn't *say* anything: there is no particular proposition p that functions as both what he expressed *and* what he intended Ada to entertain.

Schiffer's theory of pleonastic propositions enables us to avoid this counterintuitive consequence. On his view, there is a proposition p that José asserts in uttering

'I'm thirsty,' one that requires José and Ada to think of José in different ways. According to the pleonastic theory, when José says to Ada, 'Yvette believes that I'm thirsty' the that-clause reference is determined by contextually salient "criteria of evaluation." While what José refers to is partly a function of the reference to José, the speaker, it is also partly a function of the aforementioned contextual features. Now the proposition he refers to here appears to be exactly what Ada would have referred to were *she* to have uttered 'Yvette believes that you are thirsty.' Again, the that-clause reference is partly determined by the reference to José, the addressee, but also by contextual features. In the former case, one crucial such feature is that José is the speaker; in the latter case, a crucial such feature is that José is the addressee. These criteria of evaluation, though different, determine one and the same referent.

Ray Buchanan's contribution provides an alternative treatment of the same puzzling phenomenon, one that is consonant with McDowell's suggestion (as well as a related suggestion by Richard Heck). Buchanan claims that there is no proposition that José says in uttering 'I'm thirsty'—nor is there a proposition Yvette refers to in uttering 'José said that I'm thirsty.' Still, this is not to give full-throated endorsement to the no-content theory. On his approach, a that-clause does refer, albeit not to a proposition, but to a proposition *type*. Buchanan thus avoids an unpalatable consequence of the no-content theory, while at the same time avoiding the need for an excursion into the ontology of pleonastic propositions.

In slightly more detail, while Buchanan agrees with the Fregean that belief is a relation to fine-grained Fregean propositions, he claims that the that-clause in the belief report 'A believes that *S*' makes reference to a proposition type, not a proposition. The report states that, for some proposition p meeting condition Ψ, A believes p (where Ψ is the referent of 'that *S*'). Again, this allows the theorist to maintain a Fregean approach to belief—all belief is belief *in* a proposition—while denying the no-content thesis. That-clauses do refer, but not, as it turns out, to the propositions that serve as the relata of the *believes* relation, but rather to proposition types. Similarly, utterances such as 'I'm hungry' do (or can) express contents, but these contents are not themselves propositions.

I.4.7 Nathan Salmon, "Constraint with Restraint"

Schiffer has had a long-standing disagreement with direct reference (DR) theorists over the contents of reports of the following form:

1. Ralph believes that George Eliot was a man.

The DR theorist maintains that 'believes' stands for a binary relation, *believes*, holding between a person and a structured Russellian proposition. Accordingly, (1) is true just in case Ralph bears *believes* to the proposition <George Eliot, *is-a-man*>. But note that it is easy to imagine a situation in which the following is true:

Ralph believes that George Eliot was a man but disbelieves that Mary Ann Evans was a man.

But, given the DR theorist's Russellian commitments, this is just to say:

Ralph believes that George Eliot was a man but disbelieves that George Eliot was a man.

And we can restate this as follows:

(P1) Ralph believes and disbelieves that George Eliot was a man.

The DR theorist is quick to point out, however, that a rational subject can have conflicting attitudes regarding a given object. All that is required is that she has distinct modes of presentation of the object—modes which she believes are non-co-presenting. If so, then the agent does not run afoul of what Schiffer calls "Frege's Constraint," stated here in two parts:

(FC-I) x is believed by y to be F iff, for some m, m is a mode of presentation of x and y believes x to be F under m.

(FC-II) For any modes of presentation m and m', if x is believed by y to be F under m and disbelieved (or not believed) by y to F under m', then y takes m and m' to present different things.

The essence of Frege's Constraint is that one can have rationally conflicting *de re* attitudes regarding an object x only when these attitudes are mediated by distinct modes of presentation of x—modes, crucially, that the agent does not take to be co-presenting. Accordingly, if we have no evidence that the agent takes the relevant modes to be co-presenting—or, if we have no evidence that only one such mode exists—then we have no challenge to the agent's rationality. The point here is that the mere existence of conflicting attitudes does not undermine DR.

A full "proof" of the consistency of (P1) with Frege's Constraint requires appeal to a simple principle, what Schiffer calls "the special-case consequence" (SCC):

(SCC) Necessarily, if A believes that x is F then x is believed by A to be F (alternatively, x is such that A believes her to be F)

This would allow the move from (P1) to (2):

2. Eliot is such that Ralph rationally believes and disbelieves her to have been a man.

According to (SCC), *de re* belief is a *special case* of *de dicto* belief. In particular, *de dicto* belief in a singular Russellian proposition $<x, F>$ can always be recast as *de re* belief involving x, to the effect that it is F. Now, since we are assuming that Ralph has two modes of presentation of Eliot, one implicated in the belief that Eliot is a man, the other implicated in the belief in its negation, then, so long as he takes the modes to present distinct individuals (which we assume he does), there is no violation of Frege's Constraint—in particular, (FC-II) is upheld—and thus no threat to his rationality follows.

However, Schiffer (2006) constructs a scenario that would seem to preclude a similarly straightforward resolution. Here we assume that, unlike Ralph, his English professor, Jane, has only one mode of presentation of Eliot. Let us assume also that she is prone to uttering things like (3)—to illustrate, perhaps, how uninformed her students are about nineteenth-century literary history:

3. Ralph believes that George Eliot was a man.

According to DR, Jane's utterance of (3) is true just in case Ralph bears the *believes* relation to the Russellian proposition <George Eliot, *is-a-man*>. But Jane is also prone to asserting things like (4)—perhaps to indicate that Ralph isn't so hopeless as to believe just anything:

4. Ralph does not believe that Mary Ann Evans was a man.

If so, then, it seems clear that the scenario is on a par with (P1) and that we can report the situation thus:

(P2) Jane rationally believes and disbelieves that Ralph believes that George Eliot was a man.

But just as (P1) is equivalent to the explicitly *de re* formulation (3), (P2) is equivalent to the explicitly *de re* formulation (5):

5. Eliot is such that Jane rationally believes and disbelieves that Ralph believes her to have been a man.

Notice, however, that while Jane here has conflicting beliefs about Eliot—Jane both believes and disbelieves that Ralph believes her, Eliot, to be a man—the conflict cannot be ameliorated by the fact that she believes, of Eliot, that she is such-and-such under one mode and that she disbelieves, of Eliot, that she is such-and-such under a distinct mode. We have stipulated that she only has one mode presenting Eliot.

The upshot is that DR fails to capture the fairly humdrum situation described by (P2). Given how the case is set up, with Jane having only a single mode of presentation of Eliot, she, Jane, is precluded from rationally believing and disbelieving that Eliot possesses the relevant property. We seem, then, to have a counterexample to DR.

Nathan Salmon's response takes issue with (SCC). He points out that (SCC) may take us from a true attribution to a false one. Consider, for example:

6. Lois believes that Clark is stronger than Clark.

(SCC) would license the following inference:

7. Clark is such that he is believed by Lois to be stronger than himself.

But this is obviously absurd. At most, (6) should permit the inference to either (8a) or (8b):

8a. Clark is such that he is believed by Lois to be stronger than Clark.
8b. Clark is such that Clark is believed by Lois to be stronger than him.

Salmon argues that (SCC) must be restricted to belief reports involving monadic predicates: in such cases, it is a matter of indifference whether or not we use the *de dicto* form or the *de re* form. The unrestricted principle, on the other hand, gives rise to unwanted entailments. And, without the unrestricted principle, the step from (P2) to (5) fails. If so, Schiffer's challenge to DR would fail as well.

I.4.8 Dorothy Edgington, "Schiffer on Indeterminacy, Vagueness, and Conditionals"

Things contains a rich and novel account of vagueness. At issue is the status of the conclusion of a garden-variety Sorites argument:

A person with $50,000,000 is rich
A person with 57¢ is not rich

(Cut)   So, there is an amount of money n such that a person with n amount of money is rich but a person with n-1¢ isn't.

The argument form is intuitively valid and the premises obviously true. Even so, just as obviously, the conclusion, (Cut), appears false—the idea that there is a sharp cutoff between rich and non-rich seems fantastic. In the face of this, one might respond that the proposition that makes (Cut) true—its witness—is either unknowable (*Epistemicism*), or possesses an indeterminate truth-value (these are, following Crispin Wright, *third possibility* views). But Schiffer argues for an alternative view: "vagueness is neither a semantic nor an epistemic notion," rather, "it is a psychological notion explicable in terms of [vagueness-related partial belief]" (*Things*, 5, 178).

One of Schiffer's central innovations in *Things* and the work leading up to it is the notion of a *vagueness-related partial belief* (VPB). While a "standard partial belief" (SPB) conforms to the probability calculus and is used to measure uncertainty or ignorance, a VPB differs. Sally might, situated in ideal conditions of observation, believe to degree 0.5 that Harry is bald and believe to degree 0.5 that Harry is thin. Were these independent beliefs that did not involve vague properties, she would believe the conjunction of the two propositions to degree 0.25. This would be so because she would be uncertain to a given degree in each of the conjuncts and the laws of probability dictate that the degree of uncertainty of the conjunction is a function of the degree of uncertainty attaching to the individual conjuncts. But what is being measured in Sally's Harry-related beliefs is not her uncertainty or lack of knowledge—there is no fact of which we can accuse her of being ignorant. As Schiffer notes, "She's *ambivalent*, but she's not *uncertain* about anything" (*Things*, 204; emphasis in text). It is this ambivalence that is constitutive of VPBs. Whatever precise degree we attach to her VPB in the conjunction, it is closer to 0.5 than to 0.25.

The concept of a VPB plays a crucial role in Schiffer's (partial) characterization of a borderline case:

(B) x is a borderline case of F *only if* an ideally situated subject could have a VPB to the effect that x is F.

While VPBs are deployed to characterize the phenomenon that defines vagueness—that of being a borderline F—it is important to emphasize that they do not "track" the property of being a borderline F. Being borderline F is a pleonastic property, a close cousin to the idea of a pleonastic proposition. This is a property whose essence is fully determined by "our property-hypostasizing linguistic and conceptual practices" (*Things*, 212). In the particular case of being borderline F, possession of the property is determined by whether or not it is possible for someone in "an unimprovable epistemic position" (Edgington) to form the VPB that the object in question is F.

Edgington presents a number of challenges to Schiffer's views on vagueness and to his related views on conditionals. One challenge concerns the notion of a VPB and its role in understanding borderline cases. As we have seen, Sally's belief that (borderline) Harry is bald does not conform to the standard rules of probability, which measure ignorance or uncertainty. And Sally is not *uncertain* about anything,

Schiffer tells us—just ambivalent. But, as Edgington warns, characterizing this particular psychological state independently of any reference to a determinate fact the state tracks is "no easy task." And reference to this state is crucial to Schiffer's project of understanding borderline cases in purely psychological terms. Moreover, as she shows, there are potential cases of borderline properties that resist a simple psychological analysis—requiring a revision to (B), above. (Field makes a similar observation.) But it is unclear whether (B) can be revised in a manner consistent with Schiffer's intentions.

Edgington also objects to the pleonastic account of borderline cases, on which the claim that x is borderline F is equated with the claim that an ideally situated agent could formulate a VPB to the effect that x is F. She writes: "A competent judgment that something is borderline red—especially one made by Schiffer's imagined ideal thinker who knows she is in an unimprovable epistemic position—is as much a response to how things are as is a competent judgement that something is red" (162).

In addition to discussing various technical aspects of Schiffer's proposal (for example, the interaction between SPBs and VPBs), Edgington provides her own diagnosis as to what goes wrong in Sorites reasoning. On her view, the argument is valid. But what the long form of the argument shows—in which every relevant instance of the premise, 'If a man with n dollars is rich, then a man with 1¢ less is also rich' is stated—is that at some point we "depart minimally from clear truth." (Cut) is true, she maintains, "not because any one of its instances is definitely true, but because many of its instances depart very slightly from definite falsity" (166). The paper ends with a criticism of Schiffer's view of conditionals, according to which they express pleonastic propositions. Here she writes, in a comment that resonates with Smith's discussion of moral cognitivism, that the "superficial appearance of expressing a proposition is not always to be taken at face value" (170).

I.4.9 Hartry Field, "Vagueness, Partial Belief, and Logic"

Field's contribution focuses on two main concerns: (1) Because (Cut) is indeterminate, Schiffer claims that the relevant Sorites argument is "neither determinately valid nor determinately invalid"—where validity is understood as *necessary truth preservation* (this, Schiffer claims, is the "ordinary definition" of validity). Field argues that Schiffer's *rationale* for denying determinate validity/invalidity to the Sorites extends to modus ponens as well. If, following Schiffer, we interpret 'valid' as *necessary truth preservation*, then, Field argues, modus ponens will not end up being determinately valid. To see this, take an instance of modus ponens in which the antecedent of the conditional is indeterminate and the consequent is false: "we're in no position to conclude that the argument even *actually* preserves truth, let alone does so *necessarily*" (177). Indeed, he shows that something stronger may be true— that "on Schiffer's 'ordinary definition' of validity, *no* argument comes out determinately valid" (178).

(2) Field argues that Schiffer does not need VPBs to characterize borderline belief states. For Schiffer, a case where we are certain that Harry is a borderline case of bald is a case where our SPB *that Harry is bald* = our SPB *that Harry not is bald* = 0. Field shows that on Schiffer's view it is also the case that our SPB *that Harry is either bald*

or not bald = 0 as well. He argues that this suffices "to undermine the sense that we are committed to belief in a fact about which we are ignorant" (182).

Field maintains that Schiffer's fundamental contribution to the debate is to show that the belief states governing borderline cases fail to conform to standard probabilistic laws. The introduction of VPBs is unnecessary and the provision of a logic governing these VPBs is, in his view, "overkill."

I.4.10 Crispin Wright, "On the Characterization of Borderline Cases"

For Wright, Schiffer's main contribution to the vagueness literature is in addressing what Wright calls the *characterization problem*: "the problem of saying what the vagueness of expressions of natural language consists in or, more specifically... the problem of saying what being a borderline case of the concept expressed by a vague expression consists in" (190). He proceeds to an evaluation of Schiffer's contribution to our understanding of this phenomenon. Wright is broadly sympathetic to Schiffer's approach, which is to some degree influenced by Wright's own work and in which the notion of a "quandary" plays a central role. (We can understand being in a quandary as roughly analogous to the state of ambivalence Sally is in with respect to the question, discussed in I.4.9, of Harry's baldness). But Wright also wants to bring attention to the differences between their accounts. One crucial difference concerns verdict exclusion (VE), the doctrine that "no polar verdict about a borderline case proposition is knowledgeable" (191). Schiffer endorses (VE); Wright rejects it. Schiffer holds that ideally situated Sally is not only ambivalent about whether or not Harry is bald, but in addition, that she would be "entirely justified in thinking that it's impossible, given the obtaining facts, for [her], or anyone else, to know whether or not Harry is bald" (Schiffer, forthcoming *b*; I've changed the example). Wright objects:

[T]o find oneself unmoved to an opinion by evidence of which one has no clear conception of a possible improvement justifies the claim that there is no knowing in the case in question only if one knows, first, that one's lack of a clear concept of a possible improvement is an indicator that there is no possible improvement... and, more crucially, second, that one's present evidence is not enough for knowledge. (197)

Wright is also critical of the central role that VPBs play in Schiffer's account of being in a borderline belief state. He provides examples of individuals who possess the concept of being a borderline *F* but whose beliefs involving such concepts are not VPBs. While Wright applauds Schiffer's focus on partial belief "in the normal attitudinal psychology of vague judgement," he adds that it is a mistake "to see it as belonging to the nature of the understanding of vague concepts to involve a disposition to partial belief of this kind, or to write it into the possession-conditions for vague concepts that one should be so inclined" (194).

I.4.11 Paul Horwich, "The Nature of Paradox"

Schiffer states that a "philosophical paradox is a set of apparently mutually incompatible propositions each of which enjoys some significant degree of plausibility when viewed on its own" (*Things*, 68). He distinguishes between two sorts of paradox:

those that admit of a "happy-face solution" and those that only admit of an "unhappy-face solution." The *happy-face solution* isolates the "odd guy out"—it's either the case that one of the propositions is found to be less than plausible after all, or the propositions are not, in fact, genuinely incompatible. Moreover, in identifying the odd guy out—the appearance of consistency, or the appearance of truth—we have "removed its patina of plausibility, so that we would never again be taken in by it" (68). The *unhappy-face solution* would involve showing that no happy-face solution exists. In addition, it "would tell us what it is about the concepts involved that explains this." Crucial to Schiffer's view is that the explanation will involve locating "a glitch in the concept or concepts involved, a tension in the underived conceptual roles that individuate those concepts" (69).

For Schiffer, it is characteristic of philosophical paradoxes that they enjoy only unhappy-face solutions. All we can do is expose the glitches and accept a suitable revision (or, in the case of a *strong* unhappy-face solution, show that no "suitable conceptual revision is possible" (198)).

In contrast, Horwich recommends an alternative, Wittgensteinian, approach. Rather than resulting from features intrinsic to our concepts, Horwich claims that philosophical paradoxes result from conceptual overgeneralization. Contrary to what Schiffer claims, argues Horwich, it is not the concepts themselves that give rise to inconsistency, but our tendency to make illicit generalizations. These tendencies might, in some cases, be due to an overly scientistic approach to philosophical problems; but in other cases "our troublesome epistemic proclivities result from perfectly normal processes of cognitive development and language learning" (223). Whatever there source, however, it is these underlying epistemic habits that lead us astray, not the concepts implicated in our generalizations.

I.4.12 Stephen Neale, "Silent Reference"

In his 1981 essay, "Indexicals and the Theory of Reference," Schiffer provided a groundbreaking analysis of speaker reference in terms of speaker meaning. On the proposed account, a speaker refers to an individual x in virtue of saying or meaning an x-dependent proposition—a proposition whose existence presupposes the existence of x.

Reducing speaker reference to speaker meaning has an obvious payoff in terms of theoretical economy. A successful reduction means that we need not add to our basic stock of meaning-theoretic notions in order to accommodate reference. But the move is significant even for those who have no particular attraction to the IBS project. Characterizing the reference relation has been a preoccupation of philosophy of language since its inception. If an adequate reduction of reference to speaker meaning exists, and if the analysis of speaker meaning is in good order, then we have made clear progress on the problem of reference. We have, in a sense, dissolved it.

To a rough approximation, Schiffer's account of referring—of referring to x in uttering σ—runs as follows:

I. S refers to x in uttering σ just in case, in uttering σ, S means a singular, x-dependent proposition.

There is more to say, however. After all, referring to x involves the use of a *referring expression*—a name, demonstrative, or indexical—to refer to x. For example, in uttering (1) I refer to Cicero by uttering a proper part of this sentence, 'Cicero':

1. Cicero was an orator.

The notion we are after here is *referring by* (or *referring by way of*). This is exemplified when a speaker, in uttering σ, makes reference to x through—"by way of"—her uttering a proper part, μ, of σ. The analysis of this type of action is as follows:

II. S refers to x in uttering σ *by way of uttering μ* just in case μ is a proper part of σ and in uttering σ S intends it to be mutual knowledge between S and A that for some relation R, $R(μ, x)$ and, at least partly on this basis, that S referred to x in uttering σ.

(R may be a relation that obtains between μ and x just when there is a pattern of usage that involves uttering sentences containing μ to assert x-dependent propositions, but this will not always be the case.)

Occasionally, there are multiple occurrences of a single referring expression in a sentence, with different occurrences referring to different individuals. For example, Paige utters (2), referring to Ada relative to the first occurrence of 'her', but referring to Gloria relative to the second occurrence of 'her':

2. Give her her keys—now!

We can say here, assuming (II), that in uttering (2) Paige refers to Ada by way of uttering 'her' but also that Paige refers to Gloria by way of uttering 'her'. But just as (I) doesn't tell us which expression in (1) is such that I used it to refer to Cicero, so (II) doesn't tell us which *occurrence* of 'her' in (2) is such that Paige used it to refer to Gloria.

In response to this lacuna, Neale defines a notion of *referring with μ, relative to an occurrence i* to accommodate *occurrences* of referential expressions within an utterance. The details of the account need not detain us here. What is crucial is that, on Neale's view, the basic notion of reference involves not merely an utterance, a speaker, an individual, and an expression ('In uttering X, S referred to y with μ'), but an utterance, a speaker, an individual, and an *occurrence* of an expression ('In uttering X, S referred to y with occurrence i of μ').

A consequence of Neale's analysis (see his **RW**) is the following. In uttering (2), Paige refers to Ada with the first occurrence of 'her'—call it 'her$_1$'—only if (among other things) it is mutual knowledge between Paige and her audience that there is some salient relation between 'her$_1$' and Ada. But this is in tension with a basic requirement of the overall IBS framework: namely, that the intentions a given proposal attributes to speakers must be psychologically real. Otherwise we have an instance of Schiffer's meaning-intention problem, cited above. After all, it might seem questionable whether speakers actually have beliefs about occurrences of expressions, let alone have expectations that their intentions with respect to such occurrences will be transparent to their hearers.

Neale, however, maintains that such attributions are plausible: "Ordinary speakers understand quite well that someone can be referring to one person by 'his' relative to its first occurrence in (3) and someone different with 'his' relative to its second occurrence" (renumbered):

3. John told Paul that Ringo thought George had hidden his drumsticks inside his guitar amplifier.

As he admits, however, things are less straightforward when we consider *aphonic reference*—reference that occurs via an unpronounced item in a sentence's syntactic structure. It is here that the analysis becomes especially difficult to reconcile with the demand for psychological plausibility.

Consider Neale's example:

4. When it's snowing, the mayor now has the authority to prohibit cycling on the streets.

Assume that Zadie utters this during a snowstorm in London. On its most natural interpretation, the utterance contains three implicit references to London:

5. When it's snowing *in London*, the mayor *of London* now has the authority to prohibit cycling on the streets *of London*.

Here, again, one might say that ordinary speakers understand quite well both that someone can be making aphonic reference to London in connection with 'snowing,' 'the mayor,' and 'the streets' and that other contexts will assign different implicit references in connection with some or all of these expressions. After all, the thought goes, an ordinary speaker would have no more trouble recovering the speaker's intentions with respect to (4) than she would with respect to (3). If so, then this gives us motivation for assigning aphonic expressions to the syntactic structure of (4). (Although this move is controversial, as Neale points out. Relevance theorists would argue that the reading provided by (5) is the result of a process of "free enrichment" of (4).)

Yet, the question of psychological plausibility arises here, and with a vengeance. Assume that there is grammatically determined aphonic reference occurring in the hypothetical utterance of (4). (For a precise definition, see Neale's RA.) Then, in uttering (4), Zadie refers to London in connection with (say) 'the mayor' only if it is *mutual knowledge* between Zadie and her audience that there is some salient relation between a given aphonic expression in (4) and London. But that there is mutual knowledge of this sort analysis seems questionable.

The IBS theorist thus faces a dilemma. Extending his account of reference to aphonics seems well motivated—even necessary, some might argue. And yet, a proper treatment appears to violate a basic IBS requirement of psychological plausibility.

I.4.13 Anita Avramides, "Abiding Intentions"

Avramides' essay, like Hofweber's, locates *Things* in the context of Schiffer's previous work, and asks why the concerns of *Meaning* and *Remnants of Meaning*—the analysis of meaning and its place in a reductive account of the propositional attitudes—are largely absent from *Things*. Part of the explanation, she suggests, concerns Schiffer's skepticism about conceptual analysis in general and the analysis of meaning in particular. She also notes that, in *Remnants,* Schiffer showed that the

Gricean (or IBS) account he previously advocated fails to fit into a reductionist program. However, Avramides argues that an intention-based account of meaning can be of value even if it does not fit neatly into such a large-scale program. As she points out, *physicalist* reduction was neither a concern in Grice's initial accounts of meaning nor in Schiffer's early attempt to analyze the concept in *Meaning*. Rather, Schiffer was engaged in an attempt to reduce semantic properties to psychological ones—a project that retains its value even if a physicalist reduction of the psychological is no longer seen as plausible. Avramides also notes Schiffer's transition, in the period between *Remnants* and *Things*, towards a "minimalist" theory of meaning. While this approach is clearly in response to the failure of the large-scale reductionism that drives papers like "Intention-Based Semantics" (1982), the failure of that program does not, as she argues, undermine the Gricean project it was designed to complete.

I.4.14 Kent Bach, "Schiffer on Russell's Theory and Referential Uses"

As is well known, on Russell's theory of descriptions, all description sentences containing incomplete descriptions turn out false. For Russell, a sentence of the form 'The F is G' is true just in case there is exactly one F, and every F is G. One common remedy is to claim that description sentences require at every context a completing property. This is "the hidden-indexical theory of descriptions" (HITD). On HITD, one is to utter 'the F is G' only if, for some salient property H, one intends to communicate the proposition that the thing that is both F and H is G.

Schiffer has dealt several blows to this view, but perhaps the most devastating is that it involves an illicit appeal to the "say-p-➤-mean-q model" to explain the referential use of incomplete definite descriptions. (See Schiffer 2005a.) On this familiar model, we explain what a speaker means in uttering a given sentence by appealing to what she thereby says, together with various contextual factors. To see the problem, consider the following application of HITD. I utter 'the guy's drunk' upon seeing the eminent philosopher Ferdinand Pergola stumbling towards the podium. This is false on the unmodified Russellian view. But it is potentially true on HITD, since, presumably, I uttered it to say that the H guy is drunk—where H is a contextually supplied property. The problem, as Schiffer makes clear, is that selecting the completing property requires knowing to whom I was referring. But then the familiar Gricean model of explanation cannot work here. The Russellian appeals to Grice to explain how HITD can be compatible with the referential use of incomplete descriptions: the hearer, we are to believe, concludes that the referential proposition was intended (or "meant") from the fact that the speaker expressed the general proposition, together with various contextual cues. But, Schiffer argues, in any plausible scenario, the hearer must first identify the referent if she has any hope of recovering the speaker's intended completion.

Bach defends Russell's unmodified theory. Not only does he deny that 'the F is G' can be used to express a referential proposition, he also denies that it can be used to express a descriptively enriched proposition of the sort posited by HITD. But then, as he points out, he must be innocent of any appeal to the "say-p-➤-mean-q model," since that model assumes that, in uttering 'the guy's drunk,' the speaker both intended to express (or "say") an enriched proposition and, in addition (and in virtue of doing the former) to convey or mean a referential, Pergola-dependent proposition. But then Schiffer's criticism will not apply.

How, then, does Bach's Russellian explain how it is that referential propositions (or enrichments of the sort posited by HITD) are routinely communicated by incomplete description sentences? Bach rejects the (implausible) suggestion that we first judge such sentences to be obviously false and then derive the intended content (we might call this the "make-as-if-to-say-p-➤-mean-q model"). Indeed, the audience "does not have to hear the entire sentence and figure out what conversationally deficient proposition it expresses before realizing that he must read something into the speaker's use of the incomplete description" (373). Rather, Bach suggests, the fact that the description is incomplete "by itself triggers any needed search for some individuating condition or some particular individual that must be identified for figuring out what the speaker means" (Ibid.).

Notes

1. Thanks to Ray Buchanan, Russell Dale, Amanda Favia, Daniel Harris, Oliver Marshall, Frank Pupa, Rosemary Twomey, and Monique Whitaker for helpful comments on an earlier draft of sections I.1–3.
2. Another important goal (not to be discussed here) was to deploy the account of speaker meaning in the analysis of Austin's notion of a speech act—an analysis that, following Strawson's suggestion, dispensed with the idea that such acts are conventional (Austin) or are governed by "constitutive rules" (Searle).
3. Fodor (1975) is also clearly concerned with meaning properties and the analysis of meaning. Earlier figures with a more metaphysical orientation would include Sellars (see, e.g., Sellars 1969) and Wittgenstein.
4. For a dissenting voice, see Avramides (1989).
5. Thanks to Russell Dale for helpful correspondence concerning the issues discussed in this paragraph.
6. See especially Field (1978), Fodor (1987), Loar (1981), Millikan (1984), Stalnaker (1984), and, of course, Schiffer (1982).
7. Note that I use "expression meaning" and "public-language meaning" interchangeably.
8. As mentioned above, Schiffer claimed that the very problems addressed were based on false presuppositions (1987: 270).
9. Another key theme of *Remnants* and subsequent work is that a compositional semantics for natural languages is not required to explain our capacity for understanding novel sentences. This has no bearing on the naturalization project, however: Schiffer's alternative explanation is itself naturalistically acceptable.
10. Johnston (1988) recommends a positive response to the pessimistic conclusions of *Remnants* as well. He sketches a "minimalist" account of belief reports and meaning ascriptions—one according to which "Meaning has no hidden and substantial nature for a theory to uncover" (38).
11. Schiffer (1972) adds the extra condition that it be mutually known between S and A that (a) to (c) obtain. (Mutual knowledge is discussed in I.2.2.1, below.) This crucial addition addresses a challenge to the sufficiency of (a) to (c) in Strawson (1964).
12. Grice himself attempted to provide such an account (see Grice 1968), but Schiffer (1972: 134 and *passim*) argues persuasively that Grice's account must fail.

13. To simplify exposition, I here ignore the fact that many other populations (the Haitians, the Québécois, etc.) speak French. In addition, I assume that the French-speaking population of France speaks precisely the same dialect. Finally, I mean by 'French' the French language as it is now spoken. None of the points made in what follows depends on these simplifying assumptions.
14. See also Lewis (1969) and (1975) on common knowledge. Although Lewis and Schiffer arrived at their accounts separately, they each describe "essentially the same notion" (Schiffer forthcoming a).
15. In *The Descent of Man*, Darwin speculates that language originated in something along the lines suggested by Schiffer. "Since monkeys certainly understand much that is said to them by man, and when wild, utter signal-cries of danger to their fellows; and since fowls give distinct warnings for danger on the ground, or in the sky from hawks (both, as well as a third cry, intelligible to dogs), may not an unusually wise ape-like animal have imitated the growl of a beast of prey, and thus have told his fellow-monkeys the nature of the expected danger? This would have been the first step in the formation of language" (Darwin 1879/ 2004: 110–11; quoted in Skyrms 2004: 57).
16. See also the discussion in Lewis (1969: 176–7, 194–202), (1975: 168–9 and *passim*) and (1993).
17. We might call this the "Meaning-meaning" principle, as it defines the meaning-p-among-G relation partly in terms of the meaning-in-L relation.
18. To be tokened in one's "belief box" is Schiffer's metaphor for being tokened with the functional profile of a belief.
19. See Lewis (1975, 1992); Schiffer (1993, 1994, 2003, forthcoming a); Hawthorne (1989); Ray (1995); Dale (1996). The problem, as Lewis (1992) notes, is a variant of the problem of rule following as described in Kripke (1982).
20. The idea of a compositional supervenience theory is introduced in Schiffer (1991) to show that the productivity of *NE*—the fact that each of the infinitely many sentences generated by its syntax has a meaning—does not require the assumption (*contra* Fodor 1989) that there is a compositional meaning theory for *NE* (see below, this section).
21. I here borrow liberally from Schiffer's own account as presented in (1994: 297).
22. In contemporary terms, we might say that the belief property must be *grounded* in the possession of a more basic property. On grounding, see Fine (2001).
23. Jackson and Pettit (1988, 1990) develop an important response to the negative conclusion of *Remnants*, defending a version of so-called commonsense functionalism, the variety of functionalism on which folk psychology is the "theory" that correctly specifies the functional roles that constitute our beliefs and desires. On their view, psychological explanation is a form of "program explanation": a belief property may "program for" a certain behavioral effect without causing it (1990: 108). See Schiffer (1987: 28–40) for Schiffer's original critique of commonsense functionalism and *Things*, pp. 345–7 for his objection to Jackson and Pettit's proposal.
24. While Schiffer argued against the possibility of a functionalist account of belief properties, he did not take these arguments to rule out the possibility of an account of the belief *relation*, and thus of the "belief box" metaphor, in functionalist terms.
25. The account in I.2.2.3 is post-*Remnants*.
26. According to Schiffer, knowledge of meaning is not, on this view, propositional knowledge—knowledge-that—but knowledge-how (*Things*, 105–10). This way of characterizing the current proposal seems unnecessarily tendentious.

Bibliography

Avramides, A. (1989). *Meaning and Mind*. Cambridge: MIT Press.
Bennett, J. (1976). *Linguistic Behavior*. Cambridge: Cambridge University Press.
Dale, R. (1996). *The Theory of Meaning*. Doctoral Dissertation, The Graduate Center, CUNY.
Darwin, C. (1879/2004). *The Descent of Man*. London: Penguin.
Field, H. (1978). "Mental Representation." *Erkenntnis* 13: 9–61.
Fine, K. (2001). "The Question of Realism." *Philosophers' Imprint*. 1. 1: 30.
Fodor, J. (1975). *The Language of Thought*. New York: Thomas Y. Crowell.
Fodor, J. (1987). *Psychosemantics: The Problem of Meaning in the Philosophy of Mind*. Cambridge: MIT.
Fodor, J. (1989). "Stephen Schiffer's Dark Night of the Soul: A Review of *Remnants of Meaning*." *Philosophy and Phenomenological Research* 50: 409–23; reprinted in *A Theory of Content and Other Essays*. Cambridge: MIT Press, 1990.
Grice, H. P. (1957). "Meaning." *The Philosophical Review* 66: 377–88; reprinted in Grice (1989).
Grice, H. P. (1968). "Utterer's Meaning, Sentence Meaning, and Word Meaning." *Foundations of Language* 4: 225–42; reprinted in Grice (1989).
Grice, P. (1989). *Studies in the Way of Words*. Cambridge: Harvard University Press.
Harman, G. (1973). "Language, Thought, and Communication." *Minnesota Studies in the Philosophy of Science* 7: 270–98.
Hawthorne, John (1989). "A Note on 'Languages and Language'." *Australasian Journal of Philosophy* 68: 116–18.
Jackson, F. and P. Pettit (1988). "Functionalism and Broad Content." *Mind* 97: 381–400.
Jackson, F. and P. Pettit (1990). "Program Explanation: A General Perspective." *Analysis* 50: 107–17.
Johnston, M. (1988). "The End of the Theory of Meaning." *Mind and Language* 3: 28–42.
Kripke, S. (1982). *Wittgenstein on Rules And Private Language*. Cambridge: Harvard University Press.
Lewis, D. (1969). *Convention*. Cambridge: Harvard University Press.
Lewis, D. (1975). "Languages and Language." In K. Gunderson (ed.), *Language, Mind and Knowledge*. Minneapolis: University of Minnesota Press.
Lewis, D. (1992). "Meaning without Use: Reply to Hawthorne." *Australasian Journal of Philosophy* 70: 106–10.
Loar, B. (1981). *Mind and Meaning*. Cambridge: Cambridge University Press.
McDowell, J. (1984). "*De Re* Senses." *The Philosophical Quarterly* 34: 283–94.
Millikan, R. (1984). *Language, Thought, and Other Biological Categories*. Cambridge: MIT Press.
Ray, G. (1995). "Thinking in L." *Noûs* 29: 378–96.
Schiffer, S. (1972). *Meaning*. Oxford: Oxford University Press.
Schiffer, S. (1981). "Indexicals and the Theory of Reference." *Synthese* 49: 43–100.
Schiffer, S. (1982). "Intention-Based Semantics." *Notre Dame Journal of Formal Logic* 23: 119–56.
Schiffer, S. (1987). *Remnants of Meaning*. Cambridge: MIT Press.
Schiffer, S. (1991). "Does Mentalese have a Compositional Semantics?" In B. Loewer and G. Rey (eds.), *Meaning in Mind: Fodor and His Critics*. Oxford: Blackwell.
Schiffer, S. (1993). "Actual-Language Relations." *Philosophical Perspectives* 7: 231–58.
Schiffer, S. (1994). "A Paradox of Meaning." *Noûs* 28: 279–324.
Schiffer, S. (2003). *The Things We Mean*. Oxford: Clarendon Press.
Schiffer, S. (2005a). "Russell's Theory of Definite Descriptions." *Mind* 114: 1135–83.

Schiffer, S. (2005b). "What Reference Has to Tell Us about Meaning." In J. Branquinho (ed.), *Conteúdo e Cognição. Anais da série de seminários de Filosofia Analítica*. Lisbon: Centro de Filosofia da Universidade de Lisboa.

Schiffer, S. (2006). "A Problem for Direct Reference Theories of Belief Reports." *Noûs* 40: 361–8.

Schiffer, S. (Forthcoming *a*). "Intention and Convention in the Theory of Meaning." In B. Hale, C. Wright and A. Miller (eds.), *A Companion to the Philosophy of Language*, 2nd Edition. Malden, MA: John Wiley & Sons, Inc.

Schiffer, S. (Forthcoming *b*). "Quandary and Intuitionism: Crispin Wright on Vagueness." In A. Miller (ed.), *Logic, Language and Mathematics: Essays for Crispin Wright Volume II*. Oxford: Oxford University Press.

Sellars, W. (1969). "Language as Thought and as Communication." *Philosophy and Phenomenological Research* 29: 506–27.

Skyrms, B. (2004). *The Stag Hunt and the Evolution of Social Structure*. New York: Cambridge University Press.

Stalnaker, R. (1984). *Inquiry*. Cambridge: MIT.

Strawson, P. F. (1964). "Intention and Convention in Speech Acts." *Philosophical Review* 73: 439–60.

1
Easy Ontology and its Consequences

Amie L. Thomasson

While Stephen Schiffer is best known for his work in the theory of meaning, his recent work in developing a pleonastic account of propositions (and other entities) also leads to major, game-changing results in both first-order ontology and meta-ontology. This paper aims to clarify what these consequences are and why they are so important.

Over the past several decades, there has been a great resurgence in debates about what exists. Quine was thought to have defeated Carnap and eliminated the threat of positivism, and a euphoric period of serious metaphysics followed, in which debates about the existence of various entities have proliferated—including not only traditional debates about the existence of God or free will, but new debates about whether common-sense entities such as persons or artefacts exist, as well as debates about whether philosophical entities such as propositions, states of affairs, temporal parts, or mereological sums exist. Participants in these debates typically assume that their disputes are substantive, and insist that they cannot be addressed by conceptual or linguistic means. Yet they also deny that they can be resolved by straightforward empirical means—making them questions for philosophers, not scientists. Call 'serious ontology' the view that assumes that there are existence questions of this nature—which cannot be resolved either by linguistic/conceptual or straightforward empirical means, and so are (in Theodore Sider's words) "epistemically metaphysical" (2011: 87).

In my view, the biggest threat to this metaphysical party comes from a view I have elsewhere called the 'easy' approach to ontology—a view prominently developed in Schiffer's arguments for 'pleonastic' propositions, properties, fictional characters, states, and events (1994, 1996, 2003). Another version of the approach appears in the neo-Fregean's arguments for the existence of numbers (Wright 1983, Hale and Wright 2001, 2009). Taking off from Schiffer's work, I have also made use of the approach in my arguments for fictional characters, social and cultural objects, and ordinary objects such as tables and chairs (2007a). Although details differ, the basic idea shared by these views is that questions about the existence of certain entities may be easily answered by making trivial inferences from undisputed truths. So, for example, we may begin from the undisputed truth that this shirt is red, infer that the shirt has the property of redness, and so conclude that there is a property (namely, redness), answering the ontological question about the existence of properties.

I will begin by drawing out these three different forms of easy ontology, showing their interrelations, and then go on to discuss their consequences. In its initial development the approach was largely aimed at solving non-metaphysical problems: Hale and Wright were concerned largely with epistemic problems about our knowledge of mathematical and other abstract entities, while Schiffer applied the approach to address problems within the theory of meaning. But the approach also has major consequences for both ontology and meta-ontology. Where first-order ontology is concerned, the approach generally leads us to positive answers to disputed existence questions, leading us to accept that numbers, propositions, properties, etc. exist. Both defenders and critics of the approach often assume that the entities we come to accept on the basis of trivial inferences are in some sense 'cheap' or 'lightweight,' or that the existence claims should be taken as somehow deflated. I will argue, however, that this is a mistake: that the proper way of reading the first-order outcome of easy arguments is as giving us a simple, out and out realism about the entities in question. (Nonetheless, there remain differences between this realism and classical Platonist views, as I will make clear.)

Perhaps even more significant than the first-order consequences, however, are the consequences such an approach has at the meta-ontological level. For wherever debates about existence may be resolved so easily, serious ontological debates about the subject must be confused, out of place. Thus the view leads to the conclusion that something is wrong with the serious ontological debates that have dominated metaphysics after Quine—not because the disputants are talking past each other or speaking nonsense, or because the questions have no answers, but rather because the questions can be answered so straightforwardly. I will close by arguing that while the approach may be the most important threat to serious metaphysics, it is also extremely promising as a way of dissolving mysteries and clarifying the epistemology of metaphysics.

1.1 Three Forms of Easy Ontology

The idea that certain ontological debates may be easily resolved by way of trivial inferences from uncontroversial truths is familiar from recent debates about numbers (Wright 1983, Hale 1988, Hale and Wright 2001, 2009) and about propositions (Schiffer 1994, 2003). But it is only recently that these diverse uses of trivial inferences have come to be seen as parts of a unified approach to ontological questions.[1] As it has come to be recognized as a general approach, interest in and sympathy for the idea that existence questions may be answered easily has slowly been growing. Even many serious metaphysicians including Kit Fine, Ross Cameron, and Jonathan Schaffer, have begun to accept that existence questions, asked in ordinary English, may be answered easily in much the way that the deflationist suggests, and that as a result metaphysics must turn its attention to other issues.[2]

The view has been developed in distinct ways by neo-Fregeans in philosophy of mathematics, by Schiffer in his discussions of various pleonastic entities, and by myself in defence of ordinary objects. In the philosophy of mathematics, neo-Fregeans have argued that the existence of numbers can be inferred from an uncontroversial truth that begins by making no use of the number concept, by simply making use of a conceptual truth (Hume's principle: The number of ns=the number of ms iff the ns and the ms are equinumerous). So, for example, we may argue as follows:

> Uncontroversial truth: The cups and the saucers are equinumerous
>
> Conceptual truth: The number of ns=the number of ms iff the ns and the ms are equinumerous
>
> Derived claim: The number of cups=the number of saucers

But since the derived claim is a true identity claim, they hold, we are entitled to conclude that the terms in it ('the number of cups' and 'the number of saucers') refer, and so that there are numbers. Thus we get a resolution to an ancient ontological problem by starting from an uncontroversial truth that does not make use of the disputed concept <number> or make reference to the disputed entities (numbers) at all.

The most important work in developing an easy route to answering a variety of existence questions has been undertaken by Schiffer (1994, 1996, 2003), who also broadens the target entities to which it is applied, including such entities as propositions, properties, events, states, and fictional characters. In Schiffer's terms, we can begin with an undisputed truth, and then engage in a pleonastic "something from nothing inference," to reach a truth that is intuitively redundant with respect to the first, yet leaves us with (apparently new) ontological commitments to the disputed entities.

In each case, an undisputed claim in which there is no mention of an entity of type J (and no use of the concept J or any supposed to be co-referential with it) may be combined with an analytic or conceptual truth that functions as what Schiffer calls a "transformation rule," to give us a derived claim that apparently entails the existence of Js (numbers, propositions, events, possible worlds...)—thus settling what seemed like serious disputed ontological questions easily by trivial inferences from undisputed truths. So for example (making the intervening steps somewhat more explicit than Schiffer (2003) does), we can move from:

- Undisputed claim: Snow is white.
- Conceptual truth: If P then <that P> is true.
- Derived claim: <That snow is white> is true.
- Ontological claim: There is a proposition (namely <that snow is white>).

Or from:

- Undisputed claim: Jane was born on a Tuesday.
- Conceptual truth: If P was born on D, then P's birth occurred on D.
- Derived claim: Jane's birth occurred on a Tuesday.
- Ontological claim: There is an event (namely of Jane's birth).

There is one important variation to point out here: while, in the above cases, the undisputed claim is an empirical truth, in other cases one may make the relevant inferences from a conceptual truth. So, for example, Schiffer argues that we may move from 'Necessarily, there are dogs or there are not dogs,' to 'Necessarily, there are things that have the property of being a dog or there are not things that have the property of being a dog,' and from there to 'Necessarily, the property of being a dog is or is not instantiated,' to 'Necessarily, the property of being a dog exists' (cf. Schiffer 2003: 66)—but in this case the inferences seem to rely on no empirical truth. The fact that one may come to legitimately infer the existence of certain entities regardless of the empirical facts in the world (relevant to whether such a sentence is true or false) suggests a reason such entities are often thought of as independent from the empirical world, along with a deflated way of understanding that intuition.

While the pleonastic and neo-Fregean views have much in common, there are also some notable differences between them. One perhaps superficial difference is that the neo-Fregeans employ an equivalence principle, Hume's Principle, in reaching their ontological conclusions, whereas Schiffer's pleonastic inferences take the form of $S \to \exists x(Fx)$,[3] only requiring one-way entailments from the uncontroversial premise to the derived claim. This makes it clear that we can formulate easy ontological arguments even where we do not have an equivalence principle available (as we might not in cases where the candidates for S may be diverse and not fully enumerable). Nonetheless, the neo-Fregean only makes use of the right-to-left direction of the equivalence principle ('If the ms and ns are equinumerous, then the number of ns=the number of ms') in reaching the ontological conclusion, so there seems no reason to think that the neo-Fregean relies on there being an equivalence principle rather than a simple one-way entailment in order to reach the ontological conclusion.

Secondly, the derived claim of the neo-Fregean has the form of an identity statement, and it is because it has the structure of an identity statement that Hale and Wright insist that the terms in it must refer, and thus that we are licensed to say that numbers exist (2009: 202). By contrast, Schiffer's derived claims do not have to take the form of an identity statement, and he makes no use of that idea in reaching the ontological conclusion that there are the disputed entities.[4] Instead, the introduced singular term may figure in other kinds of sentence in the derived claim, e.g. the singular propositional term '<that snow is white>' figures in the derived claim '<that snow is white> is true,' and the singular event term 'Jane's birth' appears in the true derived claim 'Jane's birth occurred on a Tuesday'—and both singular terms (as Schiffer insists) seem guaranteed to refer. Thus from these derived claims it seems we are still licensed to make the inferences to the ontological conclusions that there are propositions and that there are births. Given these differences, it seems that a Schifferian can easily accept the neo-Fregean's trivial inferences from 'the cups and saucers are equinumerous' to 'the number of cups=the number of saucers' to 'there is a number.' But it is not so clear whether or not a neo-Fregean would be equally happy to accept all of Schiffer's arguments to ontological conclusions—many of which don't go by way of a true identity statement. This hinges on whether they would be willing to accept existential entailments from derived claims that do not take the form of identity statements. They make use of the fact that theirs is an identity statement in arguing that we are licensed to infer that the terms in it refer, for they treat identity statements as paradigmatic reference-demanding statements (Hale and Wright 2009: 202). But of course this does not mean that they are the *only* sort of reference-demanding atomic statements. In any case, Schiffer's pleonastic approach can be seen as a generalization of the neo-Fregean approach in the sense that he can accept their arguments for the disputed entities and capture them in his terms, though it is not clear whether a neo-Fregean would accept all of Schiffer's arguments.

In much the same way, the easy approach to ontology I have developed and defended elsewhere may be seen as a third route to getting easy answers to ontological questions, which generalizes Schiffer's approach. First, it generalizes it by showing that it may even be applied to resolve debates about the existence of ordinary concrete objects.[5] The question 'Are there tables,' for example (I have argued (2007a)) may be straightforwardly answered by beginning from a claim that is not a point of controversy between realists and eliminativists—that there are particles arranged tablewise. The 'arranged tablewise' locution is supposed to help the eliminativist paraphrase talk putatively about tables, and so mimics the truth conditions for table-talk as closely as possible. Eliminativists understand 'arranged tablewise' roughly as follows: particles are arranged tablewise if they are arranged (in part by the work of an artisan or factory, etc. with the right sorts of intentions) in such a way that they are bonded together in a fashion that enables them to jointly perform the characteristic functions of tables, at a height to accommodate a seated person eating, and so on (see van Inwagen 1990, 105 and 109). With that much in place, we can make the following trivial inference:

- Uncontroversial claim: There are particles arranged tablewise.

But the following seems to be a conceptual truth:

- Conceptual truth: If there are particles arranged tablewise, then there is a table.

That is, where there is what eliminativists would call a situation in which particles are arranged tablewise, that seems sufficient to guarantee that the application conditions for the ordinary concept <table> are met. Thus we can, by trivial inferences, move to:

- Derived/ontological claim: There is a table.

In short, those who have mastered the ordinary concept of <table>, as well as the philosophical concept of <particles arranged tablewise> are entitled to make the inference from the undisputed truth 'there are particles arranged tablewise' to the ontological claim that there are tables.[6] In this way, ontological debates about the existence of ordinary concrete objects may be settled just as 'easily' as debates about disputed abstracta, events, etc.—by a generalization of the same method.

The form of easy approach that I have defended also broadens the applicability of the approach in another sense. While all three forms of easy ontology accept that at least some existence questions may be answered by making trivial inferences from uncontroversial truths, I allow that in some cases we do not even need to begin from an uncontroversial truth in order to easily answer an existence question. According to the deflationary approach to existence questions I have argued for elsewhere (2007a, 2008, 2014), it is a fundamental rule of use for the term 'refers' (as a monadic predicate) that a sortal concept <K> refers iff Ks exist. Sortal terms and concepts, I have argued, are associated with application conditions: a well-formed sortal term 'K' refers if the application conditions for <K> are fulfilled.[7] Application conditions are among the semantic rules of use for the terms we master, which enable competent speakers to evaluate actual and hypothetical situations as ones in which the associated concept <K> would or would not be properly applied. As a result, existence questions of the form 'Do Ks exist?' can be addressed by determining whether the application conditions for <K> are fulfilled.

With that much in place, we can see the trivial inferences used in making easy ontological arguments as cases in which, given the rules of use for the sortal concept in question, the application conditions for <K> are *guaranteed* to be fulfilled given the truth of some other sentence not involving <K> or any co-referring concept. We can see the conceptual truths made use of in the trivial arguments as articulations of rules of use for the introduced noun term ('number,' 'property,' 'event,'...) that guarantee that the application conditions for the introduced noun are fulfilled, provided that the uncontroversial claim is true. That is why the truth of the uncontroversial sentence licenses us to infer 'there is a K.' This enables us to see, in all of these cases, how competent speakers may make use of their conceptual mastery, often combined with empirical knowledge (whether knowledge arrived at by looking around the restaurant, by knowing that snow is white, that Jane was born on a Tuesday, or that the cups and saucers are equinumerous) to arrive easily at the conclusions that there are things of the relevant sort. In cases in which we can infer the existence of the relevant entities from a merely conceptual truth (and require no empirical truth), we may say that the application conditions for the new term are null; they are guaranteed to be fulfilled *simpliciter*. Or, if it seems awkward to even speak of these terms as having application conditions (given that they are guaranteed to refer), we can instead speak of these terms merely as having introduction rules rather than application conditions. (Terms such as 'property' and 'proposition' may have distinct meanings even if both have null application conditions, given differences in their inferential role—including differences in their introduction rules.) In the other cases, in which a term has substantive application conditions (not guaranteed to be fulfilled), we can say that the general introduction rule is expressed in the conceptual truth that guarantees the truth of the ontological claim *provided the application conditions are met* (where the latter, in turn, is guaranteed given the truth of the uncontroversial claim—which is not itself a conceptual truth).

This deflationary approach to existence questions then leaves us with two important results: first, we can gain a general view of why the inferences that seem so trivial are indeed valid—since the truth of the uncontroversial claim guarantees that the application conditions for the introduced noun term are fulfilled. Secondly, we can see that in some cases we may easily answer existence questions (by making use of empirical work and conceptual competence) even without making use of an uncontroversial truth to begin from in making a trivial inference. For example, while I have argued that ontological debates about the existence of tables may be resolved by trivial inferences from the uncontested truth that there are particles arranged tablewise, we need not have mastered the concept of <particles arranged tablewise> to make the inference and conclude that tables exist. Someone who lacks the concept of being <arranged tablewise> (or of <particle>) of course could not use the above uncontroversial claim to infer the existence of tables. But it seems that anyone who possesses the concept <table> is entitled, upon veridically perceiving my dining room, to conclude that tables exist—even if she does not begin from a separate uncontroversial truth in making an inference to that conclusion. On the generalized version of the view, we can accept that a competent speaker is no less entitled, using her conceptual competence, to infer 'there is a table' from veridically observing my dining room (and so observing that the application conditions for the concept are fulfilled) than she is to infer 'there is a property' from knowing the truth of an uncontroversial claim such as 'Beyoncé's dress is red.'

Generalizing the approach in this way enables us to see how existence questions may be easily answered (by employing conceptual competence) even in cases in which there is no 'uncontroversial truth' that we can state in terms omitting the concept K (or any co-referring concept) and from which we can make a trivial inference. This also brings other advantages. For if we require the truth of an uncontroversial claim as the basis for resolving the ontological dispute, then there is some hazard that more serious-minded metaphysicians will take the uncontroversial claim to be the only one which is 'really true' or which properly matches the 'logical structure of the world' and the like (this is a move that Hale and Wright reject in any case (2009)). But if we do not require that we start from an uncontroversial truth (stated in terms that don't involve the concept K (or any co-referring concept)), we do not foster any illusion that there is a more basic, more ontologically apt way of *describing* the situation that might encourage the thought that an ontological claim expressed using the newly introduced noun can be viewed as a mere manner of speaking or something other than a straightforward and literal truth.

Each of these three easy ontological positions thus relies on less in making easy ontological arguments than the view that came before it. While the classic neo-Fregean position makes use of a true identity statement in arguing that the terms refer, and so that there are the relevant entities, Schiffer does not require a true identity statement. But while he doesn't require that we begin from an *identity* statement, he does (like the neo-Fregean) start from an uncontroversial true statement (S) (not involving the disputed concept or a co-referential one) to use in the trivial inference that takes us to the ontological conclusion. By contrast, I do not even require that there is any true conceptually distinct statement in order to easily arrive at the disputed ontological conclusion making use just of our conceptual competence and (sometimes) empirical knowledge. Nonetheless, all may still be classified as 'easy' approaches insofar as they allow that we may answer certain ontological questions using trivial inferences from uncontroversial truths. Perhaps more importantly, all forms of the view hold that we need nothing more than conceptual work and (sometimes) empirical knowledge to resolve the questions of ontology to which they are applied—nothing 'epistemically metaphysical' is required.

1.2 First-Order Result: Simple Realism

Making use of the easy approach to ontology (in whatever form) leads directly to first-order consequences about what we say exists: typically, it leads to affirming the existence of the disputed entities. For in most of the hotly disputed cases, uncontested truths may lead us via pleonastic or trivial inferences to conclude that the controversial entities (numbers, propositions, properties, etc.) exist.

But it is often thought that if we can arrive at ontological conclusions via these trivial inferences, the objects we now say exist can't themselves be very substantial:

they must be somehow reduced in ontological standing, mere shadows of language, or else the existence claim itself must be reduced in standing from that of more serious existence claims. Schiffer himself often talks this way, speaking of the ontology that results—an ontology of what he calls "pleonastic" entities—as a kind of 'cheap' ontology (1994: 304), and suggests that the entities we become committed to are "ontologically shallow" (1994: 304), or "thin and inconsequential" (2003: 62). In acknowledging their existence, he writes, we are "merely playing along with the language games that introduce these notions"; their existence should be treated in a "suitably deflationary, or minimalist, manner" (1994: 305).[8] Propositions, for example, are mere "shadows of sentences" (1996: 153), and are said to be "not as ontologically and conceptually independent of us as rocks and electrons...there is a sense in which they're products of our linguistic or conceptual practices, a sense in which properties and propositions are mind- or language-created entities" (1996: 153). Hofweber paraphrases Schiffer's view as holding that these are "second-class entities, whose existence is guaranteed merely by talking a certain way" (2007: 5).

I have argued elsewhere (2001) against saying that the entities to which we become committed are in any sense mind- or language-created or dependent, and Schiffer himself, at the end of the day, seems to want to avoid commitment to this—he explicitly denies the conceptualist view that "properties are creations of our conceptual or linguistic practices," since properties exist in every possible world, whereas the same is not the case for our conceptual and linguistic practices (2003: 66).

But I also think there is more to be said here. Despite my admiration for Schiffer's work in showing how trivial inferences may lead us to ontological commitments, I think we should not suggest that the entities to which we become committed via trivial inferences are in general "thin and inconsequential," "ontologically shallow," or that their existence is somehow to be understood in a deflationary manner. Instead, we should simply say that such entities exist—full stop—and adopt a simple realist view of them. Let me explain.

Schiffer's claims that so-called pleonastic entities have a diminished ontological status seem to come from three observations:

1. Epistemology: such entities have a "diminished epistemological status" in that to learn of the existence of properties, propositions, or states, one need only be inducted into the language games involving these terms; whereas the same is not the case for cats, trees, or volcanoes (2003: 62).
2. Causality: pleonastic entities are said to be inconsequential in the sense that adding the relevant concepts to a prior theory merely "conservatively extends' that theory,"[9] and so "does nothing to alter that theory's take on the pre-existing causal order" (2003: 63).
3. Modality: the natures of pleonastic entities are determined by our linguistic and conceptual practices, in such a way that there is no more to their natures than is determined by our practices; they have no "hidden nature for empirical investigation to unearth" (2003: 66).

In each case, Schiffer writes as if there is an important difference between the "shallowness" of pleonastic entities to which we may become committed via such trivial inferences, and the "depth" of "more robust" natural entities like trees. In the epistemological case, he contrasts pleonastic and non-pleonastic entities on grounds that learning of the existence of physical entities such as electrons requires substantive discovery, while to learn of the existence of propositions, for example, it is necessary and sufficient simply to adopt the relevant language game that takes us from, e.g. 'The apple is red' to 'That the apple is red is true' (Schiffer 1994: 307).

But on my view the contrast here is misleading. For—depending on what uncontested truths we have to start from—we may be able to answer questions about the existence of trees no less easily than questions about the existence of events or properties. If we began in a metaphysical debate from the uncontested truth that certain particles were arranged treewise, we could go on to make use of our conceptual competence that entitles us to accept that if there are particles arranged treewise, there is a tree, and from there infer the existence of trees. The fact that we may come to know of the existence of certain things by undertaking trivial inferences does not show that the entities themselves are in any way epistemically diminished or ontologically shallow—or that there is some crucial difference between them and regular old concreta like trees. In each case one may move from knowledge of an uncontested truth that doesn't make any use of the new concept (or any concept supposed to be co-referential with it) to easily acquire knowledge of the existence of the new kind of entity.

Regarding causality, Schiffer again suggests that there is a contrast between concepts like <property> or <proposition>, and concepts like <wishdate>, or presumably like <person>, <volcano>, or <electron>. For the former are causally inconsequential—their addition conservatively extends a theory, but the latter are not. But again I think that this is, at the least, misleading. The question of whether a given concept is a conservative extension is a *relative* matter: relative to the prior theory accepted. Once we have a thing-language that enables us to say that the notebook is red, we may indeed conservatively extend it by adding the notion of a property; and in general, all that Schiffer says about the notions of property, proposition, etc. being conservative extensions of our language as considered without their introduction stand. But as I have argued, we can also use trivial inferences to acquire commitment to tables and trees, if we start (in a metaphysical dispute) from an undisputed claim such as 'there are particles arranged volcanowise'—because (to alter Schiffer 2003: 52) "to have the practice [of using the term 'volcano'] is to have the *concept* [<volcano>], and *it is a conceptual truth—*a truth knowable a priori via command of the concept*—that the existence of* **volcanoes** is guaranteed whenever there are particles arranged volcanowise." The concept of <volcano> would not conservatively extend a prior theory that had no grip on exploding lava-filled peaks, but it would conservatively extend a prior theory that made empirical claims couched in the language of particles being arranged volcanowise. And the same could be said for other concepts of concreta. This undermines the claimed contrast, and perhaps more importantly, provides a reminder that the fact that a term conservatively extends a prior theory does not show that the entities referred to by the term are 'inconsequential' in the sense of *lacking* causal powers: it doesn't show anything about the causal or ontological standing of the entities referred to. Instead, (as the original definition also has it) it only shows that the addition of the relevant concept is inconsequential to the theory's *standing empirical commitments*, whatever those may be.

The modal case requires a bit more discussion. Schiffer draws a similar contrast regarding the natures of the objects concerned: to learn about the natures of electrons or trees one must undertake substantive investigations into the things themselves. By contrast, he says, to learn all there is to know about the nature of propositions, properties, or other pleonastic entities one must only study the language games by means of which they are deposited in our ontology (Schiffer 1996: 159). Thus, pleonastic entities are said to have "no hidden and substantial nature for a theory to uncover" (Johnston 1988: 38); "there is nothing more to the natures of these things than these little language games determine" (Schiffer 1994: 305)—a point that is supposed to contrast them with more 'robust' physical or concrete entities (Johnston 1988: 38).

But as I have argued elsewhere (2007b) (but cannot separately argue for here), the point about the natures of entities being determined by our linguistic or conceptual practices is one that applies quite generally—not just to entities such as properties and propositions. In each case (as I have argued) talk of the *most basic* modal features determining the 'natures' of the entities to be referred is the object-language correlate of rules of use for the term, and the route to discovering these basic modal features goes via conceptual competence, not deep metaphysical investigation. Whether we are talking trees, persons, or propositions, the *most basic* modal facts (I have argued (2007b)) are object-language correlates of the rules of use for the term and can be known by competent speakers capable of making use of their conceptual competence and reasoning.

It seems then in general that there are no across-the-board differences to be drawn between entities the existence of which we may infer by undertaking trivial inferences from an uncontroversial truth and those we cannot. Whether we may infer the existence of a given sort of entity K via trivial inferences depends to a great extent on what language or theory, and what uncontested truths stated in that language, we have from which we may make the relevant inference. So, for example, it is true enough that <tree> and <table> are not pleonastic concepts in our actual (non-philosophical) English language, and if we do not have terminology such as 'particles arranged tablewise' we may (depending on what other terms or concepts we have) not be able to trivially infer that tables exist from any uncontested truth stateable in that language without the concept <table>. If we add the terminology of n-wise arrangements, however, we may make the trivial inference. But whether we have such terms as 'particles arranged tablewise' in our language cannot make a difference to what ontological standing *tables themselves* have—to whether tables are in any sense 'shallow' entities or not. So we should not be looking for a difference in ontological standing of *entities* that we can versus cannot (or do versus do not) become committed to by trivial inferences. We may be able to distinguish which concepts are pleonastic additions to a given language, and which are not, but there seems to be no absolute answer to whether or not the entities referred to by a given concept are pleonastic.

None of this is to deny that there may be important epistemic, modal, and causal differences between, say, trees and propositions—indeed Schiffer may have put his finger on some crucial differences between entities of these sorts. But the difference to be drawn is not one in ontological 'shallowness' versus 'depth' of those entities we may/may not infer the existence of through trivial inferences. Instead, the significant contrast seems to be between entities the existence of which we may infer given the truth of an undisputed *empirical truth*, and entities the existence of which we may infer from a *conceptual truth*.[10] For in the first case, it does require some empirical work to discover the existence of the relevant entities: we must know that some uncontroversial empirical claim that can be fed into the rule is *true* to know that the entities exist (e.g. we must know that some particles are arranged volcanowise to infer the existence of volcanoes). In the latter case, by contrast, no empirical work is required (we may infer that the proposition <that snow is white> exists, regardless of whether or not snow is white).

Regarding causation, we may again suspect that where the existence of the questioned entities must be inferred from an *empirical* truth, the entities may have causal impact; but where it may be inferred from a mere conceptual truth, they do not. Event concepts such as <heart attack> are supposed to be pleonastic concepts: we may infer the existence of heart attacks from an empirical truth as follows: from 'Smith's heart stopped beating' we are licensed to infer 'Smith had a heart attack' and so that there are events (namely of heart attacks). But while <heart attack> may conservatively extend a prior theory that only made reference to hearts and their beating, we should not conclude that heart attacks lack causal efficacy or are causally inconsequential in any other sense. Nonetheless, pure abstracta such as propositions and numbers may plausibly be thought to lack causal efficacy altogether. But even if entities such as numbers, properties, and propositions, the existence of which we may infer from a conceptual truth, entirely lack causal impact, we cannot assume that the same holds true of those entities the existence of which we infer trivially from an empirical truth.

We can find a similar contrast where modal features are concerned. If we must begin from an empirical truth to make the relevant inference to the existence of the new entities, then while the most *basic* modal features of the entities to be referred to are object-language correlates of the rules of use for the relevant terms, talk of their natures may also be deferential to the world in ways that enable us to fill in the details of more particular modal properties via empirical investigation. So, for example, it may be knowable simply to anyone competent in use of the term 'paper' that a piece of paper cannot survive being burned to ashes, but we may go on to discover exactly what temperatures lead paper to burn, and thus lead to its destruction—thereby learning more about the 'nature' of paper. There doesn't seem to be any comparable role for empirical work in learning about the natures of those entities whose existence we may infer from a conceptual truth. As a result, there may indeed be less to learn about the natures of propositions and properties than about the natures of volcanoes, trees, or tigers; and what is learned in the first case may be learned by purely conceptual means, whereas in the latter case empirical work is also involved.

I have argued that we should not attribute a difference in the ontological standing to entities on the basis of whether or not we (may) become committed to them via trivial inferences. Whatever differences do arise between particular cases (say, those of trees versus propositions) are better attributed to differences between those cases in which one requires an empirical truth versus merely a conceptual truth to infer their existence. But in any case we should deny that the entities we are committed to (by either of those sorts of inference) are ontologically deflated or exist in some second-class way. The conceptual truths that underwrite the trivial inferences should be seen as articulations of rules of use for the concept in question.[11] We may think of them as if they were rules to introduce the new concept to a language that began without any co-referring concept (though of course that is merely as-if, and not to make actual claims about etymology. As Schiffer says, it is *as though* someone introduced the relevant notions in part by giving us these something-from-nothing transformations (1994: 306)).

If we take seriously the idea that the conceptual truths that enable us to make the trivial something-from-nothing inferences are object-language articulations of rules of use for the sortal term 'N' used in the conclusion, then we should not say anything less than that Ns exist (in the only sense that 'N' has) in the conclusion. As long as the terms <property> or <number> are being used in their standard sense, we may easily answer the existence question in the affirmative—and simply say that these things exist, full stop. But then we end up in each case being realists about the questioned entities by affirming that there are properties, propositions, numbers, etc. not in some reduced or quasi-sense, but rather *in the only sense these terms have*. This is thus a straightforward, out and out, realism about the entities in question. And so, properly understood, the view should be characterized not as the position that the *entities* accepted are deflated or have some 'second-class' status. What is deflated instead is the *ontological debates* about the entities (more on that in section 1.3 below). Thus, to be clear, I call the first-order position that results from the easy approach 'simple realism,' and the meta-ontological position that results 'deflationism.'[12]

I have argued above that we should retain pleonastic arguments for the existence of disputed entities, but give up the idea that they exist in some reduced, deflated, or quasi- sense, affirming instead a simple realism about each of the entities in question. If we go that route, what do we give up? Some might be attracted to the idea that these disputed entities are 'shallow' or exist in only some 'deflated' sense because they think that will sit more easily with a naturalistic ontology. But that does not seem to be Schiffer's own motivation—his motives instead come from concerns within the theory of meaning, particularly the need for a theory of propositions that would treat them as unstructured and fine-grained, and knowable a priori through conceptual means. We lose none of this, however, by giving up the rhetoric of treating them as entities with a second-rate, 'deflated' ontological status or sort of existence.

For example, Schiffer uses the pleonastic conception to defend the idea that we can avoid treating propositions as compositionally determined. For the practices determine all there is to know about the natures of propositions, and the "practices determinative of their nature determine, in the trivial way sketched, that our sentences express propositions, but they do not determine, and are consistent with its not being the case, that those propositions are compositionally determined" (1994, 308).[13] That motive, however, is not at all undermined by the amendments suggested below. For although on this view we should simply say that propositions exist (full stop—not that they exist in some deflated sense), it remains the case that all there is to their natures is determined by our linguistic and conceptual practices. If, as Schiffer argues and as seems plausible, these practices leave open the issue of whether propositions are compositionally determined, then we may retain the suggested solution to the paradox of meaning, and similarly retain the other benefits sought by treating propositions as pleonastic entities.

But if we do allow that the easy approach to ontology typically leads to a simple realism about the disputed entities, not to a view on which these things are some sort of second-class entities or exist in some sort of deflated sense, another question arises. How does the simple realist view that results really differ from traditional Platonist views, if both accept that the disputed entities exist?

While the realism we typically get about entities such as properties, propositions, artefacts, organisms, and the like resembles traditional realism on the surface, there is also a sense in which the form of realism that results from our trivial arguments differs importantly from standard realisms, such as Platonism regarding numbers or properties. The sort of realism the easy approach leaves us with says there are the disputed objects alright, but does not treat them as 'posits' or as 'explanatory' of our talk, the truth of our sentences, our knowledge, or anything of the sort. To mark the difference I will call the first 'simple realism' and the second 'explanatory' or 'heavyweight' realism.

The motivations for realisms vary, but especially among those post-Quinean metaphysicians who see themselves as building a best 'theory,' the motivations typically include the claim that 'positing' the relevant entities provides some 'explanatory' benefit.[14] The Platonist, for example, invokes numbers to help us explain our number talk, its objectivity, its usefulness in science, and the like. The heavyweight realist about properties holds that the existence of properties may 'explain' what it is that two things may have in common, and so on. But while the simple realist accepts that there are such entities, she denies that these are deep explanatory ontological posits; instead, the existence of the entities in question is a trivial consequence of the truth of other (uncontroversial) sentences.

Not only does the simple realist not need to appeal to explanatory power or the like to justify her acceptance of the relevant entities, she *cannot* do so. Any attempt to do so would yield only a dormitive virtue explanation. Consider the classic dormitive virtue explanation from Moliere: Q: 'Why do poppies make us sleepy?' A: 'Because they have the dormitive virtue.' Now, if saying that something has the dormitive virtue is just a fancy way of saying they make us sleepy, it may be perfectly true to say that poppies have the dormitive virtue. The joke lies in the fact, however, that if A is just a fancier way of restating the fact that poppies *do* make us sleepy and so is redundant, it clearly cannot (as it purports to do) provide any *explanation* of the fact that poppies make us sleepy—it just restates it in different terms. Put more precisely, and cohesively with the prior observations, if an existence claim is derived by trivial inferences from an uncontroversial claim, it cannot contribute any *more* explanatory power than we got from the uncontroversial claim itself. So either 'poppies make us sleepy' or 'poppies have the dormitive virtue' may explain other facts—such as 'Why did Dorothy fall asleep after walking through that field?' And similarly, either 'Particles arranged baseballwise hit the window' or 'A baseball hit the window' may explain why the window shattered. But in neither case do we gain explanatory power by shifting from the first expression to the second (which contains a new noun term)—so 'positing' a referent for the noun term can't be thought to contribute any explanatory power.

So similarly, on the simple realist's view (as contrasted with the explanatory realist's view), we can move from 'The house is red' to 'There is a property, redness, that the house has.' But we cannot use the latter to *explain* why the house is red—it is just a redundant way of restating the former (introducing a new noun term for a property). So on the simple realist view, there are the disputed entities all right, but these are not 'posits' that are parts of 'theories,' the inclusion of which is justified by their explanatory power. Instead, we can simply see that there are guaranteed to be such things given the truth of an uncontroversial sentence.[15]

A further consequence is that the easy ontologist cannot embrace any kind of truthmaker theory according to which we posit a certain ontology (as opposed to rival ontologies) in order to *explain* what it is that makes our sentences true. On the deflationary approach, neither properties and numbers nor trees or electrons can be thought of as ontological 'posits' used to 'explain' what makes a sentence like 'the house is red,' 'there is a tree in the courtyard,' or 'an electron was emitted' true. This is of course not to deny the equivalence: that 'there is a tree in the courtyard' is true iff there is a tree in the courtyard; it is only to deny that it is *explanatory*. Nor is to deny that other sorts of explanation involving appeal to trees or electrons are perfectly legitimate, e.g. we may explain why there are leaves all over the courtyard by saying that there is a tree there suffering from a disease; we may explain why an atom changed its charge by saying that it emitted an electron. And the rejection of a certain kind of heavyweight truthmaker theory, of course, is not to deny that the world makes our sentences true or false all right—and were it different the sentence would be false. The point is merely that we should not think of claims in philosophical ontology as theoretical posits to explain the truth of our sentences: philosophical ontology, on this view, is not theoretical in any sense that involves *explanation*.

The view above may also be seen as distinct from typical Platonist views of *abstract entities* in another sense: the heavyweight Platonist thinks of numbers or properties as discoverable entities that may have discoverable modal properties (Schiffer 2003: 65). But on the above view, this is also mistaken, for talk of the modal properties of these entities (the existence of which we may infer from a conceptual truth) is seen as just an object-language reflection of the rules of use for the term, and there is (as Schiffer insists) no more to discover about the natures of numbers, properties, and other entities whose existence we may infer from conceptual truths than may be acquired through analysing our linguistic and conceptual practices.

1.3 Second-Order Result: Meta-Ontological Deflationism

The easy approach to existence questions not only leads to a first-order simple realism about most disputed entities; easy ontological approaches of any kind also lead to the controversial meta-ontological position that something is wrong with many of the *serious* ontological debates that have been earnestly engaged in over the past fifty years or so.

As mentioned at the outset, serious ontology assumes that there are existence questions that are 'epistemically metaphysical' in the sense of being neither resolvable by conceptual/linguistic nor straightforward empirical means, and that must be approached through substantive metaphysical debate. The biggest threat to serious ontology has long been thought to lie in the idea (popularized by Hilary Putnam (1987) and Eli Hirsch (2002)) that the quantifier does, or could, vary in meaning in such a way that the disputants in debates about what exists are merely speaking past each other—rendering the apparent debate a merely verbal dispute.

But the easy approach to ontology gives us a view on which something is wrong with ontological debates—one on which "there are no questions that are fit to debate in the manner of the ontologists" (Sider 2009: 386), but which does not say that disputants are talking past each other, each uttering truths in their own language, or engaging in "different—and equally good—ways to talk" (Sider 2009: 386). For although given the easy approach the disputed existence questions are meaningful and answerable (generally in the positive), they turn out to be answerable so trivially that the 'serious' debates about these issues that have so exercised metaphysicians in recent decades seem misguided and pointless. Thus the easy approach to ontology presents a threat to serious metaphysics that is quite distinct from the threat presented by quantifier variance. While serious metaphysicians have focused on defending their work by attacking quantifier variance (van Inwagen 1998, 2009; Sider 2009), those arguments do nothing to defend serious metaphysics against the idea that ontological questions may be answered easily.

Given the threat that the easy approach presents to ongoing debates in ontology, it is no surprise that it has been subjected to a great many objections. Unfortunately, there is not space here to respond to the objections, but it may be useful to mention briefly where the main objections—and responses to them—may be found. Some hold that such views involve commitment to 'too many objects' or magically defining things into existence.[16] Worries have also been raised that the trivial inferences used are in 'bad company' with other inferences that lead to obvious problems, such as conflict with known facts or contradiction.[17] Others raise suspicions against the idea that there are the conceptual truths needed to underwrite the trivial inferences.[18] Still others hold that the inferences do not give us serious ontological conclusions because either they are to be read as implicitly in the context of a pretense operator[19] or because they involve a distinct use of the quantifier from one that is genuinely ontologically committing.[20]

1.4 Clarifying the Epistemology of Metaphysics

Although the easy approach to ontology may be felt as a threat by serious ontologists and faces a number of challenges, working to show how it may overcome those challenges is well worth the effort. For the approach also brings great attractions that can be best seen by those without commitment to the debates of serious metaphysics. Most crucially, it shows great promise for resolving various epistemic mysteries.

One epistemic attraction that has been much discussed by neo-Fregeans is the ability to demystify our knowledge of numbers and other abstracta. As Hale and Wright put it, the view is motivated by its ability to "tackle directly the question how propositional thought about such objects is possible and how it can be knowledgeable" (2009: 178). For given the trivial inferences that take us to claims about abstracta, we can see how speakers may acquire knowledge of these things by knowing the uncontroversial truths and mastering the rules of use for the terms that entitle them to make inferences from those uncontroversial truths to the existence of numbers and the like. We can thus avoid the epistemic problems the traditional Platonist faces in saying how we can 'come into contact with' and thereby come to acquire knowledge of abstracta. The view also enables us to accept that there are the relevant entities without the ontological difficulties incurred by Platonists who treat them as explanatory posits (see also my 2007a (especially Chapters 9 and 10) and 2009b).

Even more important is its ability to clarify the epistemology of ontology itself. For serious metaphysics faces an epistemic crisis. The debates undertaken and positions defended in serious ontology have proliferated at an alarming rate, with nothing like convergence on the truth to show for the efforts of the best minds in metaphysics, nor even any agreement about how such debates could be resolved. The serious metaphysician insists that ontological questions cannot be directly resolved empirically, and however apparently counter-intuitive their position is, serious ontologists typically emphasize that their ontology does not conflict with any empirical facts or observations. But the disputants also insist that ontological questions cannot be answered by linguistic or conceptual means—that is what is supposed to make the questions serious metaphysical questions. Thus serious ontology leaves us with a mystery about how we could possibly come to know who was right in these ontological debates, or what the answers to our existence questions are. Some metaphysicians seem little concerned with this. So, for example, Sider writes:

The epistemology of metaphysics is far from clear; this any metaphysician should concede. For what it's worth, as a general epistemology of metaphysics I prefer the vague, vaguely Quinean, thought that metaphysics is continuous with science. We employ many of the same criteria—whatever those are—for theory choice within metaphysics that we employ outside of metaphysics. Admittedly, those criteria give less clear guidance in metaphysics than elsewhere; but there is no harm in following this argument where it leads: metaphysical inquiry is by its nature comparatively speculative and uncertain. (2011: 12)

But this response may be too blithe: Unlike in the case of most scientific theories, most metaphysical theories are empirically equivalent. Moreover, differing ontological theories often involve simply trading one theoretical virtue for another, and so cannot be resolved by appealing to whichever theory has the most theoretic virtues. The difficulties here are formidable indeed, and have led to increasing debates at the meta-ontological level about whether these first-order disputes are merely verbal, somehow ill-formed or unresolvable.

The easy approach to ontology enables us to lay to rest seemingly endless debates about the existence of entities of various sorts, and to clarify the methodology of metaphysics (at least that part of it that is concerned with existence questions). For we are able to answer existence questions in ways that cohere with what we want to say in the ordinary business of life, but in answering them we need to rely on nothing more mysterious than straightforward empirical and conceptual methods. Wherever the easy approach to existence questions may be applied, we have room to defend the view that those existence questions that are meaningfully asked may be answered straightforwardly by conceptual and (often) empirical work, involving nothing 'epistemically metaphysical' nor any distinctively *philosophical* enterprise of figuring out *what (really) exists*. Empirical work may be needed to know the answer to the undisputed truth, but that is non-mysterious, and in any case it is usually not very fancy empirical work. (It may be as simple as seeing that the shirt is red.) In other cases (where the inference may be made from a conceptual truth) we needn't even undertake empirical work, but only exploit our conceptual competence and reasoning ability to come to know the ontological truth.

So while the easy approach may be a threat to serious metaphysics, it is extremely promising as a way of resolving the epistemic difficulties of metaphysics: it is a view that retains the "epistemic high-ground" (in the words of Sider) over the more mysterious epistemology of serious metaphysics.[21] Thus the impact of the easy approach to ontology pioneered by Schiffer has impact far broader than in the theory of meaning: it may not only easily resolve a great many first-order ontological debates; it also may present the biggest threat to serious ontology, and the greatest hope for clarifying the epistemology of metaphysics.[22]

Notes

1. For a characterization and defense of the general approach see Schiffer (2003) and my (2007a, 2009a, 2009b). The approach is also given a general characterization and criticized in Yablo (2001, 2005) and Hofweber (2005a, 2007).
2. Kit Fine accepts that many existence questions may be trivially answered, for example: "Thus given the evident fact that there is a prime number greater than 2, it trivially follows that there is a number" (2009: 158), and says that "the question of whether there are numbers is a mathematical question...that is to be settled on the basis of purely mathematical considerations and the question of whether there are chairs or tables is an everyday matter that is to be settled on the basis of common observation" (2009: 158). Fine concludes that the Quinean quantificational approach to ontology is ill-conceived, and that the primary question for ontology should not be 'what exists' or 'what is there' but rather 'how do things stand in reality' (2009: 172). Ross Cameron (2010) accepts that a sentence like 'tables exist' may be made true, for example, by simples properly arranged. But he suggests that metaphysicians may address a deeper question: what is there *really*, where what *really* exists is only whatever entities serve to ground the truth of our English sentences (2010). Finally, Jonathan Schaffer (2009) endorses easy ontological arguments, accepting that debates about the existence of numbers, properties, mereological sums, and the like "are *trivial*, in that the *entities in question obviously do exist*" (2009: 357). He argues that the proper questions for metaphysics are instead 'what is fundamental?' and 'what grounds what?' I will not examine these alternative suggestions here.
3. More fully and properly, Schiffer says that $S \rightarrow \exists x(Fx)$ is a something from nothing f-entailment claim iff "(i) its antecedent is metaphysically possible but doesn't *logically* entail either its consequent or any statement of the form '$\exists x(x=a)$,' where 'a' refers to an F, and (ii) the concept of an F is such that if there are Fs, then $S > \exists x(Fx)$" (2003: 56-7).
4. Schiffer also makes it explicit that pleonastic concepts for Fs may be introduced without there being any non-trivial criterion of identity for Fs. (2003: 63, *n*.14)
5. Hale (1988: 11) notes that the argument form is general and that the procedure may apply to concrete as well as abstract objects, but does not elaborate or go on to apply the approach to concreta.

6. Importantly, tables are not *identified with* particles arranged tablewise—so we do not have a co-referential concept in the undisputed truth. Particles arranged tablewise cannot be identified with tables: first, it seems inappropriate to identify a plurality with an individual; second, even if we shifted to a collection of particles arranged tablewise, these would have different identity conditions from tables.
7. The constraints on well-formedness include, for example, the requirement that the term also be associated with co-application conditions that do not lead to contradiction.
8. This way of speaking has also led some to think that the ontological commitments we get out of the trivial inferences are in some sense merely fictional or pretenseful (as we 'play along with' the relevant language game) (Yablo 2001, 2005). I have argued elsewhere (2013b) that this is a mistake.
9. Where, roughly, a theory T′ conservatively extends a theory T if T′ doesn't have any consequences that would be stateable in the vocabulary of T that aren't already logically entailed by T (see Schiffer 2003: 54–61 for discussion and refinements).
10. In terminology I used earlier (2001), the difference is between those concepts that are *relatively* minimal versus *absolutely* minimal.
11. Carnap similarly emphasizes that it is the rules that introduce the concept or term <property> or <number> that license us to make the trivial inferences to the ontological conclusion (1950: 208–10). Schiffer himself makes a similar point, arguing that we can get knowledge of things like properties that exist independently of a linguistic or conceptual practice merely by engaging in that practice, "Because to engage in the practice is to have the concept of a property, and to have the concept of a property is to know a priori the conceptual truths that devolve from that concept" (2003: 62). Neo-Fregeans similarly take equivalence principles such as Hume's Principle to function as implicit definitions of the introduced sortal concept (Hale and Wright 2009: 179). I have argued elsewhere (2016) that the easy approach is the natural heir to Carnap's treatment of internal existence questions (the only sort of existence questions he held to be sensible theoretical questions).
12. That is not to say, however, that the easy approach to existence questions leaves us accepting the existence of purported objects of absolutely any kind, including such (putative) things as phlogiston and witches. See Schiffer (1996: 152) and my (2009b).
13. And by avoiding the view that propositions are compositionally determined, we may hope to resolve the paradox of meaning that arises from accepting:

    1. That-clauses refer to propositions
    2. The reference of a that-clause is determined by its syntax and the references its words have in it
    3. There is no tenable account of the compositional determination of that-clause reference consistent with (1) and (2) (1994: 279)

    For we may reject the commitment to compositionality expressed in (2).
14. Even I talked this way sometimes in *Fiction and Metaphysics* (1999). I hadn't yet become reflective about meta-ontology, and so was participating in the dominant game. I take it all back.
15. This of course is not to deny that talk of propositions may *figure in* causal explanations— or even that the ability to engage in proposition talk may be crucially important in explaining our behavior or knowledge by testimony (see Schiffer 2003, Chapter 8). But the role of propositions in explanations of behavior may, as Schiffer suggests, be like the role of numbers in scientific explanations (2003: 334). We may say that Sally went to the mall because she thought her friends would be there, or that the bridge collapsed because the maximum number of tons it could hold was 250. But in neither case does 'positing' the existence of propositions or numbers 'explain' the observed fact in the way that positing

the presence of mice in my attic would explain the holes chewed in my camping gear (assuming one did not already posit particles arranged mousewise!). The use instead may, as McCracken (2009, Chapter 4) argues, be a pragmatic usefulness of proposition-talk or number-talk in our explanations.

16. See Yablo (2000), Bennett (2009). For responses see my (2007a, Chapter 3), (2009b), and (2015, Chapter 6).
17. Linnebo (2009a) gives a good overview. Versions of the bad company objection are raised by Field (1984) and Eklund (2006). For replies see Hale and Wright (2001), Schiffer (2003), Linnebo (2009b), and my (2015, Chapter 8).
18. The most influential criticisms of the idea that there are analytic or conceptual truths are found in Quine (1951/1953) and in Williamson (2007). For replies to Quine see Strawson and Grice (1956) and my (2007a, Chapter 2). For replies to Williamson see my (2015, Chapter 7).
19. See Yablo (2001, 2005); for response see my (2013b).
20. See Hofweber (2005a, 2005b, 2007); for response see my (2015, Chapter 9) and (2015, Chapter 5).
21. Sider (2011) argues that although the easy ontologist aims for the epistemic high ground, she cannot retain it, for she too is committed to a serious ontological position: that the world lacks a certain kind of structure. I respond to this line of argument in my (2015, Chapter 10).
22. My thanks go to Nurbay Irmak for his help with editing and preparing this manuscript. Thanks also to Gary Ostertag for helpful comments on an earlier draft.

Bibliography

Bennett, K. (2009). "Composition, Colocation, and Metaontology." In Chalmers et al.
Cameron, R. (2010). "Quantification, Naturalness and Ontology." In *New Waves in Metaphysics*, edited by A. Hazlett, New York: Palgrave-Macmillan.
Carnap, R. (1950). "Empiricism, Semantics, and Ontology." Reprinted in *Meaning and Necessity*, Second edition. Chicago: University of Chicago Press, 1956.
Chalmers, D. J., D. Manley, and R. Wasserman (eds.) (2009). *Metametaphysics: New Essays on the Foundations of Ontology*. Oxford: Oxford University Press.
Eklund, M. (2006). "Neo-Fregean Ontology." *Philosophical Perspectives* 20: 95–121.
Field, H. (1984). "Critical Notice of Wright's *Frege's Conception of Numbers as Objects*." *Canadian Journal of Philosophy* 14: 637–62.
Fine, K. (2009). "The Question of Ontology." In Chalmers et al.
Hale, B. (1988). *Abstract Objects*. Oxford: Blackwell.
Hale, B. and C. Wright (2001). *The Reason's Proper Study: Essays towards a Neo-Fregean Philosophy of Mathematics*. Oxford: Clarendon Press.
Hale, B. and C. Wright (2009). "The Metaontology of Abstraction." In Chalmers et al.
Hirsch, E. (2002). "Quantifier Variance and Realism." In *Realism and Relativism. Philosophical Issues* 12, edited by E. Sosa and E. Villanueva, Oxford: Blackwell: 51–73.
Hofweber, T. (2005a). "A Puzzle about Ontology." *Noûs* 39: 256–83.
Hofweber, T. (2005b). "Number Determiners, Numbers, and Arithmetic." *Philosophical Review* 114: 179–225.
Hofweber, T. (2007). "Innocent Statements and their Metaphysically Loaded Counterparts." *Philosophers' Imprint* 7: 1–33.
Johnston, M. (1988). "The End of the Theory of Meaning." *Mind and Language* 3: 28–63.
Linnebo, O. (2009a). "Introduction." *Synthese* 170: 321–9.

Linnebo, O. (2009b). "Bad Company Tamed." *Synthese* 170: 371–91.
McCracken, M. (2009). *Prospects for a Deflationary Account of the Ontology of Propositions.* Doctoral Dissertation, Open Access Dissertations. Paper 368.
Putnam, H. (1987). *The Many Faces of Realism.* La Salle, IL: Open Court.
Quine, W. V. O. (1951/1953). "Two Dogmas of Empiricism." In *From a Logical Point of View.* Cambridge: Harvard University Press.
Schaffer, J. (2009). "On What Grounds What." In Chalmers et al.
Schiffer, S. (1994). "A Paradox of Meaning." *Noûs* 28: 279–324.
Schiffer, S. (1996). "Language-Created Language-Independent Entities." *Philosophical Topics* 24: 149–67.
Schiffer, S. (2003). *The Things We Mean.* Oxford: Clarendon Press.
Sider, T. (2009). "Ontological Realism." In Chalmers et al.
Sider, T. (2011). *Writing the Book of the World.* Oxford: Oxford University Press.
Strawson, P. F. and H. P. Grice (1956). "In Defense of a Dogma." *Philosophical Review* 65 (2): 141–58.
Thomasson, A. (1999). *Fiction and Metaphysics.* Cambridge: Cambridge University Press.
Thomasson, A. (2001). "Ontological Minimalism." *American Philosophical Quarterly* 38: 319–31.
Thomasson, A. (2007a). *Ordinary Objects.* New York: Oxford University Press.
Thomasson, A. (2007b). "Modal Normativism and the Methods of Metaphysics." *Philosophical Topics* 35: 135–60.
Thomasson, A. (2008). "Existence Questions." *Philosophical Studies* 141: 63–78.
Thomasson, A. (2009a). "Answerable and Unanswerable Questions." In Chalmers et al.
Thomasson, A. (2009b). "The Easy Approach to Ontology." *Axiomathes* 19: 1–15.
Thomasson, A. (2013a). "The Easy Approach to Ontology: A Defense." In *Philosophical Methods,* edited by M. Haug, London: Routledge.
Thomasson, A. (2013b). "Fictionalism versus Deflationism." *Mind* 122: 1023–51.
Thomasson, A. (2014). "Deflationism in Semantics and Metaphysics." In *Metasemantics,* edited by A. Burgess and B. Sherman, Oxford: Oxford University Press.
Thomasson, A. (2015). *Ontology Made Easy.* New York: Oxford Universiry Press.
Thomasson, A. (2016). "Carnap and the Prospects for Easy Ontology." In *Ontology after Carnap,* edited by S. Blatti and S. LaPointe, Oxford: Oxford University Press.
Van Inwagen, P. (1990). *Material Beings.* Ithaca, New York: Cornell University Press.
Van Inwagen, P. (1998). "Metaontology." *Erkenntnis* 48: 233–50.
Van Inwagen, P. (2009). "Being, Existence and Ontological Commitment." In Chalmers et al.
Williamson, T. (2007). *The Philosophy of Philosophy.* Oxford: Blackwell.
Wright, C. (1983). *Frege's Conception of Numbers as Objects.* Aberdeen: Aberdeen University Press.
Yablo, S. (2000). "A Priority and Existence." In *New Essays on the A Priori,* edited by P. Boghossian and C. Peacocke, Oxford: Oxford University Press.
Yablo, S. (2001). "Go Figure: A Path through Fictionalism." *Midwest Studies in Philosophy* 25: 72–102.
Yablo, S. (2005). "The Myth of the Seven." In *Fictionalism in Metaphysics,* edited by M. E. Kalderon, Oxford: Oxford University Press.

2
From *Remnants* to *Things,* and Back Again

Thomas Hofweber

2.1 Introduction

When I was a student in Germany in the early nineties I had the good fortune to come across a copy of Stephen Schiffer's book *Remnants of Meaning*. While the spirit in the local philosophy department was that it would be premature to read anything published after 1950 unless one first had a good understanding of the differences between Wittgenstein's early, middle, and late periods, Schiffer's book provided a very refreshing and accessible fast-track to the contemporary debates in the philosophy of language, and a vivid portrayal of what it is like to struggle with these issues. I learned a tremendous amount from studying this book.

But besides all that, *Remnants of Meaning* seemed to me then, and still seems to me now, to contain a deep and important insight, one that is widely neglected and underappreciated to this day. It is the insight that that-clauses are first and foremost clauses, not referring expressions, and thus they do not refer to propositions or anything else. This insight has profound consequences in a number of areas in philosophy, and spelling out how to understand it involves a number of subtle philosophical issues that lead away from what is agreed upon among many philosophers of language these days. But this insight is so widely neglected that, I'm afraid, even Schiffer himself started to neglect it. When I had a chance to meet Schiffer in person a year or so after studying his book, I was surprised to find out that he had already changed his mind, in particular about what seemed to me to be the deep insight. He now held that that-clauses do refer to propositions after all, but propositions are a kind of second-class entity. This new view is developed in his recent book *The Things We Mean*. As a view about that-clauses and propositions it is a big change from *Remnants of Meaning*, or *Remnants* from now on. To me it was never really clear what made Schiffer change his mind. The official reasons he gives in *The Things We Mean*, or *Things* for short, don't strike me as very good reasons. Not that there weren't plenty of problems with his view in *Remnants*, but it wasn't them that got Schiffer to switch sides.

In the following I would like to look at one important aspect of Schiffer's views in *Remnants* and in *Things*, and what Schiffer's official reasons are for his change of mind. I will argue that those reasons aren't very good, but that there are a number of problems with his view in *Remnants* as well as with his view in *Things*. In fact, some of the problems are the same. I will argue, however, that the problems from *Remnants* have a solution, and I will outline what I take the solution to be. Here I take the liberty to refer to some of my own papers where these ideas have been developed. We can avoid the problems from *Remnants*, but the problems with *Things* are more serious.*

2.2 From Remnants to Things

When Schiffer changed his mind between writing *Remnants* and *Things*, it wasn't his first time. He also changed his mind between writing his first book *Meaning* and his second book, *Remnants*. But that time Schiffer gave a detailed criticism of the view of his earlier book in his new book. A whole chapter in *Remnants* is devoted to the failures of the research program he used to subscribe to, and the book in general is set up as a refutation of his earlier views. But in *Things* Schiffer spends only about two and a half pages (pp. 89–92) explaining why he changed his mind. While I find the criticism of his first book in his second convincing, I can't say the same for the criticism of his second book in his third. We will have to have a closer look at what happened.

Both *Remnants* and *Things* are complex books covering many different topics. And both contain a variety of theories that are not of central concern for us here. As far as I can see, most of these theories are independent of whether one holds a view of that-clauses and propositions as in *Remnants* or as in *Things*. We will focus on where these two books differ most directly: the question whether that-clauses refer to propositions, and whether there are such things as propositions or meanings. To do this, let me first outline Schiffer's view on the matter in *Remnants*, then his new view about this in *Things*, and finally, what his official reason for the change is.

2.2.1 Remnants

Schiffer's view in *Remnants* is basically the following: there is no way to accommodate belief ascriptions in a compositional semantic theory. To do so would require treating them relationally, as a relation between a believer and what they believe. The second relatum would have to be what a that-clause refers to, and that reference would have to be compositionally determined by the relevant expressions that occur in the that-clause. But after looking at the available options, Schiffer concludes that this can't be done. Thus natural languages don't have compositional semantic theories after all, he concludes, and that-clauses don't refer to propositions. They are non-referring expressions instead. Nonetheless, quantification into a that-clause position is possible, and various inferences involving such quantifiers are valid. But this quantification is different from quantification over objects and has to be understood as substitutional quantification. In addition, Schiffer gave an ingenious account of how language understanding can work without a compositional semantics by outlining a non-inferential approach to language understanding in which a compositional semantics plays no role.[1]

2.2.2 Things

In *Things* Schiffer agrees with his former self that one can't construct the referent of a that-clause from the referents of the expressions that occur in it and the way they are put together. But this doesn't mean that that-clauses don't refer, it just means they don't refer to structured entities, and they don't refer to entities that can be identified with entities that are constructed out of other entities. But nonetheless, he now holds, they do refer. They refer to *sui generis* entities instead: pleonastic propositions. They are pleonastic in the sense that, according to Schiffer, their existence is guaranteed by something-from-nothing transformations, like

1. a. Fido is a dog.
   b. Thus that Fido is a dog is true.

We can introduce a that-clause apparently without change of truth conditions, and according to Schiffer's new view, this guarantees that there is an entity that the that-clause refers to. This view of pleonastic entities is modified to rule out certain problematic cases, and Schiffer adds the condition that the introduction of these entities has to be a conservative extension[2] of what we can conclude without them. I won't discuss this aspect of his view here, though. Thus, overall, that-clauses refer, they refer to propositions, but these are pleonastic entities, *sui generis* entities whose existence is guaranteed by talking about them in something-from-nothing transformations. Propositions exist just as you and I do, and quantification over them is just plain old objectual quantification.

2.2.3 Schiffer's change of heart

Although there are many instances in which Schiffer agrees with himself across time, the transition from a no-reference theory to a reference theory of that-clauses is almost a 180-degree turn.[3] Many of the things that Schiffer says in the rest of *Things* seem to me to be just as good with the old theory of propositions from *Remnants*, though the details of this claim are debatable. So, why did Schiffer change his mind?

As I said above, Schiffer is surprisingly brief in explaining this transition. His official reason is spelled out in *Things* on pages 89–92. He says: 'The reason I switched from the no-reference, non-objectual quantification line to my present view... was that I came to think that if that was the solution, then what the hell was the problem?' (*Things*, 90). Schiffer then imagines a debate between his former, *Remnants*, self, and his present, *Things*, self about the reality of properties. They both agree that there are properties they both have, that Fido has the property of being a dog, etc., but they disagree whether or not properties exist, that is, whether or not there is an ontology of properties.

'What came to unsettle me were two related things. The first was that I couldn't see either how that dispute could have a determinate resolution or what the cash-value of the dispute really amounted to. Relative to all our agreement, what could the further question about existence amount to such that it could be answered?... The second thing that moved me was the realization that whatever established the truth of statements ostensibly about properties and propositions, and whatever allowed us to know the truths those statements expressed, would establish the existence and nature of properties and propositions '... (*Things*, 91)

I find these reasons puzzling. On the first, I don't see why one can't make sense of the idea that, even though two people agree on the truth value of most sentences talking about propositions, they still disagree on what they do when they talk about propositions. This situation strikes me as no different than a dispute between a cognitivist and a non-cognitivist in ethics, or any dispute about realism, or even a dispute between someone who holds that names are descriptions and someone that holds that they are not. In each case these people will not disagree about the ordinary statements involving names or talk about what to do, but on what we do when we talk that way. To be sure in each case it is a substantial philosophical project to work out what the philosophical difference comes down to, but this applies to most areas in philosophy. In Schiffer's case, the difference is one of the semantic function of that-clauses and certain uses of quantifiers. This is a disagreement about semantics, and it seems to me it makes just as much sense as any other disagreement in semantics. Furthermore, it is a symmetric situation. If this disagreement makes no sense, then either the two views are the same, or none of them makes any sense. But since Schiffer changed his mind from the old view to the new one, there is a real issue to change one's mind about. But in any case, doubts about the legitimacy of the debate between the two views are no reason to go from one view in the debate to the other. And I found the second reason unconvincing as well. The no-reference theory of that-clauses or property nominalizations can say quite a bit about what makes sentences in which non-referring terms occur true. I won't get into what can or should be said about this now, but we will discuss it below in section 2.5.3.

Although Schiffer's reasons for rejecting the view in *Remnants* are unconvincing to me, there are plenty of problems with his view in that book, and there are also plenty of problems with his view in *Things*. It seems to me that these are real problems, but that the ones from *Remnants* can be solved. And we can see what kinds of considerations allows us to decide between these kinds of views, and that in the end *Remnants* wins over *Things*.

2.3 The Real Problems with *Remnants*

There are a number of problems with the view that Schiffer held in *Remnants*. Not that these are devastating problems, but they at least require one to say more than what was said in *Remnants*. I will focus on the ones that strike me as particularly central for a defense of a no-reference theory of that-clauses, and related expressions.

2.3.1 Quantification

According to *Remnants*, quantification over propositions is substitutional quantification, but quantification over objects is not. That is to say, the quantifiers in the following two sentences are different:

2. Everything he believes is true.
3. Everything he eats is tasty.

But this requires an account of how that can be so. After all, isn't it the same word 'everything' that occurs in both examples? And why should we think that quantifiers are different when they range over one domain, propositions, than over another, food, say? It isn't enough to say that the former quantifier can be interpreted as a substitutional one. The question rather is: is this the correct interpretation, and how can it be that what appears to be one and the same word sometimes has one interpretation, and sometimes another? Whatever story one wants to tell here, it will have to be told as a story about the semantics of our ordinary use of the word 'everything' and similar quantified expressions.

2.3.2 Inexpressibility

In *Remnants* Schiffer held that quantification over propositions is substitutional quantification, but as he notes himself in a footnote,[4] this can't be quite the whole story. Substitutional quantifiers need substitution instances, but sometimes it seems that quantification over propositions doesn't have such instances, at least not with sentences of our own language as the substitution class. For example:

4. There are propositions not expressible in present-day English.

most likely is true, but the quantifier in it can't be understood as a substitutional quantifier with the sentences of present day English as the substitution class. Any instance of the quantifier involves an expressible proposition. When Schiffer discusses this in the above mentioned footnote he suggests that quantifiers over propositions are neither objectual nor substitutional, and that we shouldn't expect that such quantifiers are nicely captured by quantifiers in formal languages. But this just raises the question more vividly how such quantifiers are supposed to be understood.

But besides the technicalities about quantification, there is also a deeper issue. According to the no-reference theory, propositions do not form a language-independent domain of entities, since propositions are not entities at all, and thus in particular not language-independent entities. Still, talk about propositions nonetheless makes sense. But when we talk about propositions we don't talk about them in a referential sense of 'about,' but in a different, more innocent sense. Let's distinguish a referential sense of 'about' from a topical sense. In the former one is referring to what one is talking about. For this to be so, the relevant expressions in the sentences one uses in this discourse have to be referential expressions. In the latter, topical sense, however, this is not required. Here what one is talking about is simply the topic of one's conversation. In this sense one can talk about aliens, even if there are none. And in this sense it is no problem for the believer in the no-reference theory to hold that we can talk about propositions. Using the that-clause 'that Fido is a dog' I can talk about the proposition that Fido is a dog. Talk about propositions thus makes sense on either theory. But when we talk about inexpressible propositions things get more difficult for the no-reference theory. How can we understand the apparent truth of:

5. Some propositions which are not expressible in English are expressible in French, but others are not.

There is no domain over which this quantifier ranges, since there are no propositions out there to form such a domain. How can the no-reference theory understand this? There is no similar problem for expressible propositions, since the no-reference theory can hold that quantifiers over expressible propositions are somehow derivative on the instances (of course, the details of how this is to be understood more precisely would have to be worked out on such a proposal).

Thus, besides any technicalities about quantifiers, inexpressible propositions seem to be at odds with the no-reference theory of that-clauses. To me, this is ultimately the most important problem for any no-reference theory. In fact, it even reoccurs as a problem in Schiffer's present theory, as we will see below.

2.3.3 That-clauses outside of belief ascriptions

Schiffer's discussion of that-clauses in *Remnants* focused on that-clauses in belief ascriptions, and other propositional attitude ascriptions. But there is much more to that-clauses than that, and some of the occurrences of that-clauses are outside of attitude ascriptions. Besides ordinary cases like:

6. That Schiffer changed his mind is surprising.

we also have the something-from-nothing transformations, which seem to be rather telling about that-clauses. Such clauses can be introduced apparently without change of truth conditions from virtually any statement:

7. a. Fido is a dog.
   b. Thus, that Fido is a dog is true.
   c. Thus, there is something which is true, namely that Fido is a dog.

Any account of the function of that-clauses will have to say what is going on in such inferences. Schiffer will take this more seriously in *Things*, but in *Remnants* it doesn't play a crucial role. In any case, it isn't clear how we should understand such inferences and that-clauses.

2.3.4 The argument for the no-reference theory

Schiffer's argument in *Remnants* for the no-reference theory is rather indirect: If that-clauses refer then their referent has to be compositionally determined by the semantic values of the parts of the that-clause, assuming that natural languages have a compositional semantics. But, he argued, there is no way to assign that-clauses their referent meeting these conditions. Thus that-clauses don't refer, and natural languages don't have a compositional semantics. This does not strike me as a very powerful argument. To the contrary, it seems to me that whether or not that-clauses refer is independent of whether or not natural languages have a compositional semantics. In fact, whether or not an expression refers is quite independent of how it is treated in contemporary compositional semantic theories.

To see this, consider the use of semantic values in semantic theories, for example ones that use higher type objects as semantic values, like Montague Grammar and related approaches. In such semantic theories every expression gets a semantic value, whether or not it refers. Words like 'very' or 'most' or 'Peter' all have semantic values, although the first two are not referring expression. In addition, referring expressions usually don't get their referents as their semantic values. To be able to accommodate complex noun phrases, like 'Peter and some woman,' the semantic value of a proper name gets 'type raised' to the same kind of semantic value that a quantifier has. The semantic value of 'Peter' might be the set of all the properties that Peter has, but that is not what 'Peter' refers to. The referent is still Peter, and he has to have some proper relationship to the semantic value of 'Peter,' so that the truth conditions overall come out correctly. But all that is required is such a relationship, not that the referent and the semantic value are the same.

And similarly for that-clauses. Even if we could have a compositional semantics for that-clauses, it wouldn't mean that they refer. Even if we can assign them semantic values that capture their contribution to the truth conditions, it would not mean that these semantic values are the referents of that-clauses, i.e. propositions, nor that that-clauses are referring expressions. Schiffer's arguments that a compositional semantics has to treat belief ascriptions relationally, as a relation between a believer and what they believe, thus is only partly correct. It might well be correct that the only way to get a compositional semantics for belief ascriptions is to assign a relation as the semantic value to 'believes,' and to assign a semantic value to the term for the believer, and another semantic value to the that-clause that specifies what is believed. But this is not enough to establish the claim which is intended by Schiffer, namely that the that-clause is a referential singular term.[5] It only shows that in a compositional semantics that-clauses have to get their own semantic values. But that doesn't show that they are referential.

And, analogously, even if there is no compositional semantics for that-clauses, it doesn't mean that that-clauses don't refer. They might refer, although their referent is not semantically compositionally determined. So, these two issues are independent of each other. Thus Schiffer actually does not have a good argument in *Remnants* that that-clauses don't refer. Much of his discussion in that book is focused on the failure to accommodate belief ascriptions in a compositional semantic theory, but this issue is actually independent of the question whether or not that-clauses refer.[6]

This raises the question how we are to decide whether an expression is a referring expression. An argument for or against it can't come from the treatment of that-clauses in a compositional semantics. It rather has to come from some other feature of that-clauses. As it turns out, there are some good arguments that that-clauses don't refer, but in Schiffer's work they only appear in *Things*. There, of course, they are arguments against his view, and he accordingly rejects them. But as we will see below, these arguments are more powerful than he takes them to be.

Before we have a look to see whether these problems can be solved on a no-reference theory, let's look at how things stand with *Things*.

2.4 The Trouble with *Things*

If a no-reference theory is a coherent option for the semantics of that-clauses then the question becomes what reason we might have to think it is wrong, and thus what reason we have to think that a reference theory is correct. As far as I can tell, there are two lines of argument in *Things* that aim to establish that that-clauses refer and that propositions exist. One is based on an analogy, the other is based on a certain view about the relationship between syntax and semantics. Both strike me as unsuccessful. In fact, it seems that Schiffer slightly changed his mind while writing *Things* about which of the two is best for understanding propositions as pleonastic entities. He uses two really quite different kinds of considerations to support his view, one he had used before in some papers written between *Remnants* and *Things*,[7] and another one which is first explicit in *Things*, as far as I know, and which, I think, is really to be preferred, but still problematic.

The first consideration is the analogy between that-clauses and names for fictional characters. According to Schiffer, there are two ways to talk about fictional characters. One is the use of a fictional name in the fiction. In such a use the name doesn't refer to anything. But once we step back and talk about the fictional character in that fiction we succeed in referring to something. This is a case of a pleonastic entity, one that we succeed in picking out just by starting to use a term that aims to refer. The same holds, Schiffer claims, when we start to use that-clauses or other terms that are introduced in something-from-nothing transformations. But this story to me isn't very satisfying. First, there are many important differences between fictional characters and propositions. Fictional characters, on this story, are supposed to supervene on someone writing the fiction. But nothing analogous to this can be true for propositions, as Schiffer himself notes, since propositions, if they exist at all, have to exist necessarily and at all times. They supervene on our talking about them only if they supervene on birds flying as well. Since they exist necessarily and timelessly, they supervene on everything if they supervene on anything. Secondly, the story about fictional characters Schiffer tells and more or less takes for granted is very controversial, and I for one would not subscribe to it. It is not at all clear that when we talk about the fictional characters in a story we are succeeding in referring to an entity. Alternatively, for example, we might just use the same non-referring fictional name, say 'Sherlock Holmes,' but aposit 'the fictional character' next to it, which wouldn't affect the function of the name.

The second consideration Schiffer uses to support his view of that-clauses as referring to pleonastic entities is basically an adoption of Frege's account of numbers as logical objects. Frege held that we can see that numbers are objects since we can introduce sentences with singular terms for numbers in them apparently without change of truth conditions from sentences that don't contain such singular terms. The argument, ultimately, that these singular terms are referring expressions, and that they do succeed in referring to numbers, is what is often called *the syntactic priority thesis*. This is the thesis that what it is to be an object is only to be understood as that which a singular term stands for. Thus the apparently semantic category of an object is to be understood as derivative of the apparently syntactic category of a singular term. Singular terms in true sentences do succeed in referring to objects since that's just what it is to be a referring term and what it is to be an object.[8] This Fregean line, it seems to me, is really what Schiffer's view relies on. And it is better suited to his view than the analogy with fictional characters. And although this line is somewhat popular in the philosophy of mathematics, it relies on a mistaken view in the philosophy of language. It is the view that there is one and only one semantic function of syntactically singular terms. The neo-Fregeans never provide evidence for it of the kind that seems to be required to hold it, namely evidence from syntax, semantics, and their relationship. Rather they disguise what ultimately is a very controversial view about the relationship between syntax and semantics as a deep philosophical insight about the relationship between language and the world. But as a view about the relationship between syntax and semantics it is very controversial, to say the least, and false, in my opinion. I will present one case below where it doesn't hold. Singular terms have a variety of different semantic functions, only one of them is to refer to an object. To settle this issue requires a detailed study of various cases in natural language. The neo-Fregeans never provide such arguments, and thus I don't think we should believe them that there is only one semantic function of syntactically singular terms. Now, Schiffer doesn't defend the syntactic priority thesis as such, but in effect his Fregean argument for that-clauses being referring expressions relies on it. And because of this I think it should be rejected.

Schiffer's position in *Things* also faces some other problems. For one, his new view just as his old view has a problem with inexpressible propositions. This problem is not unfamiliar to neo-Fregeans about mathematics. The neo-Fregeans about arithmetic don't have to worry about there being more numbers than there are singular terms for them. Every natural number is denoted by a singular term in our language. But once we get to the real numbers this is not so any more. But how can the Fregean, who holds onto the syntactic priority thesis, endorse that there are more (pleonastic) objects than there are singular terms for them? Wasn't the syntactic category of a singular term supposed to be more basic than that of an object? And wasn't that the basis of the argument that the singular terms denote at all? How can there be objects then that remain undenoted? This points to a tension in the Frege-inspired line that introduces pleonastic objects, one that might be overcome, but it certainly is worthy of some more attention. In fact, Hale and Wright list this problem in the appendix of *The Reason's Proper Study* as problem 4 in their list of 18 problems that neo-Fregeans face.[9] They call it the *Problem of Plentitude*.

And similarly for Schiffer. How can there be propositions that aren't denoted by a that-clause? Schiffer addresses this problem all too briefly in a paragraph, discussing properties:

Finally, what about inexpressible properties?... My view here is that we can make sense of such properties just by virtue of our ability to make sense of there being a language—an enrichment of our own language or a completely different language—in which such properties are expressible. (*Things*, 71)

This answer does not strike me as satisfactory. It is not clear that we are making sense of there being inexpressible properties when we make sense of there being an enrichment of our language. True enough, we can make sense of our language containing more words in its vocabulary, but that doesn't guarantee that these words express more than what could be expressed before. This way we don't make sense that there are inexpressible propositions, just that there are more words in our language. Even when we imagine that these new words mean something different from what our other words mean we still don't imagine that we can express more propositions, since what the new word means might be the same as what a combination of old words mean. What we really imagine in the situation in Schiffer's quote is that there is a language in which more propositions are expressible than in our language. And that is, we imagine that there are more propositions than the ones expressible in our language, and a language that expresses them. But it is not at all clear whether this is compatible with Schiffer's view in *Things*. Are we imagining something coherent when we do this, if Schiffer is right? This is of course perfectly coherent on a view of propositions that takes them to be language-independent entities, but neither Schiffer's old view nor his new view are like that. The problem of inexpressible propositions is much more serious than Schiffer's brief discussion makes it out to be.

So, do we have to go back to propositions as forming a language-independent domain of entities? I will suggest in the following that we can in fact solve the problems from *Remnants*, and that a no-reference theory is defensible, and correct.

2.5 Solving the Problems from *Remnants*

The problems discussed above for Schiffer's version of the no-reference theory in *Remnants* can be solved. I will outline in this section how I think they should be solved. I won't be able to spell out the solutions outlined below in detail, of course, but I will refer to some papers where these solutions are developed in more detail.

2.5.1 Quantification

Most expressions in natural language have a variety of closely connected meanings, that is, they are polysemous. Paradigmatically this is true of verbs, for example 'get,' which can mean many different things in English, as for example in

8. Before I get home I should get some beer to get drunk.

But there is a false picture that was handed down to us from the early days of the philosophy of language, which we could call *the myth of the logical skeleton*. This myth says that although most expressions in natural language are somewhat soft, vague, and polysemous, there is a hard skeleton which is different, and on which the rest of language is built. This skeleton consists of the logical expressions, which are the bones and which hold up the rest of language as its core. But that the expressions we know from propositional logic are not like that is nowadays universally agreed upon. Take words like 'and' or 'if.' 'And' is not just a sentential connective as in propositional logic. It can combine verbs or noun phrases, and it can have collective or distributive readings. Conditionals are not at all the Boolean connective we encounter in logic, and similarly for other "logical constants." And the same is true for quantifiers, or so it seems to me. Quantifiers are polysemous just like most other expressions, and they can make different contributions to the truth conditions of a sentence in which they occur. That this is so can be seen quite independently of issues about that-clauses. Quantifiers have at least two different readings. On one of them they range over a domain of entities, whatever they may be. According to this *domain conditions reading*, the contribution that the quantifier makes to the truth conditions is that the domain of entities satisfies a certain condition, depending on what quantifier it is and what the rest of the sentence is like. But besides this reading there is at least one further one. It is the one where we use the quantifier for its inferential role. On this *inferential role reading* the quantified sentence inferentially relates to quantifier-free sentences, and how this relationship goes will depend on which quantifier it is, and where it occurs. In languages like ours these two readings come apart in truth conditions, although they coincide in truth conditions in simpler languages, describing a simpler world. If every object in the domain of discourse is denoted by a term, and every term in the language denotes an object in the domain of discourse, then inferential role and domain conditions coincide with respect to truth conditions. But our language and our world are not like that. Still, we have a need for both uses of quantifiers, and polysemous quantifiers give us both, with different contributions to the truth conditions from different readings of one and the same quantifier. This view is developed in more detail in Hofweber (2000) and Hofweber (2005b).

If this is so then we can see how one and the same word 'everything' in our above examples 2. and 3. can range over food in one case and over propositions in the other, even though it makes quite a different contribution to the truth conditions. It can then be that when talking about food we use the quantifier in its domain conditions reading, since we want to make a claim about whatever food is out there in the domain of discourse, whereas when we are talking about propositions we want to inferentially relate the sentence we uttered to any instance of the quantifier. In fact, we are thereby endorsing every instance. These two uses of the quantifiers thus are available generally, to any kind of quantification, over food, propositions, people, and so on. It will have to be a feature of particular uses of the quantifiers that accounts for it having one or the other reading that the quantifier can have.

The inferential role reading of the quantifier is closely related to a substitutional interpretation, but also subtly different. These similarities and differences are discussed in the papers cited above. Similarly, the domain conditions reading corresponds to an objectual interpretation of the quantifier. But understanding them this way we can see how one and the same quantifier can do both of these things, and we can see that this is so independently of any issues about ontology.

Even though the motivation for the two readings of the quantifiers does not come from ontology, that there are these two readings has consequences for ontology. In fact, it follows that ontological questions like

9. Are there propositions?

and their answers

10. There are propositions.

themselves have two readings each. On one of them it is trivially true that there are propositions, and on the other it is not. Take (10), and assume that it contains a quantifier over propositions. On the inferential role reading of this quantifier it follows trivially from anything using the something-from-nothing transformations. Or take (9). This question has two readings, one using a quantifier in its inferential role reading, the other using it in its domain conditions reading. In the inferential role reading it is trivially answered by (10) when it, too, is used in its inferential role reading. But on the other, domain conditions reading of (9) this is not so. This reading of the question is only answered by (10) in its domain conditions reading, but to get that is not trivial and it is not established in the something-from-nothing transformations. All this gives us a version of Carnap's internal–external distinction about questions about what there is, and in fact it seems to me that any version of a no-reference theory will ultimately have to take recourse to such a distinction. This is discussed in more detail in Hofweber (2005b).

2.5.2 Inexpressibility

The most serious problem for any no-reference theory of that-clauses, and any theory that holds that propositions are not language-independent entities, which includes Schiffer's theory in *Things*, is the inexpressibility worry. How can we make sense that there are propositions that are not expressible with any sentence? The key to understanding this requires a closer look at what motivates us into thinking that there are inexpressible propositions. And to understand this it helps to make some distinctions. Fix a particular language for the following, like present-day English. Let's call a proposition *speaker expressible* if there is some context such that a speaker can express that proposition with an utterance of a sentence in that context. Let's call a proposition *language expressible* if there is a sentence such that every utterance of that sentence expresses that proposition, no matter what the context. The language expressible propositions are basically the ones that can be expressed with the utterance of a sentence that does not contain any context sensitive elements in it. The speaker expressible ones are the ones expressible with utterances of sentences that contain context sensitive elements, and any context is allowed. The language expressible and speaker expressible propositions come apart in a language like contemporary English. For example, not every object is denoted by a term in this language. If O is such an undenoted object then the proposition that Bill Clinton is heavier than O is not language expressible. But it is speaker expressible in a context where the speaker has O available for demonstrative reference, and utters the sentence 'Clinton is heavier than this.'

In Hofweber (2006a) I argue that this difference between what is language expressible and what is speaker expressible in arbitrary contexts is essentially used in the arguments that have been offered to motivate that there are inexpressible propositions. Since no direct example of an inexpressible proposition can be given, arguments for there being such propositions have to be indirect. But there are good arguments that show that not all propositions are language expressible in contemporary English. They refute a simple substitutional account of quantification over propositions according to which the substitution class consists of context insensitive sentences of one's own language. For every proposition there would have to be a context insensitive sentence in contemporary English that expresses it, which is the substitution instance that makes a quantified statement true. Since this isn't so, context sensitive expressions have to be accommodated somehow. But it is not at all clear how one could have something like a substitutional quantifier that allows for context sensitive sentences to be in the substitution class, since after all the contexts that are needed to give demonstratives their values aren't part of the substitution class. But a version of an inferential role reading of quantifiers over propositions can accommodate this, or so I argued in Hofweber (2006a). The key here is to understand how context sensitive expressions figure into the inferential role of quantifiers over propositions or properties, and how this can be captured in an account of the truth conditions of such quantifiers that sees them still only as inferential quantifiers, without a domain of entities over which they range. I won't repeat the only slightly technical details here, but I believe that this can be done satisfactorily, and that this modified account of inferential quantifiers can accommodate all good arguments for their being inexpressible propositions. On the resulting view there are different senses of 'inexpressible' to be distinguished, and there are no inexpressible propositions in one sense of 'inexpressible,' but there are inexpressible propositions in another sense of 'inexpressible.' Every proposition is expressible in the sense of 'can be expressed with a sentence in some context or other,' but not every proposition is expressible in the sense of 'can be expressed with a sentence without context sensitive elements in it.' Quantification over propositions has to be understood as generalizing over the instances with context sensitive expressions in them[10] and this is perfectly compatible with the no-reference theory of that-clauses. There are also a number of positive consequences to this account, in particular how we should understand change in expressive power in a language over time, but I won't get into them here. The details of all this are in Hofweber (2006a).

If this view of expressibility is correct then it solves the problems that the no-reference theory has with inexpressible propositions. Incidentally, it can also be used to rid Schiffer's new theory of its problems with inexpressible propositions. It alone won't help us to decide between these two theories, but it removes the apparent advantage that theories have that hold that propositions are language-independent entities, only some of which might be expressed by any particular language, while some might not be expressible in any language whatsoever.

2.5.3 *That-clauses outside of belief ascriptions*

If that-clauses in belief ascriptions don't refer then what do they do? The easy answer is that instead of referring to something which is the content of the belief, they merely specify what the content of the belief is. Saying what the content of a belief is can be done without referring to a content. But there are questions left for the use of that-clauses that go beyond that. One of them concerns that-clauses outside of belief ascriptions in general, but here the same options apply for both approaches. With regard to:

6. That Schiffer changed his mind is surprising.

one theory says that the that-clause refers to what is surprising, the other says that the that-clause specifies what is surprising. But for both theories there is one phenomenon that goes beyond that and which needs some more explanation. That-clauses, as well as some other phrases like property nominalization and number words, can be introduced as singular terms apparently without change of truth conditions. This feature takes center stage in Schiffer's theory in *Things*, where it is crucial that these new singular terms are referring, since after all, being introduced this way is constitutive of the entities that we end up referring to, according to *Things*. But this account of the something-from-nothing transformation seems to me to miss an important aspect they have, one that ultimately speaks in favor of the no-reference theory. Consider again the something-from-nothing transformations, or as we will also call them, the transition from an *innocent statement*, a statement that seems to have nothing to do with metaphysics, to one of its *metaphysically loaded counterparts*:

11. a. Fido is a dog.
     b. Thus: That Fido is a dog is true.
     c. (Or:) Thus: Fido has the property of being a dog.

This can also been done with numbers:

12. a. Jupiter has four moons.
     b. Thus: The number of moons of Jupiter is four.

In fact, the latter example goes back to Frege's *Grundlagen* (Frege 1884), and just like the other two pairs above, it is puzzling in a number of ways. For one, it contains new singular terms, but nonetheless seems to be equivalent to the original sentence. How can this equivalence then be so obvious, in particular how can it be obvious to ordinary speakers of English without metaphysical opinions on the existence of properties and propositions? Schiffer's new theory of pleonastic propositions and properties can attempt to explain this, but it doesn't quite seem to work as smoothly for numbers. In the case of numbers we get the number word 'four' as a new singular term, but contrary to the properties and propositions cases, it was already present in the innocent statement. But there it occurred in an apparently quite different syntactic category, as an adjective or determiner, as in 'four moons.' But this gives rise to another puzzle. How are we to understand that what appears to be the same word 'four' is both an adjective or determiner, as well as a singular term? Usually adjectives or determiners cannot appear as singular terms without resulting in ungrammaticality. But why can 'four' do this?[11]

The solution to this puzzle is revealed once we look at the function that these loaded counterparts have in actual communication. After all, one might think that since they are truth conditionally equivalent to the innocent statements there would be little use for them in communication, and that it would make little difference whether one uttered the innocent statement or the loaded counterpart. They have the same truth conditions, after all. But there is an important and instructive difference between them. This difference is analogous to the one between an ordinary statement and a clefted sentence:

13. a. Schiffer changed his mind.
     b. It is Schiffer who changed his mind.

They are obviously truth conditionally equivalent, but there is an important difference between them nonetheless. The unclefted sentence (13a) communicates the information neutrally, whereas the clefted sentence (13b) communicates it with a certain emphasis, structure, or focus. This effect can also be achieved with intonation, as in

14. SCHIFFER changed his mind.

However, above we achieve it with a certain syntactic structure. In Hofweber (2005b) and Hofweber (2007a) I have argued that the same effect is achieved with the loaded counterparts. In addition, I have argued that the only way to understand how a certain syntactic structure can give rise to this focus effect without any special intonation is to understand the new singular terms as non-referring. I won't repeat the arguments here, and in exchange I won't expect you to believe me. But if this is onto something then we can have a quite different understanding of the something-from-nothing transformations. They are not the constitutive transformation for new pleonastic entities, but rather they move from presenting certain information neutrally, without focus, to a way to present the same information with a focus.

2.5.4 The argument for the no-reference theory

If it is correct, as I claimed above, that having or not having a compositional semantics for belief ascriptions is independent of whether or not that-clauses refer, then the question becomes how we can decide whether or not that-clauses refer. Even if that-clauses have semantic values in a certain semantic theory, it doesn't mean that they refer to these semantic values, nor does it mean that they refer at all. So, how are we to decide about reference?

One thing that we have let slide throughout this chapter is the question whether 'reference' is really the proper term even if that-clauses have as their semantic function to 'pick out' propositions. If that-clauses refer in the same sense in which names refer, and if we take it for granted that reference so understood is fundamentally different from quantification, then that-clauses would certainly be unusual in that they are syntactically complex referring expressions, a rarity, if it exists at all.[12] But we don't have to settle this issue here. We can agree that according to the reference theory, broadly understood, that-clauses have the semantic function to pick out an entity, and this entity is what a proposition is. So, how can we decide whether that-clauses have the semantic function to pick out an entity?

The best way to decide this is to see directly whether or not that-clauses behave in the way that we would expect for phrases that have the semantic function of picking out an entity. For example, we could see if they exhibit scope ambiguities, and if they do, we could argue that they are quantifiers, which paradigmatically exhibit scope ambiguities. And to see if they are referential we should see if they behave like referential terms. The best way to do this is to see if all that matters for their contribution to the truth conditions is what entity they pick out, and not how it is picked out. This is a feature paradigmatically true of referring expressions, with the usual exceptions of indirect or opaque contexts. Thus the test for referentiality to consider is whether that-clauses can be substituted for other terms that pick out the same entity. If yes, it is evidence for their being referential, if not, it is evidence against them being referential. But as is well known, that-clauses fail this test. If that-clauses like 'that Slovenia will win the World Cup' refer at all then they refer to propositions, in this case the proposition that Slovenia will win the World Cup. But 'the proposition that Slovenia will win the World Cup' also refers to that very same proposition. However, these two phrases are not substitutable for each other without change of truth conditions:

15. Jane fears that Slovenia will win the World Cup.
16. Jane fears the proposition that Slovenia will win the Word Cup.

Both of these fears are unfounded, but they are different. The first because Slovenia can't win the 2006 World Cup in Germany, since they didn't even qualify, coming up short in their qualifying group behind Italy and Norway.[13] The second, however, is no fear about the World Cup, but proposition phobia, fear of propositions themselves. The truth conditions of these two sentences thus differ, since one can be true while the other one is false, and thus that-clauses can't be referring expressions.

This argument isn't found in *Remnants*, but it is discussed explicitly in *Things*, using the above World Cup example. But in *Things* it is an argument against Schiffer's then present view and he accordingly rejects the argument. Schiffer's reason for rejecting it is that he rejects the substitution principle itself. It is not true that two co-referring terms can always be substituted without change of truth conditions, he argues, and the example that shows that this is so is apposition. Schiffer says:

There are clearly non-trick contexts where co-referring terms can't be substituted *salva veritate*. For example, if Pavarotti is the greatest tenor, we still can't substitute 'the greatest tenor' for 'Pavarotti' in
 The Italian singer Pavarotti never sings Wagner.
since
 The Italian singer the greatest tenor never sings Wagner.
isn't even well formed. (*Things*, 93)

I don't think this answer can defuse the above argument that that-clauses don't refer.[14] We should distinguish two kinds of substitution failures. First, *syntactic substitution failure* occurs when we substitute an (allegedly) referring expression for one that refers to the same object, but we thereby change a grammatical sentence to an ungrammatical one. Secondly, there is *semantic substitution failure*. It occurs when we substitute an (allegedly) referring expression for a co referring one, we preserve grammaticality, but we change the truth conditions. Schiffer's Pavarotti case is one of syntactic substitution failure. However, there is a perfectly good explanation why it occurs, and the fact that it occurs doesn't help the referentialist to explain how semantic substitution failure can occur.

Two expressions can stand for the same object, but have different syntactic properties. For example, 'Pavarotti' and 'the greatest tenor' are different in that the latter starts with the determiner 'the,' whereas the former does not. This difference is enough to explain why on some occurrences one of them is grammatical but the other in the same position is not. Apposition with a phrase that itself starts with a determiner is one example of this. 'The Italian singer' also starts with 'the,' and these two determiners clash when occurring that close to each other in the same noun phrase, as in 'the Italian singer the greatest tenor.' That they clash has a purely syntactic explanation, though I won't attempt to give it. 'The Italian singer Pavarotti' doesn't exhibit this clash of determiners, and it is thus grammatical. And so are 'my friend the greatest tenor' and 'my friend Pavarotti,' and so on. But that this can be so, that co-referring terms can have different syntactic features, is no reason not to be worried about semantic substitution failure. Semantic substitution failure still is incompatible with a referential understanding of the relevant terms. And it is exactly what occurs in the World Cup examples above. Both sentences are grammatical, but their truth conditions differ. This can't be so on the reference theory, and pointing out that co-referring expressions can have different syntactic properties doesn't help explain how that can be so after all.[15]

The no-reference theory is not threatened by the substitution failures. That two non-referring expressions can't be substituted for one another is no surprise, although it gives rise to the question what precisely the difference between them is. But substitution can't be expected on the no-reference theory, though it should be expected on the reference theory, unless we have a syntactic explanation why grammaticality is not preserved. But since this is not the case in our examples involving that-clauses, the argument against the reference theory stands. In fact, it is a prime example of the kind of argument that is suitable to decide between a reference and a no-reference theory. Substitution failure thus speaks for the no-reference theory.

2.6 Conclusion

I have argued that the reasons that moved Schiffer to change his mind between writing *Remnants* and *Things* shouldn't have moved him to do so. In addition, I hope to have at least outlined some of the main ideas that seem to me to allow one to have a coherent no-reference theory of that-clauses. But, of course, there is much more to say about all this. There are many linguistic issues that need to be addressed, and there are philosophical issues that we barely touched on. But besides all this, I have my money on the no-reference theory, and thus I think Schiffer's second of his three books was closest to the truth when it comes to that-clauses and propositions, at least in its vision, if not always in its letter. I learned a tremendous amount from studying Schiffer's books, but we honor our teachers by disagreeing with them. Although I admire Schiffer's work equally over the years, I honor him more now than I did ten years ago.[16]

Notes

* Editor's note: This paper was submitted in 2006, as one of the first for this volume. Although it still represents the author's views, the delay in publication accounts for the fact that more recent work, including his own, is not cited here. Many of the themes of the paper are discussed in more detail in his *Ontology and the Ambitions of Metaphysics* (Hofweber, 2016).
1. See also Schiffer (1991).
2. 'Conservative extension' is a technical term from proof theory. A theory T_2 is a conservative extension of a theory T_1 iff the vocabulary of T_2 includes all the vocabulary of T_1 and any theorem that can be proven in T_2 that uses only the vocabulary of T_1 can already be proven in T_1. This has to be slightly adjusted for the present purpose, and in *Things* Schiffer discusses this in some more detail.
3. It would be a full 180-degree turn if Schiffer held that propositions are just some plain old Platonic entities, completely independent of language. That they are pleonastic preserves some of the spirit of *Remnants*, but also some of its problems, as we will see below.
4. Footnote 6 of chapter 8 in *Remnants*, p. 288f.
5. See also Schiffer (1992).

6. See Hofweber (2007b) for more on this.
7. For example, in Schiffer (1996).
8. Schiffer puts it slightly differently on pp. 77-9 of *Things*, but I think this captures the spirit of Frege's approach.
9. See Hale and Wright (2001: 422).
10. See Hofweber (2006a) on how this can be done.
11. The answer suggested below is only a partial answer to this question, since it only covers one case. A more general answer is given in Hofweber (2005a).
12. Complex demonstratives are another, controversial candidate for a complex referring expression.
13. And as events have unfolded since I wrote the above, it became even harder. By now, unfortunately, Italy has won the World Cup.
14. The following objection to Schiffer's account is also found in Hofweber (2006b).
15. A different attempt to explain this is King (2002) who holds that different syntactic arguments trigger different readings of the verb. King thereby aims to explain both the syntactic substitution failure, as well as the 'objectification effect' (see Moltmann 2003). I don't think that King's account can save the referentiality of that-clauses, but it helps to defend a weaker thesis: that that-clauses have propositions as semantic values. But this thesis, I argued above, is independent of the referentiality of that-clauses, and requires a specification of 'proposition' as something other than 'whatever that-clauses refer to.' For more on the substitution arguments against the thesis that that-clauses refer, see Moltmann (2003), which contains lots of interesting data. Moltmann's own theory inspired by these examples is that 'believes' expresses a multi-relation that has a variable number of relata, and that relates a believer to the constituents of the that-clause.
16. Thanks to Russell Dale and Gary Ostertag for many helpful comments on an earlier draft.

Bibliography

Frege, G. (1884). *Die Grundlagen der Arithmetik: eine logisch mathematische Untersuchung über den Begriff der Zahl*. Breslau: W. Koebner.
Hale, B. and C. Wright. (2001). *The Reason's Proper Study*. Oxford: Oxford University Press.
Hofweber, T. (2000). "Quantification and Non-existent Objects." In *Empty Names, Fiction, and the Puzzles of Non-Existence*, edited by A. Everett and T. Hofweber, Stanford: CSLI Publications.
Hofweber, T. (2005a). "Number Determiners, Numbers, and Arithmetic." *The Philosophical Review* 114 (2): 179-225.
Hofweber, T. (2005b). "A Puzzle about Ontology." *Noûs* 39: 256-83.
Hofweber, T. (2006a). "Inexpressible Properties and Propositions." In *Oxford Studies in Metaphysics*, volume 2, edited by D. Zimmerman, New York: Oxford University Press.
Hofweber, T. (2006b). "Schiffer's New Theory of Propositions." *Philosophy and Phenomenological Research* 73: 211-17.
Hofweber, T. (2007a). "Innocent Statements and Their Metaphysically Loaded Counterparts." *Philosophers' Imprint* 7 (1).
Hofweber, T. (2007b). 'Semantic Facts and Semantic Values.' Unpublished manuscript.
Hofweber, T. (2016). *Ontology and the Ambitions of Metaphysics*. Oxford: Oxford University Press.
King, J. (2002). "Designating Propositions." *Philosophical Review* 111 (3): 341-71.
Moltmann, F. (2003). "Propositional Attitudes without Propositions." *Synthese* 35 (1): 77-118.
Schiffer, S. (1972). *Meaning*. Oxford: Oxford University Press.

Schiffer, S. (1987). *Remnants of Meaning*. Cambridge, MA: MIT Press.
Schiffer, S. (1991). "Does Mentalese Have a Compositional Semantics?" In *Meaning in Mind: Fodor and his Critics*, edited by G. Rey and B. Loewer, Oxford: Blackwell.
Schiffer, S. (1992). "Belief Ascription." *Journal of Philosophy* 89: 499–521.
Schiffer, S. (1996). "Language-Created, Language-Independent Entities." *Philosophical Topics* 24: 149–67.
Schiffer, S. (2003). *The Things We Mean*. Oxford: Clarendon University Press.

3
Objects of Thought

Ian Rumfitt

So mußte es kommen, ich hab' es gewollt;
Ich hasse ein Leben behaglich entrollt;
Und schlängen die Wellen den ächzenden Kahn,
Ich preise doch immer die eigene Bahn.

from Johann Mayrhofer (1787–1836),
Der Schiffer

3.1

The particular course that Stephen Schiffer has steered has led him to think as hard as any living philosopher about the content of our thoughts and utterances, and about the sentences we use to ascribe that content. Much of his writing in this area elaborates competing accounts of the intuitive validity of such simple inferences as "Harold believes that there is life on Venus, and so does Fiona; so, there is something that they both believe—to wit, that there is life on Venus" (see Schiffer 2003: 12). In *Remnants of Meaning* (1987), Schiffer took a Priorean line on inferences of this kind. Our sample inference is formally valid, being an instance of existential generalization, but "the existential quantification in the conclusion is a kind of *non-objectual* quantification" (2003: 90), and the that-clause which the quantifier replaces is not a singular term. I call this approach 'Priorean' for it was first systematically expounded in Arthur Prior's posthumously published monograph, *Objects of Thought*.[1] According to Prior,

phrases such as 'fears that' and 'thinks that' are predicates at the left and connectives at the right, in the quite precise sense that if the right-hand gap is filled by an actual sentence what remains with a left-hand gap is simply a one-place predicate (e.g. '—fears that there will be a nuclear war'), while if the left-hand gap is filled with an actual name what remains with a right-hand gap is precisely a one-place connective (to employ a reasonable logical barbarism), e.g. '*X* believes that—'. This expression is of the same logical type as 'It is not the case that—'. (Prior 1971: 19)

The parsing 'Harold / believes that / there is life on Venus' promises to liberate us from "the whole idea that ['*X* believes that *P*'] has to express a relation between *X* and anything whatever" (Prior 1971: 16) and hence from the idea that the quantifier in 'There is something Harold and Fiona both believe' ranges over objects (propositions) that can stand as *relata* in ascriptions of content. On Prior's view, the sort of quantification expressed here could more perspicuously be rendered using the non-nominal quantificational forms 'however things may be' and 'there is a way things may be' and the corresponding variables or pro-sentences 'things are so' or 'things are that way.'[2] Thus the conclusion of our inference might be expressed less misleadingly as 'There is a way things may be—to wit, as they are when there is life on Venus—such that both Harold and Fiona believe that things are that way.'

In *The Things We Mean* (2003), his most recent attempt to grapple with these issues, Schiffer abandons the Priorean line for a more familiar view according to which expressions in the form 'that *P*' are singular terms, and quantification into the position they occupy is objectual quantification. In the passage which explains and justifies his change of mind, Schiffer focuses on the parallel problem for properties, and leaves the reader to reconstruct the corresponding explanation for the case of propositions. But a sympathetic reconstruction would, I think, run as follows:

> Imagine a dispute between my old [Priorean] self and a realist about propositions. She and I agree that the proposition that Fido is a dog is true, and that there are many propositions that she and I both believe. We disagree on just one thing: she affirms while I deny that propositions exist. What came to unsettle me were two related things. The first was that I couldn't see either how that dispute could have a determinate resolution or what the cash-value of the dispute really amounted to. Relative to all the agreement, what could the further question about existence amount to such that it could be answered? I didn't see that this could have a happy answer, and it even seemed to me that the only concept of existence I had any grip on made it pretty difficult to deny the existence of propositions given all I wanted to say about them. The second thing to move me was the realization that whatever established the truth of statements ostensibly about propositions, and whatever allowed us to know the truths those statements expressed, would establish the existence and nature of propositions, and would explain our ability to have knowledge of those things, if those statements really were about the abstract entities they're ostensibly about. Putting all this together yields the pleonastic conception of propositions. (Schiffer 2003: 91, with alterations)

This pleonastic conception is the conception of propositions that Schiffer now recommends.

Unlike Schiffer, I do discern a substantial issue which separates the parties here: namely, whether our way of ascribing beliefs is disciplined enough to sustain judgements of identity and distinctness about their contents. Objectual quantification is quantification over objects, and the mark of objects is that it makes sense to ask whether object *a* is identical with object *b*. So we shall be able to quantify objectually over propositions only if it makes sense to ask whether the proposition that *P* is identical with the proposition that *Q*. Such questions will make sense only if we have some idea how to answer them in favourable cases. With non-objectual quantification, by contrast, the corresponding question makes no sense, as our rendering nicely brings out: the result of concatenating two variables or pro-sentences with the sign of identity is not even well formed (*'Things are so is identical with things are that way').[3]

In this chapter, I want to explore this issue by elaborating Schiffer's account (sections 3.2–3.3) and then arguing for three theses. First, that Schiffer's theory of pleonastic propositions does not by itself give us the resources to make sense of the question of propositional identity (section 3.4). Second, that making sense of the question involves constructing at least a rudimentary philosophical theory: the resources to ground judgements of identity and distinctness among propositions are not latent or implicit in our ordinary practices of ascribing beliefs but will come (if they come at all) from an attempt to regiment those practices for certain theoretical purposes (section 3.4). I then examine in some detail the regimentation that Frege proposed for his, specifically logical, purposes (sections 3.5–3.6). If it is to sustain the claim that propositions (what Frege called *Gedanken*) are objects, a regimentation must ensure that identity between propositions is reflexive, symmetric, transitive, and a congruence relation. My third thesis is that Frege's theory achieves this in certain special circumstances that were of interest to him (section 3.7), but that his account does not extend to provide for propositional identity more generally (section 3.8). I conclude that it is an open question whether the sort of theory Schiffer now espouses is as widely applicable as he wants it to be.

3.2

Schiffer recommends his pleonastic conception of propositions as the best way—perhaps the only way—of sustaining "a theory of belief reports which appears at face value to be correct; it's the default theory that must be defeated if it's not to be accepted" (11). (Henceforward, unadorned page references are to Schiffer 2003.) According to this 'face-value theory,' a simple belief report in the form '*A* believes that *S*' is "true just in case the referent of the '*A*' term stands in the belief relation to the proposition to which the 'that *S*' term refers" (12). Thus a simple report "consists of a two-place transitive verb flanked by slots for two singular argument terms" (12). This way of parsing simple reports is precisely the one Prior had rejected.

Prior notwithstanding, I think that Schiffer is right to accord to this parsing 'default' status. There are certainly some sentences in which 'believes' functions as a transitive verb—for example, 'John believes the rumour about Ted,' 'the jury disbelieved the witness's testimony'—so we shall get a simpler account of the verb's valency if we can also classify its occurrences in simple reports as transitive. By itself, this consideration is far from being decisive in favour of the face-value theory. The theory takes the second *relatum* in a simple report to be a proposition: an abstract object with no spatial location (14) nor, presumably, any temporal duration. By contrast, the rumour about Ted might be rife in Oxford but yet to reach London, and the witness's testimony might have taken up all of Tuesday afternoon. There are, however, a few sentences in which 'believes' is not only incontestably transitive but appears to relate to a proposition. Thus in 'Fred believes Einstein's Law,' 'believes' is grammatically transitive, and 'Einstein's Law' appears to be a singular term standing for a certain proposition. Moreover, the inference 'Fred believes Einstein's Law; Einstein's Law is that $E = mc^2$; so Fred believes that $E = mc^2$' seems to be an instance of the substitution of identicals.

All the same, it is worth noting that there are other forms of belief report than '*A* believes that *P*,' forms which do not even appear to be relational. One can say with Schiffer 'Harold believes that there is life on Venus.' But one can get the same message across by saying simply 'Harold believes there is life on Venus' or 'There is, Harold believes, life on Venus,' or even 'There is life on Venus, Harold believes.' In the last two cases especially, there is no temptation to parse the sentence as placing Harold in relation to a proposition, or to anything else. Rather, the final or parenthetical 'Harold believes' serves to indicate that the sentence 'There is life on Venus' is not an assertion on the speaker's own account, but is an utterance telling the hearer how (in this respect) Harold believes things to be. The reporter puts himself in Harold's shoes and speaks as Harold might, were he to speak his mind (in English) about the question of life on Venus. By themselves, these coordinate forms of belief ascriptions (as a linguist would call them) do not threaten Schiffer's analysis of reports in the form '*A* believes that *S*.' Different forms of report have to be analysed on their merits, and there is no reason why one analysis should fit all of them. But the coordinate ascriptions are ubiquitous, and just as common in everyday speech as the form on which Schiffer focuses, so we shall in the end want an account of the relation between 'Harold believes that there is life on Venus' (which purportedly places Harold in relation to a proposition) and 'There is, Harold believes, life on Venus,' which apparently does not. This Schiffer does not provide.

With this lacuna in mind, we may turn to Schiffer's own way of vindicating the face-value theory, which invokes his conception of propositions as pleonastic entities. A pleonastic entity is an entity that falls under a pleonastic concept; and a pleonastic concept is the concept of an *F* which implies true something-from-nothing *F*-entailment claims (57). As for this last notion,

Where '⇒' expresses metaphysical entailment, $S \Rightarrow \exists x Fx$ is a *something-from-nothing F-entailment claim* iff (i) its antecedent is metaphysically possible but doesn't *logically* entail either its consequent or any statement of the form '$\exists x\ (x=\alpha)$', where 'α' refers to an *F*, and (ii) the concept of an *F* is such that if there are *F*s, then $S \Rightarrow \exists x Fx$. (56–7)

So far, this is merely definitional: Schiffer's substantial claim is that many philosophically perplexing items are pleonastic entities that arise from appropriate something-from-nothing entailment claims. Thus fictional characters are pleonastic entities because it is a conceptual truth that, if there are fictional characters, then 'Joyce wrote a novel in which he used the name "Buck Mulligan" in the pretending way characteristic of fiction' entails 'Joyce created the fictional character Buck Mulligan' and hence 'There is at least one fictional character' (51). Properties are pleonastic entities because it is a conceptual truth that, if there are properties, then 'Lassie is a dog' entails 'Lassie has the property of being a dog' and hence 'There is at least one property' (61). And propositions are pleonastic entities because it is a conceptual truth that, if there are propositions, then 'Lassie is a dog' entails 'That Lassie is a dog is true' (sc., 'The proposition that Lassie is a dog is true') and hence 'There is at least one proposition' (71).

I think that Schiffer makes a slip in taking the something-from-nothing entailment associated with propositions to be the trivial entailment from *S* to 'the proposition that *S* is true.'[4] It seems fair to say that, for Schiffer, propositions are *essentially* contents of beliefs. Propositions may also be the contents of utterances (see for example 87–8), but they come into his philosophizing in the first place *as* the contents of beliefs. Given that propositions are essentially contents of beliefs, one would expect someone who proposes a pleonastic treatment of them to select, as the associated something-from-nothing entailment, an inference that brings out their role as the contents of beliefs. The entailment that Schiffer chooses, however, signally fails to do this. An arbitrary sentence 'S' will entail the corresponding sentence 'The proposition that S is true' if the words 'the proposition that S' are taken to refer to the truth-value of 'S', and if the predicate 'is true' is understood to apply to the truth-value True. (More exactly, there will be an entailment if the words 'the proposition that S' are understood to refer, with respect to a possible world w, to the truth-value True if the sentence 'S' is true with respect to w, and to the truth-value False otherwise.) No one, however, would imagine that truth-values could serve as contents of belief. My beliefs that grass is green, and that Bismarck resigned as Chancellor of Germany in March 1890, share a truth-value, but they have utterly distinct contents.

This is, I think, merely a slip on Schiffer's part, which may be rectified by choosing a different something-from-nothing entailment. And we may make a choice which provides the sought-after account of the relationship between transitive belief reports, such as 'Harold believes (the proposition) that there is life on Venus,' and the corresponding coordinate form 'There is life on Venus, Harold believes.' As we have noted, the latter ascription does not even purport to refer to a proposition: it simply says (in one respect) how Harold believes things to be. I suggest, then, that we take the inference from which pleonastic propositions are generated to be that from 'P, A believes' to 'A believes the proposition that P.' This inference is a something-from-nothing entailment in Schiffer's sense. Because it does not even purport to refer to a proposition, an ascription in the form 'P, A believes' carries no commitment to propositions. However, assuming that propositions exist, if the non-committal ascription 'P, A believes' is true, then so must be the corresponding relational report 'A believes the proposition that P.' But this entailment forces propositions to have a far finer grain than Schiffer's original choice, and thereby makes them more plausible candidates to be contents of beliefs. I hope Schiffer may accept this proposal as a friendly amendment to his theory.

3.3

Although he uses his theory of pleonastic propositions to sustain the face-value analysis of simple reports, Schiffer is clear that such reports differ in some fundamental ways from other sorts of relational statement. Perhaps the most important difference is this. In order to assess whether an utterance of 'Henri admires Picasso' is true, we typically draw on our knowledge of whom the speaker is referring to by the names 'Henri' and 'Picasso,' as well as our knowledge of what it takes for a pair of things to satisfy the relational predicate 'admires' (73). Our identifying knowledge of the names' referents is in general prior to, and partly explains, our knowledge of the utterance's truth conditions. With reports, things are the other way around. "The referent of the belief report's that-clause isn't a factor in determining the contextually determined criteria of evaluation for the belief report but is itself determined by those criteria" (75). So:

If we were evaluating an utterance of 'Ralph admires her' we would first determine the referent of 'her' and that would in turn complete the determination of the criteria for evaluating the statement. In evaluating the statement made in the utterance of ['Ralph believes that George Eliot was a woman'], however, we first implicitly fix the criteria for evaluating the statement, and that is what fixes the referent of the that-clause. (75)

I agree that any acceptable account must respect this difference between belief reports and (for example) attributions of admiration. It is utterly implausible to suppose that assessing a report involves making a prior identification of the proposition to which the reporter is referring.

What, though, remains of the face-value theory once this point is granted? According to the theory, a simple report is a relational statement. But what is the 'cash value' of this claim once it has been admitted that reports are assessed in a quite different way from other relational statements? I raised this question when responding to an earlier exposition of Schiffer's account, and he was kind enough to reply in *The Things We Mean* (79, n.27). Perplexity on this score will be allayed, he now suggests, once we recognize that, for many other statements involving reference to abstract objects, their assessment as true or false precedes the identification of the relevant object. The example he cites is the Fregean treatment of statements of number (*Zahlangaben*). In order to establish that there are four gospels, one does not need to identify an object as the cardinal number four: it suffices to show that there are gospels a, b, c, and d which are pairwise distinct and such that every gospel is one of them. All the same, the inference from 'There are exactly n As' (where 'n' is a numerical adjective and 'A' is a count noun) to 'the number of As = the number n' (where 'the number n' is a singular term) is a something-from-nothing entailment in Schiffer's sense: given that there are cardinal numbers, 'there are exactly four gospels' entails 'the number of gospels = the number four.' Against Dummett, Schiffer insists that the possibility of coming to know that the number of gospels is identical with the number four simply by counting the gospels, and without identifying any object as the number four, does not gainsay the Fregean thesis that 'the number of gospels = the number four' is a statement of identity. "Dummett is right that the criteria of evaluation for arithmetical sentences don't invoke numerical objects; his mistake is to think this entails that numerals aren't genuine singular terms whose referents are numbers" (79).

Although the matter is controversial and delicate, I think that Schiffer is right against Dummett here.[5] Accordingly, I find the analogy with statements of number helpful in understanding what the cash value of the claim that belief reports are relational is supposed to be. Closer examination of the analogy, though, reveals a large hole in Schiffer's defence of the face-value theory.

For what sustains Frege's thesis that 'the number of gospels = the number four' is a statement of identity? On Frege's theory, the (cardinal) number of As (the number 'belonging' to the As, as he puts it) will be identical with the number of Bs if and only if there are just as many As as there are Bs. There are just as many gospels as there are symphonies by Brahms; so the number of gospels is identical with the number of Brahms's symphonies. There are fewer gospels than there are platonic solids; so the number of gospels is less than the number of platonic solids. The principle on which Frege relies here is universally accepted, but it qualifies as a criterion of identity only because the relation that obtains when there are just as many As as there are Bs—the relation of 'equinumerosity' between the relevant Fregean concepts—is an equivalence relation. Only because this is so does the criterion cohere with the laws of identity, which require *it* to be an equivalence relation. Indeed, something stronger is required to sustain the Fregean claim that numbers are objects: equinumerosity must be a congruence relation for a whole range of mathematically interesting properties of concepts. Consider for example the second-level property that the As have (collectively) if they cannot be sorted without remainder into equal-sized sub-groups unless those sub-groups are singletons. Then, if there are just as many As as there are Bs, the Bs will (collectively) have the same property. Given Frege's criterion of numerical identity, the As will have this second-level property if and only if the number of As possesses the first-level property that we call 'being prime.' So by learning the techniques for calculating whether a given natural number is prime, we can discover whether any As to which that number belongs has the specified second-level property. Frege held that it was applicability alone that raised pure mathematics from a game to a science. By treating cardinal numbers as objects—that is, by taking at face value the grammatical similarities between numerals and ordinary singular terms—we enable the construction of a simple theory in which properties of numbers are expressed by first-level predicates, but which is readily applicable to determine mathematically interesting higher-level properties of ordinary empirical concepts. The resulting combination of theoretical simplicity and wide applicability is the best argument for treating numbers as objects.

3.4

What, though, is supposed to sustain the corresponding thesis about the contents of belief? Is there an equivalence relation among beliefs which ensures that the laws of identity will not be violated if we treat contents as objects? Our ordinary practices of ascribing beliefs do not immediately yield up such a relation. Let us call a non-defective[6] utterance of a declarative sentence a *saying*, and let us say that a saying v R-relates to a saying u ('R' for 'reports') if and only if there is a belief which u would be properly understood as expressing, and which v could truly report. A saying truly reports a belief if a simple report in which the saying follows the complementizing 'that' would be a true report of the belief in question. Thus a saying v that is my utterance of the English sentence 'The earth moves' R-relates to a saying u that is Galileo's utterance of the Italian sentence 'Si muove la terra.' There is a belief—Galileo's belief that the earth moves—which u is properly understood as expressing, and which v could truly report: for I could truly report this belief of Galileo's by saying 'Galileo believes that the earth moves.'

One might hope that this relation R would be an equivalence relation; abstraction on it would then yield up contents for beliefs (or at least, for those beliefs expressible by sayings) somewhat as abstraction on equinumerosity yields up cardinal numbers for concepts.[7] But R is not an equivalence relation. Or at least, it is not an equivalence relation if we share Schiffer's Fregean intuitions about the truth of belief reports.[8] For suppose that, unknown to the Baron, Octavian is in fact identical with Mariandel. And then consider the following three sayings: u, which is an utterance by the Baron of 'Octavian lives in Vienna'; v, which is an utterance by the Baron of 'Mariandel lives in Vienna'; and *w*, which is an utterance by Octavian (*alias* Mariandel) of 'I live in Vienna.' It is clear that *w* reports *u*: Octavian could truly report the belief that *u* would be taken to express by saying 'The Baron believes that I live in Vienna.' It is only marginally less clear that *w* reports *v*: since Octavian *is* Mariandel, he can also truly report the belief that *v* would be taken to express by saying 'The Baron believes that I live in Vienna.' On a Fregean view of the matter, however, *v* does not report *u*: the belief that the Baron expresses by saying 'Octavian lives in Vienna' is not his belief that Mariandel lives in Vienna, for although the names 'Octavian' and 'Mariandel' share a reference, the Baron associates them with distinct modes of presentation. These relations between *u*, *v*, and *w*, however, preclude *R*'s being an equivalence relation. If it were an equivalence, then by symmetry '*w* reports *v*' would entail '*v* reports *w*,' which could combine with '*w* reports *u*' to yield '*v* reports *u*' by transitivity. As we have seen, though, a theorist with Schiffer's Fregean predilections is committed to denying that *v* reports *u*. So such a theorist is committed to denying that *R* is an equivalence relation.

Since I share those predilections, I take seriously the problem that this result poses for the hypothesis that contents of beliefs are Fregean objects. By itself, the result does not preclude identifying a kind of object that can serve as the contents of beliefs: given a relation that is not an equivalence relation, there are many ways of defining from it one that is. The result shows, though, that in order to find such a relation we shall have to engage in more philosophical theorizing than Schiffer's discussion might lead one to expect. He rightly stresses that on any sane version of the face-value theory, the identification of propositions as the objects referred to by that-clauses will depend on the criteria for assessing simple belief reports as true or false. But what the case brings out is that our ordinary criteria for making those assessments will need to be refined and tightened if they are to yield an equivalence relation that can serve as the basis for an abstraction. I have nothing against the project of refining and tightening our ordinary criteria, but there is no reason to suppose that there is a uniquely favoured way of doing this: different equivalence relations will correspond to different ways of determining the notion of a belief's content, ways that serve different purposes.[9] Further, if the enterprise of defining a suitable equivalence relation is to be more than an intellectual parlour game, we must start with some indication of the purpose that a particular determination of content is intended to serve, and then seek an equivalence relation that ensures the resulting class of propositions really does serve it.

3.5

Frege's own writings provide a striking illustration of the interest and difficulty of this enterprise.

Many Fregean texts indicate a necessary condition for two sayings to share a content (to 'express one thought'). In 'Über Sinn und Bedeutung,' for example, Frege grounds his claim that the thought in the saying 'The Morning Star is a body illuminated by the Sun' differs from that in 'The Evening Star is a body illuminated by the Sun' by saying simply "anybody who did not know that the Evening Star is the Morning Star might hold the one thought to be true, the other false" (Frege 1892: 32). Presumably, somebody holds the thought 'in' a saying to be true when he both grasps the thought in the saying and takes that saying to be true. So we may recast the condition here so that truth applies to sayings rather than thoughts:

> If somebody can 'grasp' two sayings even though, for all he knows, one is true and the other false, then the sayings do not express a single thought."

Contraposing, we reach the following necessary condition for two sayings to express one thought:

> (N) If two sayings express one thought, then nobody can 'grasp' both sayings without being in a position to know that they share a truth-value.

It is easy to see why a logician should wish to employ a notion of content that respects condition (N). Logical deduction is important primarily because it is a way of gaining knowledge: given knowledge of an argument's premises, a thinker who reasons in accordance with logical rules can come to attain knowledge of its conclusion. Philosophical discussions of how such gain in knowledge is possible typically invoke the metaphor of a thinker taking inferential 'steps' from one thought to the next. If we can find a criterion for the identity of thoughts that respects (N), we may hope to cash out this metaphor.

Before we can cash out that metaphor, we need a sufficient condition for sameness of thought. Can the condition in (N) also serve as such? I think not. We want a sufficient condition that can serve as a criterion for sameness of content: that is, we want something that can (at least in favourable cases) be applied to yield knowledge that two sayings express one thought. The condition in (N) cannot so serve: knowledge that two sayings express one thought grounds knowledge that no one can grasp both sayings without knowing that they share a truth-value, not *vice versa*. It is not possible to run through all the possible circumstances in which people who grasp both sayings might find themselves, and check that in each case they will know that the sayings share a truth-value. Treating the condition in (N) as a criterion for the identity of thoughts would be as absurd as taking Leibniz's Law to be the criterion for the identity of planets. Since the planet Hesperus *is* the planet Phosphorus, Hesperus and Phosphorus will share all their properties. But one cannot come to know the identity by running through all the properties of Hesperus, and Phosphorus, and noting at the end that the properties are the same. Rather, one comes to know that Hesperus is identical with Phosphorus by applying the specific, substantial criteria for planetary identity; one may then infer from what one has come to know that Hesperus and Phosphorus share all their properties.

Frege himself never contemplated using the condition in (N) as a criterion for sameness of thought expressed. His clearest attempt to state such a criterion is found in his letter to Husserl of 9 December 1906. Earlier in their correspondence, Husserl had appealed to a notion of 'congruence' between sentences, which prompted Frege to complain that without a definition the congruence of two sentences could be debated without resolution "for a hundred years." Frege now claims

> that the only possible means of deciding whether sentence *A* expresses the same thought as sentence *B* is the following, in which I assume that neither of the two sentences contains a logically evident component in its sense. If both the assumption that the content of *A* is false

and that of B is true, and the assumption that the content of A is true and that of B false, lead to a logical contradiction, and if this can be established without needing to know whether the content of A or B is true or false, and without needing to appeal to anything other than purely logical laws, then nothing can belong to the content of A, as far as it is capable of being judged true or false, which does not also belong to the content of B. For there would be no reason for any such surplus in the content of <A> and according to the presupposition above, such a surplus would not be logically evident either. In the same way, given our assumption, nothing can belong to the content of B, as far as it is capable of being judged true or false, except what also belongs to the content of A. Thus what is capable of being judged true or false in the contents of A and B is identical, and this alone is of concern to logic, and this is what I call the thought expressed by both A and B. (Frege 1976: 105–6 = Frege 1980: 70–1)

In other words, logically interdeducible sentences—or, better, sayings—that contain no logically evident components will express a single thought.

Clear as it may be, the criterion offered to Husserl faces a serious problem as a sufficient condition for the identity of Fregean thoughts: it is inconsistent with the necessary condition (N). For let us consider a saying u of the words 'Nothing is both a man and immortal' and a saying v of the words 'Everything is either not a man or is mortal.' Since either one of these sayings may be derived from the other, and since neither contains any logically evident component, they will express the same thought by the criterion proposed to Husserl. Yet somebody could surely 'grasp' the sayings without seeing that they are interdeducible, and thus might 'hold the one thought to be true and the other to be false.' According to condition (N), however, this entails that they express distinct thoughts, contrary to the result delivered by the criterion.

Earlier in 1906, Frege had formulated a sufficient condition for sameness of thought expressed which, while it belongs to the same family as that given to Husserl, differs precisely in trying to accommodate considerations of cognitive value:

Two sentences A and B can stand in such a relation that anyone who recognises the content of A as true must also recognise the content of B as true without further ado (*ohne weiteres*), and conversely that anyone who accepts the content of B must immediately (*unmittelbar*) accept that of A (*equipollence*). It is assumed here that there is no difficulty in grasping the contents of A and B. The sentences need not be equivalent in every respect. For example, one may possess what we call a poetic air, while the other may lack this...One has to separate off from the content of a sentence the part that alone can be accepted as true or rejected as false. I call this part the thought expressed in the sentence. It is the same in equipollent sentences of the kind given above. (Frege 1969: 213–14 = Frege 1979: 197–8)

How are we to understand the adverbial phrases 'without further ado' and 'immediately' as they are used in this passage? The answer is implicit in the *reductio* Frege attempts of the supposition that a sentence's 'poetic aura' belongs to the part of its content that may be evaluated as true or as false. The argument starts from the assumption that of two equipollent sentences, A and B, one (A) may possess a poetic aura that the other lacks, and that this aura is a feature or part of the sentence's 'content' on some generous understanding of that term. If, though, the hypothesized aura of A belonged to what was proclaimed to be true in an assertion of A, "then it could not be an immediate consequence of anyone's accepting the content of B that he should accept that of *A*" (Frege 1969: 213 = Frege 1979: 197). This is clearly intended to contradict the initial assumption that *A* and *B* are equipollent, but it does so only if its being an immediate consequence of anyone's accepting the content of *B* that he should accept that of *A* is a necessary condition for their equipollence. This determines the requisite gloss on Frege's criterion: two sentences will be equipollent just in case each is an immediate consequence of the other.

Equipollence, when so defined, may appear to offer a solution to our problem about the identification of thoughts. Somebody may accept 'Nothing is both a man and immortal' without *immediately* accepting 'Everything is either not a man or is mortal.' Thus sayings *u* and *v* above are not equipollent, so the passage does not entail the problematical conclusion that they express the same thought. More generally, one might hope to reconcile the criterion with (*N*) by arguing that, when each of two sayings is an immediate consequence of the other, nobody will be able to hold one to be true and the other to be false. But even if this claim could be defended, a fatal problem looms. The definition of equipollence is supposed to legitimate Frege's talk of *the* thought expressed by a saying; that thought, he tells us, may be identified as that which "is the same in equipollent sentences of the kind given above." But to do this, equipollence must be an equivalence relation: if it is not, then there is no reason to suppose that there is a category of objects precisely one of which will attach to all the members of a class of equipollent sayings. Now equipollence as it has been explained here is certainly symmetrical; we may hope also to ensure reflexivity by specifying a sense in which each saying is an immediate consequence of itself. But however the notion of immediacy may be precisely determined, equipollence is not transitive. If *B* is an immediate consequence of *A*, and *C* is an immediate consequence of *B*, *C* need not be an *immediate* consequence of *A*. For while *C* will surely be a consequence of *A*, that consequence might be mediated by *B*. Equipollence, then, is not an equivalence relation, and cannot provide the basis for Frege's talk of *the* thought (in the singular) expressed by a saying.

3.6

Transitivity failed because 'immediately' was glossed in terms of immediate consequence. But the formula "somebody who recognizes the content of *A* as true must also recognize the content of *B* as true without further ado" suggests a rather different idea. The test for equipollence, it may be suggested, should not be that one can infer *B* from *A* (and conversely) in a single step, but rather that grasping the contents of utterances of these sentences *already* requires knowing that they share a truth-value. This is a different idea, for when grasp of content already requires such knowledge, there will be no room for an inference (even by a single step) from *A* to *B* or conversely. For the knowledge must be attained before one is in a position to make inferences whose contents could be expressed using the sentences *A* or *B*.

How might this alternative elucidation of the equipollence relation be spelled out? Let us say that two sayings are *manifestly isomorphic* if anybody who grasps both will recognize that one can be got from the other by substituting one or more simple component expressions for others. Thus the sayings 'The Morning Star is a body illuminated by the Sun' and 'The Evening Star is a body illuminated by the Sun' form a manifestly isomorphic pair, as do 'Some Greek is cultured' and 'Some Hellene is brave.' Where the sayings u and v are manifestly isomorphic, let us also say that a simple part w of u *corresponds* to a simple part y of v if these parts occupy the same place in the structure that is common to u and v. Thus, among the component utterances of the examples just given, 'the Morning Star' corresponds to 'the Evening Star,' as do 'Greek' to 'Hellene' and 'ξ is cultured' to 'ξ is brave.' Now, at least to a first approximation, 'grasping' a simple utterance may be taken to consist in knowing what its speaker expects a hearer to know about what (in the relevant sentential context) the utterance refers to.[10] Let us say, then, that two simple components of sayings are *equipollent* if anyone who knows what he is expected to know about their references (in the relevant contexts) will know that they coincide in reference. On this definition, the mark of equipollent simple utterances is that knowledge that they coincide in reference is required in order to grasp them.

With these preliminaries in place, let us deem two complete sayings to be *equipollent* if and only if (a) they are manifestly isomorphic and (b) their corresponding simple components are equipollent. Since a saying's truth-value is left undisturbed by a substitution in which a component is replaced by an expression which shares its reference, anyone who grasps two equipollent sayings is in a position simply to *see* that they coincide in truth-value. No inference is needed to establish that coincidence. When so defined, then, equipollence captures the idea of sayings so related that all who grasp them are in a position to know "without further ado" that they coincide in truth-value. The hypothesis for which I now wish to argue is that it is this relationship of equipollence which underpins most of Frege's judgements as to the identity or distinctness of the thoughts which sayings express.[11]

In the first place, the hypothesis explains why Frege held that "the construction of the sentence out of parts of sentences corresponds to the construction of a thought out of parts of thoughts" so that "the structure of the sentence can serve as a picture of the structure of the thought" (Frege 1969: 243 = Frege 1979: 225; compare Frege 1969: 262 = Frege 1979: 243). If the structure of a sentence (or, better, of a saying) reflects the structure of the thought that it expresses, then two sayings which express the same thought must be alike in structure. So under this doctrine, a necessary condition for two sayings to express one thought is that they should be isomorphic. We can now explain why Frege should have imposed this condition. If one is to see— without inference—that sayings match each other in truth-value, then they must be manifestly isomorphic. But if two sayings are manifestly isomorphic, they must certainly be isomorphic.

In the second place, the hypothesis explains why Frege should have taken (N) to be a necessary condition for sayings to express one thought. As we have seen, anyone who grasps the content of two equipollent sayings is, just on that account, in a position to know that they coincide in truth-value. So if we can truly say of someone who grasps two sayings that, for all he knows, one may be true while the other is false, then the sayings in question will not be equipollent. On the hypothesis, then, Frege is right to conclude in such a case that they express distinct thoughts.

Third, our explanation of equipollence, as it obtains between simple parts of sayings, fits those passages where Frege adjudicates questions of sameness of sense between sub-sentential utterances. Most of these passages concern utterances of proper names, and a typical (but unusually fully described) case is presented in 'Der Gedanke':

> Suppose... that Herbert Garner knows that Dr Gustav Lauben was born on 13 September 1875 in NN and this is not true of anyone else; suppose, however, that he does not know where Dr Lauben now lives nor indeed anything else about him. On the other hand, suppose Leo Peter does not know that Dr Lauben was born on 13 September 1875 in NN. Then as far as the proper name 'Dr Gustav Lauben' is concerned, Herbert Garner and Leo Peter do not speak the same language, although they do in fact refer to the same man with this name; for they do not know that they are doing so. Therefore Herbert Garner does not associate the same thought with the sentence 'Dr Gustav Lauben has been wounded' as Leo Peter wants to express with it. (Frege 1918: 65)

Frege's talk of Garner and Peter "not speaking the same language so far as the name 'Dr Lauben' is concerned" is florid, but the last sentence quoted shows how we are to understand it. Utterances of this name that come from Garner's mouth, and utterances that issue from Peter's mouth, contribute differently to the exchange of thoughts between them because "although they do in fact refer to the same man with this name, they do not know that they are doing so." Since they do not know that they use the name 'Dr Lauben' to refer to the same man, Garner cannot expect any listener to know that his (Garner's) uses of the name share their reference with Peter's uses of it. (Neither can Peter expect any of his listeners to know that his (Peter's) uses of the name share their reference with Garner's uses.) Accordingly, an utterance of the name by one of them will fail our test for equipollence with an equiform utterance by the other. Our hypothesis, then, explains why Frege is right to conclude that these utterances contribute differently to an exchange of thoughts.

It also accounts for the rather simpler example Frege gave when explaining the distinction between the sense and reference of a proper name to Peano:

> I say that the two names ['Morning Star' and 'Evening Star'] have the same reference but not the same sense, and that is shown by this, that a speaker need not know anything about the coincidence in reference, as most people ignorant of astronomy will not, in fact, know anything about it; but the speaker will have to connect a sense with the name<s> if he is not to be babbling senselessly. (Frege 1976: 196 = Frege 1980: 127)

If Frege's speaker is not to be babbling senselessly when he uses the names 'Morning Star' and 'Evening Star,' then he must know what he is talking about when he uses them. In other words, he must know, of the planet Venus, that the name 'Morning Star' designates it, and that the name 'Evening Star' does. Moreover, if in using these names a speaker intends to convey his thought to an audience, he must expect that audience to know what he is using the names to refer to. Frege observes, though, that the speaker may nevertheless not know that the two coincide in reference, and in such a case he will hardly expect his audience to know this. In such a case, the speaker's uses of the name 'Morning Star' will fail our test for equipollence with his uses of the name 'Evening Star.' Our hypothesis can explain, then, why Frege concludes that in such a case the utterances are not equipollent, even though they share a reference.

Some may still look askance at the suggested account of equipollence as a reconstruction of Frege's criterion for sayings to express one thought. Whether a speaker expects a hearer to know that one utterance coincides in reference with another will be highly sensitive to what the parties know about each other's state of knowledge. So whether two sayings are equipollent will be correspondingly sensitive to fine features of the conversational context in which the sayings occur. But while this may disturb some of the applications which other philosophers have hoped to make of Fregean thoughts, it is no objection to the proposed interpretation, for Frege himself recognizes that the identity of thoughts exhibits exactly this sensitivity. At another point in 'Der Gedanke,' he invites his readers to

> consider the following case. Dr Gustav Lauben says 'I have been wounded.' Leo Peter hears this and remarks some days later, 'Dr Gustav Lauben has been wounded.' Does this sentence express the same thought that Dr Lauben himself uttered? [α] Suppose that Rudolph Lingens was present when Dr Lauben spoke and now hears what Leo Peter has to say. If the same thought is uttered by Dr Lauben and by Leo Peter, then Rudolph Lingens, who is fully master of the English language and remembers what Dr Lauben said in his presence, must now know at once from Leo Peter's report that he is speaking of the very same thing. But knowledge of the language is a special thing when proper names are involved. It can easily be that only a few people associate a determinate thought with the sentence 'Dr Lauben was wounded.' For a complete understanding in the case described, one will need to know the expression 'Dr Gustav Lauben.' Now if both Leo Peter and Rudolph Lingens understand by 'Dr Gustav Lauben' the doctor who is the only doctor who lives in a house known to both of them, then they both understand the sentence in the same way; they associate the same thought with it. [β] But it is also possible that Rudolph Lingens does not know Dr Lauben personally and does not know that it was Dr Lauben who recently said 'I have been wounded.' In this case Rudolph Lingens cannot know that the same thing is in question. For this reason, I say in this latter case: the thought which Leo Peter publicly expresses is not the same as that which Dr Lauben uttered. (Frege 1918: 65, with Greek letters interpolated)

In discussing case (α), Frege does not directly answer the question that he raises about it—namely, whether Lauben's utterance of 'I have been wounded' expresses the same thought as Peter's utterance of 'Dr Gustav Lauben has been wounded.' However, the implied contrast between cases (α) and (β) suggests forcibly that the intended answer in the former case is 'yes,' and this interpretation is confirmed by a passage in the unpublished 'Logik' of 1897. Discussing there the type sentence 'ich friere' ('I am cold'), Frege remarks that, "it is not necessary that the person who feels cold should himself give voice to the thought that he feels cold [as he may do by uttering 'ich friere,' 'I am cold']. Another person can also do this, by designating the person who feels cold by name."[12] Comparing the two passages, it is natural to understand case (α) as describing one possible circumstance in which this happens, i.e., as describing a case in which Lauben's utterance of 'I have been wounded' expresses the same thought as Peter's utterance of 'Lauben has been wounded.'

The proposed reconstruction explains why this description is right. We are plainly intended to envisage case (α) as one where Lingens knows to whom Peter is referring using the name 'Dr Gustav Lauben' only by virtue of knowing that Peter is referring to the man whom they had both heard say 'I have been wounded.' We are to suppose, in other words, that Lingens must bring his memory of the previous conversation to bear if he is to know to whom Peter is referring when he uses the name 'Dr Gustav Lauben.' If Lingens must confess that, for all he knows, Peter may have been referring to someone other than the man whom they both heard say 'I have been wounded,' then in the circumstances described he will not know of whom Peter is speaking in using 'Dr Lauben.' But in that case, Lingens will not know what he is expected to know about the reference of Peter's use of the name 'Dr Lauben' unless he knows that this utterance shares a reference with Dr Lauben's own utterance of the pronoun 'I.' Accordingly, these utterances pass our test for being equipollent. Moreover, Lauben's saying is manifestly isomorphic to Peter's, so the complete sayings will qualify as equipollent too. Hence, if equipollence (as defined here) is the criterion for sameness of thought, Frege is right to conclude—as the passage forcibly suggests that he did conclude—that in case (α) Lauben's saying expresses the same thought as Peter's.

Things are quite different in case (β). Frege does not specify the knowledge that underpins Lingens' understanding of the name 'Dr Lauben' in the latter case. But since Lingens "does not know Dr Lauben personally and does not know that it was Dr Lauben who recently said 'I have been wounded,'" he will not be expected to know that Peter's utterance of 'Dr Lauben' shares a reference with Lauben's utterance of the pronoun 'I.' By our test, then, the expressions contribute differently to an exchange of thoughts between Peter and Lingens, and Frege is quite right to "say in this latter case [that] the thought which Leo Peter publicly expresses is not the same as that which Dr Lauben uttered."

The contrast between the two cases shows how the identity of thoughts exchanged can depend on what a speaker and his audience know about each other. Leo Peter's words 'Dr Lauben has been wounded' have the same reference and the same conventional linguistic meaning in Frege's case (α) as they have in case (β). All the same, different thoughts are expressed in the two cases. The difference results from the differences in the common knowledge, concerning the reference of the name 'Dr Lauben,' that Peter and Lingens are imagined to have in the two cases. Frege's own discussion makes it clear, then, that the identity of thoughts is not determined solely by the combination of conventional linguistic meaning and the contextual determination of references.[13]

3.7

Well grounded in the texts as it may be, the proposed explanation of equipollence will vindicate Frege's talk of "the thought in a saying," and thereby unlock the gates to his third realm, only if it yields an equivalence relation. Since two sayings are equipollent when anybody who grasps both is thereby in a position to know that they coincide in truth-value, the relation is patently reflexive and symmetric. The question is whether it is transitive.

When equipollence is a relation on domains of a special kind—a kind of special interest to Frege—it is, I now argue, transitive, and hence an equivalence relation. For suppose the relevant domain comprises the sayings that are the premises and conclusion of an argument that is being assessed for deductive validity; or suppose that the domain comprises sayings that are being tested for logical consistency. A characteristic of sayings in such domains is that some of their simple parts will be equipollent in the sense specified in section 3.6. Someone who grasps the argument 'Hesperus is bright; Hesperus is Phosphorus; therefore Phosphorus is bright' is expected to know that the two occurrences of the name 'Hesperus' share a reference, and similarly for the two occurrences of 'Phosphorus.' (Indeed, as Kit Fine has argued,[14] logic would be crippled if we could not take it for granted that some occurrences of proper names (say) share a reference: any attempt to prove that they do would lead to an infinite regress.) Since some of the sayings in the domains we are considering will be manifestly isomorphic, some complete sayings in those domains will also be equipollent.

The important point for the present, however, is that in the particular domains we are considering, equipollent utterances may be assumed to form chains: where we have, say, three occurrences of the name 'Hesperus' in an argument, a hearer will be expected to know not merely that the first occurrence is equipollent with the second and the second is equipollent with the third, but also that all three occurrences share a reference. So long as each equipollent pair is part of such a chain, the relation will be transitive. So, in the special domains with which we are concerned, equipollence may be assumed to be an equivalence relation.

Even when they formulate arguments in a natural language, logicians habitually try to render these equipollence chains perspicuous by ensuring that simple utterances are equiform when and only when they are equipollent. Thus logicians eschew 'elegant variation,' in which a speaker uses different words while expecting his hearers to know that the reference is shared. Moreover, they do not baulk at using neologisms to replace equiform words that are not equipollent: in discussing Kripke's 'puzzle about belief,' for instance, a case where it is not assumed to be known whether different occurrences of 'Paderewski' share a reference, they may express the crucial point of ignorance as whether Paderewski-the-pianist is identical with Paderewski-the-statesman.

This very mild regimentation of argumentative discourse is the first step towards the construction of fully formalized languages, of which Frege's *Begriffsschrift* was the earliest example. As he stressed from the start, that symbolism was intended to be a means for expressing content, and not merely a calculus for evaluating the validity of inferences. And, at least within the confines of a single use of it, equiform inscriptions in the formalism are assumed to have a constant reference. If I render a vernacular argument as the sequent 'Fa; Gb; so $Fa \wedge Gb$' it is simply assumed—taken for granted—that the occurrences of the singular term 'a' stand for the same object, that the two occurrences of the predicate letter 'F' are true of the same objects, and so forth. Within the formalized language itself, there is no way of raising the question whether (for example) one occurrence of the letter 'a' stands for the same object as another.

This means that there will be a precise relationship between equipollence in the domains we are now concerned with, and the use of equiform expressions in a Fregean formalized language. In rendering an argument into such a language, one will translate simple utterances using the same simple symbol just when they are equipollent in the specified sense. For suppose first that two simple utterances are equipollent. Then anybody who 'grasps' them will be assumed to know that they share a reference, so it would be erroneous to employ distinct formal symbols (the letters 'a' and 'b' as it might be) in translating the two utterances. Why? Well, since knowledge of the coincidence in reference is taken for granted, the vernacular argument being translated will fail to justify it, even though coincidence in reference may be required for the argument's soundness. Under a translation in which distinct symbols replace equipollent utterances, then, the argument may be made to appear to be incomplete or lacunose when in fact it is not. For any piece of reasoning rests on some presuppositions, and an argument should not be faulted for failing to justify what it presupposes.

Conversely, when the two vernacular utterances are not equipollent, a hearer may grasp the sayings in which they figure without knowing that they share a reference. Accordingly, he can—without betraying any lack of grasp of the utterances—sensibly raise the question of whether they share a reference. (Even if he knows that they do in fact share a reference, he can still question whether the argument's proponent has shown that they do.) The raising of that question, however, is precluded if the utterances are rendered using the same symbolic letter. For in a formalized language of Frege's type, there is and can be no issue of whether $a = a$.

When arguments are rendered in a formalized language in such a way that formal equiformity matches vernacular equipollence, the rendering comes to depict the way simple vernacular utterances contribute to an exchange of thoughts. The translator shows that two such utterances are equipollent by rendering them using the same symbol, and he shows that they are not equipollent by using different symbols. Trite as it may be, this point is the key to exposing the flaw in a famous objection to one of Frege's arguments for his claim that names which share a reference might yet contribute differently to an exchange of thoughts.

The argument that I have in mind emerges clearly in a draft of a letter to Jourdain that Frege wrote in January 1914. He there presents a case in which a single mountain is called 'Aphla' by those who live to its south, and is called 'Ateb' by those who live to its north; it is not common knowledge that these names share a bearer. By applying his condition (N), Frege is able to show that "what is said in the sentence 'Ateb is Aphla' is certainly not the same thing as the content of the sentence 'Ateb is Ateb'" (Frege 1976: 128 = Frege 1980: 80). He goes on:

Now if what corresponded to the name 'Aphla' as part of the thought were the reference of the name, i.e., the mountain itself, then this would be the same in both thoughts. The thought expressed in the sentence 'Ateb is Aphla' would have to coincide with the one in 'Ateb is Ateb,' which is not at all the case. What corresponds to the name 'Ateb' as part of the thought must therefore be different from what corresponds to the name 'Aphla' as part of the thought. (Frege 1976: 128 = Frege 1980: 80)

Like Schiffer (27–30), I am suspicious of Frege's doctrine that thoughts have parts. But the argument just quoted really needs only two much weaker claims. First, that the non-equipollence of two manifestly isomorphic sayings, both of which predicate a single attribute of a single thing, calls for explanation. Second, that the best explanation will advert to the lack of a suitable semantic relation between corresponding parts of the two sayings.

It was against this second claim that Hilary Putnam once mounted an interesting attack. The sayings 'Ateb is Aphla' and 'Ateb is Ateb' meet our condition for manifest isomorphism. But there is another respect in which they differ in structure and, Putnam suggested, this difference can explain their not being equipollent without any need to posit any difference in sense between the component names:

> Consider, for the moment, a simpler example (a variant of the famous 'paradox of analysis'): 'Greek' and 'Hellene' are synonymous. But 'All Greeks are Greeks' and 'All Greeks are Hellenes' do not *feel* quite like synonyms. But what has changed? Did we not obtain the second sentence from the first by 'putting equals for equals'? The answer is that the *logical structure* has changed. The first sentence has the form 'All F are F,' while the second has the form 'All F are G'—and these are wholly distinct... This suggests the following revision of the [compositional] principle: The sense of sentence is a function of the sense of its parts *and of its logical structure*. (Putnam 1954: 118)

We may account, in other words, for the fact that a saying s of 'Ateb is identical with Aphla' is not equipollent with a saying t of 'Ateb is identical with Ateb' by citing the fact that t is an instance of the schema 'α is identical with α,' while s is not.

Putnam's objection to Frege cuts little ice as it stands, for even if it is cogent, its force can be evaded simply by changing the example. Condition (N) also establishes that a saying, u, of 'Aphla is at least 5000 metres high' is not equipollent with a saying v of 'Ateb is at least 5000 metres high.' These sayings, however, instantiate the same logical schemata, so Putnam's explanation cannot account for their not being equipollent. The complaint against Frege will be merely that, in focusing on statements of identity, he chose an unfortunate sort of example. In an interesting paper, however, William Taschek has proposed a way of extending Putnam's explanation so that it covers these cases (Taschek 1995). Because u and v instantiate the same schemata, they are alike in what Taschek calls their *local* logical structure. However, an argument's validity may depend upon the way in which expressions recur in *different* sentences. Accordingly, we shall need in any case a more sensitive notion of logical structure defined, not in terms of a single sentence's being, or not being, an instance of a schema, but in terms of a plurality of sentences' being corresponding instances of a number of schemata. Taschek captures such a notion by stipulating that the sentences S and S' will have the same *global* logical structure

> just in case for all logical schemata X and Z and any sentence S^*, S and S^* are corresponding instances of X and Z (respectively) if and only if S' and S^* are corresponding instances of X and Z (respectively). (Taschek 1995: 84)

Sentences differing in local structure will differ in global structure, so Putnam's explanation of the difference between s and t is preserved. However, sentences alike in local structure may differ in global structure, so differences in global logical structure can account for differences in cognitive value which Putnam's theory is unable to explain. Thus, u and v, although alike in local structure, differ in global structure, because u and a saying w of 'Ateb is snow-capped' are corresponding instances of the schemata 'α is φ' and 'α is ψ' while v and w are not. The idea, then, is that the disturbance in global logical structure consequent upon replacing the name 'Aphla' with the name 'Ateb' accounts for the non-equipollence of u and v. There is no need to postulate different senses for the two names. We are able, Taschek concludes, "to respect the powerful theoretical considerations that support the direct reference thesis [sc., the claim that simple referring expressions that share a reference will also share a sense] without having to offend [the] deeply entrenched pre-theoretical intuitions" that led Frege himself to deny that thesis (Taschek 1995: 92).

This is, perhaps, a seductive line of argument, but we are now well placed to resist its blandishments. The fact that two vernacular sayings are not equipollent, we are told, may sometimes be explained by their differing in global logical structure. But how is it determined what the global logical structure of a vernacular saying is? How are we to determine of which logical schemata utterances are instances, or corresponding instances? A plausible answer is: by inspecting their renderings in a Fregean formalized language; for such languages are designed to render logical forms 'perspicuous.' But if my previous remarks are right about the principles of translating from a natural language into a formalized one, we can see that logical structure, whether local or global, cannot explain a failure of equipollence *independently* of such a failure on the part of sub-sentential components. If it is taken for granted in a conversation that the words 'Greek' and 'Hellene' apply to the same things, then the translator should render these words by a single predicate letter, and 'All Greeks are Hellenes' will emerge as having the same logical structure as 'All Greeks are Greeks.' The first utterance will just be a misleading way of saying that all Greeks are Greeks, so that an unmisleading translation into a formalized language will be an instance of the schema 'All x (Fx; Fx).' If on the other hand the identity of Greeks and Hellenes is not taken for granted, then the translator will use distinct symbols. At this point, however, we see the futility of trying to invoke logical schemata as a source of explanation that is *alternative* to Frege's. The schemata instantiated by the symbolic renderings of vernacular sayings will show which of their components contribute in the same way to an exchange of thoughts and which do not. But before making the translations, we shall need to find out of which pairs of components a coincidence in reference is presupposed. And to find that out is precisely to find out which pairs of components make the same contribution to the relevant exchange of thoughts.

3.8

I argued in section 3.7 that equipollence, explained as in section 3.6, is an equivalence relation across domains that comprise the sayings produced in the course of a particular deductive argument. Rather few actual sayings, however, are so produced. So we need to ask whether equipollence is an equivalence relation over sayings generally.

I claim that it is not. This can be shown in a number of ways, but perhaps the simplest way is to elaborate the case I labelled (α) when quoting from 'Der Gedanke' in section 3.6 above. In the circumstances described there, in which both Peter and Lingens heard Lauben complaining 'I have been wounded,' Peter's later utterance v of 'Dr Lauben has been wounded' is equipollent with Lauben's original complaint u. Let us suppose in addition, however, that quite unbeknownst to Peter and Lingens a second pair—let us call them Bunsen and Kirchhof—also overheard Lauben's complaint. They have never met Lauben before, and do not know his proper name, but the situation inspires them to dub him with the nickname 'Fritz.' Some days later, Bunsen says to Kirchhof, 'Fritz has been wounded,' a saying we shall label w. Now the reasoning which applied in Frege's case (α) to show that v is equipollent with u also shows that w is equipollent with u. For in this case too, we can suppose that Kirchhof will not know what he is expected to know about the reference of the name 'Fritz' unless he appreciates that it is used to refer to the man whom he and Bunsen heard say 'I have been wounded.' However, w is not equipollent with v. In order to grasp the use of the name 'Fritz' in w, a hearer must know that it shares its reference with a use of the pronoun 'I' which Bunsen and Kirchhof heard together. And in order to grasp the use of the name 'Dr Lauben' in v, a hearer must know that it shares its reference with a use of the pronoun 'I' which Peter and Lingens heard together. But in order to grasp both v and w, it is not necessary to know that the use of the pronoun 'I' which Peter and Lingens heard together is the very same use which Bunsen and Kirchhof heard together. For none of the speakers in either of the two conversations expects anyone to know this. Indeed, they do not know it themselves. Accordingly, in order to grasp both v and w, it is not necessary to know that the use of the name 'Dr Lauben' in v shares a reference with the use of the nickname 'Fritz' in w. We have, then, a situation in which v is equipollent with u and in which w is equipollent with u (so that u is equipollent with w by symmetry), but in which v is not equipollent with w. That is to say, transitivity fails, and equipollence is not an equivalence relation.

Where does all this leave the face-value theory? I should sum up as follows. There is a relation—that of equipollence, as defined in section 3.6—which is an equivalence relation over certain special, restricted domains of sayings—viz. those that form a single passage of deductive argument. Since those domains are the focus of a logician's interest, and since the Fregean thought 'in' a saying is above all else its logical content (see again Frege 1969: 213–14 = Frege 1979: 197–8), this vindicates Frege's treatment of thoughts as objects. It does not, though, vindicate the face-value theory, which posits objects as the contents of ordinary sayings and beliefs. Equipollence is not an equivalence relation over the domain of all sayings, yet the face-value theory associates propositions with sayings and beliefs quite generally, not merely those advanced in the course of deductive arguments. If there is a way of refining the definition of equipollence so that it is an equivalence relation over the wider domain, I am afraid I have missed it.

Of course, this rather inconclusive conclusion does not refute Schiffer. There may be a way of eking an equivalence relation out of our relation of equipollence. Or again, there may be a quite distinct equivalence relation that preserves the Fregean intuitions about sameness of content that Schiffer and I share. All we can really say is that the vindication of the face-value theory is incomplete, and faces a large unsolved problem. In those respects, it is like any interesting philosophical theory. And like all the best philosophical theorizing, Schiffer's work in this area directs our attention to the most pressing unsolved problems.

Notes

1. Prior (1971). Oddly, Schiffer does not cite this work in either *Remnants of Meaning* or *The Things We Mean*.
2. These forms are inspired by Wittgenstein's suggestion that the English expression 'this is how things are' can be used similarly to the propositional variables of a formal language. See *Philosophical Investigations*, Part I §134. Prior himself rendered propositional quantification in English using 'anywhether' and 'somewhether' as quantifiers and forms of 'thether' as the attendant variables. (See Prior 1971: 37–9.) But this way of talking has won few imitators, and I prefer to revert to Wittgenstein's original suggestion.
3. I fully agree with Schiffer (2003: 90) that non-objectual quantification need not be substitutional. Again, the rendering shows how: we need not assume that, however things may be, there is a sentence which says that they are that way.
4. 'Trivial,' I should say, if we ignore the wholly non-trivial problem of solving the semantic paradoxes. But, like Schiffer, I bracket that issue.
5. The best treatment of these matters that I know is Hodes (1990).
6. By which I mean *inter alia* that appropriate references are secured for any names and demonstrative expressions occurring in the sentence.
7. I say 'somewhat' for the relations abstracted over would belong to different logical levels.
8. Although Schiffer rejects Frege's theory of propositions (*Gedanken*), he describes the Fregeans' assessment of belief reports that provide the data for the theory as "commonsense intuitions" (38).
9. For an illuminating discussion of the way different theories of propositions correspond to different (and equally legitimate) determinations of the notion of a belief's content, see Moore (1999).
10. NB: both occurrences of the word 'what' in this sentence are interrogative pronouns.
11. There are some exceptions to this generalization. In particular, it does not at all fit Frege's notorious claim (1891: 10–11) that the universally quantified statement 'For all x, $x^2 - 4x = x(x - 4)$' expresses the same thought as an identity statement between value ranges. However, since that claim underpinned the fatal Basic Law V, we should not expect a rational reconstruction of Frege's criteria for sameness of sense to find houseroom for it.
12. Frege (1969: 146) = Frege (1979: 134–5). Michael Dummett regards this passage as an aberration. He deems the claim that NN's utterance of 'I am F' can express the same thought as another's utterance of 'NN is F' to be indefensible "on any view save that a name contributes to a thought only in virtue of its reference" (Dummett 1981: 119). The 'Logik' of 1897 does not adopt this view. The view contradicts the claim made there that "even though the tale of William Tell is a legend and not history and the name 'William Tell' is an apparent singular term, we cannot deny to it a sense" (Frege 1969: 141) = (Frege 1979: 130). *Contra* Dummett, however, I do not see that we need to attribute any confusion to Frege on this score. The doctrine that a name contributes something other than its reference to a thought is not threatened by the claim that there are certain rather special conversational circumstances in which the utterance of a proper name may share its sense with an utterance of the pronoun 'I.'
13. This conclusion has also been reached, in a different way, by Tyler Burge. See his 1990.
14. In the John Locke lectures he gave at Oxford in 2003, published as Fine (2007).

Bibliography

Burge, T. (1990). "Frege on Sense and Linguistic Meaning." In *The Analytic Tradition*, edited by D. Bell and N. Cooper, Oxford: Blackwell: 30–60.

Dummett, M. A. E. (1981). *The Interpretation of Frege's Philosophy*. London: Duckworth.

Fine, K. (2007). *Semantic Relationism*. Malden, MA: Blackwell.

Frege, F. L. G. (1892). "Über Sinn und Bedeutung." *Zeitschrift für Philosophie und philosophische Kritik* 100: 25–50.

Frege, F. L. G. (1918). "Der Gedanke." *Beiträge zur Philosophie des deutschen Idealismus* 2: 58–77.

Frege, F. L. G. (1969). *Nachgelassene Schriften*. Edited by H. Hermes et al. Hamburg: Felix Meiner.

Frege, F. L. G. (1976). *Wissenschaftliche Briefwechsel*. Edited by G. Gabriel et al. Hamburg: Felix Meiner.

Frege, F. L. G. (1979). *Posthumous Writings*. Translated by P. Long and R. White. Oxford: Blackwell.

Frege, F. L. G. (1980). *Philosophical and Mathematical Correspondence*. Edited by B. McGuinness and translated by H. Kaal. Oxford: Blackwell.

Hodes, H. T. (1990). "Where Do the Natural Numbers Come From?" *Synthèse* 84: 347–407.

Moore, J. G. (1999). "Propositions without Identity." *Noûs* 33: 1–29.

Prior, A. N. (1971). *Objects of Thought*. Oxford: Clarendon Press.

Putnam, H. W. (1954). "Synonymity and the Analysis of Belief Sentences." *Analysis* 14: 114–22.

Schiffer, S. R. (1987). *Remnants of Meaning*. Cambridge, MA: MIT Press.

Schiffer, S. R. (2003). *The Things We Mean*. Oxford: Clarendon Press.

Taschek, W. W. (1995). "Belief, Substitution, and Logical Structure." *Noûs* 29: 71–85.

4

Schiffer's Unhappy-Face Solution to a Puzzle about Moral Judgement

Michael Smith

In the first two chapters of *The Things We Mean* Stephen Schiffer defends the following claims.[1]

(i) *The things that we believe to be true are the very same things as the things that we mean when we state (say/assert) things.*

(ii) *The things we mean when we state (say/assert) things are propositions.*

(iii) *The concept of a proposition is a pleonastic concept,*

where, according to Schiffer, the concept of an F is pleonastic just in case the concept itself licenses entailments of the form: $S \Rightarrow \exists x Fx$. These are what he calls "something-from-nothing" entailments and the various practices in which such entailments are made are what he calls "hypostatizing practices" (57). The concept of a proposition is pleonastic, according to this definition, because it licenses the move from a claim like 'Fido is a dog,' a claim containing only the singular term 'Fido' referring to Fido, to the claim 'It is true that Fido is a dog,' which is a claim that contains the singular term 'that Fido is a dog' referring to the proposition that Fido is a dog.

(iv) *Propositions are pleonastic entities,*

as anything that falls under a pleonastic concept is, by definition, a pleonastic entity. And

(v) *The nature of propositions, as pleonastic entities, is fully determined by the hypostatizing practices that are constitutive of the concept of a proposition together with those necessary a priori truths that are applicable to things of any kind.*

Schiffer's idea is thus that propositions are entities, but that they are entities of a particularly insubstantial kind, as they have no hidden nature waiting to be discovered by a theory (63). Everything there is to know about propositions is right there on the surface, deducible from the hypostatizing practices constitutive of the concept—moves like that from 'Fido is a dog' to 'It is true that Fido is a dog'—and from the other necessary a priori truths that apply to things of all kinds.

As Schiffer points out, the theory of pleonastic propositions looks to have far-reaching consequences both in the theory of meaning and elsewhere in philosophy, consequences he explores more fully in subsequent chapters of *The Things We Mean*. One of these concerns a familiar puzzle in the theory of meaning that is confronted more often by meta-ethicists than by specialist philosophers of language. The puzzle is prompted by the Janus-faced nature of moral judgements, for while certain features of such judgements point in one direction, suggesting that they are expressions of cognitive states, other features point in the opposite direction, suggesting that they are expressions of non-cognitive states.[2] The puzzle in the theory of meaning is to give an account of what we mean when we make moral judgements that somehow makes sense of their Janus-faced nature.

Schiffer's solution to this puzzle comes in three parts. The first part consists of an argument in favour of cognitivism based on the theory of pleonastic propositions; the second part consists of a supplementary suggestion about the content of moral judgement that, as he sees things, explains why theorists have been tempted by non-cognitivism; and the third part consists of a consequence Schiffer draws about the truth-value of moral judgements, a consequence that he believes to be forced upon us by what he says in the second part: the consequence is that moral claims are indeterminate in truth-value, which is why he dubs his an unhappy-face solution to the puzzle. In what follows I will present and examine all three parts of Schiffer's solution. My hope is to prompt him to say more about the nature of both pleonastic propositions and moral judgement.

4.1 The First Part of Schiffer's Solution to the Puzzle: The Argument for Cognitivism

According to Schiffer, the theory of pleonastic propositions tells decisively in favour of cognitivism rather than non-cognitivism. Here is the relevant passage:

The two sentences

(a) Eating animals is a source of protein
(b) Eating animals is wrong

appear to be semantically on a par, and the *cognitivist* is the theorist who says they really are on a par. The *non-cognitivist* agrees that (a) and (b) appear to be on a par but adds that in this case appearances are misleading. Normative sentences like (b) are masqueraders; the kind of meaning they actually have is different from the kind they appear to have—namely, the kind of meaning (a) in fact has. Now, whatever kind of meaning sentences like (a) have, it is what defines cognitivism. So what kind of meaning do sentences like (a) have? The...meaning of a sentence is determined by two things: the kind of speech act the literal speaker must perform in uttering the sentence on its own, and the kind of propositional content those speech acts must have. If we assume, as I have been assuming, that stating and believing are relations to propositions, then, as regards (a), the literal speaker who utters it on its own must be *stating (saying/asserting) that eating animals is a source of protein*, where the proposition *that eating animals is a source of protein* is both truth-evaluable and something one might believe. It is truth-evaluable in that it is true iff eating animals is a source of protein, and false iff eating animals isn't a source of protein. By the criterion this implies, cognitivism is true if the meaning of (b) is determined by its being the case that the literal speaker uttering it on its own must be *stating (saying/asserting) that eating animals is wrong*, where the proposition *that eating animals is wrong* is both truth-evaluable and something one might believe (and believe in exactly the same sense in which one believes that eating animals is a source of protein). The doctrine of pleonastic propositions clearly entails cognitivism. (241–2)

The argument goes by very quickly at the end, so let's make the premises fully explicit.

The overarching question is whether 'Eating animals is wrong' has the same kind of meaning as 'Eating animals is a source of protein.' Schiffer points out that if it does, then cognitivism is true, for the kind of meaning that 'Eating animals is a source of protein' has is the kind of meaning that guarantees that the states of mind expressed by sincere utterances of such sentences are beliefs. Earlier on in the book, however, Schiffer has argued that the meaning of a sentence is fixed by the kind of speech act performed by those who utter such a sentence on its own plus the kind of propositional content that such a speech act has. So the question whether 'Eating animals is wrong' and 'Eating animals is a source of protein' have the same kind of meaning reduces to the question whether these are similar in each case.

Schiffer's answer to this question is that they are. When people use the sentence 'Eating animals is wrong' on its own, much as when they use the sentence 'Eating animals is a source of protein' on its own, *they make a statement*: in the one case they state *that eating animals is a source of protein*, in the other they state *that eating animals is wrong*. It therefore follows that the meaning enjoyed by the two sentences is given by the very same kind of thing, namely, a *pleonastic proposition*, for a pleonastic proposition is both what people state when they state things and what they mean by their statements. This follows more or less immediately because there is no distinction to be made in the kinds of hypostatizing practices that are in play in the two cases, where these hypostatizing practices are some among the many such practices that are constitutive of the concept of a proposition as a pleonastic entity. Just as there is a practice of saying things like 'I believe that eating animals is a source of protein,' 'It is true that eating animals is a source of protein,' 'Let me state quite categorically that eating animals is a source of protein,' and so on, so there is equally a practice of saying things like 'I believe that eating animals is wrong,' 'It is true that eating animals is wrong,' 'Let me state quite categorically that eating animals is wrong,' and so on. The kind of meaning enjoyed by the sentence 'Eating animals is wrong,' a meaning supplied by a pleonastic proposition, is thus on all fours with the kind of meaning enjoyed by the sentence 'Eating animals is a source of protein.' This is why Schiffer concludes that the doctrine of pleonastic propositions "clearly entails cognitivism." Since I want to refer back to this conclusion later—that cognitivism follows from the theory of pleonastic propositions—I will call it 'Schiffer's Conclusion.'

Schiffer does, however, more or less immediately go on to admit that the argument he gives for Schiffer's Conclusion would fail if 'statement' was being used ambiguously. Consider those who use the sentence 'Eating animals is a source of protein' on its own. Suppose that, when we say that they use the sentence to state that eating animals is a source of protein, we mean one thing by 'state,' the sense in play in (i) above—this is the sense that plays a defining role in the concept of a pleonastic proposition—but when we say that the sentence 'Eating animals is wrong' is used on its own to state that eating animals is wrong, we use 'state' in a different sense. In that case, though the meaning of 'Eating animals is a source of protein' would turn out to be a pleonastic proposition, the meaning of 'Eating animals is wrong' would not. So an important question to ask is whether there is such an ambiguity, and, unsurprisingly, non-cognitivists famously argue that there is. The argument is, in effect, that though statements in the first sense—the sense which is in play in the definition of a proposition—are indeed expressions of beliefs (look again at (i)), statements in the other sense are not, but are rather expressions of wants (or, as Schiffer calls them, "conations").

The argument non-cognitivists give for this conclusion is the argument Schiffer calls the "Argument from Internalism." He formulates the argument thus:

(1) Necessarily, one who accepts the judgement that she morally ought not to X has some conation against her X-ing.
(2) If there are moral propositions, then for a person to accept that she morally ought not to X is for her to believe the proposition that she morally ought not to X is true.
(3) But such a belief is consistent with a person's not having any conation against her X-ing.
(4) ∴ There are no moral propositions. (240)

I will have more to say about this argument presently, but, in anticipation, note that at the end of his discussion of this argument Schiffer says that he "rejects the conclusion of this valid argument" (243). The issue, as he sees it, is thus to identify the faulty premise. He cannot reject (2), for that follows directly from the theory of pleonastic propositions (again, see (i) above). Moreover, he tells us that premise (1) "seems right" (243). So this leaves him with (3), the motivation for which he explains thus:

Premiss (3) derives its plausibility from the cogency of a familiar Humean worry. If there are moral propositions, as the cognitivist claims, then to believe that acts of a certain kind are wrong is just to believe that acts of that kind have a certain objective property, and, the worry goes, such a belief would be consistent with one's feeling any way at all about whether anything has that property. A belief that a certain fact obtains, Hume held, may cause a certain conation, but having the belief can never entail that conation. (242–3)

Though he doesn't explain why, Schiffer plainly doesn't share Hume's worry, so he rejects (3). The non-cognitivist's crucial argument therefore fails. So, at any rate, Schiffer concludes.

Schiffer's discussion of the Argument from Internalism is revealing in the light of Schiffer's Conclusion which, to repeat, is that *cognitivism follows from the theory of pleonastic propositions*. For, as is, I hope, already clear, his own discussion of the Argument from Internalism suggests that we should reject Schiffer's Conclusion. This is because, according to that discussion, the theory of pleonastic propositions is itself *neutral* on the issue of cognitivism versus non-cognitivism. This might not be immediately evident, so it might be helpful if we slightly reformulate the Argument from Internalism so as to make its bearing on both the issue of ambiguity of 'state' and the theory of pleonastic propositions more vivid (I will call this the 'Argument*'):

(1*) Necessarily, one who states that she morally ought not to X wants to refrain from X-ing.

(2*) If there were moral propositions, then a person who states that she morally ought not to X would be expressing her belief that the proposition that she morally ought not to X is true.
(3*) There are no propositions p and q such that, when someone believes that p, she wants that q.
(4*) ∴ There are no moral propositions.

Though the Argument* does not differ in any substantive way from the version of the Argument from Internalism that Schiffer originally spelled out, it serves to make it clear both why the theory of pleonastic propositions is itself neutral on the issue of cognitivism versus non-cognitivism and why we should suppose that 'state' is ambiguous.

According to (i), when we state things, the things that we state are things that we believe. But what we learn from the Argument* is that there is a sense of 'state' in which we can state that someone morally ought to act in a certain way where the thing stated is not something that we believe. There is, after all, as the Argument* brings out, no moral proposition to be either believed or stated in the sense in play in (i). The premises of the Argument* and (i) are therefore inconsistent, and the obvious way to make them consistent is to suppose that 'state' is ambiguous: (i) must use 'state' in a sense quite different from the way in which 'state' is used in (1*). Moreover, this would seem to be a reasonable conclusion to draw despite the fact that none of the premises make any assumptions about the nature of propositions. In other words, reflection on the Argument* in the light of (i) seems to show that there are no moral propositions *whatever our theory of propositions*.

The crucial premise in the Argument*, much as in Schiffer's original presentation of the Argument from Internalism, is (3*). (3*) purports to state a necessary a priori truth about the relationship between the ways things are on the one hand, and our beliefs and wants on the other. It says that no matter how any particular person believes things to be and no matter how they want things to be, there is always the possibility that someone could have exactly the same beliefs but different wants. Since, according to (3*), this is supposed to be both necessary and knowable a priori, it purports to serve as a constraint on what propositions there can be. Moreover, since (3*) would seem to make no assumptions about the nature of propositions, it purports to serve as such a constraint on any theory of propositions, including the theory of propositions as pleonastic entities.

Nor is Schiffer in a position to baulk at this. For remember that, as he himself tells us (see (v) above), the nature of propositions, as pleonastic entities, is fully determined by the hypostatizing practices that are constitutive of the concept of a proposition together with those necessary a priori truths that are applicable to things of any kind. To be sure, what Schiffer had in mind when he said this were necessary a priori truths such as that, if x=y, then whatever property x has, y has, and vice versa (63). But it is difficult to see how he could plausibly resist admitting that a necessary a priori truth like (3*), assuming for a moment that it is indeed a necessary a priori truth, similarly partially determines the concept of a proposition as well.

If this right, however, then, far from being inconsistent with the theory of pleonastic propositions, the Argument from Internalism itself turns out to be a potentially crucial element in a full spelling out of that theory. For, assuming for a moment that (3*) really is a necessary a priori truth, the Argument*, in conjunction with (i)—the platitude that when we state things what we state is the same sort of thing as what we believe—enables us to identify the crucial ambiguity in what it is to state things, and hence enables us to uncover the way in which the crucial necessary a priori truth, (3*), further constrains what pleonastic propositions there can be. This version of the theory of pleonastic propositions, however, the version that is constrained by (3*), is a version according to which we should be non-cognitivists about moral judgements. So Schiffer's Conclusion—his claim that the theory of pleonastic propositions entails cognitivism—is false. What entails cognitivism about moral judgement is, at best, a *particular version* of the pleonastic theory of propositions: the version that we get by denying that (3*) does state a necessary a priori truth.

So far I have been concerned to show that Schiffer's Conclusion is false. But I want now to turn to the more substantive issue. Suppose, for a moment, that we should accept some version of the pleonastic theory of propositions. Should we accept the version that we get by denying (3*)—this is Schiffer's preferred version of the theory, the version that entails cognitivism about moral judgement—or should we instead accept the version that we get by constraining our pleonastic theory of propositions by (3*)? If we should accept the latter version, then, if Schiffer is correct that the other premises in the Argument* should be accepted, we thereby commit ourselves to non-cognitivism about moral judgement. I want now to argue that, if we were to accept any version of the pleonastic theory of propositions at all, we should accept the version that is constrained by (3*). So not only is Schiffer's Conclusion false, but Schiffer himself should be a non-cognitivist about moral judgement, not a cognitivist.

The reason we should accept the version of the pleonastic theory that is constrained by (3*) is—surprise, surprise—because (3*) is itself so plausible: there really is no belief whose possession entails the possession of a want. To be sure, some theorists deny not only the plausibility of this claim, but insist that it is motivated by a dubious metaphysical prejudice. This seems to be John McDowell's view, for example, when he complains that it amounts to an imposition of the view that the world is "motivationally inert" (17).[3] Schiffer also seems to think that Hume's worry is similarly metaphysically motivated, for he describes him as worried about how, if "to believe that acts of a certain kind are wrong is just to believe that acts of that kind have *a certain objective property*" (my emphasis), such a belief could entail a want. But the complaint is plainly wrong, as (3*) is a claim about the relationship between the things that we can believe about the world and the things that we can want about the world no matter what those things are, not a claim about the relationship between what we can believe about the world and what we can want about the world given some controversial assumptions about the metaphysical status of certain of the things that we can believe and want.

In terms familiar from Hume, the idea behind (3*) is that, since our beliefs and wants are distinct existences, so we can always separate them, at least modally. But if we can separate them, modally, then our beliefs cannot entail our wants (or, more cautiously, no particular belief can entail any particular want). Moreover, note that we can explain this idea in much less abstract and more commonsensical terms. For suppose that there were moral propositions and that possession of the belief that one morally ought to ϕ did entail that one wants to ϕ. In that case, someone who at a certain time has this belief and want, but then over time loses that want—perhaps he becomes depressed and simply loses all interest in doing what he believes he morally ought to do—must thereby lose the belief as well. If possession of the belief entails possession of the want, then simply by losing the want the agent must, somehow, lose the belief. But why would no longer wanting to φ, under these circumstances, entail that he no longer believes that he morally ought to φ?

Loss of the want means that the agent is no longer in a state with the functional role of a want: that is, that he is no longer disposed to ψ when he believes that ψ-ing affords him an opportunity to φ, and the like. Loss of the belief, by contrast, like loss of any belief, means that he is no longer in a state with the functional role of belief: that is, in this case, that he is no longer disposed to infer the proposition that he morally ought to φ—and, remember, we are simply assuming for the sake of argument that there is such a proposition for the time being—from the propositions from which it follows, and no longer disposed to infer from it to the propositions it entails, and the like. But these two states of mind—being in a state with the functional role of that belief but not in a state with the functional role of that want—look to be quite independent of each other. Someone could be in the one but not the other, or be in both, or be in neither.

To be sure, some belief and desire might contingently co-vary. As a matter of fact, loss of some desire might come along with or even cause loss of some belief. One way in which this could be so is if possession of the desire made salient certain features of something, features whose salience would be lost if the desire were to go and whose salience is crucial to belief. But it seems at least possible that such patterns of salience could survive loss of the desire—the connection imagined is, after all, causal, not logical—and hence it seems at least possible that one could be in the belief state but not the desire state. So the upshot would appear to be that if there were moral propositions then we would have no alternative but to give up premise (1*) of the Argument*: no alternative but to give up the claim that someone who states that she morally ought not to X wants to refrain from X-ing.[4]

But now suppose that there are no moral propositions and that what someone who states that she morally ought not to X is doing is expressing her desire to refrain from X-ing. In that case there would be no problem at all in understanding how (1*) could be true. For the reason why someone who states that she morally ought not to X wants to refrain from X-ing is because wanting to refrain from X-ing is the very psychological state that she expresses when she states that she morally ought not to X. In that case it would hardly be surprising that someone who loses her want to refrain from X-ing is no longer in the psychological state that she expresses when she states that she morally ought to X. For, to repeat, that want is the psychological state that she expresses.

The upshot is that non-cognitivists have a ready response to Schiffer's initial argument for cognitivism. They should say that although he lays out some reasons for thinking that the literal speaker who says 'Eating animals is wrong' states that eating animals is wrong in exactly the same sense of 'states' as the literal speaker states that eating animals is a source of protein when he says 'Eating animals is a source of protein'—and hence though he lays out some reasons for thinking that both express their beliefs that some pleonastic proposition is true—further reflection prompted by the Argument from Internalism reveals that, by contrast with the latter case, there is no pleonastic proposition for the literal speaker who says 'Eating animals is wrong' to state or believe. Though the hypostatizing practices constitutive of the concept of being wrong are a lot like the hypostatizing practices constitutive of the concept of being a source of protein, the practices are in fact subtly different. This is what we learn by attending to (3*). The Argument from Internalism therefore reveals that 'state' is ambiguous. It suggests a crucial constraint on what pleonastic propositions there can be.[5]

4.2 The Second Part of Schiffer's Solution to the Puzzle: The Suggestion about Content

Schiffer might justly complain that the argument given at the end of the preceding section fails to take into account a suggestion he makes about the content of our moral judgements. If this suggestion is correct, he might say that far from it being plausible to suppose that there are no propositions p and q such that, when someone believes that p, she wants that q, he in effect provides examples of such propositions. So let's consider this hypothetical complaint.

At a certain point, Schiffer provides an account of two conditions governing a concept of his own invention: the concept W. Though he admits that there are some differences between the concept W and our moral concepts, he insists that the conditions governing the two are very similar. If he is right about this then the concept W, so defined, suffices to give the lie to what was said in the preceding section. For the concept W must be fit to figure in the contents of an agent's beliefs and, in virtue of figuring in those contents, it must thereby guarantee that those beliefs have a connection with an agent's wants like that specified in premise (1) of the Argument from Internalism. Propositions specified using the concept W must therefore be counterexamples to (3*), the claim that there are no propositions p and q such that, when someone believes that p, she wants that q. We therefore need to examine Schiffer's somewhat oblique suggestion about the content of our moral beliefs with some care.

Here is Schiffer's suggestion:

In Bob's conceptual scheme, the concept W is governed by the following two conditions.

(a) W, by its very nature, is a concept that Bob applies to some things and withholds from others, but in order for Bob to believe that α is W, there must be some non-normative concept N such that Bob also believes both that α is N and that being N entails being W.

(b) It isn't required that N be any particular concept; N can be anything, provided certain conditions are met. These conditions pertain to what Bob wants; for example, Bob should want not to live in a world in which people do anything that is N. (256)

Once we appreciate that there can be a concept governed by these two conditions, Schiffer claims, we see, among other things, "how internalism is compatible with cognitivism" (258).

I am not completely sure that I understand the concept W. The problem I have lies in understanding in what way, exactly, a concept might be governed by condition (*b*). Imagine that there is a slightly different concept, W*, which is governed by condition (*a*), just like the concept W, but which instead of being governed by (*b*), is governed by the slightly different condition (*b**):

(*b**) It isn't required that N be any particular concept; N can be anything, provided certain conditions are met. These conditions pertain to what *Bob's wife* wants; for example, *Bob's wife* should want not to live in a world in which people do anything that is N.

When Bob applies a concept that meets conditions (a) and (b*) to α, he must be thinking that α has a property that he conceptualizes, *inter alia*, in terms of his wife's wants. That is to say, at least roughly, he must be thinking that α has N where N is a property of the actions that are performed by people in those possible worlds in which his wife does not want to live. The reason for this is simply stated: there is no way for facts about what Bob's wife wants to fix the conceptual role of Bob's concept W* except by way of being represented as such. The upshot is thus that, even though the *truth* of the claim that α is W* requires simply that α bears a certain relation to things that his wife wants, for Bob to *believe* that α is W*, he must *believe* that α bears that relation to the things his wife wants, where this is read *de dicto*.

But now suppose that we understand condition (*b*) in exactly the same way as we've just understood condition (*b**). In that case, when Bob applies W to α, he must be thinking that α has a property that he conceptualizes, *inter alia*, in terms of his own wants. That is to say, again very roughly speaking, that Bob must be thinking that α has N where N is a property of the actions performed by people in those possible worlds in which he does not want to live. As before, though the truth of the claim that α is W requires simply that α bears a certain relation to the things he wants, for Bob to believe that α is W he must believe that α bears that relation to the things he wants. Unfortunately, however, if this is the right way of thinking about the concept W—if Bob's wants partially fix the conceptual role of the concept W by being represented as such—then Schiffer's oblique suggestion about the content of our moral judgements evidently fails to deliver the goods.

To repeat, Schiffer claims that reflection on the concept W shows us that cognitivism is compatible with internalism. But note that Bob's belief that α has N, where N is a property that bears a certain relation to things he wants—this, remember, is what we must suppose Bob to believe when he applies W to α—could be false in virtue of Bob's having *misrepresented* his own wants. He might believe that N is a property that bears a certain relation to things he wants but be mistaken about what it is that he does want. It is, after all, a contingent matter that we want what we want and our beliefs about such things, though usually very reliable, are fallible. Consider the possible worlds in which Bob's belief is false because he is mistaken about what he wants. In those possible worlds Bob believes that α has N, where N is a property that bears a certain relation to things he wants, but he does not have those wants. Yet if there are possible worlds in which Bob has the belief but doesn't have the wants, then it follows that Bob's having that belief doesn't entail that he has those wants. So, contrary to what Schiffer tells us, his suggestion about the content of our moral judgements—his suggestion that our moral concepts are a lot like the concept W, and hence that what goes for W judgements goes for moral judgements too—does not show how cognitivism could be compatible with internalism. On the contrary, his suggestion provides a vivid illustration of the problem that a cognitivist faces when he tries to make his view square with the truth of internalism.

I said that I am not completely sure that I understand the concept W. This is because there is an alternative way of understanding that concept. By contrast to the interpretation just suggested, when Bob deploys the concept W, on the alternative way of understanding the concept, he is not representing his own wants. Rather, his wants themselves partially control his deployment of that very concept. Of course, this presents us with a puzzle, for how are we to suppose that his wants manage to do that? Here what we need is some crucial difference between the role that Bob's wants can play, as regards Bob's deployment of a concept, and the role that Bob's wife's wants can play, as regards Bob's deployment of a concept. The natural suggestion, of course, is that, when Bob applies W to α, he can simultaneously express his belief that α has N and express his wants regarding N. Bob's wife's wants, by contrast, cannot similarly be expressed by Bob when he deploys his concept. On the alternative way of understanding the concept, then, Bob's wants partially control his deployment of the concept W in virtue of the fact that his deployment of that concept is, *inter alia*, an expression of his wants regarding N.

At a certain point Schiffer hints that this might in fact be his view. He says, for example, that although the account he gives entails a kind of cognitivism, it follows from his account that cognitivism isn't "true in an entirely full-blooded sense" (257). The reason, he tells us, is that, according to his view,

> ...one's conative attitudes enter into the determinants of the non-normative notions on which the application of one's moral concepts will be taken to supervene. Since these conative attitudes are essential to one's having moral concepts, it further follows that the meaning of 'wrong' in one's *lingua mentis* (as it were) is unlike that of predicates which express non-normative concepts in that the former partly supervenes on *conative* facts. (258–9)

The initial idea in this passage—that "conative attitudes enter into the determinants of the non-normative notions on which the application of one's moral concepts will be taken to supervene"—sounds like the claim that facts about one's conative attitudes enter into the truth conditions of the moral claims one makes. This is the idea behind the first interpretation of the concept W, the interpretation we considered earlier. This is a version of cognitivism, indeed it is a full-blooded version, but as we have seen it doesn't entail internalism. But as the passage goes on the idea seems to be quite different. For Schiffer tells us that "conative attitudes are essential to one's having moral concepts"—in other words, that conative attitudes enter into an account of the *possession* conditions of moral concepts, not their *application* conditions—and the natural way to interpret this claim is by taking deployment of those concepts in thought to amount to *manifestations* or *expressions* of those conative attitudes themselves. This is indeed to give up on a full-blooded version of cognitivism.

However, if this is the right way of thinking about the concept W—if Bob's application of the concept W to α is a matter of his both believing that α has N and his expressing his wants regarding N—then Schiffer's suggestion once again fails to deliver the goods. This time, however, the suggestion fails to deliver the goods because, even though his view is, *inter alia*, a version of cognitivism, the respect in which his view is a version of cognitivism is irrelevant to the demonstration of the compatibility of his view with internalism. What he offers, according to this interpretation, is a hybrid theory according to which an agent's judgement that α has W is the expression of both a belief—the belief that α has N—and also the expression of his wants concerning N. This view is compatible with internalism alright: Bob's believing that α has N and his wanting what he wants about N entails that he has those wants concerning N. But it is compatible with internalism in virtue of the fact that one element in the hybrid theory is simply equivalent to non-cognitivism. The cognitivist element in the hybrid theory is irrelevant to the explanation of compatibility. The explanation derives entirely from the non-cognitivist element.

4.3 The Third Part of Schiffer's Solution to the Puzzle: A Consequence about the Truth-Value of Moral Judgements

Schiffer draws a further conclusion about the truth-value of moral judgements from his discussion of the similarity between our ordinary moral concepts and the concept W. The conclusion is that our moral beliefs are subject to two kinds of indeterminacy. This is why he dubs his an unhappy-face solution to the puzzle. It is an unhappy-face solution because it runs contrary to the expectation we have that the best solution to the puzzle will make it turn out that at least some of our moral beliefs are determinately true, an expectation we have because we ordinarily believe that there are at least some determinately true moral propositions.

In order to appreciate the two kinds of indeterminacy Schiffer has in mind, we need to remind ourselves of the difference between what he calls "standard partial belief" (SPB) and "vagueness-related partial belief" (VPB). To use Schiffer's own examples, suppose Sally believes that Beetlebomb will win the Kentucky Derby to degree 0.5 and that she also believes that Lithuania will win the World Cup to degree 0.5. The explanation of these partial beliefs is that there is a "gap between the partially believed proposition and her evidence for it" (204). Putting her in more ideal epistemic circumstances for forming such beliefs would result in a change in her credence levels. As a consequence, the rational degree of belief for Sally to have in the conjunction—that Beetlebomb will win the Kentucky Derby and Lithuania will win the World Cup—is 0.25. Strengthening the proposition widens the gap. These partial beliefs are SPBs and it is the characteristic mark of such SPBs that they rationally combine in this fashion.

But now suppose that Sally watches someone plucking hair from Tom Cruise's head (for those who are culturally challenged: at least at the time of writing this paper, Tom Cruise had a lot of hair). At the very point at which he has lost so much hair that he is a paradigm borderline case of someone who is bald, Sally believes to degree 0.5 that he is bald. But, Schiffer tells us, this degree of belief has nothing to do with a gap between the partially believed proposition and the evidence possessed for it, for the degree of belief would remain unchanged even if we put Sally in ideal circumstances for forming such beliefs, equipping her with all of the evidence she could possibly require. The degree of this partial belief—this VPB—has nothing to do with uncertainty, but has rather to do with *ambivalence*. As a result, Schiffer tells us, one difference between such VPBs and SPBs is the way in which they rationally combine. Suppose that Tom is simultaneously losing weight and that, at the very moment at which he is paradigm borderline case of someone who is bald, he is also a paradigm borderline case of someone who is thin, and so Sally believes to degree 0.5 that Tom is thin too. Schiffer tells us that the rational degree of belief for Sally to have in the conjunction—that Tom is bald and thin—is 0.5, not 0.25.

With this distinction between SPBs and VPBs in mind, let's now consider the two kinds of indeterminacy to which Schiffer thinks our moral beliefs are subject. As we will see, the indeterminacy is of the kind characteristic of VPBs.

The first kind of indeterminacy is simply the sort of indeterminacy manifested in borderline vague propositions. Thus, suppose the value of 'N' Bob settles on entails the property of being a lie. Then the proposition that Jane's calling Bob a Republican was W may be indeterminate simply because Jane's utterance was a borderline case of a lie and thus, by Bob's lights, a borderline case of a W act.

The second kind of indeterminacy is that, for any given relevant non-normative concept N, it may be indeterminate whether being N entails being W, where this isn't a matter of the vagueness of N or W. Indeed, independently of any account of indeterminacy it ought to be intuitively clear given the set-up that, for any N, the proposition that being N entails being W must be indeterminate. For suppose that the operative non-normative concept for Bob is N^*, whereas for Carla, whose concept W is also governed by (*a*) and (*b*), the operative non-normative concept requires her to believe that being N^* does not entail being W. Given the conditions governing the role of W, it is patently absurd to suppose that either Bob or Carla has the determinately true belief in their dispute about whether being N^* entails being W. And this is just the verdict my VPB-account of indeterminacy yields. For any non-normative concept N, Bob may, even under epistemically ideal conditions, believe to any degree that being N entails being W, and these beliefs will perforce be VPBs. Thus, for any non-normative concept N, someone can v*-believe [MS: in other words, someone can have vagueness-related partial belief formed under ideal epistemic circumstances] to any positive degree less than 1 that being N entails being W, and therefore the proposition that being N entails being W is indeterminate. (257)

Though the argument given pertains to propositions about which acts are W, given that Schiffer claims our moral concepts are similar to the concept W, the conclusion he draws about propositions about which acts are W is a conclusion he draws about moral propositions too. The conclusion is that propositions about which acts are W, and so by analogy moral propositions, are subject to two kinds of indeterminacy. But it is plainly the second kind of indeterminacy that is the more striking.

The first kind of indeterminacy depends on the vagueness of the propositions which Bob takes to entail W, and perhaps also on the vagueness associated with whether any particular psychological state is one of Bob's wants. This kind of indeterminacy, by its nature, will affect only some propositions about W acts. By analogy, this kind of indeterminacy will affect only some, but not all, moral propositions. The second kind of indeterminacy is, however, different, because it looks bound to infect *every* W proposition, even those where there is no vagueness associated with the features which are supposed to entail W, and even when there is no vagueness associated with whether or not the relevant psychological state is one of Bob's wants. The second kind of indeterminacy results simply from the fact that there may be disagreements among people, all of whom possess the concept W, about which features entail W, disagreements which will remain even under ideal epistemic conditions. Likewise, then, by analogy, the second kind of indeterminacy will infect every moral proposition.

This really is a striking conclusion if it follows. For it means that, contrary to ordinary belief, there are no determinately true moral propositions. But does it follow? As we saw in the previous section, there are at least two ways to understand the concept W. According to one, W is best understood as a *hybrid* concept, one whose application gives rise to judgements that are in part cognitive (the part which amounts to the ascription of N) and in part non-cognitive (the part which amounts to an expression of the ascriber's want not to live in a world in which people perform actions which are N). But part of the attraction of such a non-cognitivist analysis of W judgements is precisely that it enables us to avoid concluding, on the basis of the existence of disagreements in ideal epistemic circumstances about matters such as whether N entails W, that there is some sort of indeterminacy involved. They enable us to avoid this conclusion because since, strictly speaking, there are no W propositions, it follows that W judgements are not truth apt, and it also follows that claims such as that N entails W are not truth-apt either. Such judgements and claims are rather best understood, *inter alia*, in non-cognitive terms: as expressions of the wants of those who make such judgements and claims. The mere fact that two people, in epistemically ideal circumstances, refuse to express their wants about similar matters puts no pressure on them to be *ambivalent*. It rather underscores the differences in the wants that they express.

The other alternative is to understand W claims as, in effect, claims a speaker makes about the relationship in which acts stand to his own wants. But if this is the right way to understand the concept W, then it seems simply wrong for Schiffer to insist that "it is patently absurd to suppose that either Bob or Carla has the determinately true belief in their dispute about whether being N^* entails being W." If the truth of what Bob says requires N^* to stand in a certain relationship to his wants, and if the truth of what Carla says requires N^* to stand in a certain relationship to her wants, then, since the truth conditions of their two claims are different, they might both be making claims that are determinately false, or both be making claims that are determinately true, notwithstanding the fact that they wouldn't make the same claims under ideal epistemic circumstances. Let me explain.

Suppose that when Bob ascribes W to an act the truth of his ascription requires that there is some non-normative feature possessed by that act, where that non-normative feature is possessed by the acts performed by people in those possible worlds in which he, Bob, *actually* wants not to live. The supposition, in other words, is that when Schiffer spelled out condition (*b*) governing W—the condition that states that N must be some feature that bears a certain relation to Bob's wants—he meant us to read this condition as containing an implicit 'actually.' The supposition doesn't seem unwarranted, given that Schiffer presumably meant to spell out a concept which Bob would happily apply to acts which have N^*, even if those acts are performed in possible worlds in which he, Bob, just so happens to be indifferent to acts that have N^*. The idea is that W would still apply to such N^* acts in such worlds because N^* still bears the right kind of relation to Bob's *actual* wants, never mind about whether it bears the right kind of relation to the wants he has in those worlds.[6]

With this supposition in place, it may well be determinately true that N^* entails W. N^* is, after all, by hypothesis a non-normative feature of those acts that are performed in the possible worlds in which Bob *actually* wants not to live. It may therefore be determinately true that some act has that feature, and, if it is, then it is determinately true that every possible world in which people perform acts that are N^* is a possible world in which he, Bob, actually wants not to live. Bob's claim that N^* entails W may therefore itself be determinately true. The mere fact that Carla's contrary claim may also be determinately true is neither here nor there. It presents us with no more of a puzzle than the fact that 'I want that p' may be determinately true when said under ideal epistemic conditions by Bob and determinately false when said under such conditions by Carla. So understood Schiffer's turns out to be a happy-face solution to the puzzle.

Schiffer might, of course, object to the supposition that his account of the two conditions governing the conceptual role of W implicitly takes the wants in question to be *actual* wants. But now suppose that that supposition is false. In that case the best way of understanding W is by supposing that, when Bob and Carla ascribe W to acts, they each implicitly assume that the wants on which their W ascriptions depend are wants that are possessed *necessarily* by anyone who is so much as capable of forming wants about features of acts. This, after all, would explain why they have different views about whether or not N^* entails W; for each of them would mistakenly be taking their own contingently possessed wants to be guides to the wants that are necessarily possessed by everyone. This assumption, though it also goes beyond anything that Schiffer explicitly says in spelling out (*a*) and (*b*), would therefore seem to provide a fairly natural explanation of a concept's being governed by those two conditions if they are to be read as making no mention of *actual* wants.

But of course, if we understand Bob's and Carla's W ascriptions in this way, it turns out that both of their W ascriptions are determinately false. Indeed, all W ascriptions are determinately false for the simple reason that they all presuppose something false, namely, that there are wants that are possessed necessarily. Schiffer's argument for the indeterminacy of W propositions, and his argument for the indeterminacy of all moral propositions by analogy, thus fails on this interpretation as well. This time, however, it turns out that the criticism of his argument doesn't support the conclusion that he is in fact in a position to offer an alternative happy-face solution to the puzzle. The criticism suggests instead that the solution to the puzzle to which he is committed is an even more unhappy-face solution than he imagines. Not only is he committed to denying that there are at least some determinately true moral propositions, he is committed to the claim that all moral propositions are determinately false.

To sum up: Schiffer draws a further conclusion about the truth-value of moral judgements from his discussion of the similarity between our ordinary moral concepts and the concept W. The conclusion is that moral judgements are subject to two kinds of indeterminacy. But we saw in the previous section that there are at least two different ways in which we might interpret what Schiffer tells us about W concepts. In this section we have seen that, no matter in which of these ways we interpret what he tells us about W concepts, Schiffer's argument for the indeterminacy of moral judgements fails.

4.4 Conclusion

As I said at the outset, Schiffer claims that his theory of pleonastic propositions provides us with a novel solution to a familiar puzzle in meta-ethics about the status of moral judgements. The puzzle is whether we should interpret moral judgements as expressions of cognitive states or non-cognitive states. But, having now considered the bearing of the theory of pleonastic propositions on that puzzle, it seems to me that we should conclude that the theory leaves everything pretty much as it was. Perhaps this simply reveals the extent to which I, at any rate, have failed to grasp the crucial nature of pleonastic propositions or the meta-ethical lessons that we are supposed to learn from them. If so, then this essay will have served its purpose if it prompts Schiffer to clarify that crucial nature and the bearing of the fact that propositions have this nature on the puzzle about moral judgements that he discusses.[7]

Notes

1. In what follows, otherwise unexplained page references are to Schiffer (2003).
2. For more on this see Smith (1994).
3. McDowell (1978).
4. Note that it wouldn't help to suggest that it is part of the functional role of the belief that one morally ought to ϕ to produce in the agent a want to ϕ. Indeed, far from supporting the conclusion that the belief that one morally ought to ϕ entails the desire to ϕ, this suggestion would entail that the two states are indeed distinct existences. For their co-instantiation would require that the agent possesses and exercises relevant rational capacities. This suggestion would thus also entail that (1*) is false. (Compare: when p and q are a priori connected, but unobviously so, it may be part of the functional role of the belief that p to produce in an agent the belief that q, but, this fact about the functional role of the belief that p notwithstanding, an agent could still believe that p without believing that q. The two beliefs would in that case still be distinct existences, for their co-instantiation would require that the agent possesses and exercises relevant rational capacities.) For more on this, see Smith (1998).
5. For more on this see Jackson, Oppy, and Smith (1994).
6. A similar line of thought might lead us to conclude that, when Schiffer spelled out condition (b), he meant us to read it as containing an implicit 'now.' After all, he presumably meant to spell out a concept which Bob would happily apply to acts that have N^*, even if those acts are performed at some time at which he, Bob, just so happens to be indifferent to acts that have N^*. The idea is that W would still apply to such N^* acts at such times because N^* would still bear the right kind of relation to the wants Bob has *now*, never mind whether it bears the right kind of relation to the wants he has at those other times. However, I will ignore this further complication in what follows.
7. Many thanks to Gary Ostertag for his very helpful comments on a draft of this paper.

Bibliography

Jackson, F., G. Oppy, and M. Smith. (1994). "Minimalism and Truth-Aptness." *Mind* 103: 287–302; reprinted in F. Jackson, P. Pettit, and M. Smith, *Mind, Morality and Explanation: Selected Collaborations*. Oxford: Clarendon Press, 2004.

McDowell, J. (1978). "Are Moral Requirements Hypothetical Imperatives?'" *Proceedings of the Aristotelian Society, Supplementary Volume* 52: 13–29.

Schiffer, S. (2003). *The Things We Mean*. Oxford: Clarendon Press.

Smith, M. (1994). *The Moral Problem*. Oxford: Blackwell.

Smith, M. (1998). "The Possibility of Philosophy of Action." In *Human Action, Deliberation and Causation*, edited by J. Bransen and S. Cuypers, Dordrecht: Kluwer Academic Publishers; reprinted in M. Smith, *Ethics and the A Priori: Selected Essays on Moral Psychology and Meta-Ethics*. New York: Cambridge University Press, 2004.

5
Propositional Platitudes

Gary Ostertag

In *The Things We Mean*, Stephen Schiffer defends a face-value theory of belief reports, sentences exemplifying the following form:

1. *A* believes that *S*.

He calls it a "face-value theory" because it enjoys a default status: we abandon it, if at all, not because a competitor emerges that somehow ranks even higher on the scale of intuitive correctness, but because the theory itself is shown to face insurmountable difficulties (or requires patches whose complexity would detract from its intuitive appeal).

Schiffer's statement of the theory is concise: Sentences exemplifying (1)

are true just in case the referent of the '*A*' term stands in the belief relation to the proposition to which the 'that *S*' term refers. (12)[1]

The theory can be seen to involve two claims:

BIN 'believes' stands for a *binary* relation, holding between a believer and a thing believed; equivalently, that (1) has the logical form *aRb*.

PROP The things believed (and, by extension, asserted, doubted, desired, etc.) are propositions.

Let's briefly consider these in order.

The central motivations for BIN are twofold: assuming it allows us explain intuitively valid inferences involving both quantification into that-clause position and substitution of co-referential that-clauses. In addition, "given that '*A*' and 'that *S*' in (1) hold places for singular terms, and given that the only other word in (1) is 'believes,' it would take a very strong motivation, not yet supplied, to treat 'believes' as there functioning as anything other than a two-place predicate" (13).

Wherein does PROP derive its default status? According to BIN, the that-clause in 'Russell believed that Moore was honest' has a referent—*that Moore was honest*. And there are a number of things we know about *that Moore was honest*: it is an abstract, mind- and language-independent entity that has truth conditions and, what is more, has them essentially (unlike the *sentence* 'Moore was honest') and absolutely (its truth at a world not being relative to any additional parameter). But to say all this—that the relevant entity is abstract, mind- and language-independent, possessing truth conditions, and possessing them essentially and absolutely—is to say, according to usage standard among philosophers, that it is a *proposition*.

Before evaluating the face-value theory, we must see whether there exists an acceptable completion of the theory—one that goes beyond the features just enumerated in characterizing the key notion of a proposition. Schiffer considers and rejects the familiar Russellian and Fregean theories of propositions. He also considers, and rejects, a package that takes Russellian propositions to function as the referents of that-clauses but which violates the requirement that 'believes' express a binary relation. (The theory—the hidden-indexical theory—is, however, rejected on independent grounds.) This paves the way for the theory of pleonastic propositions; this view, according to Schiffer, is the correct completion of the face-value theory. Pleonastic propositions are entities seemingly tailor-made for their role as completers of the face-value theory, having no nature independent of their truth conditions and their function as the referents of that-clauses. But they are not in fact specially designed for this purpose, as he is quick to point out: "I aim to be revealing the nature of the propositions we believe, the actual referents of that-clauses, not inventing a new species of abstract entity assembled to do a certain job" (49).

In what follows, I will raise questions about this combination—about whether the theory of pleonastic propositions is a viable completion of the face-value theory. My goal here is not, however, to make trouble for the face-value theory—at least not directly. But if I am right that the current package must be rejected, then, assuming that Schiffer is correct in rejecting Fregean and Russellian theories of propositions, the prospects for the face-value theory are bleak.

Before turning to the pleonastic theory, I will consider the hidden-indexical theory—the approach that Schiffer at one time held to be the most promising attempt to accommodate belief reports within a compositional semantics. The pleonastic theory is, in my view, an attempt to address certain problems besetting the hidden-indexical theory, and its virtues are best seen in the context of these problems.

5.1 The Hidden-Indexical Theory and its Problems

The Russellian completion of the face-value theory takes that-clauses to refer to *Russellian propositions*—ordered pairs of objects (or sequences) and properties (or relations). For the Russellian, the proposition that George Eliot wrote *Middlemarch* just *is* the proposition that Mary Ann Evans wrote *Middlemarch*; to believe one is to believe the other. But then the reports 'Ralph believes that George Eliot wrote *Middlemarch*' and 'Ralph believes that Mary Ann Evans wrote *Middlemarch*' are equivalent.

This result is disturbing, since it is at variance with speakers' truth-value intuitions. A central motivation for the hidden-indexical theory (henceforth, 'HIT') is to retain the idea that that-clauses refer to Russellian propositions while avoiding the undesirable consequence that substitution of co-referential terms within that-clauses preserves truth-value. This dovetails with a related concern, which is to accommodate the context-sensitivity of belief reports. As Schiffer observed early on, one and the same report can be true in one context and yet false in the next, even holding the references of the terms fixed and assuming no changes in the subject's beliefs. For example, in "The Basis of Reference" he wrote of "the misconception that sentences which ascribe *de re* attitudes... express determinate propositions and are therefore true or false *qua* sentence-types and apart from context" (1978: 202–3).[2] A virtue of HIT—which is in fact already sketched in the aforementioned paper—is that it can make sense of this context-dependency.

HIT analyses *believes* as a ternary relation holding among a believer, a proposition, and a propositional mode of presentation. The element that context supplies is not a token mode of presentation, but a *condition* on modes of presentation. Accordingly, Schiffer construes belief reports as containing an implicit quantifier, binding the hidden mode-of-presentation position in the belief relation and restricted by a contextually supplied condition or property. (2)'s logical form is thus given by (3):

2. Lois believes that Kent flies.
3. $\exists m$ ($\Phi^* m$ & Lois Believes <Kent, *being a flier*> under m)

That is, Lois believes <Kent, *being a flier*> under a mode of presentation meeting (contextually provided) condition Φ^*. As indicated, what varies across context is the implicitly referred-to mode-of-presentation type. In one context, (2) will introduce a mild-mannered-reporter-presenting type, in another context, a nerdy-suitor-presenting type (yielding, relative to the Superman fiction, a falsehood in both cases).[3,4]

Schiffer has argued that this strategy must fail: "it is doubtful," he writes "that speakers are in a position to mean what the hidden-indexical theory requires them to mean" (1994: 286). The hidden-indexical theory, that is, has a *meaning-intention problem*. In fact, it has *two* meaning-intention problems: Recognition Failure and the Identification Problem, as I'll call them.

Recognition Failure runs as follows: If (3) is the correct analysis of (2), then what I say in uttering (2) is that Lois believes the proposition that Kent flies under a mode of presentation of the Φ^*-variety, where Φ^* is a contextually determined mode-of-presentation type—perhaps one that applies to a particular mode of presentation just in case it is mild-mannered-reporter-involving. But I must confess not recognizing in myself any such intention. Moreover, although my audience has understood me perfectly well, she does not recognize me as having uttered (2) with the relevant intention either. But then the hidden-indexical theory appears incompatible with basic facts about speakers' meaning intentions.

One might respond that Recognition Failure wrongly assumes that my intentions must be available to introspection. Perhaps my communicative intentions are (partly) unconscious; perhaps my audience's grasping them is (partly) an unconscious matter as well. If so, then the fact that I fail to recognize myself as having certain intentions when asserting (2) is not a particularly telling objection to the hidden-indexical theory.

While this is a plausible line of response, it fails to address the *Identification Problem*. This problem runs as follows. In any realistic case, there will be several competing mode-of-presentation properties, each of which, considered on its own, *could* serve as a plausible characterization of the speaker's intention, yet none of which can lay claim to being the particular completion that she intends. In such a case, the speaker cannot rationally expect her audience to identify a particular completing property as (part of) what she intends to convey in uttering (2). The

HIT advocate might at this point double down and say that this just shows that the content of the utterance must be indeterminate, and offer the following proposal: for each contextually relevant completing instance p of (3), the speaker, in uttering (2), indeterminately meant p. The suggestion is problematic: we have no independent reason to suppose that a speaker's meaning intention with respect to such an utterance is, in the normal course of things, indeterminate—even though, in the normal course of things, such an utterance would fail to determine a unique property. We can conclude, then, that the appeal to tacit intentions, while reasonable as a response to Recognition Failure, is a non-starter when it comes to the Identification Problem. If it is implausible to maintain that the belief reporter consciously intends a particular completion, to the exclusion of the others, it is equally implausible to maintain that she *unconsciously* does so. Moreover, the suggestion that her meaning intention is indeterminate seems *ad hoc*.

Finally, the current proposal faces what Schiffer calls a *logical-form problem*. On the hidden-indexical theory, *believes* is a ternary relation holding among a believer A, a proposition p, and a (suppressed) third relatum—a mode of presentation m of p. This analysis is in direct conflict with the face-value theory, according to which *believes* is a binary relation holding between A and p. (Although, as I have mentioned in footnote 4, one of the selling points of the hidden-indexical theory is that it provides an equally natural accommodation of intuitively valid inferences involving quantification into that-clause position.)

Schiffer (1992), (1996) argues persuasively that there is no solid syntactic evidence for, and significant syntactic evidence against, the claim that (2) contains a concealed mode-of-presentation parameter. One might point to the existence of (4) as evidence for such a parameter:

4. Lois believes that Kent flies under mode of presentation m/in way w.

But Schiffer is unmoved. As he writes, "this is no ordinary-language specification but technical jargon" (1992: 518). In addition, he argues, m in the prepositional phrase 'under...m' no more specifies an argument position in the *believes* relation than 'the mistletoe' in (5) specifies an argument position in the *kissed* relation:

5. Carmelina kissed Ralph under the mistletoe.

In each case we have an adverbial modifier, or adjunct.[5]

The hidden-indexical theory thus faces two significant challenges, one regarding the meaning intentions of belief reporters, the other regarding the logical form of belief reports. It is partly with these concerns in mind that Schiffer developed the theory of pleonastic propositions. Pleonastic propositions incorporate ways of thinking about objects, and thus possess the fineness of grain characteristic of Fregean propositions. Possession of this latter feature obviates the need for a mode-of-presentation slot in the belief relation, thereby allowing for conformity with the face-value theory. Yet, the pleonastic theory differs from the Fregean approach in two significant and related respects: propositions are unstructured;[6] the that-clauses that refer to them are not amenable to a compositional analysis.[7]

What sort of entities are pleonastic propositions? What are their individuation conditions? The next section will address these questions.

5.2 The Theory of Pleonastic Propositions

According to the pleonastic theory, propositions are the "shadows of sentences" (71). Propositions exist because of a linguistic practice that licenses certain inferences—what Schiffer calls "something-from-nothing transformations." These take us from (e.g.) 'Lassie is a dog' to 'that Lassie is a dog is true.' While they can be conjured into existence with disarming ease, it is equally important to note that the existence of pleonastic propositions amounts to nothing more than that such transformations are available. The following remark is illuminating:

> The doctrine of pleonastic propositions and properties is merely, so to speak, a hypostatization of what I used to say when I denied that there were such things as properties and propositions—except 'pleonastically speaking' as I said even then. (91)

However, with respect to individuation there is more to propositions than can be gleaned from the above-displayed transformation. While the *existence* of the proposition that Lassie is a dog is a straightforward enough matter, we are also in need of an account of when something is, and when it is not, identical to this proposition. Schiffer's proposal is appropriately non-inflationary: propositions have no features that transcend our practices of assertion and attitude reporting.

> More specifically, the propositions we believe enjoy no more intrinsic conditions of individuation than those provided by their truth conditions and the requirements for believing those propositions that are determined by the criteria for truth-evaluating belief reports in which reference is made to them. (86)

Yet, even if we accept that there is nothing to a proposition over and above its truth conditions and what is required by its role as referent of a that-clause in attitude reports, certain issues remain—namely, how seriously are we to take our intuitions regarding truth conditions and that-clause reference? If one utterly disregards say, substitutivity intuitions, one might take the that-clauses in (2) and (6) to co-refer; if one takes these intuitions seriously, then one takes them to refer to distinct propositions.

6. Lois believes that Superman flies.

Schiffer takes normal utterances of these reports to make reference to distinct propositions. The upshot is that pleonastic propositions are, like Fregean propositions, fine-grained (although, unlike such propositions, unstructured; see note 6).

As indicated, Schiffer's doctrine of pleonastic propositions is intimately related to his novel account of the semantics of that-clauses. Indeed, while Schiffer claims that propositions are the "shadows of sentences" one could say, with equal justice, that so far as his discussion is concerned, they are 'the shadows of that-clauses.' We now turn to some central features of his account.

Schiffer notes a striking disanalogy between that-clause reference and paradigm singular-term reference. Ordinarily, we determine whether a relational sentence aRb is true by first identifying the things referred to and then determining whether they are related in the appropriate manner. If they are, then the sentence is true; if not, the sentence is false. We determine whether 'Ralph loves Alice' is true by identifying the respective referents and then determining whether the former bears *loves* to the latter. Things are different with 'Ralph believes that Ed loves Trixie,' even though it also asserts a binary relation, this time between a man and a proposition. In this case, we first assess the truth conditions of the whole and then determine what 'that Ed loves Trixie' must refer to in order for the sentence to be true, relative to the context of utterance. A that-clause is thus unlike other syntactically complex singular terms, where reference is determined once we fix the referential properties of the component expressions (e.g., 'his mother,' 'Mary's first husband,' etc.). In the case of that-clauses, fixing the references of the component expressions will fail to determine the reference of the that-clause itself.[8] More is needed, according to Schiffer: "what fixes the referent of a that-clause are the criteria for truth-evaluating the belief report" (81). In what follows, I'll refer to this view, according to which that-clause reference supervenes on the truth conditions (at the utterance context) of the containing attitude report, as 'the top-down approach.'

The top-down approach applies to τ just in case: (*i*) τ refers, (*ii*) τ has constituents that refer, and (*iii*) fixing the references of τ's constituents fails to fix τ's reference.

The top-down approach is at odds with the familiar *bottom-up account*, according to which the reference of a that-clause τ is fixed by the referential properties of its syntactic constituents (both articulated and unarticulated). The top-down approach doesn't quite work in reverse—the referential properties of τ's constituents are not fixed by the reference of τ. Still, the important point is that the referential properties of τ's constituents do not fix τ's reference. But then, what does?

The short answer is: the contextually determined "criteria of evaluation" associated with the containing utterance fix τ's reference. Of course, these criteria cannot be of the familiar bottom-up variety, since this would collapse the difference between the two approaches. But then what are these criteria, and what reason do we have (besides the above-cited disanalogy between that-clauses and other complex singular terms) for thinking that they are not fully determined by the referential properties of the constituent expressions?

The answer requires us to attend to another contrast Schiffer draws. A common approach takes the context-sensitivity of (2) to derive, in some way or other, from the context-sensitivity of its contained that-clause. On most versions of the story, this would involve an assimilation of 'Harold believes that Claudia Schiffer teaches philosophy at NYU,' to 'Claudia Schiffer teaches *there*.' In both of these sentences, it would seem, the speaker intends to refer to a contextually salient object and, accordingly, uses a context-sensitive device to do so: in the case of the latter sentence, the speaker refers to NYU in the process of telling his audience where it is that Claudia Schiffer teaches; in the case of the former, the speaker refers to a given contextually available proposition in the process of telling his audience what it is that Harold believes. Schiffer rejects this familiar idea. He claims that it is "difficult to find in oneself referential intentions that would determine a particular one of the Claudia-Schiffer-teaches-philosophy-at-NYU propositions" (81). Rather, the referent of the that-clause is determined by "what the speaker and audience mutually take to be essential to the truth-value of the belief report" (81). As an example of a feature mutually deemed to be essential to the truth conditions of 'Harold believes that Claudia Schiffer teaches philosophy at NYU' he mentions the subject's acquaintance with the names occurring in the content sentence. While it may or may not be the case that Harold's assent to 'Claudia Schiffer teaches philosophy at NYU' *is* relevant to the truth of the utterance (this is something that the context establishes), if it is, then it "is an individuating feature of the proposition to which the utterance of the that-clause refers" (81).

These considerations regarding that-clause reference dovetail: First we have an intuitive asymmetry between that-clauses and other complex singular terms. In the former case, reference is determined in a top-down manner, in the latter determination is bottom-up. In addition—relative to the common assumption that 'that *S*' is a context-sensitive expression—that-clauses are unlike other context-sensitive singular terms, simple or complex: in the case of that-clauses, contextually determined criteria of evaluation—rather than the speaker's referential intentions—determine reference. In assertively uttering 'Claudia Schiffer teaches there,' part of what I intend is for the relevant context-sensitive singular term to refer to a contextually identifiable location. But it is certainly stretching things to maintain that in assertively uttering 'Harold believes that Claudia Schiffer teaches at NYU' I intend the relevant context-sensitive singular term to refer to a contextually identifiable proposition. After all, try as I might, I can find in myself no such referential intention.

Schiffer does not comment on precisely how the pleonastic theory avoids the meaning-intention problem. But what he does say provides the basis of a response. As he indicates, the criteria of evaluation relevant to determining the reference of a that-clause token τ involve requirements on how the items referred to in τ are to be thought of. Thus, what the speaker intends to refer to in uttering τ is a proposition involving contextually relevant ways of thinking of the items referred to in τ. In the ideal case, her referential intention with respect to τ is something a rational, well-informed agent would be able to recover, given as evidence the utterance and surrounding context. In addition, following Stephen Neale (2004), we can claim that when the case falls short of the ideal—when the speaker's referential intentions are not fully grasped by the hearer—attempting to resolve the question to whom or what the speaker was referring is pointless. In sum: relative to the ideal case there can be no serious disagreement as to what the speaker referred referring to in uttering τ. Moreover, nothing is to be gained by concerning ourselves with how to characterize the situation when the speaker's intentions fail to be recognized.

Thus, we have a possible response to a variant of the Identification Problem—one focused on the speaker's referential intentions as opposed to her meaning-intentions.

Of course, it does not follow that the speaker will be able to enumerate the various requirements implicitly made, even in the ideal setting: "[T]he that-clause in a particular utterance of 'Ralph believes that George Eliot was a man' may refer to a proposition that, intuitively speaking, requires thinking of George Eliot as a famous author, *along with various other George Eliot related things not so easily articulated...*" (83; emphasis added). But then the advocate of the pleonastic theory can respond that it is implausible to expect that the speaker would in each case recognize a verbalization of her intentions in uttering 'Ralph believes that George Eliot was a man' as capturing those very intentions, even when this verbalization is in fact accurate. If so, Recognition Failure may not be a genuine problem for the current proposal—it is only a problem if we maintain an unreasonably exacting requirement on what it is to possess a referential intention.

There are two things to say in response. First, and most obviously, this solution to the meaning-intention problem would seem unavailable to the pleonastic theorist, since, as we have seen, he would deny that we can assimilate (say) 'Harold believes that Claudia Schiffer teaches philosophy at NYU' to 'Claudia Schiffer teaches there.' That is, while a speaker typically utters the latter with the intention of getting his audience to recognize his intention to refer to a salient institution or location, a speaker will not typically utter the former with the intention of getting his audience to recognize his intention to refer to a salient proposition. Second, if it is no longer a requirement that a speaker's referential intentions be transparent to him—as the above proposal has it—then it should no longer be a requirement that the speaker's *meaning intentions* be transparent to him either. But, if so, the meaning-intention problem should cease to be a problem for HIT as well. So, if we're keeping score, the pleonastic theory seems no better off than HIT on the matter of the meaning-intention problem.

More needs to be said, then, if we are to take the pleonastic theory as marking an advance over the hidden-indexical theory with respect to the meaning-intention problem.[9] Before proceeding, it is also worth mentioning an apparent tension between the top-down approach and data involving propositional anaphora. Take the following exchange:

A: Oswald acted alone.
B: I doubt that's true.

It seems that top-down determination is contraindicated by the presence of the anaphoric pronoun. B's utterance seems to be on all fours with 'That's expensive' or 'She's friendly.' Intuitively, B's response is true just in case a contextually salient item—namely, what A said—is doubted by B. If so, then we have a case of bottom-up determination. B's response demands a reading on which the anaphoric pronoun derives its interpretation from the proposition expressed by A's utterance. But such an interpretation seems flatly incompatible with the top-down approach.[10]

I now turn to questions that inevitably arise with respect to theories in the Fregean mold. The criteria of evaluation determined by an utterance of (6) (assuming the Superman fiction) will likely require that 'that Superman flies' refers to a proposition involving a way of thinking of Superman that presents him as a superhero. There are, however, familiar difficulties in assigning truth conditions to belief reports in a manner that respects both their fineness of grain and their object-dependency. The next section presents these difficulties as well as Schiffer's responses.

5.3 Pleonastic Propositions and *de re* Belief Reports

Schiffer's theory is avowedly Fregean is spirit. As we have seen, the criteria of evaluation associated with a hypothetical utterance of (6) will yield a fine-grained proposition as the referent of its that-clause, one that incorporates a way of thinking of Superman. At the same time, the referred-to proposition is object-dependent— true at a world w only if Superman exists at w and flies at w. A requirement on any broadly Fregean theory is to accommodate these two apparently conflicting features. Schiffer provides an elegant way of showing how they can be reconciled. This section will indicate in more detail the problem facing such Fregean views and describe Schiffer's solution.

To get clear on the problem, consider an utterance of the following (said of Superman):

7. Lois believes that he flies.

On Schiffer's view, the pronoun plays a "contextual role in determining the proposition to which (3)'s that-clause refers" (85).[11] More generally, he holds that the role of a referring expression in a token that-clause is not limited to contributing a referent; it also partly individuates a way of thinking of the referent. In addition to referring to Superman, the term chosen will thus help determine which proposition the containing that-clause refers to at the context. This is particularly clear when we consider proper names: one choice yields a false report, (2), another yields a true one, (6):

2. Lois believes that Kent flies.
6. Lois believes that Superman flies.

The upshot is that we must avoid viewing (7) as an open sentence, such as (8):

8. Lois believes that x flies.

While an utterance of, say, 'he flies' is adequately analysed in terms of the open sentence 'x flies' (relative to an assignment of the referred-to individual to x) an analysis of (7) in terms of (8) (similarly relativized) is not acceptable. Construed thus, it would be both true *and* false of one and the same individual.

So far, so straightforward. However, as Schiffer observes, ordinary language licenses the move from the relevant utterance of (7) to (9):

9. There is someone, namely Superman, such that Lois believes that he flies.

(Or, more colloquially: 'Superman is believed by Lois to fly.') This raises a question: if we cannot quantify into the position marked by 'he' in (7) with an objectual quantifier, how can we permit the inference to (9)? After all, the inference would seem to require that 'he' as it occurs in (9) functions as a variable bound by the antecedent quantifier, and this provides good evidence for thinking that 'he' as it occurs in (7) is best construed as a genuine variable, *à la* (8).

Schiffer's response is that we understand this putative example of quantifying into belief reports in terms of (10):[12]

10. There is someone, namely Superman, such that, for some object-dependent proposition p that's true iff he flies, Lois believes p.[13]

Note that this maneuver helps Schiffer avoid a potential difficulty. Consider an utterance of (11) (said of Superman):

11. Lois doesn't believe that he flies.

Ordinary language allows an inference from (11) to (12), one that parallels the one from (7) to (9):

12. There is someone, namely Superman, such that Lois does not believe that he flies.

But now, from (9) and (12), we seem to have the conclusion:

> 13. There is someone, namely Superman, such that Lois does and does not believe that he flies.

And this would certainly be a mark against the analysis.[14]

Yet, it is unclear why Schiffer thinks the conclusion follows. (13) does *not* follow from (9) and (12), if they are to be analysed in the manner Schiffer recommends—namely, in terms of (10) and (14):

> 14. There is someone, namely Superman, such that, for some object-dependent proposition p that's true iff he flies, Lois does not believe p.

(10) and (14), taken together, fail to yield a contradiction. In particular, the relevant analysis of (13), namely (15), is *not* a consequence of (10) and (14):

> 15. There is someone, namely Superman, such that, for some object-dependent proposition p that's true iff he flies, Lois both believes p and does not believe p.

Schiffer's strategy thus neatly avoids contradiction.[15] In effect, (10) and (14) are of the form 'something is F and G' and 'something is F and *not-G*,' respectively, and this will never entail 'something is F and both G and *not-G*.'

A mystery remains: if both (7) and (11) are true of Superman, it would seem that (13) must follow, the mutual consistency of (10) and (14) notwithstanding. I will now show why this is a mistake.

Schiffer denies that "it follows from the truth of (7) that Superman has the property expressed by the open sentence... 'Lois believes that x flies'" (85). As we have seen, he is committed to saying this, since the falsity of (2) would equally entail that Superman *doesn't* have this property, yielding a contradiction. As he writes:

> In that [technical] sense, my view is that (8) ['Lois believes that x flies'] *is not an open sentence*, since it expresses no property, and this because the occurrence of 'he' in (7) does more than refer to Superman in the sense in which I allow; it also plays its contextual role in determining the proposition to which (7)'s that-clause refers. (85; emphasis added)

Yet, even if we take Schiffer at his word that (8) is not an open sentence in "the technical sense," we are still owed an answer to the question as to how it is to be understood. Schiffer wants to claim that the relevant utterance of (7) is Superman-involving and at the same time deny that it expresses a property *of* Superman. Let's see how this can be accomplished.

It will facilitate our understanding of his proposal if we deviate ever so slightly from Schiffer's presentation and replace (8) with an alternative quasi-formal sentence, one for which there is less of a compulsion to take the relevant position as bindable by an external quantifier, or open to free substitution of co-referring terms:

> 16. Lois believes that μ flies.

Here is how we are to understand (16): although (*i*) the (object-dependent) proposition it expresses is partly determined by the object "assigned" to μ, nonetheless (*ii*) the μ position prohibits free substitution of co-referring expressions and is, consequently, not bindable by an external quantifier.[16]

An open sentence Fx is true, relative to an assignment of o to x, iff o is in the extension of F. What is needed is a parallel truth condition for the pseudo-open sentence (16), relative to an assignment of Superman to μ. Schiffer's suggestion is that (16) is true just in case Lois believes an object-dependent proposition that's true iff Superman flies (85). Since (16) has no independent meaning, it makes most sense to construe this claim as deriving from the following contextual definition:

17. Lois believes that μ flies, relative to an assignment of Superman to μ $=_{def}$ Lois believes an object-dependent proposition that's true iff Superman flies.

While this suggestion is consistent with what Schiffer writes, and makes sense of an otherwise puzzling feature of his discussion, the proposal is my own and not necessarily something he would endorse. Still, I will proceed for present purposes as though this were part of the official view.

I take the definiendum in (17), 'Lois believes that μ flies, relative to an assignment of Superman to μ,' to be the formal counterpart of 'Lois believes that he flies, said of Superman.' The latter is of course but one form that *de re* belief attribution takes in ordinary English. Each variant, however, is to be handled in a similar manner: That is, (17) can be adapted to accommodate 'Superman is believed by Lois to fly,' 'Superman is such that Lois believes that he flies,' (2) and (6). In each case, the specific form is eliminated, so to speak, in favor of a sentence that quantifies over propositions.

The idea that Schiffer is contextually defining (16) sits well with what he has to say about the relation between (10) and (8):

On my view, we don't explain the truth of ['there is someone such that Lois believes that he flies'] by saying that someone satisfies ['Lois believes that x flies']; rather, we explain its truth in terms of Lois's believing an object-dependent proposition to the effect that so-and-so flies. (85)

The conventional idea is that what makes the sentence 'A believes a proposition that's true iff S' true—what *explains* its truth—is that it has a true instance, for example, that A believes that S. Schiffer here reverses the order of explanation for cases of *de re* attributions. The belief report is true *not* because A bears the *believes* relation to the proposition that S. Rather, it is true because, for some object-dependent p that's true iff S, A believes p.

But while the conventional order of explanation does not require any revision to our understanding either of the belief report or its existential generalization, the reverse order does. In particular, it requires that the belief report be *defined* in terms of the generalization. Otherwise we would have the perverse situation in which a singular statement, that a is F, is made true because something (meeting such-and-such conditions) is F—for example, a situation in which 'Fido barks' is made true by the fact that some dog who has the same owner as Fido barks. The situation can only be made intelligible if what appears to be a singular statement is in fact contextually defined by the generalization.

In a *de re* attribution such as (6), an object-dependent proposition is expressed—in the particular case of (6), a proposition that "wouldn't have existed had Superman not existed and [which] is therefore partly individuated with respect to Superman" (84–5). And yet, the proposition is fine-grained, as witnessed by the fact that free substitution of co-referring terms in the scope of 'believes' fails. Schiffer's approach to *de re* belief reports such as (6) is novel in that it meets apparently conflicting desiderata—respecting their object-dependency on the one hand while keeping sight of their fineness of grain on the other—without abandoning the idea that that-clauses are referential singular terms, as in the proposals of Kaplan (1968) and Forbes (1990).

While Schiffer provides an elegant treatment of *de re* belief, there is, I will argue, a pragmatic story that must accompany Schiffer's theory. The next section describes this accompanying account and then tries to make trouble for it.

5.4 Disbelief and Disagreement

As indicated, Schiffer's account nicely accommodates two seemingly conflicting requirements on a theory of belief reports: to respect their opacity while at the same time accommodating their object-dependency. Still, I have reservations about how the theory handles reports of disbelief. In this section, I will develop these reservations.

Before proceeding, it will be important to look once more at the truth conditions he assigns to belief reports. Recall that on Schiffer's view, (6) is true just in case Lois believes an object-dependent proposition that's true iff Superman flies. Semi-formally:

18. For some p that's true just in case Superman flies, Lois believes p.

Consider then a negative belief report, a sentence exemplifying 'A doesn't believe that S' or variants thereof. We have the option of (19)—the negation of (18)—and (20):

19. $\neg$(For some p that's true just in case Superman flies, Lois believes p)

20. For some p that's true just in case Superman flies, $\neg$(Lois believes p).

Taking a negative belief report to have as its default reading (20) as opposed to (19) makes sense, since this allows an informed, rational speaker to avoid contradicting herself in assertively uttering 'Lois believes that Superman flies but doesn't believe that Kent flies.'[17] According to the current strategy, this is true just in case, for some object-dependent proposition p that's true just in case Superman flies, Lois believes p *and* for some object-dependent proposition q with the same truth conditions, Lois does *not* believe q. And this conjunction is consistent.

One initial problem with this approach is that two speakers, uttering apparently conflicting belief reports, cannot disagree. If Ralph utters (7), referring to Superman, and Jane vehemently objects, assertively uttering (11), then, appearances to the contrary, they do not contradict one another.

7. Lois believes that he flies.

11. I have to disagree: Lois doesn't believe that he flies.

Ralph has said something that is true just in case, for some proposition p with truth condition q, Lois believes p; whereas Jane has said something that is true just in case, for some proposition r with truth condition q, Lois does *not* believe r. These assertions are consistent. But it certainly looks as if Jane has simply asserted something incompatible with what Ralph asserted.

Can we make room for the possibility that negative belief reports at least on some occasions assert (19) and on others (20)? This would allow for the possibility of genuine disagreement.

One principled way to achieve this is as follows. On some occasions a speaker, in uttering (11), intentionally contradicts the proposition expressed by a previous utterance of (7). She thus asserts a proposition whose truth conditions are captured by the relevant instance of (19). On other occasions, the speaker, in uttering (11), points out that Lois fails to believe an object-dependent proposition of a certain sort (one true just in case Superman flies), pointedly avoiding disagreement. She thus asserts a proposition whose truth conditions are captured by the relevant instance of (20).

It seems, then, that (11) can have as its default reading neither (19) nor (20). Some pragmatic story has to be in the offing, one that determines which of (19) and (20) is intended at a given context. In Ostertag (2005) I suggested the following as the required pragmatic rule:

(C) A belief reporter communicates (20) in uttering 'Lois doesn't believe that Superman flies' when it is common knowledge that Lois believes some object-dependent proposition that's true iff Superman flies; otherwise, she communicates (19).

According to (C), a speaker, in uttering (11), asserts the proposition that, for some object-dependent proposition *p* that's true iff Superman flies, Lois does not believe *p*, only when it is common knowledge that Lois *already* believes a proposition with the relevant truth conditions. If it is not common knowledge that she has such a belief, then the speaker asserts that there is no object-dependent proposition, true just when Superman flies, that Lois believes. (C) is motivated by consideration similar to those recommending Grice's Maxim of Quantity—by the requirement that my utterance be sufficiently informative for the conversational purposes at hand. If Jane has reason to believe that Lois believes a certain Superman-flies proposition, then, in uttering (11) Jane merely claims (all things being equal) that Lois also withholds belief in a Superman-flies proposition. On the other hand, if she has no reason to believe that Lois believes a Superman-flies proposition, then she would be justified in denying that Lois believes *any* Superman-flies proposition. Indeed, given the assumption that she is being maximally informative, for Jane to claim in such a circumstance that Lois merely withholds belief in a Superman-flies proposition would falsely implicate that she, Jane, knows less than she does.

But there is a counterexample to this proposal, as I noted in Ostertag (2005). Assume that Lois meets Kent prior to meeting (or having any knowledge of) his Superman persona. In uttering (11) at this time, Jane asserts that Lois does not believe any Superman-flies proposition. This makes sense: according to (C), for Jane to assert that Lois merely withholds belief in a Superman-flies proposition would implicate that there exists a Superman-flies proposition that Lois does believe. But Jane does not believe this, so (short of a desire to mislead we have no reason to attribute to her) she would not attempt to convey it to her audience. Now move forward a few months: Lois becomes acquainted with Kent's 'Superman' persona and forms the belief (via observation) that he can fly. Jane, pointing to Superman, utters (7), thereby asserting that there exists a Superman-flies proposition that Lois believes (this is also a Kent-flies proposition). But this contradicts her earlier utterance.

That is to say, Jane, who is perfectly well informed, has no reason to mislead, and has not changed her mind on any of the relevant facts (e.g., she hasn't formed the opinion that Lois now believes that the persona she associates with the name 'Kent' has the ability to fly) contradicts herself in reporting Lois's beliefs.

It seems, then, that (C) must be rejected. If so, then the prospects for an analysis of *de re* belief reports like (7) along the lines suggested by (18) seem dim.

While it appears that the pleonastic theory cannot make sense of disagreement of the sort we have been considering, there remains an option available to the advocate of pleonastic propositions. The pleonastic theorist may take a hint from the hidden-indexical theorist and hold that the assumed utterance of (7) expresses a proposition whose truth conditions might be given as follows:

$$\exists p \, (\Phi^*(p) \, \& \, (\text{True}(p) \text{ iff Superman flies}) \, \& \, \text{Lois believes } p)$$

(where Φ^* is a contextually determined, implicitly referred-to property of propositions). If we allow disbelief reports to be enriched in this manner, then we have a way of handling disagreement, one that does not require invocating (C). For example, we can hold that a sentence of the form 'Lois doesn't believe that Kent flies' always communicates a proposition whose truth conditions might be given as follows:

$$\neg \exists p (\Phi^*(p) \, \& \, (\text{True}(p) \text{ iff Superman flies}) \, \& \, \text{Lois believes } p)$$

But then a speaker asserting 'Lois believes that Superman flies' and a speaker asserting 'Lois doesn't believe that Superman flies' can in fact disagree, so long as their respective utterances make reference to one and the same property of propositions. Moreover, a speaker who asserts 'Lois believes that Superman flies but doesn't believe that Kent flies' need not be contradicting herself, so long as the respective conjuncts make reference to different properties.

Of course, while this maneuver elegantly solves the problem we have been grappling with,[18] it inherits the central problem facing the hidden-indexical theory: the meaning-intention problem. If it is implausible to suppose that a speaker makes implicit reference to a mode-of-presentation type in uttering a belief report, it is hardly more plausible to suppose that she makes implicit reference to a proposition type. The worry posed by reports of disbelief thus seem to elude an easy fix.

5.5 Conclusion

One primary goal of *The Things We Mean* is to provide a completion for the face-value theory. The recommended completion is the theory of pleonastic propositions: a theory that delivers Fregean truth conditions but which departs from conventional Fregean (and neo-Fregean) approaches in denying both that propositions are structured and that that-clause reference is compositional. While Schiffer's Frege-inspired approach is an advance over the versions of Kaplan, Forbes, and others, it is vulnerable to a serious problem involving negative belief reports.

Assuming that Schiffer's arguments against conventional Fregean and Russellian completions are conclusive, this raises a question as to whether the theory has an adequate completion, or even whether the demands it makes can be consistently met. Perhaps the best option at this point is to reconsider another Schifferian proposal—the hidden-indexical theory—one that I think he may have dismissed prematurely. But it would be rash to do so before hearing Stephen's response.[19]

Notes

1. Parenthetical references are to *The Things We Mean* (Schiffer 2003).
2. See also (Schiffer 1977: 31 and *passim*).
3. How, precisely, does context supply a mode-of-presentation type? Schiffer doesn't say much about this, but he seems to hold that the only relevant contextual parameter is the speaker's intention. Of course, this puts into relief a significant problem the theory faces. As we'll see, HIT must attribute intentions to speakers that they don't take themselves, even on reflection, to possess. See Schiffer (1992: 513), (1994: 287), (2003: 40–1).
4. Although HIT fails to comport with the face-value theory's logical-form requirement, it was originally motivated by the same data that motivated the face-value theory: to explain the standard inferences involving quantification into that-clause position. See, however, Salmon (1995) and *Things*, p. 41 for some problems facing HIT in this connection.
5. See Schiffer (1992: 518–19) on diagnostics for adicity. A more recent discussion is Stanley (2000).

    It should be noted that even if Schiffer's argument here is successful, the possibility remains that (2) can be used to say something stronger than its linguistic meaning determines at the context. Although the argument structure of (2) involves only a believer and a proposition, one could maintain (following contextualists such as Recanati 2004 and others) that a mode of presentation (or type thereof) can be supplied at the context of utterance by a process of free enrichment. Just as one can argue that what is said by a given utterance of 'It's raining' contains a location as an unarticulated constituent—a constituent not mandated by the argument structure of *rains*—so one can argue that what is said by a given utterance of (2) contains a propositional mode of presentation (or type thereof) as an unarticulated constituent—a constituent not mandated by the argument structure of *believes*. This move would allow one to maintain the essence (if not the letter) of the hidden-indexical theory—that what is said by an utterance of (2) will often involve a mode-of-presentation, or a type of mode-of-presentation—while avoiding implausible commitments regarding (2)'s logical form or literal meaning. (Of course, if this view is adopted, then the name becomes misleading, since there are no 'indexicals' at logical form to speak of.)

    Schiffer partly acknowledges such a possibility:

    > To be sure, one could utter ['Lois believes that Kent flies under mode of presentation *m*'] and mean [that for some *m* of such-and-such type, Lois believes that Kent flies under *m*], but this would be an instance of a speaker's meaning more than her utterance literally meant... [T]he hidden-indexical theory *is about the literal meaning of belief ascriptions*, and such ascriptions can require, as part of their literal meaning, an implicit quantification over modes of presentation only if modes of presentation function as arguments of the belief relation. (1996: 96; emphasis added)

    As I've indicated, there is another construal of "a speaker's meaning more than her utterance literally means," one on which a speaker can use a sentence *S* not simply to *mean* more, but to *say* more, than *S* literally means.

6. In chapter 1 of *Things*, Schiffer mounts a general argument against theories of structured propositions, based on an anti-Fregean argument due to Adam Pautz, subsequently published in Pautz 2008 (see especially 2003: 27–30). The general idea is that, according to any such theory, Fregean or Russellian, 'barks' as it occurs in 'Ralph believes that Fido barks' is a singular term, one whose referent is a constituent of the referent of 'that Fido barks.' If so, then the quoted sentence should allow us to conclude that, for some *x*, Ralph believes that Fido *x*. Since this is absurd, such theories must be rejected. Hence, the correct completion of the face-value theory must be one according to which propositions are unstructured. See King (2007: 103–11) for a critique of Schiffer's argument.
7. See the discussion of the top-down approach, below.
8. This might be readily conceded even by theorists who reject any disanalogy between 'Ed loves Trixie' and 'Ralph believes that Ed loves Trixie.' For example, unless context fixes the sense in which Ada is said to be ready, a contextualist would deny that the that-clause in 'Carlos believes that Ada is ready' secures a referent. Since addressing these cases would needlessly complicate the discussion, I set them aside in what follows.
9. The careful discussion in Buchanan (2012: 15–16) brings up related concerns.
10. One might respond that, since neither of the above examples involves that-clauses, they show nothing about the top-down approach as applied to belief reports involving that-clauses—the focus, after all, of the pleonastic theory. This is strictly speaking true, but it doesn't leave the theorist in a comfortable position. It would be unsatisfying if the only role for pleonastic propositions in a theory of belief ascription is as the referents of embedded that-clauses, and that a complete theory would require both pleonastic and non-pleonastic propositions.
11. Here and in what follows I change the numbering in the quotations to conform to the numbering in the text.
12. To forestall a potential objection, it should be noted that Schiffer takes (10) to be providing the truth conditions of (9) and its variants, not as offering an account of what someone *says* or *asserts* in assertively uttering that sentence. It is not therefore an objection to the analysis that a speaker does not recognize herself as quantifying over propositions in uttering (9). A parallel with Russell's theory of descriptions might help here. Russell does not claim that someone who utters 'the tallest building is in Dubai' thereby *says* or *asserts* that that there is exactly one building taller than any others and that any such building is in Dubai. Russell is merely saying *when* that sentence is true and can remain agnostic about what, precisely, its content is. Schiffer can remain similarly agnostic about what (9) can be used to say. The parallel with Russell will be elaborated on in what follows.
13. Schiffer uses the material biconditional here, where something stronger would seem necessary. I might believe an object-dependent proposition that is true just in case Superman flies without believing a Superman-dependent proposition. For example, the object-dependent proposition that the only son of Jor-El flies is true just in case Superman flies; yet it is not a Superman-dependent proposition. I can believe the former without believing an instance of the latter.

    An easy fix is to require that the biconditional be necessary. Another fix, which does not require this extra apparatus, is simply to restrict the quantifier to Superman-dependent propositions, thus:

    There is someone, namely Superman, such that, for some Superman-dependent proposition *p* that's true iff he flies, Lois believes *p*.

14. Kaplan (1968) provides a related analysis, one which handily avoids contradiction; see also Forbes (1990).

15. As indicated, Schiffer claims that the there is an entailment from (9) and (12) to (13), and remarks that it presents a "slight awkwardness" for his view (85). If I am right, there is no such entailment on his view, and so no need to explain away the awkwardness.
16. Of course, if μ in (16) is to mimic 'he' in (7), it must be bindable by English quantifier phrases such as 'someone is such that...' But this is merely surface grammar. The apparent binding that occurs in (9) is contextually defined in terms of (10), and in (10) the only genuine variables occur outside of that-clauses.
17. This is the strategy adopted by Salmon (1986). For discussion, see Saul (1998) and Ostertag (2005).
18. This overstates the case a bit. I argue in Ostertag (2005: 589–93) that the hidden-indexical theory is vulnerable to a variation on the same problem.
19. Ancestors of this paper were presented at a conference honoring the work of Stephen Schiffer in Pécs, Hungary, in May 2007 and at a colloquium at UMass-Amherst in February 2009. I'd like to thank the audiences on those occasions for helpful feedback. I have also presented some of this material at seminars at UMass-Amherst and at The Graduate Center, CUNY, and would like to thank the participants in those seminars for suggestions and helpful criticism. Ray Buchanan, Russell Dale, Frank Pupa, and Stephen gave helpful comments on earlier drafts of this chapter, for which I'm grateful. I'm also indebted to Ray for our ongoing conversations about the topics in this chapter and for his advice, helpful criticism, and ongoing encouragement.

Bibliography

Buchanan, R. (2012). "Is Belief a Propositional Attitude?" *Philosophers Imprint* 12 (1).
Forbes, G. (1990). "The Indispensability of Sinn." *Philosophical Review* 99: 535–63.
Kaplan, D. (1968–69). "Quantifying in." *Synthese* 19: 178–214.
King, J. (2007). *The Nature and Structure of Content*. Oxford: Oxford University Press.
Neale, S. (2004). "This, That, and the Other." In *Descriptions and Beyond*, edited by M. Reimer and A. Bezuidenhout, Oxford. Clarendon Press.
Ostertag, G. (2005). "A Puzzle about Disbelief." *Journal of Philosophy* 102: 573–93.
Pautz, A. (2008). "An Argument Against Fregean That-Clause Semantics." *Philosophical Studies* 138: 335–47.
Recanati, F. (2004). *Literal Meaning*. Cambridge: Cambridge University Press.
Salmon, N. (1986). *Frege's Puzzle*. Cambridge: MIT.
Salmon, N. (1995). "Being of Two Minds: Belief with Doubt," *Noûs* 29: 1–20.
Saul, J. (1998). "The Pragmatics of Attitude Ascription." *Philosophical Studies* 92: 363–89.
Schiffer, S. (1977). "Naming and Knowing." *Midwest Studies in Philosophy* 2: 28–41.
Schiffer, S. (1978). "The Basis of Reference." *Erkenntnis* 13: 171–206.
Schiffer, S. (1992). "Belief Ascription." *Journal of Philosophy* 89: 499–521.
Schiffer, S. (1994). "A Paradox of Meaning." *Noûs* 28: 279–324.
Schiffer, S. (1996). "The Hidden-Indexical Theory's Logical-Form Problem: A Rejoinder." *Analysis* 56: 92–7.
Schiffer, S. (2003). *The Things We Mean*. Oxford: Clarendon Press.
Stanley, J. (2000). "Context and Logical Form." *Linguistics and Philosophy* 23/4: 391–434.

…

6

Schiffer's Puzzle
A Kind of Fregean Response

Ray Buchanan

In 'What Reference Has to Tell Us about Meaning,' Stephen Schiffer argues that many of the objects of our beliefs, and the contents of our assertoric speech acts, have what he calls *the relativity feature*.[1] A proposition has the relativity feature just in case it is an object-dependent proposition "the entertainment of which requires different people, or the same person at different times or places, to think of [the relevant object] in different ways" (129).[2] But as no Fregean or Russellian proposition can possibly have such a feature, we must either (*i*) give up on these traditional theories of propositional content in favor of an account that can allow for the relativity feature, or else (*ii*) explain why the things we believe, and say, oftentimes *seem* to have this feature even though they, in fact, do not. Schiffer pursues the former option; in what follows, I pursue the latter.

The particular response to the puzzle posed by the relativity feature that I will sketch is one that I suspect Schiffer himself might have once been tempted to make; a response that will (I hope) be of interest to any theorist sympathetic to the view that the contents of our beliefs are fine-grained, Fregean propositions.[3] To be clear, however, my goal in trying to explain away the relativity feature is *not* to vindicate the traditional Fregean account of content and communication: like Schiffer, I believe that account to be problematic. As we will see, even if we assume the metaphysical thesis that *believing* is fundamentally a relation between agents and Fregean propositions, there is considerable pressure for denying that such propositions are either the contents of our assertoric speech acts, or the things we refer to, or specify, by that-clauses in belief-reports. In response to Schiffer's puzzle the proponent of the Fregean metaphysics of beliefs should, I argue, hold that that the things we assert, and the referents of that-clauses, are not Fregean propositions, but rather *kinds* thereof.

6.1 The Relativity Feature

If I sincerely and literally utter (1), I will have said that I am hungry, and, in so doing, made manifest a certain belief of mine—a belief I would report using (3):

1. I am hungry.
2. By uttering (1), I said that I am hungry.
3. I believe that I am hungry.

If you understand my utterance, you will entertain what I said. Supposing you are prepared to take my word on the matter, you will come to have a certain belief regarding me as well—a belief that I would report using (4):

4. You believe that I am hungry.

Prima facie, there is something—namely, *that I am hungry*—that I said by uttering (1), and that we both believe. We can start to appreciate Schiffer's puzzle by trying to get clearer on what, exactly, this 'something' is.

Proponents of *the face-value theory* will agree that the 'something' in question is a proposition—an abstract, mind- and language-independent entity that has truth-conditions essentially and without relativization to anything else.[4] According to these theorists, both propositional attitude reports and reports of assertoric speech acts express relations between agents and propositions referred to, or specified by, that-clauses. More specifically, a face-value theorist is committed to the following two (interrelated, but separable) theses:

> *The Semantic Thesis*: In a literal utterance of a report of the form 'S believes/says that *p*' the that-clause functions as a *referential singular term*, the semantic value of which is a proposition, the report being true just in case the proposition is something S believes or asserts.[5]
>
> *The Metaphysical Thesis*: Believing, saying, and meaning are genuinely *propositional* attitudes—relations between agents and propositions.

If these theses are correct, the says-that report in (2) is true just in case I stand in the saying-relation to the proposition specified by 'that I am hungry' (at the context); likewise, the belief-report in (4) is true if, and only if, you stand in the belief relation to that same proposition.

Let's provisionally follow the face-value theorist in accepting both of the foregoing theses, and that the that-clause in (2)–(4) specifies the proposition that I said by uttering (1). Now supposing the 'something' in question is a proposition specified by the relevant that-clause, we would still like to know what kind of proposition it is.

Though proponents of the face-value theory might disagree among themselves regarding any number of further issues, they will (or at least should) agree that in (1)–(4) the proposition in question is an *object-dependent proposition*—a proposition the truth-conditions of which can only be specified by mentioning the particular object(s) that it concerns. Plausibly, what I said in uttering (1) is something true at a world *w* just in case, at *w*, Ray Buchanan has the property of being hungry.

So far, so good. Things start to get puzzling, however, when we notice that—seemingly—in order for me to believe, or entertain, that I am hungry it is not enough for me merely to have a thought concerning some individual that happens to be me (perhaps, a thought concerning that guy in the mirror across from me in the restaurant that I do not recognize to be me). Rather, I must think of myself *as such*—that is, in a distinctively first-person, self-conscious way, a way that neither you nor anyone else can think of me. Insofar as this object-dependent proposition that I am hungry seems to require me, but not you, to think of me in a first-person way, it has what Schiffer calls *the relativity feature*.

The relativity feature also seems to be exhibited by just about any utterance involving a demonstrative. Suppose that on your suggestion I am visiting our favorite local art gallery to check out a new sculpture entitled *D'Odeurs et de Chatouilles*. While standing in front of the sculpture, I call you and say:

5. That sculpture is magnificent!

Supposing that I am speaking literally, and being sincere in so doing, I will have both said and expressed my belief that *that sculpture is magnificent*—a belief that you share. Plausibly, what I said, and what we both believe, is an object-dependent proposition concerning a particular sculpture, *s*. Prima facie, in order for me to believe, or even entertain, that proposition I must think of *s* under an occurrent perceptual demonstrative mode of presentation, but not so for you: if anything, you must think of *s* under a memory-based mode of presentation, since you are not at the moment positioned to see it. Hence, what I said in uttering (5), and what we both believe, seems to have the relativity feature.

The foregoing two examples are cases in which different agents (seemingly) must think of the same object in different ways in order to entertain a certain object-dependent proposition. There are, however, also cases in which we seem to have an object-dependent proposition, concerning some specific object *o*, that requires the *same agent*, at different times or places, to think of *o* under different 'modes of presentation' (more about this possibility momentarily).

In presenting such an example, we would do well to first get a little bit clearer on what we might call the *semantic content* of an utterance, and how that relates to 'what is said.' Following Schiffer, let's take the context-invariant meaning, or *character**, of a sentence-type σ to be a constraint on "what a speaker must mean in uttering [σ], if she's to be speaking literally" (131), a constraint that we might, in turn, think of as a propositional 'form,' or *propositional-type*.[6] For example, by uttering (6), I might mean both (i) that David is not ready for our dance party, and (ii) that we should postpone the dance party for one more round of drinks:

6. David isn't ready.

But though I meant (ii) by uttering (6), we should have no temptation to claim that this is something I *stated*, or *literally meant* by uttering (6). Intuitively, (i) 'fits,' or is 'consonant with' the character* of the sentence-type displayed in (6) in a way that (ii) is not. Following Schiffer, let's say that when the meaning of the sentence σ is a proposition-type Ψ, and a speaker S means some proposition q of the type Ψ in an unembedded utterance of σ, then q is the **semantic content** of S's utterance of σ (131). Moreover, let's also follow Schiffer in holding that if q is the semantic content of S's utterance of σ, then, necessarily, q is *among* the things S **said** by σ. Note that it does **not** follow from the fact that the speaker can truly be reported as having said that p by uttering σ, that p is the semantic content of that utterance. For example, in a conversation in which it is mutual knowledge between me and you that David is wearing sneakers, I might truly report the bouncer as having said *that David will not be let in to the club*, by uttering (7):

7. No one wearing sneakers will be let in the club.

though that is not the semantic content of his utterance. We should allow that even if "*p* is the semantic content of a speaker's utterance, the speaker may be correctly reported as having said another proposition *q*, if *q* is appropriately related to *p*, where there is more than one way of being 'appropriately related.'" (131). In uttering (7), I correctly reported the bouncer as having said both that no one wearing sneakers will be let in the club and that David will not be let in the club, but only the former is the semantic content of his utterance.

With these distinctions in hand, now consider the following case. Suppose that we get an email from the secretary of our distinguished colleague and X-Phi enthusiast, Pergola, in which he explains to us why Pergola will be unable to attend the faculty meeting scheduled for later this afternoon. It reads:

8. Professor Pergola is conducting experiments in the university cafeteria today.

It is plausible that the semantic content of (8) is an object-dependent proposition concerning, among other things, a particular day, *d* (a proposition that we could express tomorrow by uttering 'Professor Pergola was conducting experiments in the university yesterday'). But notice that if we read Pergola's email *today*, we have to think of *d as such* in order to entertain, or believe, that object-dependent proposition—we must think of *d* as (roughly) *this very day, the day it is now*. Supposing we re-read the email tomorrow we can, of course, entertain that same object-dependent proposition expressed by (8) once again. Seemingly, in order to entertain what Pergola's assistant expressed yesterday would now require us to think of *d* as, roughly, *the day before this very day*. Since the object-dependent proposition expressed by (8) is such that it requires agents to think of the referent of 'today' in different ways, at different times, it too seems to have Schiffer's relativity feature.

Each of the foregoing examples seems to dramatically exhibit the relativity feature, and it is easy to construct others. Schiffer claims that "the relativity feature can be had by the semantic content of an utterance involving almost any kind of singular term" (134). If the relativity feature is in fact a property of the semantic content of any utterance, then it is plausibly a property of many, if not most. Crucially, however, if the relativity feature is *ever* instantiated then both the Fregean and Direct-Reference versions of the face-value account are incorrect.

6.2 Direct Reference and the Relativity Feature

Qua face-value theorists, Direct-Reference theorists and Fregeans each accept both the semantic thesis, and the metaphysical thesis. Moreover, they are agreed that the objects of our beliefs, and the contents of our assertoric speech acts are *structured* propositions in that they are complexes with constituents, the identity and arrangement of which are determinative of their truth-conditions. They differ, however, in their respective views as to the nature of these propositional constituents. While the Direct-Reference theorist holds that a proposition is composed of the objects, properties, and relations that figure in its truth-conditions, the Fregean holds that it is composed of *modes of presentation* thereof. In this section, we will consider the relativity feature in the context of the Direct Reference account, in the next, in the context of the Fregean account.

A Direct-Reference (DR) theorist is any proponent of the face-value theory that holds that (i) the propositions we believe and assert are *Russellian* propositions—structured complexes of objects, properties, and relations, and (ii) the propositional contribution of a referring expression is exhausted by its referent; the propositional contribution of a predicate, the property it expresses. I will assume that this view, and the motivations for it forthcoming from the work of Kaplan, Salmon, Soames, and others are, more or less, familiar.

Returning to our initial example of (1)–(4), the DR theorist will hold that the semantic content of my utterance of (1) is, to a first approximation, a singular, Russellian proposition that has me, Ray Buchanan, as a constituent, as well as the property expressed by 'is hungry':

1*. <Ray Buchanan, the property of being hungry>

The DR theorist will also claim that this singular proposition is the referent of the that-clause in both (2) and (4), and, hence, both something I said, and something we both believe. Similarly, (1*) will also be claimed to be the semantic content of my literal utterances (9) and (10):

9. That guy is hungry. [Demonstrating myself in a mirror]

10. Ray Buchanan is hungry.

While the sentence-types displayed (9) and (10) might differ in character* from that displayed in (1), any utterance thereof will, according to the DR theorist, semantically express one and the same singular proposition. Further, the DR theorist will claim that, if I believe the semantic content of my utterance of (1), I thereby believe what is expressed by my utterances of (9) and (10) as well. Consequently, given that (3) is true, so too is (11):

3. I believe that I am hungry.

11. I believe that Ray Buchanan is hungry

If the that-clauses in (3) and (11) refer to the same singular proposition, these reports cannot diverge in truth-value.

As should already be clear, a singular proposition such as (1*) does not have the relativity feature. Insofar as (11) might be true even if I believe that I am not Ray (perhaps, I am suffering from amnesia), the singular proposition (1*) does not have the relativity feature. But if the DR theorist is correct, *that* proposition just is the proposition I believe if (3) is true. As such, the DR theorist must hold that what I said by uttering (1), and what we both believe if (3) and (4) are true, does not, and cannot, have the relativity feature (137). It takes little ingenuity to see that, more generally, no Russellian proposition—singular, or otherwise—can have the relativity feature.

As Schiffer points out, the DR theorist can explain away the appearance of the relativity feature only if she can explain away the very familiar worries for her view posed by Frege's puzzle (138). For example, the belief-reports in (3) and (11) can, intuitively, differ in truth-value, despite the predictions of the DR account to the contrary (again, I might have undergone amnesia and forgotten that I am Ray

Buchanan). Accounting for the mismatch between her theory's predictions and the intuitions of competent speakers regarding the truth-conditions of belief-reports such as (3) and (11) is only part of the challenge faced by the DR theorist. To appreciate one especially pressing such further worry, suppose that while we are at the restaurant, I mistake the mirror just to our left for a clear window. Gesturing towards a man in the mirror that I do not recognize to be me, I sincerely, literally, and competently utter (12):

12. I do not believe that he is hungry, but I believe that I am hungry.

For the DR theorist, however, (12) is an explicit contradiction, equivalent to (13):

13. I do not believe that I am hungry, but I believe that I am hungry.

The DR theorist must explain not only how it is possible for an utterance such as (13) to be literally true, she must also make it plausible that a competent, reflective speaker might *rationally* assert such a contradiction (138). This is no easy task.[7]

Like Schiffer, I am skeptical that the DR theorist can ultimately give a plausible response to the problems posed by Frege-cases, and, as such, that she can explain away the appearance of the relativity feature either. For now, I will follow Schiffer in taking it as a working hypothesis that the apparent counter-examples are genuine and that, as such, direct-reference semantics "can't be part of any correct way of explaining away the relativity feature" (139). Moreover, I will further assume that the difficulties facing the DR-theorists show that the truth-conditions of belief-reports such as (13) are, in some sense, and in some cases, 'sensitive' to the *modes of presentation* under which an agent thinks of the objects and properties which her belief concerns. In the meanwhile, I encourage fans of direct reference semantics to be patient—the view I will eventually sketch in response to Schiffer's puzzle has the wherewithal to reconstruct singular, Russellian propositions when, and where, we might find a need for them.

6.3 Fregeans and the Relativity Feature

In contrast to the DR theorist, Fregeans hold that the propositional objects of our beliefs and the contents of our assertions must be individuated in terms of the *modes of presentation* under which we think of the objects, properties, and relations that figure in their truth-conditions. According to the Fregean, an agent might (rationally) have multiple beliefs to the effect that a particular object x is F which nevertheless differ in propositional content. A Fregean can allow, for example, that Lois Lane's belief that Superman lives in Metropolis can (contra the DR-theorist) differ in content from her belief that Clark Kent lives in Metropolis (which in turn, might differ in content from her belief that that guy on TV lives in Metropolis, even if that guy is Superman/Clark). Likewise, a Fregean can, and will, claim that I might truly utter 'I do not believe that he is hungry, but I believe that I am hungry' so long as the two that-clauses refer to distinct modes of presentation (MOP) involving propositions. This is a good thing.

While Fregean accounts come in many varieties, these theorists will agree—or at least should agree—that whatever else MOPs might be, they must meet the following two constraints:

> *Frege's Constraint*: Necessarily, if m is a MOP under which a minimally rational person x believes a thing to be F, then it is not the case that x also believes y not to be F under m. If x believes y to be F and also believes y not to be F, then there are distinct MOPs m and m' such that x believes y to be F under m and disbelieves y to be F under m'.
>
> *The Criterion of Sameness*: If m is a complete MOP, then one cannot have two beliefs such that (1) both are beliefs that a thing x is F under m, and such that the two beliefs differ in internal functional role. (Schiffer 1978: 180–1)

Here, the *functional role of a belief* is intended to pick out what we might call the 'internal' functional profile of a belief state—i.e., the relations, actual and counterfactual, which that state bears to other mental states of the person which has that belief. According to the Fregean, MOPs are those components of the content of a belief that secures that it has a functional role in accord with the foregoing constraints. Of course, the Fregean will ultimately have to provide us with a metaphysical account of what, exactly, MOPs are.[8] For our purposes, we will not worry too much about the metaphysics, and simply take MOPs to be *whatever it is that plays the MOP-role*; that is, whatever it is that meets the foregoing constraints, be they *individual concepts, dossiers of information, conceptual roles of expressions in a language of thought*, or what have you.[9] For now, note that it is plausible that on any way of spelling out the notion, MOPs will likely be highly idiosyncratic and vary significantly from agent to agent. MOPs are introduced to capture an agent's *ways of thinking* of the objects, properties, and relations her belief concerns and there are, of course, many (many) cognitively non-equivalent ways of thinking of one and the same object and/or property.

Fregeans can, and should, allow that a MOP can be *irreducibly* object-, or property-, dependent, and cannot be identified, or individuated, without citing the object, or property, of which it is an MOP.[10] As Schiffer points out, a Fregean who takes this line can hold that 'the Fregean proposition <m, m'>, where m is an x-dependent mode of presentation of x, and m' is an F-ness-dependent mode of presentation of F-ness, would be...truth-conditionally equivalent to, but distinct from the direct-reference theorist's Russellian singular proposition <x, Fness>' (140). The Fregean who accepts this suggestion should claim that many of our demonstrative and/or perceptual beliefs essentially involve such object-dependent MOPs.

Returning to (1)–(4), it is clear that the Fregeans can countenance an abundance of extremely fine-grained, object-dependent propositions concerning me, Ray, to the effect that Ray is hungry. Indeed, there are as many such Fregean propositions as there are cognitively non-equivalent ways of thinking of me. (Within this plurality of propositions there will be a Fregean proposition that contains a first-person, self-conscious, MOP that I, and I alone, might think of myself under.) What the Fregean cannot give us, however, is a proposition with Schiffer's relativity feature. Here is Schiffer:

> If an *x*-dependent proposition has the relativity feature, then there is no one mode of presentation of *x* under which everyone who entertains the proposition must think of *x*, whenever or wherever the entertaining takes place. Fregean propositions, however, *do require each x-dependent proposition to contain a mode of presentation of x under which anyone, at any time or place, who entertains the proposition must think of x*. (140, italics mine)

Not only can the Fregean not provide us with a proposition that has Schiffer's relativity feature, the italicized requirement above makes it independently doubtful that the semantic content of (virtually) any literal utterance containing a referring expression is ever an object-dependent Fregean proposition. As Schiffer put it elsewhere, the real problem is that:

> ...while understanding what's said in an utterance typically *constrains* how the communicators must think of the things the utterance is about, it's extremely rare for such understanding to require them to think of those things in exactly the same way...what is the mode of presentation of Mexico City and the one mode of presentation of Los Angeles under which you and I are thinking of those two cities when I say to you, 'Mexico City has a much worse smog problem than Los Angeles.'?[11]

The worry here is completely general. While it is plausible enough that when I think of, say, the country singer Toby Keith, I am doing so under some or other specific MOP, it is implausible in the extreme to suppose that I might mean—literally, or otherwise—a Fregean proposition with that MOP as a constituent when I utter, say, (14):

14. Toby Keith is from Oklahoma.

Insofar as I can reasonably expect to be understood in uttering (14), I cannot mean, or intend to convey, any such proposition—how could I? On what grounds could I expect you, or anyone else, to come to recognize the particular MOP under which I think of Toby Keith on the basis of my utterance of (14), and the facts concerning the common ground between us? The things we mean, and say, are not fine-grained Fregean propositions.

Returning to Schiffer's puzzle: suffice it to say (for now), no Fregean proposition has the relativity feature. Moreover, in light of Schiffer's more general worry, I submit that Fregean propositions are not plausible candidates for being the contents of virtually any assertoric utterance, much less those that exhibit the relativity feature.

6.4 The "No-Semantic-Content" Theory

Neither Fregean propositions, nor the Russellian propositions favored by the DR theorist, have the relativity feature. In coming to appreciate why this is so, we have been reminded of some independent worries with both of these versions of the face-value theory. If we are to explain away Schiffer's relativity feature, we should try to do so in a way that does not have the problems of these familiar versions of the face-value theory. On the one hand, we would like an account of semantic content, and what is said, that allows for more fineness of grain than the account offered by the DR-theorist—an account that is, at least potentially, sensitive to how our audiences must think of the objects, and properties, our utterances concern if they are to understand us. (The hope is that such an account could allow for—among other things—the possibility that, say, a literal utterance of 'Lois believes that Superman flies, but does not believe that Kent does' could be true.) On the other hand, however, we need contents that are not nearly as fine-grained as those on offer from the proponent of the traditional Fregean account: *those* propositions are so fine-grained as to be all but incommunicable, and that is obviously not a good feature for semantic contents to have.

The prospects for giving such an account might seem extremely bleak. At this point in the dialectic, we no longer have Russellian propositions to appeal to, and we have just seen that Fregean propositions are not especially promising candidates for being semantic contents. If the Russellian is too liberal in its requirements on grasping, the Fregean is too demanding. It's too easy to share contents on the Russellian view, and too hard—almost impossible in many cases—for the Fregean.

Before we despair we should first consider a neo-Fregean response to Schiffer's puzzle concerning the relativity feature that he calls the "no-semantic-content theory":

> One way of attempting to [explain away the relativity feature]...is to deny that any proposition is the semantic content of my utterance and to hold instead that understanding the utterance requires me and my hearer to entertain different but related propositions. That is to say, as regards my utterance of 'I'm F', the no-semantic-content theory holds, first, that my literal and serious utterance of 'I'm F' has no semantic content—that is, that in uttering the sentence I'm not saying *any* proposition which conforms to the meaning of that sentence—but, second, my utterance (i) has a truth-value; (ii) is fully understood by me and my audience; (iii) is such that that understanding requires me and my audience to think of me in different ways (I, but not you, must think of me under the self-conscious mode of presentation); and (iv) does conform to the meaning of the sentence type 'I'm F' (it's just that that meaning can't be a propositional form which requires the literal speaker who utters the sentence to mean a proposition of that form). (143–4)

This response is, I submit, *the* response for the theorist who holds that the objects of our thoughts are fine-grained, Fregean proposition. In what follows, let's call any theorist who holds that (a) the objects of our cognitive attitudes are Fregean propositions, (b) but who—in the sense of the foregoing quote—denies that such propositions are the contents of our assertoric speech acts, an *enlightened Fregean* (or a 'Fregean$_E$', for short).

Hints of such an account are littered throughout the writings of neo-Fregeans.[12] McDowell, for example, claims that a proponent of Fregean propositions can, and should, deny that "communication must involve a sharing of [Fregean] thoughts between the communicator and audience" (1998: 222).[13] Rather, the Fregean should hold that successful communication requires "not shared thoughts but different thoughts that are mutually known to stand in a suitable relation of correspondence" (McDowell 1998: 222).

And while McDowell refrains from explicitly denying that literal utterances involving demonstratives, and/or indexicals, fail to have semantic content, Heck (2002) comes much closer:

> If one really wants to find something to call *the* meaning [of such an utterance], then perhaps what is common to the cognitive values the utterance has for different speakers is as good a choice as any. But why do we want to find something to call the meaning? What we (relatively) uncontroversially have are speakers who associate Thoughts [i.e., specific thought contents] with utterances and restrictions on how the different Thoughts must be related if they are to communicate successfully... (Heck 2002: 27)

(Here, Heck presumably means 'the semantic content of an utterance' in speaking of "*the* meaning" thereof, and by "thoughts" he means Fregean propositions.) For the Fregean$_E$, the problems posed by Schiffer's relativity feature are not so much a worry for the Fregean account of indexical or demonstrative *thoughts*; rather, they are problems for overly simplistic 'thought-sharing' conceptions of linguistic communication.

While McDowell, Heck, and other neo-Fregeans have been moved towards the no-semantic-content account from problems posed by indexicals and demonstratives, such an account should be of much more general appeal to the fan of Fregean propositions in light of the worry raised in section 6.3: namely, that such propositions are virtually always too fine-grained to be plausible candidates for being the contents of assertion. A fan of Fregean propositions *should* be every bit as sympathetic to the no-semantic-content account for utterances involving, say, proper names as they are for indexicals. That is, the Fregean$_E$ should hold a speaker will no more mean, or assert, a Fregean proposition by uttering, say, 'Mexico City has a much worse smog problem than Los Angeles' than she will by an utterance of (1), (5), or any other of the cases we have considered involving indexicals and demonstratives.

The fan of Fregean propositions who adopts the no-semantic-content theory will hold that successful linguistic communication can be achieved by the speaker and her audience coming to have, distinct, yet appropriately related Fregean thoughts. What exactly could this amount to? Insofar as understanding a speaker *S*'s utterance requires (at least minimally) recognizing her meaning-intentions, we are owed a story regarding *S*'s meaning intentions that allows that it is indeed possible for *S*'s audience to understand her by entertaining something suitably similar to the Fregean thought she 'had in mind' in producing her utterance. In the case of my utterance of (1), for example, the content of my meaning intention cannot simply be *that you entertain a thought suitably similar to my thought p*, where *p* is the Fregean content of my first-person thought. Recognition of *that* intention would require you to do something that Frege's account of indexical thoughts all but entails cannot be done—namely, it requires you to share the content of my private, unshareable thought. What then should the Fregean$_E$ say?

Stepping back, the Fregean$_E$ holds that many literal utterances will fail to have a 'semantic content' in the sense in which that notion was introduced in section 6.1. She will hold that, in typical cases, there is no proposition of the kind she is willing to countenance (i.e., Fregean propositions) that a speaker means, or asserts. But crucially, there is nothing to preclude her from theorizing about 'what' the speaker meant—literally, or otherwise—by an utterance so long as what is meant/asserted is not, itself, a Fregean proposition.[14] Whatever the things we mean turn out to be, they had better be such that different speakers can entertain, or believe, them in virtue of having distinct Fregean thoughts if they are going to be of help to Schiffer's worries concerning the relativity feature.

There are several possibilities here, but I'll just suggest the one to which I am most partial.[15] Consider (15):

15. Fichte was born in Upper Lusatia.

Notice that a Fregean proposition might have any number of properties. It might have the property of being Barack Obama's favorite proposition, it might have the property of being controversial among people who own pugs, and so on. A Fregean proposition might also, of course, have the complex property of being about a certain man, Fichte, and true only if he was born in Upper Lusatia. Call this property Ψ. On behalf of the Fregean$_E$, I suggest that in uttering 'Fichte was born in Upper Lusatia.' the speaker does not mean any particular Fregean proposition; rather *what* she is putting forward is Ψ. So long as her audience comes to entertain a suitably similar Fregean proposition—namely, one that *is* Ψ—on the basis of her utterance, understanding can be achieved. This thing—the *Fregean proposition-type* Ψ—is, for all intents and purposes, equivalent to the singular proposition <Fichte, the property of being born in Upper Lusatia>. But there is nothing to preclude the Fregeran$_E$ from holding that, in a particular context of utterance, the relevant proposition-type is more finely-grained: perhaps the relevant proposition-type in question is one that is just like Ψ, except further requires thinking of Fichte *by that name*, or *as a philosopher*, or what have you.

Interestingly, the Fregean$_E$ can also allow that in some cases the relevant type is not, in any sense, equivalent to a proposition of any stripe. This would occur when the speaker's audience might fully understand her utterance in virtue of coming to entertain any one, or more, Fregean propositions *which themselves have different possible worlds truth-conditions*. Elsewhere, I have argued that such cases abound.[16] But for present purposes, let's only consider the simpler cases in which each of the Fregean propositions of the relevant type have the same modal profile. In these cases, at least, we might claim that a literal utterance in which a speaker means/asserts such a Fregean proposition-type is true just in case each of the propositions of that type are themselves true.

Returning to the first example in section 6.1, the theorist who takes up the suggestion just offered might hold that in uttering (1) I literally meant a Fregean proposition-type, Φ, instantiated by all and only those Fregean propositions with the modal profile of <Ray, the property of being hungry>, intending that there be some or other thought of that type that my audience come to entertain on the basis of my utterance. Moreover, given our mutual knowledge of the character* of 'I,' it is plausible that I will further *conventionally signal* that the particular Fregean thought of the Φ-type that, as it were, 'prompted' my utterance was an essentially first-person one. In order to understand my utterance of (1) it is not enough for you to come to have a thought concerning me to the effect Ray is hungry. Additionally, you must recognize that I am, by my choice of the first-person pronoun 'I,' intentionally providing you evidence concerning the specific proposition of Φ-type that lies behind my utterance; namely, a first-person, *de se*, thought concerning myself. Hence, if you understand my utterance you will both (i) come to entertain a Fregean thought of the intended Φ-type, and (ii) recognize that the particular Fregean thought of that type that prompted my utterance was itself essentially de se. Regarding (ii), notice that you can know that I have a de se thought of the Φ-kind even if you yourself can't have the specific Fregean thought of that kind that you know to have prompted my utterance. More generally, on the suggestion on offer, what a speaker means/says is *a property of Fregean propositions*; her utterance is understood only if her audience comes to suitably entertain some one, or more, propositions that have the property in question. Such Fregean proposition-types are, as it were, 'contents' for the would-be proponent of the no-semantic-content account.

The no-semantic-content theory should (I hope) be of interest to any fan of Fregean propositions. But as we are about to see, any friend of Fregean propositions who adopts this view has much, much work to do.

6.5 Schiffer's Worry for the No-Semantic-Content View

Schiffer is skeptical that any version of the no-semantic-content line will solve his puzzle; indeed, he offers a worry that challenges the very coherence of the no-semantic-content account. The principal worry Schiffer has is how to square the claim that, for example, my utterance of 'I am hungry' does not express a (Fregean) proposition with the claim that (seemingly) there is one thing—namely, *that I am hungry*—that (i) I said by my utterance, and (ii) that we both believe (144). Reconsider (2) and (3):

2. By uttering (1), I said that I am hungry.

3. I believe that I am hungry.

Presumably, the Fregean$_E$ will hold that in (2) the that-clause does *not* refer to a Fregean proposition. The alternative view—that the that-clause in (2) *does* refer to a Fregean proposition p, but p cannot be the semantic content of my utterance of (1)—is untenable (145). The crucial question then is how *any* theorist who thinks that *believing* is a relation between agents and propositions—Fregean or otherwise— can coherently hold that the that-clause in (2) does not refer to, or specify, such a proposition. Given the parity of form between (2) and (3), such a theorist would have to also hold that the that-clause in (3) does not refer to a Fregean proposition either— for that matter, it must be that that-clauses *never* refer to the propositions we believe. The Fregean$_E$ theorist who is driven to this position must tell us how a report of the form '*A* believes that *S*' can possibly be true if the relevant that-clause does not, and cannot, specify something that A believes.

The challenge is daunting, and I am honestly not sure how to best try to address it. As far as I can see, however, the Fregean$_E$'s best response to this challenge will involve denying the presupposition of his question. That is to say, such a theorist should hold that even in true belief-reports of the form '*S* believes that p' we do **not** specify what S believes. Ever.[17]

This might initially sound like a very unpromising line of thought, but any fan of Fregean propositions should be sympathetic. Why? Recall the worry we considered in section 6.3 regarding the Fregean theory of speech act content. If the traditional Fregean theory of speech act content were correct, then a speaker who literally utters 'Toby Keith is from Oklahoma' will have asserted some, or other, proposition containing some specific MOP of Toby. This, as we saw before, is implausible. Notice, however, that an analog of this same problem arises equally with regard to belief-reports. On the traditional, face-value, Fregean account of belief-reports, a report such as (16) is correct just in case the that-clause in question refers to a Fregean proposition that is among the things the subject—in this case, my little sister, Frances—believes:

16. Frances believes that Toby Keith is from Oklahoma.

The problem here is that I can no more literally refer to a Fregean, MOP-involving proposition by the that-clause in (16) than I can mean, or say, such a proposition by uttering 'Toby Keith is from Oklahoma.' Though I know my sister very well, I do not know the particular MOP under which she thinks of Toby Keith (and this is certainly **not** because she hasn't spoken about him enough to me). But even if I did know the exact MOP under which she thinks of the famous country singer—say $MOP_{4,567}$—I would still not be in a position to refer it in uttering (16). What a speaker can refer to in the course of uttering u is constrained by what she can reasonably expect her audience to recognize her to have meant on the basis of u. In the case of (16), I have no reason whatsoever to suppose that my utterance could put my audience in a position to recognize any particular MOP of Toby that Frances is employing in her belief. (Further, my audience can perfectly well understand my utterance of (16) even if they know less than me about the exact MOP relevant to Frances's belief.) If the Fregean version of the face-value theory were correct, however, my inability to refer to any particular MOP should preclude me from being able to truly utter (16).[18]

If the foregoing objection is correct, the traditional Fregean account of belief-*reports* is in trouble. This is not, however, yet to claim that the Fregean *metaphysics* of belief fails. That is, *believing* might be a relation between an agent and a Fregean proposition even if that-clauses in true belief-reports never refer to, or specify, such propositions. How might this go?

The Fregean$_E$ accepts the metaphysical thesis that *believing* is a relation between agents and Fregean propositions. If this metaphysical thesis is correct, then (16), if true, entails that there is *something* that Frances believes, this 'something' being a Fregean proposition. But obviously, the belief-report in (16) tells us more than just this. If (16) is true, we also know quite a bit about the Fregean proposition that Frances believes: among other things, it is a Fregean proposition true at a world w just in cases Toby Keith was born in Oklahoma in w. Moreover, in a particular context, mutual knowledge concerning my sister's epistemic situation regarding Toby Keith might place further constraints on the nature of the Fregean proposition she believes—for example, that she must think of him as *a country singer*, *a gentleman of the South*, or what have you. In a sense to be presently elaborated, the neo-Fregean should claim that the that-clause in (13) serves to *indirectly, and partially, characterize* the Fregean proposition that Frances believes.[19]

Building on these observations, the proponent of the no-semantic-content theory should hold that, to a very rough and ready first approximation, the logical form of (16) is given by (16b):

16b. $\exists p\, (\Phi p\ \&\ \text{Believes}(\text{Frances}, p))$

where 'p' ranges over Fregean propositions and Φ is a contextually relevant property of such propositions. But prima facie, this suggestion makes the question regarding the semantic function of the that-clause in (16) even more puzzling. Where did the that-clause go? What contribution could 'that Toby Keith is from Oklahoma' be making to the logical form given in (13b)?

Perhaps the Fregean$_E$ will find some inspiration in a proposal by Francois Recanati (2004) according to which that-clauses are analyzed as *existential quantifiers*. According to this proposal, 'that Toby Keith is from Oklahoma' has the same type of semantic value, as for example, 'some country singer.' On standard accounts, in 'some country singer,' 'some' serves to introduce the existential quantifier, and 'country singer' then provides a restriction on the quantifier so introduced. That-clauses are claimed to function analogously: in a particular context of utterance, the embedded sentence in 'that Toby Keith is from Oklahoma' will have a certain semantic content, Φ, that serves as a restriction on the existential quantifier introduced by 'that.' The that-clause, *qua* existential quantifier, can then combine with a monadic predicate such as 'Frances believes x'—a predicate true of all and only the propositions Frances believes—to deliver the desired logical form—(16b). On this proposal, that-clauses are, in effect, treated as *properties of monadic propositional attitude properties*. In the case of (16), the that-clause is claimed to express a property instantiated by Frances just in case there is at least one proposition that she believes possessing the contextually specified property Φ. The compositional details of this suggestion might be worked out in any number of different ways.[20] For now, however, the point to focus on is this: if Recanati's suggestion is correct, the Fregean who has been led to this point will have a story regarding that-clauses that is compatible with her claim that (16b) is the logical form of (16). The existential quantification over propositions in (16b) is accounted for by the (putative) fact that that-clauses themselves *are* restricted quantifiers.

Recanati's general idea is that in a particular context of utterance the embedded sentence in 'that Toby Keith is from Oklahoma' will have a certain semantic content Φ. The that-clause then serves to quantify over propositions that *have* that semantic content. Different versions of the view will then arise depending upon what one says about the semantic content of the sentence embedded in the that-clause. For example, if one were originally sympathetic to a DR account of the semantic content of 'Toby Keith is from Oklahoma,' the relevant that-clause could be taken as quantifying over an equivalence class of Fregean propositions, all of which are true at a world w, just in case the singular proposition <Toby Keith, the property of being from Oklahoma> is true at w.

More plausibly, however, a proponent of Recanati's suggestion might allow that the semantic content of the embedded sentence is 'pragmatically enriched' in the context of utterance so as to have the force of something akin to 'Toby Keith, *the country singer*, is from Oklahoma.' This latter move would allow the theorist to claim that, for example, (16) can differ in truth-value from (17), even though Toby Keith is Mr Covel:

17. Frances believes that Mr Covel is from Oklahoma.

The general idea might be spelled out in any number of different ways. The crucial point for now is that Recanati's suggestion would, if correct, provide the proponent of Fregean propositions a story regarding the semantic function of that-clauses that is compatible with the desired logical form of (16), viz. (16b).

Unfortunately for the Fregean$_E$, Recanati's suggestion is deeply problematic when we reconsider 'the parity of form' between belief-reports such as (16)/(17), and reports of what is said, and meant:

18. Frances meant/said that Toby Keith is from Oklahoma.

If that-clauses are uniformly analysed as existential quantifiers, we should expect the logical form of (18) to be analogous to that of the desired logical form of (18) given in (18b):

18b. $\exists p\ (\Phi p\ \&\ \text{Meant/Said}(\text{Frances}, p))$

But, as Schiffer once pointed out in connection to a similar suggestion due to Graeme Forbes (1987), this prediction is unacceptable.[21] Suppose that I offer the meaning attribution in (18) on the basis of Frances's uttering 'He is from Oklahoma' while pointing to a picture of Toby wearing a cowboy hat. As we have already seen in section 6.3, Frances could not have meant any particular Fregean proposition by her utterance of 'He is from Oklahoma.' Hence, (18) should be false. More generally, given that the contents of our speech acts cannot be identified with Fregean propositions, *all* reports of the form 'S said/meant that p' should be false. But as this is not a desirable result, the Fregean$_E$ needs an alternative story regarding the semantic function of that-clauses compatible with her guiding thought that belief-reports only partially characterize the Fregean propositions we believe—an alternative story compatible with her desire to hold that (15b) is the logical form of (15), but which avoids the foregoing problem regarding attributions of meaning. She needs an account that is compatible with holding that *believing* is a relation to a Fregean proposition, but *saying*, and *meaning*, are not. What might such an account look like?

At this point, I humbly propose that we reconsider the suggestion that I made on behalf of the Fregean$_E$ regarding what we mean, and assert (section 6.4). First notice that if (i) *meaning, saying,* and the like are fundamentally relations to Fregean proposition-types, and (ii) it is (even in principle) possible to report the full content of a speech act by an attribution such as (18), it follows that the orthodox Fregean view of that-clauses is false. What then might the that-clause in a true says-that report such as (18) pick out if not a proposition? Perhaps, we should take the that-clause in (18) to be expressing a two-place relation between speaker and a *proposition-type*, say Φ, which is the semantic value of the that-clause:

18c. Says (Frances, Φ)

In this case, perhaps Φ is a property instantiated by all and only those Fregean propositions true at a world w just in case Toby Keith is from Oklahoma at w and which requires thinking of Toby as a country singer. The proponent of Fregean propositions who adopts this suggestion regarding the logical form of meaning attributions can avoid the problem we encountered for the Recanati-inspired representation of (18).

How, if at all, can the suggestion that that-clauses denote properties of Fregean propositions be squared with the desired logical form of (15), i.e., (15b)? The Fregean$_E$ might claim that the similarity between (15) and (18) is to be explained by the fact that in *both* reports the that-clause picks out a proposition-type Φ. But while 'says' can be analyzed as a two-place relation between agent and the proposition-type supplied the that-clause, 'believes' cannot. After all, according to the Fregean$_E$, the belief-relation is fundamentally a relation between agents and Fregean propositions, **not** properties thereof. In my view, the Fregean should claim that the underlying metaphysical difference between *saying* and *believing* engenders a crucial semantic difference between attributions of meaning and belief: whereas a report such as (18) is true just in case Frances stands in the saying-relation to the proposition-type Φ, (15) is true if, and only if Frances believes some one, or more propositions *of* the type Φ. 'Believes,' unlike 'says,' forces existential quantification over propositions that are *of* the type denoted by the that-clause.

To illustrate the general idea here, it is helpful to consider a singular term that explicitly seems to refer to a type (or kind). Suppose that while we are sitting in the dog park at Washington Square, I utter (19) while gesturing towards a particular English bulldog:

19. Pugs are more widespread than that type of dog.

What, if anything, have I referred to by my use of 'that type of dog?' Prima facie, I have referred to a certain *type* of dog—namely, *the English bulldog*—by way of an instance of that type. The two-place predicate '_ is more widespread than _' does not express a relation between individuals, or even pluralities of individuals, for that matter. It makes no sense to suggest that, for example, *Fido is more widespread than Spike*, or *Eighteen pugs are more widespread that seventeen bulldogs*. Rather, '_ is more widespread than _' expresses a relation between *kinds*, or *types*, of things; in the case of (19), a relation between pugs and English bulldogs.

Suppose that a bit later during our visit to the dog park, I utter (20) while gesturing towards the same English bulldog:

20. Mary owns that type of dog.

Taking (19) as our model, we would expect that my use of 'that type of dog' also refers to a certain type, or kind, of thing—namely, *the English bulldog*. Notice that in uttering (20), however, I most certainly did not claim that Mary *owns* the kind *the English bulldog*; rather, I have claimed that *there is a dog of a certain kind that Mary owns*. Assuming that both 'Mary' and 'that type of dog' are functioning as singular terms, where could the existential quantification be coming from? Presumably, the existential quantification arises from the *interaction* of 'owns' and 'that type of dog.' Oftentimes, when a type/kind-referring singular term is in direct object position of a verb that does not itself express a relation to types/kinds, such as 'owns,' an existential reading is generated. Though linguists debate on how exactly the interaction of 'owns' and the type/kind-referring singular term gives rise to the relevant existential interpretation, no one denies that the phenomenon occurs.[22] The theorist who has come this far should claim that since *believes* is itself a relation between agents and Fregean propositions (not types thereof)—a belief-report such as (15) generates existential quantification over propositions of the type specified by the that-clause. On her account, 'that'-clauses univocally denote Fregean-proposition-types; 'believes' then functions a bit like 'owns' in (20), whereas 'says,' a bit more like 'is more widespread than' in (19).

It should (I hope) be apparent why the view just sketched ought to be attractive to the theorist who thinks that Fregean propositions are the objects of our beliefs, and other of our cognitive attitudes. It should be equally apparent, however, that the view just sketched invites many (many) worries of its own. Among other things, the Fregean must give up the standard treatment of that-clauses enshrined in the face-value theory (section 6.1). Hence, the Fregean$_E$ will have to show how, if at all, her view can accommodate the data that originally motivated the face-value account of 'that'-clauses. For example, our discussion of the asymmetry between *saying* and *believing* notwithstanding, the inferences displayed on the left hand side of (A) and (B) certainly look valid:

(A)
Mary believes everything John said. $(\forall x)(\text{Said}(j, x) \rightarrow \text{Believes}(m, x))$
John said that snow is white. $\text{Said}(j, p)$
Mary believes that snow is white. $\text{Believes}(m, p)$

(B)
John said everything Mary believes. $(\forall x)(\text{Believes}(m, x) \rightarrow \text{Said}(j, x))$
Mary believes that snow is white. $\text{Believes}(m, p)$
John said that snow is white. $\text{Said}(j, p)$

If the face-value account is correct, these inferences instantiate the logical forms displayed to their right, and hence are valid. Since the Fregean$_E$ gives an asymmetric account of 'says' and 'believes,' one might reasonably wonder whether she can capture the apparent validity of such arguments. Addressing the question of how, if at all, the Fregean$_E$ can account for the validity of such arguments (and explain away the apparent validity of others) must, however, wait for another occasion.

6.6 Conclusion

We began with Schiffer's observation that many of the things we say, and believe, seem to have a certain feature that is incompatible with the traditional, face-value, Fregean and Russellian accounts of propositional content. In the course of trying to explain away the relativity feature we have been led a considerable distance from both of these traditional accounts. According to the no-semantic-content theory just sketched, *believes, entertains*, and other of our cognitive attitudes *are* relations between agents and fine-grained Fregean propositions. Fregean propositions *are not*, however, the contents of our assertoric speech acts—rather what we mean, and say, are *kinds* thereof.

While we have just seen how one might *coherently* hold such a view, more work must first be done to show that the view is, in fact, *plausible*. Since the theorist who has been led to this point must give up the face-value theory, she incurs the debt of explaining away the data that Schiffer, and others, have adduced in its favor. Given the difficulty of this task, we might need to reconsider our starting point. That is, *maybe* Schiffer is right and the relativity feature simply cannot be explained away. If so, this would mean that we would need a novel account of propositional content radically unlike the traditional versions of the face-value theory due to Frege and Russell. As it turns out, Schiffer indeed has such a view to offer, but I will let him tell you about that.*

Notes

1. 'What Reference Has to Tell Us about Meaning' was published in an excellent, but difficult to obtain volume edited by J. Branquinho entitled *Conteúdo e Cognição. Anais da série de seminários de Filosofia Analítica* in 2005. It is a true shame that Schiffer's paper is not more widely known, and more easily accessible. Like all of Schiffer's work in the theory of meaning and content, it deserves careful study from anyone with even a passing interest in these topics. Unless otherwise indicated, all subsequent references will be to this work.
2. Schiffer later 'tightens' this characterization as follows:

    A proposition p has the relativity feature iff p is an x-dependent proposition such that there are properties Φ and Ψ and ways of thinking w and w' of x such that (i) $w \neq w'$, (ii) a person who has Φ can entertain p only if she thinks of x in way w, and (iii) a person who has Ψ can only entertain p if he thinks of x in way w'. (134)

    The complications that lead Schiffer to this refinement will not concern us in what follows, and, as such, we can stick to his formulation of the relativity feature in the text.
3. In particular, the view that I will suggest is motivated, in large part, by Schiffer's work in the late 70s and early 80s in the theory of reference, especially Schiffer (1981). See fn. 12.
4. See Schiffer (2003), Chapter 1, for some of the motivations for the face-value view.
5. Here, and throughout, I am using 'believes' as the paradigmatic cognitive attitude and 'saying' and 'meaning' for the paradigmatic speech act verbs that take that-clauses as arguments.
6. See Schiffer (2003) for more on characters*. See Bach (1994), Buchanan (2012), and Neale (2004) for more on proposition-types, -templates, or "forms."
7. For some further worries regarding DR accounts of content see Schiffer (1987b), (1992), and (2006). For some DR-responses to Schiffer (2006), see Braun (2006) and Salmon (Chapter 7, this volume), as well as Schiffer's most recent response to Salmon (Chapter 18, this volume).
8. See Schiffer (1987a), Chapter 3, for some of the difficulties in saying what, exactly, MOPs are.
9. For the record, I am sympathetic to the view that MOPs are to be understood in terms of the conceptual roles of expressions in Mentalese, where conceptual role is modeled in the manner suggested by Field (1977).
10. See, for example, Bach (1994), Chapter One, Evans (1982), McDowell (1998) for more on *de re* MOPs.
11. This quote is from Schiffer's 2004 lecture notes at NYU on the material that ultimately led to the 2005 paper that we have been discussing. Also, see Heck (2002) for an excellent

discussion of this point in connection to indexicals and demonstratives (more on Heck's views on these topics momentarily).

12. Here, I have in mind theorists such as Gareth Evans (1982), Richard Heck (2002), Martin Davies (1982), Graeme Forbes (1987) and (1990), and John McDowell (1998). A would-be proponent of the no-semantic-content thesis will also find considerable inspiration in Schiffer's own 1981 paper entitled 'Indexicals and the Theory of Reference.' In that work, Schiffer argued that while the Frege/Russell theory of content is plausible as an account of "the thought in the mind of a speaker using a singular term" ('Indexicals and the Theory of Reference,' 49), it fails as an account of the things we mean, and say, by uttering sentences containing indexicals and demonstratives. Schiffer argued that while the semantic content of a literal utterance of the form 't is G' (where 't' is a referring expression) will be a singular, Russellian proposition, such a proposition is not, and could not be, the "complete content" of the belief in the mind of the speaker making that utterance. On this view—like the "enlightened Fregean" view to be sketched below—there is a fundamental asymmetry between the things we say, and mean, and the contents of our beliefs. See Neale (Chapter 12, this volume) for an interesting discussion of Schiffer's account of speaker-reference offered in that paper.
13. Schiffer (2005) also cites both the McDowell material and the quote by Heck to follow, as well.
14. Heck, as we have seen, allows for this possibility, but claims that the Fregean *does not need* any notion of semantic content (at least in utterances involving demonstratives and indexicals).
15. I develop this suggestion in my (2010) and (2012).
16. See my (2010) for such cases, and a more general argument that speaker-meaning is not a propositional attitude.
17. The primary inspiration for the suggestion that follows comes from Bach's seminal (1997) piece entitled 'Do Belief Reports Report Beliefs?' See the citations in fn. 19, as well.
18. See Schiffer (1993: 109–10) in connection to that-clause reference. See my (2012) for further discussion.
19. In addition to Bach's article cited in fn. 17, and Recanati's (2004) piece discussed below, see Graff Fara (2003), Forbes (1987), McKinsey (1994), Pollock (1982), Schiffer (1977) and (1978), and Shier (1993) and (1996) for further motivation for such a partial characterization account of propositional attitude reports.
20. On standard accounts, 'some country singer' is analysed as expressing the property:

(*) $\lambda Q \exists x[\text{Country-singer}(x) \& Q(x)]$

This second-order property—the property a property P has when P is possessed by at least one entity that is a country singer—is a generalized quantifier. If we abstract away further, we can then isolate the distinct contributions of 'some' and 'country singer' in (*) revealing that 'some' serves to introduce an existential quantifier, and 'country singer,' in effect, provides restriction on the quantifier so-introduced. On this analysis, 'some' is the following function from properties to generalized quantifiers, such as (*):

(*) $\lambda P \lambda Q \exists x[P(x) \& Q(x)]$

Modifying Recanati's suggestion for our current purposes, the suggestion would run 'Frances believes p' expresses a one-place property of propositions, a property true of all and only the Fregean propositions she believes. 'That Toby Keith is from Oklahoma' is also claimed to be a second-order property such as (a) (below). It is a property of monadic propositional attitude properties—properties, like (b), that are true of things just in case they bear the relevant propositional attitude relation to a proposition with the contextually specified property, Φ.

(a) λXλx[(∃p)(Φp & X(x,p))]
(b) λx[(∃p)(Φp & Believes(x,p))]
Thus, in (13) the embedded sentence 'Toby Keith is from Oklahoma' (plus various contextual factors) serves to specify precisely which property of propositions gets assigned to Φ. We can isolate the contribution of 'that' as follows:

(c) λφλXλx[(∃p)(φp & X(x,p))])

21. See Schiffer (1992) paper entitled 'Belief Ascription' fn. 10.
22. The relevant linguistics literature is vast. As a starting point, the introduction to *The Generic Book*, edited by Krifka et al., is especially helpful. See Carlson (1977) and Chierchia (1998) for two classic discussions of reference to kinds/types. Also see section 4 of Ostertag (2012) for a very helpful discussion of some of the complexities of type/kind referring singular terms.
*. I would like to thank Gary Ostertag, Gurpreet Rattan, David Sosa, and the members of the LOGOS group at Universitat de Barcelona with whom I discussed the material in 2012. I would, however, especially like to thank Stephen Schiffer.

When I was still an undergraduate at the University of North Carolina, Chapel Hill, I read Stephen's 1972 book *Meaning* in a tutorial with Simon Blackburn. The subsequent two semesters, I carried around a copy of Stephen's 1987 book *Remnants of Meaning*, reading it twice over before ever starting my PhD work at NYU. As an undergraduate, I distinctly remember wondering whether the author of these works could possibly be as formidable in person as he is in print. (I was so nervous to meet this Stephen Schiffer that I could hardly get myself to talk with him during my visit to NYU as a prospective student.) After many years of working with Stephen, I can confidently tell you that he is indeed every bit as philosophically formidable in person!

Stephen was an ideal teacher and dissertation advisor. I am exceptionally lucky to have had the opportunity to work with him. Through his seminars, his written work, and discussion, Stephen not only taught me how to think about issues in the theory of meaning and content; he set an example of how philosophy should be done. Thank you, Stephen.

Bibliography

Bach, K. (1994). *Thought and Reference*, expanded edition. Oxford: Clarendon Press.
Bach, K. (1997). "Do Belief Reports Report Beliefs?" *Pacific Philosophical Quarterly* 78 (3): 215–41.
Bach, K. (2001). "You Don't Say." *Synthese* 128: 15–44.
Braun, D. (2006). "Illogical, But Rational." *Noûs* 40: 376–9.
Buchanan, R. (2010). "A Puzzle About Meaning and Communication." *Noûs* 44: 340–71.
Buchanan, R. (2012). "Is Belief a Propositional Attitude?" *Philosopher's Imprint* 12: 1–20.
Carlson, G. (1977). *Reference to Kinds in English*. PhD Dissertation. University of Massachusetts, Amherst.
Chierchia, G. (1998). "Reference to Kinds across Languages." *Natural Language Semantics* 6: 339–405.
Davies, M. (1982). "Individuation and the Semantics of Demonstratives." *Journal of Philosophical Logic* 11: 287–310.
Evans, G. (1982). *The Varieties of Reference*. Oxford: Oxford University Press.
Fara, D. G. (2003). "Desire, Scope, and Tense." *Philosophical Perspectives* 17: 141–63. [Published under the name 'Delia Graff']
Field, H. (1977). "Logic, Meaning, and Conceptual Role." *Journal of Philosophy* 74: 379–408.

Forbes, G. (1987). "Indexicals and Intensionality: A Fregean Perspective." *Philosophical Review* 96: 3–31.
Forbes, G. (1990). "Indispensability of Sinn." *Philosophical Review* 99: 535–63.
Heck, R. (2002). "Do Demonstratives Have Senses?" *The Philosophers' Imprint* 2: 1–33.
Krifka, M. et al. (1995). "Genericity: An Introduction.' In *The Generic Book*, edited by F. J. Pelletier and G. Carlson, Chicago: University of Chicago Press.
McKinsey, M. (1994). "Individuating Beliefs.' *Philosophical Perspectives* 8: 143–69.
McDowell, J. (1998). "*De Re Senses*." In *Meaning, Knowledge, and Reality*, Cambridge: Harvard University Press.
Neale, S. (2004). "This, That, and the Other." In *Descriptions: Semantic and Pragmatic Perspectives*, edited by A. Bezuidenhout and M. Reimer, Oxford: Oxford University Press, 68–182.
Neale, S. (2016). "Silent Reference." [This Volume, Chapter 12.]
Ostertag, G. (2012). Critical Study: Julian Dodd. *Works of Music: An Essay in Ontology. Noûs* 4: 355–74.
Pollock, J. (1982). *Language and Thought.* Princeton: Princeton University Press.
Recanati, F. (2004). "'That'-Clauses as Existential Quantifiers." *Analysis* 64: 229–35.
Salmon, N. (1986). *Frege's Puzzle*. Cambridge, Mass.: MIT Press.
Salmon, N. (2016). "Constraint with Restraint." [Chapter 7, this Volume.]
Schiffer, S. (1972). *Meaning*. Oxford: Oxford University Press.
Schiffer, S. (1977). "Naming and Knowing." *Midwest Studies in Philosophy* 2: 28–41.
Schiffer, S. (1978). "The Basis of Reference." *Erkenntnis* 13: 171–206.
Schiffer, S. (1981). "Indexicals and the Theory of Reference." *Synthese* 49: 43–101.
Schiffer, S. (1987a). "The "Fido"-Fido Theory of Belief." *Philosophical Perspectives* 1: 455–80.
Schiffer, S. (1987b). *Remnants of Meaning*. Cambridge, Mass.: MIT Press.
Schiffer, S. (1992). 'Belief Ascription.' *The Journal of Philosophy* 89: 499–521.
Schiffer, S. (1993). "Belief Ascription and a Paradox of Meaning." *Philosophical Issues* 3: 89–121.
Schiffer, S. (2003). *The Things We Mean*. Oxford: Clarendon Press.
Schiffer, S. (2005). "What Reference Has to Tell Us about Meaning." In *Conteúdo e Cognição. Anais da série de seminários de Filosofia Analítica*, edited by J. Branquinho, Lisbon: Centro de Filosofia da Universidade de Lisboa: 129–53.
Schiffer, S. (2006). "A Problem For Direct Reference Theories Of Belief Reports." *Noûs* 40: 361–8.
Shier, D. (1993). *Russellian Non-Parallelism: Direct Reference without Anti-Individualism*. PhD dissertation, Wayne State University.
Shier, D. (1996). "Direct Reference for the Narrow Minded." *Pacific Philosophical Quarterly* 77: 225–48.

7

Constraint with Restraint

Nathan Salmon

Professor Schiffer has presented an alleged refutation of my version of Millianism, the doctrine (often alternatively called 'the theory of direct reference') that the semantic content of a name is simply the designatum.[1] Although Schiffer and I have many times disagreed, I applaud his deep and abiding commitment to argument as a primary philosophical tool. Regretting any communication failure that has occurred, I endeavor here to make clearer my earlier reply in 'Illogical Belief.'[2] I shall be skeletal, however; the interested reader is encouraged to turn to 'Illogical Belief' for detail and elaboration.

I have argued in numerous venues that to bear a propositional attitude *de re* is to bear that attitude toward the corresponding singular proposition, no more and no less. If this is right, then according to Millianism every instance of the following modal schema is true:

S: Necessarily, α Vs that ϕ_β iff α Vs of β (*de re*) that ϕ_{it},

where α is any singular term of English, V is any of a wide range of transitive English verbs of propositional attitude (including 'believe,' 'disbelieve,' 'doubt,' etc.), β is any proper name or other Millian term of English, ϕ_{it} is any English 'open sentence' in which the pronoun 'it'—alternatively 'he,' 'him,' 'she,' or 'her'—occurs as a free variable, and ϕ_β is the same as ϕ_{it} except for having occurrences of β wherever ϕ_{it} has free occurrences of the relevant pronoun.[3]

Schiffer uses the epithet 'Frege's constraint' for a principle that entails the following:

FC: Necessarily, if x rationally believes y to be F while also disbelieving (or while also merely withholding believing) y to be F, for some property or singularly propositional-functional concept F, then in so doing x takes y in differing ways, by means of particular *guises* or "modes of presentation," m and m' where m ≠ m'; furthermore, in so doing, x does not construe m and m' as guises of, or ways of taking, a single thing.

I have spent much of the past quarter century arguing for FC (or for a duly qualified version). The primary rationale for FC is that if x rationally believes y to be F while also disbelieving z to be F, then in so doing, x takes y and z to be distinct (one of them being F, the other not). Insofar as x is rational, he/she will thereby take y and z differently. This will be so even if, in fact, $y=z$. In this case, x will take y, i.e. z, in different ways. Similarly, if x rationally believes y to be F while also suspending judgment whether z is F, then ordinarily, in so doing x will take y and z differently.

Schiffer derives from these principles the conclusion that my version of Millianism is inconsistent with the possibility of a certain empirically possible state of affairs, (a). This state of affairs may be characterized as follows: Jane rationally believes, even while she is fully aware that 'George Eliot' and 'Mary Ann Evans' co-designate, both that Ralph believes that George Eliot was a man and that Ralph does not believe that Mary Ann Evans was a man. For according to Millianism, in situation (a), Jane rationally believes both the singular proposition about George Eliot, that Ralph believes she was a man, and its denial. Putting 'Jane' for α in $S(S)$, 'George Eliot' for β, 'believe' for V, and 'Ralph believes *she* was a man' for ϕ_{it}, and performing a bit of logic, one obtains the result that in (a) Eliot is believed by Jane to be such that Ralph believes she was a man. Now putting for β instead 'Mary Ann Evans' and for ϕ_{it} 'Ralph does *not* believe *she* was a man,' and drawing analogous logical inferences, one obtains as an additional result that in (a) Eliot is also rationally believed by Jane *not* to be such that Ralph believes she was a man. Thus, in (a) Jane believes Eliot to be F while also believing Eliot not to be F, for a particular property or singulary-functional concept F. Reasoning from (FC), it follows that in (a) Jane, insofar as she is rational, must take Eliot in differing ways, by means of a pair of guises that Jane does not thereby take to be of a single individual. But Jane does not do this in (a).

The *reductio* derivation is in fact fallacious. Specifically, a fallacy is committed when Schiffer erroneously "restates" the relevant half of the first premise as the thesis that every instance of the following alternative schema is true (putting 'believe' for V):

S': Necessarily, if α believes that ϕ_β, then β is believed by α to be (something/someone) such that ϕ_{it},

where α, β, ϕ_β, and ϕ_{it} are all exactly as before.[4] Contradiction is indeed derivable from (S') taken together with Millianism, FC, and the empirical possibility of (a), exactly in the manner that Schiffer sets out. This is because the relevant instance of (S') is inconsistent with the facts. The derivation might even be taken as demonstrating this—at least by the Millian's lights. Importantly, Millianism is in no way committed to (S'), not even a Millianism like my own, which is committed to (S). I am committed to the existence of counter-instances of (S').

The distinction between the *de re* constructions ⌜α believes of β that ϕ_{it}⌝ and ⌜β is believed by α to be something such that ϕ_{it}⌝ may seem excessively subtle and delicate, but in the present instance it is crucial. The latter is the passive-voice transformation of a relational predication:

α **Believes**$_r$ (β, to be something such that ϕ_{it}),

where '**Believes**$_r$' is a triadic predicate for a ternary relation between a believer x, an object y (the *res*), and importantly, a property or singulary-functional concept F that x attributes to y. Schema (S') is thus indeed a logical consequence of (S) in a special case: if the open sentence ϕ_{it} has monadic-predicational form, ⌜*It* Π⌝, where Π is a monadic predicate in which the pronoun 'it' does not occur free and whose single argument place is filled by the pronoun 'it' (or 'he' or 'she'). In this case, Π is a term for a particular property or singulary-functional concept F. If someone x believes the singular proposition expressed by ⌜It Π⌝ under the assignment of a particular value y to the variable/pronoun 'it,' then the proposition believed—that y is F—has the simple structure, <y, F>, so that y is indeed believed by x to be F.[5]

Not all *de re* beliefs about y involve the attribution of a property to y. Many singular propositions involving y have a structure considerably more complex than <y, F>. There are some propositions, expressed by complex sentences ϕ_β, such that someone might rationally believe the proposition without inferring, indeed even while doubting, the consequence expressed by ⌜β is something such that ϕ_it⌝.[6] Some of these propositions are witness to the fact that (S′) is no logical consequence of (S).

To take an example due to David Kaplan, if Quine's Ralph believes that *this man* [pointing at a fuzzy picture of Ortcutt, his face covered by a large brown hat] is taller than Ortcutt, then Ralph believes the singular proposition about Ortcutt, that he (Ortcutt) is taller than he (Ortcutt) is. According to (S), Ralph thus believes that Ortcutt is taller than Ortcutt. But Ralph does not thereby believe Ortcutt to be someone taller than himself. That is, Ortcutt is not believed by Ralph to be something z such that z is taller than z. The proposition Ralph believes has the binary-relational form: <Ortcutt, Ortcutt, *taller-than*>—or perhaps, the special monadic-predicational form: <Ortcutt, <*taller-than*, Ortcutt> >. It most definitely does not have the alternate monadic-predicational form: <Ortcutt, *being taller than oneself*>. Putting 'Ralph' for α, 'Ortcutt' for β, 'believe' for V, and '*He* is taller than *he* is' for ϕ_it, the resulting instance of (S) is true while the resulting instance of (S′) is false.[7]

Schiffer's central example exploits another such sentence ϕ_β, specifically 'Ralph does not believe that Mary Ann Evans was a man.' This expresses a singular proposition about George Eliot, that Ralph does not believe that she was a man, represented by the ordered pair <<Ralph, *believing*, <Eliot, *having been a man*>>, *being false*>. Jane rationally believes this proposition, while also believing precisely what it denies, as expressed by 'Ralph believes that George Eliot was a man' and represented by <Ralph, *believing*, <Eliot, *having been a man*>>. But Jane does not thereby both believe and disbelieve the singular proposition about Eliot, that she is believed by Ralph to have been a man, as represented by <Eliot, *being believed by Ralph to have been a man*>.

The following dialogue illustrates Jane's pertinent beliefs:

SOCRATES: "Does Ralph believe that Mary Ann Evans was a man?"
JANE: "No, he doesn't."
SOCRATES: "Does Ralph believe that George Eliot was a man?"
JANE: "Yes."
SOCRATES: "So George Eliot is someone Ralph believes was a man?"
JANE: "Yes."
SOCRATES: "What about Mary Ann Evans, then? Does Ralph also believe *she* was a man?"
JANE: "Ralph doesn't believe that *Mary Ann Evans* was a man. But you're now asking about Mary Ann Evans herself. Mary Ann Evans and George Eliot are the same person, don't you know? And Ralph does indeed believe she was a man."

SOCRATES: "Very well. Is Mary Ann Evans someone Ralph also *doesn't* believe was a man?"
JANE: "Of course not; that would be logically impossible. I just told you: Mary Ann Evans is someone Ralph *does* believe was a man."
SOCRATES: "Is George Eliot someone Ralph *doesn't* believe was a man?"
JANE: "You're not listening to me: George Eliot and Mary Ann Evans are the same person. Ralph *does* believe she was a man."

Jane's position is rational, sophisticated, even subtle. It is perfectly coherent (even if it is inconsistent, at least by Millian lights). It is essentially a part of a neo-Fregean theory of *de re* constructions. Putting 'Jane' for α, 'George Eliot' for β, 'believe' for V, and 'Ralph believes *she* was a man' for ϕ_{it}, the resulting instance of (S) is true while the resulting instance of (S') is false. Schiffer's *reductio* derivation fallaciously infers the latter from the former on its way to deriving a contradiction.

Schiffer's objection can make do without fallaciously inferring (S') from (S) if FC can be extended into the following more general principle schema, which might be called 'Frege's constraint without restraint':

FC': Necessarily, if α rationally believes of β that ϕ_{it} while also disbelieving (or merely withholding believing) of β that ϕ_{it}, then in so doing α takes β by means of differing guises, m and m'; furthermore, in so doing, α does not construe m and m' as guises of a single thing,

where α and β are English singular terms and ϕ_{it} is as before. (Schiffer proposes a related generalization.) But as remarked earlier, there are complex singular propositions about y that one can rationally believe without attributing the corresponding property to y. Someone may rationally believe and disbelieve one of these propositions without taking y to be distinct things. Given the existence of such cases, there is no obvious rationale for removing the restraint from Frege's constraint. One who urges such a sweeping extension of FC must bear the burden of providing a rationale that does not involve a fallacious inference from ⌜α believes of β that ϕ_{it}⌝ to ⌜α believes β to be something such that ϕ_{it}⌝, or its contrapositive. Indeed, the very situation (*a*) arguably yields a counter-instance. I maintain that in (*a*), Jane rationally both believes and disbelieves of George Eliot, *de re*, that Ralph believes she was a man—even though in so doing, Jane does not take Eliot to be two separate people. It is unclear how, or even whether, a neo-Fregean can plausibly avoid this conclusion.[8]

There remains a bit of a mystery: How *can* someone rationally both believe and disbelieve a singular proposition about y without thereby taking y to be distinct things? In short, given FC, how can FC' have any counter-instances?

The solution is not far to find. There is a sound substitute for Schiffer's fallacious *reductio*, an alternative derivation that relies on FC and (S) without fatally detouring through dubious generalizations. This time, putting for β the that-clause 'that George Eliot was a man' and putting for ϕ_{it} the open sentence 'It is something Ralph believes,' the relevant half of the resulting instance of (S) states that necessarily, if Jane believes that the proposition that Eliot was a man is something Ralph believes, then Jane believes of the proposition that George Eliot was a man, *de re*, that it is something Ralph believes. In situation (*a*), so Jane does. Now putting for β instead the alternative that-clause 'that Mary Ann Evans was a man' and for ϕ_{it} 'It is something Ralph does *not* believe,' the relevant half of the resulting instance of (S) states that necessarily, if Jane believes that the proposition that Mary Ann Evans was a man is something Ralph does not believe, then Jane believes of the proposition that Mary Ann Evans was a man, *de re*, that it is something Ralph does not believe. In situation (*a*), so Jane does. According to Millianism, the propositions to which Jane *de re* attributes complementary properties (being believed by Ralph and not) in (*a*) are one and the same. Reasoning from *FC*, it follows that Jane, insofar as she is rational in (*a*), must take this proposition in differing ways—not Eliot herself, but the proposition that she was a man.

In situation (*a*), so Jane does. In (*a*), she evidently mistakes this singular proposition for two altogether independent thoughts (or at least is committed to doing so), one that Ralph believes, the other (according to Jane) not. No contradiction is derived and no problem for Millianism generated. On the contrary, our conclusion solves the riddle of how, without mistaking Eliot for two distinct people, Jane can rationally both believe and disbelieve of Eliot, *de re*, that Ralph believes she was a man. Though Jane does not mistake Eliot to be distinct people, she mistakes the singular proposition that Eliot was a man to be distinct thoughts.[9]

In effect, Jane in (*a*) is a proto-Fregean, or perhaps a closet neo-Fregean. (Are we not all—at least early on?) With this new derivation, she has been outed. With a little further Socratic questioning, she will likely embrace her neo-Fregeanism with pride. (Unless Jane is very young—in which case, just how rational is she?)

Schiffer defends his objection to Millianism asserting, "...the only reasonable construal of *propositional* modes of presentation is that they are structured entities whose basic components are modes of presentation of the basic components of the Russellian propositions of which the propositional modes of presentation are modes of presentation." Since Jane does not have the requisite differing modes of presentation of Eliot (nor of the property or singular-functional concept of *having been a man*), she also does not have differing modes of presentation of the (putatively singular) proposition that Eliot was a man, as would be required by *FC*.

With all due respect, it is unreasonable to suppose that the only proposition guises are such composite constructions as Schiffer envisions. Equally unreasonable is Michael Dummett's rival thesis that propositions can be conceived of only as the senses of particular sentences.[10] Frege would rightly have insisted that these are but two among infinitely many ways in which propositions ('thoughts'), like anything else, can be presented or conceived. The singular proposition about George Eliot that she was a man might be taken or conceived as *the semantic content of the English sentence 'George Eliot was a man,'* as *the singular proposition composed of George Eliot and the concept of having been a man*, as *that of which the proposition that George Eliot was not a man is the denial,* as *the central propositional example in Stephen Schiffer's 'A Problem for a Direct-Reference Theory of Belief Reports,'* as *Jane's favorite proposition*, or in any number of alternative ways. Significantly, in particular the proposition might be taken as *Ralph's mistaken opinion about George Eliot's gender.* Jane takes the proposition in question to be both believed by Ralph and not believed by Ralph. Even the restrained constraint *FC* entails that in so doing Jane takes the proposition in differing ways—assuming she is rational and not a young child.

Assuming she is sufficiently sophisticated, Jane might take the proposition in question to invoke the concept that Ralph associates with the name 'George Eliot' (Ralph's concept of who George Eliot is), and alternatively, to invoke instead the concept that Ralph associates with 'Mary Ann Evans.' These are misconceptions—or so claims the Millian—but an incorrect way of taking something is a way of taking that thing. One great philosophical genius has thus misconceived propositions like the one in question. One hardly needs to be a philosophical genius to commit this exceedingly tempting error. But even if Jane is not sufficiently sophisticated to venture a theory, or a proto-theory, of the nature of what it is that Ralph believes and does not believe, it is enough that Jane believes p to be believed by Ralph while also disbelieving p to be believed by Ralph, for Jane thereby to take p by means of different guises. She need not take p to be a Fregean thought. In Schiffer's scenario it is enough that Jane does not take p to be a Russellian singular proposition.[11]

Notes

1. Schiffer presented his alleged problem for Millianism in "The 'Fido'-Fido Theory of Belief," in J. Tomberlin, ed., *Philosophical Perspectives, 1: Metaphysics* (Atascadero, Ca.: Ridgeview, 1987), pp. 445–80; and again two decades later in "A Problem for a Direct-Reference Theory of Belief Reports," *Noûs*, 40, 2 (2006), pp. 361–8. Here I follow the more recent presentation.
2. In J. Tomberlin, ed., *Philosophical Perspectives, 3: Philosophy of Mind and Action Theory* (Atascadero, Ca.: Ridgeview, 1989), pp. 243–85, at part VII, pp. 264–73, reprinted in my *Content, Cognition, and Communication: Philosophical Papers II* (Oxford: Oxford University Press, 2007), pp. 191–221. See also my "The Resilience of Illogical Belief," reprinted in *Content, Cognition, and Communication*, pp. 222–7. The earliest forum for our debate was a Pacific Division meeting of the American Philosophical Association in March 1987.
3. The relevant pronoun occurrences are anaphoric, hence bound, within (S) itself. On anaphoric pronouns as bound variables, see my "Pronouns as Variables," *Philosophy and Phenomenological Research*, 72, 3 (2007), pp. 656–64; preprinted in my *Metaphysics, Mathematics, and Meaning: Philosophical Papers I* (Oxford: Oxford University Press, 2005), pp. 399–406.
4. I have reformulated Schiffer's "restatement" to conform to the present notation, in a manner that accords with the intent indicated by Schiffer's applications of the schema. Schiffer commits the fallacy precisely at his step (iii) (*Remnants of Meaning* [Cambridge, MA: MIT Press, 1987], p. 364), when he derives his (c).

    As I argued in "Illogical Belief" pp. (265 7), Millianism is inessential to Schiffer's alleged problem. With a change of example to one of a sort made famous by Benson Mates, a similar derivation can be constructed without any appeal to Millianism. This consideration by itself bursts Schiffer's attempt to refute Millianism.
5. I assume here that necessarily, x believes y to be F iff x believes of y, *de re*, that it (he, she) is F. For more on this assumed equivalence, see Kaplan, "Afterthoughts" in J. Almog, J. Perry, and H. Wettstein, eds., *Themes from Kaplan* (New York: Oxford University Press, 1989), pp. 565–614, at 605–6; and my "Relational Belief," in P. Leonardi and M. Santambrogio, eds., *On Quine: New Essays* (New York: Cambridge University Press, 1995), pp. 206–28, at 214–16, 219; reprinted in *Content, Cognition, and Communication*, pp. 247–67.

    In contrast to $\ulcorner \alpha$ believes of β that $\phi_{it}\urcorner$, $\ulcorner \alpha$ **Believes**$_r$ (β, to be something such that ϕ_{it})$\urcorner$ is what David Kaplan calls a *syntactically de re* construction. *Cf.* his "Opacity," in L. E. Hahn and P. A. Schilpp, eds., *The Philosophy of W. V. Quine* (La Salle, Ill.: Open Court, 1986), pp. 229–88, at 268. The former construction is equivalent to ⌜$(\lambda\gamma)[\alpha$ **believes** $^\wedge\phi_\gamma{}^\wedge](\beta)$⌝; the latter to ⌜$(\lambda\gamma)[\alpha$ **believes** $^\wedge(\lambda\zeta)[\phi_\zeta](\gamma)^\wedge](\beta)$⌝, where '$^\wedge$' is a content-quotation mark (i.e., an indirect-discourse quotation mark) and ϕ_γ is the same as ϕ_ζ except for having free occurrences of the variable γ wherever ϕ_ζ has free occurrences of the variable ζ. Given Millianism, (S′) entails the following:

[α **believes** $^\wedge\phi_\beta{}^\wedge \supset \alpha$ **believes** $^\wedge(\lambda\gamma)[\phi_\gamma](\beta)^\wedge$],

where β is any proper name or other Millian term and ϕ_β is the same as ϕ_γ except for having free occurrences of β wherever ϕ_γ has free occurrences of γ.

6. That is, ⌜α **believes** $^\wedge\phi_\beta{}^\wedge$⌝ may be true even while ⌜α **believes** $^\wedge(\lambda\gamma)[\phi_\gamma](\beta)^\wedge$⌝ is false. *Cf.* the previous note.
7. See Kaplan, 'Opacity,' at pp. 269–72, and my "Relational Belief," especially pp. 213–14. I investigated these matters in some detail in "Reflexivity," *Notre Dame Journal of Formal Logic*, 27, 3 (July 1986), pp. 401–29, and "Reflections on Reflexivity," *Linguistics and Philosophy*, 15, 1 (February 1992), pp. 53–63; both reprinted in *Content, Cognition, and Communication*, pp. 30–64.
8. See "Relational Belief," pp. 217–18.
9. See "Relational Belief," pp. 218–19.
10. Dummett, *The Interpretation of Frege's Philosophy* (Cambridge, Mass.: Harvard University Press, 1981), at pp. 90–8. *Cf.* my "The Very Possibility of Language: A Sermon on the Consequences of Missing Church," in C. A. Anderson and M. Zeleny, eds., *Logic, Meaning, and Computation: Essays in Memory of Alonzo Church* (Dordrecht: Kluwer, 2001), pp. 573–95, especially at 578–82, 592–5; reprinted in *Metaphysics, Mathematics, and Meaning*, pp. 344–64.
11. I thank Gary Ostertag for providing me this opportunity. I thank David Braun for comments on an earlier draft. I am grateful also to Blackwell Publishing for permission to incorporate my article 'The Resilience of Illogical Belief,' *Noûs* 40 (2) (June 2006): 369–75.

8

Schiffer on Indeterminacy, Vagueness, and Conditionals

Dorothy Edgington

In *The Things We Mean* (2003), Stephen Schiffer gives a theory of indeterminate propositions. He takes vagueness to be one species of indeterminacy, and the theory of indeterminacy is applied in the following two chapters to moral propositions and conditionals respectively. It is also applied here and there to philosophical propositions like "free will is compatible with determinism" (97).[1] In Chapter 5, where the theory of indeterminacy is developed, the focus is on vagueness. "Almost every expression is to some extent vague," he says, "and we can't know the correct semantics and logic for any language until we know the correct semantics and logic for vague language. A theory of vagueness must lie at the heart of any complete theory of meaning" (78).

Most of my discussion of Schiffer's theory of indeterminacy also focuses on vagueness, but in section 8.6 I consider the application of the theory to conditionals.

8.1 Schiffer's Theory of Vagueness

Schiffer begins by setting out and criticizing a number of well-known approaches to vagueness and to the sorites paradox. Lessons emerge which motivate and shape the account to follow. In particular, he endorses and takes to be of central importance a point made by Crispin Wright in his paper 'On Being in a Quandary,' against the idea that vague propositions can take more than two 'values'—truth, falsity, or something else[2]—what he follows Wright in calling the "third possibility view." He quotes with approval this passage from Wright:

> It is quite unsatisfactory in general to represent *in*determinacy as any kind of determinate truth-status—any kind of middle situation, contrasting with both the poles (truth and falsity)—since one cannot thereby do justice to the absolutely basic datum that in general borderline cases come across as hard cases: as cases where we are baffled to choose between conflicting verdicts about which polar verdict applies, rather than as cases which we recognize as enjoying a status inconsistent with both. (Wright 2001: 70, quoted by Schiffer: 191)

In other words, says Schiffer,

> when confronted with borderline Harry we have some temptation to say that he is bald and some temptation to say that he is not bald, but [theories which postulate intermediate values]

can't account for this. If [they] were correct, we should recognise that the proposition that he's bald is neither true nor false, and therefore have no temptation to say that he's bald, or that he's not bald. (191)

Schiffer builds his theory upon this phenomenon of being pulled in opposing directions. Vagueness is to be explained in terms of a particular kind of partial belief. Vagueness, he claims, is a *psychological* notion, neither a semantic nor an epistemological one. There is what he calls 'standard partial belief' (SPB), which (when vagueness is not involved) can under idealization be taken to obey the axioms of probability theory. Then there is vagueness-related partial belief (VPB). "The crucial claim is that VPBs are those partial beliefs that can't under any idealization be identified with subjective probability" (201); that is, they do not, ideally, satisfy the probability calculus. "I will, however, assume that, like SPBs, VPBs can under suitable idealization be measured by real numbers in the interval [0, 1]," he says (202).

VPBs are illustrated by the plucking of hairs, one by one, from poor Tom's head, observed under good conditions by rational Sally. After a while the judgement that Tom isn't bald will have an "ever so slightly diminished confidence, reflecting that she believes Tom not to be bald to some degree barely less than 1" (203); and so on down.

VPBs don't satisfy the probability calculus—indeed this is their defining feature. Consider two independent propositions, 'Tom is bald' and 'Tom is thin,' both v-believed[3] to degree 0.5; their conjunction, says Schiffer, is believed to degree 0.5, not 0.25 as required by the probability calculus. Instead, we are told later, they combine according to the Łukasiewicz rules: a conjunction gets a value which is the minimum of the values of the conjuncts, a disjunction gets the maximum of the disjuncts:

$VPB(\neg p) = 1-VPB(p)$
$VPB(p\&q) = Min[VPB(p), VPB(q)]$
$VPB(p\lor q) = Max[VPB(p), VPB(q)]$[4] (218).

Here is Schiffer's defence of the conjunction rule, for 'Tom is bald and thin':

I regard this as intuitively correct, but that does not preclude a rationale. The rational believer who takes the propositions that Beetlebomb will win the Kentucky Derby and that Lithuania will win the World Cup to be independent and s-believes each to degree 0.5 will believe the conjunction of those propositions to degree 0.25, for that is the degree supported by her evidence for it. But for Sally, there is no gap between her partially believed proposition and her evidence for it; she's *ambivalent* but she's not *uncertain* about anything. For her, all the relevant facts are completely available to her; nothing more of relevance could possibly come to light. Sally can't wonder how, given her situation, the issue of Tom's baldness (or thinness) might turn out, nor will she wonder what the secret fact of the matter to which she can't have access might be. Thus, she v-believes to 0.5 that Tom is bald, that Tom is thin, and that Tom is bald and thin. (204)

A VPB* is a VPB formed under ideal epistemic conditions. In further explanation of 'ideal conditions' he distinguishes two kinds of case, the case in which the vague property supervenes on non-vague properties, and the case in which it does not. Baldness is a case of the first kind, and the fully informed person has full information about the hair situation on (e.g.) Tom's scalp. In the second kind of case—he gives the examples of pain and redness—you don't apply the concept on the basis of anything else. A sensation one knows oneself to have with certainty may be a borderline case of pain. "One's VPB that one is in pain is a VPB* if, as would normally be the case, one knows that nothing can be forthcoming to make one rationally revise one's partial belief" (213). Similarly for one's judgement that something is a borderline case of red.

Here is how he arrives at a characterization of vagueness:

(A) x is a borderline case of being F only if someone could v*-believe that x is F,

i.e., there is some possible world similar in relevant respects to the actual world in which someone v*-believes that x is F. In many cases the relevant respects are defined by the supervenience base for being F, e.g. the hair situation on Tom's scalp (208).

(A) cannot be strengthened to a necessary and sufficient condition of being borderline, simply because vagueness is not the only species of indeterminacy. Instead we have

(C): p is indeterminate iff someone could v*-believe p (209).

To pin down the special case of vagueness,

Let's say that one's VPB that x is F is *F-concept-driven* when one is in ideal circumstances for judging x to be F and one's concept of being F precludes one from s-believing to any positive degree that x is F or that x is not F and determines one to v-believe to some positive degree that x is F. Then we can say that:

(E) x is a borderline case of being F iff someone could have an F-concept driven VPB* that x is F (212).

Thus, "My account explicates indeterminacy in terms of an idealized epistemic agent whose degrees of belief in indeterminate propositions are normatively governed by quite different laws than those that govern her degrees of belief in propositions that are uncertain but regarded by the agent as determinately true or determinately false" (209). Further,

It is a *primitive and underived* feature of the conceptual role of each concept of a vague property that under certain conditions we form VPBs involving that concept, and *it is in this that vagueness consists*. To use a metaphor, what makes a property vague is simply the fact that its predicate name has an underived conceptual role that determines the name to go into a person's VPB box under certain conditions. When the sentence 'Tom is bald' goes into Sally's VPB box, it is not a response to her perception of the independently explicable fact that he's a borderline case of baldness. His being a borderline case of baldness consists in the conceptual fact, and it is *this* that accounts for the 'no-fact-of-the-matter' intuition many have about borderline cases. (212–13, his emphases)

He says "If being a borderline case were an ontological status explicable independently of VPBs or any other kind of propositional attitude, then a 'third possibility' view of indeterminacy would be correct, and I agree with Crispin Wright that no such view is correct" (211).

8.2 Critical Comments on the Story So Far

8.2.1

Let us grant for the sake of argument that there is a special class of vagueness-related partial beliefs, which register one's ambivalence about vague propositions. I shall argue that they do not and should not conform to the Łukasiewicz-Schiffer Min-Max rules for conjunctions and disjunctions; and my argument will support the view that, contra Schiffer, they do satisfy the probability calculus. I am transposing arguments I have given elsewhere (Edgington 1996) against the Min-Max rules for 'degree of closeness to clear truth,' with which Schiffer's degrees of partial belief of a rational well-informed person should be isomorphic.

I first consider a case in which the conjuncts are not independent. The Max-Min rules are indifferent to independence; and indeed Schiffer applies them to non-independent cases: p is not independent of $\neg p$, and he accepts that when $v(p) = 0.5$, $v(p \vee \neg p)$ and $v(p \& \neg p)$ are each 0.5, as the rules require.

Let v(Tom is tall) = 0.5, v(Tom is not tall) = 0.5, and let Harry be also borderline tall, but slightly less tall than Tom: let v(Harry is tall) = 0.4. Tom is taller than Harry. I have *no inclination at all* to believe that Harry is tall and Tom is not. I am not at all ambivalent or in a quandary about that: it is something I confidently judge to be definitely wrong. Yet by the Min-rule for conjunction, v(Harry is tall and Tom is not tall) = 0.4: not to be rejected out of hand.

Note that if instead we consider v(Harry is tall and Tom is tall), 0.4—the minimum of the two—would be a reasonable value. Thus we have a counterexample not only to the Min-rule for conjunction, but to the claim that the value of a conjunction is determined by the values of the conjuncts. This is to be expected on the hypothesis that VPBs have probabilistic structure: $v(p\&q) = v(p) \times v(q$ given $p)$; it is this second factor that differs in the two cases above. What value should I give to 'Tom is tall' given that Harry is tall? 1, because Tom is taller than Harry. So v(Harry is tall and Tom is tall) = 0.4. What value should I give to 'Tom is not tall' given that Harry is tall? 0, because Tom is taller than Harry. So v(Harry is tall and Tom is not tall) = 0.

Turn to the case in which the conjuncts are independent: 'Tom is bald and Tom is thin,' or 'The ball is small and red.' If each conjunct is a borderline case, for each conjunct we are pulled in opposing directions, and the numbers reflect the strength of these opposing pulls. Now the following seems reasonable: if Tom and Harry are judged bald to the same degree, 0.5, but Tom is judged thin to a higher degree than Harry is judged thin—Tom, 0.9, Harry, 0.5—then 'Tom is bald and thin' should get a higher value than 'Harry is bald and thin.' If asked to find a thin bald man, or as close to a thin bald man as I can find, Tom would be a better choice than Harry. This conflicts, of course, with the Min-rule, according to which, with these values, both conjunctions get 0.5 (even when Tom is most definitely thin, and the other values are as above, the Min-rule gives both conjunctions the same value).

Now the following two principles are compelling, and not at issue between us: if it is judged that Tom is definitely not bald, and thin to degree 0.5, it is definitely not the case that he is bald and thin; if it is judged that Tom is definitely bald and thin to degree 0.5, he is bald and thin to degree 0.5;

v(bald) = 0 and v(thin) = 0.5 → v(bald and thin) = 0.
v(bald) = 1 and v(thin) = 0.5 → v(bald and thin) = 0.5.

Keep 'thin' fixed at 0.5. As 'bald' goes from 0 to 1, 'bald and thin' should increase from 0 to 0.5. And, plausibly, equal increments in 'bald' make for equal increments in 'bald and thin'. So, when 'bald' is 0.5, the conjunction is half-way between 0 and 0.5, viz. 0.25. Note that this also accords with probabilistic structure: when the conjuncts are independent, the probability of the conjunction is their product.

I have given similar arguments about the dual case of disjunction (Edgington 1996: 304–5) and will not repeat them here. No doubt there are important differences between standard partial beliefs and vagueness-related partial beliefs (if such there be), but they need not show up in the way they interact with the logical constants.

Return to Schiffer's "rationale" for the Min-rule for conjunction, quoted above (157). The bulk of it points to differences between mere ignorance and uncertainty on the one hand, and vagueness-related ambivalence on the other. But I cannot see how this helps establish the last sentence, "Thus, she v-believes to 0.5 that Tom is bald, that Tom is thin, and that Tom is bald and thin."

8.2.2

Return to Wright's insight upon which Schiffer's theory is based. Schiffer notes that I come to a conclusion similar to Wright's. My theory employs the notion 'degree of closeness to clear truth' (Edgington 1996), which I dub 'verity.' I distance myself from some uses of the term 'degree of truth' according to which it is only at the poles that we have truth and falsity. I take this to be wrong for the following reason (which Schiffer quotes with approval): suppose 'a is red' is borderline: neither clearly true nor clearly false. It would not be definitely wrong to call it true. But it would be definitely wrong to give it a 'degree of truth' 1. Therefore, 'true' is not to be identified with degree of truth 1; and similarly for falsity. To avoid confusion with a position that equates truth with degree of truth 1, falsity with degree of truth 0, I introduced 'verity' as short for 'degree of closeness to clear truth' (compare 'credence' for 'degree of closeness to certainty').

Thus I accept Wright's conclusion—no third possible state of affairs of a proposition's being neither true nor false. But I don't take the quandary phenomenon—being pulled in opposite directions—as a basic and decisive reason for doing so; nor do I take the conclusion itself to have the status of a datum. There are intuitions that go the other way, and the matter is to be resolved in terms of the best overall account of our use of vague language. Certainly we are sometimes baffled as to how to judge a borderline case. Sometimes we shrug our shoulders and confidently judge that it is a borderline case—neither clearly true nor clearly false. An opponent might claim that a good theory of vagueness should remove the air of quandary, by showing that its source is that of wrongly taking the two polar verdicts to be exhaustive, and failing to recognize that a middle verdict is called for.

Moreover, Schiffer defines vagueness in terms of an ideal epistemic agent with v^*-beliefs, and such an agent, it seems to me, has transcended any initial bafflement: "she's not uncertain about anything. For her, all the relevant facts are completely available to her; nothing more of relevance could possibly come to light. Sally can't wonder how, given her situation, the issue of Tom's baldness... might turn out, nor will she wonder what the secret fact of the matter to which she can't have access might be" (204). Schiffer does say "She's *ambivalent*, but she's not *uncertain* about anything" (204). But I can't see such an all-knowing perfectly rational person as ambivalent; and that notion doesn't seem to do any work. She just knows she is right to judge that Tom is a borderline case (to whatever degree) of baldness.

Strictly speaking, she *is* uncertain, for she is not certain that Tom is bald. Schiffer seems to mean that she is not *merely* uncertain, in contrast with a case where there is no doubt that there is a determinate fact of the matter. But it is important to his project that the distinct psychological attitude appropriate to the case of vagueness is to be explained without appealing to the notion of a determinate fact of the matter. Rather, the explanation is meant to go the other way.

This is no easy task. Consider principle (C) above: 'p is indeterminate iff someone could v*-believe that p,' explained in terms of there being a possible world similar in relevant respects to the actual world in which someone v*-believes that p. If there are facts which human beings cannot know, I see no reason why there should not be borderline cases which human beings cannot competently judge. One famous example: what it is like to be a bat (Nagel 1974). The bat's sensory states, I take it, can arise and subside gradually, so that there can be borderline cases of the bat's being in state S. If we can't have knowledge of the clear cases, nor can we have VPB*s in the unclear cases.

Fitch's paradox of knowability,[5] or a close relative of it, also raises doubts about (C). A contradiction is derived from the claims that (1) every truth is knowable, and (2) not all truths are known. Let p be a truth which is never known to be true: '$p\&\neg Kp$' is true. Applying (1) to this truth, we get that it is possible to know that: p and no one ever knows that p. And this yields a contradiction (provided knowledge distributes over conjuncts, and knowledge entails truth).

The situation is not much better if we substitute 'It is rationally believed that,' for 'know'; for then the analogous two principles will yield that it is possible rationally to believe: p and no one ever rationally believes p. At least a minimally self-aware rational believer can hardly believe that *conjunction*.

Now apply this to VPBs. When picking wild berries, you come across one which you judge to be borderline red, i.e., you v-believe that it is red. Let's say you v*-believe that it is red. Now there are many berries just like this in colour which no one will ever see. Where x is such an unobserved berry, consider the proposition:

(Q) x is red at t and no one ever has a VPB that x is red at t.

The second conjunct is clearly true, the first is, ex hypothesi, borderline; so by Schiffer's rules, and any reasonable rules, the whole proposition (Q) is indeterminate. But no rational and minimally self-aware person could have a VPB that: x is red and no one has a VPB that x is red. I take it that no ideal epistemic agent could v-believe (Q).

Whatever one makes of these tricky arguments, there is, to my mind, an important point at issue here. Vagueness is a very simple phenomenon to grasp: red shades gradually into orange, people gradually grow old, and, as Schiffer said, almost every term in the language is to some extent infected with such vague boundaries. The concepts we profit by using are such that the world does not always deliver a clear verdict as to whether they apply. Our difficulty is not in understanding what vagueness is, but in coming to see how to handle it in reasoning and decision-making, how not to be misled down slippery slopes. I doubt if there is any illuminating analysis of the form 'x is a borderline case of F if and only if...,' and I doubt that one is needed. Hence, I do not find the attempted reduction of vagueness to a psychological phenomenon plausible. A competent judgement that something is borderline red—especially one made by Schiffer's imagined ideal thinker who knows she is in an unimprovable epistemic position—is as much a response to how things are as is a competent judgement that something is red.

The position Wright called the 'no third possibility' view, is that there are no intermediate *truth values* and hence no cases of being neither true nor false. I agree; so do some supervaluationists such as Vann McGee and Brian McLaughlin (1994), and so, of course, do epistemicists such as Timothy Williamson (1994); so does anyone who is impressed by the thought that if 'x is red' is borderline, 'it is true that x is red' is borderline, not false; and also impressed by the muddles one gets into trying to make sense of 'not true and not false.' None of us need deny that borderline cases are really, 'ontologically,' different from non-borderline cases, contra Schiffer: "If being a borderline case were an ontological status explicable independently of VPBs or any other kind of propositional attitude, then a 'third possibility' view of indeterminacy would be correct, and I agree with Crispin Wright that no such view is correct." In a broader sense than 'third truth value distinct from true and false,' everyone can accept that there are three possibilities for the application of a vague predicate F: definitely F, definitely not F, and neither, i.e., borderline F. Different theorists have different accounts of what this amounts to. The explanation may, but need not involve borderline cases being neither true nor false.

Schiffer's unduly wide reading of 'no third possibility' must explain a misattribution to me (194). After citing approvingly my argument that 'true' is not to be identified with 'degree of truth 1,' he claims that I do not live up to my intentions:

> Edgington emphasizes that degree-of-verity isn't degree-of-belief, and it seems clear from her exposition that Edgington would deny that borderline propositions are true or false. Evidently, then if, say, v(p) = .5, then p is neither true nor false, and this is enough to show that Edgington can't avoid the problem she hopes to avoid by refusing to identify degree of verity with degree of truth. For if v('Harry is bald') = .5, then it wouldn't be definitely wrong to say that it is true that Harry is bald, but Edgington must say that it would be definitely wrong. (194)

Edgington does not say that it would be definitely wrong. She argues that a disjunction can be definitely true when neither disjunct is, on this basis establishes the law of excluded middle for vague statements, and also the principle of bivalence: it is either true or false that Harry is bald, but it is not determinate which—it is not determinately true, not determinately false, but it is determinately true-or-false.

8.3 Schiffer on the Interaction between VPBs and SPBs

s(p) + s($\neg p$) = 1 when you are sure that p is determinate. v(p) + v($\neg p$) = 1 when you are sure that p is indeterminate. In these cases, the two kinds of partial belief are governed by the probability calculus, and the Łukasiewicz rules, respectively. The basic law governing the interaction of SPBs and VPBs, Schiffer tells us, is that the ideally rational agent's partial beliefs in a proposition and its negation sum to 1. That is

Basic Law (BL): $v(p) + v(\neg p) + s(p) + s(\neg p) = 1$ (219)

I have several worries about this. First: as Sally considers the series of states which progress from the definitely not bald to the definitely bald, she starts off having s (Tom is not bald) = 1. "At some point, however, Sally's judgement that Tom isn't bald will have ever so slightly diminished confidence, reflecting that she believes Tom not to be bald to some degree barely less than 1" (203). It is far-fetched to think that her s-belief suddenly drops to 0 as the first doubt enters her mind. Rather, as the first doubt enters her mind, she might have s(Tom is not bald) = 0.99. But then, if the above formula is satisfied, there's only 0.01 left over for her v-belief that Tom is not bald. This is a very weak v-belief. Yet it would seem, as the first doubt enters her mind, she is undecided between a strong s-belief that he is definitely not bald, and a strong v-belief pulling in the direction of not bald. But that is inconsistent with BL.

Secondly, it is hard to know how much classical logic survives, and how much standard probability theory survives for standard partial beliefs. Schiffer claims that the latter survives intact *except* for the fact that $s(p) + s(\neg p)$ may be less than 1 (221). I don't think that can be right. This is a basic equation of standard probability theory:

$s(p) = s(p\&q) + s(p\&\neg q)$,

an instance of the facts that (a) the probability of a disjunction of exclusive disjuncts is the sum of the probabilities of the disjuncts, and (b) p is logically equivalent to $(p\&q)\lor(p\&\neg q)$. One way in which the equation is basic is that it underlies the principle: $p(q) = p(q \text{ given } p).p(p) + p(q \text{ given } \neg p).p(\neg p)$. But the equation can't be right for Schiffer. For q may introduce vagueness when there was no indeterminacy about p. Let p be 'x is green,' and suppose I take this to be determinately true: $s(p) = 1$. Let q be 'x is dark green,' so that '$p\&\neg q$' is 'x is green but not dark green' (we could make the same point with 'tall but not very tall' and indefinitely many examples of this type). Now although definitely green, x is borderline between dark green, and green but not dark green. So my $s(p\&q) = 0$ and my $s(p\&\neg q) = 0$ (as is their disjunction). So $s(p) \neq s(p\&q) + s(p\&\neg q)$—indeed they are maximally different. So *either* known logical equivalents needn't be s-believed to the same degree, *or*, in Schiffer's scheme of things, p is not logically equivalent to $(p\&q)\lor(p\&\neg q)$. They also induce distinct v-beliefs. $v(p) = 0$ (for $s(p) = 1$); $v((p\&q)\lor(p\&\neg q)) =$ the maximum of the two = (say) 0.5. The distributive law is (a) classically valid, (b) basic to standard probability theory, and (c) validated by the Łukasiewicz rules, in that provably each side gets the same value; but it is not, it seems, to be countenanced in Schiffer's amalgam of the last two.

The above example would come out right if we used this formula instead of the usual one:

$s(p) = s(p\&q) + s(p\&\neg q) + v(p\&q) + v(p\&\neg q)$;

this would follow from:

if $s(p\&q) = 0$ then $s(p\lor q) = s(p) + s(q) + v(p) + v(q)$.

However, by substituting '¬p' for 'q' in the formula immediately above, and using BL, we could then prove that $s(p \vee \neg p) = 1$. But in the presence of vagueness, $p \vee \neg p$ is not something which should be fully believed, on Schiffer's theory.[6]

Third, here is a question prompted by the previous two considerations: if asked how confident you are that p, how do you answer? Do you give the sum of your $s(p)$ and $v(p)$? The larger of the two? Or do you reject the question as ambiguous, because there is no way of combining your VPB and your SPB, though of course you can give each? Schiffer doesn't address this explicitly, but his examples make clear that he favours the last option: "the situation is fully described by saying that Sally s-believes to degree 0.7 that Tom is bald, s-believes to degree 0 that he is not bald, v-believes to degree 0.24 that he is bald and v-believes to degree 0.06 that he is not bald" (220). He never suggests that they combine. So the terms 'degree of belief' or 'degree of confidence' are seriously ambiguous: whenever they are used, they could mean two radically different things. This is not an ambiguity which is recognized in our ordinary practice.

8.4 The Sorites

What can we learn from this framework about the Sorites paradox? The argument can be run in two equivalent ways, one way with a single quantified major premise, for instance $(\forall n)$(if a person with n cents is rich, then a person with $n-1$ cents is rich), or

$\neg(\exists n)$(a person with n cents is rich and a person with $n-1$ cents is not rich),

which, together with the premise that a person with $50 million is rich, we conclude that a person with just 37 cents is rich. Call this the short sorites. Or it can be formulated with a large number of conditional premises of the form 'If a person with n cents is rich, a person with $n-1$ cents is rich.' Call this the long sorites. We may as well stipulate that the conditional is material, that is, equivalent to 'It's not the case that: a person with n cents is rich and a person with $n-1$ cents is not rich.' The argument is classically valid, and, more to the point, intuitively compelling.

Consider the long series of material conditionals or negated conjunctions. As we depart from determinate truth, to begin with, 'n cents is rich' gets a very high value, '$n-1$ cents is not rich' a very low value, their conjunction a very low value, the negation of the conjunction a very high value. Round about the middle of the series, 'n cents is rich' gets marginally over 0.5, '$n-1$ cents is rich' gets 0.5, so '$n-1$ cents is not rich' gets 0.5, so by Schiffer's Min-rule for conjunction, 'n cents is rich and $n-1$ cents is not rich' gets 0.5 and so does its negation, the material conditional 'If n cents is rich, $n-1$ cents is rich.' From this point the premises of the long sorites increase in value again, until they are clearly true towards the end.

This is not an attractive result. Intuitively, we feel strongly that all these conditionals are clearly true. Perhaps the intuition can be explained away by noting that we tend to ignore very small departures from clear truth, and they are all at least very close to clearly true. But Schiffer's theory has some of the premises very close to clearly true, others equidistant from the clearly true and the clearly false. And that does not explain why they all equally seemed at first sight true.

In the short sorites, the universally quantified major premise 'For all n, if having n cents is rich, having $n-1$ cents is rich' is indeterminate—indeed, on Schiffer's theory, is something we should v-believe to degree 0.5, as this is the value of the lowest of its instances. We should be ambivalent about it, experiencing equal pulls for and against it.

It is indeterminate whether the major premise is true or false. Hence it is indeterminate whether the Sorites argument has true premises and a false conclusion; hence, says Schiffer, it is indeterminate whether the Sorites argument is valid. If we turn the argument round by contraposition, we have: Rich ($50m); ¬Rich (37 cents); therefore ¬($\forall n$)(Rich (n cents) → Rich ($n-1$ cents)). This argument has determinately true premises and an indeterminate conclusion; that is, it is indeterminate whether we have a counterexample to the claim that it is valid. As this applies equally to the long version, it follows that it is indeterminate whether modus ponens is valid.

Now it seems that no argument is valid on this conception of validity. Consider the argument from $p\&q$ to p, or just from p to p. Suppose it is indeterminate whether p is true or false. Then it is indeterminate whether the argument has a true premise and a false conclusion: it is compatible with the argument that the premise is true and the conclusion false. Validity has become a concept with no application.[7]

This is not a happy state of affairs. Schiffer agrees: "Shouldn't we therefore junk the theory of indeterminacy that brought about this result? I don't think so. We are just being confronted with the way in which the Sorites can't have a happy-face solution" (224).

8.5 Happy and Unhappy Faces

Let's turn to Schiffer's doctrine of happy- and unhappy-face solutions to paradoxes. For a happy-face solution to a paradox, you identify the mistaken premise or mistaken piece of reasoning, and also explain why it appeared plausible. In Schiffer's view, few if any philosophical problems have happy-face solutions. For example, the problem of free will does not have a happy-face solution. It is indeterminate which proposition in the paradox set is false, and this is because of a glitch in our concept of free will. The role of the concept has two parts which don't cohere (197).

An unhappy-face solution to a paradox will do two things. First it will explain what it is about the paradox-generating concept or concepts which precludes a happy-face solution. Second, it will tell us whether the paradox admits of a *weak* or a *strong* unhappy-face solution. A weak unhappy-face solution will tell us that while there can be no happy-face solution to the paradox, a suitable conceptual revision is possible that would be paradox-free, where a solution is 'suitable' if it can do the primary work we wanted the 'defective' concept to do. Tarski in effect offered a weak unhappy-face solution to the semantic paradoxes: a notion of truth on which the paradoxes don't arise. A strong unhappy-face solution denies that any suitable conceptual revision is possible. The sorites, according to Schiffer, doesn't even have a weak unhappy-face solution (198).

I am willing to admit that few attempted solutions to hard philosophical problems are cost free; that as Lewis (1983, x–xi) says, different philosophers may weigh the costs differently; and some may be as bad as Schiffer says. But I would dispute that there is a sharp line between happy-face and what he calls weak-unhappy-face solutions, for whether or not something requires conceptual revision is not always clear. Quite often when Schiffer says something is part of our concept of F, or "a primitive and underived feature of the conceptual role of F," I feel like saying 'speak for yourself!' He has introduced an innovative and inventive theory of a kind of belief we didn't know we had.

In my view, the reasoning in the sorites argument is valid. In the long form, each conditional (or negated conjunction) premise is at least very close to clearly true—as close as would make no difference, in most contexts. Degrees of closeness to clear truth have probabilistic structure. But, just as in the structurally similar lottery paradox and the paradox of the preface, the sheer number of tiny departures from clear truth mount up, the conclusion of a valid argument can inherit the sum of all these small departures from clear truth, and the conclusion can be definitely false. That, to my mind, is nice. Less easy to accept at first sight is the falsity of the single quantified major premise. I claim that it is false not because some one of its instances is clearly false, but because many of its instances depart minimally from clear truth. Its negation, '$(\exists n)$(having n cents is rich and having $n-1$ cents is not rich)' is true, not because any one of its instances is definitely true, but because many of its instances depart very slightly from definite falsity. (Just as a disjunction can be definitely true when neither disjunct is, so can an existentially quantified statement when no instance is.) The short sorites is puzzling because we wrongly identify what makes the major premise false. 'No single grain makes the difference between a heap and a non-heap.' If this means: no single grain makes a decisive difference—takes you from a clear heap to a clear non-heap—it is true. If it means: no single grain makes any difference at all to heapdom, it is false, though easily mistaken for a truth, because the difference any single grain makes is so small.

This solution to the sorites (Edgington 1996) is embedded in a positive theory of reasoning in vague languages, which pronounces on when, and to what extent, it is safe to argue from premises which are only close to clearly true. It parallels a theory of when and to what extent it is safe to reason from premises which are less than completely certain. I am content if, in Schiffer's terminology, this is classified as a weak unhappy-face solution.

8.6 Conditionals

8.6.1

Schiffer's theory of indeterminacy is intended to apply not only to vagueness. He argues in Chapter 6 that all moral propositions are indeterminate, and in the following chapter that conditionals are often indeterminate. I shall focus on conditionals, though some of my remarks apply equally to his claim about moral propositions; and like Schiffer I shall focus on indicative conditionals: he does make some remarks about counterfactuals at the end of the chapter, but they raise no extra problems.[8]

Schiffer gives an account of what it is for a conditional to be determinately true, or determinately false:

A→C is determinately true iff (a) both A and C are determinately true, or (b) it is determinately the case that A metaphysically or physically entails C.

A→C is determinately false iff (a) A is determinately true and C is determinately false, or (b) it is determinately the case that A metaphysically or physically entails ¬C (but not C) (282, 285).

He does not define 'metaphysical or physical entailment.'[9] About the former he says "it is that strong kind of entailment of which conceptual entailment, logical entailment and mathematical entailment are species" (282); and about the latter he gives a few examples which suggest instantiations of laws of nature; and adds that it is not necessary to try to be more precise, because the condition rarely applies to conditionals of interest to us: "the really important fact will be that indicative-conditional propositions with false antecedents which are of interest to us are all indeterminate" (283). We typically think or express indicative conditional thoughts when we don't know whether the antecedent is true, i.e., it is an open question whether the antecedent is false (and we typically think or express counterfactual conditional thoughts when we take ourselves to know that the antecedent is false). Most of the time the strong condition (b) is not satisfied. So most of the time, it is at least a live possibility that the conditional turns out to be indeterminate.

Earlier in the chapter we are told that "it is an obvious consequence of the theory of pleonastic propositions (developed earlier in the book) that there are indicative-conditional propositions" (268) and that:

every instance of the truth schema[10]
The proposition that if A, then C is true iff if A, then C
is true. (280)

This is meant to be trivial. His theory allows that conditionals are often indeterminate, and more often still, believed to some degree when as far as the believer knows, they are indeterminate. Of these indeterminate ones he says "[T]hey only have the truth conditions they get from being instances of the general truth schema" (p. 293).[11]

But the general truth schema, when applied to indeterminate propositions, seems to me of rather dubious status, on Schiffer's account of indeterminacy. Let p be indeterminate and v-believed to degree 0.5. Either one is rationally required to v-believe 'it is true that p' to the same degree, or one is not. Suppose first that one is not required to believe 'it is true that p' to the same degree. Then, as it is rationally permissible to take different attitudes to the two sides of the biconditional, the biconditional cannot be trivial or obvious.

Suppose second that one is rationally required to take the same attitude to each side of the biconditional. So when $v(p) = 0.5$, $v(\text{it is true that } p) = 0.5$; also $v(\neg p) = 0.5$, as is $v(\text{it is not true that } p)$. And, by Schiffer's rules, $v(p \text{ and it is not true that } p) = 0.5$, as is $v(\text{it is true that } p \text{ and } \neg p)$. The material conditionals 'it is true that $p \supset p$' and '$p \supset$ it is true that p,' and the material biconditional 'it is true that $p \equiv p$,' are indeterminate when p is indeterminate. Any conditional worthy of the name entails the material conditional, any biconditional worthy of the name entails the material biconditional: the determinate truth of 'If A, C' should be enough for the determinate falsity of A&¬C. (The problem with the material conditional is that it is too weak, not that it is too strong.) But we have seen that 'It is true that p and not p' and 'p and it is not true that p' are not determinately false, on Schiffer's account, when p is indeterminate. So, I submit, on any decent reading of 'if,' 'If it is true that p, then p,' and its converse, are not determinately true, on this account. So, far from indeterminate conditionals 'only having the truth conditions they get from being instances of the general truth schema,' indeterminate propositions render the general truth schema itself indeterminate. There is a tension here between Schiffer's theory of indeterminacy and Schiffer's theory of the innocuousness of the truth schema.

(Were Schiffer to use the Łukasiewicz conditional, this problem would not arise: the Lukasiewicz conditional is determinately true provided the consequent does not get a lower value than the antecedent. But it is a defect of the Łukasiewicz conditional that it may be determinately true when (A&¬C) is not determinately false. And there are other defects. For instance, when v(Tom is tall) = 0.5 and v(Jack is tall) = 0.4, 'If Jack is tall, Tom is not tall' gets value 1, i.e., is determinately true. And nowhere does Schiffer employ this conditional—indeed, it is blatantly inconsistent with the account of the conditional he develops, for according to the Lukasiewicz rule all conditionals with determinately false antecedents are determinately true.)

8.6.2

Schiffer raises this problem for his theory: we do not assess conditionals as his theory predicts. Here is his example. Ann is considering the conditional: if Snodgrass is made a partner (P), Bigshot will resign (R) (Bigshot having threatened to this effect). She thinks it 50% likely that P. She thinks it 25% likely that $P\&R$, 25% likely that $P\&\neg R$. Hence, her conditional probability for R given P is 0.5. And, Schiffer agrees, this is a good measure of her confidence in the conditional. But according to his theory, the conditional is determinately true only if $P\&R$, so she should s-believe the conditional to degree 0.25. The conditional is determinately false only if $P\&\neg R$, so she should s-believe its negation to degree 0.25. The conditional is indeterminate if $\neg P$, so in this case she should have v-beliefs in the conditional and its negation, which sum to 0.5. (Remember (BL): $v(p) + v(\neg p) + s(p) + s(\neg p) = 1$.) These don't combine with her s-belief: according to the theory, she should report her state of mind somewhat as follows: 'I am 25% certain that if P, R, and I'm ambivalent to degree x about whether if P, R.' "But that is not what we find, if Ann is like everyone else: because for her Pr(R given P) = 0.5, she'll believe $P{\rightarrow}R$ to degree 0.5" he says (286).

Further, suppose that Ann now becomes more confident that Snodgrass will be made a partner, and there are no other relevant changes in her state of information. She still thinks $P\&R$ and $P\&\neg R$ are equally likely, but now her Pr(P) is 90%. So Pr($P\&R$) and Pr($P\&\neg R$) are now each 45%. According to Schiffer's theory, the degree to which she is certain that if P, R (her s-belief, Pr($P\&R$) has increased from 25% to 45% (and the degrees which represent her ambivalence in the light of indeterminacy diminish).

The point is entirely general and will apply to all uncertain conditional judgements. No one has the combination of attitudes to a conditional which Schiffer's theory predicts. He has refuted his own theory, or combination of theories. Well, not exactly, in his view: "We have a paradox here, and like most philosophical paradoxes, it has an unhappy-face solution" (287). What we have is

an essentially ineradicable glitch in our conceptual practices. Our concept of a proposition leaves us no option but to say that there are indicative-conditional propositions, and our concept of the indicative conditional relation bestows on the proposition A→C the truth conditions already proposed.... At the same time, we evidently have the need to express conditional belief even when we don't have a need to express belief in a conditional, and somewhere along the way the indicative conditional got co-opted for that purpose. But the practice of using indicative-conditional sentences to express conditional beliefs gets conflated with the practice of uttering sentences to assert, and thereby to express belief in, the propositions they express. Infelicities result. (288)

Happily, this paradox has a weak unhappy-face solution, he tells us, and he thereby 'makes an important concession to non-cognitivists like Dorothy Edgington.'

Although we need to have and to express conditional beliefs about what's likely given the truth of this, that, or the other thing...we don't seem to have any great need for indicative-conditional propositions.... It is not at all clear what need we have for a connective ⇓ such that 'S ⇓ S'' is true iff (a) 'S and S'' is true or (b) 'S metaphysically or physically entails S'' is true. (290)[12]

I am pleased that Schiffer and I end up in close agreement on conditionals. I don't mind admitting that it is somewhat paradoxical that the way we evaluate them differs essentially from the way we evaluate propositions. The discovery that this was so was certainly puzzling, disconcerting, and surprising.[13] (But the epithet 'paradoxical' is a little euphemistic for the fact that we don't have the combination of s-beliefs and v-beliefs predicted by Schiffer's theory. No one other than Schiffer had any pre-existing conviction that we did.)

However, to allow that the primary function of a range of declarative sentences is not to express propositions, is to cast some doubt on Schiffer's theory of the pleonastic nature of propositions, which yield 'something-from-nothing inferences' from p to 'the proposition that p is true.' If it is open to philosophers to argue that appearances are misleading in the case of conditionals, it is open to philosophers to take a similar stance about other controversial cases. Towards the end of the paper with the famous footnote which gave rise to the Ramsey Test, Frank Ramsey said "The difficulty comes fundamentally from taking every sentence to be a proposition" (1929: 162). In a footnote to one of his last papers David Lewis wrote

When people in philosophy book go to the footy, they express their feelings by saying 'Boo!' or 'Hooray!' Real people use a wider range of expressive locutions. Some of them have at least the superficial form of declarative sentences: 'Leeds boot boys rule' or 'Collingwood sucks.' A (pompous) bystander might indeed respond 'That's true' or 'That's false,' but calling it doesn't make it so. Unless the sentence did after all express a true or false proposition, the bystander's response would be just a bit of make-believe. (2001: 276)

My point is not to endorse what Lewis and Ramsey say about particular cases, but to suggest, again, that the case of conditionals shows that the superficial appearance of expressing a proposition is not always to be taken at face value, and the reasons for accepting or rejecting a propositional account of a given class of sentences may be quite deep.

8.6.3

I like Schiffer's idea that there is a general notion of indeterminacy, which comes in degrees, and which applies to vagueness and conditionals (and perhaps to more besides). Of course our uncertain conditional judgements are often revisable in the light of further information, but sometimes, when all the facts are in, uncertainty, or indeterminacy, remains. I'm 90 per cent certain that you will get a black spot if you pick a red ball, that you will be cured if you have the operation, that the dog will bite you if you approach. Let's say these are perfectly rational opinions based on all the relevant information. The antecedents turn out to be false, and the judgements are reformulated as counterfactuals: I'm 90 per cent certain that you would have got a black spot if you had picked a red ball, etc. There are no facts to overturn these judgements, or to eliminate the uncertainty/indeterminacy. Their status is similar to that of a judgement about whether this borderline colour patch is red.

In my view our best account of all varieties of uncertainty/indeterminacy is in terms of probabilistic structure (and our best account, in the case of conditionals, is in terms of conditional probabilities). Probabilistic structure applies to ordinary epistemic uncertainty; it applies to forward-looking objective chance, when the past and the laws do not (according to our best theories) determine what will happen. Objective chances change with time and intervening events, and (normally) play themselves out, and finally settle down to 1 and 0, so the objective intermediate values are only temporary. In the case of vagueness, the indeterminacy arises from the looseness of fit, at the borders, between our concepts and the world. It is permanent, unchanging, does not play itself out. Similarly, for many conditionals whose antecedents turn out to be false, such as those above, the indeterminacy is ineliminable. Roy Sorensen puts the point, in a similar context, by saying probabilities such as these "are static. They are impervious to news" (Sorensen 2001: 175). The probability calculus provides the logical structure of all species of uncertainty or indeterminacy, in my view.

Notes

1. All otherwise unspecified page references are to Schiffer (2003).
2. In view of the fact that there are glut theories as well as gap theories, perhaps it is better to say: solely true, solely false, and neither of these.
3. Schiffer uses 'v-belief,' and the associated verb 'v-believe,' for (the taking of) the vagueness-related attitude to a proposition and contrasts it with 's-belief' which is a partial belief due to ordinary, non-vagueness-related uncertainty.
4. The Łukasiewicz conditional is not used.
5. This first appeared in Fitch (1963). For an overview of the extensive philosophical discussion of it, see Brogaard and Salerno (2004).
6. Further problems with BL have been discovered by John MacFarlane (2006).
7. I owe this point to Ian Rumfitt.
8. Rightly in my view, his account of indicatives and counterfactuals are closely linked.

9. He clearly can't define these notions in terms of (in an appropriate sense) necessarily true conditionals. Also it is worth remembering that validity, hence entailment, becomes highly indeterminate, on Schiffer's theory.
10. This is subject to possible qualification subject to semantic paradox, he says.
11. The same holds for moral propositions which, Schiffer claims, are all indeterminate, so only have this trivial truth condition.
12. I don't much like the label 'non-cognitivist' for I think I can accommodate conditional knowledge as well as conditional belief. Just as conditional belief does not reduce to unconditional belief that a proposition is true, so conditional knowledge does not reduce to unconditional knowledge that a proposition is true.
13. David Lewis (1976) was the first to prove that evaluating conditionals by the conditional probability of consequent given antecedent was incompatible with evaluating them by the probability of the truth of any proposition, and the result has been proved in many ways since. For some of these results see Edgington (1995, section 6).

Bibliography

Brogaard, B. and J. Salerno. (2004). "Fitch's Paradox of Knowability." *The Stanford Encyclopedia of Philosophy* (Summer 2004 edition), edited by Edward N. Zalta. URL = <http://plato.stanford.edu/archives/sum2004/entries/fitch-paradox/>.
Edgington, D. (1995). "On Conditionals." *Mind* 104: 235–329.
Edgington, D. (1996). "Vagueness by Degrees." In *Vagueness: A Reader*, edited by R. Keefe and P. Smith, Cambridge: MIT Press.
Fitch, F. B. (1963). "A Logical Analysis of Some Value Concepts." *Journal of Symbolic Logic* 28: 135–42.
Lewis, D. (1976). "Probabilities of Conditionals and Conditional Probabilities." *Philosophical Review* 85: 297–315: reprinted in his *Philosophical Papers*, Volume II. New York: Oxford University Press, 1986.
Lewis, D. (1983). *Philosophical Papers*, Volume I. New York: Oxford University Press.
Lewis, D. (2001). "Forget about the 'Correspondence Theory of Truth'." *Analysis* 61: 275–9.
MacFarlane, J. (2006). "The Things We (Sorta Kinda) Believe." *Philosophy and Phenomenological Research* 73: 218–24.
McGee, V. and B. McLaughlin. (1994). "Distinctions without a Difference." *Southern Journal of Philosophy*, 33, supplement: 203–51.
Nagel, T. (1974). "What is it Like to be a Bat?" *Philosophical Review* 83: 435–50.
Ramsey, F. P. (1929). "General Propositions and Causality." In *Philosophical Papers*, edited by D. H. Mellor, Cambridge: Cambridge University Press.
Schiffer, S. (2003). *The Things We Mean*. Oxford: Clarendon Press.
Sorensen, R. (2001). *Vagueness and Contradiction*. Oxford: Clarendon Press.
Williamson, T. (1994). *Vagueness*. London: Routledge.
Wright, C. (2001). "On Being in a Quandary: Relativism, Vagueness, Logical Revisionism." *Mind* 110: 45–98.

9

Vagueness, Partial Belief, and Logic

Hartry Field

In his recent work on vagueness and indeterminacy, and in particular in Chapter 5 of *The Things We Mean*,[1] Stephen Schiffer advances two novel theses:

> 1. Vagueness (and indeterminacy more generally) is a psychological phenomenon;
> 2. It is indeterminate whether classical logic applies in situations where vagueness matters.

He also puts forward a third thesis:

> 3. The 'uncertainty' we have about whether to believe that Harry is bald when we take him to be a borderline case is very different from ordinary uncertainty; so different as to not really deserve the term 'uncertainty.'

This last thesis is opposed to the views of 'epistemic theorists' such as Timothy Williamson,[2] but the thesis as I've stated it is probably one that most theorists of vagueness would accept. Even so, Schiffer develops it in a highly novel way, according to which there is a special kind of partial belief heretofore unrecognized.

After an introductory section reviewing some background and locating his approach with respect to some others, I will turn to the thesis about the indeterminacy of logic, move on to his version of the thesis about two kinds of 'uncertainty,' then to the thesis that vagueness is a psychological phenomenon, and then back to the thesis about the indeterminacy of logic.

I should say that Schiffer's views and the arguments that support them are extremely interesting and important, and I have probably learned more from him on this subject than I have from anyone else—from many conversations over the years, as well as from his writings. By most standards, our views are quite close; so in order to give him his fair share of abuse I will have to stress some issues that those with more radically different views may regard as relatively minor.

9.1 Background on Epistemicism and Supervaluationism

Schiffer begins his chapter by considering a number of arguments related to the Sorites paradox, one of which is essentially as follows:[3]

I A person with $50,000,000 is rich
II A person with 37¢ is not rich

So,

III There is an amount of money such that a person with that amount of money is rich but a person with 1¢ less isn't.

I'll call this *the Least Number Sorites*. (Of course, we're indulging in the fiction that richness is simply a matter of net assets; and since 'rich' is doubtless context-relative, we're imagining the context fixed.) Presumably the premises of this argument are true, and the argument is classically valid. (The conclusion is essentially a disjunction of about five billion conjunctions of form *Rich(x) and not-Rich(x−0.01)*; it follows from the premises by about that many applications of excluded middle together with and-introduction and the distributive law.) But the conclusion of the argument is *prima facie* implausible: it seems to assert a *sharp cutoff* between the rich and the non-rich, and this seems contrary to the evident vagueness of the term.

Not only is the conclusion *prima facie* implausible, it also raises some embarrassing questions, as Schiffer points out. For instance, it seems fairly clear that no one knows where this sharp cutoff is, and that sociologists could never find out the answer to that question no matter how heavily their studies were funded. And (the embarrassing part) it doesn't seem as if this inevitable ignorance can be explained in *anything like* the ways that one can explain other inevitable ignorance (e.g. about the very remote past or the fine details of what's happening inside a given black hole). Rather, the natural explanation of our inability to know the location of the cutoff is that the issue 'isn't fully factual.' But *that* explanation doesn't seem to fit with III.

Admittedly, it is very difficult to make clear sense of the claim that the location of the cutoff 'isn't fully factual.' The difficulty has led many to reluctantly conclude that *the epistemic theory* is right. According to it, there must be a sharp cutoff, even though we can never know where it is; vagueness is just a kind of inevitable ignorance. The epistemic view has it that the location of the boundary between rich and non-rich is a straightforward matter of fact; an omniscient being (one who knew all the facts) would know where the cutoff point is. *Our* inability to know the cutoff point is due to human limitations; and there is no conceptual bar to aliens from outer space knowing this fact about which we are ignorant.

Let's be clear: on the epistemic view, it isn't simply that the aliens might have a precise concept instead of our concept of richness, and know where the cutoff of that precise concept is. No, it's that they might know where the cutoff of *our* concept of richness is. (And it isn't merely that they might have a more precise concept of cutoff than we have, call it cutoff*, and know the cutoff* of our concept of richness. No, it's that they might know where the cutoff of our concept of richness is, *in our sense of cutoff*.) If only we were endowed with a special organ for detecting richness, we'd be as well off as they are. This position appears to be an almost inevitable result of accepting the validity of the Least Number Sorites (and hence, presumably, accepting its conclusion III). Schiffer is highly skeptical of the position, and I think rightly so.

He is also properly skeptical of attempts to accept the validity of the argument but avoid the epistemic theory. The most influential such attempt is called *supervaluationism.* According to it, III is perfectly acceptable but does not assert a sharp cutoff between the rich and the non-rich. In one formulation of supervaluationism, the claim to be rejected, that there is a sharp cutoff, is rather

> III$_T$ There is a number of dollars x_0 (a multiple of 0.01) such that *it is true that* a person with x_0 dollars is rich and *it is true that* a person with x_0-0.01 dollars isn't.

Obviously this would be equivalent to III if *it is true that p* were assumed equivalent to *p* (in a sense of equivalence that allows for substitutivity of equivalents in extensional contexts), but this form of supervaluationism takes *it is true that p* to be strictly stronger than *p*. According to this version of supervaluationism, not only is III perfectly acceptable, so is

> *It is true that* there is a number of dollars x_0 such that a person with x_0 dollars is rich and a person with x_0-0.01 dollars isn't.

But III$_T$, with the 'it is true that' distributed to the inside, is not acceptable: sentences of form 'a person with x dollars is rich' for which x is near to the critical x_0 are neither true nor false, i.e., neither they nor their negations are true.

In making *it is true that p* stronger than *p*, this form of supervaluationism seems to do violence to the ordinary notion of truth. But a variant form of supervaluationism avoids that, by explicating the notion of sharp cutoff not by III$_T$ but by

> III$_D$ There is a number of dollars x_0 such that *it is determinately true that* a person with x_0 dollars is rich and *it is determinately true that* a person with x_0-0.01 dollars isn't.

Supervaluationism of this form mimics that of the other form: again, III is deemed acceptable, as is

> *It is determinately true that* there is a number of dollars x_0 such that a person with x_0 dollars is rich and a person with x_0-0.01 dollars isn't;

but III$_D$ isn't deemed acceptable, and this is supposed to capture the idea that there is no sharp cutoff.

I think these two forms of supervaluations differ only verbally. Schiffer disagrees with that assessment, for reasons I don't fully understand (195–6); but it probably doesn't matter much, because he is skeptical of both forms, and his discussion suggests that neither form succeeds in its attempt to be significantly different from epistemicism.

For in the first place, it's obscure what 'determinately true' means in the III$_D$ version: as Schiffer notes, the usual supervaluationist attempts to explain it are blatantly circular. It seems to me equally obscure what 'true' means in the III$_T$ version: the usual explanation of 'true' in terms of the equivalence between 'it is true that p' and 'p' obviously is inapplicable to 'true' as used in III$_T$, and the point about the circularity of a supervaluationist explanation carries over.

In the second place and more important, it is unclear why anyone should care if in this sense of determinate truth (or special sense of truth), claims such as 'a person with x_0 dollars is rich' and 'a person with x_0-0.01 dollars isn't rich' aren't determinately true (or aren't true). *For III alone, without III$_T$ or III$_D$, suffices for a commitment to the existence of the critical value x_0*. If there is such a critical value, why can't we know it? It wouldn't be much of an explanation to say that knowledge of p requires that p be determinately true, or be true in the special sense assumed in III$_T$: for the only uncontentious requirement here is that one can't know that p unless p. If one really thinks there is a critical point x_0 satisfying III, why couldn't there be a god or an alien who had the means to reliably ascertain what this critical value is?

It's worth emphasizing that Schiffer does not object to the claim that it is indeterminate where the cutoff between rich and non-rich is: indeed, such a claim is an important part of his own theory. But he recognizes that (i) we need some explanation of indeterminacy that explains why this claim is of interest; and (ii) we need to drop our commitment to III, since that commitment undermines any interest the claim might have. I think this is exactly the right approach to take.

It's also worth emphasizing that Schiffer doesn't assert that the cutoff between the rich and the non-rich *isn't* sharp—that is, he does not assert the negation of III. Indeed, he notes (quite correctly) that though accepting the conclusion III would commit one to epistemicism or something in that ballpark, accepting the negation of III would appear to be as bad or worse.

One reason for this (the one Schiffer gives) is that unless normal quantifier and negation rules are questioned (a radical step that Schiffer shows no inclination to take), the negation of III is equivalent to

N-III For any amount of money, either a person with that amount of money is not rich or a person with 1¢ less is rich.

But that gives rise to another form of Sorites argument: N-III together with I classically imply the negation of II, and yet I is obviously true while the negation of II is obviously not. Moreover, the classical inference involved here seems intuitively to be at least as strong as the one in the Least Number Sorites: it involves only universal instantiation and 'disjunctive modus ponens' (the classically valid rule of inferring q from *not-p or q* together with p). Universal instantiation is hard to question (and can be avoided, in an alternative version of the argument). So accepting the negation of III would seem to require giving up disjunctive modus ponens (i.e. regarding it as invalid or at least not determinately valid), and that seems a high cost.

Actually this reason against accepting N-III isn't in the end one that Schiffer is entitled to, for he eventually argues (224) that (disjunctive) modus ponens *isn't* determinately valid. (I think this is a mistake, as I'll argue in the next section, but it is his view.) Because of this, it's worth mentioning another argument he might have given. The argument is that on the natural assumption that adding money doesn't destroy richness (together with the assumption, implicit in the whole discussion, that richness is just a matter of net assets), N-III implies

For any amount of money, either a person with that amount of money is not rich or a person with that amount of money is rich.

But that conclusion (generalized excluded middle) can itself be argued to lead to epistemicism or its supervaluationist variant, by a route very much like the one above: it seems to posit unknowable facts, as to whether people with x dollars in net assets are rich (even for values of x that intuitively correspond to the 'border region').[4]

So we have strong reason to reject III and strong reason to reject its negation; and we can accommodate both these reasons, by rejecting the instance of excluded middle *III or not-III*. Rejecting here doesn't mean accepting its negation; what it means, roughly, is adopting a policy that precludes accepting it. The claim that we should reject this instance of excluded middle will turn out to be pretty much equivalent to the claim that III should be regarded as neither determinately true nor determinately false, on Schiffer's eventual explication of determinateness.

So we can summarize his attitude toward the Least Number Sorites by saying that it has determinately true premises, but that it's indeterminate whether its conclusion is true. And I think this is exactly the line one ought to take.

9.2 Schiffer on the Indeterminacy of Logic

Since Schiffer takes the premises of the Least Number Sorites to be true (indeed, determinately true), but doesn't take the conclusion to be true (and indeed, assumes it not to be determinately true), it would seem natural for him to conclude that the Least Number Sorites isn't really valid, despite the fact that classical logic says it is. That is the conclusion offered by most proponents of a non-classical 'logic of vagueness.' As noted, the question of the validity of the Least Number Sorites turns on the law of excluded middle—about fifty billion applications of it, in fact, many of which are intuitively to 'borderline propositions.' So a consequence of this non-classical view is that the law of excluded middle is not unrestrictedly valid.[5]

But Schiffer insists that the proper conclusion is *not* that the Least Number Sorites or the law of excluded middle is invalid. (He strongly suggests that that would constitute what he calls a "happy-face solution" to the Sorites paradox, since it would offer a definite place where the Sorites argument goes wrong. He is quite insistent that we need an "unhappy-face solution.") He says, rather, that the question of whether the argument is valid is itself indeterminate: the argument is neither determinately valid nor determinately invalid.[6] Or rather, he says that that's so *on the common sense notion of validity*; and I believe he thinks that any notion on which the argument is determinately invalid is a merely technical notion lacking philosophical interest. In the ordinary sense of 'valid,' calling an argument valid requires not that it necessarily preserve *determinate* truth, but that it necessarily preserve *truth* (in the ordinary sense of truth in which asserting the truth of p is equivalent to asserting p). So because there is no possible case where we are in a position to say that the premises are true and that the conclusion isn't, we can't assert that the argument is invalid, we can only say that it isn't determinately valid. His conclusion would seem to be that the epistemic theory (or the disjunction of it and supervaluationism, if that is taken as a distinct theory) is not determinately false, despite his criticisms of it.[7] We shouldn't believe it, but we shouldn't disbelieve it either.

I have two points to make about this (for now—there will be a further discussion in the final section). The less interesting is that I don't think it at all clear that 'the ordinary sense' of the term 'valid' is what Schiffer takes it to be. In fact, I'm not at all clear that there is a unique 'ordinary sense': there are a bunch of different ways in which one might explicate 'valid' which happen to coincide under the assumption of classical logic (or if you like, of its determinate validity) but can come apart elsewhere, and I doubt that one of these senses is privileged as what is 'really meant' by people unaware of the distinction.[8] And even if there is a unique 'ordinary sense' of 'valid.' I don't see why we should glorify it: if there is another sense of 'valid' that is extensionally equivalent to the first under the assumption of classical logic but which may no longer be when that assumption is removed, shouldn't the important question be which of the two is more theoretically fruitful?

My second and I think more interesting point is that even if we stick to Schiffer's preferred sense of 'valid'—necessary truth preservation—it is not at all clear that the inference from I and II to III isn't determinately invalid. For what sort of necessity is involved here? Not 'metaphysical necessity,' whatever exactly that is: for the inference from 'There is water in the sink' to 'There is H_2O in the sink' preserves truth by metaphysical necessity, but is not valid. The notion of necessity that is involved, rather, is *logical* necessity. And it could certainly be argued that the fact that premises I and II are determinately true and III isn't is enough to show that *logic* doesn't require that if I and II are true then so is III, which is enough to show that *it is not logically necessary that* the inference preserves truth.

I don't say that it is *clear* that on Schiffer's 'ordinary sense' of validity, the inference in question is determinately invalid. What the above paragraph seems to me to show, rather, is that even this 'ordinary sense' is non-univocal: its application may be clear in the (determinately) classical case, but once we give up our allegiance to classical assumptions there is room to interpret the necessity claim in different ways, and the difference matters to whether we regard question of necessary truth-preservation as determinate.

It may seem that it doesn't much matter to broader issues whether the inferences are declared invalid or merely not determinately valid. Perhaps not—though from Schiffer's insistence on the latter choice over the former (e.g. 229), it is clear that *he* takes it to matter.

And one place that it *seems* to matter is to Schiffer's frequent hand-wringing about how hard it is to wear a happy face while theorizing about vagueness (pp. 196-8, 224-31). He takes it to be indeterminate whether the Least Number Sorites is invalid (and says more generally that it is indeterminate whether *any* classical inferences are invalid, a matter I'll come back to in the final section of the chapter). So he presumably also thinks that despite his criticisms of epistemicism and supervaluationism, they are not *determinately* incorrect. Standard theories of vagueness involving non-classical logics do take epistemicism and supervaluationism to be determinately incorrect. This seems to be one reason why Schiffer rejects these theories as acceptable theories of vagueness: they are too 'happy-faced.'[9] I can't say with complete confidence that this is Schiffer's reasoning, but it is a natural interpretation of his discussion.

But however we decide on these matters, there is a vastly more important issue in the vicinity. It concerns Schiffer's *rationale* for declaring that these inferences are not determinately invalid. That rationale (that validity is necessity of truth preservation) not only undermines claims of invalidity, it undermines claims of validity as well. For instance, as Schiffer himself notes (224), if we interpret 'valid' in this way then modus ponens comes out not determinately valid. Consider the argument from *A* and *If A then B* to *B*, where the "if...then" is taken as the material conditional: when *A* is indeterminate and *B* is clearly false, we're in no position to conclude that the argument even *actually* preserves truth, let alone does so *necessarily*. To me it seems odd not to declare modus ponens valid in Schiffer's theory, given that he would agree that once we've established the premises of a modus ponens we've established its conclusion.

If it were merely modus ponens that we couldn't declare valid, we could learn to live with that. But the point about the determinateness of validity claims may go far deeper than Schiffer acknowledges: it may indicate that on Schiffer's 'ordinary definition' of validity, *no* argument comes out determinately valid.

The reason is that talk of necessary truth preservation involves a conditional: necessarily, *if* the premises are true *then* so is the conclusion. The question then arises how the conditional in the truth-preservation claim is to be understood. Schiffer doesn't give the answer in this chapter, but of course it depends on the question of what kind of embeddable conditional connectives are available once you give up commitment to excluded middle.[10] And it is not obvious that any embeddable conditionals are available that would allow Schiffer to declare any inferences necessarily truth preserving, and hence valid in his ordinary sense.

For instance, one possible view[11] is that the only embeddable conditional connective that makes sense is the material conditional $p \rightarrow q$ (equivalent to *not-p or q*). (That would not preclude our making sense of conditional sentences that don't behave like material conditionals, as when I deny that if I run for president I'll win while also denying that I'll run for president: for we can say that my low 'degree of belief' that if I run for president I'll win doesn't consist in my attaching a low value to a claim that involves an embeddable conditional connective, it is simply a matter of having a low conditional degree of belief in winning given the assumption of running for president.) Now, the material conditional has the property that when its antecedent and consequent are indeterminate, it too is indeterminate[12] (where 'indeterminate' means 'neither determinately true nor determinately false'). But a claim of necessary truth-preservingness has the form 'Necessarily, if the premises are true then so is the conclusion'; and whatever the premises and conclusion are, it is always logically possible for them to be indeterminate.[13] So necessary truth-preservation, *understood in terms of the material conditional*, is something that can *never* determinately hold. Not even the inference from a sentence to itself, or from a conjunction to its conjuncts, would come out determinately valid in Schiffer's sense if we took that to be defined in terms of the material conditional.[14] And this problem is unaffected by how we interpret 'necessarily' (as long as it implies 'actually'): the problem is the commitment to *actual* truth-preservation, as defined by the material conditional.

To what extent is this a problem for Schiffer? His own view of conditionals, given in a later chapter, is not the material conditional view (nor is it a version of the conditional degree of belief view which does without an embeddable conditional). Still, it seems to give rise to a similar problem. For on his view, a conditional *if p then q* is determinately true only if it "owes its determinate truth ... to the satisfaction of a non-conditional sufficient condition for its being determinately true" (298), and in the case where the antecedent and consequent aren't both determinately true the sufficient condition must be that the antecedent "determinately metaphysically or physically entails" the consequent. Let's apply this to a conditional of form

(C)   If the premises of argument X are true then so is the conclusion, where neither the premises of X nor the conclusion of X is determinately true. (Argument X can be of any form you like, say from the premise *p* to the conclusion *p or q*; in that example, focus on the possibility that *p* and *q* are both indeterminate.) Then the view seems to say that that conditional can only be determinately true if it 'owes its determinate truth' to the determinate validity of argument X. But the validity of argument X, according to Schiffer, just *is* its necessary truth-preservingness, which can only hold if (C) is true and thus can only hold *determinately* if (C) is *determinately* true. Given this, it would seem that (C) can't be determinately true: if it were, it would have to 'owe' that determinate truth to the determinate truth of itself, which seems absurd.[15]

I think, then, that on Schiffer's own view of the conditional, his views about the determinate validity of inferences require that *no inference be determinately valid*—a conclusion that strikes me as having an intolerably high cost.

But the argument that no inference comes out determinately valid depends not only on his view about validity, but also on his view about conditionals. I myself think that there is good reason to want another kind of conditional connective when we weaken classical logic, so perhaps the point of the previous three paragraphs is not worth making too big a deal of. Even so, it seems a somewhat unfortunate feature of his account of validity that its acceptability should turn on this technical issue about conditionals.

Moreover, if the only kinds of conditionals that evade the argument of the previous two paragraphs are deemed technical devices unknown to ordinary folk, then presumably they are unavailable for understanding Schiffer's 'ordinary sense' of validity. We'd still be stuck with the conclusion that in 'the ordinary sense' of validity, no inferences are determinately valid, a conclusion that not even Schiffer wants to endorse. So if one insists that only the alleged 'ordinary sense' is of philosophical interest, perhaps one should wear a *very* unhappy face!

9.3 Schiffer on Partial Belief

I now turn to Schiffer's view that there are two different kinds of partial belief (belief that may fall short of certainty, i.e., belief to a degree that may be less than 1).

What Schiffer calls *standard partial belief* (SPB) is *initially* explained as the kind of partial belief that under suitable idealizations of logical omniscience can be identified with subjective probability; the usual laws of subjective probability constrain it, in the sense that a rational agent would try to make her degrees of belief accord with those laws to the extent possible.

What Schiffer calls *vagueness-related partial belief* (VPB) is something one has (to a non-zero degree) only to propositions that one regards as perhaps indeterminate. Imagine a person who seems to you neither a clear case of being bald nor a clear case of not being bald. Then you have a (non-zero) VPB in the claim that he is bald, and a (non-zero) VPB in the claim that he is not bald. These VPB's obey unusual laws. For instance, Schiffer thinks that if Harry is a 'paradigm borderline case' of baldness and also a 'paradigm borderline case' of thinness, then our VPB's in the following claims should all be ½:

Harry is bald
Harry is not bald
Harry is thin
Harry is not thin
Harry is bald and thin
Harry is bald and not thin
Harry is thin and not bald
Harry is not thin and not bald.

So though the last four claims are mutually exclusive in classical logic, Schiffer thinks that our vagueness-related degrees of belief in them will add to more than 1 (as Paul Horwich pointed out to me).[16] Just *why* he thinks this is something I defer for the moment; for now the point is only to illustrate how different VPB is from SPB on Schiffer's account.

The claim that there are two kinds of partial belief may seem mysterious. Is it that propositions divide into two classes, those that we have SPBs toward and those that we have VPBs toward? Even if we allowed such a division of propositions to depend on the agent and her situation, that would be a highly unpromising view, for many reasons. For instance, presumably we could conjoin (or disjoin) propositions in one class with those in the other, and if so, would our degree of belief in the conjunction (or disjunction) be an SPB or a VPB? And consider our attitude toward a person we meet who's wearing a hat; we have no idea if he's a clear case of baldness, a clear case of non-baldness, or a borderline case. In that situation, is our degree of belief that he is bald an SPB or a VPB?

Because of issues like these, Schiffer rejects the idea that there are for a given agent two classes of propositions, those she has SPBs toward and those she has VPBs toward. (That had been his view in earlier papers.) Instead he adopts the much more promising view, that toward any kind of proposition we can and typically do have both kinds of degrees of belief. In the situation with the person wearing a hat, suppose we think it 20 per cent likely that he is clearly bald, 50 per cent likely that he is clearly non-bald, and 30 per cent likely that he is borderline; ignore higher order vagueness. In that case, the SPB that he is bald is 0.2 and the SPB that he is not bald is 0.5; the VPBs that he is bald and that he is not bald are underdetermined by the description, but they are both non-zero and add to 0.3. In general, SPBs and VPBs are governed by the following laws among others:

(i) $0 \leq S(p) \leq 1$ and $0 \leq V(p) \leq 1$
(ii) $S(p) + S(not\text{-}p) + V(p) + V(not\text{-}p) = 1$
(iii) $V(p) > 0$ if and only if $V(not\text{-}p) > 0$.

(This is discussed in section 5.7 of his chapter.)

Given this, Schiffer's initial explanation of SPBs as involving the standard probability laws seems quite misleading: the fact is that in situations where vagueness may matter (i.e., where $V(p)$ and hence $V(not\text{-}p)$ are non-zero for some of the propositions that are in question), the usual laws of subjective probability may dramatically fail *for SPBs as well as for VPBs*, on Schiffer's view. In particular, the standard degrees of belief in p and its negation will add up to less than 1 in this situation. In cases where one is sure that p is a borderline case, V(p) and V(not-p) will sum to 1; so the standard degrees of belief in p and not-p will in those cases be 0.

In n. 38 (pp. 209–10) Schiffer criticizes a view of mine that uses only a single notion of degree of belief Q with the property that Q(p) and Q(not-p) can sum to less than 1, and are each 0 in cases where the agent is sure that the p is borderline (borderline true). Given that his own standard degree of belief function S has this property, I take it that the point of the criticism must be not that what I say about degree of belief is wrong but rather that it is incomplete: that it neglects another important kind of degree of belief. (Or rather, that it neglects something *that may or may not be a kind of degree of belief, but ought to be discussed while discussing degree of belief*: for Schiffer eventually concedes that VPBs may be partial beliefs only in a Pickwickian sense (232).)

Is there this other important kind of degree of belief (or degree of Pickwickian belief)? To some extent the plausibility of Schiffer's case that there is depends on his initial characterization of standard partial belief, which as we've seen he doesn't in the end believe, according to which SPBs obey the classical laws of probability (qualifications about lack of logical omniscience etc. aside). If SPBs really had to obey the standard laws, then the case for VPBs would be strong. For suppose we are faced with Harry who we take to be a clear borderline case of baldness. If there were only SPBs *and they had to obey classical laws*, we would need to believe to some degree z that Harry is bald and to degree $1-z$ that he is not, and these degrees of belief would have to function very much like our other degrees of belief, e.g. in who will win the next presidential election. Don't worry about the precision involved in assigning a particular number to our degree of belief about Harry's baldness—that problem arises even for our degrees of belief about the election, and can presumably be handled in a refinement of the theory that allows for indeterminacy in degrees of belief. Worry instead about the fact that there is a formal similarity between the partial belief in Harry's baldness and the partial belief in the election result, even though these cases intuitively seem very different. As Schiffer puts it, standard degree of belief is usually thought of as a measure of *uncertainty* or *ignorance*; but intuitively, in the case of Harry's baldness *there is no fact about which we are ignorant*. Admittedly, that intuition is not easy to make sense of, as epistemic theorists are fond of pointing out. Still, almost everyone thinks there's an important sense in which the question of Harry's baldness isn't something that we are ignorant about in the sense in which we might be ignorant of Thales' maternal grandmother's day of birth. Schiffer's claim that our attitudes are or should be VPBs rather than SPBs is supposed to capture the intuition reasonably well.

So given *Schiffer's initial characterization* of SPBs (according to which they must obey the standard laws of probability, qualifications about logical omniscience aside), it looks as if one needs VPBs to account for the fact that even though we refuse to fully believe that Harry is bald or fully believe that he is not bald, we don't think of ourselves as ignorant about anything. But given *Schiffer's actual theory*, one doesn't need VPBs to account for this. His actual theory is that in a case of certainty that Harry is borderline, our standard degrees of belief that he is bald and also that he is not bald are both 0. I believe that on his theory, our standard degree of belief that *he is either bald or not bald* is also 0 (as is our standard degree of belief that *it is not the case that he is either bald or not bald*).[17] This seems enough by itself to undermine the sense that we are committed to belief in a fact about which we are ignorant, even without introducing VPBs. What Schiffer's introduction of VPBs adds is that in this situation, we *also* have non-zero VPBs in the claim that Harry is bald and that he is not bald, which add to 1. Whatever purpose the introduction of these VPBs may serve, it doesn't seem to be needed, or to help, merely for the purpose of undercutting the idea that our situation with regard to Harry's baldness is one of ignorance.

What then does Schiffer think VPBs *are* needed for? On the basis of his criticism mentioned several paragraphs back, it seems that he thinks it's needed to reflect *the ambivalent attitude* we have in borderline cases. Suppose Harry is a pretty clear borderline case of baldness. We do nonetheless have some tendency to call Harry bald and some tendency to call him non-bald; and as more hair is removed we may have more of a tendency to call him bald, even while still thinking of him as a borderline case. I believe that Schiffer takes the ratio of our VPB in Harry's baldness to our VPB in his non-baldness to reflect the ratio of our inclination to call him bald over our inclination to call him non-bald.

There is no doubt that we do have such conflicting inclinations in borderline cases. Whether we really need a theory of VPBs to explain or characterize this seems more doubtful. I'm inclined to think that our conflicting inclinations in such cases have a lot to do with contextual shifts in how we use the term 'bald': when we have more tendency to regard Harry as bald than not bald, even while regarding him as borderline, that's because we find it more natural to shift to a standard loose enough to count him as bald than to one strong enough to exclude him. One piece of evidence for this diagnosis is that if you alter the example to make it seem indeterminate in *all* contexts—e.g., 'The minimum number of hairs required for someone to be bald is even'—then we no longer feel ambivalent, we simply reject both the claim and its negation. But I don't offer this diagnosis with total confidence; and especially given that Schiffer concedes that vagueness-related partial-belief may only be partial belief in a Pickwickian sense, there may be little to fight about here. Perhaps the only point to make is that Schiffer's assumption that there are neat compositional laws governing 'vagueness-related degrees of belief' appears under-motivated if the only role of such 'degrees of belief' is to characterize our conflicting inclinations in cases where our standard degrees of belief in a sentence and its negation add to less than 1.

Aside from this general worry about whether there are *any* neat laws concerning 'vagueness-related degrees of belief' in Schiffer's sense, I think that the particular laws that he proposes are quite unmotivated. In particular, he proposes that the VPB of a disjunction is the maximum of the VPBs of the disjuncts, and that the VPB of a conjunction is the minimum. I grant that there's no obvious reason why the principles appropriate to SPBs should apply to VBPs, but don't find these rules either intuitively evident or motivated by the conception of VPBs given two paragraphs back. In the example above, where V(Harry is bald) and V(Harry is thin) are each ½ and there is no connection between them, why should V(Harry is bald and thin) also be ½? (E.g., a shift of context to make Harry come out *both* clearly bald and clearly thin would seem harder than one to make him come out *either* clearly not bald or clearly not thin.) I just don't see any intuitive pull to his proposal.

9.4 Vagueness as a Psychological Phenomenon

Despite my doubts about the need for a notion of 'vagueness-related partial belief' and the details of Schiffer's account of it, I think that his view that standard partial belief does not obey classical laws is important to an understanding of vagueness: in particular, it is hard to see how one could have any real alternative to the epistemic view if standard degrees of belief were applicable to vague propositions and had to obey the classical laws. If the standard laws of partial belief are assumed, then (i) our degree of belief that Harry is bald and our degree of belief that he is not bald must add to 1, and (ii) our degree of belief that he is either bald or not bald must be 1. It is hard to see how accepting either of these two claims wouldn't involve a commitment to the straightforward factuality of the question of Harry's baldness; but by abandoning both, Schiffer makes room for a view on which we have no commitment to the question being factual.[18]

One might respond that claims about partial belief can at best illuminate *our beliefs about* vagueness and indeterminacy; they can say nothing about what vagueness and indeterminacy *really are*. I'd be skeptical of such a response. Nonetheless, I am even more skeptical of Schiffer's particular means of combating the response, which is to explicate indeterminacy in terms of partial belief.

More particularly, Schiffer defines a *VPB** in p as a belief state formed under ideal epistemic conditions in which the SPB in p and in *not-p* would both be zero, so that the VPB in p and in *not-p* would both be non-zero and would sum to 1. He then proposes that for it to be indeterminate[19] whether p *just is* for it to be the case that it is possible for someone to have a VPB* in p.[20]

It seems to me hard to take this proposed explication seriously:

(A) In one direction, let t be a certain time in the early history of the universe when it was far too hot for life to be possible, and let r be a certain region. Consider the claim p that in r at t there was a roundish configuration of particles, and suppose there actually was a configuration of particles in that region that was *a borderline case of* being roundish (and no configurations that were clear cases of being roundish). If one recognizes indeterminacy at all, p will clearly be an example of it. But since life was then impossible, there seems to be no serious sense in which it is possible for there to be a person in the ideal epistemic conditions required for a VPB* in this claim (given the interpretation of this required by note 20 above).

I suppose Schiffer could resist this by saying that a being who could survive the extraordinary high temperatures and observe the configuration is *logically* possible even if not physically possible, and that that's all that matters. But if so, why isn't a being who has a magical baldness detector or roundishness detector also possible in the relevant sense, so that a being without one isn't ideal? It isn't open to Schiffer to answer this by saying that claims about exact shape are determinate but claims about roundishness and baldness are often not, and that the relevant kind of possibility is one that allows for physically impossible beings with access to the determinate facts but not to the indeterminate ones. For to invoke that *in this context* would presuppose a notion of determinateness not based on the epistemic attitudes of possible agents.

(B) In the other direction, consider an intuitively determinate claim, say that Dick Cheney is wealthy. Schiffer's proposed explication requires that no one could have a VPB* that Cheney is wealthy: if someone were to have anything other than an SPB of 1 in Cheney's wealthiness, that person wouldn't be in ideal epistemic circumstances. But couldn't there be someone fully aware of Cheney's tremendous assets, who nonetheless is unsure whether to call Cheney wealthy on the ground that he has quite a bit less than Bill Gates? It is no good to respond to this by saying that such a person isn't in ideal conditions because he has incorrect views about indeterminacy; that response presupposes that the notion of indeterminacy is available independently of the ideality constraints on degrees of belief, which doesn't fit with Schiffer's proposal of using ideality of degrees of belief in explicating determinateness.

For an example with a different flavor, consider an even clearer case of a determinate truth, that Napoleon was less than six feet tall. Schiffer's proposed explication requires that no one could have a VPB* that he was less than six feet tall. But consider an extraordinarily rational Dummett-like anti-realist who believes that contingent claims about the past are all indeterminate, and in accordance with this, has only VPBs in such claims. Again, the only obvious way to defend the claim that such a philosopher is not in ideal conditions is to say that he has an incorrect theory of indeterminacy, and that defense seems unavailable in the current dialectical context since it seems to require a sense of indeterminacy not based on the epistemic attitudes of agents.[21]

In my view, Schiffer's attempt to explicate indeterminacy in terms of the psychology of ideal agents is overkill: the point that rational standard degrees of belief can depart from the laws of classical probability, in ways that allow for the standard degrees of belief in *p* and in *not-p* to sum to less than 1 and for the standard degree of belief in *p or not-p* to also be less than 1, is enough to illuminate the nature of vagueness without any such explication.

So why does Schiffer insist on an explication in terms of the agent's attitudes? He seems to argue (211) that if indeterminateness weren't explainable in terms of epistemic attitudes then a 'third possibility' view of vagueness would have to be correct, where this is defined (191) as a view on which indeterminate claims are neither true nor false. I agree with Schiffer that 'third possibility' views ought to be rejected: the claim that '*p*' is true should be regarded as equivalent to *p* itself, and the claim that '*p*' is false should be regarded as equivalent to *not-p*; so if it is indeterminate whether *p*, it is indeterminate whether '*p*' is true, and also indeterminate whether it is false.[22] But why he thinks that rejecting the explicability of indeterminacy in terms of agents' attitudes should require the view that indeterminate sentences are neither true nor false is a complete mystery to me: the definability of indeterminacy in other terms seems to have little if any bearing on the question of the relation between indeterminacy on the one hand and truth and falsity on the other.

9.5 More on Validity and the Status of Classical Logic

Schiffer's view that determinateness is a purely psychological concept does play a role for him: one of the reasons he gives against explaining validity in terms of necessary preservation of *determinate* truth is that this would make validity depend on psychological notions. This reason becomes suspect if the points made in the previous section are correct.

Putting that aside, let's return to the question of what validity should be taken to be. There is much to be said for the view that even in classical logic it should not be taken as a defined term, but as a primitive notion that governs our inferential or epistemic practices. (For instance, when we discover that the inference from p and q to r is valid, then we should ensure that our degree of belief in r is no lower than our degree of belief in the conjunction of p and q.) From this viewpoint (which is arguably implicit in natural deduction formulations of logic) we can explain why, in classical logic, we identify the valid inferences with those that, of logical necessity, preserve truth. For assuming 'disquotational' rules for truth and the usual introduction and elimination rules for conjunction, the validity of the inference from $p_1,\ldots,p_n$ to q is equivalent to the validity of the inference from $True(<p_1>)$ and ... and $True(<p_n>)$ to $True(<q>)$. And now assuming the usual introduction and elimination rules for the conditional, this is equivalent to the validity of the conditional *If True* $(<p_1>)$ *and ... and True*$(<p_n>)$ *then True*$(<q>)$. Validity of a single claim is presumably equivalent to the logical necessity of that claim, so the natural-deduction rules of classical logic plus the truth predicate *show* that valid inferences are those that of logical necessity preserve truth.

But note that this derivation will be inapplicable to any logic that doesn't contain both of the classical rules for the conditional (the introduction and elimination rules). And the fact is that *none* of the usual non-classical logics of vagueness contain both of these rules (unless one takes attempts at treating vagueness using intuitionist logic seriously). Indeed, if we are wedded to keeping the general intersubstitutivity of *True* $(<p>)$ with p, we can't possibly maintain both rules: as those familiar with Curry's Paradox know, we could then prove anything. If, as I think is the best policy in dealing with vagueness, we keep modus ponens (the elimination rule) and give up the unrestricted introduction rule for the conditional, we will accept the validity of some arguments without being able to assert that they preserve truth. It is still the case (i) that if we accept the validity of an argument then we shouldn't believe that all the premises are true without believing that the conclusion is true; and (ii) the existence of a case where all the premises are true and the conclusion isn't true would entail the argument's invalidity. But (i) and (ii) don't rule out there being cases of determinate validity and of determinate invalidity where an indeterminacy in one or more of the premises or the conclusion makes it indeterminate whether the inference preserves truth.[23]

The viewpoint I've just sketched is my preferred view of the matter: it makes certain classical inferences (e.g. the Least Number Sorites) determinately invalid. And note that it does so without defining validity in terms of determinate truth, or semantic values, or anything like that. So even if we were to agree that determinacy is a psychological notion and that the notion of validity is not to be defined in psychological terms, the approach just suggested would in no way be undermined.

I offer the above view of the matter as one possibility; I do not insist on it. Indeed I'm willing to grant Schiffer's preferred use of 'valid,' on which the valid inferences are by definition those that preserve truth of logical necessity. But let me repeat two points from section 9.2 before making some further ones:

1. It isn't obvious that classical inferences like the Least Number Sorites don't come out determinately invalid *even on Schiffer's definition*. (Similarly for the law of excluded middle). On a strong but natural reading of 'logical necessity,' they definitely fail at the goal of preserving truth *by logical necessity*.
2. Unless Schiffer uses a non-material conditional, and one different from his own preferred conditional, to define 'truth-preserving,' *no* inference will turn out determinately *valid* on Schiffer's definition. (This is so whichever way one reads the 'necessarily' in his definition.)

A further point to be made concerns Schiffer's suggestions (e.g. at several places on p. 229) that it is indeterminate whether there are *any* classical inferences that are invalid. Let us concede to Schiffer (putting aside the doubt raised in point 1 above) that in Schiffer's sense of 'valid' neither the law of excluded middle nor the Least Number Sorites are determinately invalid. Still, aren't there other determinately invalid inferences? In most non-classical logics of vagueness there is a conditional for which *if p then q* is not generally equivalent to *not-p or q* (though it is equivalent *given* the assumption that excluded middle holds for antecedent and consequent). And in most of these logics quite a few classically valid inferences involving the conditional will lead from determinate truth to determinate untruth, and hence will be clearly invalid in Schiffer's sense. For instance, in most logics for vagueness, there can be sentences *p* for which *if p then not-p* and *if not-p then p* are both determinately true;[24] but in classical logic these together imply that the earth is made of Jello. Similarly, in classical logic *p if and only if (if p then q)* implies *p and q*, but in most logics of vagueness the former can be determinately true and the latter determinately false.

I take this point to be fairly significant. The apparent 'punch' to Schiffer's claim that inferences like the Least Number Sorites aren't determinately invalid was that the epistemic view can't be determinately false. But if what I've just argued is right, then even if you concede to Schiffer that *those* classical inferences aren't determinately invalid in Schiffer's sense (a concession which, I repeat, one need not make), still there are *other* classical inferences that *will* be determinately invalid, and that is enough to make the epistemic view (and supervaluationism) determinately false.

Schiffer might resist this conclusion, by insisting that the above 'counterexamples' to classical logic involve a conditional that differs in meaning from any in classical logic: the connective of classical logic, he might say, is the material conditional (or perhaps the Schiffer conditional mentioned earlier), and none of the classical inferences involving *that* lead from determinate truth to determinate falsity. But to start with a small point, I see no obvious ground for insisting that the 'if... then' of these logics of vagueness differs in meaning from the classical conditional. After all, in these logics *if p then q* will completely coincide with *not-p or q when restricted to determinate sentences*; or, to put it another way, they are equivalent relative to the classical assumptions *p or not-p* and *q or not-q*. To insist that the classical conditional is not only equivalent to *not-p or q* relative to the classical assumption of excluded middle, but is synonymous with it (so that the equivalence persists even when the assumption of excluded middle is dropped), seems highly contentious, and I know of no plausible argument for it.

A more significant point is that were Schiffer to take this 'change of meaning' line it would have an extremely high cost: it would commit him to the conclusion that no classical inference is either determinately valid or determinately invalid in the ordinary sense. For by point 2 above, none is truth-preserving as defined by the material conditional, or as defined by the Schiffer conditional either, and the line now under consideration has it that any sense in which inferences are truth-preserving simply changes the ordinary meaning of 'truth-preserving.' No inference (whether licensed by classical logic or not) would be determinately valid, in the ordinary sense; and he strongly suggests that none is determinately invalid in this sense. The ordinary sense of validity would have become completely useless.

Notes

1. Schiffer (2003). All page references will be to this book.
2. Williamson (1994).
3. In Schiffer's version the conclusion is of form $\neg \forall x[A \rightarrow B]$ instead of $\exists x[A \wedge \neg B]$, but since he stipulates that the conditional is material and shows no tendency to dispute normal quantifier interchange rules or double-negation elimination, this difference is presumably not significant.
4. If it seems puzzling that III and its negation both lead to essentially the same problem, it may help to reflect on the negation of an instance of excluded middle: *not-(p or not-p)*. This certainly implies *not-p* (the negation of a disjunction certainly implies the negation of the first disjunct), and that in turn certainly implies *p or not-p* (a disjunction is certainly implied by its second disjunct). So the negation of an instance of excluded middle implies that instance, by reasoning that would be very hard to contest; and so if accepting an instance of excluded middle leads to problems, accepting its negation leads to the very same problems.
5. If validity is a purely formal notion, the 'unrestrictedly' is unnecessary: the view is that *no* sentence of form *p or not-p* is valid, though of course those in which the disjuncts display no relevant vagueness are true and are appropriate to use as non-logical premises in arguments. But some people may prefer to speak of those instances of excluded middle in which the disjuncts display no relevant vagueness as valid, and I have formulated the claim in the text so as to accommodate them. I doubt that there is more than a verbal issue here.
6. One sometimes hears people advocate another means of avoiding the conclusion that some classically valid arguments are invalid: they say that classical logic is not properly applied in situations where vagueness may matter. This way of 'saving' classical logic seems wholly uninteresting—one can always 'save' a logic from revision by declaring that cases that seem problematic for it aren't really in its scope—and Schiffer doesn't display any tendency to go in that direction.
7. 'Determinate' here is used not in accordance with the supervaluationist theory, but in a sense that Schiffer explains and that I will get to shortly. For now it suffices to say that to call a theory not determinately true does not imply that it isn't true, but does imply that it can't rationally be believed with certainty under ideal conditions, and that one can't rationally have even a positive *standard* degree of belief in it under ideal conditions.
8. If one of the senses *is* 'the one really meant' by the ordinary folk, I think ascertaining which one it is that has this status would require an exquisite faculty of distinguishing meaning from deep theoretical commitment or presupposition—a faculty not all that far removed from the faculty of detecting the cutoff between the rich and non-rich, whose absence the epistemic theorist bemoans.

9. I don't think this exhausts Schiffer's rationale for hand-wringing: that seems to be partly based also on his view (i) that there is a reasonably clear contrast between analysing a concept and reforming it, (ii) that the requirements for analysing it are fairly stringent, and (iii) that a philosopher should only be happy if he can analyse it.
10. I say *embeddable* conditionals because an explication of 'valid' in terms of a conditional must explain the use of 'valid' not only in atomic sentences but also in the scope of other operators.
11. Which has recently been given a vigorous defense by Tim Maudlin: *Truth and Paradox*, Oxford University Press 2004.
12. At least, this is so on Schiffer's conception of indeterminacy, on which the rules for determinate truth, determinate falsity, and indeterminacy behave compositionally as in the strong Kleene truth tables.
13. I'm assuming that the premises and conclusion are stated in a language whose only logical connectives are those under discussion in Schiffer's current chapter, namely the Kleene connectives.
14. When I made the point in a seminar a couple of years ago, I restricted it to arguments in which the conclusion is not among the premises. I'm grateful to Cian Dorr for pointing out that that restriction is completely unnecessary.
15. One might weaken Schiffer's claim a bit, by dropping the 'owe' rhetoric and simply saying that in cases where the antecedent and consequent of a conditional aren't both determinately true then the conditional is determinately true only if the antecedent "determinately metaphysically or physically entails" the consequent. That would be enough to undermine my argument that the inference from p to p or q comes out not determinately valid for Schiffer, but it would not be enough to settle that it was determinately valid on his theory. I guess you could say that that inference wouldn't be *determinately determinately* valid; no inference would.
16. Schiffer does however think that for the classical partition {p, *not-p*}, the vagueness-related degrees of belief can never sum to more than 1 (and must sum to exactly 1 when p is a clearly borderline proposition).
17. This pair of claims follows by (ii) from the claim that in clear borderline cases, V[*not-(p or not-p)*] = 1−V[*p or not-p*], which appears to be part of what's asserted in the negation law on 218. This assumes that p or *not-p* counts as borderline when p does. But since V[*p or not-p*] is taken to be the maximum of V[p] and V[*not-p*], and hence ½ in the paradigm case where V[p] is ½, I have little doubt that this is what Schiffer intends.
18. It is possible to give up (i) without giving up (ii): the resulting view has a bit of the flavor of supervaluationism. It is a slight improvement on supervaluationism, I think, in that it can be used to give non-circular content to claims about indeterminacy; and on this basis, I once advocated it: Field (2000). But I soon came to realize that the deepest problems with supervaluationism can't be avoided as long as (ii) is maintained. (For my own view on this and other matters related to this paper, see Field (2003) and Field (2004).)
19. Schiffer regards vagueness as a species of indeterminacy, so for vagueness a further condition is required; I won't discuss this.
20. Presumably when he says that it's possible for someone to have a VPB* in p, he means that it's possible for someone to do so with 'the facts as regards p itself' being as they actually are. That is, it's no objection to what he intends that even if p is perfectly determinate, it might have been the case *both that p is indeterminate and that someone had a VPB* that reflected this indeterminacy*.
21. Another worry is that the question of whether the conditions are ideal is a normative question, which obviously can't be cashed out in reliabilist terms (the frequency with which beliefs formed in these conditions are true) since we are dealing with beliefs that may be indeterminate. In a later chapter Schiffer argues that normative claims of this sort

are indeterminate. It would seem, then, that he must hold that it's indeterminate whether the conditions under which the Dummett-like philosopher adopts a high VPB in Napoleon's being less than six feet tall are ideal. From that it would seem to follow that irrespective of the quality of the anti-realist argument, this (and all other) questions about the past aren't *determinately* determinate.

22. Moreover, if Schiffer is right in claiming that the indeterminacy of *p* implies the indeterminacy of *p or not-p*, as I think he is, then it is indeterminate whether '*p*' is either true or false.

23. If it still seems weird to call an inference valid and yet refrain from asserting that it is necessarily truth-preserving, consider the following. A professional magician claims to be able to 'preserve evenness,' in the following sense: you write down whatever you like on a card, in secret, and he'll then write down a single numeral, and he claims that he will have written the name of an even number if and only if you have written at least one term standing for an even natural number. You write down 'the number of nanoseconds between the start of Ashcroft's life and the start of Falwell's,' and he writes '0.' It seems indeterminate whether he's preserved evenness. But a natural response is that once you consider cases like this, you'll see that the statement of the goal was too strong: all he really should have claimed is that *in any totally clear case of your either referring to an even number or not doing so*, he will write an even number iff you do.

24. E.g. in Łukasiewicz continuum valued logic, this will hold of any sentence with value ½. More generally, in any logic designed to not only handle vagueness but also allow for a naive truth theory in face of the paradoxes, it will hold of sentences that assert their own untruth: for if L is such a sentence, the naive truth theory will imply that $True(<L>)$ *if and only if not-True(<L>)*, so this classical contradiction will be taken to be clearly true.

Bibliography

Field, H. (2000). "Indeterminacy, Degree of Belief and Excluded Middle." *Noûs* 34: 1–30.
Field, H. (2003). "No Fact of the Matter." *Australasian Journal of Philosophy* 81: 457–80.
Field, H. (2004). "The Semantic Paradoxes and the Paradoxes of Vagueness." In *Liars and Heaps*, edited by J. C. Beall, Oxford: Oxford University Press.
Schiffer, S. (2003). *The Things We Mean*. Oxford: Clarendon Press.
Williamson, T. (1994). *Vagueness*. London: Routledge.

10

On the Characterization of Borderline Cases

Crispin Wright

It is a great pleasure to have the opportunity to contribute to this volume dedicated to the critical celebration of Stephen Schiffer's very considerable philosophical achievements. My focus will be on his recent work on vagueness.[1]

The broad direction of Schiffer's researches in this area has been to give priority to what we may call the *characterization problem*: the problem of saying what the vagueness of expressions of natural language consists in or, more specifically—since Schiffer takes it as a given that the vagueness he is targeting consists in a propensity of vague expressions to give rise to borderline cases—the problem of saying what being a borderline case of the concept expressed by a vague expression consists in. This has not been a main preoccupation of most of the work in the field since the vagueness 'boom' started in the mid-1970s. There has been a tendency to jump straight into devising semantic theories for vague languages, usually aimed at the twin desiderata of saving classical logic and dissolving the various paradoxes of vagueness, with a principal focus on the standard sorites, and occasional glances at the Forced March, and others.[2] Of course, such work has inevitably implicated commitment to broad conceptions of vagueness, and of borderline cases, of various kinds. The classical epistemicist approach, for example, conceives of borderline cases as instances whose correct classification in terms of the relevant concept is, for reasons it attempts to explain, unknowable. Semantic indeterminist approaches, by contrast, tend (often implicitly) to conceive of borderline cases as items to which the concept in question neither applies nor fails to apply and as coming about because our practice with the concept leaves it, in effect, merely partially defined and so 'gappy.' A variation on this, still semantic indeterminist, regards vagueness as consisting in a phenomenon akin to divided reference, whereby a predicate, for example, may be associated with a range of extensionally distinct *best candidates* to be the property it refers to; borderline cases are then items which exemplify some but not all of these properties. Finally some have attempted to see vagueness as constituted *in rebus*—in the world, rather than in meaning or in our ignorance: being a borderline case, so viewed, is a matter of being situated within a penumbra, as it were, like the position of a point between the light and the dark in the image cast by an intense but blurred shadow.[3] Generally speaking, however, proponents of these various kinds of view have not devoted the same degree of attention to elucidating and defending their (implicit) commitments concerning the nature of vagueness and borderline cases as they have devoted to the development of formal semantical theories, and to criticizing opposing views and attempting to address the paradoxes. Yet one would naturally suppose that the characterization problem should be a locus of developed discussion rather than one of presupposition. For until we have a properly argued account of what vagueness is, how can one possibly expect to know what kind of semantic theory for vague expressions might be best motivated, let alone how the most appropriate kind of semantic theory might assist with the disarming of the sorites paradox and other problems?

I find much to agree with in both the general approach and the details of Schiffer's work on the problems of vagueness. We concur, first and foremost, in prioritizing the question of the nature of vagueness and the characterization of borderline cases—though I confess to being a little less confident than Schiffer that it is possible, or necessary, to accomplish this in an exceptionless, biconditional formulation. We are also agreed in rejecting standard semantic indeterminist, epistemicist, and *in rebus* views, proposing instead that the characterization of vagueness will best proceed, broadly, in terms of aspects of the distinctive attitudinal psychology involved in the exercise of judgement involving vague concepts. And we are at one in repudiating 'third possibility' conceptions of borderline cases: conceptions according to which borderline case propositions—propositions ascribing a vague concept, or its contrary, to items in the borderline area of the concept in question—enjoy a status inconsistent with that of simple truth, or simple falsity. Examples of third possibility status include lack of truth value, the possession of a third truth value, the possession of any of a range of intermediate truth values, and the (dialetheist) idea that they possess both (polar) truth values.

Significant differences, though, remain. Some of the more major concern the epistemic status of borderline cases—in particular Schiffer subscribes to the widespread view of *Verdict Exclusion* (VE), viz. that (it is known that) no polar verdict about a borderline case proposition is knowledgeable. We also disagree about the kind of attitudinal psychological story to try to tell about borderline cases: Schiffer holds that it should give a central place to his notion of *vagueness-related partial belief* (VPB), although he finds some merit in my notion of *quandary*;[4] whereas I would prefer to centralize the notion of quandary, although I think there is insight contained in Schiffer's notion of VPB. Third, although neither of us is prepared straightforwardly to endorse the use of classical logic in reasoning with vague concepts, Schiffer proposes no alternative, holding merely that it is indeterminate whether certain principles of classical logic—including, strikingly, modus ponens—hold good for reasoning among vague judgements, whereas I have argued that the strongest logic justified for such reasoning would involve qualification of the law of excluded middle for atomic statements and of double negation elimination for compound ones (and so approximate an intuitionistic logic).

The considerations to follow will focus on these points of disagreement. They are offered in a spirit of collaboration, in the hope of furthering progress towards the best possible version of the broad genre of account to which Stephen and I are both drawn.[5]

10.1 Vagueness-Related Partial Belief

It is plausible enough that in the passage along the elements of a typical sorites series for a predicate F, we pass from cases where we are completely confident in the correctness of the verdict, 'F,' through a region where our satisfaction with any particular verdict is qualified and much diminished and then on to a region where confidence builds again in the contrary of the original verdict culminating, as the series progresses, in complete satisfaction once more. I think the phenomenology of whatever it is that seemingly decreases and then increases again in this way needs subtle description, and that it may not be most felicitous to regard it as a form of partial *belief*. But I don't think Schiffer fundamentally disagrees about that. What is striking is that the attitude involved, although allowing of degree, seems to differ from *standard partial belief* (SPB) or credence in a number of respects. As Schiffer observes, credences greater than 0 but less than 1 are typically based on evidence which is conceived of as falling short of the best possible evidence, and so are often attended by a conception of how the relevant evidence might be improved. They also tend to be associated with beliefs about likelihood: to believe to some quite high degree that it will rain tomorrow will tend to be to believe (absolutely) that it is quite likely that it will rain tomorrow. Neither of these features is replicated by the kind of partial satisfaction, or confidence, one may have in a verdict that applies a vague concept to a case that lies outside its polar regions but is, say, rather closer to one than the other. But the defining and single most striking feature of VPB is its apparent departure from the laws of classical probability. Classically, my confidence in the conjunction of a pair of (independent) propositions in each of which I place merely partial confidence should approximate the product of the degrees of belief thereby reposed in the conjuncts—and so, when both those degrees are quite small, should be very small. But it does not seem that we would be inclined to regard a conjunction whose conjuncts were a pair of independent propositions, each ascribing a vague property to a more or less 'central' borderline case of it, as very much less credible than its conjuncts. Indeed there seems no clear sense in which it would be rational to be any less confident about the conjunction than about the conjuncts. Imagine a cube of a metal which gradually changes color as it changes temperature—though neither as a result of the other—and suppose it comes to sit simultaneously on the borderlines between red and orange and between warm and hot. Imagine we find we have no preference for the verdict 'Cube is warm' over 'Cube is hot' and vice versa; and similarly with respect to the verdicts, 'Cube is orange' and 'Cube is red.' It does not seem likely that asked whether we would assent to 'Cube is orange and Cube is warm' we would feel any more negative about doing so than about assent to the individual conjuncts.[6] And no reason is apparent why we should.

The nature of this kind of partial confidence, or satisfaction—for in truth I am not sure how best to represent it—could certainly stand further clarification. What exactly is it that varies in degree, and how may the variation be measured? Betting behavior, a classic recourse for the explanation of the functional role of standard partial belief, is obviously inappropriate here since there is no question of an "outcome" where a borderline case is concerned—so nothing to bet on. But although it is arguable that Schiffer has (so far) left issues to do with the functional role and explanatory potential of VPB less clear than is desirable, I think it is hard to dismiss the phenomenon and that the prima facie case for its reality is strong. The question is whether it can take the weight that Schiffer wants to place upon it in his account of vagueness.

About that I continue to have misgivings. Schiffer's strategy is to try to characterize borderline cases directly in terms of the notion of VPB. More accurately, it is to characterize them in terms of the notion of VPB*—vagueness-related partial belief formed under epistemically ideal circumstances. I have already noted elsewhere[7] certain difficulties with the proposal developed in Schiffer (2003), to which Schiffer has since responded.[8] I won't pursue the detail of that particular discussion here, but will outline a more general, though related consideration.

Even if we take the notion of VPB, and its characteristically non-classical behavior, to be adequately clear, and attested for Schiffer's purposes, any claim that it is of the essence of grasping vague concepts to be prone to VPB with respect to appropriate judgements that involve them looks to be too strong on at least two counts.[9] Consider first the case of Tim. Tim passes, by any reasonable tests, as a master of a wide range of vague concepts expressible in his natural language. But he has persuaded himself, by a variety of more or less philosophically questionable moves, of the correctness of the classical epistemicist conception of vagueness. Accordingly, he conceives of each of the vague expressions in his language as expressing a property (or other appropriate form of semantic value) that actually has a completely sharply bounded extension. The effect is that although his atomic vague judgements are perfectly orthodox, he is very insistent on the use of classical logic in reasoning with vague judgements and very confident about the principle of bivalence as applied to them. Moreover, and crucially, although his satisfaction with/confidence in the vague (atomic) judgements that he makes varies in degree after the broad manner of VPB, he does—as he should—regard the conjunction of hard cases as increasing the risk of error, and so *is* prone to 'multiply down'—to reject conjunctions in cases where he is not prepared to flat out reject either of the (independent) conjuncts. It would be, I think, strained to insist that Tim's superstitions about the semantics of vague expressions are inconsistent with his perfectly well understanding them—with his fully possessing the concepts that they express. Rather he is making a *philosophical* mistake—the history of the philosophy of language is littered with such mistakes—about the kind of meanings possessed by expressions which he perfectly well understands. But if that is the right description of him, it is not of the essence of a grasp of vague concepts to enter into attitudes of VPB towards certain judgements involving them.

Alternatively, consider Hugh, an individual who is *maximally opinionated*.[10] Hugh's opinions know no half measures. If he takes a view about anything, he takes it with complete conviction. Yet the pattern and spread of his judgements involving vague concepts are otherwise normal. Thus, in the borderline region, of some concept, he sometimes has no view, or returns a verdict inconsistent with one he has given before—in which case he takes the line that what he said before was 'completely wrong.' He may even display signs of hesitancy in judging borderline cases—but if he finally overcomes it and is moved to judgement, that judgement is once again completely confident. In short, while the extensional profile of Hugh's judgements involving vague concepts is normal, there is none of the phenomenology of partial belief. And again, it would seem an overreaction to the case to view this psychological quirk as calling into question Hugh's grasp of the concepts concerned.

I think these cases show that while Schiffer is correct to have emphasized the role of something akin to partial belief in the normal attitudinal psychology of vague judgement—and deserves credit for the insight that this kind of partial belief may, perfectly rationally, display the non-classical features he emphasizes—it is wrong to see it as belonging to the nature of the understanding of vague concepts to involve a disposition to partial belief of this kind, or to write it into the possession-conditions for vague concepts that one should be so inclined.

10.2 Verdict Exclusion

'Verdict' is here a term of art. A *verdict* about a statement involving a vague concept is a judgement that it takes one in particular of the two polar values, true and false. The thesis of *Verdict Exclusion* (VE) is that for borderline cases of the concept concerned, no such verdict can be an expression of knowledge. Concerning VE itself, three possible views are relevant: (i) that it is known to be false—so known that knowledgeable verdicts, of truth or falsity respectively, are possible for, say, predications of a vague concept of its borderline cases; (ii) that it is known to be true—so known that borderline cases are cases where knowledge of the relevant kind of verdict is impossible; and (iii) agnosticism—that neither view about the status of VE is mandated. Schiffer's view is (ii), a contention that he finds intuitive and regards as enforced in any case by the role of VPB in the individuation of borderline cases.[11] I, by contrast, believe that the correct stance overall is (iii): we should be agnostic about the possibility of knowledgeable verdicts in borderline cases.

The disagreement is crucial. Verdict Exclusion is no less a nodal issue for the proper characterization of vagueness than Third Possibility, in whose rejection Schiffer and I, as noted, concur. In my view, a repudiation of both Third Possibility and Verdict Exclusion—that is, a rejection of both theses as *unjustified*—belongs with a more general *liberal* stance concerning the epistemic nature of borderline cases. In this section, I will outline some motivations for liberalism and defend it against certain objections, including some of Schiffer's. However, what I take to be Schiffer's principal reason for endorsing VE—and hence for rejecting liberalism—has to do with his conception of VPB as independently excluding potentially knowledgeable *belief*.[12] The issues around that impress me as very difficult, and I must reserve discussion of them for another occasion.

Schiffer and I are both impressed by the datum that ordinary speakers do not treat the borderline area of a vague distinction as one where competence mandates silence or suppression of any inclination to offer a verdict, however qualified. If something is on the borderline between red and orange, say, it won't call your competence with those concepts—or your eyes—into question if you are inclined to describe it as red, or for that matter as orange. One is *entitled*, if one is so moved, to a verdict in the borderline area, so entitled—presumably—to the opinion which that verdict expresses.

A perhaps more forceful expression of this entitlement intuition—since free of any demand on one's preferred understanding of 'borderline cases'—is this. Consider any typical soritical series running from clear instances of F to clear instances of non-F by steps small enough to service a sorites paradox as plausible as any. Then—this is the intuition—there will be no element of this series about which it is *mandatory* to return neither the verdict 'F' nor the verdict 'non-F.' A polar verdict is always permissible provided it is sincere; there are no cases that mandate a third possibility type of response. If someone prefers to understand 'borderline case' in such a way that the knowledge that something is a borderline case ought to inhibit any verdict, then a way of expressing the entitlement intuition is that there are no clear— definite—borderline cases in a typical sorites series. The clear cases on the other hand are those where only one polar verdict is permissible.

Liberalism is the simplest theoretical accommodation of the entitlement intuition. It is the view that it is always permissible to return a verdict about a borderline case simply because it is—in a sense we need to clarify—*open* what to think about such cases and open, indeed, whether in thinking one thing in particular, you are knowledgeable. This openness is, at a minimum, what goes with agnosticism about Third Possibility and Verdict Exclusion respectively: if neither thesis is justified, there is no call to stifle aspects of our natural practice and inclinations to judgement that would be inappropriate if they were true.[13]

Let me quickly summarize some considerations which I take to support liberalism and then—in the next section—respond to some objections to it. First, to emphasize the implausibility of the idea of a datum of Third Possibility. If Third Possibility were known to obtain, even if in just one case, we would know that any polar opinion about that case was mistaken. But we do not behave as though we think we know any such thing: someone who returns a (perhaps suitably qualified) polar verdict about a borderline case is never thereby automatically treated as revealing a mistake, or incompetence—rather we feel, to repeat, that they are, *ceteris paribus*, precisely entitled to their opinion. The manifestations of judgement of borderline cases include hesitation, inability to form an opinion, weakness of opinion, instability of opinion, and conflict among judges whose competence is not in question. But convergence in patterns of hesitation, or non-opinion, still less any sense that 'no opinion' is sometimes the uniquely appropriate response, is at best contingently (and doubtfully) involved. Mastery of a vague concept seems to involve no essential exercise of a concept of any kind of third possibility.

Now to Verdict Exclusion. If VE were known to obtain, even if in just one case, we would know that any polar opinion about that case was, whatever else, not the product of a successful feat of cognition. It would be something caused, no doubt, by relevant features of the case but not a fitting cognitive response to them. And if VE were known to obtain generally in the borderline area, then our propensity to verdicts—albeit weak and unstable verdicts—about cases lying within it would seem to amount to no more than a kind of cognitive incontinence. It seems that to know such a thing about opinions one is inclined to form should have the effect of undermining them. So knowledge of Verdict Exclusion is also in tension with the entitlement intuition. Our sense is that no matter what case in a sorites series we consider, it is consistent with full perceptual and conceptual competence if someone takes a (perhaps suitably qualified but) polar view of it. There are no cases, even towards the 'middle,' where it is *eo ipso* incompetent to have a (suitably qualified) polar view. However a presumption of knowledgeability—or at least warrant—is a condition of rational opinion: for a rational judge, judging that P is judging that P is what one *ought* to think. But one who thinks that VE is known says in effect that we know that there is no mandate for opinion in some cases in a sorites series—there is, in borderline cases, nothing that ought to be thought. In such cases, thinking that P is what one ought to think, is therefore *mistaken*. VE thus has the effect that opinions which, according to the entitlement intuition, are consistent with competence, are ungrounded and hence *not* competent. If VE is part of the best theory of vagueness, then the best theory is one according to which our actual practice in all but definite cases is irrational/incompetent. It is hard to envisage that a *best* theory should have that feature.

Finally, there are difficulties for VE involved in its interaction with principles of *Evidential Constraint* (EC). The best formulation of the latter for any particular type of judgement is doubtless going to be controversial. But EC is undeniably intuitive for secondary qualities generally and for a wide class of predicates of casual observation—'heap,' 'bald,' etc.—that foster sorites paradoxes. We are not, intuitively, up for the idea of baldness that cannot be recognized as such in principle, or heaps whose heaphood would elude the detection of even the most fortunately situated judge. Yet if Verdict Exclusion were known to obtain, even if in just one case, we would know that EC—in the form of the two conditionals:

If P, then it is feasible to know P

If not-P, then it is feasible to know not-P

—would have to fail in that case (on pain of the obvious contradiction).

This, it seems to me, is simply too strong a result to swallow. Maybe EC is controversial,[14] and perhaps it is implausible for certain vague expressions.[15] But it is already a problem if it is not implausible for all—since our knowledge of VE is being supposed to be characteristic of borderline cases without exception: if VE and EC are (known to be) inconsistent, the plausibility of taking VE to be known for an arbitrary vague predicate, say, is hostage to that of taking it that we actually know that EC fails for it. The proponent of VE owes an explanation of what he takes the content of this knowledge to be. And if it is, as naturally construed, that colors, baldness, heaps, and so on can all be undetectable, even under unimprovable conditions of observation, then I do not think we do know anything of the sort, for a very wide class of vague concepts.[16]

10.3 Stabilizing Liberalism

On the other side, there are a number of more or less intuitive objections to liberalism, some amounting to direct arguments for VE. While the matter requires a much fuller treatment than I have space for here, I'll try to address at least some of the anti-liberal considerations known to me and point up some of the issues on which further clarity is needed.

Schiffer himself[17] offers two intuitive thoughts on behalf of VE. The first, very simply, is that

> it's as much of a platitude to say that
>
> If someone knows that S, then it's determinately true that S
>
> as it is to say that
>
> If someone knows that S, then S.[18]

Assuming the standard kind of characterization of S's being borderline, viz. that it is neither determinately true that S nor determinately true that not-S, it follows that no one ever knows a borderline S. But I reply that Schiffer's platitude is clearly that only if 'determinately' carries the sense of a kind of particle of emphasis, like 'actually' in one common kind of use, or 'indeed.' When it is so understood, to characterize a borderline case for S as a situation where it is neither determinately true that S nor determinately true that not-S is, in effect, to endorse Third Possibility—which Schiffer does not.

Schiffer's second intuitive thought invites us to reflect

> on one's epistemic position when confronted with what one knows to be a borderline proposition. Suppose that you are holding a ball in your hands in circumstances that are as good as you can conceive of them getting for judging the ball's color. You are certain you know what color the ball is, whether or not you have a word for that color in your vocabulary; you know that you have mastery of the concept of red; and you know with certainty that the color you know the ball to have is not one you can now justifiably say either is or is not red. Furthermore, you cannot even *conceive* of how, given all you know, you could come to have warrant for judging either that the ball is red, or that it isn't red. You rightly take yourself to be in the best possible position to verify whether or not the ball is red, and you can't imagine what you could conceivably find out that would give you knowledge that the ball was, or wasn't, red. Given all that, I would think that you would be entirely justified in thinking that it's impossible, given the obtaining facts, for you, or anyone else, to know whether or not the ball is red. Examples involving any other sorites-prone concept can be used to make the same point.[19]

I think the portion of this up to but excluding the last two sentences nicely characterizes some of the phenomenology of quandary.[20] It is indeed in such a situation hard to conceive of any improvement in one's epistemic position which one could foresee would sway the balance. But to find oneself unmoved to an opinion by evidence of which one has no clear conception of a possible improvement justifies the claim that there is no knowing in the case in question only if one knows, first, that one's lack of a clear concept of a possible improvement is an indicator that there is no possible improvement—which raises interesting issues which I will not here go into—and, more crucially, second, that one's present evidence is not enough for knowledge: that had one been moved to a verdict on the basis of the very same experience and collateral beliefs, one's present quandary discloses that being so moved would have been inappropriate, rather than the other way round. But you don't know that. Had you in the same circumstances been moved—marginally—to the opinion that the ball is red, it would go with that opinion to think that coming to no view in the same circumstances would—marginally—underplay the evidence. Do you know now that that would be an inappropriate reaction?

Here next is an argument[21] that purports to commit liberalism to an actual contradiction. Suppose that Aye and Nay come to different (but suitably qualified) polar verdicts about a borderline case of F. Liberalism—specifically, agnosticism about VE—seems committed to saying that it is not known that Aye is not knowledgeable, and it is not known that Nay is not knowledgeable. But this pair of claims, given only uncontroversial proof-theoretic properties of knowledge, is unstable. For the latter claim seems to imply that

$\sim K(\sim K\sim(Fk))$,

and the former that

$\sim K(\sim K(Fk))$

And from these, given factivity and closure for 'K,' we get, by elementary moves, that

$\sim K(Fk)$ & $\sim K\sim(Fk)$

So: on the—apparently—liberal supposition that it is not known that either polar verdict is not knowledgeable, we appear to have shown that neither polar verdict *is* knowledgeable! This conclusion will go for all polar disagreements about borderline cases. So in no such disagreement is any knowledgeable opinion involved, just as VE requires, and contrary to liberalism.

I think the right reaction to this objection is that it points up the need for a distinction in the interpretation of the various occurrences of the operator 'K.' Liberalism indeed cannot be coherently expressed otherwise. But what distinction? The general idea is that we try to be open to the possibility that any particular opinion about a borderline case may be knowledgeable, including both one's own, if one has one, and that, possibly conflicting, of others. But obviously, if Aye's opinion is that P, then she ought to think that anyone who thinks otherwise is wrong, so not knowledgeable. What liberalism requires is that, consistently with thinking that he doesn't know, Aye should somehow nevertheless allow that Nay *could* be knowledgeable, even thinking what he actually does in the world as it actually is. What is the modality there?

It's the same as that whereby, when you hold any opinion of which you are not entirely sure, you may concede, consistently with retaining that opinion, that you *could* be wrong. I carefully count the marbles in a bag, and get a largish number. If I am right about the number, then given the way I arrived at my belief—by a careful count—it seems reasonable to say that I know what it is. But perhaps you nag me that even careful counts can involve error when largish numbers are involved, and I am thereby moved to concede that I could be wrong. What is the content of that concession? It had better not be tantamount to the admission that I *do not* know—after all, my belief may be true and formed by careful execution of a reliable, indeed canonical method. So the concession needs to be weaker. But nor does it seem entirely happy to view me as admitting that I do not know that I know; for if we are understanding knowledge in enough of an externalist way to allow that I may still *actually* know the number of marbles in the bag, the thought invites itself that I may still (so to say, externally) actually know that I know that I do. A better suggestion is that what I concede is *the right to claim* to know. I opine that P but I do not claim to know that P, though nor do I admit that I do not know it.

So, let's try that distinction in the context of Aye and Nay: Aye's opinion that P commits her to holding that Nay does not know not-P; but Nay's knowing not-P is nevertheless consistent with everything that Aye regards herself as *in position to claim to know*—since she does not regard herself as in position to claim to know P. Nay's knowing not-P is a possibility for Aye in that somewhat qualified sense of epistemic possibility. Again, this is not the same as saying that it is consistent with everything Aye *in fact* knows—not if one thing she may in fact know is P.

The crucial thing is thus that, when moved to a verdict in the borderline area, one is in no position to *claim to know* (although still in position to consider that one may know). This requires, to stress, that the things which one is in position to claim to know are a potentially narrower class than those which in fact one does know. Indeed it requires, I readily acknowledge, a more general account of the notion of one's 'being in position to claim' and an explanation of its potential to carry a narrower extension than one's actual knowledge. I do believe in the good standing of and need for such a notion, but I cannot argue for that here.[22]

To review the original argument in the light of this distinction. Let 'RP' express that one is in position to claim to know P. Then the ingredients in the liberal supposition become

$\sim$R($\sim$K$\sim$P), and
$\sim$R($\sim$KP)

Given that R is closed, (and K factive) we still get

$\sim$RP and $\sim$R$\sim$P

But that is now no problem—just the (agnostic) result that no one is in position to claim knowledge of a verdict in a borderline case.

To summarize, both the following liberal-seeming claims—

1. No one is in position to know that any polar verdict about a borderline case is, just in virtue of its subject matter and specific polarity, not knowledgeable.

2. No one should commit themselves to thinking that any particular polar verdict about a borderline case is, just in virtue of its subject matter and specific polarity, not knowledgeable.

—are incoherent and are no part of the commitments of liberalism. The first commits one who endorses it to the premises of the Aye-Nay reductio. The second is inconsistent with the entitlement intuition, since anyone who takes a polar view of a borderline case naturally commits themselves to thinking that the opposing view is false, and therefore not knowledgeable. What, I am suggesting, *is* a commitment of liberalism is this:

3. No one is in position to claim to know that any polar verdict about a borderline case is, just in virtue of its subject matter and specific polarity, not knowledgeable.

We are entitled, when so moved, to have polar opinions about borderline cases. When we do, we are committed to thinking that such contrary opinions are not true, and so not knowledgeable. But we are in no position to claim to know that a given such opinion is not true, or not knowledgeable. And we are also in no position to claim to know that a given such opinion is true, or is knowledgeable.

There is one final powerful-looking extant argument in favour of VE, and hence antithetical to liberalism. It is Timothy Williamson's argument that inexact knowledge requires a *margin for error*, with the latter notion understood in such a way as to entail that cases within a fixed margin of difference from a case known to be F are likewise F. This enforces the negation of the claim that all the EC-conditionals of the form,

If Fk, then it is feasible to know that Fk,

for k an element in a given sorites series, are true.[23] It does not, except classically, enforce the idea that some in particular are false; it does not, except classically, even preclude thinking that there is none that is false; nor does it force us to conceive of the falsity of such a conditional as consisting in the F-ness of the relevant k but unfeasibility of knowledge that Fk. There is therefore a project, for those, like the present author, for whom intuitionistic distinctions will be respected in the logic of choice for vague statements, of exploring whether or the extent to which Williamson's argument might somehow be stopped short of full-out contradiction with liberalism. But my own expectation is that something will have to give here. Williamson's proposal is driven by two thoughts: (i) that knowledge requires reliability of the relevant method of belief formation, and (ii) that in creatures of limited powers of discrimination, reliable detection of a characteristic will be compromised if changes too slight for them to discriminate can make the difference between its applying and its failing to apply. There is evident merit in both thoughts. Where there may be room for maneuver is over whether, as best understood, they properly combine to enforce the general truth of Williamson's putative corollary, that cases within a fixed margin of difference from a case known to be F are likewise F. But the matter needs a careful separate treatment—something I cannot embark on here.[24]

Specific arguments apart, it is clear that there is a strong intuitive pull, felt by many philosophers of very different theoretical predispositions about vagueness, to accept VE. What is the root of it? One motivation, undoubtedly, is the intuitive predilection for Third Possibility conceptions of borderline cases. Another is the questionable idea that knowledge requires subjective certainty, coupled with the thought that the borderline region is one of often tentative, uncertain opinion. A third would regard the characteristic instability of opinions in the borderline region as disqualifying them as knowledge—but that wouldn't justify the modal component in VE: those drawn to it are unlikely to feel any better about a verdict about a borderline case which just happened to be stable. My guess is that the single most powerful pretheoretic motive for endorsement of VE is the idea that the opposed contention, that knowledge in borderline cases is possible, owes a concrete conception of a number of matters that present as moot, to say the least—indeed as imponderable. What kind of fact could it be that a case on the borderline of 'red' is actually red? Won't one need recourse to something approaching the epistemicist's idea of inscrutable semantic mechanisms linking the predicate to a property of which we may have no adequate conception to make sense of such a fact? And if one goes in that direction, what would make an opinion that happened to coincide with the fact knowledgeable?

In short, it looks as though a worked out denial of VE will involve all the problems that discourage most from endorsing epistemicism, together with the additional baggage of explaining how the kind of sublimated facts in which epistemicism believes are in principle open to knowledge. But *if* this is the primary, most basic motive for endorsing VE, it should come with a sense of liberation to realize that a justifiable recoil from this cluster of issues and problems should actually motivate no such thing. We are not, in denying that VE is justified, affirming its negation. We incur none of the distinctive obligations of that affirmation. The liberal view is that we do not know VE; but nor do we claim to know that knowledge is possible in the borderline area. We have, accordingly, no obligation to provide a further account of the facts of which it would be knowledge or of how knowledge of them might be reached.

10.4 Quandary and the Characterization Problem

I turn to the question of whether the notion of quandary might be usefully deployed to address the characterization problem. An early decision needs to be taken about the form in which to try to address the problem, since there are several interrelated questions here. They include:

(1) In what does the vagueness of a vague expression consist?
(2) What is a borderline case object/item?
(3) What is a borderline proposition?

One natural proposal is to try to answer (3) first, after which the answers to questions (1) and (2) can respectively consist in elaboration of these two basic thoughts:

(1) That the vagueness of E consists in the fact that its presence in token utterances results, in certain circumstances, in their expression of borderline propositions;
(2) That a borderline case item is the subject of a borderline proposition.

The following remarks are offered under the aegis of this natural proposal.

In earlier work, I characterized the notion of a quandary as follows:[25]

Proposition P presents a thinker T with a Quandary in circumstances (of evaluation) C^{26} if and only if, in C,

(i) T does not know whether or not P
(ii) T does not know any way of knowing whether or not P
(iii) T does not know that there is any way of knowing whether or not P
(iv) T does not know that it is (metaphysically) possible to know whether or not P

I also suggested that it would be wrong to add

(v) T knows that it is not (metaphysically) possible to know whether or not P

for reasons included in and elaborated upon by the discussion of the preceding sections. It is a consequence of the proposal *sans* clause (v) that the less cognitively adept a thinker, the easier it will be to confront her with quandary—since she only has not to know various things. Indeed she doesn't even have to be able to wonder whether or not P. Clearly there is therefore no prospect of capturing the notion of a borderline proposition by reference to the propensities of actual thinkers to be put in quandary by it. We will need to consider thinkers of some degree of conceptual and cognitive sophistication.

A first shot at a characterization in terms of quandary of a borderline proposition might run as follows:

> P is borderline in circumstances C iff a conceptually and perceptually fully competent thinker T could be put in quandary by P in C

The intuitive thought is that, while quandary is never a mandated response to a borderline situation, it is always a *possible* one quite consistently with full and proper cognitive functioning and grasp of all relevant concepts. In a clear case, by contrast, to fall into quandary is *not* consistent with full and proper cognitive functioning in appropriate respects together with grasp of all relevant concepts, since the clear cases mandate a verdict. Notice that this strategy of characterization grants that quandary is not a characteristic mental state associated with the appraisal of a borderline proposition—not if 'characteristic' means widespread and typical. It is the *possibility* of quandary, consistently with full competence in all relevant respects, that is crucial, not the actual prevalence of it.

The first shot characterization, however, is still manifestly insufficient. The problem is that there are non vagueness-related quandaries. A thinker of arbitrary conceptual and perceptual—indeed, mathematical—competence may very well meet all four clauses with respect to Goldbach's Conjecture, for example: a proposition in which there is no relevant form of vagueness, and which accordingly has no claim to be a borderline proposition. And moral dilemmas hold out the prospect of another region of quandary: finding myself in a situation in which all possible courses of action conflict with one or another of my values, I may consider myself apprised of all relevant non-moral facts and quite reasonably be perfectly agnostic about the prospects of adjudicating between the competing values concerned. In that case P, i.e., some proposition of the form 'A is the best thing to do in the circumstances,' may very well present me with a quandary. True, there are almost certain to be vague concepts involved in P; but it seems likely to be a misdiagnosis of the source of the quandary posed by a moral dilemma to locate it there.

Goldbach's conjecture and the wider class of propositions that it represents—propositions, whether or not mathematical, for which we have no assurance of decidability—are, I think, easy to exclude by a well-motivated modification of the first shot proposal. What is striking about these cases is that quandary is mandated—a fully competent thinker *ought* to regard Goldbach as presenting a quandary. That is in crucial contrast to the situation of borderline cases, at least as construed by liberalism. So it looks as though the first shot should be followed by a second shot beginning like this:

P is borderline in circumstances C iff

(i) a conceptually and perceptually fully competent thinker T *could*, consistently with those competences, be put in quandary by P in C; and
(ii) Such a T is not *required* to be put in quandary by P in C; and...

—though only so beginning, since something now needs to be added to address the quandary of moral dilemma. There are other possible quandaries too: if one is persuaded of the possibility of faultless disagreement in matters of taste, for example, there looks to be potential for quandary in the situation of a bystander considering which of the protagonists in such a disagreement may be right.

There is now a tactical issue. We could proceed by trying to track through all possible varieties of quandary, hoping to find a clause for each to distinguish it from the vagueness-related cases. But it is not clear what degree of insight might be expected along that path. Better, if we can, to say something which captures the nature of vagueness-related quandary in one cast, as it were, thereby systematically contrasting it with all the other kinds. How might that be accomplished?

Here is a tempting thought: perhaps this is the place to re-invoke VPB. It is not implausible that either of the conflicting claims in a moral dilemma might—by one for whom it is not a dilemma—be endorsed as strongly as you like without any necessary implication of some form of incompetence. Likewise for the ingredient claims in a putatively faultless disagreement on a matter of taste. But can any thinker who is fully competent in relevant respects endorse a verdict about a vague judgement strongly—as strongly as you like—which, for another relevantly fully competent thinker, presents a quandary? In a borderline case, where quandary is consistent with competence, must not that fact surface in at least some, perhaps quite significant degree of qualification in the confidence of one who, as according to liberalism she is entitled, endorses a verdict? If so, we can add to the second shot along the following lines:

(iii) T is required to repose at most a relatively low degree of confidence VPB in P (or its negation) in C,

and hope thereby to have at least the overall shape of a successful characterization (even if further refinement will certainly be needed).

However, there is, if an earlier point is correct, a problem for this—the same problem caused by our friend Hugh and the possibility of 'maximal opinionation' for the general idea that VBP is a (non-contingently) characteristic mental state of vague judgement. If maximal opinionation is consistent with mastery of vague concepts, VPB is at most contingently so characteristic—and the requirement proposed in clause (iii) as formulated is not a requirement. I see no way round this objection at present.

What we should like to propose would be a clause that captured the idea that in borderline cases, a thinker who is put into quandary will be so *because of* the nature of the prevailing circumstances of evaluation and the vagueness of the judgement concerned: the quandary is an upshot of the vagueness. But of course to say that would be to surrender the project of accounting for the nature of vagueness in terms of the propensity to induce quandary in fully competent thinkers—rather we will have slipped into thinking of vagueness as an underlying cause of the attitude of quandary, whose nature will therefore have to be explained independently.[27]

Surely, though, the basic thought has to be right that it goes with the nature of the kind of vagueness we are concerned with that quandary may be induced without demanding explanation by defective cognitive or conceptual competence. And when quandary is so induced, it is presumably induced by *something*. The project of attempting a broadly attitudinal-psychological response to the characterization problem means that we cannot rest content with an account of the cause that involves an unreconstructed appeal to the vagueness of the proposition concerned. But it may quite properly appeal to a certain kind of characteristic property of the relevant circumstances of evaluation—if we can find one. And surely we can. The very form of the sorites paradox itself provides the means. All the vague concepts with which we are concerned are, after all, sorites-prone—that defines the kind of vagueness with which we are concerned. And every sorites paradox involves gradual change in the values of some parameter, Π, with the following characteristic: that there is a finite strict ordering of such values whose early instances provide for clear cases of F and whose later ones for clear cases of its contrary. The kind of quandary distinctive of vagueness is one induced by this process of gradual change—or more accurately, since quandary is not restricted to soritical contexts, one induced, in the circumstances in question, by the value for the relevant parameter taken by the object of the judgement that presents a quandary. Call such a parameter a *parameter of supervenience* for F. For *bald*, a parameter of supervenience will be number and distribution of hairs on the scalp; for *heap of sand*, a parameter of supervenience will be number and arrangement of grains of sand; for *red*, a parameter of supervenience will be color. I take it these ideas are sufficiently clear for the present purpose.

Perhaps, then, the following clauses point in a potentially profitable direction:

P is borderline in circumstances C iff P configures some concept F for which Π is a parameter of supervenience such that

(i) A conceptually and perceptually fully competent thinker T *could* be put in quandary for P in C by the value taken by Π in C; and

(ii) A conceptually and perceptually fully competent thinker T is not *required* to be put in quandary for P in C.

However, it is important to keep in mind the general pressures from which this proposal springs. In general there is no hope, I think, of a successful characterization of vagueness in terms of the attitudinal states of those who make vague judgements unless we include *some* form of causal constraint on the provenance of these states. Any successful such account will therefore be bipartite: it will proffer some putatively distinctive attitudinal feature(s) of vague judgement and it will tie significant instantiations of it/them to causes that are somehow an essential feature of the broader landscape of vague judgement. What I have suggested in this section is merely a rather simple-minded illustration of this model: the selected distinctive feature is the association of vagueness with judgemental paralysis in certain circumstances—glossed as quandary—and the relevant feature of the broader landscape is the value taken by the parameter, gradually shifting in a suitable sorites paradox, on which instantiation and non-instantiation of the relevant vague concept supervenes.

It remains to observe that if VPB is a well-conceived phenomenon at all—which I do not doubt—then there has of course to be scope for other versions of this general form of bipartite proposal which seek to centralize it, rather than quandary as characterized. Such versions will presumably be more congenial to Schiffer and may well have advantages. I regard the area as very open.

10.5 The Logic of Vagueness

There is no immediate connection between the proposal that borderline cases should somehow be characterized in terms of a certain distinctive kind of partial belief and a treatment of the sorites paradox. Schiffer effects one by proposing a simple set of characterizations of the degrees of VPB—degrees of V-credibility—that a rational subject will assign to compounds of vague statements on the basis of the degree of V-credibility that she assigns to their constituents. The matrices he proposes follow the pattern of Łukasiewicz's tables for infinitely many valued logics. Thus the V-credibility of a negation is 1 minus the V-credibility of the negated statement; the V-credibility of a conjunction is the minimum of the V-credibilities of its conjuncts; and the V-credibility of a disjunction is the maximum of those of the disjuncts. The universal and existential quantifiers respectively take the greatest lower bound and least upper bound of the V-credibilities possessed by their instances.

Now consider a sorites paradox, with a major premise taken in the form, $\sim(\exists x)(Fx$ & $\sim Fx')$. Classically (and intuitionistically) this forms an inconsistent triad with the two minor premises, F0 and $\sim Fk$, with k selected so as to ensure that the latter is effectively incontrovertible, while F0 is beyond dispute. So it is natural to think that first base for any solution must be to acknowledge that the sorites reasoning reduces the major premise to absurdity and so demonstrates $\sim\sim(\exists x)(Fx$ & $\sim Fx')$. The question is then how to block the classical entailment of the unwelcome 'unpalatable existential,' $(\exists x)(Fx$ & $\sim Fx')$, or somehow make out that it is not really unpalatable. The landscape changes, however, with Schiffer's proposals. This becomes clear if we ask what degree of V-credibility attaches to the unpalatable existential. It will be the maximum of the V-credibilities of the k instances: conjunctions of the form Fx & $\sim Fx'$, whose V-credibility in turn will be the minimum of those of their conjuncts. In the polar regions this will be very low, since one or the other conjunct will be roundly disbelieved. But the figure will climb as one enters the borderline region, culminating, at least in principle, with a V-credibility of, or very close to 0.5 (though never higher.) So the unpalatable existential, and hence also its negation—the major premise for the paradox—will also have V-credibility very close to 0.5. The upshot is that, according to the Łukasiewicz-style matrices, both are paradigms of indeterminacy.

Is that a good result? It may seem not—after all, the major premise is very plausible; that is why we had a paradox. So don't we want it to turn out to have quite a high VPB? Well, yes—inasmuch as we want to explain the plausibility of the major premise (in particular, its plausibility over its negation) but—you might suppose—also no, since we have to fault it somehow. Suppose—as I take it Schiffer intends—that the computation we have just sketched is meant to be normative: to deliver a measure of VPB that it is *rational* to have. Had the computation delivered the result that the major premise did have quite a high VPB, then the account would be saying that we *ought* to accept it over its negation—in effect, confirming the rational acceptability of the premises of the paradox! So it is good that we don't get that result. But as it is, the result is that rationally there is absolutely nothing to choose between the major premise of the sorites and its negation. That leaves the pull that the premise exerts on us—which is the whole source of the paradox—as unexplained, indeed as irrational. And surely, one may protest, it is not irrational—after all, the negation is tantamount to assertion of the existence of a sharp cutoff, i.e., a denial of the vagueness of F in the series in question, which is a datum of the problem.

Why on Schiffer's account does the negative existential form of the major premise for the sorites attract us? Rationally, if his matrices for VPB are on the right lines, we should find nothing to favour it over its negation. I am not sure how Schiffer sees the options here. One thing he can say is that we are under no pressure to choose—since the law of excluded middle, conceived as a general schema, is foursquare indeterminate too (an exercise for the reader). That suggests the following diagnostic: the major premise attracts us because acceptance of its negation repels. But the truth is that there is no rational pressure to accept either if the law of excluded middle is indeterminate. However, this leaves unexplained why the unpalatable existential is unpalatable. For if it really is tantamount to a denial of the vagueness of F in the series in question, it is false, not indeterminate. And if it isn't, the repulsiveness of that denial doesn't explain its unpalatability.

How exactly, in any case, does getting in position to regard the major premise as indeterminate dispose of the paradox? It may seem obvious: the paradox was that we seemed driven to a contradiction from acceptable premises—the contradiction, e.g., that a man with exactly 37 cents both is not—of course—and is—by the sorites—rich. Now, since one of the sorites premises turns out to be indeterminate, we are no longer under any pressure to accept one of the components in the contradiction.

What is salient, though—and of course Schiffer is absolutely aware of and explicit about this—is that that cannot be his whole story. There is a commitment in his account to a kind of over-kill. Not merely have we disposed of the acceptability of the major premise. We have also got into a position where we have to regard it as *indeterminate whether the sorites reasoning is valid*. For since the minor premise is true, and the conclusion is false, and since—at least for Schiffer—the indeterminacy of P is to be consistent with the truth of P, the situation is one where it is consistent with everything we know that the sorites premises are both true and its conclusion false—so it's consistent with everything we know that it is an invalid argument. A corollary, as Schiffer observes, is that—since we may run the sorites just using hundreds of special conditional premises instead of the usual major premise—we have to regard the validity of modus ponens as an indeterminate issue too! Is this something that can be lived with?

There may be some temptation to reply that Schiffer's account treats the validity of modus ponens, or other classical rules, as indeterminate only when we are involved with indeterminate premises and/or conclusions. Elsewhere there is no problem. But I don't think such an attempt to ring-fence the singularity makes sense. Validity—at least, classical validity—turns on compossibilities of truth-value. If certain argument patterns have instances involving indeterminate premises and false conclusions—or more graphically, true premises and indeterminate conclusions[28]—then they are not known to be truth-preserving. So why should we trust them anywhere? And in any case, don't we need reliable rules in terms of which to bring out the commitments of a thinker who takes a view—however qualified—on an indeterminate issue?

I have little space to pursue this fundamental matter further. To be sure Schiffer's predicament—if that is what it is—is a function of his choice of the Łukasiewicz-style matrices, and they have independent discomforts in this setting; for example, they mispredict the level of partial belief in which normal thinkers will repose in conjunctions of vague but incompatible conjuncts, and they predict variations in the V-credibility of conjunctions of the form, Fk and ~Fk', k and k' adjacent in a sorites series, which are surely not empirically confirmed—one would expect a uniformly low valuation, irrespective of the place in the series of k.[29] But the point I would like to emphasize in closing is that the position for which Schiffer proposes to settle is one in which he has, given other things he accepts, to doubt that certain classically valid inferences are *knowledge-preserving*. The inference for example, from F0 and ~Fk, for suitably 'distant' k, to the relevant unpalatable existential is classically valid and has—one would suppose—known premises. But the conclusion, on Schiffer's calculation, is indeterminate—so cannot be claimed to be known. Moreover, if with Schiffer, we accept (VE), we will have to say that it cannot be known. In that case—whatever the situation with truth—classical validity fails to preserve knowledge. Strikingly, that is, in effect, exactly the intuitionists' complaint about it: that it permits the derivation from warranted premises of conclusions for which there is no warrant—in particular, none elicitable from the warrant for the premises and the derivation. My own treatment of this agenda is precisely fashioned around argument for and consequences of the thesis that classical logic is epistemically non-conservative where vagueness is concerned. Schiffer's views commit him to the same. What he has yet to provide is his own account of the shape a logic should assume to remedy the defect.

10.6 Conclusion

The forgoing has concentrated on points of disagreement and difference. It would be entirely inappropriate to end on anything but a note of admiration for the work I have been commenting on. For the philosopher who wishes to better understand the nature of linguistic competence and linguistic representation, vagueness presents challenges of exceptional importance and the greatest intellectual difficulty. Stephen Schiffer has responded to these challenges with a rare mix of breadth of philosophical vision, resourcefulness, and dialectical and technical expertise. I look forward to the products of his continuing engagement.[30]

Notes

1. See Schiffer (1998), (2000a), (2000b), (2003), (2006), and (forthcoming). Schiffer's focus, of course, is on *soritical* vagueness—the kind of vagueness that is characteristic of expressions that are prone to give rise to a sorites paradox. Other linguistic phenomena that are sometimes described as involving vagueness include generality (lack of specificity), partial definition, family resemblances, and criterial conflicts. I am concerned only with soritical vagueness in what follows.
2. For example, the so-called Problem of the Many (for a definitive overview, see Weatherson 2003).
3. As far as I am aware, no one has attempted a fully general view of vagueness along these lines.
4. More accurately, he finds merit in a notion of quandary in whose characterization his notion of VPB plays a central role, and which is accordingly rather different from mine.

5. My own views are principally developed (and developing) in Wright (2001), (2003a), (2003b), and (2007).
6. As Elia Zardini has emphasized to me in conversation, however, Schiffer's point is served merely if any lowering of satisfaction in the conjunction is (appreciably) less than would correspond to the 'multiplication.'
7. Wright (2006).
8. Schiffer (2006).
9. I take Schiffer to be suggesting such a claim in his (2006) though it is another question whether he needs to.
10. I am indebted here to Elia Zardini.
11. See Schiffer (forthcoming), sections 6 and 7.
12. I take his view to be that the sort of qualified acceptance involved in VPB-ing P to some significantly greater degree than not-P is categorically unsuited to serve as the doxastic ingredient in knowledge.
13. In refusing to affirm that no verdict about a borderline case can be knowledgeable, the liberal does not, of course, intend to exempt such verdicts from other normal controls on knowledge ascription—the point is only: we have no justification for thinking that knowledgeability is excluded just by a verdict's concerning a borderline case.
14. It is, of course, in tension everywhere with Williamson's thesis (in 2000a) that knowledge is subject to margins of error in a sense that requires that knowing that P holds of circumstances C entails that any case within some fixed margin of difference of C is also a case where P holds. I'll come back to this below (in section 10.3).
15. Schiffer (forthcoming) suggests 'brave.'
16. Schiffer (forthcoming) suggests that the motivation for EC confuses the above conditionals with the (in the relevant, plausible cases) acceptable weakenings:

    If *Definitely* P, then it is feasible to know P
    If *Definitely* not-P, then it is feasible to know not-P

    This is no help, however without a developed account of the difference in the truth conditions of the original and weakened formulations, and a story about how exactly the original versions are supposed to fail. Recall that, as noted in the main text, even the supposition that we do not know that the original conditionals fail is inconsistent with the claim that (VE) is known.

    Here is a related point, due to Zardini. Consider the claim—with which the epistemicist is comfortable, though not, I would imagine, Schiffer—that some nth case in the series is such that either it is F (say, looks red) and we cannot feasibly know that, or it is not-F and that we cannot feasibly know that. Formally,

    $(\exists n)\{(Fn \ \& \sim \text{it is feasible to know } (Fn)) \vee (\sim Fn \ \& \sim \text{it is feasible to know } (\sim Fn))\}$

    That is something which, if we do not believe that there is any such n, we may very well want to *deny*. Intuitionistically and classically, the denial is equivalent to:

    $(*)(\forall n)\{\sim(Fn \ \& \sim \text{it is feasible to know } (Fn)) \ \& \sim(\sim Fn \ \& \sim \text{it is feasible to know } (\sim Fn))\}$

    And (*) is already enough to yield aporia when conjoined with VE. VE is inconsistent with the denial that there are any elements in a sorites series for *looks red* which look red but cannot be known to do so, or which don't look red and cannot be known to do that. If (*pace* the epistemicist) one can rationally doubt there are any such elements, one cannot coherently endorse VE.
17. Schiffer (forthcoming).
18. Schiffer (forthcoming).
19. Schiffer (forthcoming).

20. Although the bit about knowing "with certainty that the color you know the ball to have is not one you can now justifiably say either is or is not red" is too strong.
21. From Rosenkranz (2005).
22. It is argued for in Wright (2008).
23. We assume that each successive element in the sorites lies within the relevant margin of difference of its predecessor.
24. Useful discussion bearing on the issue may be found in Mott (1998), Williamson (2000b), and Egré (2006).
25. Wright (2001).
26. The relativity to circumstances of evaluation is for the obvious reason: the very same proposition can be a quandary in one set of circumstances and clearly true in another. But the relativity might be compounded for vagueness-unrelated reasons if one's conception of proposition allows propositional truth to be relative to time, or standards, etc.
27. Schiffer confronts an exactly analogous problem when he speaks of VPB* as 'F-concept driven' in borderline cases—for development of the challenge, see my (2006). Schiffer responds in Schiffer (2006).
28. Consider the inference from the minor premise and negation of the conclusion of the sorites to the negation of the major premise.
29. Elia Zardini has suggested in discussion that a restriction of the Łukasiewicz clauses to independent propositions would be a natural and attractive way of trying to get around these awkwardnesses (assuming a case can be made that ~Fk′ is relevantly negatively dependent on Fk).
30. I am most grateful to Elia Zardini for detailed comments on the penultimate draft, and to him and other members of the Arché Vagueness project for feedback on various of the ideas herein canvassed at various project seminars over the last few years.

Bibliography

Egré, P. (2006). "Reliability, Margin for Error and Self-Knowledge." In *New Waves in Epistemology*, edited by V. Hendricks and D. Pritchard, Aldershott: Ashgate.
Mott, P. (1998). "Margins for Error and the Sorites Paradox." *The Philosophical Quarterly* 48: 494–504.
Rosenkranz, S. (2005). "Knowledge in Borderline Cases." *Analysis* 65: 49–55.
Schiffer, S. (1998). "Two Issues of Vagueness." *The Monist* 88: 193–214.
Schiffer, S. (2000a). "Vagueness and Partial Belief." *Philosophical Issues* 10: 220–57.
Schiffer, S. (2000b). "Replies to Commentators." *Philosophical Issues* 10: 321–43.
Schiffer, S. (2003). *The Things We Mean*. Oxford: Clarendon Press.
Schiffer, S. (2006). 'Replies.' *Philosophy and Phenomenological Research* 72: 233–43.
Schiffer, S. (Forthcoming). "Quandary and Intuitionism: Crispin Wright on Vagueness." In *Logic, Language and Mathematics: Essays for Crispin Wright Volume II*, edited by A. Miller, Oxford: Oxford University Press.
Weatherson, B. (2003). "The Problem of the Many." *The Stanford Encyclopaedia of Philosophy* at http://plato.stanford.edu/entries/problem-of-many/.
Williamson, T. (2000a). *Knowledge and Its Limits*. Oxford: Oxford University Press.
Williamson, T. (2000b). "Margins for Error: A Reply." *The Philosophical Quarterly* 50: 76–81.
Wright, C. (2001). "On Being in a Quandary: Relativism, Vagueness, Logical Revisionism." *Mind* 110: 45–98.
Wright, C. (2003a). "Vagueness: A Fifth Column Approach." In *Liars & Heaps: New Essays on Paradox*, edited by J. C Beall and M. Glanzberg, Oxford: Oxford University Press.

Wright, C. (2003b). "Rosenkranz on Quandary, Vagueness and Intuitionism." *Mind* 112: 465–74.

Wright, C. (2006). "Vagueness-related Partial Belief and the Constitution of Borderline Cases." *Philosophy and Phenomenological Research* 72: 225–32.

Wright, C. (2007). "'Wang's Paradox'." In *The Philosophy of Michael Dummett*, edited by R. E. Auxier and L. E. Hahn, Chicago: Open Court.

Wright, C. (2008). "Externalism and Scepticism." *Journal of Philosophy* 105: 501–17 (special number on *Epistemic Norms*, edited by J. Collins and C. Peacocke).

11
The Nature of Paradox

Paul Horwich

11.1 Introduction

It's a matter of reasonable dispute whether or not philosophy is exhausted by paradoxes and the efforts to resolve them. Followers of Wittgenstein may say that it is—that there is nothing more for us to do, *qua* philosophers, than recognize and rectify the bad habits of thought that issue in such conceptual entanglements. But even those who would reject that radically anti-theoretical view of our subject might agree on the crucial role of paradox in exposing the notions we need to be theorizing about.

Given their undoubted importance, one would expect to find a considerable literature on the nature of paradoxes, addressing such general issues as what exactly they are, how they arise, whether to distinguish significantly different kinds, whether solutions can always be identified, etc. But in fact such discussions are few and far between. A refreshing exception, however, is the theory of paradox sketched by Stephen Schiffer in his book, *The Things We Mean*.[1] My plan for this chapter is to describe that theory and to assess it in comparison with a couple of quite different accounts of the matter.

11.2 What is a Paradox?

A paradox is an assembly of apparently reasonable considerations that engenders conflicting inclinations about what to believe, and hence a form of cognitive tension. On the one hand, we feel we have sufficient reason to be confident of the truth of a certain proposition. Either it's 'evident', or 'obvious common sense,' or we have a persuasive argument in favor of it. But, on the other hand—and in full awareness of that basis for belief—we also see, or think we see, compelling grounds for denying the proposition.[2]

In contrast, there is usually nothing at all paradoxical in having some reason to think *that p* and some reason to doubt it (e.g. hearing opposite forecasts as to whether it will rain tomorrow morning). For we will typically have little trouble in arriving at a fairly definite level of credence (perhaps 50:50) in light of the combined, total evidence. Similarly, we may be convinced of the truth of a certain proposition and then discover, without paradox, that something it entails is false. There is no cognitive tension if, given this surprising discovery, we are prepared to let go of our initial conviction.

For instance, the idea of "a barber who shaves all and only those who don't shave themselves" does not engender paradox—not even (as Schiffer supposes on p. 68) a very mild one. For, although we may uncritically accept that there is (or could be) such a barber, the demonstration that this would be self-contradictory will normally suffice to eliminate that belief. There was never, to begin with, anything to be said in favor of it; never anything that might continue to incline us to hang on to it and make its falsity seem puzzling to us.

But now consider a 25,000-mile piece of rope wrapped snuggly around the equator (ignoring the bumps and the water); then imagine it being lengthened by just one yard; and ask yourself, if the rope—given the extra bit—were lifted from the earth's surface by a slight constant amount (the same all around), how much would that amount roughly be? Surely, some indiscernible, miniscule distance, wouldn't you think? And we might find it impossible to free ourselves from that intuition, even in the face of the simple mathematical proof that the correct answer is *six inches*.[3] In which case we have a paradox: there is no synthesis of the conflicting considerations; neither extinguishes the other; so we remain somewhat torn between them.

Or consider Olber's paradox. He demonstrated, given the prevailing assumption (in 1823) of there being infinitely many, uniformly distributed stars, that the night sky should be as bright as day! If this had been regarded as a straightforward refutation of the 'infinite star hypothesis,' there would have been no paradox. But since physicists found that hypothesis too attractive to abandon—but could find nothing wrong with Olber's reasoning—the conditions for cognitive tension, for genuine paradox, were present. As it happened there *was* a mistake in that reasoning—a mistake whose detection resolved the paradox. It was an unremarked assumption that each star remains at a more-or-less constant distance from the Earth. But in fact the universe is expanding, the stars are receding from us. And that is why, despite there being infinitely many of them, they don't manage to light up the night sky.

Turning now to *philosophical* paradoxes, their peculiarity is (to a first approximation) that the considerations on which they turn are a priori.

For example, in opposition to what we normally take for granted about our perceptual abilities, there is the Cartesian rationale for skepticism: namely, that someone's beliefs about what's happening around her are justified only if she can discount the possibility that she is dreaming (or—in Putnam's version of the problem—that she's a mere 'brain in a vat' whose sensations are stimulated artificially). But since these bizarre possibilities are perfectly consistent with everything in her experience, she *can't* rule them out. So she has no genuine knowledge of the external world, no real right to believe anything about it!

Equally perturbing is the paradox of free will versus determinism. We are obviously capable of voluntary action, of freely choosing to do one thing rather than another. But it also seems obvious that an act is *not* truly free if it is causally determined by events beyond the agent's control; and there is a distinct possibility that this is invariably so; for the laws of nature may be such that whatever happens at any given time is fixed by events that took place hundreds of years beforehand!

These observations and examples suggest something like Schiffer's general characterization of the phenomenon:

A philosophical paradox is a set of apparently mutually incompatible propositions each of which enjoys some significant degree of plausibility when viewed on its own. (68)

But various additions and amendments to this formulation are needed. For:

(a) It does not articulate what is special about *philosophical* paradoxes.
(b) It identifies a paradox with a set of incompatible *propositions*; whereas we should be focused on conflicts amongst propositional *attitudes* (e.g. *believing* a given proposition, yet simultaneously *doubting* it).
(c) There need be nothing irrational or paradoxical in attributing a "significant" degree of plausibility (elsewhere, he says "non-negligible") to A and also to not-A. Or, even more obviously, to 'K_1 won't win the lottery,' 'K_2 won't win,...,' and 'K_{10000} won't win.'[4]
(d) It shouldn't be supposed that each of the conflicting propositions in a paradox is *actually* plausible, i.e. *really* rational to believe. For we surely don't take it that the contradiction they engender is genuinely supported. '*Seemingly plausible*' would be better.
(e) It isn't relevant to the creation of a paradox that each one of the conflicting propositions seems reasonable to believe 'when viewed on its own.' For, clearly, one ought never ignore the surrounding epistemic context. What's crucial for paradox, rather, is that even when the other propositions, and the considerations appearing to favor them, *are* taken into account, we are *still* left with a clash of plausibility assessments.

For these reasons I prefer a characterization that runs along the lines that I suggested at the outset: a philosophical paradox is a battery of a priori considerations that engenders conflicting epistemic inclinations.[5]

11.3 How Do Philosophical Paradoxes Arise, and What Can Be Done to Resolve Them?

I'd like to consider three distinct accounts: one suggested by Schiffer, which blames paradoxes on "glitchy" concepts; a second diagnosis, due to Wittgenstein, which stresses irrationally stubborn over-generalization; and a third—I'll pin it on Quine—for which the causes of paradox are conflicts amongst our fundamental habits of reasoning.

Let me begin with Schiffer's proposal:

...a *happy-face solution* to a philosophical paradox would do two things. First it would identify the odd guy out: it would tell us that the apparently incompatible propositions were not really incompatible, or that a certain one of the plausible propositions wasn't the truth it appeared to be; and secondly, it would, in unmasking the odd guy out, do so in a way that removed its patina of plausibility, so that we would never again be taken in by it. (68)

For example, a happy-face solution to Descartes' epistemological paradox would either supply reasoning by which the 'dreaming hypothesis' can and should be ruled out, or it would convincingly identify the mistake we were making in assuming that the rationality of beliefs about the outside world requires such reasoning, or it would explain away the naïve idea that most of our observational beliefs are perfectly legitimate.

But what classical philosophical problem enjoys a happy-face solution? The trouble in each case is that while any given 'solution' offers an identification of the odd guy out, none succeeds in removing from it its patina of plausibility.... it seems clear that none of them truly enjoys a happy-face solution. (68–9)

However (continues Schiffer) even if this is so—even if the classical paradoxes cannot be definitively solved in a fully satisfying way—there's still *something* that can be done to ameliorate our puzzlement:

An unhappy-face solution to a paradox would do two things. First, it would tell us that there can be no determinately correct complete identification of the odd guy(s) out; and secondly, it would tell us what it is about the concepts involved that explains this. In each case, the explanation will find a glitch in the concept or concepts involved, a tension in the underived conceptual roles that individuate those concepts. (69)

This 'tension' arises when the various 'deployment instructions' that fix a given concept direct us (in certain circumstances) to maintain a variety of mutually incompatible propositions. And since our concept is dictating that we must maintain each of these things, none of them can be *determinately* false. In the case, for example, of the epistemic concept, JUSTIFIED, one of the constituting rules requires that if someone has a 'looks red' experience then we are to apply that concept, without further ado, to his tentative belief that something out there really is red. But the other rules dictate, in opposition to this, that such justification would have to rest on his entitlement to maintain, 'Whatever looks red probably is red,' which—since it is general and contingent—could not qualify as 'justified' in the absence of empirical support; yet it's hard to see how he might provide such support, since he could not, without circularity, take for granted the legitimacy of the perceptual beliefs that would be needed.

In this sort of unhappy condition, what can be done to relieve our discontent? Schiffer distinguishes two possibilities:

A *weak* unhappy-face solution to any paradox will tell us that... a suitable conceptual revision is possible that would be paradox free, where a conceptual revision is 'suitable' if it can do the primary work we wanted the 'defective' concept to do... A *strong* unhappy-face solution denies that any suitable conceptual revision is possible. (198)

We'll assess the merits of this package of ideas in a minute. But, before that, I'd like to briefly describe a couple of alternative of approaches.

One of them—which I attribute to Wittgenstein—places responsibility for philosophical paradox on our tendency to over-generalize:

The man who is philosophically puzzled sees a law in the way a word is used, and, trying to apply this law consistently, comes up against paradoxical results. (1958: 27)

For example: typically, beliefs are termed 'justified' only if when they are based on plausible reasoning; so one might be inclined to conclude that justification *necessarily* involves argumentative backing; but the premises of such arguments will have to be justified; hence each justification will engender an infinite regress; so justified belief turns out to be impossible. Similarly, the statements we normally encounter trivially specify their own truth conditions—e.g. 'The claim that bats snore is true if and only if bats snore'; so we might presume that *all* statements must obey that law; hence the liar paradoxes.

Wittgenstein holds that paradox-inducing over-generalizations often derive from an exaggeration of linguistic analogies. For instance, we might be struck by the resemblances in use between the word 'true' and empirical predicates such as 'inflammable' or 'magnetic'; thereby come to expect a substantive answer to the question, 'What is truth?'; and then feel puzzled when no satisfactory answer can be found. Similarly, we might over-stretch the analogies between numerals and names of planets, or between temporal terminology and spatial terminology, or between sensation terms (like 'pain') and observation terms (like 'red'). We might therefore, in each of these cases, wrongly attribute to the former concepts characteristics that are possessed by the latter. And we might thus become convinced by theses that lead into paradox.

Evidently, when that is so, our way out will be a matter of unearthing such errors:

Our investigation is therefore a grammatical one. Such an investigation sheds light on our problems by clearing misunderstandings away. Misunderstandings concerning the use of words, caused, among other things, by certain analogies between the forms of expression in different regions of language. (Wittgenstein 1953: 90)

These are, of course, not empirical problems; they are solved, rather, by looking into the workings of our language, and in such a way as to make us recognise those workings; in despite of an urge to misunderstand them. The problems are solved, not by giving new information, but by arranging what we have already known. Philosophy is a battle against the bewitchment of our intelligence by means of language. (Wittgenstein 1953: 109)

The central idea might be put as follows. Philosophical paradoxes result from *mistakes*, from blameworthy failures to obey our own basic norms of reasoning. More specifically, our extrapolations from prominent patterns of linguistic activity are often inaccurate—deriving from an unreasonable demand for theoretical simplicity. We must learn to see that the norms of correct word-use are (and need to be) both complex and heterogeneous.[6]

Before turning to an assessment of the competing approaches just outlined—Schiffer's and Wittgenstein's—there is a third prima facie reasonable proposal about the source of paradox that I would like to get onto the table—namely, that the serious, philosophically troublesome ones issue from conflicts amongst our *most basic* habits of reasoning. For want of being able to think of anyone more appropriate, I'll associate Quine with this suggestion. For he says:

An antinomy [= *serious paradox (PH)*] produces a self-contradiction by accepted ways of reasoning. It establishes that some tacit and trusted pattern of reasoning must be made explicit and henceforward be avoided or revised.[7]

To be more explicit, our third candidate theory is that hard philosophical paradoxes result from the fact that in certain rare circumstances (perhaps merely hypothetical) one of our *fundamental* epistemic habits clashes (or would clash) with others, pulling us in opposite directions. Resolution is a matter, not of somehow *demonstrating* that one or another of these proclivities is irrational (for, after all, they are *basic*), but of one of them simply being less powerful and being adjusted to bring it into harmony with the others. The upshot is a change in the fundamental rules of reason that we implicitly follow.

Thus we have three competing accounts of the origin of philosophical paradoxes. And, of course, we might be eclectic: we might come to think that some belong in one of these three categories, and the rest in the others (or in just one of the others). Let me turn now to an appraisal of their relative merits.

11.4 Critique of Schiffer's 'Glitchy Concepts' Theory of Philosophical Paradox

Here again, in a nutshell, is Schiffer's proposal. Every classical philosophical paradox is caused by a concept (perhaps more than one) that is *defective*, in that its possession conditions incline us (in certain circumstances) towards incompatible beliefs; therefore, we can never hope to arrive at a happy-face solution, which would succeed in identifying, and protecting us against the particular mistake that gave an air of plausibility to what is in fact a determinately false proposition; rather, such problems must be disposed of via some form of more-or-less radical conceptual revision.

But various concerns about this perspective come to mind:

First reservation

It would appear, on the contrary, that many long-standing philosophical paradoxes *can* be fully resolved. For, very often, the "patina of plausibility" possessed by their operative assumptions *can* be shown to be illusory—sufficient reason *can* be given for regarding some one of them as, in fact, *im*plausible; and a good explanation can be found for why, despite that reason, it still seems (or initially seemed) eminently plausible. No doubt, in each such case, some philosophers (perhaps many) will remain unpersuaded—unconvinced by the solution. And such recalcitrance certainly calls for explanation. But it does not impugn the fact that a certain 'false appearance of plausibility' has been exposed as such.

Here are a few examples:

(a) Hempel's ravens

We're disposed to accept each of these mutually contradictory propositions: (1) Any hypothesis of the form, 'All A's are B' is confirmed by observing that a known A is also B; (2) Whatever confirms a hypothesis also confirms logically equivalent hypotheses; and (3) 'All ravens are black' is *not* confirmed by observing that a known non-black thing is not a raven.

But this paradox may be dealt with by making it plausible that the third proposition is strictly speaking false, and that we were inclined to accept it only because we were failing to distinguish between no confirmation at all and a negligibly slight degree of confirmation. To that end, a Bayesian representation of the situation vindicates two relevant intuitions: *first* that, since 'All ravens are black' *entails* that a known non-black thing will turn out not to be a raven, the correctness of such a prediction *will* confirm that hypothesis; and *second* that, since the vast majority of things in the world are not ravens, this predictive success would be extremely unsurprising and unimpressive, and could increase our previous level of confidence in the hypothesis by only a trivial amount. A happy-face solution![8]

(b) Negative existentials

Consider any sentence composed of just a singular term and a simple or complex predicate. Surely, its condition for being true is that the singular term refer to an object and that this object possess the property designated by the predicate. But, in that case, the combination of 'Atlantis' with 'does not exist' cannot be true. But it *is* true!

What are we to think? Well, a pretty obvious way out of this problem is to reject the proposed truth condition as overly general. We should not have forgotten that certain statements are *false* in virtue of the failure of their subject-terms to refer to anything (e.g. 'Vulcan is a planet whose orbit is between Mercury and the sun'), and therefore that the negations of such statements will be *true*, despite the presence within them of 'empty' names. In particular, since 'Atlantis exists' is false, its denial is true.

Granted, this move does not settle all outstanding issues. We are still left with the task of devising an alternative general account of truth conditions—an account that will be more complicated, yet more adequate, than the simplistic theory that engendered the tension. But an unanswered theoretical question is one thing, and a paradox another![9]

(c) Agrippan skepticism

Contrary to what we all naively assume, *justified* belief (hence, *knowledge*) appears to be impossible! For any such belief would need to be derived from premises that would themselves have to be justified. But these would in turn have to rest on justified premises, and so on. An unimplementable regress!

But the problem here stems simply from the seductiveness of equating *justification* with *argumentative support*. We can see, on reflection, that *not* all rational commitments are taken to obtain their rationality from arguments based on more fundamental rational commitments. Especially obvious examples are provided by observational beliefs (e.g. *that this is red*, or alternatively *that this looks red*). And it's pretty clear that no change in our concept of JUSTIFIED BELIEF comes from our appreciating that it applies—and always did apply—to beliefs, like these, that are not the product of reasoning.[10]

(d) Normativity

The conviction that torture is wrong is enough, all by itself, to induce some reluctance to torture. But surely the world contains no fact with the odd property that a mere awareness of its existence is intrinsically motivating. So there can be nothing to make it true that torture is wrong. So torture is not wrong![11]

The main flaw here, it would seem, is that once again we have been guilty of overgeneralization. No doubt most facts do not have that peculiar property. Empirical causal-explanatory facts certainly don't. Arithmetical facts don't, etc. But, if—as is indeed plausible—our conviction that torture is wrong is intrinsically motivating, then the extrapolation to *normative* facts is clearly a mistake. For we have no real choice but to acknowledge their existence. After all: a normative fact is simply a true normative proposition. So if we believe (as we do) that torture is wrong, we can trivially infer the truth of the proposition that torture is wrong; and we thereby commit ourselves to the fact at issue.[12]

(e) Zeno

In order to get from A to B, an object must first traverse half the distance between these two locations, then half the remaining distance, then half the remaining distance, and so on, *ad infinitum*. So motion is impossible!

But why not, instead, take at face value the observed existence of moving objects? Why not then infer, in light of Zeno's ingenious way of dividing up any given motion, that, surprisingly, there is in fact no limit to the number of non-overlapping 'events' that can occur within a finite time? Modern mathematics helps us to see *how* this could be so. But *that* it's so should have been clear all along.

(f) Free will versus determinism

Science gives us reason to suspect that every physical event (including, for example, the raising of an arm) is necessitated by things that took place long before human life evolved. But, in that case, we must be mistaken in supposing—as we do in everyday life—that human actions tend to be *free*, and that we can justifiably hold people *responsible* for what they do.

However, our normal naïve attitude is, very roughly speaking, to regard an act as un-free only when its causes bypass any deliberation or decision by the agent. Thus we do *not* intuitively think—as presupposed in the paradoxical argument—that no externally caused action can be voluntary. Rather, we think (roughly) that if a decision results from a normal process of deliberation and leads, in the normal way, to the act decided upon, then that act is free—and it doesn't matter if the deliberative process was itself somehow caused by external events.

Granted, there is considerable fuzziness in this characterization of our concept of FREE ACT. And there may very well be arcane counter-examples to it. Moreover we'd have difficulty, I imagine, in massaging it into fairly exact conditions that are necessary and sufficient for an act to be free and for the agent to be subject to praise or blame for it. But such residual theoretical questions do not constitute a paradox. Our initial cognitive tension is dissolved once we see, as we easily can, that the general argument against free action is clearly fallacious.

In light of these various examples—and others could easily be supplied[13]—one surely cannot say of the classical philosophical paradoxes that none of their superficially appealing premises can have their "patina of plausibility" removed on the basis of rational considerations, and therefore that "none of them enjoys a happy-face solution." Indeed, it's far from clear that there are *any* paradoxes of that peculiarly intractable kind.

I'm not, of course, claiming that the solutions I've just sketched are widely embraced. My claim is merely that they are correct. Certainly, they *might* become generally accepted, and I myself believe, for the reasons given, that they *should* be.

Second reservation

On the face of it, none of these proposed solutions would, if adopted, involve conceptual revision. Therefore, even if—contrary to what I've been suggesting—Schiffer were right that one cannot undermine the apparent plausibility of any of the premises of a classical paradox, we would have to demur from his particular explanation of this inability: namely that our acceptance of the conflicting premises is tied to the deployment of certain operative concepts.

Third reservation

Even commitments that *are* tied to the exercise of concepts might nonetheless be rationally abandoned; their first impression of plausibility may easily be dispelled.

Consider, for example, Russell's famous set-theoretic paradox, which derives from the initially reasonable-looking general assumption that something is a member of the set of fs just in case it is an f. And suppose that our concept of set calls for us to make this assumption. Nonetheless, its "patina of plausibility" is explained away by (a) remembering that generalizations are always somewhat risky—so we were never really in a position to insist that the full schema simply *must* be correct, and (b) observing that, after all—as we might well have feared from the outset—there do turn out to be counter-examples to it. What could be less than fully satisfying about a solution that, on this basis, recognizes the unacceptability of that general principle and hence puts aside the concept of set whose identity is tied to endorsing it?

Moreover, there's nothing at all unusual here. For conceptual change is a normal and familiar feature of progress in the sciences. —We regularly replace our theories with better ones without caring, or even always noticing, whether somewhat different concepts are thereby introduced.[14] So it clearly not the case that the prospect of having to shelve currently deployed concepts makes it peculiarly difficult to criticize the assumptions that are tied to them.

Nor is it the case that if a concept is "glitchy" in Schiffer's sense (—if it is engendered by inconsistent commitments) then no particular one of these commitments can be determinately mistaken—i.e. identified as the false one which ought to be given up.

To see this, it is useful to distinguish between *positively deploying* a concept and merely *possessing* it—between, on the one hand, engaging in the special conceptual practice which brings the concept into play, and, on the other hand, merely being aware of that practice, not endorsing it, but nonetheless appreciating the role of the concept within it. For example, in doing and accepting arithmetic we positively deploy the number concepts. But a skeptic about arithmetic is surely able to *understand* those of us who maintain '1+2=3.' So he, no less than us, possesses the salient concepts—presumably, in virtue of appreciating their distinctive roles within the practice.[15]

Therefore, if the special commitments that call for a given concept turn out to be mutually inconsistent and to engender paradox, the resulting abandonment of one or more of those commitments will imply, *not* that the associated concept disappears from our repertoire, but simply that it is no longer positively deployed. Whatever conceptual activities are required merely to *possess* it will invariably be much too weak to yield paradox.[16]

But if this is right, the critic of a set of commitments—even when they are concept engendering—will have all the resources he needs to assess their relative epistemic merits and may well reach the objective conclusion that a certain one of them mistaken.

Fourth reservation

My final gripe concerns Schiffer's claim to have explained, via his account, why strikingly many philosophical paradoxes remain contentious despite the hundreds of years of attention that have been devoted to them. He suggests that this frustrating situation is just what one would expect given the assumption he is recommending: namely that, in these cases, the paradox-inducing combinations of commitments are required by our concepts.

But, as we have just seen, that assumption is in fact perfectly consistent with a determinate identification of which of the clashing commitments is the irrational one, the one to be abandoned or altered.

Moreover, even if (contrary to this suggestion) certain paradox-premises *were*, on account of their being essential to our present concepts, especially resistant to revision—precluding happy-face solutions—that would not account for the phenomenon to be explained: namely, the inability of us philosophers to lay certain paradoxes permanently to rest. What it would lead us to expect, rather, is the existence of widespread agreement on the frequent need for unhappy-face solutions, and, in each such case, on the particular solution of that type that ought to be accepted. But in fact there is no such agreement. What we actually observe is that different philosophers endorse different approaches, debates are frequent and searching, yet consensus fails to emerge. And Schiffer's theory leaves us in the dark as to why that should be so.

I've expressed four reservations about this theory. One was that paradoxes appear to involve identifiable mistakes. Another was that many paradox-inducing assumptions are typically not concept engendering. The third was that even if they were, that would not make them difficult to assess and revise. And the final point was that, since "glitchy concepts" can perfectly well be generally recognized as such, their invocation doesn't help us to understand why so many of the most ancient philosophical paradoxes are still very much with us, in that every alleged solution is controversial. (Of course, it remains to be seen whether the Wittgensteinian or Quinean approaches can do any better on this score.)

11.5 The 'Over-Generalization' Approach

In contrast with Schiffer's 'concept-based' theory, Wittgenstein's central thought, as we've seen, is that a philosophical paradox issues from *fallacious reasoning*. His idea, more specifically, is that by extrapolating irresponsibly from paradigm cases in which a term is deployed we have a tendency to wrongly persuade ourselves of some overly general principle about its proper application. We might come to think, for example, that *no* belief can be justified unless it is derived by a good argument from justified assumptions; that *no* state of affairs can be such that our awareness of it is intrinsically motivating; that a person's state of knowing some fact must *always* be explicable in terms of the existence of that fact; . . . ; and so on.

But notice that the mere tendency to over-generalize is not enough to get us into trouble. For we might be quite ready to abandon our extreme conclusions on being reminded of the conflicting facts—in which case no cognitive tensions will emerge. Paradox can take hold only when that readiness is absent, only when we refuse to let go of our theory, despite the mass of counter-evidence.

So the question arises as to *why* we are prone, when engaged in philosophical reflection, not only to embrace overly general conclusions, but to resist giving them up in the face of such strongly opposing considerations.

Wittgenstein's answer is that we tend to have a *scientistic* attitude towards philosophy: we search for simple theories, we expect them to hold, we hope thereby for discoveries that are interesting—even dramatically counterintuitive—and we feel that such results must be obtainable in principle if our subject is to be worthwhile. It is this perspective, he says, that yields a dismissive response to putative counter-examples. For, when a neat general thesis is supported by a range of prominent cases, then our faith in simplicity and our appetite for surprising discoveries unite to encourage the conviction that the thesis is likely to hold in *every* case—even when there are glaring indications to the contrary. Thus, it can seem, for example, that justification should quite generally be identified with argumentative support (yielding the remarkable result that no one knows anything); and that if an action was caused—no matter how—then it cannot have been free (yielding the stunning conclusion that no one is ever responsible for anything).

Now, what's wrong with this attitude, according to Wittgenstein, is that it's only in science that we seek and obtain *theoretical profundity*; and only in that context—as something to be expected at an *underlying level*—does simplicity function legitimately as a vital methodological desideratum. Other domains of assertion—for example, urban planning, friendly advice, film criticism, holiday postcards, attributions of knowledge and responsibility—serve quite different social purposes for us; such practices and their implicit assumptions may well be messy and disorganized in comparison with a decent science; but that doesn't mean that there is anything the matter with them. A concept with complex, vague, disjunctive application conditions is not likely to appear in a deep law of nature; but in other areas such concepts may be just what we want (NB 'family resemblance' terms). Moreover, even within science there is a need for notions of quite different kinds—only some are the special-purpose theoretical ideas introduced for the sake of specific explanations and predictions; others (e.g. logical concepts) are part of the general apparatus—needed whatever explanations or predictions are being attempted.

Thus, our fundamental error is to extend, beyond its legitimate range, the desideratum of *simplicity in scientific theorizing*; to become wedded to the idea that the norms governing our everyday linguistic/conceptual activity 'surely' cannot be a disjointed, convoluted mess—either in part, or as a whole; and to think rather that for each word there must be a fairly simple basic rule dictating its proper use, and that the collection of these rules will have to display a fairly uniform structure. Consequently, we are easily seduced into paradox-inducing over-generalizations by what are, in fact, rather limited linguistic regularities and analogies.

So the moral Wittgenstein draws is that we must beware against this error—we must resist the alluring but incorrect idea that a priori reflection on our conceptual activity is capable of producing elegant and revolutionary theories. From this deflationary outlook on philosophy our exaggerated extrapolations will be more readily recognizable as such.

Having recognized such a mistake—having thereby identified the solution to a certain paradox, we might still feel a degree of discomfort. For we may be unsure that our response is 'fully adequate,' in providing the *best* way of constraining our initial over-generalization. Maybe there's a better replacement, which hasn't been noticed?

However, it is important to distinguish between, on the one hand, defusing the tense bafflement that is the defining feature of a paradox and, on the other hand, answering the further *theoretical* questions that may remain. The first of these things is a matter of un-convincing oneself of a certain thought—learning not to insist on it. The second is a matter of figuring out what to think instead. Thus we might come to see that our assumption about how some word ought to be used is simplistic; so we might abandon it, thereby eliminating a certain paradoxical conflict. But it will be a further job—not essential for getting rid of that paradox—to work out what the right alternative assumption would be.[17]

Another reason that our solution might leave us feeling a bit disgruntled is that we remain somewhat under the spell of scientism—a little sorry that things aren't as nice and simple as we had previously thought they were. What a shame that we can't have the full, unrestricted truth-schema! So the happy grin may be tempered.

Of course, many of our colleagues will be more than disgruntled—they will be entirely unconvinced. But this is not to acknowledge that the paradox is still in some sense unresolved. Nor is it any indication that the needed change in our thinking is a change of *concepts*. The real reason that our problems are rarely settled to everyone's satisfaction—the reason that the sort of progress displayed in physics and biology is seldom encountered in philosophy—is, ironically, the yearning for philosophy to resemble a science in delivering simple theories and satisfying discoveries. For such ambitions, as we've seen, are typically both the initial source of a paradox and the cause of our inability to agree on the right way out of it.[18,19]

11.6 Conflicting Fundamental Epistemic Rules

Now, one might make the following Quinean objection against this Wittgensteinian approach—against the suggestion that paradoxes are induced by our reprehensible failure to reason as our basic epistemic rules dictate we should. One might observe that many cases of problematic generalization in philosophy don't strike us (even in light of the paradoxes they engender) as foolishly irrational, as moves that violate our own principles. The problems appear to reside, *not* in a failure to *abide* by those basic rules, but in the *rules themselves* and the dispositions underlying them.

Consider again the liar paradox. It is quite natural for us to want to accept *every* instance of '<p> is true ↔ p.' Similarly, there is no 'bad philosophical methodology' in the almost universal inclination to assume (as in note 13) that if you remove one grain of sand from a heap, what remains will still qualify as a heap. But neither of these tempting assumptions can be coherently combined with the principles of classical logic—which are no less easy to relinquish. In such cases we might find it impossible to achieve a stable epistemic attitude—even after considerable reflection on where we could be going wrong. We are pulled in opposite directions, and neither side emerges as the indisputable victor. So we remain stuck in a state of epistemic limbo. Or, alternatively, although one side turns out to be stronger, and the need to escape from paralysis leads us to go in that direction, the conflicting inclination is not entirely quelled, and so we continue to feel guilty and discontented. A real resolution would therefore require some *alteration* in our basic epistemic rules—the elimination of certain fundamental dispositions. Yet this may not be possible; they may all be too ingrained, too innate, to be changed.

I think we must agree that there is an important grain of truth in these misgivings. Specifically, we should concede that not *all* philosophical paradoxes are merely the perverse artifacts of scientism. Sometimes our troublesome epistemic proclivities result from perfectly normal processes of cognitive development and language learning.

In light of this concession we might distinguish between two kinds of paradox: the *artificial* and the *natural*. And we might be tempted to suppose that only cases of the first kind can be blamed, à la Wittgenstein, on scientistic irrationality. When it comes to the second kind, it might seem, we are in the grip of basic habits for which we cannot be held responsible.[20]

But this assessment lets us off the hook much too easily. To see why, consider again Russell's idea of "the set whose members are all and only those sets that are not members of themselves." This engenders paradox because the proof that there cannot, on pain of contradiction, be such a set stands in tension with our strong natural inclination to accept the generalization that *every* meaningful predicate specifies a set—that for *any* given condition (including 'being a set that isn't a member of itself') there exists the set of those things that satisfies that condition (although in some cases it will merely be the so-called *empty set*).

Our investment in this generalization ('the full comprehension schema') may be so great that we feel there must be *some* error in the alleged proof-of-contradiction (despite our inability to identify one). However, our final acceptance that there is indeed no such set is an acknowledgement that we had been unreasonable—*not* in believing something that turned out to be untenable, but in irrationally insisting on something that we could have, and ought to have, always recognized as uncertain. We were *overconfidently* over-generalizing.

Of course, since none of the commitments that together engender a natural paradox is an independently identifiable blunder, it will typically be far from obvious which of them ought to be modified—which of them is the *over*-generalization. For example, the tension of Russell's paradox—the clash between the apparently irresistible attractions of classical logic and an unrestricted comprehension schema—is relieved once we come to understand that these commitments are not written in stone—that one or the other of them can (indeed must) be reined in.[21] Still, we are left with the non-trivial problems of deciding which it should be and on what alterations ought to be made.

Now one might feel that the paradox has not been well and truly dealt with until these further questions have been answered. And I don't wish to quibble about the proper use of 'well and truly dealt with.' However, terminology aside, we have seen that it is important to separate—here and elsewhere—the two very different kinds of issue that any paradox will engender. Their trademark conceptual tensions and resulting perplexities are dissolved by the recognition that they are in part the product of our obstinacy, of our unwillingness to let go of entrenched ways of thinking, of our tendency to construe that entrenchment as an infallible insight into the truth. But even after all of this has sunk in—so that the paradoxical perplexity is gone—there will remain the problem of determining *which* general assumptions are *over*-general and how they should be rectified—i.e., what the right levels of generalization ought to be. This is a problem of theory construction—quite different from paradox resolution, with a distinct methodology and distinct presuppositions.[22]

Returning to the question of whether certain paradoxes are the inevitable and forgivable products of conflicting irresistible dispositions, I think we can now see that, in point of fact, we are never in that predicament. The inclination to generalize (in such a way as to provoke doxastic tension) is actually never so strong that we can't curb it. Rather, we learn from our paradoxes where the limits of extrapolation ought to lie; and we can perfectly well control ourselves accordingly. Although *certain* generalizing proclivities may indeed be overwhelming (e.g. innate survival mechanisms inhibiting us from what has proved sickening or painful in the past), the reasoning-tendencies that lead us into philosophical paradox, however naturally, don't appear to have that depth and power. Rather, we recognize from the outset (especially in theoretical areas) that the jump to a generalization should be made with caution. The proper rule of thumb is something like: 'By all means go for it; but don't get too attached; keep an eye out for counter-examples; and don't be shocked when they turn up.' There's no foolish irrationality in our extrapolations, provided they are conducted in this tentative spirit. The irrationality consists in over-confidence, in being inappropriately wedded to the results. Only then do we fall into paradox.

11.7 Concluding Moral

Some may say, "It's not my fault—my concepts made me do it." For others the excuse is, "I was merely obeying innate epistemic orders." But I've been arguing (with Wittgenstein) that we ought to take full responsibility for the conceptual entanglements to which we are prone in doing philosophy. We can and should learn how to avoid them.[23]

Notes

1. Schiffer (2003).
2. We may think of a paradoxical tension as residing in conflicting *convictions* about what there is sufficient reason to believe, rather than *conflicting inclinations* about what to believe; for the former will engender the latter.
3. The circumference of a circle is 2π times its radius. So a lengthening of the circumference by some amount correlates with an elongation of the radius by roughly one sixth of that amount.
4. The so-called *lottery paradox* resides *not* merely in finding each of these claims highly plausible, but in sliding to the conclusion that their *conjunction* is plausible. For that is clearly inconsistent with what we know to be the case: namely, that there will be a winner.
5. This criterion—like Schiffer's, I suppose—is intended merely to point us in roughly the right direction. An exact account of what philosophical paradoxes are is likely to rest on an understanding of what is distinctive about the way in which they arise. And that is the understanding we will be striving to achieve in the remainder of this chapter. Thus one should not imagine that an accurate definition of 'philosophical paradox' must *already* be available in order for us to be in a position to investigate the underlying nature of that phenomenon.
6. Let me emphasize that my concern here is with the intrinsic merits of this view of paradoxes (elaborated further in section 11.4) and not with the accuracy of its attribution to Wittgenstein. It seems to me, rightly or wrongly, that the view is in fact contained in his later writings—see especially his *Philosophical Investigations*, paragraphs 109-33—and I feel obliged to give credit where I believe credit is due. But I acknowledge that his actual ideas on this topic may well be more nuanced that my brief account of it here would suggest, and that they may have evolved somewhat, even within the period of his later philosophy.
7. Quine (1966: 7). It should be noted that some of his other remarks in that essay are suggestive of Schiffer's position. Concerning the principle, '"f" is true of x ↔ fx', which

Quine thinks must be abandoned to avoid the 'heterological' paradox (obtained by replacing 'f' with 'is not true of itself' and replacing 'x' with the quote-name "'is not true of itself'"), he says:

> Yet so faithfully does the principle reflect what we mean in calling adjectives true of things that we cannot abandon it without abjuring the very expression 'true of' as pernicious nonsense. (7–8)

And he might be read as supposing (like Schiffer) that this explains why we find the principle so hard to give up. However, such a position would not sit well with his skepticism about meaning!

It's also worth noting that Quine doesn't say outright that, in the case of serious paradoxes, the conflicting patterns of reasoning are *fundamental*. However, only if that is so can it be that none of them is straightforwardly recognizable as mistaken (by reference to more basic rules).

These are the reasons for which I hesitate to attribute the third approach to Quine.

8. See C. G. Hempel (1945). For more on the above Bayesian solution, see Horwich (1982: 54–63) and Horwich (2004).
9. See Lambert (2002).
10. For discussion of Agrippa's regress-of-justification argument, see Williams (2001), Chapter 5, esp. pp. 61–3.

    Once we have allowed ourselves to acknowledge the existence of beliefs that are unsupported yet nonetheless rational, it would be arbitrary to insist that this special class be restricted to *observational* beliefs. And also it would be undesirable; since that restriction would still leave us with further epistemological paradoxes (e.g. the 'brain in a vat' argument, mentioned on p. 212). Rather, we should be primed to recognize as additional members of the special class whatever else may be needed to defuse those paradoxes too (—perhaps, for example, that what *seems* red probably *is* red, and that if all observed emerald have been green then it's not unlikely that the next one will turn out to be green). Thus, other skeptical paradoxes will also have happy-face solutions.

    As we'd expect, Schiffer disagrees. His alternative "glitchy concept" account of these problems is presented in Schiffer (1995/6).
11. This is a rendition of John Mackie's reason for supposing that moral facts would have be so queer that there probably aren't any. See Mackie (1977).
12. For more on this expressivist-emotivist conception of normativity, see Blackburn (1993), Gibbard (2003), and Horwich (2010a).
13. It seems to me that the *sorites* paradox, too, has a solution that turns on the exposure of over-generalization (though I admit that this solution is especially far from being generally recognized as such).

    The notorious problem is this. It seems unquestionable that if a single grain is removed from a heap of sand, we will still be left with a heap; but unless that assumption is suspended we can infer, by repeated applications of it, that zero grains will be enough for a heap!

    So—initial appearances to the contrary—the assumption must in fact be wrong; and our problem becomes that of understanding why it can seem so obviously right.

    The explanation (I would suggest) stems from the fact that there can be no *intuitively clear* case of a heap of sand being transformed into a non-heap by removal of just one grain. So intuition pushes us to conclude that there is *no case at all*. But, on reflection, this step is fallacious. For, on the one hand, it is in the very nature of a vague concept that its application to things within a certain range (the 'borderline' cases) be irremediably uncertain and controversial. Yet, on the other hand, the initially cited, step-by-step, reductio argument demonstrates that somewhere in that range there *must* be a sudden transition from 'enough for a heap' to 'not enough.' Therefore, the fact that 'intuition' cannot identify that transition point is precisely what we should expect, *even relative to the hypothesis that there really is such a point*. So that fact is a very bad reason for rejecting this hypothesis.

For further discussion of this approach see Chapter 4 ("The Sharpness of Vague Terms") of Horwich (2005). Schiffer's divergent account of the sorites argument is an application of his general theory of paradox. It is to be found in Chapter 5 of *The Things We Mean*.

14. For example, it may well be that the concept expressed by 'mass' changed as we went from Newtonian Mechanics to Relativity Theory; and that the concept expressed by 'number' was modified by our move from basic arithmetic to complex analysis.

15. The distinction sketched here may be clarified by analogy with a well-known view, developed by Russell, Carnap, Ramsey, and Lewis, about how the meanings of scientific theoretical terms are fixed. In the case of 'neutrino,' for example, their idea (roughly speaking) is that, whereas its meaning (the concept, NEUTRINO) is positively deployed by those who accept neutrino-theory, 'T(n),' someone might question the substance of this theory, yet nonetheless mean the same as everyone else by the word, 'neutrino.' Therefore—they suggest—our meaning what we do by it requires merely our recognition of how 'n' is deployed in 'T(n).' And they take this recognition to be constituted by a *conditional* commitment to accept 'T(n)' *if* we were to accept *something* of the form, 'T(Φ).' For further discussion, see Horwich (2010b: 197–223).

16. To illustrate, consider the liar paradox, which derives from combining classical logic with the general schema, "<p> is true $\leftrightarrow$ p." And suppose we favor a solution that involves restricting the application of this schema. What then happens to our original concept of truth? It might be supposed that we can no longer possess precisely that concept, since we no longer assume what must be assumed in order to possess it—namely, the unrestricted truth schema. But I am suggesting, rather, that mere *possession* of the naive concept requires nothing more than an appreciation of the role of truth in that schema—which might be represented as a *conditional* endorsement of the schema, i.e., as a commitment to accept its instances *provided* that one accepts *some* general schema of the form, '<p> is $\Phi \leftrightarrow$ p.' In that case the solution to the paradox is to violate that proviso. But we retain our conditional commitment; so we continue to possess the old concept.

Granted, such a solution does involve a *kind* of conceptual change. For in transferring our allegiance to a restricted schema we are beginning to *positively deploy* a somewhat different concept of truth. But this doesn't mean that the old concept is no longer *possessed*. Nor does it mean that our initial basic mistake was that of having allowed the old notion into our conceptual repertoire. Our basic mistake was to have *positively deployed* that notion—i.e. to have thought, as a result of over-generalization, that some schema of the above unrestricted form was correct. Thus it is far from obvious that *possession* of the naïve concept of truth requires acceptance of a schema that will need to be given up if the liar-contradictions are to be avoided.

17. Examples from earlier in this chapter are (i) that our escape from the paradox of negative existentials left the problem of coming up with a *more adequate* general account of truth conditions; and (ii) our escape from the paradox of free will left the question of what *are* the conditions in which an act is free.

It's worth noting that Wittgenstein himself displays little interest in these residual theoretical issues. For him, they are, at best, *technical* questions in the formal or empirical sciences. The state of mind associated with not (yet) being able to answer them is a matter of *ignorance* rather than *puzzlement*—hence not *distinctively* philosophical. And at worst

they are the product of a confused and pointless application of the norms of scientific theory-construction beyond their proper domain.
18. For further discussion of the grounds for Wittgenstein's opposition to scientistic philosophical theorizing, see Horwich (2012) and Horwich (2016).
19. Schiffer thinks it is implausible to suppose that the classical paradoxes actually do have objectively correct solutions, given that intelligent and rational philosophers have not managed, after such a long time, to converge on what they are. But, in the first place, although I am claiming that there are determinate solutions—i.e. objectively correct ways of escaping from conceptual tensions—I am not claiming that what I called "the residual theoretical questions" tend to have determinate answers. In the second place, I believe that the Wittgensteinian explanation of why philosophy fails to resolve paradoxes expeditiously succeeds in making plausible what might otherwise seem implausible. In the third place, such pervasive blind spots would not be unique in our intellectual history:— from an atheist's point of view the persistence of religious belief is a further example. And, in the fourth place, Schiffer's own account would equally entail the state of affairs he finds implausible (namely, that for each classical paradox there is a determinately correct way of responding to it): for he thinks that one ought to appreciate that happy-face solutions are not to be had, even though there is clearly no consensus on this point.
20. Some further examples of *natural* paradoxes would appear to be Russell's paradox of naïve set theory, Newcomb's problem, and the ship of Theseus.
21. A third option would be to recommend accepting this particular contradiction, and to diagnose the paradox as stemming from an over-generalization of the obvious unacceptability of *most* contradictions. Some such "dialethic" response appears to be what Wittgenstein is suggesting (for the case of the liar paradox) in one of his discussions with Turing in 1938 (published in Wittgenstein 1976; see lectures 21 and 22). I thank Gary Ostertag for bringing that discussion to my attention.
22. The familiar methodology of empirical theory construction emphasizes consistency with what is known, global simplicity, conservativeness, and explanatory power. Amongst the presuppositions of its application within a priori domains are, first, that it is legitimate to extend those norms in that way and, second, that the theories that will result from doing so will constitute knowledge that is worth having. As we saw in note 17, Wittgenstein regarded these presuppositions as quite dubious.
23. This essay—which appeared as Chapter 11 of Horwich (2010)—was in fact written for the present volume, and also for a conference in honor of Stephen Schiffer that was held in Pecs, Hungary on 14–15 May 2007. I would like to thank Gary Ostertag for very helpful advice on how to improve an early draft of it, and Stephen himself for his critical responses to my talk at the conference. I am grateful also for the questions and comments I received from Paul Boghossian, Alexi Burgess, Dean Chapman, Yasuo Deguchi, Philippe Keller, Jakob Rosen, and from others who attended presentations of this material: at the University of Pecs, the University of Geneva (February 2007), the University of Kyoto (May 2007), the University of Connecticut (November 2007), and New York University (February 2008).

Bibliography

Blackburn, S. (1993). *Essays in Quasi Realism*. Oxford: Oxford University Press.
Gibbard, A. (2003). *Thinking How to Live*. Cambridge: Harvard University Press.
Hempel, C. G. (1945). "Studies in the Logic of Confirmation." *Mind* 54: 1–26, 97–121; reprinted in *Studies in the Logic of Confirmation*. New York: Free Press, 1965.

Horwich, P. (1982). *Probability and Evidence*. Clarendon: Cambridge University Press.
Horwich, P. (2004). "Wittgensteinian Bayesianism." In *From a Deflationary Point of View*. Oxford: Clarendon Press.
Horwich, P. (2005). *Reflections on Meaning*. Oxford: Clarendon Press.
Horwich, P. (2010a). "The Motive Power of Evaluative Concepts." In *Truth—Meaning—Reality*, Oxford: Oxford University Press, pp. 167–95.
Horwich, P. (2010b). "Ungrounded Reason." In *Truth—Meaning—Reality*, Oxford: Oxford University Press, pp. 197–223.
Horwich, P. (2016). "Wittgenstein's Global Deflationism" in H. Cappelen, T. Szabó Gendler, and J. Hawthorne (eds.) *The Oxford Handbook of Philosophical Methodology*. Oxford: Oxford University Press.
Lambert, K. (2002). *Free Logic: Selected Essays*. Clarendon: Cambridge University Press.
Mackie, J. L. (1977). *Ethics: Inventing Right and Wrong*. London: Viking Press.
Quine, W. V. (1966). "The Ways of Paradox." In *The Ways of Paradox and Other Essays*. New York: Random House.
Schiffer, S. (1995/6). "Contextualist Solutions to Scepticism." *Proceedings of the Aristotelian Society* 96: 317–33.
Schiffer, S. (2003). *The Things We Mean*. Oxford: Clarendon Press.
Williams, M. (2001). *Problems of Knowledge*. Oxford: Oxford University Press.
Wittgenstein, L. (1953). *Philosophical Investigations*, edited by G. E. M. Anscombe and R. Rhees, translated by G. E. M. Anscombe, Oxford: Blackwell.
Wittgenstein, L. (1958). *The Blue and Brown Books*. Oxford: Blackwell.
Wittgenstein, L. (1976). *Wittgenstein's Lectures on the Foundations of Mathematics*, edited by Cora Diamond, Sussex: The Harvester Press.

12
Silent Reference

Stephen Neale

12.1 Introduction

Debates about the strength of *schiff* are as heated today as they were in Oxford's halcyon days of palaeopragmatics. Is it a contracted *schif and only schif*, as Strawson maintained? Or is it equivalent to the non-commutative *schif and only if*, as Grice suggested (tentatively), the illusion of anything stronger attributable to conversational implicature? Both recognized that *schiff and only schiff* harboured an infinite regress. And both saw the apocryphal *schiff and only if* as frivolous. But with the arrival in Oxford of advanced American technology, the quest began for a regress in *schif and only schif*. And it fell to one (remarkably named) Stephen Schiffer, to provide a proof and *ibs so fucto* crush all compositional and commutative pretensions.[1]

It is a pleasure and a privilege to contribute to this volume celebrating Stephen's work. He has been a great friend and philosophical interlocutor for two decades, and I have learned much from his work and his constructive criticisms of my own, particularly in immensely enjoyable seminars we have taught together as joint CUNY/NYU courses. A topic that has bubbled away in those seminars is what Schiffer originally called *implicit reference* (often discussed under Schiffer's later regrettable, label, *hidden indexicality*). Implicit reference is a controversial topic for two reasons. Firstly, it has been used in attempts to addressed puzzles about knowledge, truth, moral relativism, objectivity, aesthetic judgment, necessity, attitude ascriptions, and seemingly incomplete nominal and adjectival expressions (most famously, definite descriptions). The driving idea is that felicitous uses of certain expressions involve implicit reference to such things as epistemic standards, moralities, possible worlds, modes of presentation, moral codes, personal tastes, locations, quantifier domains, and comparison classes. Secondly, it has been used to cast doubt on a widely held thesis about natural language that I'll call TCS for "truth-conditional semantics":

(TCS) For every declarative sentence x with all lexical, structural, anaphoric and prosodic ambiguities resolved, the truth conditions of what is said (or the proposition expressed) by x, relative to an occasion or context of utterance are wholly determined by (i) the meanings of the individual words in x, (ii) prosodic features of x, (iii) principles of semantic composition that reflect x's syntactic structure and prosody, and (iv) the systematic effects of a pre-established set of features of the occasion or context of utterance (exploited by the meanings of indexical expressions).[2]

Rejections of TCS often come by way of theses couched in local idioms. In Sperber and Wilson's (1986) terms, the proposition expressed may be underdetermined (or underspecified) by the mechanical interactions of (i)–(iv); in Perry's (1986) terms, it may contain unarticulated constituents.[3] In Schiffer's (1981) terms, it may have constituents referred to implicitly. To endorse implicit reference, in the sense in which I shall define it here, is to acknowledge that underdetermination and unarticulated constituents are very real. But it is to do more than that. Implicit reference is a narrowly defined species of speaker reference; speaker reference is a species of speaker meaning; speaker meaning is action performed with higher-order, audience-directed intentions; and acts of meaning are material events under intentional descriptions.

With clear pictures of precisely what implicit reference is and what capacities are needed to sustain it, licensed by an underlying metaphysics of expressions and utterances, we get a better fix on the content of TCS, on how to separate constitutive, epistemic, and causal determination of content—which are frequently conflated in the literature—and on the relevance and force of appeals to context, conversational topic, conversational maxims, relevance, salience, and phonologically empty expressions to content determination in all three senses. And all of this gives us a clearer picture of what is involved in producing a semantic theory that is empirically substantive in the sense of forming part of an explanation of how we are able to express and communicate our thoughts so efficiently just by producing certain types of audible sounds and visible marks and movements. Syntactic, semantic, and pragmatic theories are empirically substantive only to the extent that they can play such a rôle, and the technical notions theorists define and deploy have empirical content only to the extent that empirically substantive theories appeal to them.

Schiffer first wrote about implicit reference in 'Naming and Knowing' (1977). He entertained (and went on to refute) a theory according to which speakers reporting beliefs refer implicitly to *mode of presentation types* that bear on the truth conditions of what is said. In 'Indexicals and the Theory of Reference' (1981), he went on to define implicit reference in terms of a broader notion of speaker reference, itself defined in terms of speaker meaning, which he had defined in *Meaning* (1972), a landmark book in which he advanced the intention-based theory of meaning initiated and explored by Paul Grice (1957, 1968, 1969). In recent years, he has sharpened his original objection to the implicit reference theory of belief reports and transposed it into objections to other implicit reference theories.[4] His attitude to implicit reference, as he characterizes it, is strikingly similar to Grice's (1981: 187) attitude to conversational implicature: (1) its existence is an explicable feature of the ordinary use of natural language; (2) to ignore it is to risk misunderstanding what certain philosophical theses entail (or at least presuppose); and (3) to avoid "any kind of sloppy use of this philosophical tool", certain antecedently specifiable conditions must be met (Grice 1981: 187). The difference is that while confirmation of the presence of a conversational implicature can indicate that a philosophical thesis entails *less* than originally thought, confirmation of the presence of implicit reference can indicate that it entails *more*. On Schiffer's account, the antecedent condition is straightforward: speakers can refer only to kinds of things they have thoughts about. Extant implicit reference accounts of knowledge, aesthetic judgment, attitude ascriptions and definite descriptions simply fail to meet this condition.

My concern in this essay is less with these particular theories than it is with the nature of implicit reference itself (construed as an important type of what I shall call *silent* reference) and with a host of maddeningly intertwined questions in metaphysics, semantics, pragmatics, formatics, syntax, phonology and psychology that it raises, questions whose answers bear on core concerns in the philosophy of language, linguistics, and cognitive science.

By zooming in on the sorts of reflections that initially prompted proto-theoretic talk of implicit reference, displaying them against a background picture of interlocking theories of expression meaning, speaker meaning, and utterance interpretation, and by sharply distinguishing and carefully relating constitutive, epistemic, and causal notions of determination, I shall articulate a notion of implicit reference that I take to have a place in a theory of reference that is empirically substantive in virtue of the contribution it makes to answering a Master Question in the study of language and communication. The first steps, taken in sections 12.2 and 12.3, involve clarifying terminology, making a few preliminary distinctions, and teasing apart different notions of meaning and reference, some of which are fused in intuitive notions. Ultimately, the theoretical notions we gravitate towards will earn their keep not by conforming to our proto-theoretic intuitions or to ordinary uses of words like 'word', 'mean', 'say', or 'refer'—which certainly help us get *started*—but in virtue of their roles within theories that are empirically substantive. Ordinary usage might be where we *begin*, but there is no reason to think that that is where we will end up.

12.2 Things that Mean

12.2.1 Speaker meaning

Suppose a teacher asks the children in a class, 'Who threw that paper plane?' One child says, 'Tom threw it.' Another says 'He did,' pointing at Tom. A third merely points at Tom but does not speak. All three children *meant* that Tom threw the paper plane. We have three cases here of what Grice (1957) calls *utterer's meaning* and Schiffer (1972) calls *speaker meaning*, though the third child did not actually speak or utter anything, in any ordinary sense. Philosophers have gravitated towards Schiffer's label, so it is the one I shall use here. The three children in the class were all *speakers* in this special technical sense. Each performed an act of *speaker meaning*: each *did something* and in so doing *meant* something. (See section 12.5.)

12.2.2 Expression meaning

Two of the three acts of speaker meaning exploited *linguistic meaning* or *expression meaning*, as I shall call it. (I use 'expression' throughout as a generic term for words, phrases, and sentences. I also use 'words' as a generic: the second child uttered the words 'He did', for example.) The words 'he' and 'did' have meanings that transcend particular utterances, their "standing" meanings as Dennis Stampe dubbed them, meanings that the second child exploited when uttering the sentence 'He did.' The child could have uttered a less "elliptical" sentence such as 'He did it,' 'He threw it,' or, pedantically, 'He threw the paper plane.' But in the context of the teacher's question, a simple 'He did' was a perfectly good way for the child to assert something that is true iff Tom threw the paper plane. Part of the explanation of this fact is that the child *also* exploited the meanings of the words 'threw', 'that', 'paper' and 'plane' which *the teacher* used. (In a different context, the same child might use 'He did' to assert something that is true iff Paul hid the chalk.)

When it comes to articulating a theory of language that can form part of a theory of how we manage to communicate like this, it is not obvious what either form of meaning exploitation consists in. One problem is unclarity about what constitutes the meaning of a word; another is what constitutes *being* a word. But whatever words are, whatever meanings are, and whatever the relevant types of exploitation consist in, we know this: both the meaning of a word and the syntactic position it occupies in a given sentence constrain what we can hope to assert using that sentence. So it has seemed perfectly natural to say that *sentences* have meanings too, and that their meanings are determined by principles respecting their syntactic structures and the meanings of the words of which they are composed. A *compositional semantics* is a theory that specifies precisely how the meanings of complex expressions (e.g. sentences) are related to the meanings of their parts, drawing upon a *lexical semantics*, which specifies the meanings of atomic expressions (roughly, words). (See section 12.11.)

12.2.3 Non-natural meaning

Expression meaning and speaker meaning are species of what Grice (1957) calls *non-natural* meaning, which is to be contrasted with the *natural* meaning we talk about when we say such things as 'Those rings mean (indicate) that this tree is more than a hundred years old.' The vague idea that non-natural meaning is to be explained in terms of natural meaning has spawned divergent and sometimes very precise theories about the place of language and symbolic representation in the natural world, drawing heavily on ideas about natural functions and behavioural regularities, correlations, or coordinations.[5] But this has had no discernible impact on how philosophers concerned with speaker meaning and expression meaning view the prospects of investigating one without investigating the other.

Many semanticists hold that a compositional semantics can be constructed without worrying about the intellectual horror of a theory of speaker meaning. A semantic theory, so the story goes, is a formally tractable object that provides a systematic explanation of an indefinitely large number of precise facts about natural language, thereby constituting the core of a story about the systematic ways in which we use language to state things that are true or false (and do much else that is parasitic on this activity). A theory of speaker meaning is very different, so the story continues: it concerns a morass of facts about the roles beliefs, desires, intentions, perceptions, memories, and social relations play in our attempts to communicate with one another.

The Gricean takes a different line. Speaker meaning is the most *basic* notion of non-natural meaning, the notion in terms of which any other empirically significant notions, including expression meaning, must be explained. And what a speaker means on a given occasion by uttering something is wholly constituted by certain *intentions* with which he produced the utterance. For the moment, it is enough to note that (i) we can readily and straightforwardly describe what speakers mean in very many cases—the three children all meant that Tom threw the paper plane, for example—and (ii) there are cases of speaker meaning that do not involve the use of natural language—one of the children merely pointed at Tom. (See section 12.5.)

12.2.4 Expressions and utterances of expressions

A distinction between expression *types* and expression *tokens* is often invoked in discussions of language. An expression token is meant to be a physical entity that instantiates (or tokens) an expression type, a non-physical entity, by virtue of possessing some formal property that involves resemblance to something or other. What we really need here is a not a distinction between two notions of an expression but an appreciation of the difference between talking about a given expression and talking about particular *utterances* of that expression. Utterances are physical events that take time. Expressions themselves are *abstractions* over them, abstract artefacts brought into existence by sufficiently many physical artefacts we have produced: utterances and signings (which are events) and inscriptions (which are objects). But having utterances of expressions on the table has brought with it semantic temptation, in the form of *utterance meaning*. See section 12.6.

12.2.5 Utterance Meaning?

In the literature—in philosophy, linguistics, cognitive science, ethology, and beyond—there is a good deal of talk about the meanings of *utterances*. And some philosophers are explicit that they take the meanings of *utterances* of expressions—rather than the meanings of expressions—to be the objects of semantic composition. In fact, there is something of a schism between what we can call expression-semantics and utterance-semantics. But putting a few cards on the table immediately will forestall potential confusion. First, there are technical difficulties involved in semantically composing purported utterance meanings, difficulties that do not arise when composing expression meanings. Second, it is unclear that there is a theoretically significant notion of utterance meaning construed as a form of non-natural meaning distinct from expression meaning and speaker meaning. Certainly some invocations of utterance meaning are the products of confusion.[6] Statements purporting to be about *utterance meaning* are, I maintain, either (a) cloaked statements about expression meaning, speaker meaning or natural meaning, or else (b) statements that involve fatal conflations of at least two of these notions. A compositional semantic theory forming part of an account of how humans communicate with language must be an expression-semantics, a theory built on the idea that the objects of semantic composition are the meanings of *expressions* (relativized to contexts or utterances, to be sure) not the meanings of *utterances* of expressions. (Mutatis mutandis for utterance-reference. See section 12.11.)

12.3 Varieties and Vehicles of Reference

Ideally, we would like to have a notion of implicit reference that has the potential to be empirically substantive and does justice to some sort of intuitive, proto-theoretic notion motivating discussions in the literature. But perhaps there is no single notion that satisfies both conditions at once. Perhaps investigation will reveal *several* substantive notions that are fused in any intuitive notion, notions that play importantly different theoretical roles. Thoughts of this kind are familiar from attempts to say what a *word*, a *sentence*, or an *utterance* is, or what *meaning*, *saying*, *referring*, or *knowing* are. But ultimately the definitions we gravitate towards earn their keep not by yielding results that conform to our proto-theoretic intuitions or to ordinary uses of words like 'word', 'sentence', 'mean', 'say', 'refer', and 'know'—which certainly help us get *started*—but in virtue of their roles within theories that are empirically substantive. It should occasion no surprise that as the notions evolve to play various theoretical roles there will be divergences between ordinary and theoretical usage of key terms.

12.3.1 Speaker Reference

The acts of speaker meaning performed by the three children in class are also acts of *speaker reference*. Each child meant something *about Tom*, namely that *he* threw the paper plane. So each child *referred* to Tom. The way I just introduced speaker reference employs Schiffer's (1981) wonderfully simple definition. Speaker reference is just *object-dependent* speaker meaning. So each child performed an act of speaker meaning that was also an act of speaker reference (not a separate act). (See sections 12.8 and 12.9.)

12.3.2 Expression Reference

Two of these acts exploited expression meaning. Should we also say they exploited *expression* reference (or *semantic* reference, as it is often called), understood as the notion employed by the compositional machinery of truth-conditional semantic theories, a notion that Geach (1962) and Kripke (1977) have argued is importantly different from speaker reference?[7] Or should we, as I have suggested elsewhere, reject the idea of a primitive notion of expression reference, align ourselves with Strawson (1950) and Linsky (1963), and wager that a compositional semantics doing justice to the way natural language works will take the reference of an expression x, as uttered on a given occasion, to be whatever the *speaker* is referring to with x on that occasion?[8]

I see no reason to change my mind (though proper names raise thorny issues). Even if the first child, who answered 'Tom did it', exploited a self-standing reference relation between the name 'Tom' and Tom—which is far from clear—the second child, who uttered 'He did,' certainly did *not* exploit a self-standing reference relation between the pronoun 'he' and Tom.[9] The second child referred to Tom *with* 'he' (exploiting the word's ordinary *meaning*, not its reference), and it is this fact, I maintain, that underpins any theoretically significant talk within compositional semantics of 'he' referring to anything, relative to this occasion of utterance. Whenever the operations of a compositional semantics appears to be sensitive to the reference of a given expression e, as used on a given occasion, this is only because those operations are, at bottom, sensitive to whatever the *speaker* is referring to with e on that occasion. To put the point another way, the idea of a serious distinction between speaker reference and expression reference is illusory. The notion of expression reference that a compositional semantics needs is just speaker reference, a definable species of speaker meaning, itself definable in terms of speakers' communicative intentions. Moreover, fundamental facts about beliefs and intentions explain why speaker reference is "rigid" in a perfectly intelligible sense that itself explains what we have become accustomed to call the *rigidity* of referring expressions, in Kripke's (1972, 1980) sense. (See section 12.11.)

But I'm jumping ahead. For the moment, it is enough to notice that (i) we can readily and straightforwardly describe what speakers are referring to in very many cases—the three children all referred to Tom, for example—and (ii) there are cases of speaker reference that do not involve the use of natural language—the third child's pointing at Tom.

12.3.3 Utterance Reference?

Just as there are philosophers and linguists who talk about utterance meaning, so there are those who talk about utterance *reference*. In a non-philosophical discussion of the second child's utterance of 'He did,' no-one is likely to ask, "Was it the *child* or the *pronoun* that referred to Tom?" But if the question were dropped in (from above, as it were), if pressed to answer, a discussant might say, "I suppose it was the combination." And it is perhaps thoughts of this sort that have led some theorists to posit a theoretical notion of reference that is different from traditional notions of expression reference and speaker reference, a notion that can replace the former in theories of semantic composition, a notion of *utterance* reference. Advocates will say that from the point of view of semantic theory the correct answer to the question "Was it the *child* or the *pronoun* that referred to Tom?" is "Neither. It was the utterance. The child's utterance of the pronoun, that is." In principle, then, we have three distinct *vehicles* of reference to contend with:

(a) *Speaker reference*: What a given speaker refers to in uttering expression *e* on a specific occasion;
(b) *Expression reference*: What *e* itself refers to (relative to a given context);
(c) *Utterance reference*: What a given utterance of *e* refers to.

The key notion I maintain, is speaker reference. It's fine for a theory of semantic composition to operate on what it takes to be the references of expressions, but that's only because what determines the reference of an expression in the relevant sense is what the speaker is referring to with it. (See section 12.11.)

Talk about utterance reference is another matter. Firstly, there are technical difficulties involved in semantically composing properties of utterances which become acute in connection with some cases of implicit reference. Secondly, statements purporting to be about utterance reference appear to be wholly dispensable because they are either (a) cloaked statements about expression reference, speaker reference or natural meaning, or else (b) statements that conflate at least two of these notions.

12.3.4 Silent Reference

In section 12.9, I provide a taxonomy of around a dozen theoretically significant forms of *speaker reference*. For now, I shall provide only a few pointers, with just enough detail to get things moving. In accord with my title, I begin with silent reference (which turns out to be a hodge-podge of six forms of silent reference in the eventual taxonomy).

The child who pointed at Tom performed an act of speaker reference that can be classified more narrowly as an act of *silent* reference. This particular type of silent reference is not my primary focus here (though it will surface on occasion). First, it does not involve uttering *words*, and the cases of silent reference of most interest to the debates in the philosophy of language and linguistics are those in which the meanings of words still play key roles, for they are the cases that bear on the viability TCS. Second, although the case does not involve uttering words, it is closely associated with cases that *do*, for example the case of *explicit* speaker reference involving the second child's demonstrative utterance of 'he did.''. The cases of silent reference that will be of primary interest here are those in which a speaker refers to something not merely silently but *implicitly*, in a sense that needs to be characterized quite carefully.

12.3.5 Implicit Reference

For the moment, let's say the following, more or less in line with Schiffer (1981): in uttering something, *x*, a speaker, *S*, refers to something, *o*, implicitly if (1) *S* refers to *o* in uttering *x*, and (2) there is no part of *x with which S* referred to *o* (ignoring for now the question of what sort of thing *x* is). An utterance of the following would involve implicit reference to a location or jurisdiction:

(1) It is illegal to sell alcohol to anyone under twenty-one years old.

A speaker using (1) to say something about New York State would be referring implicitly to the state and saying something true. Equally, a speaker using (1) to say something about England would be referring implicitly to England and saying something false.

12.3.6 Aphonic Reference

In much of the literature, a good deal of what I want to call implicit reference is called *hidden indexicality*, a label introduced by Schiffer, with its regrettable connotation of indexical expressions lurking somewhere in (or perhaps behind) the branches and leaves of, syntactic trees. Some theories of natural language syntax do in fact postulate expressions that are often described as "phonologically null", "phonetically unrealized", "unvocalized" or "unpronounced", expressions whose presence in sentences is to be revealed by work in generative syntax. To say these expressions are merely "unpronounced" or "unvocalized" suggests, wrongly, that speakers have a *choice* as to whether or not to pronounce them. And to call them "empty categories" is to conflate expressions and syntactic categories—unless it is stipulated in advance that there cannot be distinct aphonics belonging to the same syntactic category. In line with earlier work, I'll call them *aphonic* expressions, or just *aphonics*, for short, a label that is meant to capture the fact that I am talking about individual expressions that are unpronounced and unheard *by their nature*, expressions that instrinsically lack phonological features or instructions for pronunciation.[10] Schiffer is keen to distance himself from this regrettable connotation.[11] Perhaps *some* cases of implicit reference should be explained, in part, by the presence of indexical aphonic referring expressions in sentences, but it is no part of what Schiffer meant by 'hidden indexical' that every case does so. If there are cases of implicit reference that are explained in part by the presence of aphonics in sentences, let's say these cases involve *aphonic reference* (reference with an aphonic expression), which we can contrast with ordinary cases of phonic reference (reference with a phonic expression) i.e. explicit speaker reference. So, conceptually, aphonic reference will be a special case of implicit reference. And it is an empirical question whether all cases of implicit reference are, in fact, cases of aphonic reference.

Once we introduce aphonic reference, we must be particularly careful about the distinction between sentences and utterances of sentences. Sentences have words (and phrases) as parts, *utterances* of sentences have *utterances* of words (and phrases) as parts. To entertain the idea of aphonic referring expressions is to entertain the idea of sentences having proper parts to which no proper part of any *utterance* of those sentences corresponds.

12.3.7 Indirect Meaning

Suppose you are one of a group of people invited to my home for dinner. It is midnight. The other guests have gone. I want you to leave, but I do not want to be *direct* about that, so I say, 'I'm tired.' I mean *two* things—it's my example, so I get to stipulate this. I mean that I'm tired; but I also mean that you should leave now. Borrowing Grice's (1975) terminology, I am *saying* that I'm tired and *conversationally implicating* that you should leave. In my preferred idiom, which I shall draw upon here in order to introduce the notion of *indirect reference*, but otherwise largely eschew, I *directly* mean that I'm tired and *indirectly* mean that you should leave now.[12]

Meaning directly and meaning indirectly are broader notions than saying and conversationally implicating because they explicitly include non-linguistic cases. An example: instead of saying to you 'I'm tired,' I yawn ostentatiously. By doing so, I *directly* mean (but do not, strictly speaking, *say*) that I'm tired and *indirectly* mean (but do not, strictly speaking, *conversationally implicate*) that you should leave. Rather than exploiting *linguistic* meaning, I am now exploiting *natural* meaning in the form of a natural connection between yawning and tiredness in order to directly mean something, expecting you to recognize that I have produced an overtly *non-natural* (voluntary, intentional) imitation of a *natural* yawn.

12.3.8 Indirect Reference

Corresponding to direct and indirect speaker meaning we have direct and indirect speaker reference which must not be confused with explicit and implicit speaker reference. In the case just sketched, when I say to you, 'I'm tired,' I am referring to myself with 'I'. But somehow or other, I am also referring to *you*, for part of what I mean is that *you* should leave now. On my usage here, I am *not* referring to you implicitly, I am referring to you *indirectly*. This is because the truth conditions of what I *indirectly* mean (indeed, conversationally implicate) involve you, not the truth conditions of what I *directly* mean (indeed, say). The truth conditions of what I directly mean, however, do involve me. So we can say that I refer to myself *directly* but to you only *indirectly*.[13]

Since a speaker can say something and implicate something about the same object, we need to allow for the possibility of a speaker referring both directly and indirectly to that object. On the face of it, Grice's example of a letter of recommendation that damns with faint praise qualifies. All Grice writes is, 'Jones has wonderful handwriting and is always punctual.' Grice says (or at least *makes as if* to say) that Jones has wonderful handwriting and is always punctual, and implicates that Jones is not particularly well qualified for the position or something along those lines. (As Grice points out, there is considerable indeterminacy in the content of implicatures.) What Grice says (means directly) and what he implicates (means indirectly) *both* involve Jones; so Grice refers to Jones directly and indirectly.

12.3.9 Examples

I want now to sketch a broad range of examples that have been (or might well be) taken to involve one or another variety of silent reference, drawing upon the notions just introduced but otherwise imposing a minimum of theory, waiving syntactic and metaphysical questions about logical form, ellipsis, control vs raising, aphonics, and the nature of words, and sometimes overlooking—or intentionally blurring—for now the crucial distinction between *expressions* and *utterances* of expressions, which will figure prominently in the rest of the chapter. Similarities between some of the examples will be obvious, but there is little systematicity in the way I have ordered or labeled them—indeed, the labels are playful with use and mention, and are not intended to suggest particular syntactic, semantic, or pragmatic theses.

Yes–No Answers. This is one of Schiffer's (1981) examples. You ask me whether Truman is still alive. I say, 'No', intending this to be a perfectly adequate way (as, indeed, it should be) of telling you that Truman is not still alive. In uttering 'No', I referred to Truman, but there is no part of the expression I uttered with which I referred to him. I referred to him silently. I certainly *meant* that Truman is not still alive. And if I *said* (*directly meant*) he is not still alive, then I referred to him implicitly (rather than indirectly).

Imperatives. This is also one of Schiffer's (1981) examples. Sue says to Andy, 'Pass the caviar, please.' There is no expression with which Sue is referring to Andy. She refers to him implicitly. (Question: Does this sort of example involve rule-governed ellipsis of some sort? For example, is 'Pass the caviar, please,' an elliptical version of 'You pass the caviar, please'?)[14]

Implicit Times. Examples of this sort have been discussed by Sperber and Wilson (1986). I might say, 'I've had an afternoon nap,' to tell you that I've had an afternoon nap *today*. I might say, 'I've had a flu shot,' to tell you that I've had a flu shot *this year*. I might say, 'I've had measles,' to tell you that I've had measles *in my lifetime*. In each of these cases, I refer implicitly to some period of time, but there is no expression with which I refer to it (unless the tense morpheme functions as some sort of indexical that speakers use to refer to time periods).

Implicit Locations. Examples involving implicit locations have been discussed by Perry (1986), Schiffer (1992). and many others.[15] Here is Schiffer (I've changed the names to names beginning with the letters 'S' and 'A' to conform to the rest of the chapter, 'S' (suggesting 'speaker') and 'A' (suggesting 'addressee', 'audience' or 'auditor')):

Andy calls Sue in Chicago and asks about the weather. Sue replies, 'It's raining.' Here Sue refers to Chicago, and this by virtue of the fact that in uttering 'It's raining', she means that it is raining in Chicago. In other words, Sue counts as having referred to Chicago because the proposition she meant is about Chicago. Notice that there is no difficulty whatever in ascribing to S the propositional speech act in question: Sue clearly intended Andy to believe that it was raining in Chicago, and she is quite prepared to tell you that this is what she meant, what she implicitly said, and what she intended be to be informed of. Because these things are so clear, Sue's utterance is a paradigm of implicit reference. (1992: 512)

Similar examples can be constructed by replacing 'raining' by 'foggy', 'humid', 'minus 4 degrees Celsius', '6 Beaufort', 'warming up', 'Tuesday', 'midnight', 'winter', 'illegal to ϕ', 'customary to ϕ', 'quiet', 'noisy', 'relaxing'. We regularly leave locations implicit, particularly in narratives or histories in which a location has already been mentioned. ('Nero stamped out public drunkenness'—in Rome, but not in Gaul. 'It is illegal for anyone under twenty-one to buy alcohol'—in the US, but not in Britain.) (Question: Is a relativist approach to such examples viable, one according to which the proposition that it's snowing right now is true relative to Chicago but false relative to Tucson?)

Implicit Restrictions. This sort of example has been a staple of discussions of implicit reference since at least Strawson's (1950) 'On Referring'. It is similar to the previous two, but has interesting things in common with the several that follow. We can provide a simple example by modifying Schiffer's example involving 'It's raining':

Andy and Sue live in Chicago. They are discussing local politics and Andy asks Sue what issues will be important to her in next year's mayoral elections. (No candidates have yet emerged but the current mayor has declared categorically that he will not run.) Sue says, 'I want the next mayor to advocate gun control.' Here Sue refers to Chicago, and this by virtue of the fact that in uttering 'I want the next mayor to advocate gun control', she means that she wants the next mayor *of Chicago* to advocate gun control. In other words, Sue counts as having referred to Chicago because the proposition she meant is (in part) about Chicago. Notice that there is no difficulty whatever in ascribing to Sue the propositional speech act in question: Sue clearly intended Andy to believe that she wants the next mayor of Chicago to advocate gun control, and she is quite prepared to tell you that this is what she meant, what she implicitly said, and what she intended Andy to be informed of. Because these things are so clear, Sue's utterance is a paradigm of implicit reference.

A similar example: I look inside the fridge and say, 'There's no milk,' intending this to be a perfectly adequate way (as, indeed, it should be) of telling you there is no milk *in the fridge*. There is no expression with which I refer to the fridge. I am referring to it implicitly.

Traffic (and other) Signs. A 'No Parking' sign (or the authority that places it) makes implicit reference to a location. One task of the driver is to work out *where it is*. It is no part of the meaning of 'No Parking' signs that drivers are not to park on them, or on the walls or poles to which they are attached. Often drivers are being instructed not to park somewhere in any more or less car-length space that extends to within about a car-length of a point at more or less ninety degrees to the sign, or something like that. But sometimes the location in question is more encompassing, and drivers are usually able to work it out. There need be no English words on a parking sign. In fact, sometimes the location is referred to explicitly, but the 'No Parking' element is represented by something else (see Figure 12.1):

Implicit Specificity. This is an example of a sort discussed at length by Ludlow and Neale (1991). Half a dozen people have become raucous after rather too much to drink at an embassy party. It has been made clear to three of them, Jones, Smith, and Brown, that if they want to continue receiving invitations they need to pull themselves together or retire for the night. But Jones is now in full flight. By nine o'clock, he has spilled a few drinks, gathered people around the piano to sing rugby songs, fallen over twice in full view of everyone, smashed three crystal goblets, and tried to seduce the ambassador's wife, before toppling one last time. We carry him to his car and instruct a driver to take him home. As the car pulls out, I say to you, 'Well, I know at least one person who will not be invited here again.' I don't mention Jones by name or refer to him with an indexical, demonstrative, or definite description. I refer to him indirectly.

Association. In the next example, which is pulled from *Descriptions*, there is also indirect reference:

Suppose it is common knowledge between S and A that the tallest man in the world, whoever he is, is spending the weekend with Nicola. Suppose that there is no individual o such that either S or A believes of o that o is the tallest man in the world; however, it is common knowledge between S and A that the tallest man in the world (whoever he is) is very shy and that Nicola will take him with her wherever she goes this weekend. S and A are at a party on Saturday and it is a matter of some interest to S and A whether Nicola is present. S overhears a conversation during which someone says, 'the tallest man in the world is here.' S goes over to A and says 'the tallest man in the world is here' intending to communicate that *Nicola* is here. (Neale 1990: 88)

By uttering 'the tallest man in the world is here', S *means* that Nicola is here. But S does not *say* (or directly mean) that Nicola is here, and does not refer to Nicola *with* the description 'the tallest man in the world' or any other expression. Rather, S *conversationally implicates* (or indirectly means) that Nicola is here. And in doing so, S is referring indirectly to Nicola.

Deduction. Here's a related type of example, also pulled from *Descriptions*:

Scott Soames, David Lewis, and I are the only three people in Lewis's office. Soames has never played cricket and knows that I know this... Soames wants to know whether Lewis and I have ever played cricket, so I say,

Most people in this room have played cricket

fully intending to communicate to Soames that Lewis and I have both played cricket... given his background beliefs and given the quantificational proposition expressed... Soames was able to *infer* the truth of a particular object-dependent proposition (or two object-dependent propositions). I was thus able to convey an object-dependent proposition by uttering a sentence of the form 'most *F*s are *G*s'. (Neale 1990: 88)[16]

In short, I refer *indirectly* to Lewis and to myself.

Allusion. At a hiring meeting, I say, 'The last time we hired in logic... I'm sure you don't need to be reminded.' I am alluding to, and expect you to recognize I am alluding to, Professor Gamma-Minus, whose work on paratactic hyper-implosive polar logic turned out to be a spoof. I referred *indirectly* to Professor Gamma-Minus.

Implicit Subjects. Returning now to implicit reference, I want to sketch some examples that involve more complexity. This is one that Kripke (1972, 1977) uses to illustrate a different point. In *Naming and Necessity*, he presents it as follows:

Two men glimpse someone at a distance and think they recognize him as Jones. 'What is Jones doing?' 'Raking the leaves'. If the distant leaf-raker is actually Smith, then in some sense they are referring to Smith, even though they both use 'Jones' as a name of Jones. (Kripke 1972: 343, n. 3; 1980: 25, n. 3)

By saying "they both use 'Jones' as a name of Jones" Kripke does *not* mean that in the example they both *utter* 'Jones'. The second participant *doesn't* utter it, all he says is 'Raking the leaves.' (These are the two facts I shall focus on.) All Kripke means is that in their shared language 'Jones' is a name of Jones. This is made clear in a later version of the example:

Two people see Smith in the distance and mistake him for Jones. They have a brief colloquy: 'What is Jones doing?' 'Raking the leaves.' 'Jones,' in the common language of both, is a name of Jones; it never names Smith. Yet, in some sense, on this occasion, clearly both participants in the dialogue have referred to Smith, and the second participant has said something true about the man he referred to if and only if Smith was raking the leaves (whether or not Jones was). (Kripke, 1977: 263)

Kripke's point is that despite the fact that 'Jones' is a name of Jones in the common language of the participants, they both referred to Smith ("in some sense"). Only the first participant uttered the name 'Jones'. All the second participant said was 'Raking the leaves'. So both participants referred to someone ("in some sense"). But the second managed to do so without uttering a proper name or indeed any referring expression. He referred to Smith implicitly. Perhaps aphonically.

Implicit Binding. This type of example traces back to 1960s generative grammar. Suppose I say to you

(1) Sue wants [you to drive].

(I use pairs of square brackets to delimit whole sentences or clauses, and sometimes longer noun phrases.) I refer to Sue explicitly with 'Sue' (the subject of the main verb 'want'), and I refer to you explicitly with the pronoun 'you' (the subject of the embedded verb 'drive', in its infinitival form). *Sue* is the person I say is doing the *wanting*, and *you* are the person who will be doing the *driving* (if Sue's wish is satisfied). Now suppose I say to you

(2) Sue wants [__ to drive]

where the underscore is just an annotation marking the position in (2) that 'you' occupies in (1). Again, I refer to Sue explicitly using the subject of the main verb. But this time there appears to be no expression, occupying the subject position of the embedded verb 'drive'. So, on the face of it, either there is no such position (making (1) and (2) differ *syntactically*) or else the position is unoccupied. You have no trouble grasping what I mean by uttering (2). And if you did have trouble, I might paraphrase my remark by saying

(2′) Sue wants [*Sue (herself)* to drive].

So perhaps, in the absence of an expression in the embedded subject position in (2), the syntactic and semantic conventions of English dictate that the sentence is to be understood *as if* it contained a copy of the expression occupying the subject position of the main verb. On such an account, I refer to Sue *twice* in uttering (2), once *explicitly* with the name 'Sue' (the subject of the main verb), *qua* person doing the wanting, and again *implicitly*, *qua* person who will be doing the *driving* (if her wish is satisfied). But there's a problem. If the theory is that the expression occurring as subject of the main verb is always treated *as if* it also occurred as the subject of the embedded verb, then it will make many patently false predictions. For example, it would make (3) and (3′) equivalent, and (4) and (4′) equivalent:

(3) Everyone wants to drive

(3′) Everyone wants [*everyone* to drive].

(4) Everyone but Sue wants to drive

(4′) Everyone but Sue wants [*everyone but Sue* to drive].

A more plausible (but still problematic) account emerges if we think of the syntactic and semantic conventions of English dictating that the purported absence of an expression in the embedded subject position in (2), (3), and (4) indicates that understanding the sentence requires treating that position *as if* it were occupied by a stilted 'self' understood as a *variable* bound by the subject of the main verb, as in (2″)–(4″):

(2″) Sue$_i$ wants [*self$_i$* to drive]

(3″) Everyone$_i$ wants [*self$_i$* to drive]

(4″) [Everyone but Sue]$_i$ wants [*self$_i$* to drive].[17]

I have italicized 'self' to stress its *as if*-ness here, so to speak. The subscripts on the subject noun phrase and *self* indicate that the former (*as if*) binds the latter. (The first pair of square brackets in (4″) just delimits the subject of the main verb.) So, on the reasonable assumption that we want a uniform semantics of the embedded clauses in (2″)–(4″)—just as we want a uniform semantics of 'loves herself' in 'Sue loves herself' and 'every woman loves herself'—some cases of implicit reference can be more narrowly classified as cases of implicit binding (binding being a special form of reference).

But why all the *as if*-ness? Why not explore the idea that the embedded subject position in these sentences really *is* occupied by a variable bound by the subject of the main verb, an *aphonic* variable with the same semantics as stilted-'self'. With the *as if*-ness dropped, we are free to take those occurrences of *self* in (2″)–(4″) as occurrences of this aphonic variable. On this account, there is an expression of English we do not utter or hear, the presence of which in a sentence we could signal in our theory by writing '*self*' in structural descriptions. (Linguists usually call any aphonic occupying the position *self* occupies in (2″)–(4″) PRO. PRO is meant to have certain syntactic and semantic properties not shared by other postulated aphonics. Although I introduced *self* as an aphonic with the same semantics as stilted-'self', silent *self* should not be confused with stilted-'self'. Stilted-'self' is not silent, and silent *self* is not stilted!) If explorations along these lines produced a concrete proposal, it would then be worth exploring how best to subsume it under a general account of binding. And, in fact, this has been done.[18]

The verbs 'long' and 'yearn' differ from 'want' in an interesting way, being verbs that do not permit phonics (other than stilted-'self'), to occur as the subject of the embedded verb:

(5) Sue$_i$ longs (yearns/tried/refused/decided/attempted) [*self*$_i$ to drive].

(6) Sue admits [*self*$_i$ driving without a licence].

Here *self* is bound by the subject of the main verb, 'Sue'. To borrow some jargon from syntax, the verbs in (5) are *subject control* verbs. Those in (7), by contrast, are *object control* verbs, *self* being bound by the object of the main verb, 'Andy':

(7) Sue asked (told/ordered/persuaded) Andy$_j$ [*self*$_j$ to leave the room].

More Implicit Binding. A number of sentence types commonly used in the philosophy of language also involve implicit binding. Here are two much loved by Griceans:

(8) a. Sue$_i$ meant/said that p by [*self*$_i$ uttering x]
    b. By [*self*$_i$ uttering x], Sue$_i$ meant/said that p

(9) a. Sue$_i$ referred to o in [*self*$_i$ uttering x]
    b. In [*self*$_i$ uttering x], Sue$_i$ referred to o.

Sentences of the following type are also common:

(10) Sue$_i$ used the pronoun 'he' [*self*$_i$ to refer to Andy]

On the face of it, in key respects (10) is structurally identical to the following:

(11) Sue$_i$ used her finger [*self$_i$* to refer to Andy]

(12) Sue$_i$ used an abacus [*self$_i$* to solve the problem].

The indexing I have imposed on these examples takes *self* to be bound by the subject expression, 'Sue', so I am assuming 'use' is a subject control verb. So indexed, (10) is ostensibly being used to make a statement about *speaker* reference (roughly equivalent to 'Sue used the pronoun "he" and in doing so *she* referred to Andy'). Does 'use' *have to be* a subject control verb? Is there a legitimate indexing of (10) on which 'use' is an object control verb, giving us a reading on which *self* is bound by the pronoun 'he', so that (10) is ostensibly being used to make a statement about *expression* reference (roughly equivalent to 'Sue used the pronoun "he" in such a way that *it* referred to Andy')?[19] In the absence of evidence to the contrary, I shall take (10) to be a statement about speaker reference, with the indexing I have given it. That is, I shall treat 'use' as a *subject control* verb as far as theoretical statements are concerned.[20]

12.3.10 Questions

Using a vocabulary that I shall deploy later, I am going to develop an example involving a weather report to raise some questions. Sue and Andy live in London. It's been unusually, uncomfortably hot there for the past two weeks. It's now 7.30 a.m. and the couple are eating breakfast. It's not yet hot, but Andy, who dislikes the heat, fears it will be hot again by noon. Sue picks up the newspaper. When she reaches the page containing the weather report, Andy says,

(13) How hot's it going to be today?

He could have mentioned London by name, but didn't. He could have used the indexical 'here' or a demonstrative or definite description such as 'this infernal city' or 'the city of your dreams'. But he didn't. Nonetheless, Sue correctly takes him to be asking about today's temperature *in London*. But she is more interested in the weather in Dubai, where she must fly tonight on business. She is surprised to notice that yesterday's high in Dubai was lower than yesterday's high in London, so before answering Andy's question about today's forecast for London, she says to him,

(14) It was hotter yesterday than it was in Dubai!

Her statement is true if and only if it was hotter in *London* yesterday than it was in Dubai (yesterday). Indeed, she could just as well have uttered the longer sentence (14′) instead of (14):

(14′) It was hotter in London yesterday than it was in Dubai!

But she uttered (2). And in so doing she mentioned Dubai by name. But, like Andy, she didn't mention *London* by name, and didn't use the indexical 'here' or a description to refer to it. There was no need: a few seconds earlier, Andy had just asked a question about the weather in London (though not by name). She grasped what *he* meant, and he grasped what *she* meant.

Taking the difference between (14) and (14′) at face value, for the moment, we can say that *if* Sue had uttered (14′) rather than (14), she would have referred *explicitly* to both London and Dubai (as there are proper parts of (14) with which she would have referred to London and to Dubai, viz. the names 'London' and 'Dubai'). But in fact she uttered (14), and when she did so she referred explicitly to Dubai but only *implicitly* to London (as there is no proper part of (14) with which she referred to London).

For better or worse, a number of important theoretical choices have been made by the way I have described Sue's utterance of (14). The relevant issues raise questions whose answers are not always obvious. For the moment, I'll just state them, leaving potential answers until we have the pieces needed to make certain distinctions.

Determination. The first question to ask is a metaphysical one:

(Q1) What constitutively determines what a speaker refers to implicitly in uttering a sentence on a given occasion?

It does not follow from the mere fact that Sue was *in London* when she uttered (14) that she meant it was hotter *in London* yesterday than it was in Dubai. In fact, it is neither necessary nor sufficient for a speaker to be in London to mean this by uttering (14). Consider a case where Sue is in Berlin talking on the telephone to Andy in London. He has been complaining about the unusual, uncomfortable heat in London. She sympathizes, says she has just seen the international weather on CNN, and then utters (14). She means that it was hotter yesterday *in London* than it was in Dubai, and if all goes well Andy recognizes this. So being in London is not necessary. Nor is it sufficient: the same case reveals that being located in *x* does not suffice for a speaker uttering (14) to mean that it was hotter *in x* yesterday than it was in Dubai. For anyone who has absorbed points made by Grice, Schiffer, and Donnellan, the answer to (Q1) is clear: (a) the place Sue refers to implicitly in uttering (14) is constitutively determined by her *communicative intention* in uttering it, an intention whose *fulfilment* (but not identity), consists in its being recognized by Andy (*qua* addressee); (b) the *formation* of that intention is constrained by Sue's knowledge of the words she is using and by certain beliefs she has (or assumptions she is making) about Andy, the context, the topic of conversation, and probably other things, for the simple reason that she cannot have the requisite communicative intention unless she thinks there is a good chance Andy will recognize it; and (c) Andy's knowledge of the words Sue is using and certain beliefs he has (or assumptions he is making) about Sue *qua* speaker), the context, the topic of conversation and probably other things, will play rôles in his reaching a conclusion about what Sue means, on this occasion, by uttering (14).

Individuation. Let's continue with Sue and Andy at breakfast. While reading the newspaper, Sue comes across a story about new powers granted to the mayor of London. She decides to tell Andy:

(15) When it's snowing, the mayor now has the authority to prohibit cycling on the streets.

What Sue means by uttering (15) is that when it's snowing *in London*, the mayor *of London* now has the authority to prohibit cycling on the streets *of London*. (She does not mean that when it's snowing *in Brighton*, the mayor *of London* now has the authority to prohibit cycling on the streets *of Brighton*, for example, though it's not hard to imagine a situation in which someone might mean precisely this by uttering (15).) Instead of uttering (15), Sue *could* have uttered (15′), (15″), or (15‴), which contain, respectively, one, two, and three occurrences of 'London':

(15′) When it's snowing *in London*, the mayor now has the authority to prohibit cycling on the streets.

(15″) When it's snowing *in London*, the mayor *of London* now has the authority to prohibit cycling on the streets

(15‴) When it's snowing *in London*, the mayor *of London* now has the authority to prohibit cycling on the streets *of London*.

On the face of it, acts of explicit reference can be counted by counting the occurrences of referring expressions in the sentence uttered. Had Sue opted for (15‴) instead of (15), she would have referred explicitly to London three times (with 'London'). If she had opted for (15″), she would have referred explicitly to London twice. If she had opted for (15′), she would have referred explicitly to London just once. But she opted for (15), and so did not refer *explicitly* to London at all. She referred to London implicitly. But *how many times did she do that*? Three times? Or just once? If, in uttering (15′) she would have referred explicitly to London once, does this mean she would have referred *implicitly* to London twice? And if, in uttering (15″), she would have referred explicitly to London twice, does this mean she would have referred *implicitly* to London only once? Or do these questions betray a misunderstanding of the notion of implicit reference, a misunderstanding based on seeing every act of implicit reference as corresponding to an act of explicit reference that *would* have been made if a referring expression had been used?

The underlying question that needs answering is this:

(Q2) Can we count acts of *implicit* reference this straightforwardly? (Can we do it by counting seeming *absences* of potential referring expressions, for example?)

Aphonics. Countenancing the possibility of sentences containing phonologically unrealized expressions suggests this question:

(Q3) If a speaker refers to something o implicitly in uttering a *sentence*, x, could a key part of the explanation be that there is a syntactic position in x occupied by an *aphonic* term the speaker is using to refer to o?

If the answer to the previous question is affirmative, we can ask another:

(Q4) How plausible is the thesis that in *every* case in which the speaker refers to something implicitly, there is a syntactic position in the sentence the speaker uttered that is occupied by an *aphonic* term the speaker is using to refer to that thing?

Composition. A related question is this:

(Q5) If, in uttering a sentence x, the speaker refers to o with an aphonic term e occupying a position i in x, does a compositional semantic theory do its job by treating e itself as referring to o (relative to position i in x)?

Logical Form. Related to these questions is another question about syntax:

(Q6) Does positing the existence of an aphonic in a sentence require positing a level of syntactic representation such as LF ("Logical Form") distinct from surface form?

Mandate. What are we going to say about referring implicitly in uttering a sentence x if we reject the idea that x contains a (relevant) aphonic? The general question might be put like this:

(Q7) If it is not the presence of an aphonic in a given sentence x that mandates implicit reference, what is it about X, or about an utterance of x, that *does* mandate it?

Semantics. There is a serious schism in the philosophy of language between those who take the compositional semantic machinery to operate on contents of *expressions* (relative to contexts) and those who take it to operate on the contents of *utterances* of expressions. The issue is forced by the existence of indexical and demonstrative expressions. Practitioners of traditional *expression*-semantics will talk about (e.g.) the contents of the *words* 'I' and 'meditate' relative to a context, and invoke compositional machinery that serves up the proposition expressed by the *sentence* 'I meditate' relative to that context. Practitioners of *utterance*-semantics will talk about (e.g.) the contents of the specific *utterances* of the words 'I' and 'meditate' making up a particular utterance of 'I meditate', and invoke compositional machinery that serves up the proposition expressed by the composite utterance of the sentence 'I meditate'. The respective bearers of content are very different beasts. Expressions are abstract entities (abstract *artifacts*), whereas utterances are acts, hence material events (under intentional descriptions). In many settings, philosophers can afford to be agnostic about whether they are assuming expression-semantics or utterance-semantics. But implicit reference is most certainly *not* one of those settings. Inevitably, we are going to be forced to talk about the *parts* of both sentences and utterances, and if we are going to entertain the possibility of sentences containing aphonics, then as a matter of definition we are going to be entertaining the possibility of a *sentence x* containing a part to which no part of any *utterance* of x corresponds.[21] So one question we would like to see answered is this:

(Q8) What constraints do accounts of implicit reference and expression-semantics place on one another?

(Q9) What constraints do accounts of implicit reference and utterance-semantics place on one another?

Rigidity. Let's return to Sue's utterance of (14) to Andy:

(14) It was hotter yesterday than it was in Dubai!

I said that what Sue said is true if and only if it was hotter in *London* yesterday than it was in Dubai (yesterday), noting that she could just as well have uttered (14′):

(14′) It was hotter in London yesterday than it was in Dubai!

The proper names 'London' and 'Dubai' are rigid designators in Kripke's (1972) sense. 'London' refers to the same thing with respect to every possible world in which the thing it refers to with respect to this world exists, namely London. So we need to answer the following questions:

(Q10) How do we explain the fact that the truth conditions are the same whether Sue utters (14) or (14')?

(Q11) Is the moral of the example that rigidity is only *derivatively* a property of proper names and other referring expressions, the underlying property being a property of acts of speaker reference?[22]

(Q12) Or is the moral that (14) contains a rigid aphonic referring expression with which Sue refers to London?

Psychology. Suppose the answer to (Q1) is that the speaker's referential intentions determine what a speaker refers to implicitly. The following question now arises:

(Q13) Can we make sense of the idea that speakers have referential intentions in connection with *aphonics* in the sentences they are uttering? (Might speakers have *implicit* intentions, as they are said by Chomskyans to have implicit knowledge of the presence of aphonics in sentences?)

Ignorance. What Sue refers to implicitly in uttering (14) or (15) is a *place*; and places are things ordinary speakers *recognize* they are talking about. Furthermore, speakers have at their disposal ordinary terms *with which* they can refer to those things *explicitly* (e.g. 'London' or 'here'). But the same cannot be said about, say, *modes of presentation*, as Schiffer has stressed. Most speakers have never heard or thought about them, and they do not have at their disposal ordinary terms with which they can refer to them explicitly. Following Schiffer (1977), a number of people have attempted to solve puzzles about beliefs and belief reports by appealing to theories according to which reporting a belief involves implicitly referring to a mode of presentation (or type thereof). So the following question needs to be addressed:

(Q14) Can a speaker refer implicitly to something he or she does not know about, such as a mode of presentation?

12.4 Methodological and Terminological Issues

12.4.1 Intuitions

Theoretical notions and distinctions often have a basis in intuition, and early uses of the terms we select for potentially theoretical notions often have a basis in intuitions about pre-theoretical usage of those terms. There is no special class of philosophical uses of the words 'intuition' and 'intuitive'. There are all sorts of uses, some easier to explain or more useful than others.[23] There is nothing mysterious in my usage above. I'm using 'intuitions' to cover fast, pretty reliable judgments (some more malleable than others) that human evolution and our individual life histories have, in various proportions, tuned us to make because of advantages they bestow, judgments we are normally not in the habit of justifying because (i) sufficiently similar judgments we have made in the past have tended to be beneficial to us (as far as we know), and (ii) our being tuned to make such judgments enables us to react to certain things sufficiently quickly that there is neither the time nor the need—once we've acted it's too late—to justify the judgment.[24] Within any individual, judgments of this sort surely lie on several sliding scales, speed, strength, and robustness being obvious dimensions. Many of them likely form clusters on those scales, some clusters quite reasonably called the products of proto-theories, particularly when they concern objects or events studied in a field in which the judger has received some form of training. A seasoned archaeologist who has worked on excavations in Crete for decades will have less trouble than the undergraduate on his first dig classifying certain walls, pots, or even sherds as, say, Minoan. Her expert judgments might have the hallmarks of cognitive reflexes and she, unlike the novice, might be able to classify fifty sherds a minute with reasonable accuracy. When it comes to our intuitive judgments about language, if we have acquired language in the usual way then by the time we are in our teens we are in a position analogous to that of an archaeologist who has received a solid training and gained a decent amount of experience in the field. That means there is room for some "improvement", or more "sophistication", or at least more "harmony" with the judgments others make. And if we go into philosophy or linguistics and so spend a lot of time thinking about truth conditions, rigidity, grammaticality, and speaker meaning, it is inevitable we will, by dint of training, exposure, and conscious shifts, develop more robust and more refined intuitions about the applications of words of philosophical significance, for example the verbs 'mean', 'refer', 'say', 'know', and 'believe', or the nouns 'meaning', 'intention', 'word', and 'sentence'.

This goes a good way towards explaining why we see ourselves, as philosophers, working with a theory of X that can be regarded as connected to an earlier prototheory of X, without being hostage to pre-, proto-, or semi-theoretic judgments or to "ordinary", "common", "intuitively correct", or even "somewhat sophisticated" uses of key words. Formulating substantive theories often involves replacing or sharpening the loose, proto-, or semi-theoretical notions lurking behind the questions that motivate our early investigations. But philosophical investigations have to begin *somewhere*, and, in the early stages, familiar language will be used, and it is hardly surprising that formulations of questions about language and communication have relied heavily on both immediate reactions to, and more sustained reflections on, uses of the words listed in the previous paragraph, or that considerable effort has gone into defining and sharpening the notions these words are meant to get at in theoretical talk.

12.4.2 Theoretical Notions

We cannot take it for granted that we have reached a point where the theoretical notions and terms widely used in philosophical debates about language and communication are clear and precise enough to sustain intelligible empirical theses and debates. The number of technical and semi-technical notions invoked has increased greatly over the past thirty years or so, and it is perhaps a good time for serious philosophical reflection on the coherence and utility of many of the notions themselves. Ultimately, notions of meaning, saying, referring, and so on are substantive only to the extent that they play rôles in explaining empirical facts or phenomena. The intuitive satisfaction we might find in a distinction between two notions—speaker meaning and expression meaning, for example, or saying and conversationally implicating—does not guarantee we have mastered theoretically significant concepts that will have coherent rôles in theories of the facts or phenomena we are trying to explain.

To get close to having such concepts we would need to do at least two things. First, we would need to provide clear statements of the substantive questions and the empirical facts we are proposing to explain. (If we are unable to do this, we have no rejoinder to claims that we are just philosophers spinning our wheels.) Second, we would need to characterize with some precision the invoked notions and the *relations* they bear to one another and to other theoretical notions in a well-grounded, nexus of notions needed to formulate clear and substantive theses about language and communication.

Perhaps under the influence of linguists, philosophers seem to have become increasingly prone to thinking that they can "do semantics" without worrying about constitutive accounts of the principal theoretical notions a semantic theory employs. It is hard to gauge how much of this stems from the belief that questions about constitution can be put off "for now" and how much from the belief that addressing them *at all* evinces attachment to an outmoded style of philosophy that has no bearing on the empirical study of language. (Fashionable talk of "metasemantics" as something quite distinct from semantics may have bolstered both beliefs.) But the idea that we can investigate the semantics and syntax of natural language seriously without paying attention to these questions is surely absurd. Theories of the semantics of particular expressions or linguistic constructions can be at most as substantive as the explanatory frameworks within which they can be intelligibly placed, and without a grounded nexus of defined theoretical concepts there can be no such framework. A semantics without philosophical foundations is no semantics at all. At most it is clever wheel-spinning. So before examining implicit reference in detail, I want to articulate a framework within which key questions can be formulated and addressed cogently.

12.4.3 A Master Question

Much work in linguistics and the philosophy of language assumes from the outset (1) that expressions have *representational properties*, or *meanings*, and (2) that the principal objective is providing a specification of these meanings, part of which will take the form of a compositional semantics, a theory that explains precisely how the meanings of complex expressions are related to their syntactic structures and the meanings of their parts.

An important philosophical question is left unanswered by a theory of semantic composition, a constitutive question in metaphysics and the philosophy of language: In virtue of what facts does an expression mean whatever it means? (Or, in common jargon, what constitutes (i.e. constitutively determines) the meaning of an expression? For a non-atomic expression x the answer seems straightforward: in virtue of facts about x's syntax and the meanings of x's parts. But in virtue of what facts does an atomic expression (roughly, a word) mean whatever it means? What constitutively determines its meaning? On pain of circularity, the answer cannot be that an atomic expression means whatever it means in virtue of its contribution to the meanings of expressions of which it is a constituent. So a compositional semantics can hardly be the bedrock upon which work on language and communication rests. There will be empirical substance to a given semantic theory only to the extent that the meanings invoked by the theory can figure in explanations of empirical facts and phenomena. (Similarly for syntactic theories, for example.) To some extent, any substantive specification of the relevant facts and phenomena (and of the questions we need to answer to explain them) will be shaped by, and evolve in response to, considerations that emerge only in the course of theorizing. But it cannot be seriously doubted that central among what needs explaining are systematic features of our linguistic behavior and the nature of the *cognitive* processes and states involved in utterance *formation* (studied by what I call *formatics*) and utterance *interpretation* (studied by *pragmatics*), where these are taken to be connected in some way to the *physiological* processes and states involved in utterance *production* and utterance *perception*.[25] There are no *other* empirical facts or phenomena that a semantic theory (or, for that matter, a syntactic theory) could help explain, so a semantic (or syntactic) theory that does not potentially figure in an explanation of the facts and phenomena just mentioned must be devoid of substance.

Perhaps the preceding remarks sound too theory-laden to be compelling. But we can use pre-theoretic—or at least proto-theoretic—language to state the key point in terms of a *Master Question* that takes for granted none of the technology of contemporary theorizing deployed (and argued about) so regularly by philosophers, linguists, and cognitive scientists in the course of addressing specific questions about language and communication. A semantic (pragmatic, formatic, syntactic, morphological, phonological) theory is substantive only to the extent that it can be construed as part of a larger—*much* larger—theory that potentially answers a question we might state in a preliminary way as follows:

> **Master Question**: What general facts about our cognitive states and processes, about particular physical circumstances and social relations, about the various noises, bodily movements, and marks we are capable of producing, and about acts of producing or displaying them, explain the fact that *by* producing or displaying them we can communicate to others information about the external world or about our own beliefs, desires, plans, hopes, fears, feelings etc., express or sharpen our thoughts, and create or discharge obligations, and do such things so efficiently (i.e. so quickly, systematically, and consistently)?

In our attempts to express ourselves or communicate, sometimes things go horribly, embarrassingly wrong, of course; but the striking fact is how often they *don't*, and this is a large part of what needs to be explained.

All substantive work in formatics, pragmatics semantics, syntax, morphology, and phonology of natural language is hostage to this Master Question. An important task for philosophy is the construction of an architecture within which the Master Question (henceforth MQ) can be tackled. If we have been going about things in the right way in recent years, then that architecture will be one within which we can, in principle, produce and suspend many interlocking syntactic, semantic, and pragmatic proposals with which we are familiar. But (a) neither the architecture nor any familiar theory we end up suspending within it needs to be *mentioned* in order to say what MQ *is*, and (b) if a particular proposal in semantics (syntax, etc.) cannot be construed as part of an answer to MQ then there is nothing that proposal is *about*.

I do not mean to suggest that MQ itself contains no hint of theory. Proto-philosophical reflection and proto-theoretical classification lie behind substantive questions—inquiry has to begin somewhere, after all—and doubling back to put anything "proto" on a sounder footing (once things get moving) is itself part of the process of mature theorizing. (In the present case, we anticipate discovering ways of saying usefully what sorts of things noises, marks, gestures, information, communication, beliefs, desires, plans, commitments, hopes, fears, feelings, cognitive states, and social relations are, or at least appealing to conceptions of them that seem robust enough to occasion no deep concerns.)

12.4.4 Content

The Master Question mentions noises, marks, and bodily movements but not linguistic expressions or meanings. Yet obviously the lion's share of the efficiency the question mentions resides in the use of linguistic expressions, and ridicule awaits anyone who thinks the question can be answered without invoking a notion of expression meaning. The efficiency the use of expressions affords revolves around (1) the fact that the noises, marks and bodily movements MQ mentions are the *perceptible proxies* of expressions, and (2) the fact that expressions themselves have certain relatively stable properties, their *semantic* properties or *meanings*. (It does not follow that the perceptible proxies have meanings, a point that will be important later.)

Although the verb 'mean', does not occur in the statement of the Master Question, the verbs 'express' and 'communicate' do. So does the noun 'information', and it seems plausible that explicating the relevant notion of information will require (i) invoking a notion of *content* relevant to the individuation of certain types of mental states (e.g. beliefs) and acts of communication, and (ii) providing, for any mental state and any object, event, or state of affairs, *x*, an account of when a mental state is *about x*. So the existence of mental states and a robust notion of *aboutness* are both assumed by MQ.

There is a popular view in the philosophy of mind that having a belief (or some other propositional attitude) is, or at least involves, standing in a specific type of computational relation to a "sentence" of Mentalese (the Language of Thought), a "language" whose representational properties or "semantics" cognitive science is trying to explicate. But the popularity of a view of the mind that helps itself to terms like 'sentence', 'language', and 'semantics' is hardly a reason to claim that a notion of linguistic meaning is smuggled into all talk of mental states. Nor is popular talk of beliefs and mental states *referring* to things (objects, truth conditions, states of affairs, or whatever). (Mercifully, we have not yet been subjected to talk of mental states *saying* things!) For it was already enough to say that beliefs *have* content, *have* truth conditions, or *represent* states of affairs. Nothing is gained by adding that they *refer* to (or *say*) these things. The point carries over to sub-propositional contents. There is no upside to saying that beliefs (or their parts, if they have them) *refer* to things they are *about*. My belief that Wellington is the capital of New Zealand is a belief *about* Wellington, *about* New Zealand, and (perhaps) *about* a particular state of affairs that involves them both. To restate this by saying that my belief (or part of it) *refers* to Wellington, New Zealand, and a state of affairs is hardly progress. We already have the vocabulary we need without dragging in the verb 'refer'—which is already used in talk of *persons* and *words* (and, in some theories, utterances) referring to things. The Master Question does *not* assume the existence of entities that *refer* to things; it just assumes something pretty uncontroversial: the existence of mental states that are *about* things. (Similarly, talk of a person *referring mentally* to something is hardly progress from natural and less misleading talk of a person *thinking about* a thing.)

12.4.5 Meaning and interpreting

Although the verb 'mean' does not occur in the Master Question, two *reciprocal activities* are assumed that we are naturally inclined to describe using precisely this verb:

(1) Someone, S, *meaning* something by doing something, x, on a particular occasion

(2) Someone *reaching a conclusion* about what S means by doing x on that occasion.

So before even floating the idea of theories about systems of noises, marks, or gestures that have meaning, we have been led to the idea of a *person* meaning something by doing something, and into distinguishing (1) theories that concern *acts of meaning*, and (2) theories that concern "*acts*" *of interpreting acts of meaning*.

This is the starting point for many philosophers in their thinking about language and communication.[26] Is there any commitment in this to the view that language evolved for communication or the view that the function (or purpose) of language is communication, as is sometimes claimed? Matters are more complex than is usually assumed, I think, and I will not attempt to answer the questions here. Suffice to say, answering MQ requires explaining both linguistic communication and linguistic self-expression. (My suspicion is that we shall be unable to provide an explanation of one independently of providing an explanation of the other because both depend upon recursion.)

We sometimes communicate with one another in ways that do not involve anything usefully called a *language* (which we might, as a first shot, equate with a special *system* of noises, marks, or gestures). And it cannot be discounted that an account of non-linguistic communication will shape an account of linguistic communication, or that an account of the interpretation of human behavior quite generally will shape an account of interpreting communicative behavior. We reflexively generate hypotheses about the things we perceive—objects, situation, events, actions, phenomena, whatever. This includes especially the behavior of conspecifics, which often enough we take to be backed by reasons. To interpret an action is just to form a hypothesis about the *intentions* behind it, the intentions that *explain* it.[27] When the interpreter has done that—and ceases to revise the hypothesis—the interpretive problem is taken to be solved. As it is often put, interpreting behavior is a form of *mindreading*, construed as the capacity non-demonstratively to infer the mental states of others (e.g. their beliefs, goals, intentions) from their behavior. The behavior in question will be compatible with all sorts of different hypotheses about the intentions behind it—a standard case of an empirical hypothesis being underdetermined by the available evidence.

Interpreting *communicative* behavior is a special case of mindreading.[28] We form hypotheses about the intentions behind communicative behavior. Certain of these intentions count as communicative intentions (in a sense that needs to be elucidated); and a hypothesis about the content of a communicative intention someone has in performing a certain act is a hypothesis about what the person *meant* by performing that act. Communicative behavior, like any other, is compatible with all sorts of different hypotheses about the intentions behind it. And, to this extent, there is no guarantee the interpretation an audience comes up with will capture what the performer of the act meant. Interpretation always involves a risk, and to that extent so does attempting to communicate.

Communicative behavior involving the use of language is not magically exempted from all of this. The interpreter's *goal*—what he or she appears to be *built* to do—is the same whether interpreting linguistic or non-linguistic communicative behavior: identifying what the performer meant by engaging in it. Nonetheless, interpreting an utterance of a sentence belonging to a language one knows is surely *a special case of the aforementioned special case* of mindreading. The interpreter's largely tacit grasp of the language used will play a major rôle in the utterance interpretation processes, just as it will play a major rôle in the utterance formation process. But there is still no guarantee the interpretation an interpreter comes up with will capture what the speaker meant. Communication still involves risk on both sides.

A last point about speaker meaning and expression meaning. It is almost always speaker meaning that interests us in ordinary conversation and in many other situations in which we encounter proxies for expressions in our daily lives. That is, typically, we care more about what *people* mean than about what their *words* mean. To say this is not to deny that there are times when the exact words are important—when we read Acts of Parliament, statutes, or constitutions, for example; when listening to trial testimony; when reading novels and (especially) poetry, where imagery or feelings may be connected to uses of particular words or strings of words (often in ways we have difficulty explaining prosaically). Nor is it to deny the obvious fact that we attribute meaning when we encounter (what we take to be) inscriptions of words and have no idea who produced them; or when we look at (what we take to be) inscriptions (or pixel formations) that we know have been generated by a computer; or when we see seeming inscriptions of words in the sand and know they have been formed by nothing more than the wind. But in much of daily life words are *means to ends* and, importantly, so are their *meanings*. Only in special cases are we interested in word meanings *per se*. Canonically, when we encounter utterances, signings, and inscriptions of expressions, the largely non-conscious cognitive operations that serve up hypotheses about what *people* mean involve registering (if only subdoxastically) the meanings of the words used. But it is a striking fact that much of the time we do not retain the exact forms of words that speakers, signers, and writers use, even when we remember what we took those people to *mean*.

I am going to enforce strictly the distinction between what a person S means by doing x and what S *communicates* by doing x. To call an intention a *communicative* intention is to say it is a specific type of higher-order audience-directed intention characteristic of acts of meaning. The existence of such an intention no more guarantees its fulfillment than the existence of any other intention does. By doing something, x, S *communicates* to A that p only if S *means* that p (by doing x) and A *interprets* S as meaning that p (by doing x).

We can draw a parallel distinction between interpretation and understanding. A *understands* what S means (by doing x) only if what A interprets S as meaning (by doing x) is what S in fact means (by doing x). So if A fails to understand, then S fails to *communicate*. (More fully: If A fails to understand that S means that p (by doing x), then S fails to *communicate* to A that p (by doing x).) If A fails to understand what S means because A interprets S as meaning something other than p, then A *misunderstands* S. To understand is to interpret and get it right; to misunderstand is to interpret and get it wrong. (Notice we can say everything we need to say without talking about *misinterpreting*. So I hereby declare that if I use 'misinterpret' anywhere, it is to be understood as if it were 'misunderstand'.)

In summary, we can talk about a speaker *meaning* something by doing x, and about someone—typically someone else—*interpreting* the speaker as meaning something by doing x. When things go well, the interpreter *identifies* what the speaker *means*. In such cases, the interpreter understands and the speaker communicates. So *communicating* stands to *meaning* as *understanding* stands to *interpreting*:

	Actor	Intended Interpreter
Act/Activity	Meaning	Interpreting
Goal	Communicating	Understanding.

In what follows, I shall adhere to this usage strictly so as to avoid certain pitfalls.[29]

12.5 Gricean Underpinnings

With Schiffer, I maintain that any useful account of what *referring* is and of what *referring expressions* are must emerge from the sort of Gricean framework for semantic explanation that he did so much to advance in the 1970s and early 1980s.[30] The assumption driving this work is that the representational content of psychological states is more basic than the representational content of either natural language sentences (which are abstract objects) or the noises, marks and bodily movements that "token" them (which are material objects and events).

12.5.1 Aims

The overarching Gricean aim was to reduce *semantic* notions to psychological notions such as belief and intention. (Grice himself appears to have been happy with a functionalist account of psychological states.) The procedure was to produce a nexus of defined notions needed to theorize clearly about meaning. The most basic of these notions, for Grice, was not expression meaning but speaker meaning (or *utterer's occasion-meaning*, as he came to call it). Acts of speaker meaning are acts of attempted communication, hence acts performed with intentions to affect the psychological states of others. So the first task for the Gricean is to define speaker meaning by characterizing the nature of these intentions. Expression meaning is then to be defined in terms of speaker meaning.[31]

Schiffer (1972, 1981, 1982) has pushed the Gricean project further than anyone, providing detailed definitions not only of *speaker meaning* and *expression meaning*, but also of *speaker reference* and *expression reference*. Grice's own attempts to bring referential notions into the intentional fold can be discerned only dimly in his published work—mostly from scattered remarks in Grice (1969, 1978, 1981, 1989).

However Grice and Schiffer were construing their definitions of speaker meaning, sentence meaning, and saying between 1948 and 1972, they are best understood today as statements in *metaphysics*, as attempts to provide *constitutive accounts* of key notions. It is pointless understanding them as conceptual analyses, as attempts to define intuitive notions, or as attempts to provide *synonyms* for, or *semantic analyses* of, the verbs 'mean', 'say', 'imply', and 'refer' as they are used in ordinary English (despite appearances fostered by seemingly remorseless appeals to theorists' intuitions). They are ultimately *stipulative*, earning their keep not by yielding results that conform to pre-theoretic intuitions or ordinary uses of terms—though this is where we have to *start*—but in virtue of their interlocking rôles in theories that intended to be part of an answer to the Master Question.[32] The same is true of theoretically significant notions of *word, sentence, utterance*, and so on. Ordinary usage is where we begin, but it should occasion no surprise that as the notions evolve to play theoretical rôles there will be divergences between ordinary and theoretical uses.

Notoriously, Schiffer later went on to reject the most ambitious thesis: that expression meaning is definable in terms of speaker meaning.[33] But, contrary to what some commentators have concluded, Schiffer did not throw out the intentionalist baby with the reductive bathwater. To abandon the idea that linguistic meaning can be reduced in this way is not to abandon either (a) the idea that a theoretically robust account of *speaker meaning* (at least for central or canonical cases) *can* be provided without appealing to any other notion of meaning and *cannot* be provided except in terms of speakers' intentions, or (b) the idea that a theoretically robust account of expression meaning *cannot* be provided without appealing to the systematic rôles that expressions play in acts of *speaker* meaning (or the idea that a theoretically robust account of expression reference *cannot* be provided without appealing to the systematic rôles that expressions play in acts of speaker reference, itself understood in terms of speaker meaning). In certain key respects, then, Schiffer remains an intentionalist—which is why he still places such stock in intention-based objections to specific implicit reference proposals. Indeed, I think he is as mystified as I am by the fact that (a) and (b) have not become virtually *axiomatic* in the philosophical study of natural language and human communication.

The basic features of the Gricean program are set out below. The definitions are deliberately simpler than many of those Grice, Schiffer and others have articulated as they are intended only to give the shape of the program. Some will be replaced by more precise definitions later.

12.5.2 Meaning

Speaker Meaning. The most basic notion of meaning is that of *someone* (a "speaker") meaning something by *doing something* on a given occasion. This is the notion in terms of which expression meaning and all other public-language semantic notions are defined. (Among these are notions such as *saying, implying, referring*, and entailment.) Grice's basic definition of speaker meaning is this:

> By doing something, x, someone, S, *meant* that p iff (roughly) for some audience, A, S did x intending to produce some specific response in A via A's recognizing that S did x intending to produce that response in A.

This type of intention is a *meaning intention*, or *M-intention*, for short, often also called a communicative intention (though some care must be taken as Sperber and Wilson (1995) call the importantly weaker intentions they focus on communicative intentions). So the analysans can be abbreviated to

> S did x *M-intending* to produce a specific response in A.

No assumption is made in the definition about the nature of x. A speaker may mean something by doing x without the *act*, the *product* of the act, or any *part* of either (the act or its product) meaning anything. Specifying *what* S meant by doing x requires specifying the M-intended response. For many cases, the relevant instantiation will have the following form:

> By doing something, x, S, meant *that p* iff (roughly) for some audience, A, S did x M-intending A to think that p.[34]

In order to deal all sorts of apparent counterexamples, Grice, Strawson, Schiffer, and others explored dozens of refinements of this type of definition. (For Schiffer's refinement, which invokes a notion of *mutual knowledge*, see §8.1) Assuming something along these lines can be filled out, an explanatory notion of speaker meaning will have been defined (at least for central or canonical cases) that makes no appeal to any other notion of meaning.[35]

Expression Meaning. An explanatory notion of *expression meaning*—more generally, *utterance-type meaning*—is to be defined without appealing to any notion of meaning other than speaker meaning. The driving idea is that a theory of the meanings of the expressions in a language amounts to a theory of self-perpetuating regularities for performing acts of speaker meaning by uttering those expressions, or at least efficiency-based correlations between expressions and what speakers mean by uttering them. (Ultimately, the meaning of a *sentence x* can be viewed as something that *constrains* (without fully determining) not just what a speaker can mean by *uttering x* but, more narrowly, what he can *say* in uttering it. See below.)

12.5.3 Referring

Speaker Reference. The key insight here is due to Schiffer: singular reference is just singular speaker meaning.[36]

In doing x, S referred to o iff in doing x, S meant something the content of which is a singular, o-dependent proposition (a proposition with o-dependent truth conditions).

(So a *referential* intention is just a singular (object-dependent) M-intention.) It is in terms of this basic notion of speaker reference—which assumes nothing linguistic and no semantic notion other than speaker meaning—that all other notions of reference are to be defined.[37]

Expression Reference. An explanatory notion of *expression reference* (more generally, *utterance-type* reference) can be non-circularly defined in terms of correlations between the productions of utterance-types and what speakers refer to in producing them, correlations that can be defined without appeal to any other notion of reference or any notion of meaning other than speaker meaning.[38]

Referring Expressions. We can call the different sorts of expressions for which there are such correlations *referring expressions*. And we can distinguish different *sorts* of referring expressions in terms of different *types* of correlations—some may refer only relative to features of the context of utterance, for example.

12.5.4 Saying

Saying. The Gricean idea is that *saying* something is a special form of *meaning* something:

In uttering a sentence x (of language L), S said that p iff (1) the proposition that p conforms to the meaning of x (in L), and (2) S *meant* that p by uttering x.[39]

So S cannot say that p without *meaning* that p. This is ultimately a stipulative definition, remember, not an attempt to provide a *synonym* for, or a *semantic analysis* of one use of the verb 'say' in ordinary English.[40]

12.5.5 Playing

Play-saying. On Grice's account, sometimes the speaker only *makes as if* to say, i.e. *openly feigns* saying something. This fact plays a crucial role in his theory of conversational implicature. A provisional definition of what I shall call *play-saying* might take the following form:

In uttering an expression x (of language L), S *play-said* that p iff (1) the proposition that p conforms to the meaning of x (in L) and (2) in uttering x, S *play-meant* that p.

Play-meaning. Again, a provisional definition:

In doing x, S *play-meant* that p iff (1) in doing x, S meant *something* but did *not* mean that p, and (2) S expected A's reaching a conclusion about what S meant to proceed via A's belief that S did *not* mean that p.

12.5.6 Implicating

Conversational Implicature. S can *mean* that q without *saying* that q. For example, S may say (or play-say) that p and thereby *conversationally implicate* that q. Crucially, the *M*-intention that determines what S implicates by saying (or play-saying) whatever it is S says (or play-says) in uttering x is *ontologically dependent* upon the M-intention that determines what S says (or play-says) in uttering x. Pulling together what Grice says about speaker meaning, calculability and cancellability, we get roughly the following definition of conversational implicature:

> In saying (or play-saying) that p in uttering x, S *conversationally implicated* that q iff (roughly) (1) S expected A to recognize that S meant that q at least partly on the basis of (a) recognizing that S said (or play-said) that p and (b) presuming that S was observing the conversational maxims (or at least the Cooperative Principle), and (2) S can consistently (albeit dishonestly) deny that he meant that q without denying that he said (or play-said) that p.

S can also play-implicate. In a provisional definition, clause (1) would invoke *play-meaning* that q.

12.5.7 Act composition?

The fact that *saying* (something) and *referring* (to something) both involve *meaning* (something), precludes reading too much of theoretical significance into the intuitive idea that the simplest way of saying involves *referring* and *predicating*. A referential intention is no more than an object-dependent *communicative intention*: for S to *refer* to o in uttering x is just for S to *mean* something in uttering x and for the content of what S means to be an o-dependent *proposition*. (Referring is singular speaker meaning.) And what S means in uttering x is propositional, so *full propositional content is already involved in anything we are calling an act of referring*, it is not something that is attained only when an act of referring is composed with an act of predicating.[41] So the Gricean rejects the claim that a basic act of saying something (in uttering x) is composed of two "sub-acts", a *self-standing act of referring* to something (in uttering x) and a *self-standing act of predicating* something of that thing (in uttering x). (Since *all* acts of meaning are also acts of predicating, and *all* acts of predicating are *eo ipso* acts of meaning, *all* acts of referring are also acts of predicating.) Anything the Gricean calls an act of *saying* is an act of meaning *of a certain type*, the details of which will be provided by the definition of saying. (That is, *all* acts of saying are *eo ipso* acts of meaning, but only *some* acts of meaning are acts of saying.)

Cases of implicit reference reinforce the point. Suppose S utters (1) and means that it's snowing in London (at the time of utterance):

(1) It's snowing in London.

For the sake of argument, suppose that in the course of uttering (1), S performs a self-standing act of referring to London, an act temporally coincident with S's uttering of 'London' (and that somehow this act combines with a self-standing act of predication temporally coincident with S's uttering of the rest of the sentence. So far, so good. (I doubt it, but let that pass.) But now what are we to say about a case in which S utters (2) and means that it's snowing in London (at the time of utterance):

(2) It's snowing.

When did the self-standing act of referring to London take place? There is no sensible answer to this question, and this just confirms there is something as deeply wrong in the idea of self-standing, sub-propositional acts of referring as there is in the idea of self-standing, sub-propositional referential intentions.

12.5.8 Intention composition?

What goes for acts of meaning goes for the communicative intentions with which they are performed. Anything the Gricean calls a *referential* intention is just a singular communicative intention. (That is, *all* referential intentions are *eo ipso* communicative intentions, but only *some* communicative intentions are referential intentions because in principle the content of what a speaker means may be an object-independent proposition.) There is no commitment in this picture to the bizarre idea that a self-standing referential intention composes in some way with a self-standing predicational intention to produce a communicative intention. So the Gricean rejects the claim that the communicative intention *S* has in saying something (or even just *meaning* something) is composed of two "sub-intentions", a *self-standing referential intention* and a *self-standing predicational intention*.

12.6 Metaphysics

Intuitively, we think of certain parts of an utterance of a sentence as corresponding to parts of that sentence. But talking about implicit reference forces us to consider the possibility of aphonic reference, to take seriously the idea that we utter sentences containing words we do *not* utter, words that have no phonetic realization. So if we are going to talk seriously about implicit reference, we need accounts of (1) what sentences and words are, (2) what utterances and their parts are, and (3) the facts in virtue of which a given utterance is an utterance of a given word or sentence.

12.6.1 Words

What sorts of entities are expressions? This is a notoriously difficult question, one that talk of sets, types, tokens, forms, shapes, patterns, sounds, properties, universals, stereotypes, templates, causal chains, and space-time worms has hitherto done little to illuminate. Just as it is doubtful that the notions of meaning, referring, and saying needed to theorize about language will correspond to ordinary uses of the verbs 'mean', 'refer', and 'say', so too it is doubtful that the notions of word and sentence we need will correspond to ordinary uses of the nouns 'word' and 'sentence'.

It is often said that expressions must be abstract objects because they are not among things we perceive with the senses—we perceive objects and events, and these include inscriptions, utterances, and signings of expressions. But we can say more about *words*. They are abstract *artifacts*, along with such things as laws, practices, conventions, and social hierarchies.[42] Utterances and inscriptions (of words and sentences) are *concreta* we bring into existence. Words are *abstracta* we bring into existence by means of our actions, and destroy by means of other actions or just by inaction. If a word fails to get uttered for long enough and if all inscriptions (and other recordings) of it are destroyed, the word will pass out of existence. Surely this has happened. There is a common and consistent theoretical usage of 'word' that comports with all of this. Four examples illustrate the usage, and together they provide a reasonable characterization of what a word is.

(1) There are approximately a quarter of a million *words* in English.
(2) When you and I both say, 'I need lunch', we are uttering the *same three words*, and uttering the *same sentence*. We aren't producing the same *utterance*. So: *three* words, *two* utterances, *one* sentence, *no* problem. *Mutatis mutandis* if we both write 'I need lunch' on a piece of card (two *inscriptions* instead of two utterances).
(3) The sentence 'The cat ate the mouse' contains *four* words. It contains five *positions* in which words *occur*. But just four words *occur* in the sentence because the word 'the' *occurs* in two of those five *positions*. More concisely: the word 'the' *occurs* twice in that sentence. There are two *occurrences* of the *word* 'the' in the *sentence*.
(4) A semantic theory has two components. The lexical component specifies the meanings of individual *words*. The compositional component specifies the meanings of *sentences* on the basis of the meanings of the *words* they contain and principles respecting their syntactic configurations.

In non-theoretical contexts, we might well say "There are *five* words in the sentence 'The cat ate the mouse'." But so what? We know what people are trying to get across with such locutions, and they are doing it perfectly well using the word 'word' in a way that differs from our theoretical usage. I do it myself. I tell students in my seminar that their final papers must contain "no more that 6000 words." I rightly complain when one of them turns in a paper that I say to him "contains 36,000 words". And I do not take seriously this rejoinder: "It contains only 907 words in the theoretical sense of 'word' you have been talking about in the seminar, the theoretical sense that is the *subject matter* of my paper!" There is no need to talk about word-types and word-tokens to describe the situation clearly: (i) When I said students' papers were to contain "no more than 6000 words", I was talking about the maximum number of *inscriptions* of words there should be on the paper handed in. (ii) There were 36,000 *inscriptions* of words on the paper the student handed in. (iii) Each of the 36,000 inscriptions was an inscription of one of 907 *words*. (iv) Quite a large number of those 907 *words* were inscribed more than once. How is it progress to redescribe the situation as follows? (i') When I said students' papers were to contain "no more than 6000 words", I was talking about *word-tokens* not *word-types*. (ii') There were 36,000 *word-tokens* on the paper the student handed in. (iii') Each of the 36,000 *word-tokens* in the student's paper instantiated one of 907 *word-types*. (iv') Quite a large number of those 907 *word-types* were instantiated by more than one *word-token*. From the point of view of theorizing, we do not need to countenance two different notions of word—word-type and word-token. There are just *words* (which are abstract artifacts) and their *perceptible proxies*, utterances, signings, and inscriptions.[43]

An inscription or utterance of a word is no more a *word* than a transcription or a recording of a speech is a *speech*, than a photograph or a picture of a horse is a *horse*. Inscriptions, utterances, signings, transcriptions, recordings, photographs, and pictures are proxies, deputies, representations. It is of no philosophical moment that someone might point at an inscription of a word may say, "I don't know what this word means", just as it is of no moment that someone holding a transcription of a speech may say, "I'll put the speech on your desk", or that a salesman showing a customer a photograph of a car may say, "If you buy this car, we insure it for free for the first year."

12.6.2 Word and medium

I hold that words are medium-relative. Every word is a word in some language, and every language is a language in some medium. Words of English are intrinsically words of a *spoken* language (even though some people can produce and perceive only inscriptions of them). And words of American Sign Language (ASL) are intrinsically words of a *signed* language. It is a contingent fact that there is a writing system (orthography) for English. The writing system is a method of representing English words (and thereby larger units) by making inscriptions.[44] In a sense we can make more precise later, an inscription is a transposition of something temporal into something spatial. ASL is *not* a system for representing English words.[45] (It is *not* the gestural counterpart of the writing system for English, for example). It is a distinct language whose syntax, morphology, phonology,[46] and syllables do not reflect the syntax, phonology, morphology, and syllables of English. To render an English sentence in ASL is no less *translating* than is rendering an English sentence in French. (However, some words of English are "borrowed" by ASL through the fingerspelling of orthographic representations of those words. American and British English are mutually intelligible, but American Sign Language and British Sign Language (BSL) are *not*, despite the similarity of social connections signers of the two signed languages bear to speakers of more or less the same spoken language (with more or less the same associated writing system).[47] Fingerspelling aside, we can no more talk about signing an English sentence in ASL than we can talk about uttering an ASL sentence in English or uttering an English sentence in German (or, with Neddie Seagoon, sliding down a ship's rope in French to avoid detection at Calais).[48] So we can think of uttering an English sentence or signing an ASL sentence as *first*-order activities, producing an inscription of an English sentence as a *second*-order activity, and using Morse or (uncontracted) Braille to produce representations of English sentences as *third*-order activities, Morse and Braille being systems for representing inscriptions, which themselves represent English sentences.[49]

What the two first-order activities mentioned have in common is *action produced to be perceived and interpreted*. To utter or sign a word or sentence is to perform an act. Of course, so is inscribing a sentence, but typically it is the inscription, the *product* of the act, not the inscribing itself that is perceived and interpreted, and inscriptions are objects. And if there *is* an action that is interpreted in connection with an inscription, it is typically the *displaying* of an inscription rather than the original inscribing.

12.6.3 Utterances, signings, and inscriptions

Expressions, unlike utterances and inscriptions of expressions, are usually taken to be abstract objects. I regard *words* as abstract *artifacts* along with such things as laws, practices, conventions, and social hierarchies, things we bring into existence by our actions (and destroy by other actions or by inaction). We don't see or hear expressions any more than we see or hear laws, conventions, and so on. (1) We see objects and events. Among these are objects and events that we bring about. Among those objects we bring about are *inscriptions* of English expressions. Among those events we bring about are *signings* of ASL expressions. (2) We hear sounds, acoustic events. Among these are events we bring about, which include utterances of English expressions. So utterances, signings, and inscriptions are all things we *produce, encounter,* and *interpret*. By *producing* them, we *mean* things. And our goal in *interpreting* them is to *identify* what people mean by producing them.

The differences between objects and events are summarized lucidly by David Wiggins:

> ...objects are conceptualized in our experience as occupying space but not time, and as existing whole *through* time... An event does not persist in the way a continuant does—that is through time, gaining and losing new parts. A continuant has spatial parts, and to find the whole continuant you have only to explore its boundary at a time. An event has temporal parts, and to find the whole event you must trace it through its historical beginning to its historical end. An event does not have spatial parts in any way that is to be compared with (or understood by reference to) its relation to its temporal parts... *Material object* and *event* are in some sense duals. (Wiggins, 1980: 25-6)

Duals indeed: objects *endure*, whereas events *occur* (happen, take place, unfold in time); objects are *continuants* (they persist through time), whereas events are *occurrents* (they take time, have durations); objects *occupy* spatial locations, whereas events *occur in* them; objects have reasonably clear *spatial* (but less clear temporal) boundaries and parts, whereas events have reasonably clear *temporal* (but less clear spatial) boundaries; the parts of objects are further objects, whereas the parts of events are further events.[50] (To acknowledge this duality is not to deny an intrinsic dependence. Without objects to *participate in* them, arguably there are no events; and without events *in which to participate*, arguably there are no objects. So, arguably, the ontology of objects and events is a dependent duality.)

Utterances, signings and inscriptions are all spatio-temporal particulars. Unlike inscriptions, utterances and signings of expressions are *acts* we perform, hence concrete *events* (under intentional descriptions).[51] They are *occurrents*: they occur in spatial locations (but do not occupy them), they happen, take place, take time, have durations (but do not endure or persist though time), and have reasonably clear temporal (but less clear spatial) boundaries. Their proper parts are just more concrete events (though not all of these sub-events are interesting).

Utterances exploit vocalization, sound, and hearing (studied by *articulatory, acoustic,* and *auditory* phonetics, respectively), whereas signings exploit gesture, space, and vision. Utterances and signings of expressions are alike in being acts performed to serve as *perceptible proxies* for expressions. (This is perfectly consistent with the idea that a great number of individual expressions of spoken and signed languages come into existence by way of utterances and signings.) Utterances are *articulatory-acoustic-auditory* proxies, signings are *kinetic-spatial-visual* proxies. If utterances and signings of expressions did not stand proxy for expressions, they would not be able to function in the ways they do in speakers' and signers' dealings with one another. When it comes to utterances and signings of whole sentences, a key element of the explanation is the fact that some events that are parts of an utterance or signing of a sentence correspond to words in the sentence uttered or signed—though the correspondence may well be more complex than a linear mapping from parts of one to parts of the other. An utterance of the sentence 'The cat sat on the mat' will contain, as proper parts, two *utterances* of the word 'the', each corresponding to a distinct *occurrence* of the word 'the' in the sentence.[52] (*Mutatis mutandis* for a signing of an ASL sentence that contains two occurrences of the same word.) However, there is some *abstraction* involved in saying this because in ordinary connected speech and signing there are no sharp boundaries—whether in articulation, acoustics, or auditory experience, in the case of speech, or in kinesis, space, or visual experience, in the case of signings—between what we are taking to be the various sub-utterances or sub-signings because of such things as assimilation. (The abstraction itself is quite complex. In the case of an utterance of a sentence, we do no justice to the relationship the sound bears to the sentence if we fail to appreciate phonological abstraction from the phonetic, morphological abstraction from the phonological, and syntactic abstraction from the morphological. *Mutatis mutandis* for the relationship between the bodily movement and the sentence being signed.)

Besides being the products of a second-order activity, inscriptions are quite different from utterances and signings. They are concrete *objects*, *continuants*, albeit typically discontinuous.[53] They endure (but not occur, happen, or take place); they persist through time (but do not take time); they occupy spatial locations (but do not occur in them); they have reasonably clear spatial boundaries; their proper parts are further objects. Like signings, inscriptions exploit *space* and *vision*. But whereas signings exploit *motion*, inscriptions exploit *stasis* and *shape*. With sparklers and skywriting, we would need to talk about acts of inscribing and ephemeral inscriptions, though often there is no point at which the whole inscription exists. To keep things manageable, I shall ignore such cases.

I shall also ignore cases of displaying inscriptions of sentences. One type of example would be the chair of a conference session holding up to the speaker a piece of paper upon which he has just written 'five minutes'. Another would be a homeless person overtly holding up before a passerby a piece of card upon which 'Please help me', a card that he has used repeatedly for some days. Displayings of inscriptions are individual intentional acts, like utterances and signings. They occur, happen, take place, unfold in time, take time, and have durations and reasonably clear temporal boundaries; they occur in spatial locations; and their proper parts are further events. (The case of a homeless person just leaving the sign in front of him and not engaging passersby strains this idea, of course, as does the displaying of an official sign that reads 'No Parking'.)

I said earlier that an inscription is a transposition of something temporal into something spatial. We can be more precise now: an inscription of a sentence x is a linear segmentation in space of *objects*, corresponding to a linear segmentation in time of *events*—an utterance of x. And in a (roughly) phonemic system of inscription (such as the one we use to write English) orthographic segmentation is an approximate tracking of phonemic segmentation: the linear *spatial* sequencing of the objects in an inscription tracks the linear *temporal* sequencing of events in an utterance. Unlike an uttering or signing of a sentence, a displaying of an inscription of a sentence typically does not have parts that correspond to parts of the sentence inscribed. It is the *inscription* being displayed that has parts, and those parts typically correspond to parts of the sentence inscribed.

Grice talks about what he regards as a "convenient act-object ambiguity" (sometimes called a process-product ambiguity) in our use of 'utterance'. Act-object ambiguities certainly exist in English, most obviously with gerundive nominals such as 'painting' and 'drawing'. When we come across 'painting' or 'drawing' in a text, we can usually tell whether the author is talking about an act or an object—or, for that matter, the *activity*, which is not the same thing as any object or any particular act.[54] An *act* of painting or drawing can result in an *object*—a painting or drawing. The act may *take* an hour, but the object produced might *endure* for a century. Similarly for the non-gerundive nominal 'inscription' (though an act of inscription might also be called as act of inscribing). If there is, in the philosophical literature, a genuinely intelligible application of 'utterance' to *objects* rather than acts, we can just use the gerundive form 'uttering' when and only when talking about acts. (The count noun 'uttering' would be shorthand for 'act of uttering', and the ungainly plural 'utterings' shorthand for 'acts of uttering'. Similarly for 'signings', 'inscribings', and 'displayings'.) I'll stick to 'utterance', but I might on occasion use 'uttering' as a noun to stress that it's an act I'm talking about.

Utterances and inscriptions of words are often lumped together as "tokens" of word "types" in what are said to be Peirce's senses. But in order to avoid crossing wires, I'm going to introduce the gerundive noun 'tokening' into the discussion temporarily. Just as I've been using 'expression' as a harmless catch-all term for words, phrases, and sentences, I'll use 'tokening' as a harmless catch-all term for utterances, signings, inscriptions, and nothing else (at least for now). So two distinct *signings* of an ASL expression x are two distinct *tokenings* of x; and two *utterances* and two *inscriptions* of an English expression y are four distinct *tokenings* of y.

12.6.4 Utterance identity

The following questions need to be distinguished:

(1) In virtue of what facts is a given utterance an acoustic proxy for a given word?
(2) What properties of utterances of words enable them to function as acoustic proxies for those words?

The answer to question (2) will doubtless mention types of acoustic, articulatory, and auditory properties. But it does not follow that the answer to question (1) will. Question (1) is a constitutive question, while question (2) is a question in cognitive psychology, informed by work in acoustic, articulatory, and auditory phonetics.

Unsurprisingly, my own answer to question (1) is intention-based. I won't defend my position here but it is roughly this: To utter an expression e is (very roughly) to perform an act u that exploits the mechanics of articulation to produce a sound sequence whose acoustic properties are to provide a basis for the interpreter's perception of auditory properties, which are to provide a basis upon which the interpreter is to recognize that the speaker intends u to be an utterance of e. Relative to a few reasonable assumptions, this effectively means that an utterance u produced by S on a given occasion is an utterance of expression e iff S intended u to be an utterance of e.[55]

12.6.5 Propositions

For several reasons, I am going to assume Kaplan's (1978a, 1989a) Russellian propositions throughout: it is well known; it meshes with Kaplan's notions of content and expression reference, which will be important later; it makes it easy to talk about implicit reference in terms of constituents of propositions; and it is frequently used by Schiffer himself in discussions of reference.[56]

Following Kaplan, then, propositions are structured entities whose atomic parts are objects and properties (and whose non-atomic parts are structured entities whose atomic parts are objects and properties).[57] Propositions are assumed to have structure in much the same way that sentences do. And just as n-ary sequences (ordered n-tuples) can be used to specify the structures of sentences (typically using square rather than regular or angled brackets), so they can be used to represent propositions. The proposition that Sue meditates has Sue and the property of meditating as atomic constituents and can be represented as

<SUE, MEDITATES>

which has the obvious truth condition: it is true iff Sue meditates. It is a *singular* proposition because it has 'Sue' herself as a constituent. The proposition that some F is G, by contrast, is a general proposition whose atomic constituents are property of being F, the property of being G, and the second-order SOME relation (which holds between two properties iff the intersection of their extensions is non-empty), the, which can be represented as

≪SOME, F>, G>.

Assuming a Russellian account of descriptions, the proposition that the F is G is a general proposition whose atomic constituents are the property of being F, the property of being G, and the second-order THE relation (which holds between two properties F and G iff everything in the extension of F is in the extension of G and exactly one thing is in the extension of F) which can be represented as

≪THE, F>, G>.

Nothing that bears on my project here turns on assuming this conception of a proposition. But it's a convenient conception for talking about implicit reference, as we shall see. There is one aspect of Kaplan's conception of propositions that I shall not go along with here. Following Frege, propositions are standardly taken to have their truth-values eternally. But in Kaplan's semantics, a proposition can have different truth-values at different times.[58] I'll assume the standard view.

12.7 Determination

12.7.1 Three projects

Grice's work has provided the foundations upon which researchers have attempted to construct empirical theories of utterance interpretation, sometimes called *pragmatic* theories. Since the basic communicative goals of speakers and interpreters are reciprocal—*being understood* and *understanding*, respectively—it is natural to think the ideas providing the foundations of an interpreter-side *pragmatic* theory can also provide the foundations of a speaker-side *formatic* theory (construed an empirical theory of utterance formation). It has been largely Grice's theory of *conversation* and his theory of *conversational implicature*—the two should not be conflated—that have provided the impetus for work in pragmatics (and for what little work there has been in formatics). Three important assumptions run through much of this work. The first is that the goal of ordinary utterance interpretation is identifying what speakers *mean* by uttering what they do. The second is that what a speaker, S, means by uttering something, x, on a given occasion, is determined by certain intentions with which S uttered x. And the third is that what the speaker means is roughly divisible into what the speaker *says* in uttering x and what he or she *conversationally implicates.*[59]

But it is important to appreciate that a theory of speaker meaning of the sort Grice, Schiffer, and others have attempted to provide, is at bottom, a theory of the *metaphysics* of meaning. The definitions of speaker meaning that Griceans have articulated, examined, refuted, and refined are meant to specify what is *constitutive* of speaker meaning, of the facts *in virtue of which* someone who does such-and-such on a given occasion thereby means that so-and-so. And an adequate definition is meant to have a rightful place in a well-grounded nexus of notions needed to formulate clear and substantive theses about language and communication.[60]

It is to Sperber and Wilson that we can turn for the most serious and sustained attempts to use Grice's ideas as the base upon which to construct a *pragmatic* theory. In their hands, Grice's rational reconstruction of the type of argument an audience should be capable of constructing to verify the presence and content of a conversational implicature is at best something that points in the direction of a theory of non-demonstrative inferences that need to be characterized in terms of brute facts about human cognition. So pragmatics, for Sperber and Wilson, is straightforwardly part of cognitive science. Appreciating this difference in interests is vital to clear-headed theorizing in both pragmatics and the underlying philosophy of language and metaphysics, particularly when discussing implicit reference, as we shall see soon enough. The difference was something I tried to bring out in my 1992 review of Grice's *Studies in the Way of Words*, where I stressed

[the] distinction between (i) accounts of what S said and what S meant by uttering x and (ii) accounts of how hearers recover what S said and what S meant by uttering x.... What S meant by uttering x is determined solely by S's communicative intentions; but of course the *formation* of genuine communicative intentions by S is constrained by S's expectations: S cannot be said to utter x M-intending A to ϕ if S thinks that there is very little or no hope that S's production of x will result in A ϕ-ing.... S's conceptions of such things as the context of utterance, the topic of conversation, background information, and A's ability to work out what S is up to may all play rôles in the *formation* of S's intentions; but this does not undermine the view that what determines what S means are S's communicative intentions. (Neale, 1992: 552–3)[61]

(I am using 'communicative intention', 'M-intention', and 'meaning intention' interchangeably.) There are four basic points about speaker meaning here. (I'll put aside *saying* for a while.)

(1) The first point is straightforward but often missed:

the need to separate [A] the *metaphysical* question concerning what determines (or fixes) what S means and [B] the *epistemological* question concerning what is used by those other than S to identify what S means (a question to be answered by a theory of interpretation). (Neale 2005: 180)[62]

(2) Assuming the answer to [A] is "the communicative intentions with which S uttered *x*", [A] and [B] must both be separated from a third question:

[C] the *aetiological* question of what bears on the *formation* of the communicative intentions that determine the content of what S means by uttering *x*.

The Gricean recognizes that [A]–[C] are conceptually distinct but also that their answers will be *mutually constraining* because of the reciprocal nature of the goals S and A have by virtue of (i) their rôles in communicative situations and (ii) the cognitive asymmetry of their situations with respect to S's communicative intentions.[63] This is something I shall spell out in a moment.

(3) The third basic point about speaker meaning here is that "the context of utterance, the topic of conversation, and background information" play no rôle in answering either [B] or [C]. In an answer to [C], all the work is all done by "S's conceptions of such things" and S's conception of "A's ability to work out what S is up to", for it is these conceptions that "may...play rôles in the *formation* of S's [communicative] intentions".[64] Quite generally, it is S's *own cognitive life* that fuels and constrains the formation of S's meaning intentions. (If a certain version of *externalism* is true, then community standards, causal chains, and divisions of linguistic labour may certainly bear on the *contents* of some of S's mental states, including the contents of certain intentions S forms; but that does not mean these things themselves bear on the *formation* of intentions having those contents. The only things that bear on that are things happening in S's head.) Similarly, in an answer to [B], there will be rôles for A's conceptions of "the context of utterance, the topic of conversation, and background information" as well, of course, as "A's ability to work out what S is up". I elaborate below.

(4) A point regularly missed in legal and literary theory, and sometime in philosophy, is that "the *formation* of genuine communicative intentions by S is constrained by S's expectations". The precise nature of the constraint is something I discuss later.

12.7.2 Metaphysics: constitutive determination

Unfortunately, in much of the literature on intention-based theories of meaning, questions [A]–[C] are not always clearly separated, or when they are their mutually constraining nature is simply overlooked. One reason for this seems to be the conflation of different notions of "determination" when talking about content, the failure to appreciate that [A] is about a *constitutive* notion of determination, [B] is about an *epistemic* notion, and [C] is about an *aetiological* notion, as I shall call it. [A]–[C] can be refined as follows:

(CQ) In virtue of what facts does someone, S, mean whatever he or she means by uttering something, x, on a given occasion?

(EQ) What sorts of information, what principles, and what types of cognitive states and processes are involved in the (typically spontaneous) arrival in the mind of an interpreter of a (typically resilient) conclusion about what S means by uttering x on that occasion?

(AQ) What sorts of information, what principles, and what types of cognitive states and processes are involved in the formation of the communicative intentions S has in uttering x on that occasion?

(Since the constitutive, epistemic, and aetiological questions are questions in metaphysics, pragmatics, and formatics, respectively, it won't hurt if I sometimes call them the metaphysical, pragmatic, and formatic questions.)

CQ is a question in metaphysics about the *nature* of something, a question about the constitutive determination (or constitution) of the content of an act of speaker meaning. An answer to CQ is a *theory of speaker meaning*. The classical Gricean answer—that the content of what S *means* by uttering something x (or, more generally, doing something) on a given occasion is wholly determined by the communicative intentions S had in uttering x—makes no mention of an addressee's interpretive abilities, and no mention of such things as the context of utterance, the topic of conversation, background information, discourse structure, salience, relevance, conversational maxims, pragmatic inference, social conventions, norms, or practices, community standards, expert opinions, and causal chains. Even linguistic meaning is left out, and that has baffled people who have run together two or more of CQ, EQ, and AQ. (See below.)

One is certainly free to debate the *correctness* of the intentionalist answer to CQ. But it would be a mistake to complain that the answer *smuggles in* facts about S's addressee or about the context of utterance, the topic of conversation, background information, discourse structure, salience, relevance, conversational maxims, pragmatic inference, etc. To think such facts *are* smuggled in is to conflate constitutive determination with either epistemic or aetiological determination. (See below.)

12.7.3 Pragmatics: epistemic determination

EQ is not a question about the nature of speaker meaning, it's a question about the *identification* or *recovery*, or *epistemic determination* of speaker meaning by an interpreter, a question in pragmatics, the study of utterance interpretation, and thereby a question in cognitive psychology. Sometimes interpreters fail to identify what the speaker means. They may recover nothing; or they may get it wrong, "recover" the wrong thing, so to speak. So, strictly speaking, pragmatics concerns itself with the sorts of information, the principles, and types of cognitive states and processes involved in *reaching conclusions* about speaker meaning, conclusions that are typically resilient and formed spontaneously as the outputs of cognitive mechanisms that are quite likely tailored to the recovery of communicative intentions. So one would expect an answer to EQ to make reference to at least the following:

(1) An assumed linguistic meaning of x, as constitutively determined by the conventions of the language to which x belongs (which may or may not be explained in terms of regularities in speaker meaning).
(2) The contents of perceptual states and memory.
(3) All manner of beliefs and expectations (including especially beliefs about the speaker).
(4) Cognitive processes and principles governing the identification, evaluation and integration of information arriving from various channels and sources (including especially information deriving from (1)–(3)).

A pragmatic theory, then, will specify the *fully general component* of an explanation of how interpreters reach the conclusions they do about what speakers mean by uttering whatever speakers utter on given occasions, whilst accommodating the fact that, in any individual case, there will be much that is *not* general or systematic but local or specific.

There is no obvious delimitation of the mental states whose informational contents are alluded to in (3) above.[65] In principle, in any particular case, all sorts of information might be exploited by A in the process of reaching a conclusion about what S means, including (but certainly not restricted to) information flowing from what I shall call A's *assessments* of (i.e. perceptions, conceptions, or estimations of, and beliefs and expectations about) such things as those on the following list, which I'll call £:

- the topic of conversation;
- the general nature of the discourse;
- the extent to which S can be assumed to believe that S and A share specialized knowledge of what is being discussed;
- the relative salience for S of objects in the immediate environment;
- the relevance to S of certain types of information;
- prior conversations with S or people who know S;
- S's general knowledge; S's general intelligence; the extent to which S can be presumed to be a rational, cooperative speaker;
- S's conception of power relations involving S and A;
- S's fluency in the language to which x belongs;
- the extent to which S can be assumed to be operating in accordance with various norms, conventions, practices, maxims, canons, and community standards;
- the extent to which S is a stickler for accurate or careful wording;
- the extent to which S's choice of language (in general, or given the topic at hand) can be presumed to be affected by emotional, cultural, social, or political considerations.

In principle, A's assessments of any item on £ could play a rôle in A's reaching a particular conclusion about what S means on a given occasion by uttering x. And £ is not even close to exhaustive.

Despite the very different natures of CQ and EQ, carelessness with the verbs 'determine' and 'establish' can lead to their conflation. Consider the following statement of a seemingly interesting question:

(5) How is what S means in uttering x on a given occasion determined?

Someone using this form of words could be asking either of two questions, one about *constitutive* determination, the other about the process of *epistemic* determination:

(5′) What (*constitutively*) *determines* what S means by uttering X on a given occasion?

(5″) What is involved in an interpreter's (*epistemically*) *determining* what S means by uttering X on a given occasion?

But (5′) and (5″) are just casual ways of asking CQ and EQ, respectively, the former being a question about constitutive determination, the latter a question about epistemic determination.[66]

When philosophers and linguists start throwing around expressions like 'context', 'background', 'discourse structure', 'salience', 'relevance', or 'conversational maxims' in their discussions of "determining" the content of what S means, we must be on guard. The concepts behind some of these expressions might well secure rôles in the *epistemic* determination of the content of what S means, i.e. rôles in a cognitive theory of utterance interpretation. But it does not follow that they also play rôles in the *constitutive* determination of what S means.

12.7.4 Formatics: aetiological determination

Like EQ, AQ is ultimately a question in cognitive psychology, but a question to be answered by what I call a *formatic* theory, a theory of *utterance formation*. (Such a theory should no more be confused with a theory of utterance *production* than a pragmatic theory of utterance *interpretation* should be confused with a theory of utterance *perception*.) A formatic theory is a theory of the sorts of information, the principles, and the types of cognitive states and processes leading to a *pairing* of a particular sentence (or smaller expression) x, with a particular proposition—the one that is the content of S's communicative intention in uttering x.[67] (There is no assumption here that S begins with a propositional content he intends to communicate and then mentally searches for words that he believes will, if uttered in the present circumstances, have the best chance of communicating it. More plausibly [in many cases at least], S has a general idea of what he wants to communicate and this gets sharpened as different forms of words are considered. Furthermore, the idea that there is some specific proposition that is the content of the speaker's communicative intention must be seen as an idealization. Often there will be indeterminacy as to precise content. When it comes to the content of conversational implicatures, this is something that Grice (1975) acknowledges. And as Buchanan and Ostertag (2005) and Wilson and Sperber (2012) and others have pointed out, indeterminacy extends to what is said, particularly in so far as it includes implicit reference.) So a formatic theory will specify the *fully general component* of an explanation of how speakers come to form the communicative intentions they do, whilst accommodating the fact that, in any individual case, there will be much that is *not* general or systematic but utterly local or specific.

To cut a long story short, one would expect an answer to AQ to make reference to the speaker-side analogues of (1)–(4) above, including the speaker-side analogues of the things on list £. To the extent that S's assessments of anything δ that bears on the formation of S's communicative intentions, let us say that δ is an *aetiological determinant* of the content of S's communicative intentions and that δ *aetiologically determines* (together with many other things) those intentions. Importantly, it does not follow from δ's being a *aetiological* determinant of a particular communicative intention S has in uttering x on a given occasion that δ is a *constitutive* determinant of what S means by uttering x on that occasion.

So once again, we must be on guard when philosophers and linguists begin throwing around expressions like 'context', 'background', 'discourse structure', 'salience', 'relevance', or 'conversational maxims' in their discussion of "determining" the content of what S means. The concepts behind some of these expressions might well secure rôles in the *aetiological* determination (or constraining) of the content of what S means, i.e. rôles in a cognitive theory of utterance formation. But it does not follow that they also play rôles in the *constitutive* determination of what S means.

12.7.5 The relation between formatics and pragmatics

A theory of *communication* includes a theory of the cognitive processes involved in utterance interpretation (pragmatics), and a theory of the cognitive processes involved in utterance planning and formation (formatics). Where a *pragmatic* theory will specify the fully general component of an explanation of how interpreters form the hypotheses they do about what speakers mean by uttering whatever they utter on given occasions, a *formatic* theory will specify the fully general component of an explanation of how speakers come to form the communicative intentions they do (both theories accommodating the fact that, in any individual case, there will be much that is *not* general or systematic but local or specific).

The relation between formatics and pragmatics is as straightforward as the reciprocal relation between speakers and their intended interpreters: the latter seek to *understand* and former seek to *be understood*, and both parties operate in accordance with this implicit assumption unless there is good reason not to. Meaning and interpreting stand to one another in much the same way that selling and buying stand to one another. For the most part, we operate on the assumption that various sorts of transactions will put us in a position to better do the things we want or need to do. (There are pathological cases, of course, in both economic and linguistic transactions—the person whose principle desire is to keep as much money as possible in a box under the bed; the person whose main desire is to use money to amass more of it, with no apparent further aim; the person who talks just for the sake of talking—but this does not detract from the overall utility of thinking about communication in a transactional way.) So it is not surprising that the vocabulary of economics has always appealed to those working in the intentional-inferential tradition. We find talk of linguistic "transactions", talk of talk "exchanges" ("exchange" of words and "exchanges" of information, some more "valuable" than others), and talk of "trade-offs" between "expenditure" of cognitive effort and "richness" of cognitive "rewards".[68] Among the goods we produce are marks, sounds, and gestures; utterances, inscriptions, and signings. Restricting attention to things we produce intentionally, 'producer' and 'consumer' are useful modality-neutral words we can use to label people performing acts of meaning and acts of interpreting.

The two sides of communication—the sending and receiving, the producing and consuming—are inextricably bound.

(The overarching relationship between a formatic theory and a pragmatic theory seems relatively straightforward, each mirroring or inverting the other, so to speak. But the relations they bear to a *semantic* theory are a matter of intense debate, much turning on whether a semantic theory can be understood as a theory about what speakers tacitly know or understand about the languages they speak.)

There is no prospect of explaining an interpreter's capacity to interpret a speaker without explaining a speaker's capacity to exploit the interpreter's capacity, and vice versa. Speakers and interpreters are intentional agents with *reciprocal* goals: interpreters seek to *understand* and speakers seek to be *understood*. And both sides operate in accordance with this tacit assumption unless there is good reason not to, and also in accordance with the tacit assumption that their respective ways of operating are mutually sustaining. So answers to CQ, EQ, and AQ will place constraints on one another, despite being quite different sorts of questions. And it is a virtue of Gricean theories that CQ, EQ, and AQ are not conflated while the proffered answers are nonetheless tightly interlocked. What S means by uttering x on a given occasion is constitutively determined by S's communicative intentions in uttering x; but the fact that it was x that S uttered is partly a function of S's presumptions about what might be expected to impinge upon A's effort to identify those intentions. CQ, EQ, and AQ fit together thus:

The question of what **constitutively** determines what S meant by uttering something (on a given occasion) and the question of what is involved in **epistemically** determining (ascertaining, identifying, or at least arriving at a conclusion about) what S meant by uttering it are conceptually distinct, even though the formation of the communicative intentions that **constitutively** determine what S meant is typically **aetiologically** determined, in part, by S's conceptions of the sorts of things S may reasonably presume to be potentially involved in A's **epistemically** determining what S meant.

12.7.6 Farewell to Transcendent Meaning

It is important to appreciate that in a formatic theory no appeal is made to anyone's actual ability to grasp a speaker's communicative intention. The work is all done by "S's *conceptions* [emphasis added] of such things as the context of utterance, the topic of conversation, background information, and A's ability to work out what S is up to for it is these conceptions that play rôles in the *formation* of S's communicative intentions" (Neale, 1992: 552–3). Quite generally, it is S's own cognitive life that fuels the formation of S's communicative intentions. (If a certain version of *externalism* is true, then community standards, causal chains, and divisions of linguistic labor may certainly bear on the *contents* of some of S's mental states, including the contents of intentions S forms; but that does not mean these things themselves bear on the *formation* of intentions that have those contents.)

Conceptually, (i) and (ii) are distinct:

(i) What S meant by uttering x (on a given occasion)
(ii) What S's addressee A took S to mean by uttering x (on that occasion).

When things go well, (i) and (ii) coincide. When they don't, it's too bad. But no philosophical puzzle results when (i) ≠ (ii), when, for example, S meant that p, but A took S to mean p'. In particular, it does not follow that there is some *third* thing—some *participant-transcendent* speaker meaning!—for which the proposition that p and the proposition that p' are competing candidates.[69] Perhaps S or A, or both, could have *done better* in the circumstances. Perhaps S could have chosen slightly better words, and if he'd uttered x' (instead of x), perhaps A would have taken him to mean that p (rather than p'). Perhaps A wasn't listening as carefully as he should have been, and if he had been he would have taken S to mean that p (rather than p').

There is *some* third thing theorists can talk about, but it is not something for which (i) and (ii) are *candidates*:

(iii) What a reasonable, attentive, informed interpreter would take S to have meant by uttering x (on that occasion).

When we construct pragmatic theories, theories of utterance interpretation, we cannot help thinking in terms of (iii). But that's because a pragmatic theory is an idealized theory of the *epistemic* determination of what speakers mean, not a theory of its *constitutive* determination. Similarly, when we construct formatic theories, theories of utterance planning, we cannot help thinking in terms of (iv):

(iv) What a reasonable, attentive, informed speaker would have meant by uttering x (on that occasion).

And that's because a formatic theory is an idealized theory of the *aetiological* determination of the communicative intentions with which speakers produce their utterances.

12.7.7 The formatic and pragmatic rôles of expression meaning

So where does *expression meaning* fit into this account of speaker meaning? The short answer is that although it plays no rôle whatsoever in answering CQ, it plays rôles in answering both EQ and AQ. Schiffer has it exactly right when he says,

what a speaker means supervenes entirely on her communicative intentions, regardless of what the sentence she utters means ... while speaker-meaning isn't a function of sentence-meaning, but only of communicative intentions, the rôle of sentence-meaning is to make known the speaker's communicative intentions: the hearer is intended to rely on her knowledge of what the sentence means in order to infer what the speaker meant in uttering the sentence. (Schiffer, 2006: 57)

Knowledge of the meaning of (6) isn't the *only* thing S intends A to rely on in reaching a conclusion about what S means. Suppose S utters (6):

(6) I think everyone is here.

S and A both recognize that no fact about (6) itself will tell A who is speaking, where exactly S intends by 'here', what S intends to be the reach of 'everyone', whether S is being ironic, speaking literally, or speaking metaphorically, or what S is conversationally implicating (if anything). A *pragmatic* theory concerns itself with the sorts of information and types of cognitive states and processes involved in interpreters forming hypotheses about what speakers mean. And the information in question includes information about linguistic meaning—which the Gricean sees as constitutively determined by conventions explained in terms of regularities in speaker meaning—and a whole lot more. Similarly, a *formatic* theory concerns itself with the sorts of information and the types of cognitive states and processes involved in *pairing* a particular utterance type, x, with the particular proposition that is the content of S's communicative intention in uttering x. Again, the information in question includes information about linguistic meaning (and a whole a lot more). To reiterate, the relation between formatics and pragmatics is as straightforward as the reciprocal relation between speakers and their intended interpreters: the latter seek to understand and former seek to be understood. Where a *pragmatic* theory specifies the fully general component of an explanation of how interpreters form the hypotheses they do about what speakers mean by uttering whatever speakers utter on given occasions, a *formatic* theory will specify the fully general component of an explanation of how speakers come to form the communicative intentions they do (both theories accommodating the fact that, in any individual case, there will be much that is *not* general or systematic but local or specific).[70]

12.7.8 *The formatic and pragmatic rôles of context*

So where does *context* fit into this picture of speaker meaning? The short answer—which should sound familiar—is that although it plays no rôle whatsoever in answering CQ, it plays rôles in answering both EQ and AQ. The point is appreciated by Kent Bach:

It is one thing for something to be determined by context in the sense of being *ascertained* on the basis of contextual information and quite another for it to be determined by context in the sense of being *fixed* by contextual factors (*epistemic* vs. *constitutive* determination). (2000: 271)

In the crucial respect, context is just like linguistic meaning: the interpreter uses it as evidence in reaching a conclusion about the content of what the speaker means. Since this use of context is part of a story about the epistemic determination of that content, we call this its *pragmatic* (or *epistemic*) rôle in the overall picture.

The speaker's use of context is reciprocal: it is part of a story about the utterance's causal history, a story about the pairing of x and with that content, a story about the aetiology of a communicative intention. Call this the *formatic* (or *aetiological*) rôle of context. In conclusion, context plays no rôle in the *constitutive* determination of the content of what the speaker means by uttering x, for that is wholly determined by the communicative intentions S had in uttering x.

12.7.9 *Formatics: constraints on communicative intentions*

Communicative intentions cannot be formed on a whim. I mentioned an epistemic constraint earlier:

the *formation* of genuine communicative intentions by S is constrained by S's *expectations* [emphasis added]: S cannot be said to utter x M-intending A to ϕ if S thinks that there is very little or no hope that S's production of x will result in A ϕ-ing. (Neale 1992: 552)

The expectations I am talking about here are simply *beliefs about the future*—beliefs about the likelihood of one's communicative intentions being *recognized*.

I have been told many times that the constraint I mention on the formation of communicative intentions is an arbitrary one *theorists* impose in order to deflect charge of Humpty-Dumptyism and counterexamples to a Gricean account of speaker meaning or an intentional account of statutory interpretation. The charge is utterly baseless. The constraint is a consequence of an epistemic constraint on intentions *quite generally*. Grice and Schiffer provide brief statements about the nature of the constraint in question. According to Grice: "it is in general true that one cannot have intentions to achieve results which one sees no chance of achieving" (Grice 1969: 158; 1989: 98). The negation-modal combinations 'cannot' and 'no chance', and the epistemic character of 'see no chance' make this a tricky remark to interpret univocally. If the epistemic character comes from the verb 'see' rather than from the modal 'chance', then reading 'if ϕ then ψ' as a strict biconditional, the condition Grice is stating appears to be one of the following (by contraposition):

(1) S intends to ϕ only if $\neg(S$ believes $\neg(S$ can $\phi))$

(2) S intends to ϕ only if S believes $(S$ can $\phi)$.

(2) imposes a stronger condition on intending than (1) does. Evidently Grice (1971) came to think that even (2) is not strong enough. There is, he claims, a serious infelicity involved in saying "I intend to ϕ, but I might not ϕ", and he suggests this is due to the fact that S's intending to ϕ requires S's "having no doubt" or "being sure" that S will ϕ. (1971: 266).[71] So Grice's condition is effectively (3):

(3) S intends to ϕ only if S believes $(S$ will $\phi)$.[72]

Schiffer's (1972) version of the epistemic constraint is weaker: "In general, one cannot do an act x with the intention of bringing about a certain result if one knows or believes that one will not thereby bring about that result" (Schiffer 1972: 69). This is effectively (4):

(4) S intends to ϕ only if $\neg(S$ believes $\neg(S$ will $\phi))$

Whichever of (1)–(4) we go with, there appear to be complications. Donnellan, brings out two. First, he says that

> Intentions...are essentially connected with expectations. Ask someone to flap his arms with the intention of flying. In response he can certainly wave his arms up and down .... But this is not to do it with the intention of flying. Nor does it seem to me that a normal adult in normal circumstances can flap his arms and in doing so really have that intention. Perhaps one can, by a stretch of the imagination, conceive of someone (a child, say, who has seen birds flying) doing this. But such a person—the child, for example—would have expectations not shared with us. (Donnellan, 1968: 212)

In a footnote, he suggests the precise connection between intentions and expectations is more complex:

> I have, I think, oversimplified ... What we can do with a certain intention not only depends upon expectations, but also upon the possibility of *other means* [emphasis added] of

accomplishing the same end and upon *incentives* [emphasis added]. A man in the water from a sinking ship might move his arms with the intention of swimming a hundred miles to shore, if that is the only hope, even though he has no rational expectation of doing it. But is it open to an ordinary man at the beach to strike out with that intention? (Donnellan, 1968: 212, n. 10)

Schiffer thinks the moral of such examples is that

... while [it] is generally the case [that one cannot do something with the intention of bringing about a certain result if one knows or believes that one will not thereby bring about that result], it is not necessarily the case. A person trapped in a burning building might leap from a seventh floor window with the intention of saving his life. Somewhat analogously, it is not uncommon to try to convince someone that *p* despite its being virtually certain that one will fail. (Schiffer, 1972: 69)

Harman, disagrees:

But, if the person who leaps from the seventh floor does not believe that he will save his life, he does not leap with the simple intention of saving his life. He leaps, perhaps, intending to save his life *if he can*. He leaps in the *hope* of saving his life. If he tells himself that he intends in this way to save his life, he speaks bravely but inaccurately. (Harman, 1974: 228-9)

I'm inclined to think the weak modal constraint, (1) above, is quite strong enough if understood correctly. My own formulation makes reference to what the agent *believes to be impossible*, with the modality left unspecified:

The formation of genuine intentions is severely constrained by beliefs. I cannot intend to become a prime number, intend to digest my food through my lungs on alternate Tuesdays, or swim from New York to Sydney because (roughly) I cannot intend *what I believe to be impossible*. (Neale 2005: 181)

In any particular case, some non-empty class of modalities will be relevant to producing a sensible interpretation, so Donnellan's talk of "the possibility of other means" of accomplishing the same end and his talk of reward possibilities fall into place when discussing the sorts of emergency counterexamples that Donnellan and Schiffer have produced without resorting to a stronger constraint such as (2) or (4).[73] This is the constraint I shall now assume.

Let us turn now to communicative intentions. A communicative intention is not something *similar to* an ordinary intention but more complex. It *is* an ordinary intention, but it has a complex *content*. To say that it is higher-order is just to say that its content includes other mental states. To say that it is audience-involving is just to say that its content includes a specific audience. In fact, the content of a communicative intention includes the mental states of a specific audience, including certain mental states of the audience that include mental states of the speaker. And of course it has as part of its content that the audience recognize that the speaker intends the audience to have a certain cognitive reaction via recognizing that that speaker intends the audience to have that reaction. Furthermore, unlike most intentions, communicative intentions are *ephemeral*. I may have had a long-standing intention to visit Egypt—for twenty years, let us suppose. I may reflect on this intention, think about things that have so far precluded me from going (time, money, political unrest, etc.). I may even make sketchy plans I might be able to implement next year, thinking this is finally the year I can go. Communicative intentions are not like this.

What this all means is that my modal constraint on intentions has considerable bite when it comes to communicative intentions. For S to form a genuine communicative intention, S must, in effect, quickly *pair* a proposition and a sentence x in a special way: S must think that by uttering x, S will likely get his audience, A, to recognize that S intends A to think that p (for example) at least partly on the basis of recognizing that S uttered x intending A to think that p. The formation of such an intention is constrained by S's beliefs. If S believes A will not recognize that S intends A to think that p, for example, then S doesn't communicatively intend A to believe that p, so S does not mean that p by uttering x. As Grice says, "Success... requires those to whom communications or near communications are addressed to be capable in the circumstances of having certain thoughts and drawing certain conclusions" (Grice 1969: 158; 1989: 98–9). Assuming this is something a rational speaker S appreciates, and assuming S is being cooperative, if what S means by uttering x on a given occasion is determined by the communicative intentions S has in uttering x, then S cannot mean that p by uttering x if S believes it is impossible for his audience A (or at least any rational, reasonably well-informed interpreter in A's shoes) to construe S as meaning that p by uttering x.[74] Donnellan puts the basic point well in his response to the claim that intention-based accounts of meaning and reference succumb to Humpty-Dumptyism:

whether [the speaker] can form [an intention involving recognition on the part of his audience of his intention] may depend upon what expectations he has about his audience and their ability to grasp his intention. It does not follow, then, from this analysis that speakers might, out of the blue, mean anything at all by any utterance. And the existence of an established practice may be usually required for speakers to have the right expectations. (Donnellan, 1968: 212)

Expression meaning gets into the picture as follows: The psychological processes involved in the formation of any communicative intention with which S utters x, and in A's reaching a conclusion about the content of that intention are constrained by what S and A take to be x's meaning (if it has one) and (in the absence of indication to the contrary) by general principles governing cooperative behavior that S and A mutually assume S is observing in uttering x.

12.8 Schiffer's Theory of Reference

I turn now to Schiffer's (1981) work on reference, which is far and away the most sophisticated in the Gricean tradition to date.

12.8.1 Speaker meaning

Consider the following definition of speaker meaning, which is essentially Grice's:

(GM) In doing x, S, meant that p iff (roughly) for some audience, A, S did x intending to activate in A the belief that p via A's recognition that S did x intending A to think that p.

In the light of the metaphysics sketched earlier, we need to tidy up the format of such definitions. The apparent variable x appears in GM as part of the phrase 'do x' (with suitable tense and aspect). But what does x range over? That's an infelicitous question because x is not straightforwardly a variable in (GM). We often talk about "doing things", and all of the following count as cases of *doing x* in the sense relevant to understanding GM: *uttering a sentence, pointing at something, nodding, frowning, and banging a fist on the table*. So it is not x but the *entire phrase* 'do x' (with suitable tense and aspect) that is functioning as the variable in GM. This means there is no reason we could nor reformulate (1) using 'x-ing' rather than 'doing x'. But to avoid crossed wire let's use ϕ-ing:

(GM') In ϕ-ing, S, meant that p iff (roughly) for some audience, A, S ϕ-ed intending to activate in A the belief that p via A's recognition that S ϕ-ed intending A to think that p.

Schiffer's account of speaker meaning assumes a notion of mutual knowledge:[75]

(SM) In doing x, *S meant* that p iff for some audience A and relation R, S did x intending S and A to mutually know that $R(x, p)$ and, on the basis of this, that S did x primarily intending A to think that p.

There are three points to notice about SM:

(i) It makes no assumption about the nature of R. As Schiffer puts it, "R may be any relation which S thinks will do the job... [though] pretty clearly, some relations are better than others" (1981: 65). And one task of an intention-based theory of meaning is to spell out those relations—some of which may well involve *conventions*, or *self-perpetuating correlations*, within some group of people to which S belongs—without appealing to any undefined notion of *expression meaning*, and without appealing to what I earlier called the pragmatic or formatic rôles of either linguistic meaning or context.

The other two points concern '$R(x, p)$':

(ii) '$R(x, p)$' contains an occurrence of x that does not occur as part of the variable phrase 'do x', which is the real variable phrase. So if we simply replace all occurrences of 'do x' by 'ϕ' in SM (if we replace doing x' by 'ϕ-ing', and 'did x' by 'ϕ-ed') we are still left with an occurrence of x.

(iii), 'p' is not functioning in '$R(x, p)$' in the same way that it's functioning in the phrases 'meant that p' and 'think that p'. In the last two, we can replace 'p' by a sentence. In '$R(x, p)$' we cannot replace 'p' by a sentence. It's as if Schiffer wants to use both 'that p' and 'p' as alternative names of *the proposition that p*, but that's not possible because they are not of the same grammatical category. The fix is easy: replace the occurrence of 'p' in '$R(x, p)$' by 'the proposition that p' or by 'that p', at least assuming that 'that p' is a name of the proposition that p. But just in case there turns out to be a problem with that idea, let's just stipulate that 'p^*' is a name of the proposition that p and use it in place of the infelicitous 'p' in '$R(x, p)$'. So, dealing with both problems at once we get the following:

(SM') By ϕ-ing, *S meant* that p iff for some audience A and relation R, S ϕ-ed intending S and A to mutually know that $R(S$'s ϕ-ing, $p^*)$ and, on the basis of this, that S ϕ-ed primarily intending A to think that p.

This allows for the possibility (without requiring) that S and A mutually know that R holds between S's ϕ-ing and p^* because there is some relation R' that they mutually know holds between ϕ-ing (in general) and p^*.

12.8.2 Speaker reference

Schiffer saw that speaker reference, when stripped down, is just *singular speaker meaning*. Simplifying and adjusting to comport with **SM'**, his definition of the basic notion of speaker reference (and, indeed, the most basic of all referential notions) amounts to this:

> (**SR**) In ϕ-ing, *S referred* to *o* iff what *S meant* by ϕ-ing is an *o*-dependent proposition (a singular proposition that has *o* as a constituent).[76]

As with **SM'**, no assumption is made in **SR** about the nature of R, and no mention is made of the pragmatic or formatic rôles of either linguistic meaning or context.

Of course, the following question is unanswered: In virtue of what fact is a speaker's meaning intention about *o* rather than something else? But this does not mean the original question has not been answered, even answered satisfactorily, in the context in which it was asked. But it does mean we have brought out a question about *thought* content that needs answering.

12.8.3 A Narrower Notion

Schiffer defines a narrower notion of speaker reference that he calls *referring-by*. The definition comes to this:

> (**SB**) In ϕ-ing, *S referred* to *o by* (*way of*) ψ-ing iff (1) S's ψ-ing was a proper part of S's ϕ-ing, and (2) for some audience A and some relation R, S intended S and A to *mutually know* that R(S's ψ-ing, *o*) and, at least partly on the basis of this, that S referred to *o* in ϕ-ing.[77]

(This allows for the possibility [without requiring] that it is mutual knowledge between S and A that R holds between S's ψ-ing and *o* because it is mutual knowledge between S and A that some relation R' holds between ψ-ing (in general) and *o*.) Again, some relations will be better than others for making known one's referential intentions and we can conjecture that a handful of different relations will suffice for the cases of most interest (relations correlated in fairly systematic ways with a handful of significant [and definable] classes of referring expressions.) Although **SB** does not assume that either ϕ-ing or ψ-ing involve the use of language, obviously the cases of principal interest are those in which S's ϕ-ing is S's utterance of some expression (e.g. a sentence), and S's ψ-ing is S's utterance of some sub-expression (e.g. a name or a pronoun). Suppose Sue utters sentence (1):

(1) I admire him.

And suppose that in doing so she means that she admires Andy. Then we can say that, in uttering (1), Sue referred to herself by uttering 'I' and that she referred to 'Andy' by uttering 'him'.

12.8.4 Implicit Reference

Schiffer provides a *sufficient* condition for referring implicitly which amounts to this:

> (SI) In ϕ-ing, S referred to o *implicitly* if (i) S referred to o and (ii) S's ϕ-ing properly contained no ψ-ing by S such that S *referred* to o *by* (*way of*) ψ-ing.

There are several reasons why SI isn't quite what I need. Firstly, it does not exclude cases of what I earlier called *indirect* reference (nor was it Schiffer's intention to do so). Secondly, it does not assume that either ϕ-ing or ψ-ing involve the use of language (nor was it Schiffer's intention that it should). If, by ostentatiously holding his nose as B passes, S means that B is obnoxious, then, according to SI, S referred to B implicitly. Relatedly, in order to make room for cases of implicit reference that some theorists wish to classify as aphonic reference (see below) and in order to mesh with a favoured way of construing semantic composition, the definition I want needs to talk about parts of *expressions* rather than parts of *utterances*.

12.9 Referring: The Key Notions

12.9.1 Referring Explicitly

I need to define a narrower form of speaker reference that is specific to the use of language. That means helping myself to notions such as *language, sentence,* and *word*. My principal aims now are to define a notion of speaker reference that can be used to characterize theoretically tractable notions of implicit and aphonic reference and to explain why the only notion of expression reference we need is one that makes it *de jure* identical to one of the narrower forms of speaker reference I shall define.

Since the same expression may occur more than once in a single sentence, we need to mention *occurrences* of expressions in sentences to get the definition right. And in order to forge a proper link between speaker reference and expression reference (to the extent such a notion is needed), we need to talk about occurrences of expressions in the right way. Classical semantics does not talk about the semantic properties of *occurrences* of expressions, it talks about the semantic properties of *expressions* relative to their occurrences (or relative to particular syntactic positions they occupy). The following seems like a good place to start, where e is an expression that occurs at least once in expression x:

> (RW) In uttering x, S referred to o *with* e, relative to its i-th occurrence in x, iff for some audience A and relation R, S intended A to recognize that $R(e, x, i, o)$ and, at least partly on the basis of this, that S referred to o in uttering x.

Notice that if RW is correct, referring to something with an expression requires having propositional attitudes about it relative to a position it occupies. Is that psychologically plausible? I think so. Ordinary speakers understand quite well that someone can be referring to one person by 'his' relative to its first occurrence in (2) and someone different with 'his' relative to its second occurrence:

(2) John told Paul that Ringo thought George had hidden his drumsticks inside his guitar amplifier.

They might not state it quite like that, but that's irrelevant.

We can now provide a simple definition of explicit reference (phonic reference, reference with a phonic):

(RE) In uttering x, S referred to o *explicitly* iff there is a *phonic* in x with which S referred to o.

Suppose Sue utters sentence (3) in the course of a conversation:

(3) Andy told him to call him.

And suppose that in so doing Sue means that Andy told John to call him, Andy. Then we can say that, in uttering (3), Sue referred explicitly to Andy and John. She referred to Andy with 'Andy' (relative to its sole occurrence in (3)) and also with 'him' (relative to its *second* occurrence in (3)), and she referred to John with 'him' (relative to its *first* occurrence in (3)).

It will do no harm on occasion to use 'mean by' as a synonym for 'refer with' or 'refer using'. So, for example, I'm happy to use the following interchangeably:

S referred to o with e (e.g. Sue referred to Andy with 'he')

S referred to o using e (e.g. Sue referred to Andy using 'he')

S meant o by e (e.g. Sue meant Andy by 'he').

In fact, I think it would be a good thing to retire 'refer' and make do with 'mean'.

12.9.2 Farewell to transcendent reference

Conceptually, (i) and (ii) are distinct:

(i) What/whom S referred to with e (or meant by e)

(ii) What S's addressee A took S to refer to with e (or mean by e).

When things go well, (i) and (ii) coincide. When they don't, it's too bad. But as stressed in in Neale (2005), no philosophical puzzle results when (i) $\neq$ (ii), when S referred to o with e but A took S to be referring to o', for example. In particular, there is no *third* thing—some *participant-transcendent* speaker reference!—for which o and o' are competing candidates. Perhaps S or A, or both, could have *done better* in the circumstances. Perhaps S could have chosen a slightly better expression, and if he'd uttered e' (instead of e), A would have taken him to be referring to o (rather than to o'). Perhaps A wasn't listening as carefully as he should have been, and if he had been he would have taken S to be referring to o (rather than to o').

As with speaker meaning, there is *some* third thing *theorists* can talk about, though it is not something for which the other two things are *candidates*:

(iii) What a reasonable, attentive interpreter would take S to be referring to with e (or to mean by e).

When we construct pragmatic theories, theories of utterance interpretation, we cannot help thinking in terms of (iii). But that's because a pragmatic theory is an idealized theory of the *epistemic* determination of what speakers mean and refer to, not a theory of the *constitutive* determination of these things. Similarly, when we construct formatic theories, theories of utterance formation, we cannot help thinking in terms of (iv):

(iv) What a reasonable, attentive speaker would be referring to with *e* (or would mean by *e*).

And that's because a formatic theory is an idealized theory of the *aetiological* determination of the meaning intentions, including referential intentions, with which speakers produce their utterances.

Given the importance of separating the roles of (i)-(iv) in our thinking about reference, surely we have spilled far too much ink on cases discussed by Linsky (1967), Donnellan (1966), Kripke (1977), and Kaplan (1989) in which uses of definite descriptions, proper names, and demonstratives involve one or another type of epistemic problem on the part of interlocutors. Referring is often said to be like hitting a target with an arrow. We can certainly distinguish (i′) and (ii′):

(i′) The thing S intended/meant to hit with an arrow (on a given occasion)

(ii′) The thing someone else, A, took S to intend/mean to hit with that arrow (on that occasion).

In some cases, (i′) and (ii′) coincide. But no philosophical puzzle results when they don't, when, for example, S intended/meant to hit o with the arrow, but A took S to intend/mean to hit o' with that arrow. In particular, there is no *third* thing for which o and o' are competing candidates—they are not competing candidates for what S actually *did* hit with the arrow, for example, which might have been be o''.

In the light of these considerations, it is hard to get excited about some of the cases philosophers have contrived to differentiate the predictions made by specific theories about what a speaker refers to (or about what a given expression refers to) in a given case. In a famous example of Kaplan's, unbeknownst to him the picture of Rudolph Carnap that usually hangs on the wall behind him has been replaced by one of Spiro Agnew. What does Kaplan refer to when he points, without looking, to the area of the wall where the picture of Agnew now hangs, where the picture of Carnap usually hangs, and says 'That is a picture of one of the greatest philosophers of the twentieth century'? Call the picture of Carnap o. Kaplan has seen o, on the wall behind his desk many times, let us suppose, and he has various singular beliefs about o, including the belief that it is on the wall behind him. Moreover, his communicative intention concerns o, so the answer to the question is clear: Kaplan is referring to o. The fact that his addressee might (though need not) think he is referring to the picture of Agnew, call it o', is completely irrelevant. As is the fact that a reasonable, attentive interpreter might (but need not) take him to be referring to o'. (Sometimes you refer to o and *everyone else* thinks you are referring to o'. Life's tough. But not so tough that we can't have an intentional account of what speakers refer to with demonstratives.) It's easy to construct more complex versions of the story. Suppose o usually hangs on the wall to Kaplan's *left*. As in the original version, o has been replaced by o'. Kaplan sees o' in his peripheral vision and assumes it is o. Here Kaplan has a false belief about o and a false belief about o'. Does he have referential intentions (i.e. singular meaning intentions) about both objects? Perhaps. But what seems important is that his *primary* meaning intention concerns *o*, the picture about which he has a good number of beliefs, the picture that is *of* someone he believes to be one of the greatest philosophers of the twentieth century.

To the extent that we are going to need a theory of the reference of a demonstrative itself, I see no problem saying that, relative to a context, a demonstrative refers to whatever the speaker in that context is referring to with it. (See below.)

12.9.3 *Referring Silently*

A sufficient condition for silent reference, in my sense:

(**RS**) In uttering *x*, S referred to *o silently* if S referred to *o* but there is no phonic in *x with which* S referred to *o*.

12.9.4 *Referring Implicitly*

We can now replace Schiffer's sufficient condition for referring implicitly, **SI**, with an expression-based condition of the sort I want:

(**RI**) In uttering *x*, S referred to *o implicitly* if (i) the truth conditions of what S said (or play-said) are *o*-involving, and (ii) there is no phonic in *x with which* S referred to *o*.

Clause Three points. First, clause (i) also characterizes what I take to be a *necessary* condition on implicit reference, so cases of what I have been calling indirect reference (to be defined later) will be excluded.

Second, there is no need to specify that S referred to *o*: if the conditions of what S said (or play-said) are *o*-involving, then so are the truth conditions of what *S meant*. Third, we need to allow for the possibility of a speaker's referring explicitly and implicitly to the same thing, so conjoining the sufficient condition specified in **RI** with the necessary condition I mentioned falls short of providing necessary and sufficient conditions. This raises questions I shall discuss in a moment.

If, in uttering (4), Sue meant that it snowed *in London* this morning

(4) It snowed this morning

then she referred implicitly to London. Once aphonic reference is defined, a clear and interesting question can be stated: did Sue refer to London aphonically (referring aphonically being a narrower notion than referring silently, on my usage). And clear general theses can be stated, for example that *all* implicit reference is aphonic reference, that *some* is, or that *none* is

12.9.5 *Referring Aphonically*

Recall the metaphysics sketched earlier. Expressions are abstract objects. The parts of expressions are expressions. The expression 'him' is part of the expression 'loves him', which is part of the expression 'she loves him'. By contrast, *utterances* of expressions are material events. Events take place in time, they have durations. The parts of events are events. Among the parts of utterances are utterances. An utterance of 'she loves him' has as one of its more interesting parts an utterance of 'loves him', which has as one of its more interesting parts an utterance of 'him'. Utterances of 'she loves him', 'loves him' and 'him', unlike the expressions of which they are utterances, take place in time, they have durations.

As a matter of definition, there can be no utterances of *aphonic* expressions. But there can be utterances of expressions that *contain* aphonic expressions as proper parts. That is (using square brackets to indicate enough constituent structure to reassure the reader there is nothing paradoxical here),

(UA) [An *utterance* of [an *expression* that contains an aphonic]] does not contain an *utterance* of that aphonic (or any other aphonic).

So **RW** allows for the possibility that a speaker can refer to something *with* an expression *e* without *uttering e*. The theorist who maintains that sentence (4) contains an aphonic referring expression, *e*, might wish to say that Sue referred to London *with e* (without commitment to the absurd idea that Sue *uttered e*).

Although **RI** and **RI'** fall short of providing necessary and sufficient conditions for implicit reference, we can provide necessary and sufficient conditions for implicit reference effected by aphonic reference:

(**RA**) In uttering *x*, *S* referred to *o* aphonically iff there is an occurrence *i* of an aphonic *e* in *x* such that *S* referred to *o with e*, relative to its *i*-th occurrence in *x*.

Since **RA** appeals to the notion defined in **RW**, referring aphonically requires having propositional attitudes about an aphonic (relative to a position or occurrence). Prima facie, this is a problem for the very idea of referring with an aphonic. I'll come back to it.

12.9.6 *Referring Indirectly*

Finally, we can define indirect reference, in my narrow sense:

(**RJ**) In uttering *x*, *S* referred to *o indirectly* iff (i) there is no phonic or aphonic in *x* *with which S* referred to *o*, (ii) the truth conditions of what *S* conversationally implicated are *o*-involving.

12.9.7 *The Rigidity of Implicit Reference*

Let's return to the story of Sue and Andy in London. Sue is reading the newspaper. Andy has asked about today's weather forecast. Before answering, Sue glances at the world weather and says

(5) It was hotter yesterday than it was in Dubai!

Sue refers to London but there is no expression in (5) with which she does this. And, as I said earlier, (a) what she said is true—the truth conditions of what she said obtain—if and only if it was hotter in *London* yesterday than it was in Dubai (yesterday), and (b) she could have uttered (5') and said the same thing:

(5') It was hotter in London yesterday than it was in Dubai!

The fact that there would have been no difference in the truth conditions of what Sue said had she used (5') reveals something important. In a famous passage in the preface to *Naming and Necessity*, Kripke (1980) characterizes rigidity in terms of truth conditions (truth in actual and counterfactual circumstances). The example he uses contains a proper name ('Aristotle') but the characterization of rigidity itself makes no explicit mention of reference. Moreover, as I have pointed out elsewhere, the passage in which the characterization occurs is easily transposed to cover cases of implicit reference.[78] Here is the transposition for Sue's utterance of (5):

A proper understanding of what Sue said in uttering (5) involves an understanding both of the (extensionally correct) conditions under which what she said is in fact true, *and* of the conditions under which a counterfactual course of history, resembling the actual course of history in some respects but not in others, is correctly (partially) described by what Sue said. There is a certain place x—*viz.* the British city we call 'London'—and a certain place y—*viz.* the city in the United Arab Emirates we call 'Dubai'—such that, as a matter of fact, what Sue said in uttering (5) is true if and only if yesterday, it was hotter in x yesterday than it was in y. The rigidity thesis I hold is simply—subtle points aside—that the same paradigm applies to the truth conditions of what Sue said as it describes *counterfactual* situations. That is, what Sue said correctly (but only partially) describes a counterfactual situation if and only if yesterday it would have been hotter in x than it would have been in y had that situation obtained.

So we have rigid reference to London but no expression which refers to London or with which Sue refers to London. However, it might be argued that Sue is referring to London with an *aphonic* expression that is a constituent of (5)—an expression that serves much the same overall functional purpose as 'here' or 'in London'—and that this aphonic is rigid. But of course, this position does not seem to be forced on us. If, as I have suggested, expression reference is just speaker reference seen through the eyes of the machinery of semantic composition, then we can say that what we have become accustomed to calling the rigidity of a referring expression simply reflects a fact about speaker reference. With some terminological licence, we can say that *speakers refer rigidly*, with or without referring expressions, in a perfectly well understood sense of rigidity extracted from the above transposition of Kripke's characterization in terms of truth conditions, i.e. in terms of truth in actual and counterfactual situations.

12.9.8 The Roots of Rigidity

The reasons speakers refer rigidly are not hard to find if we reflect on our ordinary conception of reality and the nature of the information about it that we seek to represent and communicate. I have talked about this elsewhere, so I can be brief here.[79] Ordinarily we conceive of the world as containing *individual objects* (e.g. material objects, persons, and other living things), three-dimensional continuants that persist through time. And these objects have several interesting features that are important from the perspective of our attempts to cope with and represent aspects of the world. Our beliefs about these objects change, and so do the properties of the objects themselves, but not always in tandem. Typically, all but a small number of the properties of objects are known to us, but we construe them as possessing many *further properties* of which we are unaware, but some of which we could become aware of. So our beliefs about them may change as we learn. Often enough, we seek to establish whether or not our beliefs about them are correct, with a view to keeping our beliefs up to date, as it were. And, typically, the beliefs in question, whether true or false, are still beliefs *about* those objects, rather than about whichever objects just happen to fit them best, qualitatively—which is not to say we may *never* be confused about which objects we are thinking about. Putting aside theoretical entities (e.g. mathematical entities), objects *change* over time. But the *objects* themselves remain identical through changes; they persist through time as entities that are wholly present at different times despite possessing many of their properties only temporarily and contingently—which is not to say that there are *no* properties that an object must possess throughout its history.

On the perfectly reasonable assumption that such objects play important roles in our attempts to understand and organize our experiences and deal with our surroundings, it would be odd if these features of objects were not respected in our acts of communicating information about them, and so in our acts of *referring* to them. The things we refer to are things we *keep track* of, things we take to have different properties at different *times*, things we take to have the potential to have (or to have had) properties different from those they *actually* have. So when we refer to them, we refer *rigidly* (modally and temporally). In short, speaker reference is rigid because the *beliefs* and *intentions* behind it are rigid—in a perfectly good sense of 'rigid': they provide a cognitive grip on three-dimensional continuants in a dynamic and contingent world.

Referring expressions facilitate acts of rigid *speaker* reference. If the rigidity of natural language referring expressions is rooted in the rigidity of acts of referring, which is itself rooted in the rigidity of thought, it is not obvious that a theory of referring will need to invoke the notion of referring *non-rigidly*, and so it is not self-evident that it will need to invoke the notion of a *non-rigid* referring expression.[80] Non-rigid referring expressions would not serve any useful and lasting purpose for creatures with our ordinary experiences, needs, desires, and interests. If you like, they are selected against. This does not mean that we cannot choose to introduce them into theoretical discourse by way of stipulation if the need arises, for example in formal languages used in mathematics, computing, and physics, or into the enhanced segment of natural language used to do the relevant metatheory. The concept of a non-rigid referring expression is a perfectly coherent one, but it is an empirical question as to whether natural language *naturally* avails itself of such expressions.[81] The fact that we have the intellectual capacity to stipulate them into existence for certain theoretical purposes is neither here nor there.[82]

12.9.9 *Referring Multiply*

Sue continues reading the newspaper. She comes across a story in about new powers granted to the mayor of London. She decides to tell Andy and utters (6):

(6) The mayor now has the authority to prohibit cycling on the streets when it's snowing.

What Sue means by uttering (6) is that the mayor *of London* now has the authority to prohibit cycling on the streets *of London* when it's snowing *in London*. And according to RI, Sue is referring implicitly to London. But *how many times* did Sue refer to London (implicitly) in uttering (6)? Given the way I just described what she means, it is tempting to say *three* times. But what if she had uttered (7)—as perhaps only a philosopher or logician would—with 'its' and 'there' functioning as variables bound by 'London'?

(7) London is such that its mayor now has the authority to prohibit cycling on its streets when it's snowing there.

The sentences (6) and (7) are clearly not synonymous. There is nothing about the semantics of (6) dictating that it can be used to say something true only when there is a place x such that the mayor *of x* now has the authority to prohibit cycling on the streets *of x* when it's snowing in x. In bizarre political circumstances—in the context of a discussion of the absurdity of a government directive giving the mayor of London sweeping new powers including the control of traffic in *Brighton*, for example—Sue might, by uttering (6), mean that when it's snowing *in Brighton*, the mayor *of London* now has the authority to prohibit cycling on the streets *of Brighton*; or (worse, I suppose) that the mayor *of London* now has the authority to prohibit cycling on the streets *of Brighton* when it's snowing *in London*. In these two cases, Sue would be referring implicitly to both Brighton and London. But the cases differ from one another in an interesting way. It is initially tempting to say that the difference is in how many times Sue would be referring to Brighton and how many times she would be referring to London. That is, it is tempting to say she would be referring twice to Brighton and once to London in the first case, but twice to London and once to Brighton in the second case.

Let's return to the original case in which Sue refers only to London in uttering (6). She *could* do the same thing by uttering (6'), (6''), or (6'''), which contain, respectively, one, two, and three occurrences of 'London':

(6') The mayor now has the authority to prohibit cycling on the streets when it's snowing *in London*.

(6'') The mayor *of London* now has the authority to prohibit cycling on the streets when it's snowing *in London*,

(6''') The mayor *of London* now has the authority to prohibit cycling on the streets *of London* when it's snowing *in London*,

If she utters (6'), (6''), or (6'''), she refers to London explicitly (because in each case she refers to London with 'London'). Intuitively, we also seem to want to say that in uttering (6') or (6''), but not (6'''), Sue also refers to London *implicitly*. But **RI** is silent on this matter, being merely a sufficient condition that is not met—there *is* a phonic in (6') or (6'') with which Sue refers to London. (The necessary condition I added is met as the truth conditions of what Sue said involve London.) Changing 'if' to 'iff' in **RI** would mean that Sue does *not* refer to London implicitly in uttering (6') or (6''), which is not the result we want.

If Sue utters (6''') instead of (6), she refers to London *three times* explicitly (with 'London'), each time corresponding to an occurrence of 'London' in (6'''). Does saying this commit us to saying that her acts of explicitly referring to London are temporally sequenced, that it is *when* producing an individual utterance of 'London' that exactly one of those acts of explicit reference is taking place? Does it mean that on a Kaplanian account of structured propositions, the proposition that is the content of what Sue says by uttering (6''') contains *three* "occurrences" of London itself (or whatever the metaphysical counterparts of occurrences are), i.e. it contains London itself in three distinct positions?

If Sue opts for (6″) instead of (6), she refers to London only *twice* explicitly, each time corresponding to an occurrence of 'London' in (6″). But how many times does Sue refer to London *altogether* in uttering (6″)? If we say she refers to it twice explicitly, shouldn't we also say that she refers to it once *implicitly*? (After all, isn't the proposition that is the content of what she means identical to the one that is the content of what she means when she utters (6)?) But what are we to say about *when* she refers to it implicitly? After she has already referred to it explicitly? Right after she utters 'streets'?

If Sue had opts for (6′) instead of (6), she refers to London explicitly just *once*. Does this mean that she would have referred *implicitly* to London *twice*? If so, does that mean it makes sense to ask about the temporal sequencing of her acts of *implicit* reference in uttering (6′) just as we can ask about the temporal order of her acts of *explicit* reference in uttering (6″) or (6‴)? Does it mean we can count acts of *implicit* reference Sue performed in uttering sentences (6)-(6‴) by counting seeming *absences* of 'London' in sentences (6), (6′), and (6″) when compared with sentence (6‴)? Or do such questions reveal an intrinsic difficulty in treating implicit reference on the model of explicit reference?

Perhaps we should drop talk of *how many times* Sue refers implicitly to London in uttering (6) to Andy. Perhaps we should just say that she refers implicitly to London and does not refer implicitly to anywhere else, and that the truth conditions of what she says are just those of what she says if she utters (7). Similarly, if she opts for (6′) or (6″), she refers implicitly to London, but in uttering (6′) she refers to London explicitly once and in uttering (6″) does this twice.

12.10 What Is Said

12.10.1 Said by what?

Prima facie, implicit reference poses a serious threat to any compositional semantic theory whose viability consists, at least in part, in composing the truth conditions of a sentence on the basis of the meanings and references of its parts and their syntactic organization. Prima facie, implicit reference is incompatible with the thesis I earlier called TCS:

> (TCS) For every declarative sentence x with all lexical, structural, anaphoric and prosodic ambiguities resolved, the truth conditions of what is said (or the proposition expressed) by x, relative to an occasion or context of utterance, are wholly constitutively determined by (i) the meanings of the individual words in x, (ii) prosodic features of x, (iii) principles of semantic composition that reflect x's syntactic structure and prosody, and (iv) the systematic effects of a pre-established set of features of the occasion or context of utterance (exploited by the meanings of indexical expressions).

The viability of TCS—or theses very close to it—has been a topic of great debate in philosophy. However, it is not clear that all participants in these debates have been engaging with one another cogently. One problem is a possible difference of focus that can be obscured by the sheepishly passive nominal 'what is said'. "Said by *what*?" one might well ask. What is the entity that *says* something, in the requisite sense, when someone utters a sentence on a given occasion? The speaker? The utterance? The sentence? Does it matter? In principle, we have three notions of reference to contend with:

(a) *Sentence saying*: What sentence x said relative to a given context or utterance.
(b) *Utterance saying*: What a given utterance of x said.
(c) *Speaker saying*: What a speaker said in uttering x on a given occasion.

Any given theorist might simply *define* a technical sense of 'say' in connection with an expansion of one of these three forms and then *stipulate* that expansions of the other two are to be treated as stylistic variants. (The expansions of (a) and (b) will have to make explicit mention of S, who is implicit at present, via the word 'utterance'.) But that is not what theorists have done, and their allegiance to one or other type of locution seems to indicate what it is they are trying to characterize with talk of what is said.

When Grice and Schiffer talk about saying, for example, they consistently talk about what a *speaker* says in uttering x, and for good reason: for them, a speaker's *saying* something in uttering x, is a special case of a speaker's *meaning* something by uttering x. So, like the Gricean notion of speaker meaning it assumes, the Gricean notion of saying is *psychological*—to say something by uttering x is to have *a meaning intention* in uttering x—the whole idea being to articulate a notion of saying that can play a rôle in a theory forming part of an answer to the Master Question. And it is for this reason that Grice—contrary to what some people have argued—allowed for the possibility of implicit reference.

When philosophers talk about saying in connection with *semantic composition*, however, they tend to talk either about what *sentences* say (relative to occasions of use, utterances, contexts of utterance, or whatever) or about what *utterances of sentences* say depending upon whether the theorist is assuming a traditional semantic theory that composes the semantic values of *expressions*, or a theory that composes the semantic values of *utterances of expressions*. Theories that compose the semantic values of expressions (suitably relativized) involve quite different commitments from theories that compose the semantic values of utterances of expressions, and these commitments bear on how implicit reference is to be explained and whether compositional semantics needs aphonic referring expressions.

12.10.2 *The Gricean notion*

A number of influential philosophers and linguists who accept the existence of implicit reference (or, more generally, unarticulated constituents) claim that Grice cannot be counted among their ranks because his conception of what is said is so closely tied to sentence meaning.[83] But such claims involve (a) misunderstanding what Grice is claiming in the passage they typically present as evidence, (b) failure to take into account Grice's explicit account of the relation between *saying* that p and *meaning* that p, (c) mistakenly inferring a general thesis on the basis of examples that Grice tried to explain in terms of conversational implicature, and (d) overlooking Grice's (1981) own implicit reference theory of incomplete definite descriptions, which he saw as an integral component of a response to Strawson's (1950) Argument from Incompleteness against Russell's Theory of Descriptions.

Certainly Grice did not make the case that there is implicit reference at work in all of the cases that Schiffer, Sperber and Wilson, Carston, or Recanati have examined. But it does not follow from this, or from the fact that Grice put forward a conversational implicature account of properties of certain uses of 'and', that he rejected the existence of implicit reference.

For Grice, saying and implicating are both things *speakers* do. At the beginning of 'Logic and Conversation', he tells us that "I shall, for the time being at least, have to assume to a considerable extent an intuitive understanding of the meaning of *say*" (1975: 44; 1989: 24–5), adding that "in the sense in which I am using the word 'say', I intend what someone has said to be closely related to the conventional meaning of the words (the sentence) which he has uttered" (1975: 44; 1989: 25).[84] This "favored, and maybe in some degree artificial, sense" of 'say' (1968: 225; 1989: 118) might well diverge occasionally from an intuitive sense, but it is one Grice "expect[s] to be of greater theoretical utility than some other sense of 'say' would be" (1989: 121). In the favored sense, in uttering x, S does not *say* that p unless S *means* that p, for what S *says* in uttering x is effectively that portion of what S *means* by uttering x that conforms to x's standing (or unrelativized) meaning.[85] As Schiffer puts it,

(SS) In uttering sentence x, S said that p iff (1) S meant that p, and (2) the proposition that p conforms to the standing meaning of x.[86]

In effect, then, the standing meaning of a sentence x is something that *constrains* (without fully determining) what a speaker can say by uttering x. The hard work comes in spelling out precisely what the standing meaning of an expression is—a Kaplanian *character*?—and what it takes for a proposition to conform to a sentence's standing meaning.

Some of what Grice says about reference sheds more light on this. He brings together saying and pronouns in the following oft-quoted passage:

In the sense in which I am using the word 'say', I intend what someone has said to be *closely related* [emphasis added] to the conventional meaning of the words (the sentence) which he has uttered. Suppose someone to have uttered the sentence 'He is in the grip of a vice.' Given a knowledge of the English language, but no knowledge of the circumstances of the utterance, one would know *something* [emphasis added] about what the speaker had said, on the assumption that he was speaking standard English, and speaking literally. One would know that he had said, about some particular male person or animal x, that at the time of the utterance (whatever that was), either (1) x was unable to rid himself of a certain kind of bad character trait or (2) some part of x's person was caught in a certain kind of tool or instrument (approximate account, of course). But for a full *identification* [emphasis added] of what the speaker had said, one would need to know (a) the identity of x, (b) the time of utterance, and (c) the meaning, on the particular occasion of utterance, of the phrase *in the grip of vice* [a decision between (1) and (2)]. (1975: 44; 1989: 25)

It would be an egregious error to claim the passage shows that on Grice's account, implicit reference has no bearing on what is said.

(i) In the first sentence of the passage, Grice is making a constitutive point of epistemic significance. He was almost pathologically cautious in his wording, and it is striking that he says "closely related to" and not "largely determined by" conventional meaning. (On Grice's account, *S says* that *p* only if *S means* that *p*.)

(ii) In the remainder of the passage, Grice is talking straightforwardly about *epistemic* determination. Contrary to what many people who quote the passage seem to think, Grice is *not* making the *constitutive* claim that *what S says* on a given occasion by uttering a sentence *x* is determined by the meaning of *x* and various contextual coordinates. He is claiming that an interpreter's knowledge of English will carry him *only so far* in attempting to *identify* (*epistemically determine*) what the speaker has said. If the interpreter has "no knowledge of the circumstances of the utterance" but can take it for granted that the speaker (whoever that was) was speaking literally and using standard English, given the interpreter's knowledge of English he would know "*something* [emphasis added] about what the speaker had said". Among the things the interpreter would *not* know about what the speaker said are (a) who the speaker was referring to with 'he', (b) the time the speaker was referring to (which is standardly the time the utterance takes place), and (c) which of the two meanings of 'in the grip of a vice' the speaker intended. These things all have to be *inferred* by the interpreter. And if Grice's theory of conversation can throw light on how interpreters identify conversational implicatures it can certainly throw light on the (typically) easier task of identifying who speakers are referring to with personal pronouns and the like.

In Grice's (1969b, 1970, 1975, 1981) discussions of definite descriptions, we get more information about what is said, and also find Grice committing himself to the view that there exist cases of implicit reference.

(1) Grice says his use of 'say' leaves it open whether two people who, in 1967, knew that Harold Wilson was the British prime minister, said the same thing when one uttered 'Harold Wilson is a great man' and the other 'The British Prime Minister is a great man' (1975: 45; 1989: 26). In effect, then, he leaves it open whether (some) definite descriptions are (sometimes) referring expressions and whether the content of what is said is a singular proposition (which presumably it would have to be if Grice's two speakers from 1967 said the same thing).

(2) Grice (1969b) invokes his distinction between what *S says* and what *S means* in defending a Russellian account of definite descriptions and argues that the cases Donnellan (1966) used with a view to demonstrating that *speaker reference* accompanying the use of a definite description can have an impact on what is said, demonstrate no such thing. Descriptions, he says, "have no relevant systematic duplicity of meaning; their meaning is given by a Russellian account" (1969b: 143) Since there is no impact, according to Grice, on what is said, in the terminology of the present paper Donnellan's cases must involve *indirect* rather than implicit reference. This leads to serious trouble because Grice also effectively commits himself to the view that speakers do refer to things *with* descriptions.

(3) Grice (1981) presents an implicit reference theory of incomplete definite descriptions:

Consider utterances of such a sentence as 'The book on the table is not open.' As there are, obviously, many books on tables in the world, if we are to treat such a sentence as being of the form 'The F is not G' and as being, on that account, ripe for Russellian expansion, we might do well to treat it as exemplifying the more specific form 'The F which is ϕ is not G', where 'ϕ' represents an epithet to be identified in a particular context of utterance ('ϕ' being a sort of *quasi-demonstrative* [emphasis added]). Standardly, to identify the reference of 'ϕ' for a particular utterance of 'The book on the table is (not) open', a hearer would proceed via the identification of a particular book as being a good *candidate* for being the book meant, and would identify the reference of 'ϕ' by finding in the candidate a feature, for example, that of being in this room, which could be used to yield a composite epithet ('book on the table in this room'), which would in turn fill the bill of being an epithet which the speaker had in mind as being uniquely satisfied by the book selected as candidate. If the hearer fails to find a suitable reference for 'ϕ' in relation to the selected candidate, then he would, normally, seek another candidate. So determining the reference of 'ϕ' would standardly involve determining what feature the speaker might have in mind as being uniquely instantiated by an actual object, and this in turn would standardly involve satisfying oneself that some particular feature actually is uniquely satisfied by a particular actual object (e.g. a particular book). (Grice, 1981: 276-7)

Although Grice does not use the verb 'say' in this passage in connection with what the speaker does, it is hard to see how to read his talk of the *form* 'The F is not G', when ripe for *Russellian expansion*, exemplifying the *form* 'The F which is ϕ is not G', "where 'ϕ' represents an epithet to be identified in a particular context of utterance ('ϕ' being a sort of *quasi-demonstrative*)" as anything but a proposal about the content of what the speaker says, i.e. an *implicit reference* proposal.

Despite Grice's objective, his remarks here provide much of what is needed for what I shall call the *Argument from Priority* for a *referential* semantics for definite descriptions. The argument I have in mind is stated clearly by Schiffer (2005):

when a definite description is used referentially, a hearer cannot even identify *candidate* descriptive propositions except on the basis of knowing that to which the speaker was referring in uttering the definite description, and this is incompatible with the claim that the Russellian theory *explains* the referential uses. (2005: 88)

So, where Grice takes the identification by A of the intended implicit content to proceed via A's identification of a particular F as being a good *candidate* for being the F that S meant, and then A's satisfying himself that the candidate possesses some property that S could reasonably be thought to believe is possessed by no other F, Schiffer holds that A's identification of a *candidate property* that S could reasonably be thought to believe is possessed by no F other than the one S meant must proceed via A's identification of the F that S meant. Whoever is right about the details, the moral Schiffer draws is surely right: A's identification of a property that no F other than the one S meant possesses plays no explanatory rôle whatsoever; it is an epicycle whose sole objective is to ensure that incomplete descriptions used referentially do not constitute counterexamples to a unitary Russellian theory of descriptions.

Grice says, "unanswered questions remain" about his "reliance (without much exposition) on a favoured notion of 'saying' which needs to be further elucidated"

(1989: 86–7). But, taken together, (i) his discussions of examples involving pronouns and descriptions, (ii) his taking what S *says* in uttering *x* to be that portion of what S *means* by uttering *x* that conforms to *x*'s meaning, (iii) his taking what S means by uttering *x* to be determined by the communicative intentions S had in uttering *x*, and (iv) his intention to cash out the meaning of *x* in terms of self-perpetuating correlations between utterances of *x* and what speakers mean by uttering *x* gives us a better understanding of Grice's notion of saying than we have of some competing notions and an indication of its rôle in a theory forming part of an answer to the Master Question.

12.10.3 *The Kaplanian notion*

Kaplan's semantic theory uses a technical notion of what is said by a *sentence*.[87] This is not surprising, given that the theory is rooted in the formal semantics (model theory) for a formal language containing demonstrative and other indexical expressions, a *logic of demonstratives*, as Kaplan calls it.

Kaplan distinguishes two forms of expression meaning, *character* and *content*. Expressions have *contents* relative to (or *in*) *contexts*.[88] The content of a singular referring expression *e* (in context *c*), is the object to which *e refers* (in *c*). The content of a sentence *x* (in *c*) is a *proposition*—the proposition the sentence expresses (in *c*). It is this, the proposition expressed by a sentence *x* (in *c*) that Kaplan identifies with *what is said* by *x* (in *c*). (For that reason, I shall allow myself to talk about *constituents of what is said* when talking about constituents of propositions expressed.)

We need to distinguish contexts in the *intuitive* sense of situations in which real people (with beliefs, desires, intentions, fears, interests, biases, and so on) produce utterances—the things I have been calling *contexts of utterance, occasions of utterance*, or *utterance situations*—and contexts in the *technical* sense within Kaplan's theory, which are *n*-ary sequences whose entries include those things in the situation of utterance upon which the *contents* of words might depend—everything apart from their *meanings* that is. Kaplan's characters, are functions from contexts to contents.[89] Putting the pieces together, a context is an *n*-ary sequence whose entries are exhausted by objects representing those facets of occasions of utterance that *characters* of certain words *systematically exploit*, hence facets to which the *contents* of those words are *systematically sensitive*.

The character of 'I' is just a function that takes a context *c* as its argument and returns the speaker in *c* as the word's content, in *c*.[90] The character of 'here' is a function that takes a context *c* as its argument and returns *c*'s location as the word's content. To know the character of 'I' is to know that, canonically, the speaker or writer uses it to refer to himself or herself, and this is something I know about the word 'I' just by virtue of being a competent speaker. So the content of an *atomic* expression *e* (in a context *c*) is determined by *e*'s character. And the content (in *c*) of a *complex* expression *x* is determined by (i) the contents (in *c*) of *x*'s atomic expressions, and (ii) rules of content composition that determine the content (in *c*) of a complex expression *Y* from (a) the contents (in *c*) of *y*'s parts and (b) *y*'s syntactic structure.[91]

I said earlier that I'll follow Kaplan in taking propositions to be structured entities whose atomic parts are objects and properties (and whose non-atomic parts are structured entities whose atomic parts are objects and properties). The connection with Kaplan's semantics is straightforward. Propositions have structure, in much the same way that sentences and ordered *n*-tuples do, and the objects and properties that are their atomic constituents are the things that atomic *referring expressions* and *predicates* have as their contents, in contexts. So the content of 'Sue resides in London' (in *c*) is the singular proposition that Sue resides in London, which has Sue, London, and the property of residing-in as atomic constituents (these being the contents (in *c*) of 'Sue', 'London', and 'resides in', respectively).

I have said nothing about the characters of demonstrative expressions yet ('this', 'that', 'this *F*', 'that *F*', 'he', and 'she', relative to some uses). Before looking at them, at the limitations of Kaplan's theory, and at Kaplan's notion of what is said, we need to look at how semantic composition works and at the difference between the traditional composition of *expression*-contents and the composition of *utterance*-contents, a difference that has a bearing on how we think about character and content in connection with implicit reference and especially aphonic reference, if it exists.

For all I've said so far, it's not obvious how there could be a substantive disagreement about the truth conditions of "what is said" between (1) a theorist talking about what a *speaker* says by uttering a given sentence on a given occasion and (2) a theorist talking about what that *sentence* says relative to a context, construed as modelling that occasion of utterance. If there is no single notion of "what is said" about whose content they genuinely disagree, there are two important consequences, one for each party, the combination of which seems to have cancelled both out in the minds of many theorists. First, it underscores the need for those who talk about what *speakers* say (state, explicate) not to overstate what the impact of implicit reference on "what is said" demonstrates about the utility of a theory whose compositional machinery delivers the content of what *sentences* say, relative to contexts. Second, it underscores the need for those who talk about what *sentences* say, relative to contexts, to explain why *that* notion of saying has a rôle to play in a theory forming part of an answer to the Master Question—unless it is meant to coincide with the Gricean notion. (The overtly psychological and communicative characteristics of the Gricean notion were, from the outset, meant to equip it with the properties it needs to play such a rôle.) Perhaps, as theories develop, we will discover the need for both notions of saying. Or perhaps they will ultimately coalesce, extensionally, Kaplanians and Griceans finding themselves talking about the same thing from two different perspectives, one centered on facts about *sentences* being used, the other on facts about the intentions (or other mental states) of competent *users* of those sentences.

12.11 The Composition of Content

12.11.1 *Expression semantics*

Theorists who talk about saying and referring in broadly Kaplanian terms, take the compositional component of a semantic theory to compose *expression*-contents. (To say this is not to deny that when discussing a particular utterance of a sentence they are happy to talk about the content of the utterance or the content of the sentence-context pair. It's to say that as far as the *formal machinery* of their semantic theories are concerned, composition is on the contents of expressions, relative to (or "in") contexts, not on, say, utterances.) The overall picture is as follows (for the time being I shall artificially restrict attention to sentences in which no expression occurs more than once):

(1) What is said by a declarative sentence x in a context c (which models an occasion of utterance) is wholly determined by

  (i) The contents (in c) of the expressions that are x's atomic constituents, and
  (ii) Rules of content composition that wholly determine the content (in c) of a complex expression y on the basis of y's syntactic structure the contents (in c) of y's constituents.

(2) The content (in c) of each atomic part of e of x is wholly determined by a proprietary rule (a *character*) specifying e's content (in a context), a rule represented by a function from contexts to contents.

(3) If e is a genuine singular referring expression, e's content (in c) = e's reference (in c).

Since a theory of this sort composes *expression* contents, call it a *compositional expression semantics*.[92] When we come to look at implicit reference and aphonics, the following consequence of (1)–(3) will be important:

(4) If x is a sentence containing a singular referring expression e, the reference of e (in c) is a constituent of *what is said* by x (in c).

12.11.2 Utterance semantics

A fair number of philosophers assume (and very occasionally argue) that indexicality and other forms of context-sensitivity require us to attribute semantic content not to expressions, relative to contexts, but to *utterances* of expressions (or expression *tokens*). Since a theory of this sort composes utterance contents, I'll call it a *compositional utterance semantics*.

Things are a little more complicated for utterance semantics than they are for expression-semantics, as we need to talk about those parts of a single utterance of a sentence x—presumably temporal parts—that are themselves utterances of constituents of x (I continue with the artificial restriction to sentences in which no expression occurs more than once):

(1′) What is said by a given utterance $u[x]$ of a declarative sentence x is wholly determined by

  (i) The contents of those parts of $u[x]$ that are utterances of x's atomic constituents, and
  (ii) Rules of content composition that wholly determine the content of an utterance $u[y]$ of a complex expression y on the basis of y's syntactic structure and the contents of those parts of $u[y]$ that are utterances of constituents of y.

(2′) The content of each part of $u[x]$ that is an utterance of an atomic constituent e of x is wholly determined by a proprietary rule (a *character*) specifying $u[e]$'s content, a rule represented by a function from utterances to contents.

(3′) If $u[e]$ is an utterance of a singular referring expression e, $u[e]$'s content = $u[e]$'s reference.

When we come to look at implicit reference and aphonics, the following consequence of (1′)–(3′) will be important:

(4′) If $u[x]$ is an utterance of a sentence x and has as one of its parts an utterance $u[e]$ of an expression e that is a genuine singular referring expression in x, the reference of $u[e]$ is a constituent of *what is said* by $u[x]$.

12.11.3 *The shady characters of demonstratives*

According to Kaplan's original theory,

Some of the indexicals require, in order to determine their referents, an associated demonstration: typically, though not invariably, a (visual) presentation of a local object discriminated by a pointing. These indexicals are the true demonstratives, and 'that' is their paradigm. The demonstra*tive* (an expression) refers to that which the demon*stration* demonstrates. I call that which is demonstrated the 'demonstratum'.... The linguistic rules which govern the use of the true demonstratives 'that', 'he', etc., are not sufficient to determine their referent in all contexts of use. Something else—an associated demonstration—must be provided. The linguistic rules assume that such a demonstration accompanies each (demonstrative) use of a demonstrative. (1989a: 490)

The idea seems to be that that the *character* of a "true demonstrative" specifies that the "associated demonstration" determines the content of a demonstrative in a context. Two objections to this idea strike me as fatal. First, sometimes there is no demonstration as none is needed. (As Evans (1985) observes, a soldier who faints in the heat at a parade while the rest of his company remain standing to attention makes himself salient and an easy referent for 'he'—'He must be dehydrated', an observer might say.) Second, a demonstration is an act, and acts are individuated in part by the *intentions* with which they are performed. Demonstrating *o* involves more than simply having one's arm and forefinger extended and lined up with *o*. *S*'s arm and forefinger might be extended in this way towards a wall while asleep in a darkened room, and when *S* mutters in his sleep, 'That's good', he can hardly be credited with demonstrating and referring to the wall, and saying that the wall is nice. Without taking into account the speaker's intentions, the idea of a demonstration determining the reference of an expression falls flat. (Intentional but nonetheless lazy or vague demonstrations reinforce the point.)

So what are the characters of 'he', 'she', 'this', and 'that'? As Gareth Evans notes, "All that the conventions governing the referring expression 'he' insist upon, in any given context, is that the object referred to should be male" (1982: 312). "There is no linguistic rule which determines that a 'he' or a 'that man' refers to *x* rather than *y* in the vicinity, or that it refers to someone who has just left rather than someone who has been recently mentioned' (1985: 230–1). Any theory according to which the characters of 'he', 'she', or any other referring expression for that matter, are imbued with some principle about *salience* gets everything backwards, the confused product of conflating different notions of determination. (See section 12.5.). As Schiffer (2003, 2005) notes, in discussing uses of 'she',

The literal speaker is...constrained to refer to a female who is contextually salient with respect to the topic of conversation, but that is only because the speaker can't hope to have his referential intentions recognized unless his audience can single out a particular female as the most likely candidate for being the referent. (2003: 122)

We do not even have to say that [its character] constrains the speaker to refer to a contextually salient female, since the speaker cannot intend to refer to a particular female unless he expects his hearer to recognize to which female he is referring, and the expectation of such recognition itself entails that the speaker takes the referent to have an appropriate salience. (2005: 1141)

And the formation of genuine communicative intentions (of which referential intentions are a species) is subject to some serious constraints.

Let's stick with speaker reference for a moment. At a certain point in a conversation we are having, you suggest inviting Sue to give the keynote lecture at a conference we are organizing. I say to you,

(1) She gave a brilliant lecture at the Graduate Center last year.

Suppose I mean that *Sue* gave a brilliant lecture at the Graduate Center last year. I have the relevant communicative intention. The content of that proposition is a singular proposition that has Sue as a constituent. I am referring to Sue with 'she', in the sense of **RW**. The formation of my communicative intention in uttering (1) is constrained by my grasp of the conventions governing the referring use of 'she'. So if I had not thought that the female I planned to talk about was not salient enough, in the context, to be recognized as such, I simply could not have formed the requisite referential intention. This is not something built into the meaning of 'she'! It's far more basic than that.

Suppose you took me to be referring to Sue with 'she'. How did you reach that conclusion? In such an everyday situation, something like the following is a reasonable sketch of an answer: you assumed that my utterance was intended as a contribution to the discussion we were having about Sue and Ann; you had just asked me whether we should invite Sue to give the keynote lecture at the conference we are organising, and you are confident I heard and understood your remark; so the evidence strongly suggested to you that I was referring to Sue, that my intention was to be talking about Sue.[93] This has nothing to do with you knowing, by virtue of knowing the meaning of 'she', that I must be referring to a *salient* female! (Of course, this answer does not constitute a *theory*: it is merely a set of statements about [some of] the *local* evidence you draw upon in interpreting my remark.) This reinforces an important point I made earlier: the interpreter's *objective* is establishing what the speaker means, and in this particular case, the route to that involves establishing who I'm referring to with 'she'.

But notice, officially we have not answered the questions the advocate of Kaplanian expression semantics needs to answer:

(i) What does the pronoun 'she' refer to, relative to a context?
(ii) What is the character of 'she'?
(iii) Since a context is an *n*-ary sequence whose entries are objects representing those facets of occasions of utterance that *characters* of certain words systematically exploit, hence facets to which the *contents* of those words are systematically sensitive, what is the relevant object that is to be added to a

context to provide something the character of 'she' will exploit i.e. take as an argument for which it will return the content of 'she', in that context?

(i) Given that I referred to Sue with 'she', in uttering (1), and given that you, the interpreter, had as an objective establishing who I was referring to, if we can generalize from this case the only plausible answer to question (i) is that, in c, 'she' refers to whichever female the *speaker* in c is referring to.

(ii) What about the character of 'she'. Schiffer suggests the only hope for the Kaplanian is something like "that function that maps ... 'she' [relative to a context c] onto x just in case x is the female to whom the speaker [in c] intended to refer [with it]" (2005: 1141). But even this has problems, as we can see by addressing question (iii).

(iii) Suppose for the moment that a context is a sequence (s, t, p, w), the first element of which is its speaker, the second its time, the third its location, and the fourth its world. There are two important points to note.

>   (a) The first three elements of a context are those facets of an occasion of utterance that the *characters* of the words 'I', 'now', and 'here' exploit, the facets to which the *contents* of those words are sensitive. In any given context modelling a situation of utterance, its first element is there *because* it is (or at least represents) an utterance's *speaker*, not because it is the referent of 'I'.[94] Indeed, *the whole idea* is that the first element of a context is the referent of 'I' in that context *because* the first element of a context is (or at least represents) the utterance's *speaker*. Mutatis mutandis for the second element (the utterance's time) and 'now', and the third element (the utterance's location) and 'here'.
>
>   (b) The *contents* of 'I', 'now', and 'here' in a context c are all *elements* of c. So the character of 'I', 'now', or 'here' is not just a function from contexts to *contents*, it is also (by design?) a function from contexts to *elements of those contexts*. More precisely, the character of each of these words is a function that takes a context c as argument and returns *one of c's elements* as the word's content in c.

So what is the character of 'she'? What facet of a situation of utterance does its *character* exploit, i.e. what facet is its *content* sensitive to, what facet are we going to make the fifth element of contexts to supplement the other four s, t, p, w?

If the character of 'she' is to be a function that takes a context c as argument and returns one of c's *elements* as the content of 'she' in c (as the characters of 'I', 'now', and 'here' do), then the female that the *first* element of c is referring to with 'she' will have to be the fifth element of the context. But notice this means whereas s, t, p, w, are elements of c because they are (or at least represent), respectively, an utterance's speaker, time, place, and world, the fifth element is in there only *because* it's the female the first element of c is referring to with 'she', and not because it is a facet of the situation of utterance—the female referred to might be a thousand miles away in a lead-lined room with no wifi or telephone. So the whole theory becomes a mockery.[95]

Suppose instead we take the fifth element of contexts to be a referential intention.[96] Now we have to give up the idea that the character of 'she' is (like the characters of 'I', 'now', and 'here' do) a function that takes a context c as argument and returns one of *c*'s *elements* as the word's content in *c*, otherwise 'she' will refer in *c* to the *referential intention* the speaker in *c* has in uttering it! Furthermore, making a speaker's intention an element of a context means forsaking part of the original idea (imported from work on indexical logics) that the elements of contexts are (or correspond to) public, objective, mind-independent features of situations of utterance.

On such an account, a rather different type of character is required for 'she', one that does not have to return an element of context *c* as the content of 'she' relative to *c*. What would the character of 'she' have to look like? Schiffer (2005) has provided the answer and explained its consequences. (I have modified Schiffer's prose and definitions to reflect an *expression* semantics rather than the sort of *utterance* semantics he seems to assume, and changed 'token' to 'utterance' where it is still needed):

> ...the meaning of 'she' (very roughly speaking) merely constrains one uttering it to be referring to a female.... What fixes the referent of 'she' [relative to an utterance of it] are the speaker's referential intentions in producing that [utterance], and therefore in order for Kaplan to accommodate [utterances of] 'she', he would have to say that a speaker's referential intentions constitute one more component of those n-tuples that he construes as "contexts." [*Footnote omitted.*] The trouble with this is that there is no work for Kaplanian contexts to do once one recognizes speakers' referential intentions. The referent of a pronoun or demonstrative [relative to an utterance of it] is *always* determined by the speaker's referential intentions. If the speaker who utters 'I' does not intend to refer to herself by 'I' [relative to that utterance of it]—say, if she uttered 'I picked a peck of pickled peppers' merely to work on her elocution—then she is not speaking literally and thus 'I' does not refer to herself or to anything else [relative to that utterance], since she is not saying anything about herself or anything else. The difference between 'I' and 'she' is that the meaning of 'I' constrains the literal speaker to be referring to herself, whereas the meaning of 'she' merely constrains the speaker to be referring to a female. Kaplan's notion of "context" is superfluous. He would have done better to have said that the character of an expression...is a function that maps possible [utterances] of [it] onto contents. Then he might to a first approximation have said:
>
> The character of 'she' is that function f such that, necessarily, for any utterance τ of 'she' and any o, $f($'she', relative to $\tau) = o$ iff o is the female to whom the speaker refers with 'she'.
>
> The character of 'I' is that function f such that, necessarily, for any utterance τ of 'I' and any o, f ('I', relative to $\tau) = o$ iff $o =$ the speaker and the speaker refers to himself with 'I'. (2005: 1141)

I'll call these *shady characters*. In line with the expression semantics I have been assuming, these characters need to be transposed. So, for example, we get this for 'she':

> The character of 'she' is that function f such that for any o, any occurrence i of 'she' in any sentence x, any utterance τ of x, $f($'she', $X, i, \tau) = o$ iff o is the female to whom the speaker refers with 'she' relative to its i-th occurrence in X.

As noted earlier, originally, Kaplan (1989a) treated the reference of a demonstrative as determined by a demonstration ('typically, though not invariably, a (visual) presentation of a local object discriminated by a pointing" (1989a: 490). But later,

Kaplan (1989b) shifted to treating the reference of a perceptual demonstrative, relative to a context, as determined by a 'directing intention' (a referential intention informed by perception) and treating the demonstration as "a mere externalization of this inner intention" (1989b: 582). Commenting on this change, Schiffer says,

> Kaplan himself came to appreciate that the reference of a term like 'she' or 'that' is determined by the speaker's referential intentions and not by any reference-independent contextual factor, but it is not clear he realized that this in effect ruined his conceptions of characters as functions from *indices* to contents. For the only way of keeping indices along with the fact that reference is determined by the speaker's referential intentions is to take the referential intentions as a component of the index for 'she' et al. The trouble is that then the notion of an 'index' is rendered superfluous. (2003: 112)

I agree. To know the meaning of the word 'she' is to know that on a proper literal use the competent speaker is referring to a female. Since an expression semantics needs to take 'she', as used on a given occasion, to have a reference, it should take whatever the speaker is referring to with 'she' on a given occasion to be the reference of 'she', relative to that occasion of utterance.

To know the meaning of the word 'I' is to know that on a proper literal use the competent speaker is referring to himself or herself; so our semantics should take the reference of 'I', as used on a given occasion, to be whoever the competent user of 'I' is referring to with it? *Mutatis mutandis* for 'we', 'here', 'this', 'that', 'now', 'today', and (importantly) any *aphonic* referring expressions.

The upshot of all this is that when it comes to a demonstrative e, an adequate expression semantics will take e's reference in a context c to be identical to what the speaker in c is referring to with e. More precisely, we can say this:

> (DR) Relative to its i-th occurrence in a sentence x, what a demonstrative d refers to, in context c, is identical to whatever the speaker in c referred to with e, relative to its i-th occurrence in x.

I mentioned in section 12.6.5 that Kaplan refers to the picture of Carnap, not the picture of Spiro Agnew, when he says 'That is a picture of one of the greatest philosophers of the twentieth century' in his famous example. The picture of Carnap is the only one about which Kaplan has a relevant *singular communicative intention*. (Of course, in different elaborations of the example this might change.) So by DR, the word 'that', relative to the context (or utterance), refers to the picture of Carnap.

12.12 Aphonic Content

12.12.1 Aphonics in expression semantics

Expression semantics is perfectly consistent with the existence of aphonic referring expressions. But claiming that the phrase-marker for a given sentence x contains an aphonic e is not something to be undertaken lightly, and any such a claim will be empty unless certain conditions obtain.

Let $\Phi(f)$ be a simple sentence comprising a one-place phonic predicate Φ and a *phonic* referring expression f (an indexical pronoun such as 'I', for example). In an expression semantics, such as Kaplan's, what is said by $\Phi(f)$ (in context c) is determined by the contents of Φ and f (in c) and the relevant principles of semantic composition. The contents of the atomic constituents Φ and f (in c) are determined by their characters. The connection between content and reference lies in the fact that it is f's reference (in c) that constitutes e's content (in c). So the referent of f (in c) will be a constituent of what is said by $\Phi(f)$ (in c).

Now let e be an *aphonic* referring expression. If e is to have a content (in c), then it needs to have a character that determines it. And if the determined content is to play a role in determining the content (in c) of a sentence x containing e, then e (no less than the phonic f) must occupy a definite *syntactic position* in x in order to attract the attention of any principle of content composition. (It is *constitutive* of such principles that their operations are sensitive to the syntactic *positions* in which expressions occur.) Now consider claims of the following form about aphonics and content:

> The content of such-and-such a sentence, relative to a context, is determined in part by the content, in that context, of an aphonic expression occurring in that sentence.

Anyone can say things like this. But for claims about a purported aphonic e to have substance, at least the following four conditions on the postulated aphonic, e, must obtain:

(C1) e must belong to a specific syntactic *category*;

(C2) e must occupy specific syntactic *positions* in sentences;

(C3) e must have *character*, which maps a context, c, to e's *content*;

(C4) the content of e is something some *phonic* could have as its content in *some* context or other.

Not all of the aphonics that philosophers have postulated in explanations of implicit reference satisfy all of these conditions. One might have doubts about (C4), but put these aside for the moment.

12.12.2 *Aphonics in utterance semantics*

Utterance semantics does not fare as well with aphonics. The reason is intuitively obvious, but it will pay to articulate it precisely.

According to utterance semantics, what is said by a particular dated *utterance* of a sentence x is constitutively determined by the composition of the contents of particular dated *utterances* of the expressions that are the constituents of x (in accordance with principles of semantic composition reflecting x's syntactic structure).

(i) Let $u[\Phi(f)]$ be a particular utterance of sentence $\Phi(f)$ by S. Utterance semantics specifies the proposition expressed by $[\Phi(f)]$ by composing the contents of utterances of Φ and f by S. But not just *any* utterances of Φ and f. The relevant utterances are those that are adjacent *parts* of $u[\Phi(f)]$, which we can represent as $u[\Phi]$ and $u[f]$. Since $u[\Phi(f)]$ is an event (under an intentional description), presumably *temporal* adjacency will be the relevant notion, so we can take $u[\Phi(f)]$ to be a linear temporal sequencing of events, $u[\Phi]\frown u[f]$. Utterance-semantics, then, assumes not only that *sentences* have definite parts (as does expression-semantics, of course), but also that *utterances* of sentences have definite parts, at least some of which correspond to parts of the sentences they are utterances *of*. As such, it needs some sort of story about the metaphysics of utterances and their parts, and about the facts in virtue of which some part of $u[\Phi(f)]$—a temporal slice of it—is $u[f]$, for example.

(ii) Where do the contents of $u[\Phi]$ and $u[f]$ come from? They are functions of the characters of Φ and f. In an expression semantics, the character of f is a function that takes a *context* as its argument and returns f's content, relative to that context, as value. That is, one and the same entity, an expression, has a *character* and a *content* (in a context). In utterance semantics, by contrast, expressions have characters but *utterances* of expressions have contents. On the most straightforward account, the character of f is a function that takes an utterance of f as its argument and returns the content of that utterance as value. For example, the character of the word 'I' will be a function that takes an utterance $u[I]$ of 'I' and returns $u[I]$'s producer (the speaker) as $u[I]$'s content. (On a less straightforward account, the argument of the function that is the character of f might be the utterance of some larger expression containing f. See below.)

(iii) Now comes the trouble. For simplicity, let's pretend simple English sentences have the "flat" syntactic structures of the simple formulae of predicate logic we often use to represent them. So the usual '[[$_S$Romeo] [$_{VP}$ *loves Juliet*]]' becomes '*Loves (romeo, juliet)*'. Let $u[\Phi(e,f)]$ be a particular utterance of $\Phi(e,f)$, a simple sentence made up of a two-place predicate, Φ, and two referring expressions e and f. But let e be aphonic. While $u[\Phi(e,f)]$ has $u[f]$ as one of its parts, it does *not* have $u[e]$ as one because there is *no such thing* as $u[e]$. By definition, *there are no utterances of aphonics*. (See UA above.) If there are aphonics, and if e is one of them, then there can certainly be utterances of *sentences* containing e, but there can be no utterances of e. There can be utterances of the sentence $\Phi(e,f)$, for example, but the parts of a given utterance $u[\Phi(e,f)]$ will be just $u[\Phi]$ and $u[f]$. And this is problematic. Since the content of $u[\Phi(e,f)]$ is supposed to be wholly determined by (i) the contents of its parts and (ii) rules of content composition reflecting the syntactic structure of the sentence $\Phi(e,f)$, of which it is an utterance. $\Phi(e,f)$ has three constituents; but $u[\Phi(e,f)]$ has only *two* parts, $u[\Phi]$ and $u[f]$. So whatever the content composition rule is, its application here will take into account the content of $u[f]$ but *not* the content (or any other property) of $u[e]$ as *there is no such thing*. And this makes a mockery of the idea that e is a referring expression.

(iv) Not only can no *content* be associated with e in connection with any utterance of $\Phi(e,f)$, e itself can have no *character*. The phonic f has a character and individual *utterances* of f have contents. f's character is a function that takes $u[f]$, an individual utterance of f, and returns the content of $u[f]$. By parity of semantic composition, if the aphonic e had a character it would be a function that takes $u[e]$ to the content of $u[e]$. But there is no such thing as $u[e]$. So e has no character. (Or its character is a function with no arguments and no values.)

Suppose we modified the theory, taking the argument of the function that is meant to be e's character to be *an utterance of a sentence containing e* (rather than an utterance of e). In the case at hand, the character of e would take $[\Phi(e,f)]$ as its argument. But that's only *half* of the problem solved. What would be the content returned as value? And what would the *bearer* of that content be? The defining idea of utterance-semantics is that *utterances* have content. But there is no utterance of e, so which utterance has the content returned by the character of e when $u[\Phi(e,f)]$ is uttered? Not the non-existent $u[e]$, and not $u[f]$, whose content is "already" the value returned by the character of f when its argument is $u[f]$ (or if the proposed modification is general, when its argument is $[\Phi((e,f)])$. And not $[\Phi]$ or $u[\Phi(e,f)]$ obviously. There seem to be only two possible ways out of this:

(i) give up utterance-semantics in favour of expression semantics
(ii) deny the existence of aphonics that play any role in determining content.

A third way out seems desperate:

(iii) abandon the view that utterances of expressions are material events.

What would an utterance be? An expression *token*? But what is such a thing if not a material event (and hence an *utterance* of an expression in the original sense) or a material object (such as an *inscription* of an expression)? Perhaps it would be an abstract entity of some sort. If so, an "utterance" (in the required technical sense) of a sentence will have to have at least as much structure as the sentence it is an utterance of. But this version of "utterance semantics" would just be expression semantics with a funny name.

As far as I have been able to ascertain, there is no good argument in the literature for composing utterance contents rather than expression contents. (And as I said in sections 1 and 2, talk of "uterance meaning" tends to be symptomatic of deep confusion in any case.) So I will continue to avoid talk of utterances having contents, and with it all talk of utterances of expressions *referring* to things and all talk of utterances of sentences *saying* things.

12.12.3 The shady characters of aphonics

In each of the following examples, the purported aphonic (or the *tense* of the verb, if this turns out to provide a better theory) would refer to a particular timeframe:[97]

(1) I've had <today> an afternoon nap
(2) I've had <this year> a flu shot
(3) I've had <in my lifetime> measles.

But the only plausible story about what the aphonic (or verb tense) refers to is *whatever the speaker is referring to with it*. Transposing Schiffer's remarks about 'she', we get another shady character:

The literal speaker is... constrained to refer to a [timeframe] [that] is contextually salient with respect to the topic of conversation, but that is only because the speaker can't hope to have his referential intentions recognized unless his audience can single out a particular [timeframe] as the most likely candidate for being the referent. (transposing Schiffer 2003: 122)

We do not even have to say that [its character] constrains the speaker to refer to a contextually salient [timeframe], since the speaker cannot intend to refer to a particular [timeframe] unless he expects his hearer to recognize to which [time] he is referring, and the expectation of such recognition itself entails that the speaker takes the referent to have an appropriate salience. (transposing Schiffer 2005: 1141)

We can state the shady character of the temporal aphonic *e* (or the tense marker) as follows, in line with an expression semantics:

The character of timeframe tense marker or aphonic *e* is that function f such that for any t, any occurrence i of e in any sentence x, any utterance τ of x, $f(e, x, i, \tau) = t$ iff t is the timeframe to which the speaker refers with e relative to its i-th occurrence in x.

Examples (4) and (5) raise some interesting questions:[98]

(4) It's foggy <in London/here/there> right now

(5) It's illegal to sell alcohol to people under twenty-one <in New York State>.

Suppose there is a *locative aphonic*, as I'll call it, in these sentences and that it refers to a geophysical or geopolitical location.[99] We need to know (a) to which syntactic category it belongs and (b) where it occurs (which node immediately dominates it, what its sister node is (if any), and so on). Is it a noun phrase (on the model of 'London' or 'the capital of England')? Or does it belong to whatever syntactic category 'in London', 'here' and 'there' belong to? Or does the locative aphonic belong to some altogether different syntactic category, perhaps one that no phonic expression belongs to?

Then there's the question of whether it is present in the following sentences or whether is it "overwritten", as it were, by 'here' or 'in London'?

(6) a. It's foggy here right now

b. It's foggy in London right now

c. It's foggy here in London right now.

If the aphonic *is* overwritten, we need to know the mechanics of overwriting. If it is not, we need to know *where* it occurs in these sentences, what node immediately dominates it, and so on. These are important questions about the syntactic structures of (6a)–(6c).

How does the purported aphonic function semantically? There are two parts to this question: what is its *character*, and what sort of thing does it have for its *content* (relative to given context or utterance)? Since its content can vary across contexts, it is tempting to call *e* an indexical. But the locative aphonic does not have the character of any known phonic indexical.[100] In particular, it does not have the character of either 'here' or 'there' because a speaker inside or outside London can use (4) to say it's foggy in London right now. Its character is wholly non-perspectival, so if we take seriously, as perhaps we should, the fact that traditional talk of indexicality, deixis, and egocentricity—in the work of (e.g.) Reichenbach, Russell, Kaplan, Perry, and Evans, for example—involves various forms of perspective, it would be somewhat misleading to call the postulated locative aphonic *indexical*. So let's just call it *context-sensitive*. (On this usage, the indexical expressions in a language will be a subset of its context-sensitive expressions.) But what is the aphonic's character? Since, by hypothesis, it has no phonology, without some evidence of its existence motivated by grammatical considerations, i.e. considerations of syntactic distribution, the postulation of such an expression might seem little more than an ad-hoc attempt to cling to the thesis that every case of implicit reference is a case of aphonic reference. We can conjure up a shady character again:

> The character of the location aphonic e is that function f such that for any location l, any occurrence i of e in any sentence x, any utterance τ of x, $f(e, x, i, \tau) = x$ iff x is the location to which the speaker refers with e relative to its i-th occurrence in x.

This is not, of course, an argument against the existence of the locative aphonic. It's simply grist for the mill that *expression reference is just speaker reference with an expression*, in the sense of RW, an expression with a type of character specially suited to the task, of course. I am not saying that aphonic referring expressions with shady characters present a *technical* problem for expression semantics. They do not. And, if they exist, they are as rigid as phonic referring expressions.[101] I am simply pointing to the coherence of the view that the content of a referring expression that compositional machinery needs is just whatever the speaker is referring to with it.

12.13 Demands for Implicit Reference

12.13.1 Formal demands (aphonics)

There is implicit reference, as I have defined it, whenever the truth conditions of what is said by someone uttering a sentence x involve something the speaker did not refer to with a phonic occurring in x. The case for its existence is overwhelming. But interesting questions remain concerning the roles played in *facilitating* it by syntax and semantics.

If S refers to something aphonically in uttering sentence x, then x is of a specific *form* that demands implicit reference (if x is to be used to say something true or false). If all implicit reference is aphonic reference, then any contribution to the truth conditions of what is said stemming from implicit reference stems from speakers referring to things with aphonics. And if the assumption is correct, then implicit reference, indisputable as it is, poses no threat to TCS. So part of an explanation of the efficiency in human communication mentioned in the Master Question may well lie in the presence of aphonics in the syntactic structures of certain sentences. However, it is not clear this picture does justice to the mental states of either the speaker or the addressee, a matter I shall take up after examining Schiffer's meaning-intention problem. But first I need to consider cases of implicit reference that do not involve straightforward reference to individiuals and then contrast the formal demand for implicit reference with what I shall call *semantic* and *pragmatic* demands (either of which could, in principle, precede or trump a formal demand in the cognitive processes involved in utterance interpretation).

Consider the following examples in which an aphonic is assumed to occur as the subject of the embedded gerundive or infinitival clause (bracketed) and to be linked (in some semantically relevant way) to the subject of the main clause (indicated here by co-indexing):

(1) Sue remembers [*e* lecturing on aphonics]
(2) Sue has fond memories of [*e* lecturing on aphonics]
(3) Sue$_1$ intends/wants/expects [e_1 to lecture on aphonics].

Intuitively, someone uttering one of these sentences is (to put it incautiously for a moment) referring to the same person *twice*: as the person intending, wanting, expecting, or remembering, and as the person lecturing (or potentially lecturing). Superficially at least, the syntactic position occupied by the postulated aphonic is occupied by *phonic* expressions in (4) and (5):

(4) Sue remembers herself lecturing on aphonics
(5) Sue remembers Andy/him lecturing on aphonics.

But the advocate of the aphonic analysis is unlikely to see support for the position in this observation. Arguably, (i) the subject of 'lecturing' in (4) and (5) is *still* an aphonic, and (ii) 'herself' and 'Andy' are the direct objects of 'remembers'. (Notice the third-person pronoun in (5) appears in its accusative form, 'him', the form associated with direct and indirect object positions of verbs.) This would mean that the structures of (4) and (5) above are roughly (4′) and (5′), below, with a purported aphonic, again occurring as the subject of the embedded clause but this time linked (in the semantically relevant way) to the object of the main verb (again indicated by co-indexing):

(4′) Sue remembers herself$_2$ [e_2 lecturing on aphonics]
(5′) Sue remembers Andy$_2$/him$_2$ [e_2 lecturing on aphonics].

The syntax of a sentence places constraints on its semantics, which amounts to a set of *conditions on the truth conditions* of what can be said when that sentence is uttered. What is said by someone uttering (4) is true only if Sue—more precisely, whoever the speaker is referring to with 'Sue'—has memories of herself in which she is lecturing on aphonics. But the condition set by the semantics of (1) is stronger in an important way, as indeed Grice (1971) noticed.[102] On the account I favour (which Schiffer has criticized in seminars as over-intellectualizing what is involved), what is said by someone uttering (1) is true only if Sue (a) has memories of herself in which she is lecturing on aphonics, and (b) conceives of the agent of the remembered activity (lecturing on aphonics) as identical to herself. This is *not* a requirement for saying something true by uttering (4). So if there is an aphonic occurring as the subject of the embedded clause in (1), its semantic properties, the syntactic position it occupies, or the combination place an additional condition on what is said.

This does not mean *e* is not a referring expression of some sort. In (6) it would seem to be functioning as a bound variable:

(6) Every woman who taught at the summer institute remembers [*e* lecturing on aphonics].

Quite independently, there is good reason to think that in order to provide a unitary account of the predication involved in sentences such as (7) and (8),

(7) Sue loves her mother

(8) Every woman loves her mother

which differ only in that one has a singular referring expression as its subject while the other has a quantifier phrase, and in order to explain the existence of the so-called sloppy reading of (9),

(9) Sue loves her mother and so does Mary

we need a semantics that requires what is said when (7) is used on one of its readings to involve binding (or some equivalent form of abstraction) rather than *de jure* co-reference, for example a semantics that treats the predicate as expressing the property $(\lambda x)(x$ *loves x's mother*$)$. In the same spirit, the predicate in (1) and (6) would express the property $(\lambda x)(x$ *remembers x's lecturing on aphonics*$)$. An adequate semantics of (6) must require what is said by someone uttering it to be true only if every woman who taught at the summer institute (a) has memories of herself in which she is lecturing on aphonics, and (b) conceives of the agent of the remembered activity (lecturing on aphonics) as identical to herself. Whether the abstraction semantics just sketched does justice to this is debated.

12.13.2 *Semantic demands (saturation)*

We can certainly make sense of the possibility of implicit reference that is not formally demanded. Cases involving what Francois Recanati (2002, 2004) has called *saturation* are cases of *semantically* demanded implicit reference. Felicitous utterances of (1) certainly involve implicit reference:

(1) Citizens do not need to complete this section

Perhaps it is formally demanded. But if not—indeed even if there turn out to be syntactic grounds for *not* postulating aphonics in this sentence, and so grounds for denying formal demands for implicit reference—there would still be linguistic demands, specifically *semantic* demands. Necessarily, or so it would seem, to be a citizen, (local, native, foreigner, mayor, president, king) one has to be a citizen (etc.) of (or relative to) somewhere or something. And the standard meaning of the noun 'citizen' reflects this in a clear way. It does not shift between (1) and (1'):

(1') UK citizens do not need to complete this section.

And using it in accordance with its standard meaning requires referring to something (a geopolitical entity of some sort) if one is to express something fully propositional and say something true or false. To do this in uttering (1'), the speaker refers to the relevant entity with 'UK'. To do it in uttering (1), the speaker must refer to the relevant entity implicitly. In short, sentence (1) *semantically demands* implicit reference, even if it doesn't demand it formally.

The question for compositional semantics at this point is how the formal machinery composes implicit reference that is semantically but not formally demanded. To claim, without examining concrete proposals, that it cannot be done—that all semantically demanded implicit reference is *ipso facto* also formally demanded is just formal prejudice.

12.13.3 Pragmatic demands (enrichment)

Can we make sense of implicit reference that is not linguistically demanded? The existence of *indirect* reference suggests we can. Recall the example in which I utter the sentence 'I'm tired' and mean not only that I'm tired but also that you should leave. I refer to myself and I refer to you. But there's a difference: I refer to myself with 'I'; and the truth conditions of part of what I mean, viz. what I *say*, involve me. There is not even the semblance of an expression with which I refer to *you*. Yet the truth conditions of part of what I mean involve you—not the truth conditions of what I say, but the truth conditions of what I conversationally implicate. Moreover, there is a non-linguistic counterpart to the example, recall, that does not involve the use of words. By yawning ostentatiously I might *directly* mean (but not, strictly speaking, *say*) that I'm tired, and *indirectly* mean (but not, strictly speaking, *conversationally implicate*) that you should leave. Instead of exploiting facts about language, in such a case I am exploiting the natural connection between yawning and tiredness in order to directly mean something, expecting you to recognize that I have produced an overtly *non-natural* (voluntary, intentional) imitation of a natural yawn. But in both cases, I have also exploited the ability to infer what a speaker *indirectly* means by way of what the speaker directly means. So we know that speakers can refer to things in the absence of an expression, phonic or aphonic, with which they refer to that thing. Since there must be a perfectly good explanation of how we manage to do this without uttering words—because we *do* it—it stands to reason there must be an even better explanation of how we manage to do it when we *do* utter words, since the meanings of words and larger units containing them place constraints on the special type of direct meaning we call saying.

Unlike the meanings of 'citizen' and 'mayor', the meanings of 'child' and 'table' do not demand implicit reference. Nonetheless, it is often the case that when S uses a sentence containing such a noun, S has in mind a property "richer" than the one taken to be the noun's standard meaning, a property that A must recover in order to identify what is said. In the right circumstances, S might use sentence (2), for example,

(2) Every child has been vaccinated against rubella

and thereby say that every child *in Scotland* has been vaccinated. S referred implicitly to Scotland, but implicit reference was not *semantically* demanded. It seems to have been *pragmatically* demanded. It is not needed here to obtain a complete proposition only to get the *right* proposition. So, on the face of it, this sort of example falsifies TCS. But if as Stanley and Szabó (2000) and Stanley (2007) have argued, an aphonic occurs with every nominal, even those whose core noun is 'child' or 'table', the possibility exists of defending TCS by treating some implicit reference as formally and pragmatically demanded.[103]

12.14 The meaning-intention problem

12.14.1 Belief Ascriptions and Belief Sentences

The nouns 'ascription', 'attribution', and 'report' are used ambiguously in the literature to talk about (a) certain types of *sentences* containing words such as 'believe' and 'belief' (or other words apparently used to talk about the contents of certain types of mental states), and (b) *acts* of meaning performed by uttering such sentences.

(1) I shall use the 'belief ascription', 'attitude report', 'doubt attribution' etc. to talk only about the acts.

(2) For a reason that will emerge, I shall use 'belief sentence', 'attitude sentence' etc. narrowly to talk only about sentences containing subordinated clauses introduced by *verbs* of propositional attitude (e.g. 'Ann believes that p' is a belief sentence but 'Ann's belief that p is unfounded' is not).

12.14.2 Believing

According to Schiffer, if there is a compositional theory of the truth conditions of sentences of English, it will be an implicit reference theory "whose essential idea must have occurred to anyone who has thought seriously about the semantics of belief sentences" (1992: 500).[104] According to this theory, when speakers ascribe beliefs, they make implicit reference to *mode of presentation types*. In principle, such a theory holds out the hope of explaining the apparent substitution failures discussed by Frege and Russell, the idea being that someone can believe a proposition under one mode of presentation while disbelieving it under a second and suspending judgment under a third. Underpinning the implicit reference theory is the idea that, as Schiffer puts it, "necessarily, to have a belief about a thing is to have a belief about it under a mode of presentation" (1977: 65, 1978: 179). (Presumably, then, necessarily, to have an *intention* concerning a thing is to have an intention concerning it under a mode of presentation.)

A number of problems would arise if I did not now enforce (1) distinctions already made between various distinct notions and forms of reference, (2) the distinction between the composition of *expression* content, and the composition of *utterance* content, (3) a distinction between two importantly different notions of logical form, and (4) terminological precision when it comes to (a) *predicates* and the *relations* they express, and (b) attitude *sentences* and attitude *ascriptions*. And this means I shall need to make some adjustments to Schiffer's prose when examining his exposition of and objections to the implicit reference theory of attitude ascriptions—or, strictly speaking, the implicit reference theory of *attitude ascriptions made using attitude sentences*.

The claim that "necessarily, to have a belief about a thing is to have a belief about it under a mode of presentation" is a *constitutive* claim about the nature of belief, one that is distinct from any linguistic claim we make about the English verb 'believe': distinct from the *syntactic* claim that 'believe' is a three-place predicate and, strictly speaking, distinct from the *semantic* claim that 'believe' expresses a three-place relation, for it might be maintained that the semantics of the verb 'believe' does not do full justice to the constitution of belief.

12.14.3 Logical form

As articulated by Schiffer, the implicit reference theory takes the embedded clause 'that Fido is a dog' in

(1) Ralph believes that Fido is a dog.

to be a referring expression with which the speaker refers to the singular proposition ⟨Fido, doghood⟩" (1992: 504). And although 'believe' looks like a two-place predicate expressing a two-place relation between a believer and a proposition, according to the implicit reference theory, it expresses a three-place relation "holding among believers, Kaplan propositions, and modes of presentation of those propositions" (1992: 504).[105] Notice that it does not follow from what I just said that 'believe' is a *three-place predicate* (a wholly syntactic claim, on my use of 'predicate') only that it is a predicate (a syntactic claim) that expresses a three-place relation (a semantic claim). The following is supposed to capture the "logical form" of what is said when someone utters (1):

(1′) $\exists m \, [\phi^* m \wedge B(\text{Ralph}, \langle \text{Fido, doghood} \rangle, m)]$.[106]

Here is part of what Schiffer says by way of fleshing out the idea:

> The logical form of an utterance of [(1)] may be represented as [(1′)] where ϕ^* is an implicitly referred to and contextually determined type of mode of presentation. By a type of mode of presentation I mean merely a property of modes of presentation.... The reference to a type of mode of presentation is implicit in that, although *an utterance of* the sentence requires the speaker to be referring to a type of mode of presentation whenever the sentence is uttered, there is no word in (1) [with] which [the speaker] refers to that type. (1992: 503)

This prompts questions about what Schiffer means by 'logical form'. That no syntactic claim is intended is clear from the following passage:

> an utterance of the sentence (1) requires reference to a type of mode of presentation... This contextually determined reference to a type of mode of presentation is by a "hidden-indexical" in that there is no actual indexical in (1) that refers to it. (1992: 504)

There is no suggestion here that (1′) is a schematic rendering of the syntactician's LF for (1). The idea is, rather, that (1′) is a perspicous representation of the truth conditions of what is said that respects some aspects of the structure of sentence (1).

12.14.4 *The problem: modes of presentation*

Schiffer's meaning-intention problem exploits a purported disanalogy. The implicit reference accounts of condition reports (such as 'It's raining') and attitude reports assume some metaphysics: it is in the nature of (e.g.) raining that it takes place *somewhere*; and it is in the nature of (e.g.) believing that it takes place *under a mode of presentation*. It is in the *epistemic* realm, according to Schiffer, that something important separates the accounts. If S says something using 'It's raining' and is asked to specify *where* he is saying that it is raining, typically S can provide a clear and sensible answer. But if S says something using (1) and is asked to specify the mode of presentation type under *which* Ralph believes that Fido is a dog, typically S will have no idea what to say. I want to work through this purported contrast slowly to establish (a) precisely what Schiffer is and is not claiming, and (b) whether there is a good response the implicit reference theorist can make.

Schiffer begins as follows (I have replaced his interlocutors by S and A, making S female):

> A calls S in Chicago and asks about the weather. S replies, 'It's raining.' Here S refers to Chicago, and this by virtue of the fact that in uttering 'It's raining', she means that it is raining in Chicago. In other words, S counts as having referred to Chicago because the proposition she meant is about Chicago. Notice that there is no difficulty whatever in ascribing to S the propositional speech act in question: S clearly intended A to believe that it was raining in Chicago, and she is quite prepared to tell you that this is what she meant, what she implicitly said, and what she intended A to be informed of. Because these things are so clear, S's utterance is a paradigm of implicit reference. (1992: 512)

In order to demarcate clear battle lines and ensure that Schiffer's negative appraisal of implicit reference accounts of *incomplete definite descriptions* does not create the wrong impression, I should stress that Schiffer's point could have been made just as well with an example involving an attributive use of them:

> A and S live in Chicago. A asks S what issues will be important to her in next year's mayoral elections. (No candidates have yet emerged but the current mayor has declared categorically that he will not run.) S says, 'I want the next mayor to advocate gun control.' Here S refers to Chicago, and this by virtue of the fact that in uttering 'I want the next mayor to advocate gun control', she means that she wants the next mayor of Chicago to advocate gun control. In other words, S counts as having referred to Chicago because the proposition she meant is (in part) about Chicago. Notice that there is no difficulty whatever in ascribing to S the propositional speech act in question: S clearly intended A to believe that she wants the next mayor of Chicago to advocate gun control, and she is quite prepared to tell you that this is what she meant, what she implicitly said, and what she intended A to be informed of.[107]

Of course, interpreting attributive uses of incomplete descriptions (or other incomplete noun phrases, such as 'everyone' or 'no one') is not always this straightforward, but that is besides the point. In respect of *meaning intentions* the last two examples are on a par.

Belief ascriptions, according to Schiffer, are very different from statements made with 'It's raining' and 'I want the next mayor to advocate gun control'. Schiffer asks us to imagine that S utters (2) during a conversation about airfare bargains:

(2) Harold believes that TWA is offering a New York–Paris return fare for $318.

Here is Schiffer's argument in close to its entirety:

> According to the [implicit reference] theory, there is a property ϕ of modes of presentation of the proposition that TWA is offering a New York-Paris return fare for $318 such that S referred to ϕ in [uttering (2)]. If this is true, then, presumably, it is because S, in producing her utterance, meant some proposition about ϕ in just the way that [in the previous example involving her utterance of 'It's raining'] she meant some proposition about Chicago. But... it is doubtful that S meant any such thing [in the present example].
>
> We had no trouble saying what *Sue* meant in uttering 'It's raining': she meant that it was raining in Chicago. But what, that implies a reference to a type of mode of presentation, does S mean in uttering (2)? It must surely be

(2′) that there is something that both has ϕ and is such that Harold believes the proposition that TWA is offering a New York-Paris return fare for $318 under it.

for some particular property ϕ of modes of presentation of the proposition that TWA is offering a New York-Paris return fare for $318. *But... neither S nor her audience is aware of her meaning any such thing* [emphasis added]. [In the 'It's raining' case] S is consciously aware of both the *form* of the proposition she meant (she is aware that she meant that it is raining *in* Chicago) and the implicitly referred to *thing* the proposition is about (she is aware that she meant that it is raining in *Chicago*). But [in the TWA example] it is doubtful that the nonphilosopher S has conscious access to the form of (2′), and it is especially doubtful that she has conscious awareness of referring to any mode-of-presentation property. That is to say, if she did mean a proposition of form (2′), then *she has no conscious awareness of what property ϕ that proposition is about, and no conscious awareness, therefore, of what she meant* in uttering (2) [emphasis added].

Neither we nor S can say what mode-of-presentation property [she] referred to in [uttering] (2). Just try to say it. The referred-to property, if it exists, would be given by a completion of the form

> The property of being an *m* such that to believe the proposition *that TWA is offering a New York-Paris return fare for $318 under m* requires thinking of TWA, the offering relation, New York, Paris, the US dollar currency, the number 318 [and so on for the other components of the proposition] in ... ways, respectively.

But the non-philosopher S has no access even to this *form* of specification, and who among us can offer to replace the three dots? Now, of course, it is in principle possible to have knowledge of such a property even though one cannot specify it in the forgoing way ... for example ... knowledge of it under some quite extrinsic description. But I submit that it will be obvious on reflection that S has no such alternative way of explicitly picking out a property of modes of presentation to which she is implicitly referring in her utterance of (2). There is no sentence σ such that S can say 'I meant that σ', where 'that σ' explicitly refers to a proposition of (2′)'s form. Thus, if the [implicit reference] theory is correct, then S has no conscious awareness of what she means, or of what she is saying, in uttering (2), and this is a prima facie reason to deny that she means what the theory is committed to saying she means. (1992: 512–14)

12.14.5 *The problem: epistemic standards*

The meaning-intention problem also arises, Schiffer believes, for implicit reference theories of both knowledge claims and uses of incomplete definite descriptions. According to so-called contextualist accounts of knowledge claims, for example, speakers make implicit reference to *epistemic standards*, which Schiffer takes to be on par with making implicit reference to mode of presentation types: "No ordinary person who utters "I know that p", however articulate, would dream of telling you that what he meant and was implicitly *saying* was that he knew that p relative to such-and-such standard" (1996: 326–7).[108]

12.14.6 *The problem: nominal completions*

Similarly, implicit reference accounts of referential uses of incomplete definite descriptions such as 'the table' are vulnerable to the meaning-intention problem.

For even if there are *some* cases in which speakers *do* implicitly refer to very obvious things, the plethora of cases in which they do *not* makes Schiffer's point just as destructive for its intended target. At the very least, Schiffer can say this:

> An ordinary person who uses 'the *F*' referentially in uttering 'The *F* is *G*', however articulate, will not always be willing to say that what he meant and was implicitly saying was that an *F* that is uniquely such-and-such is *G*.

The meaning-intention problem for implicit reference theories of descriptions is just a special case of the general problem for nominals:

> An ordinary person who utters 'every *F* is *G*' (or 'no *F* is *G*'), however articulate, will not always be willing to say that what he meant and was implicitly saying was that every *F* that is such-and-such is *G* (or that no *F* that is such-and-such is *G*).

Assuming that the usual Fregean problems for belief ascriptions carry over to knowledge claims, a champion implicit reference theorist will maintain that *S* makes implict reference to *three* distinct things when uttering (3):

(3) Ralph knows the pillar-box is red.

Combining Schiffer's logical form notation with Kaplan's notation for the propositional constituents associated with uses of descriptions, the "logical form" of (3) will be something like (3'):

(3') $\exists m \exists s \exists r \, [\phi^* m \wedge \psi s \wedge \chi r \wedge K(\text{Ralph}, \langle \langle \text{THE}, \textit{pillarboxhood}, r \rangle \, \textit{red} \rangle, s, m)]$

where ϕ^* is an implicitly referred to mode of presentation type, ψ an implicitly referred to property of epistemic standards, and χ an implicitly referred to property that holds of a pillar-box.[109] Actually, it is not obvious to me there is anything in the result of combining implicit reference accounts of belief ascriptions and knowledge claims that ensures there is not something like a scope ambiguity here. (There could hardly be anything in the metaphysics of theories of modes of presentation and epistemic standards ensuring that knowing something relative to standard *s* under mode of presentation *m* is the same thing as knowing something under mode of presentation *m* relative to standard *s*.)

12.14.7 *The Deeper Problem: Aphonics*

A free-standing variant of the meaning-intention problem arises for aphonic reference accounts of implicit reference, potentially compounding the original problem. The variant, which we can call the aphonic-intention problem, concerns not the things *to* which speakers are said to be referring but the things *with* which they refer to those things. If speakers refer with aphonics then, by **RW**, they must have aphonic-involving intentions:

> (RW) In uttering *x*, *S* referred to *o with* (or *using*) *e*, relative to its *i*-th occurrence in *x*, iff for some audience *A* and relation *R*, *S* intended *A* to recognize that *R*(*e*, *x*, *i*, *o*) and, at least partly on the basis of this, that *S* referred to *o* in uttering *x*.

But is it really plausible to maintain that ordinary speakers have *any* beliefs or intentions about aphonics, let alone intentions as complex as **RW** requires? Or that syntacticians who argue emphatically against the existence of aphonics do? Ordinary speakers no more have "conscious awareness" of aphonics that they do of modes or presentation. So an implicit reference theory according to which speakers refer aphonically to mode of presentation types faces a compound problem: the theory has ordinary speakers referring *to things* they don't know about *with things* they don't know about.

The problem can be brought into sharp relief by looking at a concrete example. Stanley and Szabó (2000) present what amounts to an aphonic reference theory of nominal completions. Every nominal has associated with it an aphonic variable they represent as $f(i)$, itself composed of an individual variable, i, and a functional variable, f, so that 'every man', for example, has roughly the following structure:

(4) [every [man $f(i)$]].

Stanley and Szabó spell out their theory using the discredited picture of expressions being "assigned" or "supplied" contents by contexts, but we can flush that out in a moment. First, here's what they say:

The value of 'i' is an object provided by context, and the value of 'f' is a function provided by context that maps objects onto quantifier domains. The restriction on the quantified expression 'every man'... relative to context would then be provided by the result of applying the function that context supplies to 'f' to the object that context supplies to 'i'.... Since we are taking quantifier domains to be sets, relative to a context, what results from applying the value of 'f' to the value of 'i' is a set. Relative to a context, 'f' is assigned a function from objects to sets. Relative to a context, 'i' is assigned an object. The denotation of '[man $f(i)$]' relative to a context c is then the result of intersecting the set of men with the set that results from applying the value given to 'f' by the context c to the value given to 'i' by c. That is (suppressing reference to a model to simplify exposition), where '$[\alpha]_c$' denotes the denotation of α with respect to the context c, and '$c(\alpha)$' denotes what the context c assigns to the expression α:

[man $f(i)$] = [man] ∩ {x: $x \in c(f)(c(i))$} (2000: 251-3).[110]

If this theory is to be of empirical substance, and potentially form part of an answer to the Master Question, it must be understood as entailing that in order to identify what is said when S utters a sentence containing 'every man', A must identify the content of '$f(i)$', construed as a function of the contents of 'i' and 'f' "provided" by "context". In a fuller version of the theory, presumably Stanley and Szabó would say that 'f' and 'i' have *characters* that are functions from contexts to, respectively, functions and objects. But the characters in question would be shady. So, cleaning things up, we end up with the claim that in order to identify what is said when S utters a sentence containing 'every man', A must identify what S is referring to with '$f(i)$', via identifying what S is referring to with 'i' and 'f'. But it is utterly implausible to suppose that ordinary speakers have intentions about 'f' and 'i', intentions to be referring to functions with the former and objects with the latter.

I want now to look at a range of replies to the meaning-intention problem, the last of which is readily transposed into a reply to the aphonic-intention problem.

12.14.8 The Intention-rejection reply

According to the Intention-Rejection Reply, the meaning-intention problem arises only if it assumed that speaker meaning is defined in terms of audience-directed intentions. But this is incorrect. Certainly Schiffer stresses the point that on standard, intentional accounts of speaker meaning, S cannot mean something without intending to be *understood*: S's meaning that such-and-such involves S's intending her audience A to *recognize* that this is what she means; in which case, S's referring to something *o* involves S's intending A to recognize that she is referring to *o*. And assuming such an account of speaker meaning, the requirement that there exist some type of mode of presentation φ* such that S means that Ralph believes that TWA is offering a New York–Paris return fare for $318 under a mode of presentation of type φ cannot be satisfied unless S intends her audience to recognize that she means that Ralph believes that TWA is offering a New York–Paris return fare for $318 under a mode of presentation of type φ*. In summary, if (i) S is aware of what she means, and (ii) A understands S perfectly well, S simply does not mean what the implicit reference theory says she means.

But notice that the point about S's audience understanding her is not really necessary to generate the basic form of the meaning-intention problem—it just drills it home. Schiffer stated the basic problem without mentioning audiences explicitly earlier. Of course, his own informal talk of *what S means* is audience-invoking.[111] But this should not obscure the fact that the meaning-intention problem is not circumvented by adopting, say, Searle's (1979) audience-free but still intention-based characterization of speaker meaning. Indeed, even if one were persuaded (for some bizarre reason) that speakers' intentions play no rôle whatsoever in an account of speaker meaning, the basic problem persists because the only assumption about speaker meaning Schiffer's argument actually assumes is that speakers are *aware of what they mean*.

12.14.9 The acceptable mismatch reply

The Acceptable Mismatch Reply misses the point of the meaning-intention problem in much the same way as the Intention-Rejection Reply, but it brings out an important fact about our use of natural language and leads nicely into a third, related reply. According to the Acceptable Mismatch Reply, when, in uttering *x*, S refers to a mode of presentation type, it is not a requirement on A understanding S that there be a *single* mode of presentation type upon which S and A both fasten. Indeed, in some cases a shared mode of presentation type might be impossible. The basic point originates with Frege, at least for first-person thoughts, and is broadened to third person cases by Evans (1982), Sperber and Wilson (1986), and others:

> Two people may be able to think *of* the same man *that* he has gone, without being able to think exactly the same thought, because they might not individuate him in exactly the same way. Similarly, by saying, "He has gone" I may induce in you a thought which is similar to mine in that it predicates the same thing (that he is gone) of the same individual... It seems to us neither paradoxical nor counterintuitive to say that there are thoughts that we cannot exactly share, and that communication can be successful without resulting in an exact duplication of thoughts in communicator and audience. (Sperber and Wilson 1986: 193)

But there is no comfort in this idea for the implicit reference theorist of attitude reports—Sperber and Wilson themselves do not claim there is—because the basic form of the meaning-intention problem itself does not assume that successful communication involves mode of presentation type *replication*; it assumes only that speakers are *aware of what they mean*.

12.14.10 The indeterminacy reply

The Acceptable Mismatch Reply is closely related to the Indeterminacy Reply, according to which the meaning-intention problem amounts to no more than the bald assertion that a speaker's meaning-intentions in acts of implicit reference must be held to higher standards of *determinacy* than those in acts of explicit, phonic reference. This reply actually misses the point of the meaning-intention problem too, but I shall ignore this fact and simply show that there is no truth to the claim that Schiffer assumes higher standards of determinacy for implicit reference. The Indeterminacy Reply might be prompted by pulling together two passages from Schiffer, the first (allegedly) arguing that explicit reference involves *tolerable* indeterminacy, and the second (allegedly) motivating the idea that implicit reference involves *catastrophic* indeterminacy:

Suppose you call Ernie Lepore in New Brunswick and ask him where Jerry Fodor is. 'He's here,' Ernie replies. To what does [Ernie refer with] 'here'? To New Brunswick? To Rutgers University? To Douglas Campus? To Davison Hall? To Ernie's office? The example is underdescribed, but even if I fully describe it, there need not be a definite answer. Almost certainly, [Ernie] doesn't refer to some definite region of space. The word is being used to make a vague or indeterminate reference. (1995: 112)

[According to the implicit reference theory of "incomplete" definite descriptions, used referentially], when a speaker utters a sentence like 'The dog has fleas', then there must be some property ϕ such that she means the proposition that the thing that is uniquely a dog and ϕ has fleas. What makes this so implausible is that there will typically be a number of potentially completing descriptions that are equally salient in the context (e.g., the dog that I own, the dog we are both looking at, the spotted dog in the green chair, and so on). Consequently, it is highly implausible that there will be one such description such that the speaker intends it to be understood between her and her audience that she means a proposition containing that very description.

Now, just the same problem arises with the meaning claim required by the [implicit reference theory of attitude ascriptions]. For if a proposition is believed under one mode of presentation, then it will typically be believed under many modes of presentation. Further, each of those modes of presentation will instantiate infinitely many types of modes of presentation, many of which will be equally salient in the communicative context. This makes it extremely implausible that of all the equally salient types of ways that Ralph has of believing the proposition about TWA, S should mean—and intend to be taken to mean—a proposition about one definite one of them. (1992: 516)

Now Schiffer has been arguing *for* the theoretical importance of implicit reference for a long time, so even if he is arguing that explicit reference often involves a tolerable degree of indeterminacy (as he surely is), he can hardly be construed as motivating the idea that implicit reference *per se* engenders catastrophic indeterminacy in speaker meaning. He is simply pointing out (a) that the implicit reference theory of *belief ascriptions* leads to catastrophic indeterminacy, and (b) that this is not the *only* implicit reference theory that does so: so does the implicit reference theory of referential uses of incomplete definite descriptions. This does not commit him to saying the meaning-intention problem arises for implicit-reference theories of incomplete quantifier phrases *per se*, for that is a very natural theory to hold in connection with utterances of the following, for example (assuming the description in (7) is being used attributively):

(5) Most working people earn more than $100 a month

(6) Nero stamped out public drunkenness

(7) The next mayor will inherit a budgetary deficit.

All we find with these cases, is the usual, tolerable form of indeterminacy we found earlier.

This interpretation is supported by pulling together two earlier passages, the net result of which would have Schiffer saying the following:

> You call Ernie Lepore in New Brunswick and ask him how the weather is. "It's raining here," he replies. To what does Ernie refer? To Central New Jersey? To New Brunswick? To Douglas Campus?... Almost certainly, Ernie doesn't refer to some definite region of space. The word is being used to make a vague or indeterminate reference. Moreover, nothing would be appreciably different if Ernie had not included the word 'here', if he had replied 'It's raining,' and made a vague or indeterminate *implicit* reference. Ernie's utterance would have been a paradigm of both implicit and indeterminate reference.

In summary, although Schiffer sees implicit reference to mode of presentation types as leading to catastrophic indeterminacy in a speaker's meaning intentions, this has nothing to do with any *general* fact about implicit reference or with the *general* sort of indeterminacy that any theory of quantification (and all sorts of other theories) must be able to accommodate.

12.14.11 *The extrinsic parameters reply*

The Extrinsic Parameters Reply aims to show that facts about ordinary uses of certain expressions show the meaning-intention argument is too strong to be useful. Consider the following sentences:

(8) It's noon

(9) It's summer

(10) The train is travelling at 100 mph

(11) The collisions occurred simultaneously.

In its most simplistic form, the Extrinsic Parameters Reply is this: (i) When S uses (8), what he says is true only relative to a particular time zone; when he uses (9), only relative to a particular hemisphere, and when he uses (10) or (11), only relative to a particular rest-frame; (ii) thousands of years of speech testify to the fact that speakers and hearers can communicate perfectly well without knowing about time zones, hemispheres, or rest-frames; so (iii) the fact that speakers using these sentences are unable to describe clearly such parameters is no barrier to their having clear intentions. Similarly, (iv) the fact that speakers using belief (or knowledge) sentences are unable to describe clearly the relevant mode of presentation types (or epistemic standards) is no barrier to their having clear communicative intentions.[112]

There is much that is problematic in this train of thought, not least of which is the fact that once speakers *learn* about time zones, hemispheres and rest-frames, and learn a few additional words, they can easily describe the parameters relevant to the truth or falsity of what they are saying with (8)–(11) on particular occasions, and will, in fact, unprompted, often make explicit reference to these entities in ordinary conversation:

(8′) It's noon GMT (in London)

(9′) It's summer in the southern hemisphere.

By contrast, learning about modes of presentations for a quarter of a century has not put *me*—or, I hazard, anyone else—in a position to describe clearly the alleged mode of presentation types relevant to the truth or falsity of what I say when I utter belief sentences. (In ordinary talk, 'GMT' and 'in the southern hemisphere' are no more technical terms or theoretical jargon than 'acceleration', 'vacuum', and 'sentence' are.) There is little to comfort the implicit reference theorist of belief ascriptions in the following passages:

Consider our practices of reporting velocity. A claim that an object is moving at a certain velocity makes sense only if it is understood with respect to what the velocity is to be assessed. We say that velocity is relative to an observer, or a frame of reference—we must count something as stationary. But we articulate this additional parameter of velocity claims only when it is not obvious what is to count as stationary. We have in English a number of general-purpose constructions for articulating commonly suppressed constituents of a claim. We say, 'with respect to...' or 'relative to...' or 'in the sense that...'. The more likely the unarticulated constituent is to be unclear, the more likely it is that we have a natural way to articulate it.

In the case of belief reports, in which notions are unarticulated, we do have rough and ready ways to clarify just which notions we mean to talk about. We say, for instance, that Miles believes that Edward is a peasant in one way—the way related to the boy in front of him, not in the way related to the Prince. Or we add to the report, "that is, he thinks the boy in front of him, who really is Edward, is a peasant." Or we specify how Miles would or would not "put" his belief. Or we allude to the evidence which led Miles to form the belief, or to the actions it would be likely to bring about. Each of these devices can succeed in distinguishing among the two notions which in context can seem equally relevant, thus eliminating possible confusion about which notion we mean to talk about.

We do not, of course, have a very direct way of specifying the notions we mean to talk about in belief reports. This is due to the fact that it is almost always obvious which notion a speaker is talking about. Where it is not, we either use one of the devices just mentioned, or leave the language of belief reporting altogether and talk instead about what the agent would say or would do. (Crimmins and Perry 1989: 701)

Suppose I judge perceptually that two events happen simultaneously, and I am right. The fact that makes me right is that those two events were simultaneous relative to my certain frame of reference... The frame of reference in question is not determined by a representation in my thought, but by the broader situation in which my judgment takes place. A theorist who is analyzing the way an agent handles information and uses it to guide action may have to pay attention to factors the agent's cognitive system can safely ignore. The theorist's interest may be precisely how these factors can be ignored—how architectural or external constraints make internal representations unnecessary. It is the speed of light that allows us to get by with a two-place concept of simultaneity. It is the shortness of our arms compared to the width of time-zones that allows us to ignore the latter when we read our watches. (Perry 1993: 221)

Perry is talking here about factors *external* to us—time zones and rest-frames—about which we may be ignorant but about which we may acquire knowledge and thereby easily refine our linguistic behavior. Mode of presentation types are not like this at all. They are supposed to be things *under* which beliefs are *had*, and learning about their existence and a great deal of information about their rôles in theories of language and mind doesn't even put theorists in a position to articulate the truth conditions of the propositions they actually express on given occasions using belief sentences if the hidden-indexical theory of belief reports is true.

12.14.12 The tacit states reply

I turn finally to what Schiffer sees as the implicit reference theorist's best bet: (a) concede that S is not "consciously aware" that she means a proposition of form (2′) under any mode of presentation type, and (b) maintain that S meant such a proposition nonetheless because she *tacitly* had the requisite beliefs and intentions. A solution of this sort will likely occur to anyone already sympathetic to Loar's (1976) suggestion that both S's communicative intentions and A's recognition of them might be partly unconscious, or to Chomsky's (1980) talk of tacit knowledge of language. And such a solution suggests a similar solution to the related aphonic-intention problem.

Schiffer finds two serious problems with this reply to the meaning-intention problem:

[According to the Tacit States Reply] not only do ordinary belief ascribers have no conscious knowledge of what they are asserting, they also turn out not to have the conscious thoughts they think they have. S clearly thinks she has conscious knowledge of what she is *saying* in uttering (2). She is quite prepared to say, "Look, what I am saying, and all that I am saying, is that Ralph believes that TWA is offering a New York-Paris return fare for \$318." In other words, she thinks she is consciously aware of what she is *saying* in uttering (2), but the tacit-intention line implies that here she is in error: the only proposition she *expresses* in uttering (2)—viz., some proposition of form (2′)—is not anything of which she is conscious. What makes this error aspect of the tacit-intention proposal problematic is not merely that it riddles the propositional-attitude ascriptions of ordinary speakers with error; it also forces us to qualify our views about first-person authority in an important way. S does not have the privileged access to what she consciously means, intends, and believes in uttering (2) which one might reasonably have supposed to be part of a normal person's functional architecture. (1992: 515)[113]

(The weight Schiffer places in the second half of this passage on first-person authority about the contents of one's conscious beliefs and intentions and about what one means might bother those of a strongly anti-Cartesian disposition.) Are there problems of this sort for a tacit states reply to the aphonic-intention problem? A tacit states reply would revolve around the idea that speakers tacitly know, for any given sentence they utter what expressions it contains and which are aphonic. But if this knowedge is only tacit, speakers cannot have conscious intentions about aphonics, in which case any referential intentions speakers have about them cannot be conscious. Since referential intentions are just object-involving *meaning* intentions, Schiffer can object in much the same way he objects to the tacit states reply to the meaning-intention problem.

This raises quite general questions about the psychological status of aphonic referring expressions (and aphonics more generally) and their roles in our actual use of language when we refer to things implicitly and interpret others as doing so. One would have thought that a necessary condition for becoming linguistically competent with a phonic f, as part of normal childhood language acquisition, is encountering at least one *utterance* of f (as part of the "triggering and shaping" effect of experience, as Chomsky puts it).[114] But encountering at least one utterance of an *aphonic e* cannot be a necessary condition for becoming linguistically competent with e as there are no such utterances to encounter. However, there are utterances of *expressions that contain e*, so any story about the acquisition of aphonics will turn heavily on the child's knowledge of the grammatical categories, thematic roles, and meanings of the constituents of e-containing expressions that are uttered. But no one will become linguistically competent with *any* referring expression, phonic or aphonic, without the ability to recognize and interpret acts of meaning, the ability to infer speakers' communicative intentions, an ability that involves mechanisms of mind-reading that are functional in early infancy and active even when speakers (in the technical sense employed here) are not using language to communicate.[115] The absence of utterances of aphonics might seem to create an additional burden on the acquisition process. But presumably the range of aphonics is relatively small, being constrained by general features of natural language that are taken to be unlearned by virtue of being dictated by our shared cognitive endowment. It seems likely, then, that any account of how we refer aphonically will have a Gricean and a Chomskyan ring to it. Schiffer's work has made it possible to provide an architecture within which serious questions about aphonic reference and implicit reference can at least be stated with a degree of precision previously lacking. But we are still a long way from having an account of the syntax, semantics, metaphysics, and psychology of aphonic referrring expressions.

12.15 Conclusions

1. Particular proposals in semantic theory lack substance if they cannot be construed as potential contributions to an answer to a Master Question about dovetailed activities of meaning and interpreting.
2. Once we separate constitutive, epistemic and aetiological notions of content determination, intention-based theories of what speakers *mean*, *say*, and *refer to* in uttering sentences of natural language look considerably more plausible that is often supposed.

3. An intentional notion of *speaker* reference underpins any intelligible notion of *expression* reference, just as an intentional notion of *speaker meaning* underpins any intelligible notion of expression meaning.
4. Speaker reference is just speaker meaning with object-dependent truth conditions.
5. Speakers often refer *implicitly*. Implicit reference is a ubiquitous feature of ordinary and theoretical discourse that we need to understand if we are to do justice to any systematic account of the truth conditions of what speakers say when they speak.
6. Speakers also refer *indirectly*, for example when conversationally implicating things with object-dependent truth conditions.
7. When speakers refer, explicitly or implicitly, even indirectly, they refer *rigidly* in a perfectly intelligible sense that underpins the apparent rigidity of proper names and other referring expressions.
8. It is not clear that a compositional theory of the truth conditions of what speakers say using sentences of natural language needs to invoke an independent notion of *expression reference*. The lesson from reflections on demonstratives and indexicals is that what a theory of semantic composition takes to be the reference of a referring expression (relative to a position in a sentence being uttered) is just whatever it is the *speaker* is referring to with that expression (relative to that position in that sentence) on that occasion, in a sense that is clearly defined.
9. Some implicit reference might be *aphonic* reference in the sense that some sentences of natural language might contain aphonic expressions with which speakers refer to things.
10. The existence of aphonic expressions with which speakers refer to things is consistent with the classical semantic composition of *expression contents* but not with the composition of *utterance contents*.
11. Implicit reference theories of belief ascriptions, knowledge and incomplete nominals are threatened by Schiffer's meaning-intention problem. The theories attribute to ordinary speakers mental states they simply do not seem to possess, for example intentions and beliefs about types of modes of presentation and epistemic standards.
12. Theories that purport to explain cases of implicit reference in terms of aphonic reference must face up to an aphonic-intention problem: such theories attribute to ordinary speakers intentions and beliefs about aphonic expressions whose existence they do not know of and is debated by linguists. In effect, such theories have speakers referring *to* things they don't know about *with* things they don't know about.

Many linguists believe the postulation of aphonics has been a source of great progress in the theory of grammar over the past several decades. But at present it is hard to see how aphonic reference can be part of an answer to the Master Question until serious interdisciplinary work is done by philosophers, linguists, and cognitive scientists on difficult and (as I said at the outset) maddeningly intertwined questions in metaphysics, semantics, pragmatics, formatics, syntax, phonology, and psychology.

Notes

1. The attribution to Schiffer is controversial. It is sometimes claimed that Kripke sketched the proof *in utero* or that it is a corollary of the 1944 Kreisel-Wittgenstein proof for *shef-and-only-shef*. The latter claim is doubtful. First, it was not until the St Tropez Congress of 1968 that Kreisel proved the free logical *schif-und-önly-if* requires a separate algorithm for each satisfiable model. (*Paris Match*, July 1968.) Second, prior to Kripke's work on proper names, no one distinguished using *schiffer* (or *Schiffer*) as a name whose reference is fixed by description (the *schiff-er*, as Quine would have put it, if he could have) and using it to describe the schiffing agent in a given Kaplanian context. Third, as an esteemed logician in my own institution has observed, the date of Kripke's physical birth is hardly evidence for the priority of an alleged "Kreisenstein" proof—at least not unless a jejune form of materialism is assumed together with a theory of personal identity over time that, in terms of modal logic, may involve a technical error. Kripke's work on *schiff* remains unpublished, but evidence of (an outline of) an independent (picture of a) proof may be gleaned from (a mimeograph of) (a transcript of) an (apparently) impromptu lecture Kripke gave (without notes) in Helsinki (possibly Stockholm) in January (possibly February) 1961. The Draconian word limit imposed by the editor of this volume precludes an examination of this important topic here.
2. For some semantic theories, there is no distinction to be made between *truth conditions* and *propositions*, the latter being functions from possible states of the world to truth values. On other accounts, propositions *have* truth conditions, the former being structured and more fine-grained than the latter. For present purposes, the difference is mostly immaterial, and I shall make nothing of it except where it really matters (if it does).
3. Those who reject TCS have pulled out the literary stops in stating their positive proposals for "bridging the gap" ("taking up the slack", "making up the shortfall") between the interactions of (i)–(iv) and truth conditions: "pragmatic factors", "contextual factors", and "non-demonstrative inference" are construed as things that may "determine" ("fix", "supply", "contribute", "provide", "furnish") "parts" ("constituents", "elements", "features", "aspects") of the proposition expressed. Two ways in which they do this are usually distinguished: either (i) they "complete" ("fill gaps in") "partial" ("incomplete", "gappy") propositions, "saturate" propositional "schemas", "stabilize" propositional "radicals", "flesh out" propositional "skeletons", or perform some bluish-collar activity on propositional "templates", "molds", "dies", "stencils", or "blueprints", or else (ii) they "enrich" ("develop", "expand", "supplement") contents that are already fully propositional, by processes of "intrusion" ("encroachment", "infringement").
4. See Schiffer (1992, 1995a, 1996, 2005, 2006).
5. Dretske (1981), Godfrey-Smith (2013), Millikan (2004), Skyrms (2010).
6. For discussion, see Neale (forthcoming c).
7. Geach calls speaker reference *personal* reference. Kripke calls it *speaker's* reference and calls expression reference *semantic* reference. Whether talking about speaker reference or expression reference, I limit my talk here to *singular* reference, the sort philosophers usually associate with uses of so-called singular terms (singular referring expressions) such as proper names, pronouns, demonstratives, and descriptions.
8. See Neale (2004, 2005). Here is Strawson: "'referring'... is not something an expression does; it is something that someone can use an expression to do" (1950: 326). And Linsky: "it is the users of language who refer... and not, except in a derivative sense, the expression which they use in so doing" (1963: 74).
9. Whether or not we should say that the first child exploited the fact that 'Tom' refers to Tom is a difficult question, the answer to which turns on how proper names are individuated, which turns on a number of psychological issues that I cannot address here.

10. See Neale (2004, 2005, 2007). Other virtues of the term 'aphonic' include its brevity, an obvious contrast with 'phonic', and the fact that, like 'indexical', it may be used as either an adjective or a noun—'an aphonic indexical' and 'an indexical aphonic' are both well-formed expressions, and sometimes one is more useful dialectically than the other.
11. Schiffer originally talked about *implicit indexicality* (1977: 32, 33; 1979: 65, 66), before settling on *hidden indexicality*.
12. Grice (1961) originally talked about *stating* and *implying*. In his William James Lectures, where he refined the distinction, he talked about *saying* and *implicating*. For present purposes, I use 'implicate' as shorthand for 'conversationally implicate'. I largely ignore what Grice calls *conventional implicature*. (See Neale (1999).) My uses of 'direct(ly)' and 'indirect(ly)' are *similar* to Searle's in his talk of direct and indirect *speech acts*. Transposing, on his account if, by uttering 'I'm tired,' I *directly mean* that I am tired and *indirectly mean* that you should leave, then I performed *two* (illocutionary) acts. But what I call *acts of meaning* cannot be identified with Searle's *illocutionary acts*. In uttering, 'I'm tired,' I produce a single utterance *hence* I perform *a single* act of meaning but mean *two* things (because I have *two* communicative intentions in performing that single act). Utterances are just acts of a special type, acts of *meaning*. And acts of meaning are *individual, material events*.
13. Referring directly and indirectly, in my sense, are *speaker*-based notions. There is no intrinsic connection between a *speaker* referring directly to something with an expression, *e*, and *e* itself being a device of *direct reference* in Kaplan's technical (1989a) sense.
14. The presence of 'please' seems to preclude Sue from using 'Pass the caviar' (a) to talk about something she wants done by someone *other* than her addressee, for example in response to 'What do you want Andy to do next?', or (b) to make a prediction, for example, in response to 'What do you think Andy will do next?' But perhaps these answers are elliptical forms of 'I want Andy to pass the caviar' and 'I predict Andy will pass the caviar', respectively. The return of the performative hypothesis and generative semantics?
15. See also Schiffer (1992), Recanati (2001, 2010), and Neale (2007a).
16. With the benefit of hindsight, I think this would have been a slightly better example if I had set it up like this: Soames has never played cricket and knows that I know this; he also knows that I have played cricket and knows that I know he knows this. Soames wants to know whether Lewis has ever played cricket, so I say 'Most people in this room have played cricket', fully intending to communicate to Soames that Lewis has played cricket. I have referred indirectly to Lewis.
17. We do sometimes use 'self' as a freestanding nominal, as in 'She has found her true self' or 'note to self'.
18. For a summary, see Heim and Kratzer (1998).
19. If so, we have a familiar decision to make. If we take sentence individuation to be sensitive to binding indices, we will talk about two sentences that sound alike; if not, we will talk about a single sentence that is "ambiguous" in respect of legitimate indexings.
20. To make sure the idea is not totally off-base, let's look at isomorphic sentences containing a verb we don't care about instead of 'refer'. Consider (i)—constructed on the basis of a vignette of Searle's (1969)—where the main embedded verb is 'fool':

   (i) [The captured American soldier]$_i$ used a line of German poetry [self$_i$ to fool the Italians into thinking he was a German officer].

   The indexing I have imposed on (i) takes *self* to be bound by 'the captured American soldier', so I am assuming 'use' is a subject control verb. So indexed, (i) is ostensibly being used to make a statement about a *soldier* fooling the Italians. ("He certainly fooled them," we might say.) We can ask the same sort of question that we asked about example (10): Does 'use' *have to be* a subject control verb? Is there a legitimate indexing of the words in

(i) that gives us a reading on which *self* is bound by 'a line of German poetry', used to make a statement about *a line of German poetry* fooling the Italians? ("That line certainly fooled them," we might say.) As philosophers of language, we do not have much of a stake in this. We are specialists in the study of reference, not the study of *fooling* (I hope). So with respect to (a)–(c) below, we are in more or less the situation non-specialist ordinary speakers are in with respect to questions about speaker reference, expresson reference, and utterance reference, viz. baffled by the pedantry involved in trying to separate them:

(a) *Speaker fooling*: The soldier fooled the Italians with a line of German poetry.

(b) *Expression fooling*: Relative to the soldier's utterance, a line of German poetry fooled the Italians.

(c) *Utterance fooling*: The soldier's utterance of a line of German poetry fooled the Italians.

21. This is one reason among several for abandoning the practice of calling sentences sentence-*types* and calling utterances, signings, and inscriptions of sentences sentence-*tokens*. I shall have something to say later about the complacency the practice engenders, and about the unclarity and confusion it can create, particularly in the realm of implicit reference. I shall also defend an *intentional* and, I think, very Gricean account of the facts in virtue of which a given utterance is an utterance of a given sentence. (The mere fact that *outside* our theorizing about language, we might point to an inscription of a word and say, 'This word is...' or the fact that we might say there are 250 words on a page of text or 4000 sentences in a book is no reason to panic ourselves into thinking there are two different notions of *word* that our philosophical theories must respect, word-*types* and word-*tokens*. We can say everything we need to say about such cases perfectly well by talking about words and inscriptions of words.)

22. See Neale (2010).

23. See Cappelen (2012).

24. To the best of my knowledge, the core of this picture of intuitions is due to Michael Devitt (2006, 2010).

25. Specifying precisely what counts as data is fraught with difficulty, of course. Behavior itself, including linguistic behavior (whatever that amounts to), is sometimes included, as are robust judgments that speakers of a language make about vocalizations of symbols of that language, followed by the highly theory-laden judgments made by the relevant specialists (linguists and philosophers of language). (Compare judgments people make about ailments they have and the judgments made by medical professionals.)

26. Grice (1957, 1969, 1989), Strawson (1964), Schiffer (1972, 1981, 1982), Bach and Harnish (1979), Loar (1981), Neale (1992, 2004).

27. For detailed discussion, see Sperber and Wilson (1986/1995), Wilson (2005), Wilson and Sperber (2012).

28. For present purposes I sidestep the question of just how special or domain-specific a form of mindreading this is. For discussion, see Sperber and Wilson (2012) and Wilson (2005).

29. In *Descriptions* I was very careful to talk about a (singular) *proposition meant* rather than a (singular) *proposition communicated* when talking about referential uses of descriptions, but a number of critics missed this. The meaning-communicating distinction is still widely ignored in the literature, creating no end of confusion. Failure to respect this distinction can lead to the erroneous leap from the true claim that Griceans define speaker meaning in terms of communicative intentions to the false claim that they define meaning in terms of communication.

30. Schiffer (1972, 1981, 1982).

31. Some philosophers have followed Anscombe (1963) and others influenced by Wittgenstein in (a) disavowing intentions as mental states in terms of which intentional action can be explained and (b) turning directly to intentional acts themselves. Griceans find the

Wittgensteinian considerations invoked in (a) unpersuasive and the behavioristic underpinnings of (b) unpalatable. Schiffer informs me that his talk of intention was meant to be a temporary idealization, to be replaced eventually by roughly Bayesian talk of degrees of desire and partial belief.

32. See Grice (1974: 13) and esp. Schiffer (1981: 68). That said, when Grice wrote 'Meaning' in 1948—it did not make it into print until 1957, when Strawson, fed up with Grice's reluctance to publish it, edited the manuscript and sent it to *The Philosophical Review* on Grice's behalf—definitions of the sorts Grice was investigating were generally treated as conceptual analyses. By the time of his 1968 and 1969 publications, Grice had already begun moving away from such an understanding and saw himself as explicating theoretical notions. Quite how Grice (1971, 1974) and Schiffer (1972) were construing their definitions in the early 1970s is harder to gauge. But by the early 1980s, Schiffer (1981, 1982) was making it clear that he saw the relevant definitions as constitutive.

33. See Schiffer (1987a), esp. Ch 9.

34. Given common and even theoretical talk about "sending messages", "communicating", or "meaning" things by way of bodily adornment—for example by using makeup, wearing jewellery or badges, or just appearing dressed in certain items of clothing in certain contexts—can we isolate in a useful way what we might call acts of *self-displaying*, with a view to possibly including some of these as full-fledged acts of speaker meaning? That's a more interesting question than it seems initially, one I take up in Neale (forthcoming a).

35. Schiffer's (1972, 1983) terminology is much clearer than Grice's, about which there is (perhaps unsurprisingly) considerable confusion in the literature, even among avowed Griceans. In 'Meaning' (1957) Grice called speaker meaning *utterer's meaning*. But in his William James Lectures (which included 'Utterer's Meaning, Sentence Meaning and Word Meaning' (1968) and 'Utterer's Meaning and Intentions' (1969)), he called it *utterer's occasion-meaning*, which he distinguished from what he (somewhat misleadingly) called *utterance-type occasion-meaning* (or *the occasion meaning of an utterance-type*). To talk about utterer's occasion-meaning is to talk about what S means *by uttering x* on a given occasion. To talk about utterance-type occasion-meaning is to talk about what S means *by x* on a given occasion. In specifications of utterer's occasion-meaning what follows 'means' is a phrase of the form 'that p', whereas in specifications of utterance-type occasion-meaning what follows 'means' is in quotation marks. Compare the following (the choice of example may suggest where I'm heading):

> (i) *By uttering* 'Kennst du das Land wo die Zitronen blühen', the American soldier meant that he was a German officer.
>
> (ii) *By* 'Kennst du das Land wo die Zitronen blühen', the American soldier meant "Knowest thou the land where the lemon trees bloom."

In 'Meaning' Grice was trying to present an account of utterer's occasion-meaning (as he later called it). But in that early paper he used 'by x' where he would later use 'by uttering x'. One understandable consequence of his use of 'by x' in the early paper was that some of the purported counterexamples to his analysis that appeared in print prior to the appearance of his 1968 and 1969 papers were, in effect, purported counterexamples to an imagined analysis of something closer to utterance-type occasion-meaning. Among these purported counterexamples, I include Searle's (1969) frequently cited example of the captured American soldier who has learned by heart a poem by Goethe but otherwise has no German. Schiffer (1972) provides a very different analysis.

36. Throughout, I assume, with Schiffer (1981, 1995, 2005), Kaplan (1978a, 1989a, 1989b), Evans (1982), Salmon (1986), Neale (1990), and probably the vast majority of philosophers, that an important distinction is to be made between singular (object-dependent)

and general (object-independent) propositions, construed as the contents of singular (object-dependent) and general (object-independent) propositional attitudes.

37. Notice the difference between Schiffer's position and Bach's (2001), according to which a referential intention accompanying a use of, say, a demonstrative, is a *component* of a communicative intention. This idea, also seems to be part of the theories of speaker reference proposed by Stine (1978) and Bertolet (1987).

38. It is commonly held that a notion of expression reference is needed for semantic composition within theories that purport to compose *contents*. The contents of *expressions* (relative to contexts) are composed in popular theories of expression-based semantic composition such as those inspired by the work of Kaplan. The contents of *utterances* of expressions are composed in (less popular) theories of utterance-based semantic composition. For reasons that will emerge, I suspect *speaker reference* will suffice for such theories, 'expression reference' being no more than a label for 'speaker reference' when doing semantic composition of content. (Put another way, the only theoretically interesting notion of expression reference is just the notion of what the speaker is referring to with an expression on a given occasion.)

39. I have suggested elsewhere that clause (1) is unnecessary, that the meaning of x plays no part in constitutively determining what S says in uttering x. See Neale (2004, 2005). This may sound absurd. It should seem much less so by section 12.7.7, after I have distinguished *constitutive*, *epistemic*, and *aetiological* determination. But it raises the question of what should replace clause (1), as something is needed to separate the M-intention determining the content of what S *said* (or *directly meant*) in uttering x and the M-intention determining the content of what S *conversationally implicated* (or *indirectly meant*) by saying whatever it was S said in uttering x. The answer lies in the relative "priority" and "directness" of those contents as parts of what S *meant* by uttering x.

40. The data Grice and Schiffer mined to test potential analyses of *meaning* were, for the most part, reasonably ordinary intuitions about the truth or falsity of a *definiendum* used to describe an occasion of utterance in which a proposed *definiens* (specifying the structure and content of an audience-directed intention) seemed clearly true or clearly false. From the outset, evidently Grice thought this method of closing in on a robust and theoretically useful notion of what the speaker *means* would not be as helpful in closing in on a correspondingly useful notion of what the speaker *says*, and he has good reason to believe this: in ordinary, tutored, and semi-theoretical talk there are in fact genuine differences in the *strengths of intuitions* about, on the one hand, what S *means* and, on the other, what S *says* and *implicates*; and, of course, numerous cases in which intuitions about what S *means* are clearer and more robust than those about what S *says* were precisely what was fuelling debates in the 1940s, 50s, and 60s about the meanings of (e.g.) 'and', 'or', 'if', 'the', 'a', 'some', 'know', 'look', 'try', and 'voluntary', the very cases that provided much of the substance to, and philosophical interest in, Grice's attempt to draw a clear line between what S says and what S implicates.

41. In the course of preparing 'Term Limits Revisited' (2008) for republication in a collection of papers, I noticed that I originally wrote that acts of saying "comprise" (rather than "are") acts of referring and acts of predicating. That was not the way a good Gricean should put the point because it suggests (i) that a located, self-standing act of referring somehow composes with a located, self-standing act of predicating to produce an act of saying, and (ii) that a self-standing referential intention composes in some way with a self-standing predicational intention to produce a Gricean communicative intention, which is not the Gricean position.

42. See Neale forthcoming (b).

43. There is another, technical use of 'utterance' in some work, an utterance being a sentence-context pair. This is not what I shall understand by 'utterance' here.
44. Relative to speech, writing is a very recent phenomenon. For most of human history, no spoken language had any written form. As recently as a century ago, only a few hundred of the many thousands of languages spoken around the world had anything like a full-fledged writing system. Even today, many hundreds of the approximately 7000 languages still spoken—the number has been steadily declining for many decades—have no full-fledged writing system. The rapid spread of technology, English, and the Latin alphabet probably means that almost all spoken languages will have writing systems quite soon, partly because the number of languages will decline and partly because Latinate systems are being developed for many languages lacking writing systems.
45. ASL is the gestural-visual language used by members of the deaf community in the United States and geographically Anglophone Canada).
46. It is tempting to say 'counterpart of phonology', but the term 'phonology' is now used in connection with signed as well as spoken languages. No confusion should arise.
47. By standard measures, ASL is closer to French Sign Language (FSL) than it is to BSL. ASL and BSL share around a third of their signs, and a high proportion of the shared signs of ASL and BSL are *not* among the most commonly used in either language. Since iconicity is exploited more widely in signed languages than it is in spoken languages, more sharing and resemblance is due to iconicity in the former. According to Sandler and Lillo-Martin (2006), the same type of pronominal system is used across quite different sign languages. An object being referred to in a discourse is associated with a proprietary position in space. (If the object is present, its actual position is used; if it is not present, some other position is selected on pragmatic grounds or else arbitrarily.) Pronoun signs simply point to those positions in space already associated with objects referred to.
48. It is remarkable how many philosophers of *language* just assume that ASL is a system for representing English words by signing in much the same way that written English is a system for representing them by writing. Even those who have written about words and signing make this mistake or analogous ones. Hawthorne and Lepore (2011), for example, say "the same word can be written, uttered, signed, Brailled, or semaphored", a claim which, as Bromberger (2011) points out, "is symptomatic of an outlook on language too removed from reality to warrant any philosophic claim" (2011: 492). In a footnote, they say they mean something like "Signed English" not ASL. But as Bromberger points out, and supports with empirical facts about versions of Signed English, also known as Manually Coded English, none of them is an encoding of English; they all encode a pidgin form of ASL, and again the morphology, phonology, and syllables in play do not reflect the syntax, phonology, morphology, and syllables of English, though, by design, word order gets pushed to mirror that of English translations of sentences of ASL because the whole point of these pidgins is, as Bromberer notes, "to help communication between hearers and Deafs, and to help Deafs parse written English." (2011: 493).
49. Uncontracted braille is a system used for character-by-character transcription, each braille character standing for its printed equivalent. English Braille books are transcribed in contracted braille, in which the characters for certain printed letters encode whole words, including many favorites from intensional and indexical logic: *n* for 'not', *e* for 'every', *c* for 'can', *c't* for 'can't', *cd* for 'could', *w* for 'will', *wd* for 'would', *sh* for 'shall', *t* for 'that', *td* for 'today', *k* for 'knowledge', *s* for 'so', and *nec* for 'necessary'. (There is no contraction for 'possible'. Perhaps *n nec n* works.) Some contractions are irregular, e.g., *x* for 'it' (surely a logician's idea) and *xs* for 'its' (presumably as a bound variable).

50. There is a view sometimes called *perdurantism* or *four-dimensionalism*, according to which an object is said to have "a distinct temporal part at every instant of its existence." It is far from clear that there is an intelligible position here.
51. Although utterances and signings are intentional acts, they are not to be identified with *illocutionary* acts. It is perfectly possible to perform two distinct illocutionary acts by means of a single act of uttering or signing. The ontological status of illocutionary acts is a difficult matter. But Drestske seems to me basically right when he says

> To ask a question, a common way of describing what someone has done, is to produce meaningful sounds with a certain intention. To ask a question is not merely to have the relevant movement of the lips, tongue, and larynx produced by some internal cause, any more than to be a wound is to have the scar produced by some puncture of the skin. It is, rather, to have these vocal activities produced by a purpose, an intention, or a desire to obtain information. Unless the internal cause of speech is some such intention or purpose, the resulting behavior does not qualify as asking a question. It might, rather, be rehearsing a line in a play, reading aloud, telling a joke, or giving an example. (1977: 8)

52. There are four *words* in the sentence 'The cat sat on the mat.' But the word 'the' occurs in two *positions* so there are two *occurrences* of the word 'the' in the sentence. If expressions are abstracta, so are *occurrences* of expressions within other expressions. Utterances are *not* abstracta. So it is obviously false that there are two *utterances* of the word 'the' in the *sentence*, 'The cat sat on the mat', and if utterances are so-called "tokens" of expressions, tokens and occurrences of expressions are not at all the same thing. But an *utterance* of 'The cat sat on the mat' will contain two utterances of the word 'the', each corresponding to a different *occurrence* of 'the' in the sentence. *Mutatis mutandis* for inscriptions and occurrences.
53. Kaplan (2011) rejects the view that all inscriptions are physical objects. Inscriptions of sentences produced by writing on paper with a pen or pencil, by pushing ribbon onto paper with typewriter keys, or by writing on a blackboard with chalk are objects made up of ink or graphite or chalk. But, says Kaplan, inscriptions are not "necessarily material objects, as the cases of words incised into stone and stencils show" (2011: 512). Inscriptions taking the form of incised words are "perceivable though nonmaterial... it is the space that we perceive, not the hunk of stone" (2011: 510, n. 10). This seems wrong. An inscription can be touched as well as seen. An inscription produced by carving into stone or wood is certainly different from the other examples just mentioned in that its creation involves the *removal* of matter rather than the addition (and possible compression). When a marble grave stele is made by removing stone from a slab, neither the removed stone nor the resulting slab is the same thing as the inscription. But this does not mean "the space we perceive" is the inscription. The inscription is a discontinuous material object composed of certain of the smaller *edges* of the slab, edges locatable by *touch* but typically located by way of visible contrasts of colour and hue, mostly produced by the angle and intensity of light hitting parts of the slab, contrasts easily manipulated using artificial lights. If the incised area alone is painted (or filled with a compound of adhesive and other matter), then there are *two* inscriptions that more or less overlap (though I suppose we could instead say we have a "belt and braces" inscription).
54. Notice 'sketching' is different from 'painting' and 'drawing' in that it is not normally used of individual products because of the existence of the simple nominal 'sketch'. It can, however, be used while indicating a sketch (as in 'Look at how much John's sketching has improved').

55. To the extent that my proposal is intentional, I think it puts me on the same side of an important fence as, Bromberger (1989), Devitt (1981), Kaplan (1990, 2011), and Richard (1990). (Kaplan (2011) has done an excellent job fending off the usual arguments against intentionalist accounts of utterances and inscriptions, including specifically the arguments of Lepore and Hawthorne (2011).
56. Schiffer (1981, 1992, 1995, 2006).
57. Kaplan (1978a, 1989a), Schiffer (1981, 1992, 1995).
58. This feature has been criticized by Salmon (1986a) and by King (2003).
59. (As I've indicated, I'm going to keep the controversial notion of *conventional* implicature out of the picture.) For Grice himself, the connections between his theories of meaning, saying, conversation, and conversational implicature are clear. Importantly, nothing is either *said* or *conversationally implicated* unless it is *meant*. (See Grice (1961: 130; 1978: 120; 1989: 49) as well as the discussions in Bach (1994, 2001), Bach and Harnish (1979), Harnish (1976), Horn (1996), Levinson (1983), Loar (1981), Neale (1990, 1992, 2004), Schiffer (1972), Stalnaker (1989, 2006), Strawson (1990), and Walker (1975).) Armed with wooden interpretations of a few passages snipped from two of Grice's William James Lectures, Saul (2002) claims that this "standard" interpretation of Grice is incorrect. But the idea that *all* of these people are wrong about this is scarcely credible: many of them studied or worked with Grice, attended his seminars at Oxford or Berkeley on a regular basis, discussed meaning and implicature with him at length, or co-authored work with him—*all* of these things, in the case of Strawson. Saul's interpretations of the passages she selects involve a type of exegesis so strained and lacking in charity that it cannot but help attributing to an author views the author could not reasonably be said to hold.
60. Given how much has been written about Grice's theories, it is somewhat surprising that so little attention has been paid to (1) how Grice saw his theory of conversation figuring in explanations of what speakers *say*, and (2) how much his theory of conversation illuminates the inferential character of his theory of speaker meaning. The theory of conversation consists of (a) a collection of tentative principles (a Cooperative Principle and attendant conversational maxims enjoining truthfulness, informativeness, relevance, and perspicuity), and (b) a type of non-deductive reasoning subserving those principles that a *speaker* could reasonably expect an *interpreter* to be capable of engaging in with a view to identifying what the speaker means. The theory is meant to be a localization of a more general theory of ordinary rational interaction. But it is not *quite* as localized as some people seem to think. For example, there is no indication anywhere in Grice's work to suggest he saw these principles and the type of reasoning subserving them to have rôles *only* in explanations of what a speaker conversationally implicates. Indeed, upon reflection it is clear that Grice appreciated their rôles in connection with what a speaker *says*. Schiffer (2005), Stalnaker (1989: 527), and I appear to belong to a small minority who explicitly acknowledge the second point. Indeed, it is striking how regularly the second point is explicitly *denied* by people whose work is heavily influenced by Grice's and how little attention has been paid to the rôles the theory of conversation plays within his overall theory of meaning. An unfortunate consequence of this is that the question, which bothered Grice, of the conditions under which a given part of what a speaker *means* in uttering x is also part of what the speaker *says* in uttering x gets virtually ignored.
61. The distinction between (i) and (ii) is also emphasized by Bach (1997: 39; 1999: 72; 2000: 271; 2001: 29–30; 2005: 43), Devitt (1981: 32–6), and Fodor and Lepore (2005: 8–9). See also Neale (2004: 76; 2005: 180; 2007a: 359, n. 7; 2013, *passim*). In the quoted passage, I have changed the original 'said' and 'meant' to the present tense, as 'say' and 'mean' now seem better to my ear.

62. Again, see Bach, Devitt, Fodor and Lepore, and Neale (references are in the previous footnote). In a similar vein, see also Renfrew's (1982) emphasis on the need for archaeology to distinguish [A] the metaphysical question of the origins, nature, and evolution of intelligent behavior, [B] the epistemological question of identifying such behavior on the basis of the archaeological record, and [C] the methodological question of the framework within which we can make inferences about intelligent behavior from material culture. On the nature of the relations between pragmatic, legal, and archaeological interpretation, see Neale (forthcoming b).
63. This comes out particularly clearly in Grice's discussion of conversational implicature, which greatly illuminates his account of speaker meaning.
64. While the quoted material makes it clear that it is S's *conception* of the context of utterance, the topic of conversation, background information, and A's ability to work out what S is up to that does the theoretical work, the ellipted material slips up in mentioning "facts about the context of utterance, the topic of conversation, background information, and so on" where it should be mentioning S's *conception* of facts about the context...".
65. If Chomsky (2000) and Fodor (1983, 2001) are right, then asking for a theory of interpretation is tantamount to asking for a complete 'theory of mind' because the hypotheses that audiences form about what speakers mean are the outputs of a central all-purpose inference system that can access all manner of information from all manner of sources, making them aetiologically very unlike the outputs of cognitive modules (in Fodor's sense) such as the perceptual channels. But if Sperber and Wilson are right, they are the products of a dedicated inference system that forms "a sub-module of the mind-reading module, with its own special-purpose principles and mechanisms" Wilson (2005: 1129).
66. Specific arguments that involve conflations of CQ and EQ, as well as some involving the conflation of CQ and AQ, and conflations of EQ and AQ are discussed in detail in Neale (forthcoming b).
67. I have resisted talk of "utterance creation" and "utterance production" as both have incorrect connotations.
68. There are two pieces of economic vocabulary that I think should be resisted. Words and sentences are sometimes regarded as "coins" or "counters", and languages as the "currencies" to which they belong. I think such talk ultimately does more harm than good.
69. See Neale (2005).
70. So linguistic meaning plays no role in answering CQ—the constitutive question about what S means by uttering x. But does it play a role in answering the corresponding question about what S *says* in uttering x? In the literature—Gricean and non-Gricean— it is usually assumed that it *does*, that there is a special *constitutive* relation between expression meaning and what is said, not just aetiological and epistemic relations. In earlier work, I took the position that "what S said ... [is] determined by, and only by, certain very specific interpreter-directed intentions S had in uttering x" (2004: 78). For elaboration see Neale (forthcoming c).
71. In unpublished work, Grice (1974) rejects Davidson's suggestion that the infelicity be accounted for in terms of conversational implicature.
72. See also Audi (1973), Harman (1974), and Pears (1985). Audi suggests that intending to ϕ amounts to believing one will ϕ while having one's actions guided by a desire to ϕ. As I read Grice, he had already recognized a problem with this as he floats the idea that intending to ϕ amounts to believing that one will ϕ *on the grounds that* one desires to ϕ (1971: 278–9). This idea is criticized by Bratman (1987: 19–20) on the grounds that the epistemic component is insert.
73. This is meant to be understood as an account of the nature of intention. In a seminar we taught together at Rutgers, John Hawthorne pointed out to me it sounds like a hidden

indexical (implicit reference) account of intention attribution. To the extent it is, it may well be subject to Schiffer's meaning-intention problem, addressed in section 12.14.
74. Neale (2004: 77; 2005: 181).
75. Schiffer (1972: 30–42) originally provided a complex definition of a technical notion of mutual knowledge. For present purposes, it will be enough to say, as he does in his 1981 paper, that two people mutually know that p if each knows that p, and knows that the other knows that p. See Schiffer (1981: 96, n. 16).
76. Schiffer's definition is strikingly different from Kripke's (1977) notion of speaker's reference (which is defined in terms of his Kripke's notion of semantic reference, reversing the Gricean direction of explanation), different from earlier Grice-inspired intentional definitions given by Stine (1978), Bertolet (1987) and Bach (1992). On Stine's account, by uttering e, S referred to o iff S uttered e intending (1) that S's utterance of e bring it about that a certain audience A identify o, (2) that A recognize S's intention (1), and (3) that A's recognition of S's intention (1) shall function as at least part of A's reason for identifying o. Stine glosses the notion of *identifying* that the definition invokes as "picking out who it is one has in mind (a transparent notion for which substitutivity of identity for singular terms holds)" (1978: 323). The only constraint imposed on S's choice of e in referring to o is that S be capable of forming the intention that the use of e will enable A to identify o. Bertolet (1987) suggests trading S's intention that A identify something for S's intention to direct A's attention to something. In a similar vein, Bach takes a referential intention to be "the intention that one's audience identify, and take themselves to be intended to identify, a certain item as the referent by means of thinking of it in a certain identifiable way" (1992: 143) These accounts are problematic precisely because they appeal crucially to notions of, and awareness of, sub-propositional content. There is no space to discuss this matter here.
77. Schiffer says this is a simplification that covers only cases of what he calls *primary* reference. Suppose there are two old clocks in the house, one in the study, the other in the kitchen. A tells S he will spend the morning doing household chores, and S says,

(i) The clock in the study needs winding up.

So 'uttering (i)' will be ϕ-ing in this example. According to Schiffer, in uttering (i) in the described scenario, S refers to a certain thing (*qua* its being a clock in a certain study), and S *means* that that thing needs winding up. But S also refers to another thing (*qua* its being a study), but refers to this solely to enable A to identify the clock. As Schiffer puts it, S makes *primary* reference to the clock in the study but a *non-primary* reference to the study. The machinery of object-containing propositions is helpful here: If, in ϕ-ing, S makes primary reference to o, then o is a constituent of the proposition that is the content of what S means in ϕ-ing. But if S makes only secondary reference to o, then o need not be—and in a good many cases will not be—a constituent of that proposition; o's impact on the proceedings may be limited to the rôle S intends A's recognition that o is being referred to is to play in leading A to identify S's *primary* reference. In some cases, the thing to which S makes non-primary reference *will* turn out to be a constituent of the proposition expressed, if only because S may make primary and non-primary reference to the same thing: if S and A mutually know that Fred is the tallest person in his family, S could use the definite description 'the tallest person in Fred's family' referentially in uttering (ii) and mean that Fred is a fool:

(ii) the tallest person in Fred's family is a fool.

In so doing, S would be making non-primary reference to Fred by uttering 'Fred', non-primary reference to Fred's family by uttering 'Fred's family', and primary reference to

Fred by uttering 'the tallest person in Fred's family'. (I use this example elsewhere to demonstrate the futility of objecting to the utility of a Gödelian description merely on the grounds that it contains a referential component used to refer to the unique object satisfying the matrix of the description as a whole. See Neale (2008: 416–18).) S could also inform A of something A did not previously know by uttering (iii):

(iii) the tallest person in Fred's family is Fred.

But in such a case S would be using 'the tallest person in Fred's family' attributively.

Schiffer's distinction between primary and non-primary *reference* is intimately, but not perfectly, related to a syntactic distinction he draws between primary and non-primary *occurrences* of (purported) singular terms. An occurrence of a singular term t in a sentence x is primary iff t is not a proper constituent of an occurrence of some other singular term in x. So, in example (i) the occurrence of the noun phrase 'the clock in the study' is primary, whereas the occurrence of 'the study' is secondary. An adequate recursive definition would entail that the occurrence of 'the study' in, say, 'the pendulum inside the clock in the study is cracked' is tertiary. The machinery of object-containing propositions is helpful again: If t has a *primary* occurrence in a sentence x, then (typically) the thing, o, that S refers to by uttering t will be a constituent of the proposition that is the content of what S means by uttering x; but if t has a non-primary occurrence, then (typically) the thing o, that S refers to by uttering t will *not* be a constituent of that proposition: o's impact on the proceedings may be limited to the rôle S intends A's recognition that S is referring to o by uttering t is to play in leading A to identify what S is referring by uttering the smallest singular term $F(t)$ of which t is a proper part. $F(t)$ might be a proper constituent of some larger singular term $G(F(t))$, of course. So in sentence (1) above, the occurrence of the description 'the tallest person in Fred's family' is primary, the occurrence of the description 'Fred's family' secondary, and the occurrence of the name 'Fred' tertiary.

The relation between the syntactic notion of a primary (secondary, tertiary, ...) occurrence of a singular term and the notion of a primary (secondary, tertiary, ...) reference is similar to the one between the syntactic notion of an indicative sentence and the notion of an assertion, or the one between the syntactic notion of an interrogative sentence and the notion of a question. In a sense that intention-based semantics aims to make precise, indicative sentences have some property that makes their use "maximally efficacious", as Schiffer (1981: 66) puts it, as a means for making assertions. (The existence of expressions having this property is virtually assured, Schiffer maintains, by the need to make assertions and broadly Gricean assumptions about the nature of rational behavior and cooperative endeavors.) But in the right circumstances, indicative sentences can certainly be used to make requests. ('You're standing on my foot.') Similarly, interrogative sentences have some property that makes their use maximally efficacious as a means for asking questions. But in the right circumstances they can certainly be used to make requests. ('Do you realize you're standing on my foot?') Similarly, secondary occurrences of singular terms have some property that makes their use maximally efficacious as a means for making secondary references, but in the right circumstances, they can be used to make primary references:

A: How was the food at Maxim's the last time you ate there?

S: Excellent, though the woman who tied Mick Jagger to his chair during dessert complained about the *Nonnettes de poulet Agnès Sorel*.

78. Neale (2008).
79. See Neale (1993, 2008).
80. Of course, on some accounts, definite descriptions are non-rigid referring expressions. For present purposes, I shall just assume they have two uses, a rigid referential use and a Russellian quantificational use that is not relevant to the present discussion. For discussion, see Neale (2004, 2008).
81. See Neale (2008).
82. As Kripke has pointed out, we can certainly introduce a name into a language by description. But unlike the description used to introduce it, such a name will be rigid. It takes some effort – *conscious* effort at that – to introduce a name non-rigidly by description, if it can be done at all. Suppose I stipulate that the person who delivers my mail, *whoever he is, whatever the day of the week, wherever I happen to be living at the time, whatever the weather,* shall be called 'Nigel'. A strange stipulation; a strange 'name' to use. I can move country and Nigel will be there when I arrive at my new abode. I can kill Nigel on Tuesday, but he – or she – will be back on Wednesday. I have no escape from Nigel unless the world's postal services shut down. We are sorely tempted to say that I have introduced 'Nigel' not *by* description but as *shorthand for* a description ('the person who delivers my mail'). And, if that is so, the question of whether or not 'Nigel' is a non-rigid singular term reduces to the question of whether the description it abbreviates is a non-rigid singular term.
83. See, for example, Carston (1988, 2002), Recanati (2001, 2002, 2004), Sperber and Wilson (1995), Wilson and Sperber (2012).
84. Earlier, Grice (1961) talked about a speaker *stating* rather than *saying* something.
85. Grice (1989: 87-8), Schiffer (1972: 112-14).
86. Grice goes on to replace 'means' in his version of clause (i) by '*centrally* means' so as to exclude what S conventionally implicates. This is because he wishes to exclude from what is said anything that does not bear on its truth or falsity. In uttering 'Ann isn't here yet,' all *S says*, on Grice's account, is that Ann isn't here. *S* does not say that Ann is on her way or expected, or that someone thinks she is. Nonetheless, by using 'yet', *S* is *conventionally implicating* that someone, perhaps *S*, thinks that Ann is on her way or expected. But the truth or falsity of this suggestion has no bearing on the truth or falsity of what *S* said. Similarly, in uttering 'Ann is poor but she is honest,' all *S says* is that Ann is poor and Ann is honest. *S* does not *say* anything about the relation between poverty and honesty (or about the relation between Ann's poverty and Ann's honesty). But by using 'but' rather than 'and', *S* is conventionally implicating that someone, perhaps *S*, thinks some particular relation—contrast or unexpected co-occurrence, for example—is of conversational relevance, but the truth or falsity of the suggestion has no bearing on the truth of falsity of what *S* said. I do not mean to be endorsing this picture, I am simply specifying a condition Grice's places on saying. Grice's notion of conventional implicature is essentially Frege's notion of *colouring*. For discussion, see Neale (1999).
87. See Kaplan (1978a, 1978b, 1989a, 1989b). Kaplan occasionally lapses into saying 'what the speaker says', but the context makes it clear this is only stylistic, that he is still talking about the technical notion of saying his theory uses.
88. For certain purposes, Kaplan (1978a) is happy to talk about the content of an *utterance* of a sentence, though sometimes this is clearly shorthand for the content of a sentence relative to a context.
89. In Kaplan's *formal* theory, contents are functions from "circumstances of evaluation" to extensions. It is common to take such circumstances to be possible states of the world (though Kaplan's preferred conception of a circumstance includes a *time* along with possible state of the world, which accords with his preferred conception of a proposition

as something that can have different truth-values at different times). On such an account, contents are represented by *intensions*, so the content of a sentence, in a context, is effectively a *truth condition* as it is represented by a function from possible states of the world to truth-values (sentence extensions). That is good enough for capturing *validity*, and presumably this is why Kaplan says that structured propositions are not a part of his theory, if he means his logic of demonstratives (1989a: 496). Certainly no commitment to structured propositions as sentence contents follows from accepting Kaplan's account of character and content, which can be tailored to fit any truth-conditional semantics. But *philosophically* the idea is still that the content of a sentence is a *proposition*, where a proposition *has* a truth condition but is too fine-grained to be identified with one.

90. Kaplan actually talks about the *agent* of the context rather than the *speaker*. This is for reasons to do with logic—Kaplan does not want 'I am speaking' to come come out as a logical truth, for example. None of this matters for present purposes.

91. It is an interesting theoretical question whether there is a need for a complete semantics to compose characters. On the face of it, we might end up with two related compositional theories. Then again, it might turn out that a compositional theory of character is idle (or worse), that character is construed as a useful property only of *atomic* expressions. (King and Stanley (2005) have given good reasons for thinking this is so.) Or it might turn out that we cannot have a complete compositional theory of content that is not itself fuelled in places by deliverances of a compositional theory of character (see Braun (1994, 1996) and the objections raised by King and Stanley (2005)). These are not things to be decided in advance of serious theorizing.

92. Salmon (2005) distinguishes what he calls the *expression centered conception* of semantics and the *speech act centered conception*. I think that what he calls the *expression centered conception* is to be found motivating theories whose core is what I am calling the composition of expression-contents. But what he calls the *speech act centered conception* seems to be motivating a considerably broader range of theories than those whose core is what I am calling the composition of utterance-contents. Traditional semantic theories compose expression-contents. I suspect two things have drawn people to theories that compose utterance-contents—though I have seen neither mentioned explicitly in the literature. The first is the assumption, quite unjustified, that composing utterance-contents opens up space to accommodate all manner of content-affecting implicit reference whereas one that composes expression-contents can accommodate only a very restricted range of cases. The second is the belief that the type-token distinction provides an important part of a proper implementation of Kaplan's theory and a proper explanation of his character-content distinction: word-types have *characters*, word-tokens have *content*. But this belief is just *false*. Kaplan's semantics is all about properties of *expressions* and is completely silent on properties of *utterances* of expressions. (For those who still like type-token talk, Kaplan's semantics concerns properties [characters, contents, and more] of expression-types and is silent on properties of expression-tokens).

93. In a different setting, the following might be a more appropriate answer: you were examining the results of functional magnetic resonance imaging and polygraphs you had subjected me to during and shortly after my utterance and you have interpreted the results as evidence strongly suggesting that I was referring to Sue.

94. In Kaplan's *logic*, the first element is merely a context's *agent*. But in any context modelling a *situation of utterance*, the first element will be the utterance's *speaker*.

95. Of course, there may be more than one occurrence of 'she' in a given sentence, and the first element of c (the speaker) might be using each to refer to a different female; so the fifth

element of a context should really be a *sequence* of females—one for every occurrence of 'she' in a sentence—to which the first element of the context is referring with 'she'.
96. More precisely, a sequence of such intentions. See previous footnote.
97. See Stanley (2007) for possible implementations. If the aphonic (or tense marker) refers to an individual event, rather than timeframe, it will nonetheless be an entity with a particular temporal location (and duration).
98. For discussion, see Neale (2007a).
99. Stanley (2007) considers a more sophisticated implementation where the aphonic is an event variable. This seems rather strained for cases like 'It's noon', and 'it's autumn' and 'It's quiet'. The difference is irrelevant for my purposes here.
100. For more detail see Neale (2007a).
101. See Neale (2008) for discussion.
102. See Castañeda (1966, 1967, 1968), Chierchia (1989), Fodor (1975), Grice (1971), Higginbotham (1990), Lewis (1979), Neale (2005), Perry (1979, 1993), Salmon (1986b, 1992), and Soames (1990, 1994). The syntactic and semantic issues here are highly complex and, as far as I am aware, far from wholly resolved. However, two incontrovertible results have emerged: (i) not all pronouns are the product of syntactic transformations, and (ii) anaphora cannot be reduced to *de jure* co-reference.
103. Unfortunately, the arguments for the postulated aphonic in (2) are not terribly persuasive. See Recanati (2004), Neale (2005), Collins (2007).
104. See also Schiffer (1977, 1978, 1981, 1987b, 1995, 1996, 2005). In his earliest discussion, he calls it the "implicit indexical treatment" (1977: 66).
105. For simplicity, I follow Schiffer in suppressing a fourth, temporal relatum, the *time* at which the believer believes the proposition under the mode.
106. Exercises for the reader: (1) Under (a) the assumption that having an intention concerning a thing is having an intention concerning it under some type of mode of presentation, and (b) the assumption that all cases of implicit reference involve aphonic reference, spell out the logical form of the following with all relevant aphonics:

(i) S uttered x intending A to believe that p via A's recognizing that S uttered X intending A to believe that p.

(2) Specify the character of each aphonic in the sentence. (3) Compositionally derive the sentence's content, relative to a context.
107. In both examples, the implicit reference is to a *location*. This is not essential to the "paradigm" Schiffer is talking about. Donnellan's famous example of an attributive use of 'the murderer' would have served as well:

Two detectives S and A are looking down at Smith's mutilated corpse. They have no suspect and no clues as to who committed this act, but the state of Smith's body prompts S to say, 'The murderer is insane.' Here S implicitly refers to Smith, and this by virtue of the fact that in uttering 'The murderer is insane', she means that the murderer of Smith is insane.' In other words, S counts as having referred to Smith because the proposition she meant is (in part) about Smith. Notice that there is no difficulty whatever in ascribing to S the propositional speech act in question: S clearly intended A to believe that Smith's murderer is insane, and she is quite prepared to tell you that this is what she meant, what she implicitly said, and what she intended A to be informed of.

108. Schiffer presents a barrage of other arguments against contextualist accounts of knowledge claims.
109. Since, as Austin (1950) noted, a woman's hair might be blonde naturally but dyed red, or red naturally but bleached blonde, a contextualist might want to make room for the "way" in which something is being said to be red. I shall say no more about this.

110. I have suppressed Stanley and Szabo's ordered pair notation for the nominal.
111. However, Schiffer informs me that he believes it should ultimately be possible to expunge reference to audiences in a final definition of speaker meaning.
112. The claim that we are all relativists of a sort about truth, that no one takes propositions to be true or false absolutely because the same proposition can be true at one possible world and false at another, is the confused product of allowing oneself to be steered more by formal machinery than by the philosophical problems engendering it. To express an interest in the *truth* of a proposition is to express an interest in how things *are*: A proposition is true or false depending upon how things are. The philosopher who finds solace in construing this as talk of propositions being true or false *relative* to the way things are has no more discovered a pervasive relativism than the logician who talks of truth in a model. Within a semantic framework that appeals to the machinery of possible worlds, the surrogate for a proposition's being true ("relative to the way things are") is its being *true at the actual world*, where the actual world is conceived as one of an indefinite number of ways things could have turned out. But the perfectly sensible idea that we can, *within such frameworks*, characterize a *proposition's* being true in this way should not mislead us into thinking that because there are rôles in certain logics for talking about a *sentence's* being true/false (expressing a truth/falsehood, expressing a true/false proposition) with respect to collections of parameters ("circumstances of evaluation") that include worlds and times (and perhaps locations), that there are interesting choices to be made about *the nature of propositions*, that we are free to view "them" as true or false relative to worlds, or relative to worlds and times, or relative to worlds, times, and locations, or relative to worlds, times, locations, epistemic standards, aesthetic standards, and so on.
113. The weight Schiffer places in the second part of this passage on first-person authority about the contents of one's conscious beliefs and intentions and about what one means might bother those of a strongly anti-Cartesian disposition.
114. The situation is different for someone who has already the language and is just learning a new word. For the literate, encountering an inscription might suffice, if one had some reasonable (but potentially quite inaccurate) way of imagining a pronunciation for *f*, based on its spelling, for example, or on a set of instructions supplied by someone who knows how to pronounce it.
115. Carruthers (2013) presents a good case for thinking they are functional as early as the middle of second year of life.

Bibliography

Anscombe, G. E. M. 1963. *Intention*, second edition. Oxford: Blackwell.
Audi, R. 1973. Intending. *Journal of Philosophy* 70: 387–403.
Austin, J. L. 1950. Truth. *Proceedings of the Aristotelian Society* Suppl. 24: 111–29.
Bach, K. 1992. Intentions and Demonstrations. *Analysis* 52: 140–6.
Bach, K. 1994. *Thought and Reference*. Oxford: Oxford University Press.
Bach, K. 1999. The Semantics Pragmatics Distinction: What it is and Why It Matters. In K. Turner (ed.), *The Semantics-Pragmatics Interface From Different Points of View*. Oxford: Elsevier.
Bach, K. 2000. Quantification, Qualification and Context: A Reply to Stanley and Szabó. *Mind and Language* 15 (2&3): 262–83.
Bach, K. 2001. "You Don't Say." *Synthese* 128: 15–44.
Bach, K. and M. Harnish. 1979. *Linguistic Communication and Speech Acts*. Cambridge, MA: MIT Press.

Bertolet, R. 1987. Speaker Reference. *Philosophical Studies* 52 (2): 199–226.
Bratman, M. 1987. *Intention, Plans, and Practical Reason*. Cambridge, MA: Harvard University Press.
Braun, David. 1994. Structured Characters and Complex Demonstratives. *Philosophical Studies* 74: 193–219.
Braun, David. 1995. What Is Character? *Journal of Philosophical Logic* 24: 227–40.
Braun, David. 1996. Demonstratives and Their Linguistic Meanings. *Noûs* 30: 145–73.
Bromberger, S. 1989. Types and Token in Linguistics. In *Reflections on Chomsky*, A. George, eds., Oxford: Blackwell, pp. 58–9.
Bromberger, S. 2011. What are Words? Comments on Kaplan (1990), On Hawthorne and Lepore, and On The Issue. *The Journal of Philosophy* 108 (9): 486–503.
Buchanan, R. and G. Ostertag. 2005. Has the Problem of Incompleteness Rested on a Mistake? *Mind* 114, 456: 889–913.
Cappelen, H. 2012. *Philosophy Without Intuitions*. Oxford: Oxford University Press.
Carruthers, P. 2013. Mindreading in Infancy. *Mind and Language* 28 (2): 141–72.
Carston, R. 1988. Implicature, Explicature, and Truth-Theoretic Semantics. In *Mental Representations*, ed. R. Kempson, Cambridge: Cambridge University Press, pp. 155–81.
Castañeda, H. N. 1966. "He: A Study in the Logic of Self-Consciousness. *Ratio* 8: 130–57.
Castañeda, H. N. 1967. Indicators and Quasi-indicators. *American Philosophical Quarterly* 4: 85–100.
Castañeda, H. 1968. On the Logic of Attributions of Self-Knowledge to Others. *Journal of Philosophy* 65: 439–56.
Carston, R. 2002. *Thoughts and Utterances: The Pragmatics of Explicit Communication*. Oxford: Blackwell.
Chierchia, C. 1989. Anaphora and Attitudes De Se. In *Semantics and Contextual Expression*, eds., Renate Bartsch, J. F. A. K. van Benthem and P. van Emde Boas, Dordrecht: Foris Publications.
Chomsky, N. 1981. *Lectures on Government and Binding*. Dordrecht: Foris.
Chomsky, N. 1986. *Knowledge of Language*. New York: Praeger.
Chomsky, N. 2000. *New Horizons in the Study of Language and Mind*. Cambridge University Press: Cambridge.
Collins, J. 2007. Syntax, More or Less. *Mind* 116: 805–50.
Crimmins, M., and J. Perry. 1989. The Prince and the Phone Booth: Reporting Puzzling Beliefs. *The Journal of Philosophy* 86: 685–711.
Devitt, M. 1981. *Designation*. New York: Columbia University Press.
Devitt, M. 2006. Intuitions in Linguistics. *British Journal for the Philosophy of Science* 57 (3): 481–513.
Devitt, M. 2007. Referential Descriptions and Conversational Implicatures. *European Journal of Analytic Philosophy*.
Devitt, M. 2010. Linguistic Intuitions Revisited. *British Journal for the Philosophy of Science* 61 (4): 833–65.
Donnellan, K. 1966. Reference and Definite Descriptions. *Philosophical Review* 75: 281–304.
Donnellan, K. 1968. Putting Humpty Dumpty Together Again. *Philosophical Review* 77: 203–15.
Donnellan, K. 1979. Speaker Reference, Descriptions and Anaphora. In *Contemporary Perspectives in the Philosophy of Language*, ed. P. A. French, T. E. Uehling Jr., and H. Wettstein, Minneapolis: University of Minnesota Press.
Dretske, F. 1981. *Knowledge and the Flow of Information*. Cambridge MA: MIT Press.
Dretske, F. 1988. *Explaining Behavior*. Cambridge MA: MIT Press.
Evans, G. 1982. *The Varieties of Reference*. Oxford: Clarendon Press.

Evans, G. 1985. *Collected Papers*. Oxford: Clarendon Press.
Fodor, J. 1975. *The Language of Thought*. New York: Thomas Y. Crowell.
Fodor, J. 1983. The Modularity of Mind. Cambridge MA: MIT Press.
Fodor, J. 2001. Language, Thought and Compositionality. *Mind and Language* 16, 1: 1–15.
Fodor, J. and E. Lepore. 2005. Out of Context. *Proceedings and Addresses of the American Philosophical Association*, 78, 2: 3–20.
Geach, P. 1962. *Reference and Generality*. Ithaca, NY: Cornell University Press.
Godfrey-Smith, P. 2013. Information and Influence in Sender-receiver Models, with Applications to Animal Behavior. In *Animal Communication Theory: Information and Influence*, ed. U. Stegmann, Cambridge: Cambridge University Press.
Grice, H. P. 1957. Meaning. *Philosophical Review* 66: 377–88.
Grice, H. P. 1961. The Causal Theory of Perception. *Proceedings of the Aristotelian Society* 35 (Suppl.): 121–52.
Grice, H. P. 1968. Utterer's Meaning, Sentence Meaning and Word Meaning. *Foundations of Language* 4, 225–42.
Grice, H. P. 1969a. Utterer's Meaning and Intentions. *Philosophical Review* 78, 147–77.
Grice, H. P. 1969b. Vacuous Names. In *Word and Objections*, ed. D. Davidson and J. Hintikka, Dordrecht: Reidel, pp. 118–145.
Grice, H. P. 1971. Intention and Uncertainty. *Proceedings of the British Academy* 57: 263–79.
Grice, H. P. 1974. Reply to Davidson on 'Intending'. Unpublished manuscript.
Grice, H. P. 1975. Logic and Conversation. In *Syntax and Semantics, Vol. 3: Speech Acts*, ed. P. Cole, New York: Academic Press, pp. 41–58.
Grice, H. P. 1978. Further Notes on Logic and Conversation. In *Syntax and Semantics, Vol. 9: Pragmatics*, ed. P. Cole, New York: Academic Press, pp. 113–128.
Grice, H. P. 1981. Presupposition and Conversational Implicature. In *Radical Pragmatics*, ed. P. Cole, New York: Academic Press, pp. 183–98.
Grice, H. P. 1989. *Studies in the Way of Words*. Cambridge, MA: Harvard University Press.
Harman, G. 1986a. *Change in View*. Cambridge, MA: MIT Press.
Harman, G. 1986b. Willing and Intending. In *Philosophical Grounds of Rationality*, ed. R. E. Grandy and R. Warner, Oxford: Oxford University Press, pp. 363–80.
Harman, G. 1974. Review of Stephen Schiffer, *Meaning*. *Journal of Philosophy* 71: 224–9.
Harnish, M. 1976. Logical Form and Implicature. In *An Integrated Theory of Linguistic Ability*, ed. T. G. Bever, J. J. Katz & T. Langedoen. New York: Thomas Y. Crowell, pp. 313–92.
Heim, I. and A. Kratzer. 1998. *Semantics in Generative Grammar*. Oxford: Blackwell.
Hawthorne, J. and E Lepore. 2011. On Words. *The Journal of Philosophy*, 108, 9: 447–85.
Higginbotham, J. 1990. Reference and Control. In R. Larson, S. Iatridou, U. Lahiri and J. Higginbotham, eds., *Control and Grammar*, Dordrecht: Kluwer.
Horn, L. 1996. Presupposition and Implicature. *The Handbook of Contemporary Semantic Theory*, ed. Shalom Lappin, Oxford: Blackwell, pp. 299–319.
Kaplan, D. 1978a. Dthat. In *Syntax and Semantics, Vol. 9: Pragmatics*, ed. P. Cole, New York: Academic Press, pp. 221–43.
Kaplan, D. 1978b. On the Logic of Demonstratives. *Journal of Philosophical Logic* 8: 81–98. Reprinted in French et al. (eds.), *Contemporary Perspectives in the Philosophy of Language*, Minneapolis: University of Minnesota Press, 1979, pp. 401–12.
Kaplan, D. 1989a. Demonstratives. In *Themes From Kaplan*, ed. J. Almog et al., New York: Oxford University Press, pp. 221–43
Kaplan, D. 1989b. Afterthoughts. In *Themes From Kaplan*, ed. J. Almog et al., New York: Oxford University Press, pp. 481–563.

Kaplan, D. 1990. Words. *The Aristotelian Society*, Supplementary Volume, LXIV, pp. 93–119.
Kaplan, D. 2011. Words on Words. *The Journal of Philosophy*, 108, 9: 504–29.
King, J. 2003. Tense, Modality and Semantic Values. *Philosophical Perspectives* 17: 195–245.
King and Stanley. 2005. Semantics, Pragmatics, and the Role of Semantic Content. In *Semantics versus Pragmatics*, ed. Zoltan Szabo, Oxford: Clarendon Press, pp. 111–64.
Kripke, S. A. 1972. Naming and Necessity. In *Semantics of Natural Language*, ed. D. Davidson, and G. Harman, Dordrecht: Reidel.
Kripke, S. A. 1977. Speaker Reference and Semantic Reference. In *Contemporary Perspectives in the Philosophy of Language*, ed. P. A. French, T. E. Uehling Jr., and H. Wettstein, Minneapolis: University of Minnesota Press.
Kripke, S. A. 1980. Preface. In *Naming and Necessity*, Cambridge, MA: Harvard University Press.
Levinson, S. 1983. Pragmatics. Cambridge: Cambridge University Press.
Linsky, L. 1963. Reference and referents. In *Philosophy and Ordinary Language*, ed. C. E. Caton, Urbana: University of Illinois Press, pp. 74–89.
Loar, B. 1976. The Semantics of Singular Terms. *Philosophical Studies* 30, 6: 353–77.
Loar, B. 1981. *Mind and Meaning*. Cambridge: Cambridge University Press.
Ludlow, P. and S. Neale. 1991. Indefinite Descriptions: In Defense of Russell. *Linguistics and Philosophy* 14, 171–202.
Millikan, R. G. 2004. *Varieties of Meaning*. Cambridge: MIT Press.
Neale, S. 1990. *Descriptions*. Cambridge, MA: MIT Press.
Neale, S. 1992. Paul Grice and the Philosophy of Language. *Linguistics and Philosophy* 15: 509–59.
Neale, S. 1993a. Logical Form and LF. In *Noam Chomsky: Critical Assessments*, ed. C. Otero, London: Routledge, 1993, pp. 788–838.
Neale, S. 1993b. Term Limits. In *Philosophical Perspectives* 7: 89–114.
Neale, S. 2004. This, That, and the Other. In *Descriptions and Beyond*, ed. A. Bezuidenhout, and M. Reimer, Oxford: Oxford University Press, pp. 68–182.
Neale, S. 2005. Pragmatism and Binding. In *Semantics Versus Pragmatics*, ed. Z. Szabo, Oxford: Oxford University Press.
Neale, S. 2007a. On Location. In *Situating Semantics: Essays on the Philosophy of John Perry*, ed. M. O'Rourke, and C. Washington, Cambridge, MA: MIT Press, pp. 251–393.
Neale, S. 2007b. Heavy Hands, Magic, and Scene Reading Traps. *European Journal of Analytic Philosophy*, 3: 77–132.
Neale, S. 2008. Term Limits Revisited. In *Philosophical Perspectives* 22, 1: 375–442.
Neale, S. forthcoming a. Determining Meaning.
Neale, S. forthcoming b. *The Mythology of Context: Language, Archaeology and Law*. The Chandaria Laureate Lectures, 2010. Oxford: Oxford University Press.
Neale, S. Forthcoming c. Natural and Non-natural Meaning. *Croatian Journal of Philosophy*.
Pears, D. 1985. Intention and Belief. In *Essays on Davidson: Actions and Events*, ed. B. Vermazen and M. Hintikka, Oxford: Clarendon Press.
Perry, J. 1979. The Essential Indexical. *Noûs* 13: 13–21.
Perry, J. 1986. Thought Without Representation. *Supplementary Proceedings of the Aristotelian Society* 60: 263–83.
Perry, J. 1993. *The Problem of the Essential Indexical and Other Essays*. New York: Oxford University Press.
Quine, W. V. 1940. *Mathematical Logic*. Cambridge, MA: Harvard University Press.
Quine, W. V. 1950. *Methods of Logic*. Cambridge, MA: Harvard University Press.
Recanati, F. 2001. What is Said. *Synthese* 128: 75–91.
Recanati, F. 2002. Unarticulated Constituents. *Linguistics and Philosophy* 25: 299–345.
Recanati, F. 2004. *Literal Meaning*. Cambridge: Cambridge University Press.

Renfrew. 1982. *Towards an Archaeology of Mind.* Inaugural lecture, Cambridge University. Cambridge: Cambridge University Press.
Richard, M. 1982. Tense, Propositions, and Meanings. *Philosophical Studies* 42: 337–51.
Richard, M. 1990. *Propositional Attitudes. An Essay on Thoughts and How We Ascribe Them.* Cambridge: Cambridge University Press.
Salmon, N. 1986a. *Frege's Puzzle.* Cambridge, MA: Bradford Books, MIT Press.
Salmon, N. 1986b. Reflexivity. *Notre Dame Journal of Formal Logic* 27: 401–29.
Salmon, N. 1992. Reflections on Reflexivity. *Linguistics and Philosophy* 15: 53–63.
Salmon, N. 2005. Two Conceptions of Semantics. In *Semantics versus Pragmatics*, ed. Z. Gendler-Szabó, Oxford: Oxford University Press, pp. 317–28.
Sandler, W. and D. Lillo-Martin. 2006. *Sign Language and Linguistic Universals.* Cambridge: Cambridge University Press.
Saul, J. 2002. Speaker Meaning, What is Said, and What is Implicated. *Noûs*, 36, 2: 228–48.
Schiffer, S. 1972. *Meaning.* Oxford: Clarendon Press.
Schiffer, S. 1977. Naming and Knowing. *Midwest Studies in Philosophy* 2: 28–41.
Schiffer, S. 1978. The Basis of Reference. *Erkenntnis* 13: 171–206.
Schiffer, S. 1981. Indexicals and the Theory of Reference. *Synthese* 49: 43–100.
Schiffer, S. 1982. Intention-Based Semantics. *Notre Dame Journal of Formal Logic* 23, 2: 119–56.
Schiffer, S. 1987a. *Remnants of Meaning.* Cambridge, MA: MIT Press.
Schiffer, S. 1987b. The 'Fido'-Fido Theory. *Philosophical Perspectives* 1: 455–80.
Schiffer, S. 1988. Preface to Second edition of *Meaning.* Oxford: Clarendon Press.
Schiffer, S. 1992. Belief Ascription. *Journal of Philosophy* 89: 499–521.
Schiffer, S. 1995. Descriptions, Indexicals, and Belief Reports: Some Dilemmas (But Not the Ones You Expect). *Mind* 104: 107–31.
Schiffer, S. 1996. Contextualist Solutions to Scepticism. *Proceedings of the Aristotelian Society* 96: 317–33.
Schiffer, S. 2003. *The Things We Mean.* Oxford: Oxford University Press, 2003.
Schiffer, S. 2005. Russell's Theory of Descriptions. *Mind* 114: 1135–83.
Searle, J. 1969. *Speech Acts: An Essay in the Philosophy of Language.* Cambridge: Cambridge University Press.
Skyrms, B. 2010. *Signals.* Cambridge: Cambridge University Press.
Soames, S. 1990. Pronouns and Propositional Attitudes. *Proceedings of the Aristotelian Society* 90: 191–212.
Soames, S. 1994. Attitudes and Anaphora. *Philosophical Perspectives* 8: 251–72.
Sperber, D. and D. Wilson. 1986. *Relevance: Communication and Cognition.* Oxford: Blackwell.
Sperber, D. and D. Wilson. 1995. *Relevance: Communication and Cognition.* 2nd ed. Oxford: Blackwell.
Sperber, D. and D. Wilson. 2002. Pragmatics, Modularity and Mind-Reading. *Mind and Language* 17: 3–23.
Stalnaker, R. 1989. On Grandy on Grice. *The Journal of Philosophy*, 86, 10: 526–7.
Stalnaker, R. 2006. Saying and Meaning, Cheap Talk and Credibility. In *Game Theory and Pragmatics*, ed A. Benz, G. Jäger, R. Van Rooij, New York: Palgrave Macmillan, pp. 83–100.
Stanley, J. 2007. *Language in Context.* Oxford: Oxford University Press.
Stanley, J. and Z. Szabó. 2000. On Quantifier Domain Restriction. *Mind & Language*, 15: 219–61.
Stine, G. C. 1978. Meaning Other Than What We Say and Referring. *Philosophical Studies* 33, 4: 319–37.
Strawson, P. F. 1950. On Referring. *Mind* 59: 320–44.
Strawson, P. F. 1964. Identifying Reference and Truth-Values. *Theoria* 30: 96–118.
Strawson, P. F. 1990. Review of *Studies in the Way of Words.* Synthese, 84, 1: 153–61.

Walker, R. 1975. Conversatiopnal Implicatures. In *Meaning, Reference and Necessity*, ed. S.W. Blackburn, Cambridge: Cambridge University Press, pp. 133–81.
Wiggins, D. 1980. *Sameness and Substance*. Oxford: Blackwell.
Wilson, D. 2002. Pragmatics, Modularity and Mindreading. *Mind and Language* 17: 3–23.
Wilson, D. 2005. New Directions for Research on Pragmatics and Modularity. *Lingua* 115: 1129–46.
Wilson, D. and D. Sperber 2012. *Meaning and Relevance*. Cambridge: Cambridge University Press.

13
Abiding Intentions

Anita Avramides

13.1 Introduction

Stephen Schiffer has given the philosophical world much to ponder. Philosophy of language, philosophy of mind, metaphysics, and epistemology are where the really big issues in philosophy are to be found—and Schiffer has made his mark in all of them.

The first place that Schiffer made his mark was in the study of language, and in particular in the study of the relationship between the semantic and the psychological (Schiffer's interest in the philosophy of mind, metaphysics, and at least some questions in epistemology arguably stem from this study). Schiffer's mentor here was H. P. Grice, and, although Schiffer followed in Grice's deep footsteps, even so his mark was distinctive. Schiffer, with his clever and challenging counter-examples, was responsible—along with Brian Loar—for much of the development of Grice's work on meaning.[1] With Schiffer's help Grice's seminal work took on a very specific shape. Much of it was a shape with which Grice himself agreed—although there were notable exceptions. (Grice, for example, was never reconciled to the idea of mutual knowledge, nor to the idea of convention.) After the publication of his first book in 1972 Schiffer continued to develop his ideas in this area. In the early 1980s he incorporated Grice's work into a program of Intention Based Semantics (IBS). IBS was arguably responsible for giving Grice's work a new lease on life, and made it relevant to a new generation of philosophers. What IBS did was to make semantics amenable to a naturalist reduction. IBS gave Grice's work yet another distinct shape; it is unclear how far Grice went along with this.[2]

Despite some notable papers that did not bear directly on Grice's work, one could say that Schiffer's work had not, by the early 1980s, strayed too far from his early Gricean interests. But that was about to change. In 1987 Schiffer published his second book *Remnants of Meaning* (hereafter, *Remnants*), and this time he was not only moving away from his early interests and influences, he was excising them from his philosophical development. IBS was, as far as Schiffer was concerned, dead; it just could not be made to work. Why he came to think this is the subject matter of sections 13.2 and 13.3, below.

Once Schiffer got the taste for change, there was no stopping him. At first glance, Schiffer's third book *The Things We Mean* (hereafter, *Things*), published in 2003, does go back on many of the things he wrote in *Remnants*. After all, in *Remnants* Schiffer renounces propositions while in *Things* he re-introduces propositions— albeit pleonastic ones. And in *Remnants* Schiffer rejects compositionality while in *Things* he allows for character*. How much these are real changes of philosophical heart or just a 'mild kind' of 'chutzpah,' is not the real concern of this chapter.³ What will concern me, however, is where Schiffer's work stands vis-à-vis Grice's at the beginning of the twenty-first century.

Looking at what Schiffer has to say about Grice's work as the decades roll on is one part of what I want to do in this chapter. The other part will be concerned to suggest that Schiffer's work has taken two wrong turnings. The first is when he elaborated Grice's work within the context of IBS. There was, I shall argue, another option. The second wrong turning was in the way Schiffer understood naturalism. What I am referring to as 'wrong turnings' might be better thought of as missed opportunities. First Schiffer missed the opportunity to think of Grice's work in a certain way and then he missed the opportunity to see that what was *really* driving his work was not a commitment to IBS per se but a commitment to a certain sort of naturalism. I shall elaborate on both of these points below. What I will be suggesting is that it is possible to see more unity in Schiffer's work than is apparent. But that unity would need to be prefaced on a very different interpretation of Grice's work. Of course, this would have involved a more radical change of heart than any Schiffer has hitherto embraced.

In *Remnants* Schiffer went through what Fodor has called a "dark night of the soul" (Fodor 1989). In the course of that dark night Schiffer came, not just to doubt, but positively to reject, IBS. We can think of IBS as the two-part program that consists of (i) a Gricean account of meaning understood as a reduction of the semantical properties of natural language to the intentional properties of the mental states of speakers and hearers, and (ii) the idea that what makes it the case that someone believes that *p* is naturalistically specifiable. In Chapter 9 of *Remnants* Schiffer does not clearly separate out the two elements that compose IBS, and as a result it can be hard to discern whether IBS is being rejected because (i) is untenable, or because (ii) is untenable, or both. In a characteristic manner, what we get is what we might call 'death by overkill': Schiffer offers a wealth of argument, and it can be a little difficult to see which, if any, is the 'killing blow.'

Writing about *Remnants*, Fodor notes in one place that "it is important to Schiffer's skepticism about what he calls IBS for him to maintain that you can't give a compositional semantics for a language with the expressive power of English" (1991: 304). In another place, Fodor notes that Schiffer's loss of faith in IBS stems from a "doubt that IBS can cash its checks" (1989: 178). Schiffer has come to believe that *neither* the Gricean reduction *nor* the naturalist reduction can be carried out. Fodor, of course, begs to differ. Fodor is another prominent Gricean. What attracts Fodor to Grice's work is precisely its reductionist potential. As Fodor writes: "If the Gricean Program and the Naturalization Program can be carried through, then IBS will have solved one of the Great Metaphysical Problems: it will have found a place for meaning in the natural order. It would certainly be nice to solve a Great Metaphysical Problem [GMP]; philosophy could do with a success or two" (1989: 177). It is arguable that philosophy—unlike the sciences—is not about this kind of success, but we needn't go into that now. What is important to note is that, with an eye to solving a GMP Fodor adopts a more scientific attitude than Schiffer to the evaluation of IBS. For Fodor the motivation for IBS is empirical. As he writes at the start of his review of *Remnants*, "IBS *must* be right because there are facts about intentionality that nothing else will explain" (1989: 178). And he ends his review by adding:

So we know that IBS *must* be true. So we know that IBS *is* true. So, there's no need to throw an existential fit; *everything is going to be all right*, many current appearances to the contrary notwithstanding.

It doesn't follow, of course, that everything is going to be all right *in the near future*. In the meantime, faith is the evidence of things unseen. (1989: 191; emphasis in original)

To be fair, Fodor doesn't just rest on his faith; he also advances arguments. The arguments concentrate on a defense of IBS and of naturalism. According to Fodor, Schiffer needn't have been so pessimistic about the prospect either. Or, to be specific, Fodor believes that there is an intact argument for intentional realism that is compatible with naturalism (1989: 185).[4]

It is not my concern to adjudicate on this particular debate. What I want to explore are Schiffer's reasons for rejecting IBS. I presume he would like to solve a Great Metaphysical Problem as much as Fodor, but he is less willing to keep the faith needed to achieve this. It certainly looks as if Schiffer is less persuaded by the empirical motivation for IBS and more influenced by what Fodor calls the logico-semantical motivations (1989: 178). The logico-semantical motivations include doubts about the relational account of belief and the compositional theory of meaning. It should be noted that the first of these is something about which Schiffer has had another dark night. As I have said, in his latest book propositions make a bit of a comeback—or rather the shadows of propositions do. Schiffer calls them pleonastic propositions. In *Remnants* Schiffer gives us a wealth of argument against the relational account of belief, while in *Things* a relational account of belief is reinstated. It is rather difficult to assess where IBS stands relative to *Things*. One might think the following: although a relational account of belief is required for IBS and that account is accepted by Schiffer in *Things*, a relational account—although necessary—is not sufficient for IBS. The *reductive* side of IBS requires that the account of belief that one gives is non-circular. Does the Schiffer of *Things* think *this* is possible? Well, in order to satisfy the non-circularity requirement, the content-determining semantic properties of the objects of belief must not be public-language semantic properties. Now, either of the following is compatible with that desideratum: (i) a sententialist account of belief (just so long as the 'sentence' is one whose content can be accounted for without invoking public language semantic features); and (ii) a propositional account of belief. As Schiffer wrote in *Remnants*, "A propositional theory is prima facie very appealing to the IBS theorist. Not only are the semantic properties of propositions clearly non-public language semantic properties, but, as propositions are contents, no further theory of content is needed for them..." (14). In *Things* propositions are back, albeit only pleonastically. Can we conclude that we now have what is required for IBS? If pleonastic propositions aren't just what an IBS theorist needs, Schiffer needs to explain why. I find it curious that there is not a single mention of Grice or of IBS in *Things*. One may be excused for thinking that IBS is still something Schiffer wishes to distance himself from (there being an absence of any indication of a change of heart back in the direction of IBS); however, the *reasons* for the rejection of IBS are a not at all clear at the end of *Things*. Perhaps it is Schiffer's continued opposition to compositional semantics that is relevant here, but it would have been useful to be clear about this.

Be that as it may, I want to take things in quite another direction—away from this debate between one lapsed and one practicing Gricean. In what follows I shall leave Fodor even further behind. Where Fodor tries to persuade Schiffer back into the fold, I want to lead him further astray. I believe that going back to his philosophical roots, Schiffer may be shown a short cut to the position he reaches at the end of *Remnants*. I have in mind here what Schiffer calls his 'no-theory theory of meaning.'[5] What I will suggest is that, had he been more robust about his 'no-theory theory of meaning'—if he had followed it through a bit further—he may not have had to be quite so pessimistic about his earlier Griceanism. IBS is another matter. That, I shall argue, was the real wrong turning. To reject Griceanism because one rejects IBS is to overlook the fact that IBS always had *two* components. What linked the two components in Schiffer's mind was always reductionism. And it is reductionism that Schiffer has grown wary of. Given this, I shall suggest that the position he arrives at at the end of *Remnants* could just as well have led him to reassess his earlier interpretation of Grice's work. I expect this would be a little *too* radical for Schiffer. And I don't expect Fodor would be interested in the slightest.

Some time ago I wrote a book about Grice and about IBS.[6] The message of that book was not in the spirit of most of the work that was going on in Grice studies at the time, and those who sympathized with the message probably wondered why I chose to have any truck with Grice's work. At the time my real mentor was Davidson, and what motivated me was an attempt to see if a commitment to Davidson's work in the philosophy of language *needed* to spell the end of the Gricean program. I never thought one *had* to bring Grice on board, but I did think that his work had much that was insightful, interesting, and downright useful when it came to thinking about meaning and language. I was heartened to find that Davidson himself came, in due course, to write more about the allegiances between his work with Grice's and less about the differences. I have in mind, in particular, Davidson's work on the social aspects of language.[7] I still believe that exploring the links between the semantic and the psychological is one fruitful way of shedding light on the complex business of meaning. With his rejection of Grice's work Schiffer denies himself one fruitful way of exploring the 'no-theory theory of meaning' that he espouses (if that is the right word) at the end of *Remnants*.

Explaining how Grice's work can help with the 'no-theory' position is rather complex; I shall say something brief about it in the final section. I want to begin by talking about Grice. Earlier I said that Schiffer rejects *both* elements of IBS: Griceanism and reductive naturalism. I want to begin by introducing distinctions in both. I want to suggest that Schiffer could have held on to some version of both and still ended up where he did at the end of *Remnants*—with a 'no-theory theory of meaning.' This is not to say that IBS as Schiffer understands it is compatible with the 'no-theory' position. Given one interpretation of Grice's work and one understanding of naturalism, Schiffer's IBS follows. Given quite another interpretation of Grice's work and another understanding of naturalism, something along the lines of Schiffer's 'no-theory' may be argued to follow. The interpretation of Grice and of naturalism from which Schiffer's IBS follows is familiar from Schiffer's work. It is the alternative interpretations on which I shall concentrate here.

13.2 Griceanism

When Schiffer first began to think about meaning and Grice's approach to that issue, it was probably not the case that he was thinking about its reductive potential—not consciously, at least. Rather, I venture that he was interested in Grice's proposed analysis because it seemed so useful as a way of replying to the question with which Schiffer begins *Meaning*: "What is meaning?"[8] At that time Schiffer was drawn to the idea that meaning has something to do with (in fact, quite a lot to do with) the intentions of speakers. Even Davidson (who at one time rejected so much of Grice's work)[9] was always careful to point out the role of intentions in meaning. In one place, Davidson identified three different kinds of intention that play a part in speech; one of these he labels 'semantic intentions,' intentions that one's words have a certain meaning.[10] Of course it is one thing to hold that intentions are relevant and another to take the route that Grice and Schiffer did. My point for the moment is that, at this time, Schiffer took it that reference to intentions had an important part to play in accounting for meaning.

Schiffer begins *Remnants* with the following question about meaning: "What makes it the case that a certain utterance means what it does? By virtue of what does any mark or sound, or sequence of them, come to have a given meaning?"[11] In *Remnants* Schiffer has two things to say about the philosopher's attempt to say what meaning is. The first is this. "The philosopher's invitation to say what makes it the case that x is F is an invitation to give a correct, interesting, and noncircular completion of 'x is F iff...', and this is what cannot be done."[12] The second is this: "That we find meaning in 'snow is white' but not ' ///;;;– ,' is the result of our cognitive apparatus, of the conceptual roles of our semantic concepts and the way they are related to the way we are 'programmed' to process productions of marks and sounds."[13] I want to say something about both of Schiffer's remarks.

Let me first address the point about a "correct, interesting and non-circular completion of 'x is F'..." I am not sure an invitation to say something about what makes it the case that x is F is *automatically* an invitation to give a non-circular completion of 'x is F iff...'; I am not even sure it is necessarily an invitation to give any sort of analysis. Earlier I mentioned that there are different possible interpretations of Grice's work. I could have made a more general point. The general point is that analysis need not always be taken to be reductive analysis. In *Meaning and Mind* I pointed out that there are two ways to understand what is going on in an analysis.[14] One way is to take the right-hand side of the biconditional as giving something more basic or more fundamental than what we have on the left-hand side. But another way is to take the biconditional as providing a detailed account of the interrelations between what is mentioned on either side of it. The first gives us a reductive, and the second a reciprocal, analysis. In connection with what I called 'reciprocal analysis'

I cited G. E. Moore, who once suggested that the two uses of analysis are: first, to relieve puzzlement about some concept; and second, to make our thoughts clearer.[15] In contrast to this, John Wisdom, for example, once argued that we engage in analysis in order to reach a new level of concept, one that is more fundamental and more basic than the ones under analysis.[16] Wisdom labeled his version 'new-level analysis' and he labelled Moore's approach 'same-level analysis.' What I took from this debate between Moore and Wisdom was the idea that we can interpret the analytic biconditional in two very different ways. It is clear, both from the above quotation and from much else that he has written, that Schiffer engages in the Gricean analysis for reductive purposes. But it is one thing to espouse the reductive interpretation and quite another to write as though no other interpretation exists. Even if one agreed that the invitation to say what makes it the case that x is F is an invitation to give a completion of 'x is F iff...,' it needn't be an invitation to give a *non-circular* completion of that schema.[17] Furthermore, as I said earlier, I don't see why it needs to be taken to be an invitation to engage in any sort of analysis. Plenty of philosophers—who have had no truck with Grice's analysis—have had a go at answering the question, 'what is meaning?'

Perhaps there is some significance in the specific question Schiffer formulates. Analysis looks tailor-made to provide an answer to the question that Schiffer asked in *Meaning*, as an analysis of meaning takes the form: 'Meaning is...' Not everyone, however, believes that such a direct response to the question, 'What is meaning?' is the most fruitful. Davidson, and many following him, take the line that meaning is what a theory of meaning is a theory of. This provides what I once called an 'indirect' account of meaning.[18] Proposal of a theory of meaning looks to be even less appropriate as an answer to the question Schiffer asks in *Remnants*. The question of *Remnants*, remember, is: 'What makes it the case that a certain utterance means what it does? By virtue of what does any mark or sound, or sequence of them, come to have a given meaning?' The reason why invoking a theory of meaning looks inappropriate in response to *this* question is that, in Davidson's hands at least, the theory on offer is not necessarily a theory that could be said to be employed by speakers. For Davidson, it is sufficient that the theory provides a perspicuous representation of *what would suffice* for meaning. A theory of meaning interpreted as Davidson interprets it, looks less promising as an answer to the question, 'What makes it the case that certain marks and sounds have the meaning they have?' This said, it can sometimes look as if Davidson's commitment to semantic intentions (*vide supra*) can be used as at least the beginning of an answer to that question. Of course it may not be true to the phenomenology of language use that speaker's intentions loom large here, but Davidson replies to this objection:

I agree that the speaker does not usually 'form an express intention', and he does not 'hold a theory', but I do say that even when a speaker is speaking in accord with a socially acceptable theory he speaks with the intention of being understood in a certain way, and this intention depends on his beliefs about his audience, in particular how he believes or assumes they will understand him.... I think someone acts intentionally when there is an answer to the question what his reasons in acting were, and one can often tell what an agent's reasons were by asking whether he would have acted as he had if he had not had those reasons. (1994: 13)[19]

However one thinks it best to approach the question, 'What is meaning?', it is arguable that the question Schiffer poses in *Remnants* puts the emphasis in a different place. The question, 'What makes it the case that...?,' looks more like it is asking specifically about what it is *about the speaker* that makes it the case that certain sounds and marks have meanings. Now there always were questions about the Gricean analysis of meaning concerning the psychological reality of what was mentioned on the right-hand side of the biconditional. Some appealed to the idea of tacit knowledge. In *Remnants* Schiffer mentions the idea that speakers and their audience undergo unconscious processes that correspond to the inferential processes reflected in the analytic biconditional, only to reject the idea on the grounds that that which is unconscious must be potentially (or possibly) conscious and that this is not the case with these processes.[20] Brian Loar once appealed to the idea of implicit expectations. He wrote: "When one addresses a sentence in normal circumstances to a person who is attentive, a speaker of one's language, etc., one has many implicit expectations about the person's impending psychological states..." (1981: 248). More directly to the point, there is nothing in Schiffer's theory, among the required intentions for meaning that *p*, which it is unrealistic to count among "normal speakers' implicit expectations" (1981: 248–9). Grice (and others) had yet another suggestion for how to think of the biconditional. Grice has suggested that we think of what the analysis describes as an optimal state or ideal.[21] Indeed, judging how far we, in the actual world, fall short of this ideal may be instructive (I give an example of this below).[22] The idea of an optimal state—like the idea of what would suffice—does not look like an answer to the question, 'What makes it the case that certain marks and sounds have meaning?' Neither of the latter two responses to the psychological reality problem is mentioned by Schiffer in *Remnants* when he cites this problem as one of his reasons for abandoning IBS (and Griceanism). That he doesn't even consider these responses may indicate that he is looking for quite a different sort of response. In *Remnants* Schiffer is clear that he is thinking about a person's understanding of language as a kind of *processing*. He is looking for a response to the 'What makes it the case...' question that makes clear the process whereby an audience can go from, say, an auditory perception of an utterance to knowledge of what was said. And it may be that thinking about the Gricean biconditional in this way is doomed to failure. But, as we have seen, there are other ways of thinking about that biconditional. My conclusion here is that at least one reason that Schiffer may have had for becoming disillusioned with Grice's work has less to do with that work than with the sort of question that Schiffer now wants answered. Grice's account of meaning may still have value, so long as one is clear about what work it is doing.[23]

Thus far I have argued that while Schiffer has lost heart in the reductive potential of Grice's work on meaning, there is still some non-reductive life left in that work. Although this may not make Grice's work of interest to *Schiffer*, it does mean that we have to take his rejection of that work with a pinch of salt. It would be a mistake to conclude that Schiffer has given us reason yet to reject the analysis per se. Furthermore, I suggested that another reason that Schiffer may have lost heart in Grice's work may be due to the question he is looking to answer. As with my first point, there may be some value left in Grice's work if one changes the question.

I expect Schiffer (and others) may insist that the interest in language *processing* is not only what interests him but what should interest us all. After all, isn't this the real question? Perhaps the more purely philosophical question once made sense, but with all that has happened in linguistics and cognitive science surely philosophers should see that there is really only one question to ask. I think Grice gives the best reply to this way of thinking. One abiding interest of Grice's—one that runs throughout his work—is an interest in value. That may be a little nebulous, but Grice didn't think it necessary to expand. What he did suggest is that interpreting the analysis of meaning as an optimal state was one way of seeing how value enters into semantics.[24] I would suggest that that there is much to understand about language which has nothing (or very little) to do with the actual *processing* of auditory and visual cues. Both the analysis of meaning and the development of a theory of meaning can do something towards promoting this understanding. I see Schiffer's interest in how we process language as closely connected with his interest in reduction. My point is only that we needn't reject outright the Gricean analysis of meaning. If we shift our interests and questions we may yet find some value in that analysis.

But what about the very idea of philosophical analysis? Isn't it, in the words of Timothy Williamson, a "degenerating research program" (2000: 31)? Schiffer certainly seems to agree with Williamson. In *Remnants* Schiffer writes:

Although philosophers have been trying to give reductive analyses of philosophically interesting concepts since even before the time of Plato, there has not yet been one clear success. This is especially depressing when one compares the history of philosophy with that of the natural sciences. Is it that philosophy is still awaiting its Newton, or that much of it has been barking up the wrong tree? (263)

It is clear that, having waited for a while, Schiffer has decided that philosophy is barking up the wrong tree. In keeping with what I have been saying, I would suggest that philosophy has to be clear about the questions it is—and the questions it is not— in the business of asking. This is a rather delicate matter, and one I can only touch on in this chapter. There is a real trend in philosophy away from analysis, and it is hard to blame Schiffer for joining the trend. But it is interesting to contemplate the reasons behind the trend. Schiffer hints at stagnation (reminiscent of Paul Churchland's reason for rejecting common-sense psychological theory). But even Fodor is content to employ analysis where it suits him. For all his commitment to arguments from best explanation throughout his work in the philosophy of mind, it is easy to forget that Fodor also has a strong commitment to the Gricean analysis of meaning (albeit as part of a larger program).

One should not forget (and Schiffer should not forget) that it is not the case that the only successful analysis is one that can give watertight (i.e. counter-example proof) necessary and sufficient conditions. The thought here is not unfamiliar, but it does bear repeating. Searle put it well some time back when he wrote:

Concepts...do not have absolutely knock down necessary and sufficient conditions....But this insight into the looseness of our concepts...should not lead us into a rejection of the very enterprise of philosophical analysis; rather the conclusion to be drawn is that certain forms of analysis, especially analysis into necessary and sufficient conditions, are likely to involve (in varying degrees) idealization of the concept analysed. (Searle 1971: 55)

Searle concludes that when we come upon counter-examples to the analysis, this need not lead us to reject the analysis. There is another option, which is to say why these examples do run counter to the analysis; to give an "explanation of why and how they depart from the paradigm cases."[25] Understanding both the idealization of meaning and the problems we encounter in achieving this ideal can give us some insight into this business we call meaning.[26]

Earlier I mentioned the idea of an ideal or optimal state as a way of avoiding the problem of saying how the Gricean biconditional can represent a psychological reality. I am now mentioning the ideal or optimal state in connection with the problem of being able to give necessary and sufficient conditions for meaning that are not open to counter-example. Once again, we see that Schiffer may have been premature in his rejection of Grice's work. Perhaps there is some value in an analysis for which there are outstanding counter-examples. Let me outline what I see as one of the more important lessons that can be learned from the failure to rule out counter-examples to the sufficiency of the Gricean analysis of meaning. Schiffer himself—along with P. F. Strawson—did much to show that, with enough ingenuity, it is possible to devise situations where the given conditions for meaning are fulfilled and yet we would not say that the speaker meant anything (the conditions do not suffice for meaning). The reason, time and again, is the possibility of deceit. In response to the counter-examples, Schiffer, Strawson, and Grice each amended the original analysis (adding to its complexity) in the hopes of ruling out this deceit. Strawson feared that deceit might still creep in, and Schiffer was the one to come up with ever more complex situations where deceit could be practiced.[27] If we think of the analysis as approximating to an ideal, then we might say that the ideal of communication is not something we, mere mortals, can achieve. The reason we cannot achieve this is that we are capable of deceit. And the cleverer we are the greater the potential for exploiting situations so as to deceive. Deception, we might conclude, lies at the heart of human communication. (Consider here Grice's just-so story about how we progressed from natural to non-natural meaning.)[28] By thinking about ideals and how we fall short of them, we begin to understand something that is important about human communication. By contemplating the ideal, we learn much about sublunary arrangements.

Which isn't to deny that other questions about, for example, language processing aren't important as well. But, as Schiffer correctly says, such questions are not philosophical questions.[29] About this we might agree.

For the sake of completeness, we might also consider the several other arguments that Schiffer advances in Chapter 9 of *Remnants* against the specifics of the Gricean analysis. To be clear, these are not arguments to the effect that the analysis was aimed at the wrong question, or arguments against the very idea of analysis, but arguments aimed against specific claims entailed by the analysis or counter-examples to the analysis. As far as I can see, to use Fodor's metaphor, where Schiffer once believed that Griceanism could cash its checks, he now doubts they can. Schiffer opts to lose his faith; Fodor opts to keep it. As I see it, whether one loses ones faith or keeps to it depends upon what profit one hopes to gain. As I have explained, Schiffer's loss of faith in Griceanism goes hand-in-hand with his loss of faith in reductive naturalism. If reduction cannot be made to work, *there is no need for Grice's work*. And if there is need for that work, there is no motive to work towards cashing its checks. Fodor, in contrast to Schiffer, has lost faith in neither reductive naturalism nor Griceanism. And it is ultimately Fodor's faith in reductive naturalism that drives his faith in Griceanism. As Schiffer was once so keen to tell us: Grice offers the only viable way of reducing the semantic to the physical. Notice that the faith that Fodor keeps is not terribly high profile. I know of no papers where Fodor attempts to meet the objections and counter-examples to Grice's analysis of meaning that abound in the literature. I want to introduce another motivation for keeping the faith in Grice's work. It is not because that work offers the only way to reduce semantics, but because Grice's work shows us *a way to understand the semantic without having to resort to reduction*. My motivation clearly differs from Fodor's, as mine has nothing to do with reductive ambitions. Notice that at the heart of that reductive motivation lies an important disagreement with Schiffer. At the end of *Remnants* Schiffer holds that, as reduction is not viable, we can only say what is responsible for our semantic knowledge. That is, we can say that as a result of things happening at the physical/neural level, we have the semantic knowledge that we have; we can say no more. But this strikes me as saying that we mean what we mean because our bodies/brains process information in the ways that they do, and this is no kind of understanding at all. Schiffer, as we have seen, is pessimistic about philosophy's capacity for offering further understanding; he seems to think that all philosophers can do is clear away confusions that stand in the way of our appreciating this. But I think this not just depressing for philosophy, but also for humanity (if I may put the point a little dramatically). We not only yearn for understanding, but there is much we can understand about this business we call 'meaning.' Of course there are important things happening in our bodies and brains that make this all possible. But there is an important story to be told at the level where meaning is produced and sustained as well. That story requires that we mention intentions. The question still remains how far we can follow Grice, but we should not lose sight of his work in the attempt to gain further understanding of meaning. But of course, my motivation for still clinging to what one might call the 'remnants of Griceanism' presupposes a non-reductive interpretation of that work.

13.3 Naturalism

So much for the other interpretation of the Gricean element of IBS. I want now to turn to reductive naturalism. It is an obvious point that reduction is one thing and naturalism another. But working through the obvious can give us an interesting perspective on the progress of Schiffer's thinking. In what follows I shall work through this obvious point.

In *Remnants* Schiffer lays out various commonly held hypotheses. Amongst them is the hypothesis that there is a token-token identity thesis that Schiffer glosses as "your present belief that you are reading is a neural state-token of yours" (Schiffer's hypothesis 6), and the hypothesis that semantic and psychological facts are not irreducibly semantic or psychological, but can be revealed to be facts statable in sentences devoid of semantic, mentalistic, and intentional idioms (Schiffer's hypothesis 8).[30] Schiffer explains that hypothesis 8 goes further than hypothesis 6 as it refuses to recognize anything, of *any* ontological category, that is irreducibly semantic or psychological.[31] Schiffer once accepted both hypotheses 6 and 8.

At the end of *Remnants* Schiffer rejects hypothesis 8; but he continues to accept 6. We do well to be clear about what is being rejected. The Schiffer of the early 1980s (i.e., pre-*Remnants*) was committed to reduction. In his early paper 'Intention-Based Semantics,' Schiffer is clear that "we should not be prepared to maintain that there *are* semantic or psychological facts unless we are prepared to maintain that such facts are completely determined by, are nothing over and above, physical facts" (Schiffer 1982: 1–2). Furthermore, Schiffer maintains in that paper that "the only plausible nonmentalist account of belief, which makes determinate sense of it, is...an *extended functionalist* account."[32] Interestingly, in this early paper Schiffer identifies as his reason for rejecting irreducibly psychological facts is commitment to the following: (i) there is a complete physical explanation of every bodily movement, which provides causally necessary and sufficient conditions for the occurrence of that movement; (ii) beliefs and desires are causes of bodily movements; and (iii) "the property of being a belief is a causally necessary property of those beliefs which are, in the way typical of beliefs, causes of behavior" (1982: 18).[33] At this point in his philosophical development Schiffer holds that "it is not enough merely to suppose that particular beliefs are physical states; one needs to account for what it is about a particular physical state-token which makes it a belief" (1982: 19). The property Schiffer favors for this identification is what he calls an "extended functional property."[34] It was a commitment to extended functionalism as the way to avoid irreducible belief properties that Schiffer saw as a way to ensure that the psychological is independent of the semantical. Why? Because Schiffer did not believe "that there is any [extended functionalist] theory with respect to which belief and some [outer-language semantical] construct are...co-definable" (1982: 24). In other words, it is Schiffer's view in that early paper that extended functionalism (which is required to ensure that psychological and semantical facts are nothing over and above physical facts) cannot be made to work on the assumption of the inter-definability of the psychological and the outer-public-language semantical. This ensures that belief is not a relation to public-outer-language semantical properties. And this ensures (the possibility of) the truth of a reductive interpretation of the Gricean program.

The difficulties with this reductive naturalist program are, according to the Schiffer of *Remnants*, manifold. As we have already seen, Schiffer came to despair over the possibility of a complete counter-example-proof formulation of the Gricean biconditional (*vide supra*); he also came to despair over extended functionalism. And, relatedly, Schiffer came to despair over the possibility of giving a relational account of belief.[35] This is an example of the overkill I referred to at the outset of this chapter. In Chapter 2 of *Remnants* Schiffer shows why he now thinks that what he sometimes refers to as 'propositional-functionalism' (the functionalism of Brian Loar)[36] is in serious difficulty. The lion's share of that difficulty is concentrated around the very idea of the theory that is used to define belief and desire (taken as theoretical constructs). The Schiffer of *Remnants* has objections to all the attempts to construct this theory.[37] He also believes that there are problems with the very idea of propositions.[38]

Schiffer believes that he has hit a *cul-de-sac* in the search for a reduction. What he does at this point is a little radical. He rejects the very thing that cannot be reduced. Thus, Schiffer holds that there are no genuinely objective, language-independent belief properties and facts (a position he labels 'Ontological Physicalism'). He then couples this position with another (which he labels 'Sentential Physicalism'), which holds that there are true but irreducible belief-ascribing sentences. Given Sentential Physicalism we can say that there are true but irreducible belief-ascribing sentences, and so there are believers and '(possibly) beliefs.' However, as Ontological Physicalism commits one to holding that psychological entities are not irreducibly psychological, "believers are bodies, that is, occupiers of space, and beliefs, in humans at least, are states of the nervous system."[39] Schiffer explains that in order to understand his position one must make a clear distinction between the reduction of properties and the reduction of sentences. He points out that although each of these reductions has a strong impact on the other, things are different if one denies the existence of belief properties rather than adopt a reductive position with respect to them. Schiffer's position in *Remnants* is that one may deny the existence of belief properties and still hold that there are true belief-ascribing sentences.

As this position depends crucially on the rejection of belief properties, we do well to remind ourselves of Schiffer's argument at this point. Here it is: Firstly, if there were a genuinely objective, language-independent (non-pleonastic) belief property, then it would be expressed by a certain predicate, e.g. the property of believing that philosophers are playful would be expressed by the predicate 'believes that philosophers are playful.' If there were a genuinely objective, language-independent property of belief it would have to be non-composite. But if it *were* non-composite, its corresponding predicate would be non-composite, and that would make English unlearnable. So there are no genuinely objective, language-independent belief properties.

Now, an important question here is why Schiffer holds that, if it existed, the belief property would have to be non-composite. The answer to this is, in effect, the core thesis of *Remnants*. To hold that belief properties are non-composite is in effect to deny that belief is a relation between believers and things believed—and this is what Schiffer does in Chapters 2 through 5 of *Remnants*. So *Schiffer* is in a position to deny belief properties. So *Schiffer* is in a position to hold that, although there are no belief properties, there are true belief-ascribing sentences. I have explained the logical space into which Schiffer's position of Ontological Physicalism and Sentential Dualism fits, but one could equally have opted for eliminativism across the board. Schiffer does not choose to go this route. His reason for this is implied in a question he poses for himself:

What would justify one in denying Sentential Dualism at the cost of denying both that marks and sounds have meaning and truth values and that people have beliefs and other propositional attitudes? (For it is obvious that marks and sounds have no semantic features if the people who produce them have no beliefs and intentions.)[40]

Of course Schiffer has the likes of Quine to contend with here, but as with so many others, with Quine Schiffer begs to differ. Schiffer considers a comment by Quine to the effect that there is a connection between the acceptance of Sentential Dualism and Brentano's idea of an autonomous science of intention.[41] In support of his acceptance of Sentential Dualism Schiffer notes the distinction between reduction and realization. It is only realization that is required if one is to hold (as Schiffer *does* hold) that "physics is in some sense basic and explains all physical events."[42] One could say that realization plays the role in *Remnants* that reduction played in IBS; the Schiffer of *Remnants* believes that realization is sufficient. Sentential Dualism is Schiffer's preferred position.

Now let's be clear about what is now being rejected. The rejection of a reduction of types of belief properties is a rejection of just the position Schiffer was hoping for when he put forward IBS. The idea, to recap, was that the Gricean analysis be taken to give us a reduction of the semantic to the psychological, and that further work on the psychological would yield a reduction here are well. But, we might ask, does IBS *require* type reduction? I am not so sure. Maybe IBS was never clear about these things (or better: never explored these issues). Fodor, for one, is clear about how he understands IBS. In his review of *Remnants* Fodor identifies two doctrines which together form IBS: (i) the idea that semantic properties of natural language expressions should reduce to the intentional properties of the mental states of hearers/speakers, and (ii) the idea that "that there should be something *naturalistically specifiable* that is—as Schiffer likes to put it—*what makes it the case* that someone believes that P (call this the Naturalization Program)" (Fodor 1989: 177). In his early writing (especially in 'Intention-Based Semantics') Schiffer has a tendency to talk only about 'reduction'; Fodor, as we can see, talks of 'the naturalization programme.' *Is* there a real difference between a program of reduction and one of naturalization? There is. Both positions could be considered to be anti-Cartesian dualism, but a commitment to reduction is stronger than a commitment to naturalism. As I see it, what should be driving Schiffer's IBS is a certain sort of anti-dualism. If a certain sort of anti-dualism is what one is aiming for, then there are ways of achieving it even if one side-steps reduction (and it is possible to achieve this without having to give up on belief properties).

Notice that what the Schiffer of *Remnants* rejects are belief *properties*. He assumes "without argument that if [for example] Ava's coming to have her present belief state-token is a neural event, then that state-token which is her belief is a neural state-token."[43] In other words, he accepts token physicalism (hypothesis 6, cited above). This is directly in opposition to his earlier view (*vide supra*: "it is not enough merely to suppose that particular beliefs are physical states..."). Along with token physicalism, Schiffer accepts what he calls 'a mild supervenience thesis' which he formulates as follows: given that [for example] Ava believes that a car is coming toward her, she also believes this in every possible world that is physically indistinguishable from the actual world.[44] What Schiffer does not think one gets from this token-physicalism-cum-weak-supervenience is either a causal explanation of why people have the beliefs that they have or conditions necessary and sufficient for that belief in non-psychological and non-intentional terms.[45]

If we return to my point, above, and take on board the idea that reduction is not the only way of achieving what might be thought of as the general underlying aim of IBS (i.e. anti-dualism), then this underlying aim can be achieved if we discard reductionism in favor of token identity. As Schiffer is committed to a token identity at the end of *Remnants*, we could conclude that this work is still in the *spirit*—albeit not the letter—of IBS.

Now we may well ask why Schiffer formulates issues here in terms of reduction and not a more generalized anti-dualism. It may be thought that it is anti-dualism that *really* informs IBS. IBS need not be formulated in terms of reduction. If anti-dualism is what really informs IBS, then *as far as this is concerned* Schiffer need not give up on IBS. After all, Schiffer is still an anti-dualist. But perhaps one needs to be a little careful. Schiffer is an anti-Cartesian-Dualist but—as we have seen—he *is* a *sentential* Dualist. I think the key point for Schiffer emerges when he writes:

what is at issue is nothing less than an obnoxious metaphysical dualism of properties versus a benign dualism of conceptual roles for belief and other *predicates*. The irreducibility of belief *predicates* is an innocuous feature of their conceptual roles and implies no insupportable ontological proposition whatever.[46]

Perhaps what we should think is that it is really *physicalism* that informs IBS, rather than anti-dualism. If that were the case, then it is arguable that, as Schiffer holds to a *form* of physicalism—token physicalism—he need not have abandoned IBS on *that* account.

My question is whether one needs more than token physicalism in order to sustain IBS. The problem is that IBS isn't a doctrine that exists far beyond Schiffer and his circle. He pretty much can, and does, say what is part of IBS. And if we look at the specific doctrines that Schiffer took to support IBS, reduction of the psychological is an important part.[47] Of course, reduction requires a commitment to the properties to be reduced. The Schiffer of *Remnants* does not just reject reduction, but he rejects a commitment to the very properties to be reduced. It is the very foundations (or parameters) of IBS that are now being questioned. Schiffer has really thrown up the whole deck and decided to have a radical re-shuffle of the cards. It might be clearer to say that IBS has been pre-empted rather than rejected. It can be agreed that the letter of IBS is gone at the end of *Remnants*, but I am suggesting that its spirit remains. IBS was designed to be anti-Cartesian-dualist and physicalist—in short, naturalist. Reduction was just the method employed for reaching these goals. In so far as the Schiffer of *Remnants* is anti-Cartesian-dualist and physicalist, the spirit of IBS as a naturalist position is maintained. But now IBS is exposed as a method—a means to an end. And if we can agree that the end is more important than the means, then we can say that the spirit of IBS is alive at the end of *Remnants*.

If we go back and adopt a non-reductive interpretation of Grice's work, and add to this an anti-Cartesian, physicalist, naturalism, what we get is a way of making Grice's work relevant to the new Schiffer.[48] Dropping the specific IBS means to a naturalistic end, we can begin to see another distinctive shape for the work begun by Grice. We can now see that, by insisting on taking his later work as a rejection of his earlier work, Schiffer may be thought to have missed an opportunity—an opportunity to bring his ideas at the end of *Remnants* into line with a non-reductive interpretation of his earlier Gricean work on meaning. Or perhaps I should say that Schiffer missed the opportunity to bring his ideas at the end of *Remnants* into line with a more general 'anti-reductive' stance. It is reduction of the psychological that Schiffer has come to think won't work. This leads him to see the options available as: (i) Cartesian dualism, (ii) eliminativism, or (his preferred option), (iii) the rejection of belief properties (in anything more than a pleonastic sense). *Why can't we simply go back on the original Gricean reduction of the semantic to the psychological?* This can then be worked into a picture of meaning and mind that avoids Cartesian dualism, avoids eliminativism, and avoids the need to reject belief properties. On the plus side, it leaves room for Grice's work in an expanded anti-reductionist picture of meaning.

13.4 The No-Theory Theory of Meaning

I want to conclude by considering the position Schiffer introduces at the end of *Remnants*, the no-theory theory of meaning. I have suggested that there are ways of exploring this option that need not involve a total rejection of Grice's work on meaning. In particular I suggested that there is an interpretation of Grice's work and of what was driving IBS which—had Schiffer attended to them rather than the interpretations he favored—could have led him to the no-theory theory of meaning position with which he ends *Remnants*.

Before explaining the alternative which he may have missed, I want first to explore a little what Schiffer may have had in mind when he advocated the no-theory theory of meaning. Talk of the no-theory theory comes right at the very end of *Remnants*. And he amplifies:

What I mean is that if one were to make a list of all the things philosophers have in mind when they talk of 'theories of meaning or intentional content,' then I would claim that there are no true theories satisfying the descriptions on that list. The questions being asked in the philosophy of language that would require positive theories as answers all have false presuppositions.[49]

The first of these is a rather sweeping statement. I am reminded of the opening pages of Paul Horwich's book *Meaning*, where Horwich sets out a whole host of questions and issues that philosophers have discussed in connection with the innocent seeming question, 'What is meaning?' It is Horwich's opinion that the legacy of twentieth-century philosophy is less of a theory than a series of observations about meaning (which, in Horwich's opinion, provide "an accumulation of increasingly severe constraints on an adequate account of [meaning]").[50] In the light of Horwich's comments, one is led to ask what theories of meaning Schiffer has in mind when he comes to his conclusion that none is true. Schiffer would no doubt reply that his real point comes when we notice that questions in the philosophy of language "all have false presuppositions" (*vide supra*). What are these? Well, presumably they are the ideas that Schiffer rejects in *Remnants*: the existence of psychological properties, compositionality, and the relational account of belief. As Fodor has remarked in a slightly different connection, "The problem with this way of arguing is that it's convincing only if you have a cat for every mousehole" (Fodor 1989: 178).

I don't want to end with a question about exactly what Schiffer thinks won't work. Rather, I want to pursue the line suggested by Mark Johnston when he writes, "I share

[Schiffer's] view that a correct theory about meaning would be in a certain sense no theory but a statement of the obvious coupled with a resistance to the urge to find a hidden and substantial nature for meaning to have."[51] This is an idea familiar from the work of Wittgenstein, and Schiffer himself does mention Wittgenstein in connection with his no-theory idea.[52] Johnston himself favors a position that he calls 'minimalism,' and he is clear that what characterizes minimalism is that it follows the contours of our platitudes about meaning without reifying talk about meaning. In his discussion of minimalism Johnston highlights another important idea. According to Johnston, minimalism is "at odds with any attempt to psychologize a theory of meaning, to talk of it as implicitly known and hence such that knowledge of its propositions could be quite generally the causal explanatory basis of competence in our native language."[53] In his reply to Johnston, Schiffer agrees with Johnston and adds that "understanding the meanings of expressions is not something that lies behind and is the causal-explanatory basis of the ability to use the expression" (Schiffer 1988: 59).

With mention of causal explanations we hit up against another important and complex strand in Schiffer's work. It is a strand exposed also by Fodor in his debate with Schiffer. Schiffer is inclined to insist that what he is *really* out to deny is the relational account of belief (and positions consequent upon it). Fodor, on the other hand, thinks that the denial of a relational account of belief is less damaging to IBS than Schiffer's denial of psychological properties (Fodor: 1989: 180). As we saw earlier (section 13.1, above), Fodor is concerned to defend IBS because it can help philosophers solve a Great Metaphysical Problem. Fodor points out that what matters to IBS is Intentional Realism, and what is required for Intentional Realism is the existence of psychological properties. Now Fodor begs to differ with Schiffer over the existence of psychological properties. According to Fodor, psychological properties exist because psychological laws require that they exist and "all the evidence suggests that there are intentional psychological laws" (Fodor 1989: 180).[54] Here we reach another place where Schiffer parts company with Fodor. Schiffer does not agree that there are intentional psychological laws, so he is free to deny the existence of psychological properties. While Schiffer is busy distancing himself from Fodor and IBS, he is—as we have just seen—moving towards Johnston's form of minimalism.[55] Furthermore, it is clear that one of the important strands in *Remnants* is a denial of a causal explanatory basis of our ability to act.

Here I have reached a topic that I cannot develop in the space that remains. To do this topic justice I would need to discuss Schiffer's rejection of psychological laws and why he holds that *ceteris paribus* generalizations cannot be completed. In the course of his rejection of psychological laws in *Remnants* Schiffer writes: "Rather than conclude that there are no beliefs and desires because those concepts cannot be embedded in theorizing of a certain kind, one would do better to conclude that that is not their point."[56] A few lines earlier Schiffer suggests that the utility of psychological concepts is exhausted by their applicability to our quotidian needs; rigorous scientific theorizing, claims Schiffer, needs quite other concepts. Following this line of thought, what we get is a certain 'minimalism' that follows our psychological talk without positing psychological properties and without the hope that our psychological states can be taken to represent a causal explanation of our actions. This is a minimalism in psychology that parallels the minimalism in semantics that Johnston proposes and that Schiffer claims to accept (*vide supra*). Minimalism is another way of understanding the no-theory theory of meaning that Schiffer proposes at the end of *Remnants*. If one takes the no-theory to be a rejection of hidden structures, then we see once again that what is really driving Schiffer's thought here is an anti-reductionism. Once this anti-reductionism is established, it opens the door for further anti-reductionist positions. The relationship between the psychological and the semantical can also be viewed non-reductively. This is precisely what Grice's work on meaning can be thought to provide. This is something that Schiffer can exploit if he is careful not to throw out Grice's work on meaning altogether, when he rejects the reductive interpretation of it. Of course, Schiffer may not think that Grice's work—even considered non-reductively—is of value here. But the argument for this is not yet on the table. There is reason yet, when thinking about meaning, for clinging to what I earlier called some "remnants of Griceanism."

Notes

1. H. P. Grice's seminal work, 'Meaning' was published in 1957, and this was followed by a series of related papers (see Grice 1989a, Part I). In 1972 Schiffer published *Meaning*, the work that developed the program of work begun by Grice. Brian Loar published his extended discussion of Grice's work, *Mind and Meaning*, in 1981.
2. In his paper 'Retrospective Epilogue,' written in 1987, Grice considers the issue of reductionism and explicitly distances himself from this enterprise. See footnote 24 below.
3. Schiffer (2003: 9).
4. Fodor also doesn't like what he sees as the whiff of verificationism about Schiffer's new position. See p. 218 of *Remnants* where Schiffer suggests that we discover what is happening at the physical-neural level (where, by the way, he allows that composition is in order) by mapping formulae at the physical-neural level to sentences of a given language with a little help from our understanding of that language. This leads Fodor to respond: "But what has to be the case for us to discover that *S* isn't to the point. What's to the point is what has to be the case for *S* to *be* true" (1989: 189).
5. *Remnants*, Chapter 10.
6. Avramides (1989).
7. The references are scattered throughout much of Davidson's writing. See, for example, Davidson (1986) and (1994). In his paper 'The Structure and Content of Truth' (Davidson 1990) Davidson writes: "The influence of H. P. Grice's 'Meaning'...will be evident here" (310–11). For a discussion of the ways in which Davidson's work can be seen to be more closely aligned with Grice's, see Avramides (2001).
8. In *Meaning* Schiffer moves swiftly on to refine his question, but his opening gambit is still illuminating.
9. See, for example, Davidson (1984: 143).
10. See Davidson (1993: 298–9). In 'The second person' (Davidson 1992) Davidson writes: "My central aim is...only to emphasize, following Grice, the central role of intention in communication" (258). We see here one way in which Davidson came to align his work with that of Grice. Cf. footnote 7, above.
11. *Remnants*, 2.
12. *Remnants*, 263–4.

13. *Remnants*, 264.
14. Avramides (1989), Chapter 2, Section 3.
15. See G. E. Moore, 'The Justification of Analysis' (Moore 1966).
16. See Wisdom (1934).
17. In a 'Retrospective Epilogue' (Grice 1989b), written in 1987, Grice writes the following: "Reductive analysis might be called for to get away from unclarity not to get to some predesignated clarifiers" (351). And Grice says that he puts forward his analysis of meaning as an attempt to "get away from unclarity." Despite calling his analysis "reductive" Grice is careful to distinguish this from *reductionism* (351). It would have been clearer if he had simply dropped the word "reductive" altogether in connection with analysis. Nevertheless, his meaning is clear. A few lines earlier he insists that his is an analysis that is "unhampered" by such constraints as "avoiding circularity." In the terms I prefer, Grice clearly sees himself as proposing a reciprocal, as opposed to a reductive, analysis of meaning.
18. Avramides (1989), Chapter 1, Section 2.
19. Davidson (1994: 13). In this connection see also, Strawson (1971: 284–5).
20. See *Remnants*, Chapter 9, Section 9.5.
21. See Section III of Grice (1982). Grandy and Warner support this suggestion. See their Introduction to Grandy and Warner (1986), Section 2.
22. Grandy and Warner give this example of the use of an ideal from sailing: there is an optimal setting for sails that maximizes forward thrust but is difficult (if not impossible) to achieve when sailing due to wind shifts and changes in direction caused by the waves. See Grandy and Warner (1986: 25–6).
23. Once we begin to look at questions that drive the work, we find another curious reversal in the move from *Remants* to *Things*. As we shall see below, Schiffer moves from a position where he rejects the reality of psychological and semantic facts (*Remnants*) to one where he accepts them (*Things*). It is arguable that Schiffer has moved *back* to an interest in questions of the form, 'What is meaning?' and is, thus, closer to the work in his first book in his third book than in his second. Notice that Schiffer begins his paper 'Meanings' (Schiffer 2002) with the following,

> Do there exist such entities as *the things we mean*? If such things do exist, they are also the things we believe and assert, and thereby the things in terms of which we must understand what our words and sentences mean. The question about the existence of the things we mean and believe is the first question in the theory of linguistic and mental content, for its answer sets the agenda for the theory of content... In this chapter I assume, as a working hypothesis, that there are such things as the things we mean and believe...". (79)

This return to the question that interested him very early in his career raises once again the question I asked earlier about Schiffer's commitment to Grice's work by the time of this latest work.

24. See Grice (1982), Section III, where Grice writes,

> The general idea that I want to explore, and which seems to me to have some plausibility, is that something has been left out... in the analyses, definitions, expansions, and so on, of semantic notions, and particularly various notions of meaning. What has been left out has in fact been left out because it is something which everyone regards with horror, at least when in a scientific or theoretical frame of mind: the notion of value. (297)

25. Searle (1971: 55).
26. Cf. Grandy and Warner who write that, although we often make do with what they call "rules of thumb," we must acknowledge that "to spot exceptions and resolve conflicts as well as handle situations not covered by the rules, one needs to know what the optimum is" (Grandy and Warner 1986: 26).
27. For a summary of these problems and the proposals to counter them in the analysis see Avramides (1989), Chapter 2, Section 2.
28. See Section II of Grice (1982).
29. See, for example, *Remnants*, 271.
30. See the Introduction to *Remnants*.
31. Cf. *Remnants*, 23:

> One can be an antidualist about minds and a dualist about mental states, or an antidualist about mental states and a dualist about mental properties. The most thoroughgoing antidualism, or physicalism, is one that is antidualist with respect to all three kinds of mental entities. It will not countenance anything, of any ontological category, that is irreducibly mental, neither minds nor mental states nor mental properties.

32. For an account of extended functionalism, see Schiffer (1982: 17). Schiffer's idea of extended functionalism builds on the functionalism of Lewis, Field, and Loar. It is designed to accommodate intuitions about Twin-earth. For the purposes of this paper, what is important is *why* Schiffer opts for extended functionalism. I explain this below.
33. Schiffer elaborates: "Consider that state of mine which was my belief that a car was coming: had that state not been a belief it would not have been a cause of my stepping back." Schiffer finds this idea "palpably plausible," and believes that this idea is "evidently overlooked by those who are attracted to a *Verstehen* construal of belief-desire explanations of behavior" (130).
34. As with extended functionalism (footnote 32, above) I refer the reader to Schiffer (1982: 21 ff).
35. What Schiffer holds is that, IBS cannot be true whether or not the relational theory of propositional attitudes is true. It cannot be true if the relational theory is true because Schiffer now thinks it is not possible to find objects of belief with non-public-language semantic features. He thinks propositions won't do, sentences won't do, etc. And, since IBS *presupposes* the relational theory of propositional attitudes, it cannot be true if that is not true. Schiffer now rejects the relational theory. IBS is, therefore, caught whichever way it turns.
36. See Loar (1981).
37. Schiffer concludes *Remnants*, Chapter 2: "If believing is a relation to propositions, and if there is a specification of that relation in nonmentalistic terms, then that specification is not the product of any functionalist theory considered in this chapter" (47).
38. In *Remnants*, Chapter 3 he writes: "I thought that the only serious problem unique to the propositional theory of propositional attitudes was that, being creatures of darkness, propositions were hard to believe in. I now realize that I was wrong: the real trouble with propositions is that, even granted that they exist, propositional attitudes cannot be relations to them" (49).
39. *Remnants*, 143.
40. *Remnants*, 156.
41. See *Remnants*, 157. The passage from Quine that Schiffer is here considering is to be found in Quine's *Word and Object* (Quine 1960: 221).
42. *Remnants*, 158.
43. *Remnants*, 149.
44. *Remnants*, 165.

45. *Remnants*, 173. For more on Schiffer's commitment to causal explanation, see section 13.4, below.
46. *Remnants*, 163. Schiffer explains conceptual role thus: "The 'conceptual role' of an inner formula, we may still say, is that complex counterfactual property of the formula knowledge of which would inform one of the conditions under which the formula would occur in B [a belief box inside each human being's head]" (*Remnants*, 167).
47. If we look at the introduction to the second edition of *Meaning* Schiffer mentions two motivations for IBS. They are (i) the fact that meaning supervenes on use; and (ii) physicalism (see xii). Having mentioned physicalism, Schiffer then goes on to explain that he only means to consider physicalism *reductively* (xiii). And his reason for this is that reductive physicalism is needed to explain "how psychological facts can be used to provide correct causal explanations of physical facts." My point is that Schiffer could have stopped at physicalism, and left reductionism to one side.
48. Or at least, relevant to the Schiffer of *Remnants*.
49. *Remnants*, 265.
50. Horwich (1998: 2).
51. Johnston (1988: 42).
52. *Remnants*, 266.
53. Johnston (1988: 42; cf. 38–9).
54. Furthermore, Fodor does not think any of what he wants requires a *reduction* of psychological properties.
55. *Things* has much in common with Johnston's minimalist semantics.
56. *Remnants*, 161.

Bibliography

Avramides, A. (1989). *Meaning and Mind*. Cambridge: MIT Press.
Avramides, A. (2001). "Davidson, Grice and the Social Aspects of Language." In *Paul Grice's Heritage*, edited by G. Cosenza, Turnhout: Brepols.
Davidson, D. (1984). "Belief and the Basis of Meaning." In *Inquiries into Truth and Interpretation*, Oxford: Oxford University Press.
Davidson, D. (1986). "A Nice Derangement of Epitaphs." In *Truth and Interpretation: Perspectives on the Philosophy of Donald Davidson*, edited by E. Lepore, Oxford: Basil Blackwell.
Davidson, D. (1990). "The Structure and Content of Truth." *Journal of Philosophy* 87: 279–328.
Davidson, D. (1992). "The Second Person." *Midwest Studies in Philosophy* 17: 255–67.
Davidson, D. (1993). "Locating Literary Language." In *Literary Theory After Davidson*, edited by R. W. Dasenbrock, University Park: Pennsylvania University Press.
Davidson, D. (1994). "The Social Aspect of Language." In *The Philosophy of Michael Dummett*, edited by B. McGuinness and G. Olivieri, Dordrecht: Kluwer.
Fodor, J. (1989). "Stephen Schiffer's Dark Night of the Soul: A Review of *Remnants of Meaning*." *Philosophy and Phenomenological Research* 50: 409–23; reprinted in *A Theory of Content and Other Essays*. Cambridge: MIT Press, 1990.
Fodor, J. (1991). "Reply to Schiffer." In *Meaning in Mind: Fodor and His Critics*, edited by G. Rey and B. Loewer, Oxford: Blackwell.
Grandy, R. and R. Warner (eds.). (1986). *Philosophical Grounds of Rationality: Intentions, Categories, Ends*. Clarendon Press: Oxford.
Grice, H. P. (1957). "Meaning." *The Philosophical Review* 66: 377–88; reprinted in Grice (1989a).

Grice, H. P. (1982). "Meaning Revisited." In *Mutual Knowledge*, edited by N. V. Smith, New York: Academic Press; reprinted in Grice (1989a).
Grice, H. P. (1989a). *Studies in the Way of Words*. Cambridge: Harvard University Press.
Grice, H. P. (1989b). 'Retrospective Epilogue.' In Grice (1989a).
Horwich, P. (1998). *Meaning*. Oxford: Clarendon Press.
Johnston, M. (1988). "The End of the Theory of Meaning." *Mind and Language* 3: 28–42.
Loar, B. (1981). *Mind and Meaning*. Cambridge: Cambridge University Press.
Moore, G. E. (1966). "The Justification of Analysis." In *Moore's Lectures on Philosophy*, edited by C. Lewy, London: George Allen and Unwin.
Quine, W.V.O. (1960). *Word and Object*. Cambridge: MIT Press.
Schiffer, S. (1972). *Meaning*. Oxford: Oxford University Press; paperback edition with new introduction, 1988.
Schiffer, S. (1982). "Intention-Based Semantics." *Notre Dame Journal of Formal Logic* 23: 119–56.
Schiffer, S. (1987). *Remnants of Meaning*. Cambridge: MIT Press.
Schiffer, S. (1988). "Reply to Johnston." *Mind and Language* 3: 53–63.
Schiffer, S. (2002). "Meanings." In *Meaning and Truth*, edited by J. Keim Campbell, M. O'Rourke, and D. Shier, New York: Seven Bridges Press.
Schiffer, S. (2003). *The Things We Mean*. Oxford: Clarendon Press.
Searle, J. (1971). *Speech Acts: An Essay in the Philosophy of Language*. Cambridge: Cambridge University Press.
Strawson, P. F. (1971). "Meaning and Truth." In *Logico-Linguistic Papers*. London: Methuen.
Williamson, T. (2000). *Knowledge and Its Limits*. Oxford: Oxford University Press.
Wisdom, J. (1934). *Problems of Mind and Matter*. Cambridge: Cambridge University Press.

14

Schiffer on Russell's Theory and Referential Uses

Kent Bach

Stephen Schiffer thinks that referential uses of incomplete definite descriptions pose a devastating problem for Russell's theory of descriptions. Even if Russell's theory, or some modernized version of it, works for attributive uses, which Schiffer doubts, it fails for referential uses because "what one says...is an object-dependent non-descriptive proposition" (1180).[1] Since Russellians agree that speakers mean object-dependent propositions when using descriptions referentially, the question, as Schiffer sees it, boils down to whether such speakers also means a descriptive proposition. Schiffer maintains that Russell's theory requires this and argues that this requirement is not met, at least when the description is incomplete (not uniquely satisfied).[2]

This descriptive proposition could either be distinct from the object-dependent proposition, in which case the speaker says one thing, a general proposition, and means something else, namely the object-dependent proposition conveyed with the referential use.[3] Alternatively, the requisite descriptive proposition could be the object-dependent proposition itself. Schiffer finds serious difficulties with both options. The main trouble with the first option, which is key to what he calls the "standard Russellian response," is that it implausibly implies that referential uses are not literal. The alternative, recently endorsed by Stephen Neale (2004), avoids the non-literality problem, but it has problems of its own. I will defend a version of the standard Russellian response, but one that is not vulnerable to Schiffer's objections. Or so I hope to show.

The standard Russellian response is indeed vulnerable to certain objections, but only on assumptions it could better do without. As Schiffer portrays it, it models referential uses on the paradigm of conversational implicature (perhaps generalized). I think this is the wrong model. It misconstrues the pragmatic role of incomplete definite descriptions in referential uses; it misrepresents both the speaker's communicative intention and the hearer's inference in recognizing that intention. This model assumes that the speaker says and means some enriched proposition in uttering 'The F is G,' and it assumes the hearer's inference to the object-dependent proposition that the speaker ultimately means is routed through this enriched descriptive proposition.

Schiffer himself shares certain of the assumptions built into the standard Russellian response as he portrays it. These pertain to what makes an utterance literal and to the relation between saying something and meaning something. They lead Schiffer to take for granted that the standard Russellian response must rely on what we might call the standard Gricean model, on which referential uses involve conversational implicature. After exposing and challenging these assumptions, I will sketch a Russellian response that does without them.

Schiffer stresses that referential uses of incomplete definite descriptions are both straightforward and ubiquitous. So it could easily seem to be a black mark against Russell's theory, even though it is a theory of the meaning of description sentences rather than of their uses, that it cannot explain referential uses except by treating them as non-literal. Nevertheless, I will contend that it can accommodate referential uses despite not counting them as literal. Indeed, I will suggest that Schiffer's conception of what counts as literal is too liberal, and point out that his anti-Russellian argument depends on the implausible assumption that attributive uses, in contrast to referential uses, of incomplete descriptions are literal.

In my view referential uses of incomplete definite descriptions do not work all that differently from attributive uses, even though in the one case the speaker means an object-dependent proposition and in the other a descriptive one. Both uses are not strictly literal, and this is so even if all the lexical items in the description sentence are used literally. Once we see that both uses of incomplete descriptions are not literal and that in both cases the speaker does not mean what he says but means a pragmatic enrichment of it instead, we will be in a better position to judge what to expect and what not to demand from Russell's theory.

14.1 The Problem: Russell's Theory and Donnellan's Distinction

Russell's (1905) theory of descriptions concerns the meanings of sentences containing singular definite descriptions. The most important feature of this view is that the proposition semantically expressed by a sentence containing a description does not depend on what, if anything, satisfies the description.[4] This feature is easiest to see in the case of simple description sentences of the form 'The F is G,' as compared to sentences of the form 'a is G,' where 'a' is a logically proper name.[5] A sentence of the latter sort expresses a singular, object-dependent proposition, which has the individual a as a constituent. Suppose that a is the F, hence that a is denoted by 'the F.' Even so, a is not a constituent of the proposition expressed by 'The F is G.' This is a general, uniqueness proposition, to which 'the F' contributes a quantificational structure, not its denotation a. Unlike the proposition expressed by 'a is G,' this descriptive proposition, as Schiffer calls it, is not object-dependent. For it to be true there must be a unique F, which must be G; otherwise (whether because the unique F is not G or because there is either more than one F or no F) this proposition is false. It is a general proposition, and its truth condition does not depend on the existence or the identity of the unique F.[6] So its truth relative to a possible world in which the unique F is not the actual F requires that the unique F in that world be G (of course Russell would not have put it this way). A sentence of the form 'The F is G' may be represented, in restricted quantification notation, by '[the x: Fx] Gx,' just as 'Some F is G' and 'Every F is G' may be represented, respectively, by '[some x: Fx] Gx' and by '[every x: Fx] Gx.'[7]

Russell's theory of descriptions says nothing about how definite descriptions are used. Donnellan's (1966) referential-attributive distinction concerns that. A speaker using a description attributively intends to be talking about, to be referring only "in a weak sense" to, whichever individual satisfies the description (or, if it is incomplete, a certain completion of it). In this way, the description enters 'essentially' into the statement made, whose content is a general proposition. On the other hand, when a speaker uses a description referentially, he uses it merely "to enable his audience to pick out whom or what he is talking about and states something about that person or thing" (1966: 285). In this case the content of the statement is an object-dependent proposition. Donnellan spoke of this distinction as indicating an "ambiguity," but he was unclear on whether the ambiguity is semantic or pragmatic. He was content to observe that "a definite description occurring in one and the same sentence may, on different occasions of use, function in either way" (1966: 281).

Interestingly, Russell recognized a similar distinction regarding uses of proper names. For him a name can be used "directly" or "indirectly." When used directly, or "as a name," it serves "merely to indicate what we are speaking about; [the name] is no part of the fact asserted ... : it is merely part of the symbolism by which we express our thought" (1919: 175). Russell allowed that names can also be used indirectly, "as descriptions," observing, just as Donnellan later observed in regard to definite descriptions, "there is nothing in the phraseology to show whether they are being used in this way or as names." Donnellan's distinction closely parallels Russell's.

> [With the attributive use] if there is anything which might be identified as reference here, it is reference in a very weak sense—namely, reference to *whatever* is the one and only one F, if there is any such.... But this lack of particularity is absent from the referential use of definite descriptions precisely because the description is here merely a device for getting one's audience to pick out or think of the thing to be spoken about, a device which may serve its function even if the description is incorrect. (Donnellan 1966: 304)

In light of Russell's distinction between using a name as a name and as a description, we can easily imagine him distinguishing between using a description as a description (attributively) and using a description as a name (referentially).

For Donnellan the difference between a referential and an attributive use corresponds to the difference between asserting an object-dependent and a descriptive proposition.[8] In the referential case, the speaker has a specific individual in mind and uses the description with the intention that the hearer identify this individual and take the speaker's statement to be about that individual. As Donnellan explains, there is a "lack of particularity" in the attributive use. However, "in the referential use as opposed to the attributive, there is a *right* thing to be picked out by the audience and its being the right thing is not simply a function of its fitting the description" (Donnellan 1966: 304).

The referential/attributive distinction is between uses of descriptions. If the distinction marks a semantic ambiguity, a difference in linguistic meaning, that spells trouble for the Russellian approach. As Schiffer points out, "referential cases constitute a counterexample to the Russellian theory only if they show that 'The F is G' is *ambiguous*, as it would have to be if the content of a referential utterance is a non-descriptive, object-dependent proposition, whereas the content of an attributive utterance is a Russellian descriptive proposition" (1158).[9] This assumes that a Russellian approach works at least for attributive uses.[10] Even if it does, the fact is, as Schiffer points out, that referential uses are ubiquitous and that they strike us as literal. How can this be compatible with Russell's theory or anything like it?

14.2 The Problem of Incomplete Descriptions and the "Standard Russellian Response"

Schiffer does not argue that Russell's theory of descriptions fails for complete definite descriptions, that is, descriptions that are uniquely satisfied, such as 'the discoverer of X-rays' and 'the first mammal clone.'[11] Evidently he is satisfied that if 'the F' is complete, a sentence of the form 'The F is G' is true just in case the one and only F is G, and that in the attributive use this is what a speaker says and means in using it literally. Although Russell's theory does not explain the referential use, in which the speaker means an object-dependent proposition (about an object x, which is the F, that it is G), apparently Schiffer thinks that a straightforward Gricean account works for referential uses of complete descriptions. At least his arguments are not directed toward them. Perhaps that is because when a speaker uses a complete description and it is mutually evident between him and his audience which individual satisfies the description, the speaker cannot but intend, and cannot but be taken to intend, to be referring to that individual. So, for example, if one says, 'The author of *Waverley* was Scottish,' given that it is mutually evident that Walter Scott wrote *Waverley*, if one is reasonable and assumes one's audience is reasonable, one cannot but intend, and cannot but expect to be taken, to be referring to Scott.[12] In that case, what one means would be that Scott, the author of *Waverley*, was Scottish.

The problem that Schiffer poses for Russell's theory arises only in connection with referential uses of incomplete descriptions. But this is a serious problem, since most of the descriptions we use are incomplete, and in most cases we use them referentially. In so using them in the course of assertively uttering simple sentences of the form 'The F is G,' we mean and assert object-dependent propositions and, it would seem, do not mean or assert descriptive propositions.[13] Schiffer concludes from this that Russell's theory cannot accommodate referential uses of incomplete descriptions. He is not the first to draw this conclusion. There is a substantial literature on the problem that incomplete descriptions pose for Russell's theory since Kripke first expressed his "doubt that such descriptions can always be regarded as elliptical with some uniquely specifying condition added" (1977: 6), but Schiffer exposes this problem in a particularly forceful way.

He sketches what he takes to be the "standard Russellian response" to this problem. He does not finger specific culprits, but it is clear that he has Neale (1990) in mind. Neale himself now repudiates that approach, dismissing it as "the standard, wooden, Gricean explanation of referential usage" (2004: 173). This response is inspired by

Grice's theory of conversational implicature and his strategy of not multiplying meanings beyond necessity, as enjoined by 'Modified Occam's Razor' (Grice 1989: 47). In this way it appeals to "general mechanisms pertaining to rationality, conversation, and speaker-meaning" (1158). Schiffer illustrates the application of this strategy to the use of 'and' to implicate temporal sequence, as in a likely utterance of 'Alice got pregnant and married Bob.' Just as it is implausible in that case to suppose that 'and' is ambiguous as between logical conjunction and conjunction plus temporal order ('and then') or even causal connection ('and, as a result'),

In the same sort of way, these always-in-place pragmatic mechanisms would generate referential utterances of 'The F is G' even on the assumption that the semantic content—the proposition the literal speaker is *saying*—is, for some contextually determined property H, the descriptive proposition that the thing that is uniquely H and F is G. (1159)[14]

On this Gricean account, saying the descriptive proposition that the thing that is uniquely H and F is G is supposed to be the means by which the speaker manages to convey the object-dependent proposition of the thing in question that it is G.[15] The hearer is to recognize that the speaker means the object-dependent proposition by way of identifying this descriptive proposition.

Schiffer's main objection to the standard Russellian response is that in typical cases there will be no property, as expressed by a substitution instance of 'H', that determinately enters into what the speaker says and means and into what a rational hearer could take the speaker to mean. But, on Schiffer's rendering anyway, the standard Russellian response requires that there be some such property.[16] He objects further that this Gricean account contains the wrong ingredients for plausibly modeling the inference whereby the hearer is to identify which object the speaker is referring to, and thereby the object-dependent proposition that he means. It is not on the basis of first determining what descriptive proposition the speaker says.

In the next two sections I will take up these objections. I will argue that their effectiveness depends on a combination of assumptions that Schiffer imputes to the standard Russellian response and assumptions that he makes himself. I will call these assumptions into question and argue that a Russellian response can do without the ones that Schiffer imputes to it.

14.3 Incomplete Descriptions and Literality: Must What Is Said Be Meant?

Here is the gist of Schiffer's no-determinate-H objection.[17] When a speaker uses an incomplete description referentially, there is no determinate completer of the description's nominal that fills out what the speaker says or means. So the speaker does not say or mean any descriptive proposition, not even indeterminately. What the speaker means is a non-descriptive object-dependent proposition. Even so, Schiffer contends, the utterance is literal, and no truly Russellian theory can accommodate this fact. But is such an utterance literal?

Schiffer's no-determinate-H objection is valid all right, but that is only because of how he renders the standard Russellian response.[18] Why should the Russellian

SCHIFFER ON RUSSELL'S THEORY AND REFERENTIAL USES   369

assume that the semantic content of 'The F is G' is the proposition that the F that is H is G and that this is what is said by someone who utters the sentence? Semantically speaking, where does the 'H' come from, such that an utterance of 'The F is G' should count as literal even though the speaker does not mean that the F is G? This is a question not just for the standard Russellian response as Schiffer frames it, but a question for Schiffer himself, since he sees no problem with the inference that *if* 'the F' is incomplete and, contrary to the no-determinate-H objection, what a speaker of 'The F is G' says is a descriptive proposition, *then* this is the proposition that the F that is H is G (for some property H) and the speaker is being literal in saying it. In general, Schiffer allows that there can be elements in what is said that do not correspond to anything in the uttered sentence and that the utterance can nevertheless be literal.

It seems to me that Schiffer saddles the Russellian with assumptions that he can better do without: that the extra descriptive material ('that is H') is somehow part of what is said and that to say and mean the whole thing (that the F that is H is G) is to speak literally. This is a consequence of how Schiffer defines 'say' and 'literal.' Following Grice, he stipulates that saying something entails meaning it. That rules out saying one thing and meaning something else instead and implies that someone speaking non-literally fails to say anything.[19] Even so, he indicates that he will "use 'say' in the following stipulative way" (1160),

One *says* p in uttering σ iff one means p in uttering σ and p conforms to the, or a, character* of σ.

One speaks literally, then, if one means something that conforms to the character* of the sentence, where for Schiffer character* plays the role of linguistic meaning.[20] However, Schiffer is rather liberal on what counts as conforming. In particular, he allows that "for every *literal* utterance of 'The F is G' there is a predicate H such that, necessarily, the truth-value of that utterance is the same as that of $\exists x(\forall y((Hy \land Fy) \leftrightarrow y = x) \land Gx)$" (1138). He does not explain why meaning this should count as speaking literally, as if one had uttered 'The F that is H is G' rather than the unembellished 'The F is G.' Why should this count as conforming to the character* of the sentence actually uttered? For example, suppose that an emcee utters 'The winner gets a trip to Hawaii' and means, using 'the winner' attributively, that the winner of the raffle he is conducting gets a trip to Hawaii. If he said anything it would be this latter proposition, according to Schiffer, even though this implies that what the emcee said includes something that does not correspond to anything in the sentence he uttered.

This liberal conception of literality leads Schiffer to think that Russell's theory needs to be modified even to be plausible. Take a sentence like (1).

1. The dog growls.

Russell, of course, would maintain that (1) is simply false, independently of context, given that there is more than one dog. He would not endorse what Schiffer presents as a friendly amendment, whereby "for any utterance of (1), there is a predicate H such that, necessarily, that utterance has the same truth-value as (2).

2. $\exists x(\forall y((Hy \land Dy) \leftrightarrow y = x) \land Gx)$

where 'D' is assigned as its extension the set of dogs and 'G' the set of things that growl" (1137). The notation of restricted quantification provides a more perspicuous rendering:

2′. [the x: $Hx \land Dx$] Gx

Notice that in attributing to the Russellian the claim that (2) or (2′) is truth-conditionally equivalent to an *utterance* of (1), Schiffer has shifted from sentences to utterances. Evidently he makes this shift because incomplete description sentences like (1) "do not have context-independent truth-values" (1137). But Russell was concerned with sentences, not utterances, and was unfazed by the fact that on his theory a sentence like (1) counts as false, even if every dog growls. Moreover, Schiffer does not explain why, just because speakers of (1) are likely to mean different things in different contexts and, in particular, to be talking about different dogs, sentence (1) itself lacks a context-independent truth-value. (1) has no context-dependent constituents, aside from the tense of the verb, but tense is not the issue here. Moreover, characterizing H as "a contextually-determined supplementary property" (1137n) misleadingly suggests that this property somehow figures in the semantic content of (1) rather than in what the speaker means in uttering it. This property is contextually determined only in the loose sense of being determined by the speaker's communicative intention, which is to say that it is not really determined by the context at all. For this intention is not determined but merely rationally constrained by facts about the context, facts that the speaker can reasonably expect the hearer to take into account in recognizing his intention.[21]

Now it might be objected, just on the basis of intuition, that (1) *qua* sentence-type lacks a context-independent truth-value, that is neither true nor false independently of the context in which it is used. But Schiffer himself is leery of appeals to intuition about semantic contents (1139), and for good reason. Since seemingly semantic intuitions can be responsive to pragmatic regularities (Bach 2002, 2005) and can even count what is implicated as actually said (Nicolle and Clark 1999), we should not assume that they track semantic content.

At any rate, to see why Schiffer is being too liberal about saying and literality, consider likely utterances of (3) and (4), which, unlike (1), do not contain descriptions.

3. John has not taken a bath.
4. Jack and Jill are not engaged.

Intuitively, an utterance of (3) is true so long as John has not taken a bath that day, and an utterance of (4) is true if Jack and Jill are not engaged to each other. But if John has taken a bath at any prior time and if Jack and Jill are engaged to others, the sentences themselves are false and the utterances are not literal. Yet, so far as I can tell, for Schiffer the utterances of (3) and (4) would count as conforming to the sentences' characters*, hence as literal, and a speaker would count as saying that John has not taken a bath that day and as saying that Jack and Jill are not engaged to each other, even though part is left implicit. Similarly, I suggest, a normal utterance of (1) is not literal, and the speaker does not both say and mean that [the x: $Hx \land Dx$] Gx. Even if he *means* that, as he might if he were using 'the dog' attributively, what he *says* is that [the x: Dx] Gx.[22]

The question of what counts as a literal utterance bears on Schiffer's no-determinate-*H* objection. Having shown that in the case of (1) or any typical referential use of an incomplete description no descriptive proposition is meant, determinately or indeterminately, Schiffer proceeds to argue,

> If the Russellian theory were true of the typical cases and yet no proposition was meant in them which conformed to the characters* of the sentences uttered, then all these referential uses would in that sense be *non-literal*. But they do not strike us in that way. They seem like perfectly *straightforward* uses of 'The *F* is *G*', and there is no sense that in these cases we are not using the *words* we utter with meanings they have. It seems preposterous to deny that your saying to your spouse 'The car needs to be serviced' is an entirely *literal and straightforward* use of those *words*. (1167; my italics)

This is too hasty a conclusion. As the cases of (3) and (4) illustrate, a use of words can be straightforward without being literal. Similarly, suppose Jack says to Jill, "I don't like you, I love you." If he were speaking literally he would be denying that he likes her, but presumably he is not denying that. Yet his use of words is perfectly straightforward. The key thing to notice about this example, as well as (3) and (4), is that one can use all the words in a sentence literally and yet not be speaking literally in using the whole sentence. That is what Jack is doing. In particular, he is using 'not' (in 'don't') literally: what he means is that he does not *merely* like Jill, but he is not saying this and he is not using 'not' non-literally to mean 'not merely.' Similarly, in (4) the speaker is not using 'engaged' to mean 'engaged to each other.' These are not cases of *constituent* non-literality or figurativeness, which is what our intuitions track. Rather, they are cases of *sentence* non-literality.[23] They do not strike us as non-literal because none of their constituents are being used figuratively, but that does not show that they are literal. As hearers we can routinely interpret them in an enriched fashion without having to intuitively regard them as not literal.

Similarly, typical utterances of sentences containing incomplete definite descriptions are not literal. This is so even when the description is used attributively. Suppose, for example, a certain DA says, "The perpetrator will be identified, arrested, and prosecuted." Presumably he has some particular crime in mind but he is not using the word 'perpetrator' to mean perpetrator of the crime in question. He is using all of his words, including 'perpetrator,' literally, but his utterance is not literal as a whole.

Schiffer's anti-Russellian argument depends on his assumption that according to Russell's theory attributive uses of incomplete descriptions are literal, even though what the speaker means is a pragmatic enrichment of the sentence's semantic content. However, the Russellian should reject that assumption. Whether a speaker uses an incomplete description referentially or attributively, ordinarily he is not using it literally.[24] In neither case in uttering 'The F is G' does he mean that [the x: Fx] Gx. The difference, of course, is that in the attributive case the speaker means a descriptive proposition of the form 'The F that is H is G,' whereas in the referential case he means a non-descriptive object-dependent proposition, about the object he is using 'the F' to refer to, that it is G.[25] Either way, there is a mismatch between the Russellian semantic content of the sentence and what the speaker means in uttering it.

Now if even attributive uses of incomplete descriptions are not literal, it is no objection to Russell's theory to point out that referential uses are not literal of them either, albeit in a different way. They are both special cases of a very general phenomenon: meaning something that one does not make fully explicit. In the referential case, there must be an obviously distinguished F that the speaker intends to be speaking of. In the attributive case, there must be an obvious way of distinguishing one F.[26]

As I have argued so far, the Russellian should not concede that in using an incomplete 'the F' in uttering 'The F is G', the speaker says that the F that is H is G, even if, at least in the attributive case, that is what he means. Whether using an incomplete description referentially or attributively, the speaker is not being literal. Either way, the speaker intends the semantic information provided by the sentence to be supplemented by contextual information, information that he intends his audience to take into account, partly on the basis of taking him to intend them to do so. In either case, the content of the description can be pragmatically enriched, either by the obviously intended descriptive material or by an object that is uniquely salient. In the latter case, the object is, as it were, an unopposed candidate for being what the speaker is referring to. So it is no objection to Russell's theory that if the use is referential, what the speaker means is an object-dependent proposition, because that is not the proposition semantically expressed by the sentence that was uttered. For even if a use is attributive and what the speaker means is a descriptive proposition, that too is not the proposition semantically expressed by the uttered sentence.[27] As I will argue next, the Russellian also should not adopt a model on which the general, descriptive proposition that the F that is H is G plays any psychological role, in connection either with the formation of the speaker's intention or with the hearer's process of identifying that intention.

14.4 Incomplete Descriptions and Literality: Must What Is Said Be Represented?

According to the standard Russellian response as Schiffer portrays it, when an incomplete description is used referentially, the speaker intends the hearer to identify which object he is referring to, and thereby the object-dependent proposition he means, on the basis of what he says; and, correlatively, the hearer normally does identify that object and that proposition on that basis, that is, by first determining what proposition the speaker says. Here is how Schiffer presents the standard Russellian response's model, on which what is said figures both in what the speaker means and in the hearer's inference to what the speaker means:

Let us call this way of saying one thing and meaning another the say-p-▶-mean-q model; it is arguably also exemplified in the above example in which in uttering 'Alice got pregnant and married Bob,' the speaker says that Alice got pregnant and married Bob and also means that Alice first got pregnant and then married Bob. The standard Russellian response to the problem of referential uses of definite descriptions is best understood as the claim that referential utterances of 'The F is G' exemplify the say-p-▶-mean-q model. (1163)

Notice that although Schiffer calls this the "say-p-▷-mean-q model," by his lights to say that p entails meaning that p. So he is really saddling the standard Russellian response with a say-and-mean-p-▷-mean-q model. However, as argued in the previous section, when a speaker uses an incomplete definite description, whether referentially or attributively, he is not speaking literally. Whether or not he means that the F that is H is G, he does not *say* that the F that is H is G, and he does not *mean* that the F is G.

Notice also that in cases like this the speaker does not mean two things. This is clear with the 'and' example. The speaker does not mean that Alice got pregnant and married Bob *and* that Alice first got pregnant and then married Bob—he means just the latter (or perhaps some embellishment thereof). Similarly, whether using an incomplete 'the F' attributively or referentially, the speaker means just one thing, either the descriptive proposition that the F that is H is G or an object-dependent proposition about the object he is using 'the F' to refer to, that it is G. In neither case does he say and mean one thing and mean something else as well.

When Schiffer observes that "one problem with this intended application of the say-p-▷-mean-q model is that often when a speaker's utterance of 'The F is G' is referential, she seems not to be determinately or even indeterminately saying any descriptive proposition" (1164), he is talking about the expansive descriptive proposition that the F that is H is G. As I suggested in the previous section, the Russellian need not assume that what is said is also meant and should not suppose that what is said is this expansive descriptive proposition. What is said is simply the proposition that the F is G, i.e. that [the x: Fx] Gx.

Moreover, the Russellian need not go along with Schiffer's rendering of the say-p-▷-mean-q model and concede that the hearer has to identify what is said in order to figure out what is meant. The process is not like that of recognizing a conversational implicature by way of judging that what the speaker said is blatantly false or, if taken by itself, uninformative or irrelevant.[28] In typical cases, it will be mutually evident to the speaker and the hearer that 'the F' is incomplete, that is, there is more than one F. This will be especially so with unmodified run-of-the-mill nouns, such as 'guy,' 'car,' and 'tree,' that apply to millions of things. The hearer does not have to hear the entire sentence and figure out what conversationally deficient proposition it expresses before realizing that he must read something into the speaker's use of the incomplete description. The incompleteness of the description by itself triggers any needed search for some individuating condition or some particular individual that must be identified for figuring out what the speaker means. Ordinarily, clues that are already available, such as the topic of conversation, the physical setting, or the interests of the speaker, will be enough to enable the hearer to do this (in Gricean fashion, he will take these clues into account partly on the supposition that the speaker intends him to do so). To be sure, if such clues are insufficient, he will need to hear more, perhaps the entire sentence, including its predicative part.[29] But generally that will not be necessary. In any case, it is the incompleteness of 'the F' that triggers the search. This is because the definite article 'the' signifies totality, the nominal 'F' is singular, and it is obvious that there is more than one F.

The alternative to the standard Russellian response that I will sketch in the next section, which does not rely on the version of the say-p-▷-mean-q model laid out by Schiffer, avoids objections like this:

In clear cases in which the only proposition meant in uttering a sentence does not conform to the sentence's character*, the sentence's character* nevertheless plays an essential explanatory role in the account of how one's hearer was able to know what one meant. Quite frankly, I cannot think of a remotely plausible account of how a Russellian character* would enter into the processing that resulted in a hearer's knowing what was meant in all those referential cases if no descriptive proposition was also meant. (1168)

I have suggested why it is ordinarily the character* of the description by itself rather than the character* of the entire sentence that enters into the relevant processing. Schiffer also raises the following problem for the say-p-➤-mean-q model:

> For the model to apply, the hearer must know the speaker meant the non-descriptive object-dependent proposition on *the basis of knowing* that she determinately or indeterminately said a descriptive proposition... When a definite description is used referentially, a hearer cannot even identify *candidate* descriptive propositions except on the basis of knowing that to which the speaker was referring in uttering the definite description, and this is incompatible with the claim that the Russellian theory *explains* the referential uses. True, *if* the sole character* of 'The F is G' were as the theory requires it to be, *then* referential uses of the sentence *would* be explained by the say-p-➤-mean-q model. The fact that they are not explained by the model implies that the character* of 'The F is G' which is operative in referential cases is not as the Russellian theory requires it to be. (1168–9; italics in original)

This is not a problem for the Russellian theory if it does without the assumption (discussed in the previous section) that when a speaker uses a description referentially, he both says and means that the F that is H is G. It remains to suggest an alternative account.

14.5 Using Incomplete Descriptions Referentially

Whether using an incomplete description referentially or attributively, a speaker uttering a sentence of the form 'The F is G' says but does not mean that [the x: Fx] Gx.[30] If he is using the description attributively, he means that [the x: $Fx \wedge Hx$] Gx, where the property of being H completes the content of the description ('the x: $Fx \wedge Hx$' is uniquely satisfied). And if he is using it referentially, he means [the x: $Fx \wedge x = a$] Gx, where a is the F that he is referring to. The property of being identical to a is just another way of completing the content of the description.[31]

Moreover, the hearer need not base his inference to what the speaker means on the fact that the speaker says that [the x: Fx] Gx. Nor must the speaker intend him to make such an inference. For it is not the fact that the speaker could not plausibly be supposed to mean that [the x: Fx] Gx that triggers his inference. Rather, it is the incompleteness of the description itself, with its unfulfilled promise of uniqueness. The implication of uniqueness is generated by the presence of the definite article 'the' and the fact that the nominal 'F' is singular, together with its being obvious that there are many Fs. The task for the hearer is to identify the relevant F (in the referential case) or the relevant way of distinguishing one F (in the attributive case). A rational speaker will use an incomplete 'the F' only if he takes it to be mutually evident either that he has in mind a certain F or that he has in mind a certain way of singling out a unique F.

In the referential case, what the speaker means is that [the x: $Fx \land x = a$] Gx, even though all he says is that [the x: Fx] Gx. Suppose, for example, that he utters (5).

5. The killer is crazy.

If he says this in a situation where it is mutually obvious who the relevant killer is (in the attributive case it might be mutually obvious who the relevant victim is), he will intend the hearer to take him to be referring to that killer. Referring to him with 'the killer' is enough to single him out. Now Schiffer might object, as he does to the view of Neale's mentioned in the previous footnote, that he "can see no principled basis on which to secure that the descriptive proposition meant, assuming there is one, will contain no more descriptive material than is directly expressed by the incomplete description that is uttered" (1173), in this case 'the killer.' Schiffer grants that "what a speaker means in uttering a sentence is determined by her communicative intentions" (1173), and, for the reason Schiffer gives, it seems that there is no unique enrichment of the description 'the killer' that the speaker could reasonably intend the hearer to take him to have in mind. However, under the circumstances no embellishment of the description is needed to enable the hearer to figure out who the speaker is talking about. If more were needed, presumably the speaker would have included it. So the hearer can reasonably take the description at face value, assuming that the killer that comes to mind can only be the one the speaker has in mind.

It is noteworthy that discussions of definite descriptions tend to neglect the question of why we have occasion to use definite descriptions to refer and under what circumstances. Obviously, we use them referentially to enable our audience to pick out who or what we are talking about. Beyond this truism, consider that if we always had other means by which to refer, we would never need to use a definite description. In fact, when we wish to refer to a person or thing, under the circumstances often there is no other linguistic means available or suitable for doing it. If we want to refer to something that lacks a name or whose name is unfamiliar (to us or to our audience), is not perceptually accessible and thus not suited for being demonstrated, or has not just been mentioned, in which case a pronoun or a demonstrative will not do the job, we must resort to using a definite description. Even using a complex demonstrative (of the form 'that F') will not do the trick if there are many Fs around and it is not feasible to demonstrate the F we have in mind. That leaves using a definite description. A complete description will single out a unique object, but generally we do not have to resort to using one. An incomplete description will normally indicate the type of thing we wish to refer to, and the topic of conversation and other mutually evident contextual information give us good reason to think the hearer will know which F we intend. We then can exploit our audience's ability to take this information into account, partly on the basis that we intend them to identify the relevant F. This will work if indeed there is an obviously distinguished F for the hearer to identify as the one being referred to (in the attributive case there must be an obviously distinguished way of singling out some F). Since the speaker is using the description referentially, he need not mean any general, descriptive proposition involving some sort of completion of 'the F.' Normally he means only an object-dependent proposition about a certain uniquely salient F.

As I suggested in the previous section, the description does not play its role of helping the hearer identify the intended referent by virtue of its contribution to the descriptive proposition expressed by 'The F is G.' That is, the route the speaker takes in forming his intention to convey the object-dependent proposition that the referent a is G by uttering 'The F is G' is not via the descriptive proposition expressed by 'The F is G.' And the hearer's inferential route from hearing 'The F is G' to thinking that the speaker means the object-dependent proposition that a is G is not via this descriptive proposition. Rather, the hearer figures out that the speaker is using 'the F' to refer to a and then infers that he means that a is G.

In considering the role of an incomplete description in securing the intended reference, we should remember, as Donnellan (1966) pointed out, that the referent need not in fact be F. The uniquely salient thing that he is referring to could be something that he mistakenly takes to be F, takes the hearer to mistakenly take to be F, or takes the hearer to take him to mistakenly take to be F.[32] By the same token, there are cases in which the hearer can identify the referent, even if it is not F, by correctly taking a certain object to be something the speaker thinks is F, or thinks he thinks is F (and so on).[33] Clearly the fact that a speaker can successfully use 'the F' to refer to something that is not F requires a pragmatic explanation. And, if a pragmatic account is needed in cases where 'F' does not apply, then it would seem, as Soames has argued, that it might as well be extended to cases in which 'F' does apply (2005: 13). This consideration provides one more reason for thinking that referential uses are not literal and that it is not the obligation of Russell's theory to explain them by itself.

These cases illustrate that the important thing with referential uses is that the speaker's use of the description enables the hearer to identify something as what he is using the description to refer to, not as that which satisfies the description's nominal. Of course, if the speaker means that the F that is a is G and a is not F, then he means something that is strictly speaking false. However, since he is using 'the F' primarily to enable the hearer to identify what he is referring to, then, as Donnellan points out, practically speaking it will be enough if a is G. Although the content of 'the F' is normally part of what the speaker means, it is of secondary importance. The speaker's primary aim is to predicate something of an object.

We should observe that understanding a referential use requires more than realizing that the speaker has a certain object in mind. Consider the following comparison. Suppose a speaker has a particular F in mind but uses an *indefinite* description and utters a sentence of the form 'An F is G.' In that case, normally he would not be referring the hearer to that object. His use of the indefinite would be specific, but not referential—the hearer could know that the speaker has some object in mind but without being in a position to know which object it is and, more to the point, would not be intended to think of that object.[34] However, in using a definite description referentially, incomplete though it may be, the speaker does intend the hearer to identify a unique F as the one he is thinking of. The speaker is not using 'the F' as elliptical for 'the F that I have in mind' (or anything of the sort), and it would not be enough for the hearer to think of that thing under the description 'the thing that he the speaker has in mind.' The speaker must expect the hearer to have cognitive access to the object as well. So, in using 'the F,' with its implication of uniqueness even though it is incomplete, the speaker must intend for the hearer to identify, by a process of triangulation as it were, a certain unique thing as the distinguished F, the one he has in mind.

It is one thing for the hearer to recognize that the speaker is using a description referentially and another thing for the hearer to figure out which object he is using it to refer to. The mere fact that the description is incomplete is ordinarily enough to indicate that it is being used referentially, unless it is already evident that there is some obvious completer of 'the F,' as with anaphoric uses of definite descriptions, as in (6), and in so-called 'bridging' cases like (7):

6. If you see a man wearing a suit playing frisbee, the man is a spy.

7. I had a blowout, but the spare tire was flat.

In using an obviously incomplete description to refer, a rational speaker must use it only if it will be evident to the hearer what he is using it to refer to. Something Schiffer says about 'she' applies equally to using 'the woman' to refer: "the speaker cannot intend to refer to a particular female unless he expects the hearer to recognize to which female he is referring, and the expectation of such recognition itself entails that the speaker takes the referent to have an appropriate salience"[35] (1141).

14.6 Fregean Referentialism Instead?

In the second to last paragraph of his paper Schiffer hints at an alternative Fregean approach to definite descriptions. It is motivated by the following thought, based on certain of his earlier claims:

I am inclined to think that 'The F is G' is ambiguous, does have two characters*, *if* the Russellian theory gives the correct account of the operative character* in attributive utterances. For in that case, 'the F' can occur either as a quantifier phrase or as a singular term, and while there may well be a single kind of proposition whose members are all and only those assertable in literal utterances of 'The F is G,' the fact that the sentence's surface form would be underlain by two such disparate LFs would I think strongly suggest that two distinct characters* attach to the one surface form, 'The F is G.' But ... I for one am not confident that the Russellian theory is correct even for the attributive cases. Frege's theory, according to which definite descriptions in subject position are always singular terms, is unthreatened by attributive uses, and, while I shall now not pursue the issue, I also think a single univocal character* will accommodate both referential and attributive utterances of 'The F is G', if 'the F' functions as a singular term in both cases—that is to say, if in both cases no true or false proposition is expressed if 'the F' fails to refer. (1180)

Schiffer does not indicate whether the theory he envisages is Fregean in more robust respects, employing a notion of sense that plays such roles as determining reference and comprising cognitive significance. Also, he is doubtful that an adequate theory that is Fregean even in just the respect he mentions would be determinately true or determinately false. He acknowledges, using the sentence 'Prince Harry's first child will be a girl' to illustrate the point, that there may simply be no fact of the matter as to whether, if Prince Harry never has a child, the sentence is false or neither true nor false.

There is not much to be gained by objecting to a theory that is not spelled out but merely hinted at as a possible alternative to Russell's. Even so, I think it is appropriate to question two things Schiffer says about this envisaged 'Fregean' approach. He says both that "Frege's theory, according to which definite descriptions in subject position are always singular terms, is unthreatened by attributive uses" and that whether a description is used referentially or attributively, "no true or false proposition is expressed if 'the F' fails to refer." The first question is why Schiffer limits the application of Frege's theory to descriptions in subject position. Leaving predicative position aside, what about descriptions in non-subject argument position? It is well known that sentences containing unsatisfied descriptions in such a position are perfectly capable of being true or false. Here are two examples:

8. Russell never had breakfast with the king of France. [true]

9. In October of 1905 Russell had breakfast with the king of France. [false]

Insofar as a Fregean theory has to deny that sentences containing unsatisfied descriptions are true or false, it seems hard put to explain the obvious truth of (8) and the obvious falsity of (9). It seems arbitrary to limit the application of the Fregean theory to descriptions in subject position, but it seems that such a theory does not work for descriptions that occur elsewhere.

More importantly, one wonders, on the sort of Fregean theory Schiffer has in mind, what is it for a definite description to be a singular term and to refer whether it is used referentially or attributively. In fact, Schiffer does not explain how the Fregean approach would characterize the difference between referential and attributive uses. While Frege's theory may be "unthreatened by attributive uses," it does not seem equipped to treat referential uses differently, and Schiffer offers no hint as to how it would treat them. Moreover, what about cases like these?

10. If Queen Elizabeth got pregnant again, the baby would be a boy.

11. The engine of a perpetual motion machine would not use gasoline.

In these cases the descriptions do not seem to function as singular terms or even to purport to refer.[36] If that is correct, then either the Fregean theory Schiffer envisages would incorrectly count these descriptions as singular terms or its scope of application would not include them.

Schiffer may have more up his sleeve than he tells us, but the theory he hints at would seem to count attributive uses as referential and to treat referential uses in the same way it treats attributive uses. We need to hear much more about how this Fregean theory might go.

14.7 Summing Up

As I see it, referential uses of incomplete definite descriptions do not pose a special problem for Russell's theory of descriptions. If incomplete descriptions pose a problem for it at all, the problem is basically the same for attributive as for referential ones. In both cases a speaker using a sentence of the form 'The F is G' says but does not mean that the F is G. If he is using the description attributively, he means that the F that is H is G (where presumably 'the F that is H' is complete). And if he is using it referentially, he means that the F that is a is G, where a is the F that he is referring to. Being a is just another way of completing the content of the description.

I do not think there is a problem in either case. Schiffer thinks there is a problem because he assumes that to handle incomplete descriptions Russell's theory must concede that in uttering 'The F is G,' where 'the F' is incomplete, a speaker does not say that [the x: Fx] Gx, but says and means something more elaborate. On Schiffer's take on Russell's theory, in the attributive case the speaker says and means a descriptive proposition, and in the referential case he also means an object-dependent proposition. The latter part of this interpretation gives rise to a dilemma for the Russellian: either concede that the speaker's utterance is not literal—what he says is a descriptive proposition and what he means is not—or explain how the one proposition that he means and is literally expressed can be object-dependent as well as descriptive. I argued that we should not assume that when a speaker uses an incomplete description there is *any* proposition that he both says and means. What he says, but does not mean, is that [the x: Fx] Gx. So he is not speaking literally whether he is using the incomplete 'the F' referentially *or* attributively. If that is correct, then it is not incumbent upon Russell's theory, as a theory of the meaning of description sentences, not of their uses, to explain either use of incomplete descriptions. Both uses require pragmatic explanations.

Moreover, Russell's theory need not be encumbered with the assumption that what is said is the inferential route to what is meant. Specifically, the hearer need not base his inference to what the speaker means on the fact that he says that [the x: Fx] Gx. Nor must the speaker intend him to make such an inference. Referential uses of incomplete descriptions do not fit the model of Gricean conversational implicature, whereby the hearer is to figure out what the speaker means on the basis of what he says. It does not involve judging what is said to be blatantly false, uninformative, irrelevant, or whatever. Rather, it is the incompleteness of the description itself, with its unfulfilled promise of uniqueness, that triggers the hearer's inference as to which F the speaker is referring to.

Both referential and attributive uses of incomplete definite descriptions are special cases of the phenomenon of meaning something that one's utterance does not make fully explicit. This phenomenon is ubiquitous but is not generally recognized as a kind of non-literality. Most of the things that people mean in uttering the sentences that they do, even if they are using all of the words in the sentence literally, are pragmatic enrichments of the sentence's semantic content. To treat the problem of incompleteness as specific to uses of definite descriptions is to miss the ubiquity of this phenomenon. A proper theory of definite descriptions should not treat the distinction between complete and incomplete descriptions as a linguistic distinction and should not treat incompleteness as relevant to their semantics. The fact that a speaker who utters a sentence containing an incomplete definite description can mean different things in different contexts does not make these sentences context-sensitive. So there is no need for a Russellian theory of descriptions to build a spot for a completer into its semantic analysis of sentences containing them. Attributive as well as referential uses of incomplete definite descriptions can and should be explained pragmatically.

Notes

1. All unidentified page references are to Schiffer 2005.
2. Both the term 'incomplete' and the term 'improper' are commonly used for descriptions whose nominal is multiply satisfied, as in 'the girl,' but 'improper' is more often used as well for descriptions whose nominal is not satisfied at all, as in 'the mermaid.' Our examples will be of the first sort only.
3. For convenience I will sometimes use the awkward 'say/mean a proposition,' which sounds much worse than 'say/mean that p,' for some substitution instance of 'p.' And, for typographical convenience I will use single quotes for schemata rather than the corner quotes that sticklers might require. It will also be convenient to use 'The F is G' when I mean a sentence of that form.
4. Unless otherwise indicated, from now on I will use 'description' as short for 'singular definite description.'
5. Like Schiffer (1138), we will be limiting our attention to description sentences of this form. We will not take up cases in which descriptions contain bound pronouns, fall within the scope of modal operators or propositional attitude verbs, or occur as predicates rather than in (apparent) argument position. I believe that these and other complications do not bear on the present discussion, although they do need to be taken into account by a comprehensive theory of descriptions.
6. Semanticists sometimes characterize general propositions as ascribing higher-order properties (corresponding to restricted quantifiers) to lower-order properties, or what Russell called propositional functions.
7. This notation, which Schiffer adopts, was used by Stephen Neale (1990) to avoid the mismatch between surface grammatical form and logical form for which Russell's theory is notorious, not just in Russell's metalinguistic formulation but in modern formulations using the notation of standard first-order logic, such as '$\exists x(\forall y(Fy \leftrightarrow y=x)$ & $Gx)$.' As Neale has neatly explained (2001: 224–32), what makes descriptions "incomplete symbols" for Russell is not this mismatch, whereby they "disappear upon logical analysis," but that they introduce quantificational, variable-binding structure into the sentences in which they occur.
8. Schiffer prefers 'object-dependent (proposition)' over 'singular (proposition)' because it is neutral on the nature of propositions, whereas the latter suggests Russellian propositions, whose constituents comprise objects, properties, and relations. It makes sense to debate Russell's theory of descriptions in a way that, so far as possible, does not presuppose any particular theory of propositions.
9. If definite descriptions have referential as well as quantificational meanings, then it would seem to follow, implausibly, that the word 'the' is ambiguous. This consequence would suggest that a massive cross-linguistic coincidence is at work here (Bach 2004: 226). Otherwise, there ought to be languages with two different definite articles, one corresponding to the attributive use and one to the referential, but so far as I know, there are not.
10. There is also the view, which Schiffer toys with toward the end of his paper and I will touch on later, that definite descriptions are unambiguously referential. Frege (1892) and Strawson (1950) both held this view, though on very different grounds and within very different frameworks. A further possible, indeed actual, view (Recanati 1989 and Bezuidenhout 1997) is that definite descriptions are not semantically ambiguous but

underdetermined as between the attributive and referential uses, in the sense that sentences containing them fall short of expressing either singular or general propositions. This view is implausible for reasons spelled out by Neale (1990: 110, n. 36). See also Bach (2001a: 34–5).
11. It should be noted that containing a bound pronoun does not render a description incomplete. In 'Every child likes the relative who is most generous to him,' different people may satisfy 'the relative who is most generous to him,' but that is relative to different values of 'him.'
12. On the other hand, if someone says 'The inventor of the zipper was a genius,' they probably have no idea that Whitcomb Judson invented the zipper and, even if they do, it is likely that their audience does not and could therefore not be expected to identify who that is, in which case the speaker could not (reasonably) intend to refer to Judson.
13. From now on, when I talk about speakers using descriptions referentially to assert propositions or about what a speaker says or means in so doing, I will mean using them in the course of uttering a sentence.
14. Schiffer puts this in terms of a phrasal completion of the description rather than a domain restriction on it. These alternatives correspond to Neale's distinction between the "explicit" and the "implicit" responses to the problem of incompleteness (1990: 95; 2004: 116ff). Schiffer argues that the difference between the two is merely cosmetic, since the same property that explicitly restricts the description implicitly restricts the domain (1151–4). Both he and Neale construe both responses as aiming to give the semantic contents of sentences containing incomplete descriptions. In my view the incompleteness of a description does not affect the semantic content of sentences containing it (Bach 1994: 103), or, as Soames puts this point, "the distinction between complete and incomplete definite descriptions is nonlinguistic" (2005: 11). So, for example, it is not a semantic fact that there is more than one dog in the universe but only one even prime number.
15. Since Schiffer's takes referential uses of incomplete definite descriptions to be the source of trouble for Russell's theory, I will assume that it is not in dispute that in attributive uses the speaker means something of this form: that the F that is H is G. However, I will argue in the next section that this is not what the speaker says, in attributive as well as referential cases.
16. Schiffer raises a number of subsidiary objections to particular implementations of the standard Russellian response, but because these implementations are implausible for the reasons that Schiffer gives, there is no point in taking them up here.
17. This indeterminacy problem in connection with referential uses of incomplete descriptions was first pointed out by Kripke (1977), and Wettstein (1981) raised it for attributive uses. Schiffer (1995) first presented his version of this objection as part of a dilemma for a Russellian about descriptions who is also a direct-reference theorist about indexicals. In Schiffer 2005 he casts it, in the guise of his theory of character*, as a direct objection to the Russellian.
18. Buchanan and Ostertag (2005) would disagree. They argue that the problem of incompleteness rest on an overly restrictive conception of communication, which requires there to be a determinate property H that figures both in what the speaker means and in what the hearer understands. Their less restrictive conception escapes the problem of incompleteness all right, but it raises interesting questions of its own about just what is necessary for successful communication. (Bach and Harnish (1979: 85–9) touch on the question of what sorts of discrepancies between what the speaker intends and what the hearer infers do or do not vitiate communication.) I agree that even with attributive uses, there may be no intended completer of the description but, I have suggested, "what these cases illustrate is not a problem for Russell's theory but a common problem in communication" (Bach 2004:

222n). In any case, Buchanan and Ostertag's conception of communication deserves much more attention that I can pay it here.
19. This implication led Grice oddly to describe non-literal speakers as merely "making as if to say" something (1989: 30).
20. In what follows I will occasionally use, or quote Schiffer as using, the term 'character*' rather than '(linguistic) meaning,' but most of my points will be independent of Schiffer's theory of character*. I am not confident that they will all be—especially insofar as his is a compositional theory of character*, not content, and, in particular, on his "way of individuating propositions we cannot happily identify anything as the 'content' of a sub-sentential expression token." He goes on to say that "the meanings of sub-sentential expression types help to determine the meanings of sentence types, and they determine a relation of fit between them and propositions that might be meant in uttering sentences that have those meanings" (1142-3). It would take me too far afield to explain his theory and its motivations, and I will leave that to others to do elsewhere in this volume.
21. I develop these points about sentences vs utterances, contextual determination, and speakers' intentions in Bach (2005). Considering his critique of Kaplan (1989), it is surprising that Schiffer characterizes incomplete-description sentences as being context-dependent. In assessing Kaplan's theory based on the notion of character, he asks, "What 'contextual factors' determine the referent of the pronoun 'she' [as opposed to 'I'] in a context of utterance?" and answers,

> What fixes the referent of a token of 'she' are the speaker's referential intentions in producing that token, and therefore in order for Kaplan to accommodate 'she', he would have to say that a speaker's referential intentions constitute one more component of those n-tuples that he construes as 'contexts'. The trouble with this is that there is no work for Kaplanian contexts to do once one recognizes speakers' referential intentions. The referent of a pronoun or demonstrative is *always* determined by the speaker's referential intentions. (1141)

So if the meaning (or character) of 'she' does not determine its reference, as used in a given context, what does it do? In Schiffer's view, it "merely constrains the speaker to be referring to a female," at least if one is using it literally (and not referring to a ship).
22. Obviously I am not using 'say', as Grice and Schiffer do, to imply 'mean.' I grant that 'say' has a perfectly ordinary use on which it means the same as 'state' or 'assert' and does imply 'mean,' but it also has a narrow, locutionary sense, on which a speaker can say something without meaning it. I think we need this sense of 'say.' For further explanation and justification of this use, see Bach (2001a).
23. See Bach (1994: 69-73) for my initial explanation and justification of this distinction. In Bach (2001b) I give a variety of examples of sentence non-literality, and suggest why, even though this way of speaking loosely is ubiquitous, it is commonly overlooked.
24. Ordinarily, because there are also cases in which a speaker mistakenly believes that there is only one F when in fact there are many. He would be using the description literally, but a knowing audience would not take him literally and might look in vain for some intended completion of the description, at least if the speaker were using it attributively.
25. I have long held (Bach 1994: 124-6) that in using a description referentially, a speaker need not mean any descriptive proposition and, moreover, that this is consistent with Russell's theory.
26. The fact that both uses of incomplete definite descriptions are not literal undercuts what is sometimes called the 'historical objection' to Russell's theory. As Schiffer states it, "given the way meaning supervenes on use, we should expect that even if 'The F is G' originally had only a Russellian, description-theoretic character*, it would by now have acquired a secondary meaning, another character*, in line with the referential uses" (1167). However,

if neither use is literal, in which case neither conforms to the description-theoretic character* of 'The F is G', then this objection does not arise.

27. I suppose it might be objected that even if the attributive use of an incomplete description is not literal, the completed descriptive proposition (that the F that is H is G) is in some sense 'closer' to the (descriptive) proposition expressed by 'The F is G' than is the object-dependent proposition (about the object he is using 'the F' to refer to that it is G). For it is least a descriptive proposition. However, the mere fact that the proposition meant when an incomplete description is used attributively is a descriptive proposition does not show that it is 'more literal' than the object-dependent proposition. It might seem that the content of the description 'the F' figures in the wholly descriptive proposition in a way that it does not in the object-dependent proposition, but that is illusory. This is evident from the fact that 'the F' is not a constituent of the sentence 'The F that is H is G.' The structure of the completed description that is the subject of this sentence is not [the F][that is H] but [the[F that is H]].

28. In particular, the Russellian is not committed to the claim that because Russell's theory entails that a sentence containing an incomplete definite description in subject position is false, the hearer must (at least tacitly) take this into account and, in effect, treat the speaker's utterance as a quality implicature.

29. This applies to the case to which we, like Schiffer, have been limiting our discussion: simple description sentences, with 'the F' in (main) subject position. Obviously, descriptions can occur in any argument position, as the object of a preposition, in the place of a determiner in genitive phrases, etc.

30. The ideas about referential uses sketched here are developed more fully in Bach 2004, mainly in Points 4, 5, 11, and 12. Some appeared earlier in Bach (1994: ch. 6).

31. This view, which I defended in Bach (2004), looks similar to the view defended by Neale (2004), which Schiffer discusses in section 6 of his paper as the non-standard Russellian response. The difference is that Neale treats uses of incomplete definite descriptions, whether referential or attributive, as literal, at least if 'F' is used literally (this means, in Schiffer's terms, that the utterance conforms to the character* of the uttered sentence). In my view, on the other hand, these uses do not count as literal, since in neither case does the speaker mean that [the x: Fx] Gx.

32. It is also possible that the speaker mistakenly takes the hearer to take the intended referent to be F, or even that the speaker takes the hearer to mistakenly take him to take it to be F. This need not vitiate communication, for there may be no other plausible candidate for what the speaker has in mind.

33. For more on these aberrant cases, see Bach (1994: 126-9).

34. For more on the difference between specific and referential uses of indefinite descriptions, see Ludlow and Neale (1991) and Bach (2004: 205-6).

35. Schiffer says this in support of a nice point he makes about 'she', namely that "the meaning of 'she' (very roughly speaking) merely constrains one uttering it to be referring to a female. We do not even have to say that it constrains the speaker to refer to a contextually salient female" (1141).

36. I admit to having certain demanding views on what it takes to refer (see Bach 2006), but you do not have to share those views to agree that if the descriptions in (10) and (11) refer at all, it is only in a very weak sense.

Bibliography

Bach, K. (1994). *Thought and Reference*, expanded edition. Oxford: Clarendon Press.
Bach, K. (2001a). "You Don't Say." *Synthese* 128: 15-44.

Bach, K. (2001b). "Speaking Loosely: Sentence Nonliterality." *Midwest Studies in Philosophy*, vol. 25: *Figurative Language*, edited by P. French and H. Wettstein, Oxford: Blackwell, pp. 249-63.

Bach, K. (2002). "Seemingly Semantic Intuitions." In *Meaning and Truth*, edited by J. Keim Campbell, M. O'Rourke, and D. Shier, New York: Seven Bridges Press, pp. 21-33.

Bach, K. (2004). "Descriptions: Points of Reference." In Reimer and Bezuidenhout (2004), pp. 189-229.

Bach, K. (2005). "Context ex Machina." In *Semantic versus Pragmatics*, edited by Z. Szabó, Oxford: Oxford University Press, pp. 15-44.

Bach, K. (2006). "What Does It Take to Refer?" In *The Oxford Handbook of the Philosophy of Language*, edited by E. Lepore and B. C. Smith, Oxford: Oxford University Press, pp. 515-54.

Bach, K. and R. M. Harnish. (1979). *Linguistic Communication and Speech Acts*. Cambridge, MA: MIT Press.

Bezuidenhout, A. (1997). "Pragmatics, Semantic Underdetermination, and the Referential/Attributive Distinction." *Mind* 106: 375-410.

Buchanan, R. and G. Ostertag. (2005). "Has the Problem of Incompleteness Rested on a Mistake?" *Mind* 114: 889-913.

Donnellan, K. (1966). "Reference and Definite Descriptions." *Philosophical Review* 75: 281-304.

Frege, G. (1892/1970). "On Sense and Reference." In *Translations from the Philosophical Writings of Gottlob Frege*, edited by P. Geach and M. Black, Oxford: Blackwell.

Grice, H. P. (1989). *Studies in the Way of Words*. Cambridge: Harvard University Press.

Kaplan, D. (1989). "Demonstratives: An Essay on the Semantics, Logic, Metaphysics, and Epistemology of Demonstratives and Other Indexicals." In *Themes from Kaplan*, edited by J. Almog, J. Perry, and H. Wettstein (eds.), New York: Oxford University Press, pp. 481-563.

Kripke, S. (1977). "Speaker's Reference and Semantic Reference." *Midwest Studies in Philosophy* 2: 255-76.

Ludlow, P., and S. Neale. (1991). "Indefinite Descriptions: In Defense of Russell." *Linguistics and Philosophy* 14: 171-202.

Neale, S. (1990). *Descriptions*. Cambridge, MA: MIT Press.

Neale, S. (2001). *Facing Facts*. Oxford: Clarendon Press.

Neale, S. (2004). "This, That, and the Other." In *Descriptions and Beyond*, edited by Reimer and Bezuidenhout, pp. 68-182.

Nicolle, S. and B. Clark (1999). "Experimental Pragmatics and What Is Said: A Response to Gibbs and Moise." *Cognition* 69: 337-54.

Recanati, F. (1989). "Referential/Attributive: A Contextualist Proposal." *Philosophical Studies* 56: 217-49.

Reimer, Marga and Anne Bezuidenhout (eds.). (2004). *Descriptions and Beyond*. Oxford: Clarendon Press.

Russell, B. (1905). "On Denoting." *Mind:* 14: 479-93.

Russell, B. (1919). *Introduction to Mathematical Philosophy*. London: George Allen and Unwin.

Schiffer, S. (1995). "Descriptions, Indexicals, and Belief Reports: Some Dilemmas (But Not the Ones You Expect)." *Mind* 104: 107-31.

Schiffer, S. (2005). "Russell's Theory of Descriptions." *Mind* 114: 1135-83.

Soames, S. (2005). "Why Incomplete Definite Descriptions do not Defeat Russell's Theory of Descriptions." *Teorema* 24: 7-30.

Strawson, P. F. (1950). "On Referring." *Mind* 59: 320-44.

Wettstein, H. (1981). "Demonstrative Reference and Definite Descriptions." *Philosophical Studies* 40: 241-57.

PART V
Replies to the Essays

Stephen Schiffer

Acknowledgements

This book was conceived and executed entirely by Gary Ostertag—and at no small cost to him of time, effort, and psychological equanimity. I am extremely touched and honored by this tribute, and extremely grateful to Gary for rewarding me with it. I thank you, Gary, more than mere speech acts can convey.

  I also owe a huge debt of gratitude and appreciation to the contributors for their insightful and challenging contributions, and for taking on the task of doing them. Each contribution forced me to rethink my views, and I found writing my responses a difficult, albeit rewarding, task. In several instances I was on the verge of accepting very damaging objections to my work, only to be saved at the last moment by the realization that my job was to offer up the best responses my views permitted consonantly with my not abandoning them altogether.

PART V

Replies to the Essays

15

Pleonastic Entities
Responses to Amie Thomasson, Thomas Hofweber, Ian Rumfitt, and Michael Smith

15.1 Introduction

Central to *The Things We Mean* is the claim that there are pleonastic entities, these being things whose existence is entailed by what I call *something-from-nothing* transformations or inferences, such an inference being one in which from a premise that contains no singular term that refers to an F we can infer a conclusion that does contain a singular term that refers to an F. The claim is central because I go on to argue that the properties our predicates express are pleonastic properties and the things we believe and assert, and the things to which that-clauses in propositional-attitude and speech-act reports refer, are pleonastic propositions, and because of the use I make of those claims in attempting to resolve issues about meaning, vagueness, moral realism, conditionals, and the role of propositions in communication and in propositional-attitude explanations. It's no surprise, then, that several of the essays in this volume concern themselves to one degree or another with claims I make about the nature of pleonastic entities. What sets apart the essays in this section is their special concern with the question of whether or not there are pleonastic entities.

My one ally in this section is Amie Thomasson, a great friend of pleonastic entities. She agrees with me that something-from-nothing inferences deliver an ontological commitment to pleonastic entities, but she questions the way I characterize pleonastic entities, especially in my use of a conservative-extension criterion for being a pleonastic entity, and she claims that I didn't go far enough, in that I failed to appreciate the affinity that concepts of ordinary objects—tables, horses, volcanoes—have to the concepts I recognize as being concepts of pleonastic entities, an affinity, she has argued in a series of important publications, that can be used to display the ease with which we can show ordinary objects to exist, thereby countering the claim of the new metaphysical nihilists that ordinary objects like tables, horses, and volcanoes don't *really* exist. Since I am highly counter-suggestible by nature, in responding to Thomasson it was an effort not to disagree with her when she was agreeing with me, but I mastered that neurosis (on this occasion) and confine myself to defending the characterizations I gave of pleonastic entities and to suggesting that her easy approach to the existence of ordinary objects may be too easy, at least in the way she claims it is easy.

Remnants of Meaning argued that that-clauses weren't referring expressions and that ostensible quantification over possible objects of belief wasn't objectual quantification over anything. *The Things We Mean*, published fifteen years later, contends that that-clauses in belief reports refer to pleonastic propositions and that ostensible quantification over objects of belief is objectual quantification over those propositions. Thomas Hofweber thinks the about-face was a big mistake, but his essay is less concerned to show that my *Things* view is false than it is to point out that the little I say in *Things* about why I changed my mind falls short of justifying it and to suggest that a return to a *Remnants*-type view can be motivated by a deft use of certain notions borrowed from linguistics combined with a version of substitutional quantification he calls the "inferential role" reading of quantifiers. In my response to Hofweber I say more about what motivated my change of mind and, of course, I find disparaging things to say about his positive proposals. I'm relieved I didn't feel compelled to endure the humiliation of yet another change of mind.

Ian Rumfitt raises a quite different concern with my claims about objectual quantification over pleonastic propositions. He claims (i) that quantification over them is possible only if it makes sense to ask whether pleonastic proposition P = pleonastic proposition Q, (ii) that it makes sense to ask such questions only if we know how to answer them in favorable cases, (iii) that we can have such knowledge only if we have a criterion of identity for pleonastic proposition, and, I gather, (iv) that such a criterion would have to take the form of an abstraction principle that does for pleonastic proposition what Frege thought Hume's principle did for cardinal numbers. My response to Rumfitt is not that he has set the bar for answering questions about propositional identity too high. My response to him concedes that on my account it's not possible to know that pleonastic proposition P = pleonastic proposition Q but adds that that is no barrier to their existence or to our ability objectually to quantify over them. The point turns on an interesting feature of vagueness and bears on my account of how the references of that-clauses are contextually determined.

Chapter 6 of *Things*, "Moral Realism and Indeterminacy," challenges the theory of pleonastic properties and propositions. The challenge is this: since the theory entails that moral predicates express moral properties and moral sentences express moral propositions, the pleonastic theory evidently entails cognitivism, the claim that a moral sentence such as 'Eating animals is wrong' has the same kind of meaning as a fact-stating sentence such as 'Eating animals is a source of protein'; but cognitivism is called into questions by certain familiar arguments. One such argument, which I call the *Argument from Internalism*, claims that one can't accept the judgment that Xing is wrong unless one disfavors Xing in a certain way, but that if cognitivism is correct then to accept the judgment that Xing is wrong would just be to believe that a certain fact obtained—viz. that Xing has the property of being wrong—and, as Hume pointed out, believing that a fact obtains is compatible with feeling any way at all about it. One main point of Chapter 6 is to show that the pleonastic conception of properties and propositions is not only compatible with there being an internalist component to moral judgments but that it can be used to *explain* it. Michael Smith questions both whether I have succeeded in explaining anything and whether I've shown that the pleonastic conception of properties and propositions is compatible with Internalism about moral judgments. My response to him makes explicit the argument strategy of Chapter 6 and tries to explain why that strategy isn't undermined by the considerations he invokes.

15.2 The Easy Approach to Ontology: Response to Amie Thomasson

It is heartening to have such a resourceful philosophical ally as Amie Thomasson, and I welcome this opportunity to engage with her own "easy approach to ontology"—which I'll call *the Easy Approach*—both for the view's intrinsic interest and, more immediately, for the promise it holds of explaining, generalizing, and correcting aspects of my own "pleonastic conception" of properties, propositions, fictional characters, states, and events. In section 15.2.1 of this response I will restate the view that constitutes the core of the Easy Approach and explain the ways Thomasson either explicitly or implicitly brings the core view to bear on my pleonastic conception of the things just mentioned. In section 15.2.2 I will ask whether the core view is correct, and whether, if it is, it bears on my account of pleonastic entities in the ways Thomasson thinks it does.

15.2.1

My restatement of Thomasson's core view will use the following conventions:

- An italicized uppercase letter (e.g. *K*) is a placeholder for terms, and thus '*K*' is a placeholder for quotation-expressions such as 'table' that result by replacing *K* with a term.
- A sentence matrix using *K* or '*K*' functions in effect as a claim that every substitution instance of the matrix is true. For example,

    If '*K*' denotes, then *K*s exist

    should be read as implying

    If 'table' denotes, then tables exist.

Then the core view is as follows:

If '*K*' is a "well-formed" sortal term,[1] then '*K*' has an "application condition" *C* such that:

1) *C* is a "semantic rule of use ... which speakers master in becoming competent with applying and refusing the term";[2]

2) satisfaction of *C* entails that there is something to which '*K*' applies (i.e. something '*K*' denotes);

3) *C* is used by speakers to determine when '*K*' applies (so it can't be an application condition for '*K*' that '*K*' applies to a thing if it's a *K*).

Now, it's trivially true that *K*s exist if there is something '*K*' denotes, and this affords in principle the following easy two-step way of establishing that *K*s exist: first, discern—no doubt in the usual philosophical way of armchair conceptual, or semantic, analysis—that such-and-such condition is an application condition for '*K*'; second, point out that the condition is satisfied.

We are now positioned to understand five claims about the bearing of the Easy Approach on my account of pleonastic entities.

1. *The Easy Approach explains how something-from-nothing inferences establish the existence of pleonastic entities.* According to the account of pleonastic entities I developed in *Things* and elsewhere,[3] a pleonastic entity is one whose existence can be established by a something-from-nothing inference, that being a valid inference from a statement that involves no reference to an F or quantification over Fs to one that does involve reference to an F or quantification over Fs. So, for example, properties are pleonastic entities: from the statement

Fido is a dog,

whose only singular term is 'Fido', we may validly infer the pleonastically equivalent statement

Fido has the property of being a dog,

which contains the new singular term 'the property of being a dog,' whose referent is the property of being a dog. Now the inference

Fido is a dog.
So, Fido has the property of being a dog.

is of course not formally valid, but it is, I claimed, conceptually valid: it's a conceptual truth that if Fido is a dog, then Fido has the property of being a dog. The Easy Approach offers an explanation of why it's a conceptual truth: The rules of use that determine application conditions for sortal predicates also induce application conditions for singular referring expressions formed from those predicates. Thus, the semantic rules governing the use of 'property' secure that if Fido is a dog, then the singular term 'the property of being a dog', as it occurs in 'Fido has the property of being a dog', is bound to refer. In the same way, the semantic rules that govern state and event terms secure that "if 'Fido bit FiFi' is true, then the singular event term 'Fido's biting FiFi' is guaranteed to refer, and if 'The stair rail is rusting' is true, the singular state term 'The stair rail's state of rusting' is guaranteed to refer."[4]

2. *The Easy Approach also explains (pace Schiffer) how something-from-nothing inferences can even establish the existence of such ordinary things as tables.* Let 'there are particles arranged tablewise' mean (to a rough approximation) that there are particles

arranged (in part by the work of an artisan or factory, etc. with the right sorts of intentions) in such a way that they are bonded together in a fashion that enables them to jointly perform the characteristic functions of tables, at a height to accommodate a seated person eating, and so on.[5]

Then, Thomasson would say, it's a conceptual truth that there is a table wherever there are particles arranged tablewise, because one who has mastery of the English word 'table' and knows that there are particles arranged tablewise will *eo ipso* also know that an acceptance condition for 'table' is satisfied, thus making it possible for that person to establish that there is a table via the something-from-nothing inference

There are particles arranged tablewise.
So, there is a table.

3. *There are of course people who can apply 'table' even though they lack the concept of a subatomic particle, and this shows that 'table' has an application condition that can be used to establish the existence of tables without recourse to any something-from-nothing inference.* For example, Thomasson tells us that anyone who knows how to use 'table', and therefore has the concept of a table, "is entitled, upon veridically perceiving [Thomasson's] dining room, to conclude that tables exist—even if she does not begin from a separate uncontroversial truth in making an inference to that conclusion."[6]

4. *The easy approach undermines Schiffer's conservative-extension criterion for pleonastic entities in two important ways.* The first way, Thomasson would say, is that it undermines my motivation for the conservative-extension criterion. Suppose we stipulatively define a wishdate as "a person whose existence supervenes on someone's wishing for a date, every such wish bringing into existence a person to date."[7] Then we may ask why it is that, say,

Mary was born on a Friday

So, *Mary's birth* was on a Friday

but not

Mary wished for a date

So, Mary has a date

is a valid something-from-nothing inference? To answer this I proposed a certain refinement of the rough idea that Fs were pleonastic entities, and thus amenable to something-from-nothing inferences, just in case the result of adding the concept of an F, with its attendant something-from-nothing entailments, to a theory T would result in a theory that conservatively extends T.[8] The claim then was that whereas the concepts *property, proposition, event*, etc. pass the conservative-extension criterion, the concept *wishdate* doesn't. Thomasson, however, offers to explain the difference between events and wishdates in a different way: whereas anyone's being born is an application condition for the event sortal 'birth', someone's wishing for a date can't be an application condition for the sortal 'wishdate', and this because any application condition for 'wishdate' must include an application condition for 'person', and we know that no sort of wishing can be an application condition for that sortal. So wishdates can be ruled out without the need for a complicated conservative-extension criterion. The second way the easy approach is supposed to bear on my conservative-extension criterion is that, whereas the criterion is supposed to let in only those things I considered pleonastic entities, it in fact lets in things such as tables and volcanoes, which are supposed not to be pleonastic entities. Thomasson explains:

The question of whether a given concept is a conservative extension is a *relative* matter: relative to the prior theory accepted. Once we have a thing language that enables us to say that the notebook is red, we may indeed conservatively extend it by adding the notion of a property....

But...we can also use trivial inferences to acquire commitment to tables and trees, if we start...from an undisputed claim such as 'there are particles arranged volcanowise'.... The concept of <volcano> would not conservatively extend a prior theory that had no grip on exploding lava-filled peaks, but it would conservatively extend a prior theory that made empirical claims couched in the language of particles being arranged volcanowise. And the same could be said for other concepts of concreta. This undermines the claimed contrast [between such things as properties and such things as volcanoes] ...[9]

5. *Schiffer's discussions of pleonastic entities is liberally sprinkled with metaphors debasing the ontological status of the things he takes to be pleonastic entities— properties, propositions, fictional characters, etc.—vis-à-vis physical objects like horses and volcanoes—but the foregoing points show that ordinary physical objects and his pleonastic entities are in the same ontological boat, and that therefore his deflationary rhetoric is unwarranted.* I do say that propositions, properties et al. are not as ontologically and conceptually independent of us as rocks and electrons, and while I nowhere say that pleonastic entities other than fictional characters are language-created, I do say it's as though the concepts of pleonastic entities had been explicitly introduced via the something-from-nothing transformations that govern them. Thomasson's point is that, if she has shown, as she claims to have shown, that the existence of, say, volcanoes is conceptually entailed by there being particles arranged volcanowise, then even volcanoes are such that it is as though the concept of them had been explicitly introduced by the something-from-nothing transformation that governs the concept of a volcano.

15.2.2

There are two critical questions: Is Thomasson's core view correct? Would its being correct bear on my conception of pleonastic entities in any of the ways 1–5?

Is the core view correct? This can't be answered before we have a better sense of what "acceptance conditions" are supposed to be—better, that is, than that conveyed by my statement of the core view. There are supposed to be semantic "rules of use" for 'table' that determine an existence-entailing acceptance condition C that we can know is satisfied if we know that there are particles arranged tablewise, and an existence-entailing acceptance condition $C^\#$ that we can know is satisfied just by looking at Thomasson's dining room. Are C and $C^\#$ the same or different? I don't see how they could be the same, since Thomasson is evidently committed to saying that only C can be the premise of a conceptually valid something-from-nothing inference. In any case, there is a problem with seeing how $C^\#$ could be an acceptance condition which doesn't arise for C. This is that the concept of a table is a *functional* concept in that a thing is a table only if it was made or is used with certain intentions, but no condition which one can *see* is satisfied just by looking at Thomasson's dining room will *entail* anything about the intentions with which something satisfying the condition was made or is used. This problem doesn't arise for acceptance condition C, the condition one is supposed to know is satisfied just by knowing that there are particles arranged tablewise, for the functional condition in question is supposed to be built into the concept expressed by 'tablewise'.

C, however, confronts its own problems. For consider the inference:

> There are particles arranged tablewise.
> So, there is at least one table.

'Tablewise' is an abbreviation, and the displayed inference—which I'll call *Particles*—is the same (to a "rough approximation") as:

> There are particles arranged "(in part by the work of an artisan or factory, etc. with the right sorts of intentions) in such a way that they are bonded together in a fashion that enables them to jointly perform the characteristic functions of tables, at a height to accommodate a seated person eating, and so on."
> So, there is at least one table.

Thomasson says that Particles is conceptually valid. Yet even if it is, her concern isn't with tables but with all ordinary physical objects. This means that she must be able to replace all reference to persons, factories, and intentions in Particles with talk of particles arranged in a certain way, where the statement of the way they must be arranged makes no reference to persons, factories, or intentions. Can that be done? Well, she might say that 'particles arranged tablewise' means *particles so arranged that some subset of them would constitute a table if there are any tables*. Then Thomasson might explain that in order for particles to be so arranged, some of them must be so arranged as to constitute persons with such-and-such intentions, if there are any persons, and likewise for all the other "non-fundamental" things whose existence would be required by the existence of tables. But then it would be considerably less than obvious that there being particles arranged tablewise *would* conceptually entail that tables exist. After all, I'm competent in the use of 'table', and while I suppose that such an arrangement of particles would *metaphysically* entail the existence of a table (and of people and whatever else must exist in order for tables to exist), I'm unable to say that introspecting on my use of 'table' affords me a confident basis from which to issue claims of *conceptual* entailment. There is also another important difference between paradigm pleonastic something-from-nothing inferences, such as, on the one hand,

> Fido is a dog.
> So, it's true that Fido is a dog.

> Fido is a dog.
> So, Fido has the property of being a dog.

> FDR died in 1945.
> So, FDR's death was in 1945.

and, on the other hand, the inference

> There are particles so arranged that some subset of them would constitute a table if there are any tables.
> So, there is at least one table.

even if it's in some sense "conceptually" valid. This is that in a pleonastic something-from-nothing inference, not only does the premise contain no reference to or quantification over the pleonastic entity introduced in the conclusion, it's also the case that the pleonastic concept introduced in the conclusion doesn't even *occur* in the premise. That is as much a defining feature of pleonastic something-from-nothing inferences as the no-reference feature I used to characterize those inferences. In writing about something-from-nothing inferences I thought I didn't need to make a big deal about the no-concept feature because the no-reference feature was already a sufficient condition for being the sort of something-from-nothing inference to which I wished to draw attention, but I would have included the no-concept feature as a defining feature if it had occurred to me that inferences like Particles were possibly conceptually valid. Now, the prospect of producing a plausible version of *Particles* that doesn't invoke any ordinary-object concept strikes me as being about as promising as the prospect of reducing physical-object talk to sense-data talk when one appreciates that talk of the sense-data a normal perceiver would have in certain circumstances was to no avail unless the reference to perceivers and circumstances could be replaced with expressions that referred only to sense data.

I agree with Thomasson that tables exist, but I very much doubt that you could convince an advocate of serious ontology like Ted Sider that they do by showing him that a non-question-begging "application condition" for being a table was satisfied. She might, however, ask him which premise in his exceedingly abstruse and arcane argument is supposed to come across to us as have anything remotely like the plausibility the claim that there are tables already has for us when we confront his skeptical argument. I don't see that Thomasson has succeeded in making her core view plausible.

But suppose the core view is correct. Would it then bear on my claims about pleonastic entities in any of ways 1–5?

Claim 1 was the claim that the Easy Approach explains how something-from-nothing inferences establish the existence of pleonastic entities. Well, my explanation of the validity of something-from-nothing inferences was that the premises of those inferences conceptually entailed their conclusions; so the Easy Approach would explain the validity of something-from-nothing inferences only if it explained why those entailments were conceptual. But if the Easy Approach did explain that, then it would show that something from-nothing-inferences were available to establish the existence of tables, horses and volcanos. But that is what has been put in doubt.

Claim 2 was that, contrary to what I maintain, the Easy Approach also explains how something-from-nothing inferences can even establish the existence of such ordinary things as tables. Here there are two problems. The first is the one already labored, that Thomasson has failed to show that there are conceptually valid something-from-nothing inferences whose conclusions entail that there are ordinary objects of any kind. The second problem is that, as I stated the core of the Easy Approach, it doesn't entail that there are such something-from-nothing inferences. For the Easy Approach claims merely that ordinary-object sortal predicates have non-question-begging "application conditions,"[10] and, as Thomasson herself seems to acknowledge, that doesn't entail anything about there being conceptually valid something-from-nothing inferences to prove the existence of the ordinary objects that satisfy the application conditions.

Claim 3 was that 'table' has an application condition that can be used to establish the existence of tables without recourse to any something-from-nothing inference. But the only explanation I could find of that condition was that it was a condition one could see was satisfied by merely looking at Thomasson's dining room. But, as I remarked above, a condition one could *see* was satisfied in that way wouldn't entail that one was perceiving objects with the functional properties things must have in order to be tables. Besides, even if there were such conditions, it's difficult to see how they could help establish the existence of ordinary objects if they presupposed the existence of other kinds of ordinary objects, and, as I also remarked above, it's extremely implausible that any ordinary-object concept could have an application condition the application of which didn't require one to know antecedently that there were ordinary objects of some kind. Still, I have so little understanding of what these application conditions are supposed to be that I can't be entirely confident that the problems I've raised hit the right target.

Claim 4 was that the Easy Approach undermines my conservative-extension criterion for pleonastic entities in two ways. The first way is supposed to be that it undermines the reason I thought I needed such a criterion, which was to show that the definition I gave of a "wishdate" couldn't bring wishdates into existence. Thomasson's point was that I could have explained that, without a technical criterion, by pointing out that the concept *person* precluded its having an application condition of the sort the definition of 'wishdate' was trying to provide. Well, it is indeed true that the concept of a person precludes the definition of a wishdate from providing an application condition for *person*, but I don't see that as an as objection, since the conservative-extension criterion was in effect trying to *explain* why that was so. The second way the Easy Approach (aka "the core view") was supposed to undermine the conservative-extension criterion was that, *if* the core view was correct it would entail that ordinary objects like tables would satisfy the criterion, thus refuting my claim that the criterion would keep those guys out. Not so. The criterion would let those things in only if the existence of those things could be secured by conceptually valid something-from-nothing inferences and it's neither the case that it's plausible that there are such inferences nor that the core view entails that there are.

Claim 5 was that, because ordinary physical objects and pleonastic entities are in the same ontological boat, my invidious comparison of the ontological status of pleonastic entities with that of ordinary physical objects was based on a false assumption. I have already explained why I am not yet convinced that my assumption was false.

* * *

I appreciate and sympathize with Thomasson's attempt to provide a silver bullet against the creeping threat of the neo-nihilists. It would be very nice if one could *prove* to the likes of Cian Dorr and Ted Sider that there really do exist such things as tables, horses, and volcanoes. Failing the ability to do that, we'll just have to keep on pointing out to them that they give us no good reason to think otherwise.

15.3 Reference, Quantification, Propositions: Response to Thomas Hofweber

Necessarily, if

1. Molly and Herb are two people Phil admires,

then

2. There are two people Phil admires.

Evidently, there is an "objectual" reading of the quantifier phrase 'there are' in (2), and on that reading (2) is true only if there exist two people whom Phil admires. Does the quantifier also have a "nonobjectual" reading on which (2) doesn't entail that there *exists* anything that Phil admires? It isn't clear what this question is asking, given how little 'exist' is used in ordinary English (we say 'Dinosaurs no longer exist', but 'There is a student waiting to see you' is considerably more natural than 'There exists a student waiting to see you'), and given that philosophers, including Hofweber, who use the term in what can only be a technical sense offer little guidance to those who would like to understand what they mean by 'exists'. Anyway, let's suppose that the quantifier phrase 'there are' has what Hofweber calls a nonobjectual "inferential role" reading, a reading, he acknowledges, that is a version of substitutional quantification which permits substitution instances to have context-sensitive elements. On this substitutional, or inferential-role, reading, (2) is true if (1) is true, but the truth of (2) doesn't *per se* require the occurrences of 'Molly' and 'Herb' in (1) to have referents.

Of course, even if (2) has a reading that doesn't *per se* require that there *exists* anyone who is a friend of Phil's, whether or not (2) can *in fact* be true if there are no friends of Phil's to make it true turns wholly on whether (1) can be true if 'Molly' and 'Holly' don't refer to anything, or don't in some other way require persons as semantic values. For anyone who thinks the existence of persons is worth debating *and* that an utterance of (1) may be true, *the key question isn't about quantification, but about whether (1)'s being true requires its names in subject position to have referents*. The need to fuss about nonobjectual readings of (2) arises only when one wants to deny the existence of persons yet affirm that there may be true utterances of sentences like (1). And for a theorist who does want to deny that 'Molly' and 'Holly' need referents in order for (2) to be true, it's a good bet that her point of departure won't be a sexy new theory of the semantics of sentences like (1) that doesn't require names in subject position to refer. Her point of departure will rather be a combination of metaphysical (as opposed to semantic) reasons she takes herself to have for denying the existence of persons (perhaps she thinks that only "noncomposite" things exist) and a reluctance to deny that there can be true utterances of sentences like (1). Only if that is her point of departure will a theorist be motivated to cast about for a nonontologically committing semantics for (1), as well as a nonontologically committing reading of (2), provided she allows that there is a reading of (2) on which it's entailed by (1).

Sentences (3) and (4) are very much like (1) and (2), and they bring me to some of the difficult issues Hofweber skillfully raises.

3. *Modesty* and *humility* are two attributes Phil admires.

4. There are two attributes Phil admires.

As I understand his position, Hofweber holds that attributes (i.e. properties) don't exist, and that therefore there are no attributes to be the referents of 'modesty' and 'humility' in (3) (or anywhere else), but that (3) might nevertheless be true, and on the reading on which it might be true there is a reading of (4) that it entails. I assume that what he would say about (3) and (4) with regard to the occurrences in them of 'modesty' and 'humility' he would also say, *mutatis mutandis*, about the italicized terms in (5)–(10c) and whatever general statements they entail in which their quantifiers bind variables that occupy a position previously occupied by an italicized term in (5)–(9c):

5. Fuchsia = Harvey's favorite color.
6. Logicism = the proposition that arithmetic reduces to logic.
7. The fact that women are not permitted to drive in Saudi Arabia is outrageous.
8. 'Quantum mechanics' and 'wave mechanics' refer to *the same theory*, and 'fuchsia' is just another name for *magenta*.

9a. Frege believed *logicism*.

9b. Frege believed the proposition that arithmetic reduces to logic.

9c. Frege believed that arithmetic reduces to logic.

Hofweber's position—not to mention the one I occupied in *Remnants*—raises certain obvious questions:

a. *What reasons are there for doubting the existence of properties and propositions?* To the best of my knowledge, Hofweber hasn't been explicit about his reasons in any of his publications, but this may be because he accepts some of the well-known reasons offered by other outstanding philosophers. For example, Nelson Goodman seems merely to have been concerned "that there should not be more things dreamt of in [his] philosophy than there are in heaven or earth;"[11] Quine fretted about properties' and propositions' not having conditions of identity; Benacerraf and Field can't see how we can have knowledge or reliable beliefs about abstract objects, given that we have no direct or indirect sensory or other causal contact with them. Some contemporary philosophers dismiss properties and propositions, along with human beings, cats, rocks, and tables, because such things are left out when nature is "carved at its joints" and all that remains are things that belong to the "ultimate furniture of the universe." Much more than we might like to admit, the philosophical positions to which we are drawn are determined by psychological factors that are independent of any reasons we might have for occupying those positions, and I can't say to what extent the attachment I had to physicalism and nominalism during the first two decades of my career was due to my having as an infant philosopher imprinted on my undergraduate teacher Nelson Goodman. Of course, when I wrote *Remnants* I took myself to have reasons. I thought the Benacerraf-Field argument made a good case for skepticism about the abstract objects it targeted, but that wasn't the argument on which I explicitly relied in *Remnants* for my own skepticism about propositions and properties. One argument I had applied only to propositions, and it didn't purport to show that no propositions existed, but merely that none existed that could be the referents of that-clauses and thus the contents of propositional attitudes and speech acts (I believed that propositions were contents only if they were the referents of that-clauses in belief and speech-act reports). Consider an utterance of 'Alice believes that Harold is a dog.' I assumed that the uttered token of 'that Harold is a dog' referred to a proposition only if that proposition was determined by the that-clause's syntax and the semantic values of the word tokens that compose its embedded sentence token. I then focused on the contribution that the token of 'dog' might make to the determination of the proposition to which the that-clause token might refer. I took familiar Fregean considerations to show that the token of 'dog' can't merely contribute to the proposition the property of being a dog, despite the efforts of contemporary Russellians to show otherwise, and then I argued by elimination that no "mode of presentation" ("guise," "way of thinking") of doghood was available to be what the token of 'dog' contributes to the proposition to which the that-clause token referred. Because I couldn't see how a proposition could be determined as the referent of a that-clause token if not as a function of semantic values of its constituent word tokens, I was motivated to deny that that-clauses referred to propositions. That motivation was fortified by arguments I took to show that what compositional semantics for public languages were invoked to explain could be explained without that invocation, and I concluded, by the obvious generalization, that that-clauses didn't refer to propositions. My skepticism about the existence of properties had its roots in a skepticism about the existence of intentional properties. I thought that if there were such properties, then they played an ineliminable causal-explanatory role in true common-sense propositional-attitude explanations, as when one explains Billy's crawling under his bed by saying that he wants to find his collection of Keith Richards' cigarette butts and believes it's under his bed. I thought that if there were intentional properties (e.g. the property of believing that such-and-such), then in order to explain their causal-explanatory role in such explanations, one would have to show that they could be identified with physical or functional properties, but I thought there were good arguments to show that it was doubtful that such reductions were to be had.

I would not have switched from my *Remnants* position to my *Things* position if I hadn't thought, as I continue to think, that none of the reasons just mentioned for the nonexistence of properties and propositions were good reasons given the availability of the pleonastic conception of those entities. That point is elaborated and defended in *Things*, but because I wanted the book to be accessible to readers who hadn't read *Remnants*, the discussion in *Things* wasn't presented as a response to *Remnants*. I did, however, allude to it in the couple of pages in which I summarized my reasons for the change. In *Remnants* I spoke about the "pleonastic sense" of 'property', 'proposition', 'fact', etc. that allowed one to move back and forth between, e.g., 'Fido is a dog' and its pleonastic equivalent 'Fido has *the property of being a dog*' or 'It's true *that Fido is a dog*'. But while I allowed that the sentences containing the italicized ostensible terms may be true, I denied that they occurred as referring to or denoting anything. What I came to appreciate, in part as a result of Mark Johnston's prodding,[12] was that, given the pleonastic conception of propositions and properties, whatever allowed one to know the propositions expressed by sentences containing pleonastic occurrences of the questionable terms would also suffice to establish corresponding truths about the referents of those terms. This is what I was alluding to—too cryptically, I now appreciate—when I wrote the paragraph in *Things* (91) which sums up by saying that "the doctrine of pleonastic propositions and properties is merely, so to speak, a hypostatization of what I used to say when I denied that there were such things as properties and propositions—except 'pleonastically speaking', as I said even [in *Remnants*]," and which I also alluded to in my response to Hofweber's contribution to the 2006 symposium on *Things* in *Philosophy and Phenomenological Research* (Hofweber 2006b), where I said that part of the reason I came to reject my *Remnants* position on the existence of propositions and properties

was that I saw that what I said about pleonastic properties and propositions when I regarded ostensible reference to them as a *façon de parler* could easily be worked into a deflationary account of what it was for such things to exist, and I saw that the reasons that I and others thought they had for denying the existence of properties and propositions were answered if those things were pleonastic entities, in the way explained in *The Things We Mean*. For example, Hartry Field wondered how we could have reliable beliefs about numbers and other abstract objects, given that we have no causal or other contingent connection to them that would explain how we could have reliable beliefs about them. But that isn't a problem on the pleonastic conception of those things, since the truths about which we're reliable are seen to be [based on] conceptual truths that we know a priori [e.g. that if Fido is a dog, then Fido has the property of being a dog].[13]

Hofweber complains that many of the things I say in *Things* "seem...just as good with the old theory of propositions from *Remnants*" (56). I agree, but don't see it as an infelicity: it's a consequence of the fact that "the doctrine of pleonastic propositions and properties is merely...a hypostatization of [my *Remnants* view]" (*Things* 91). One of the things I especially came to appreciate was how details of the pleonastic conception of propositions explained how a proposition was contextually determined as the reference (or denotation) of a that-clause token without having to be determined either by the speaker's referential intentions or as a function of semantic values of the expression tokens that compose the that-clause token. I tried to spell this out in *Things* §2.4,[14] and I think that what I said there is further illuminated by the distinction I made in more recent work between the 'Fido'-Fido and 'Midtown'-Midtown models of the name-named relations.[15] In any case, my agreement here with Hofweber explains why it would be pretty much OK with me if the nonreferential, nonobjectual-quantification view of *Remnants*, or Hofweber's improved version of that line, were correct.

b. *Hofweber's position evidently implies that there may be true occurrences of sentences (3)–(9c), but only on the condition that the italicized terms in them don't contribute referents or any other kind of semantic values to the determination of the truth-values of the utterances in which they occur.* How then does he suppose that the terms in question contribute to the determination of the truth-values of the sentences containing them, or does he take them not to make any contribution? Hofweber makes two claims that bear on this question, but neither answers it. He would allow that the italicized expressions in (3)–(9b) are syntactically either names or definite descriptions, and therefore require referents (or denotations) if they are also functioning semantically as names or definite descriptions, but he says that stand-alone that-clauses—e.g. the that-clause in 'Al believes that Lola snores', as opposed to the one in 'Al believes the rumor that Lola snores'—are no kind of singular term, and that they function semantically in just the way that expressions of its syntactic category are supposed to function. That function in a sentence of the form 'A believes that S' isn't to refer to what the subject is said to believe, but instead to specify it. This, however, is puzzling for two reasons. First, because specifying what a person believes is perfectly compatible with referring to what she believes; anyone who holds that that-clauses refer to things believed will acknowledge that they also specify what agents believe. Second, to be told that that-clauses specify the contents of propositional attitudes isn't per se to be told anything about how that-clauses contribute to the determination of the truth conditions of the sentences containing them, that is to say, gives no idea what clauses must be written for that-clauses in a compositional truth theory, or even whether or not that determination can be explained in such a theory. Hofweber gives no account of the semantic import of the specifying role of that-clauses. In Remnants and elsewhere,[16] I argued that if the truth-value of a belief report was a function of its syntax and the semantic values of its constituent morphemes, then that-clauses have propositions as their semantic values, and I then argued by modus tollens that the truth-value wasn't compositionally determined in that way. That required me to come up with an account of language processing that didn't require an internally represented compositional semantics. Hofweber neither suggests something other than a proposition to be the semantic value of a belief report's that-clause nor denies that a semantic value is needed.

What about the other italicized expressions, the ones in (3)–(9b)? Hofweber offers no account of the italicized expressions as they occur in sentences like (3)–(9b). He does offer an account of what those expressions are up to semantically in other kinds of sentences, but what he says about those cases doesn't apply to (3)–(9b). Hofweber contrasts what he calls "innocent" statements such as

10. Fido is a dog.

11. Jupiter has four moons.

with what he calls their "metaphysically loaded counterparts" such as

12. That Fido is a dog is true.

13. Fido has the property of being a dog.

14. The number of moons of Jupiter is four.

(the italicized expressions are of course what make (12)–(14) "metaphysically loaded"). His account of (12)–(13) borrows and extends two notions from linguistics. In the theory of syntax deriving from Chomsky, a pronoun is said to occur in a sentence as an *expletive* (or *pleonastic*[17] or *dummy*) *pronoun* when, while a bona fide syntactic constituent of the sentence, it contributes no semantic value to the determination of the sentence's truth-value; it is, as it were, semantically idle. For example, 'it' and 'there' occur as expletive pronouns in 'It's raining' and 'There's a storm coming.' The notion of an expletive clearly extends unproblematically to expressions of any category: an expression occurs expletively in a sentence provided it's semantically idle in it. A *focus construction*, again in linguistic theory, is a way of giving part of a sentence special prominence or emphasis. In '*I* ate all the caviar' intonation is used to give the pronoun 'I' prominence, perhaps in a situation in which it's known that some rascal ate all the caviar, but not known who that rascal was. The same focus effect can be achieved syntactically in various ways, for example by a cleft construction as in 'It was I who ate all the caviar.' Hofweber's account of the "metaphysically loaded" terms in (12)–(14) invokes the notions both of the expletive use of an expression and of a focus construction. As regards the notion of an expletive, his claim is (i) that the italicized "metaphysically loaded" terms occur expletively in (12)–(14), and therefore not only don't contribute any referents to the determination of the sentences' truth-values, but don't contribute any kind of semantic value at all, and (ii) that *the only way* (12)–(14) can be true is if their italicized terms occur expletively. A corollary of this (nearly enough) is that there is no sense in which the truth of (10) or (11) necessitate the existence of properties, propositions, or numbers. As regards the notion of a focus construction, his claim is that it constructs (12) and (13) from (10), and (14) from (11), and that the effect of such transformations is to put into prominence corresponding parts or features of (10) and (11), while giving (12) and (13) the same truth-conditional meaning as (10), and (14) the same as (11), it being assumed that that meaning doesn't necessitate the existence of properties, propositions, or numbers. The significance of examples (3)–(9b) is that, even if what Hofweber says about (12)–(14) is true, it seems unable to generalize to an account of (3)–(9b) that has any chance of being true. The reason is simple: none of those sentences is pleonastically equivalent to a sentence that doesn't contain the italicized term. Perhaps Hofweber would say that there can't be true occurrences of (3)–(9b), but I doubt he would say that, and if he doesn't we need to know why there isn't a univocal account of the italicized terms which includes their use in (12)–(14).

c. *Hofweber claims that both my appeal to nonobjectual quantification in Remnants and my account of pleonastic properties and propositions in Things founder on the problem of inexpressible properties and propositions, but that his own "inferential-role" account of quantification is unthreatened by that problem.* What truth is there to this? In the first place, whatever the problem of inexpressible propositions is taken to be, I don't see that Hofweber has a better way of dealing with it than I did in *Remnants*. This is because I can't see that there is a relevant difference between the two accounts. Hofweber's account is supposed to be unthreatened by inexpressible properties and propositions because he allows for substitution instances of quantified sentences to have context-sensitive elements, and his claim is that, while "not every proposition is expressible in the sense of 'can be expressed with a sentence without context sensitive elements in it'," "every proposition is expressible in the sense of 'can be expressed with a sentence in some context or other'" (66). Well, if that is so, then the account of substitutional quantification proposed in *Remnants* is also off the hook, for it explicitly allows substitution instances to contain context-sensitive elements:

What about ineffable thoughts? Might it not be true that

Ralph is now thinking something

even though there was no true substitution-instance of the following sentence form?

Ralph is now thinking that S.

It is difficult to see how, when we appreciate that substitutions for 'S' may contain demonstratives and roundabout descriptions. Thus Ralph might report his ineffable thought by saying 'I think that she has that certain *je ne sais quoi* that no words can convey'.[18]

In the second place, "ineffable thoughts" isn't the real problem, nor is it, as Hofweber seems to think, object-dependent properties that are "inexpressible" because the objects on which they are dependent don't yet exist.[19] What I understood to be the real threat were propositions to which we might stand in the way dogs stand to the Banach-Tarski theorem. It was to propositions that were radically inexpressible in that way that I was referring when I suggested, in *Remnants*, that

> we can make sense of [a sentence such as 'There are truths that our language is inadequate to express and that we are constitutionally unable to conceive'] because we can imagine there being creatures like us, but with greater perceptual and intellectual powers, with languages that were extensions of ours, in which the alluded-to truths would be expressible. (71)

and it was in this connection that I said that 'there are' in the troublesome sentence just cited was nonobjectual but not strictly speaking substitutional. Actually—and this is something about which I should have been much more candid (and perhaps a little less confused)—the apparent appeal in *Remnants* to any form of substitutional quantification was little more than a heuristic, since if ordinary language quantifiers do have a nonobjectual reading there is no more reason to demand that it be definable than there is to demand that objectual quantification be definable. Yet whether or not there being truths that are to us as the Banach-Tarski theorem is to dogs is a problem for my *Remnants* view; it is, ironically, definitely a problem for Hofweber's view, for he says that "every proposition is expressible in the sense of 'can be expressed with a sentence in some context or other'," but if there are propositions that are inaccessible to us in the way that the Banach-Tarski theorem is inaccessible to dogs it would be false that every proposition is expressible "in the sense of 'can be expressed with a sentence in some context or other'."[20]

In the third place, and perhaps most importantly in the current context, Hofweber's claim that inexpressible properties and propositions threaten the pleonastic conception of properties and propositions is mistaken. I think three things may have led him to think that inexpressible properties and propositions were a problem for the account of properties and propositions advanced in *Things*.

(i) "The most serious problem," Hofweber writes, "for...any theory that holds that propositions are not language independent entities, which includes Schiffer's theory in *Things*, is the inexpressibility worry" (65). He doesn't say why he thinks that my view entails that propositions are not language-independent entities, nor what exactly he means by 'not language independent.' I find this surprising, since at the very beginning of *Things* I stipulatively define propositions in part as mind- and language-independent entities in that they are not themselves mental or linguistic entities (in particular, nothing anyone ever said or thought brought any proposition into existence); indeed, the proposition *that there are prime numbers* exists and is true in every possible world, *a fortiori* in worlds without thinkers or speakers. In 1996 I published an early foray into pleonastic ontology that bore the oxymoronic title "Language-Created Language-Independent Entities," and I called the pleonastic conception of properties and propositions a conceptualist *manqué* theory, since the theory aimed to have enough in it to relieve the impulse towards conceptualism without actually falling into the preposterous consequences of that theory. There I say that there is a sense in which pleonastic entities are hypostatizations of our linguistic or conceptual practices, but in saying that I was alluding to what I claim is the way in which it's only owing to our use of language that properties and propositions become individuated for us in a way that enables us to gain epistemic access to them. That was the point of my imagining a possible world exactly like ours, except that our counterparts in that world don't have the concept of a property, and therefore have no way of thinking or talking about properties, even though the properties that exist in our world also exist in that world. For when I asked what it would take to bring the inhabitants of that world up to epistemological snuff with us as regards properties, I thought it would seem intuitively plausible that "what it would take, and all that it would take, would be for them to engage in a certain manner of speaking, a certain language game—namely, our property-hypostatizing practices, in particular our property-yielding something-from-nothing transformations."[21] That view doesn't entail that "completely alien propositions" (see note 10) can't exist; merely that we couldn't have epistemic access to them without first having ways to talk about them.

(ii) Hofweber says that one consideration I use to support my view that that-clauses refer to pleonastic propositions, and what in fact that view relies on, is Frege's account of numbers as logical objects, in particular to that part of it that Crispin Wright has called *the syntactic priority thesis*, which, according to Hofweber,

is the thesis that what it is to be an object is only to be understood as that which a singular term stands for. Thus the apparently semantic category of an object is to be understood as derivative of the apparently syntactic category of a singular term. Singular terms in true sentences do succeed to refer to objects since that's just what it is to be a referring term and what it is to be an object. (61)

Hofweber further understands the syntactic priority thesis to require that for every number there be a singular term denoting it, which, he says, is why real numbers are a problem for the thesis, as there are more real numbers than there are singular terms to denote them. He takes inexpressible propositions to be a problem for my acceptance of the syntactic priority thesis because it requires that there be a that-clause for every proposition.

I demur. First, Frege's view wasn't, and wasn't used as, a basis for my view about pleonastic propositions. I didn't arrive at my view from that view,[22] nor do I even mention it in presenting my conception of pleonastic propositions until p. 77, where I mention it only to point out an important parallel between my thesis about reference to propositions in belief reports and the Frege-Wright thesis about reference to numbers in arithmetical statements. The parallel is this. Ordinarily one can't truth-evaluate an utterance containing a referentially used singular term without first determining the referent of the singular term (e.g. you can't verify an utterance of

'She loves him' without first identifying the referents of the uttered tokens of 'she' and 'him'). But I claimed that in order to truth-evaluate a belief report such as an utterance of 'Ralph believes that George Eliot was a man' one doesn't first identify the proposition to which the uttered token of the that-clause refers; rather semantic values of 'Ralph', 'believes', 'George Eliot', and 'was a man' commingle with a motley and indeterminate congeries of contextual and non-contextual factors to determine what must hold in order for the report to be true, and those contextually determined truth conditions themselves determine the proposition to which the that-clause refers.[23] The parallel with the syntactic priority thesis to which I was primarily concerned to draw attention was Wright's claim on behalf of Frege that syntactic criteria establish numerals as singular terms that will refer to numbers whenever those numerals occur referentially in true statements, and that the ordinary arithmetical criteria enable one to establish the truth of those statements without one's having first to identify anything as the reference of the numerical singular terms. Second, notwithstanding that parallel, I *don't* accept—and am not even sure I understand—the claim that "what it is to be an object is only to be understood as that which a singular term stands for" or that "the apparently semantic category of an object [sic] is to be understood as derivative of the apparently syntactic category of a singular term." Third, and most importantly, my view does not entail that every proposition must be the referent of a that-clause. I could hardly hold that, since if it were true it would have to be the case that that-clause *types* refer to propositions, and as I emphasize in *Things* it's my view that that-clause types don't have referents, since "the referent of every, or virtually every, that-clause token is contextually determined" (79). So if my view is incompatible with there being inexpressible propositions, it's not because for every proposition there is a that-clause that refers to it. In fact, if my view is incompatible with there being inexpressible propositions, it would take an argument to show that, and I've no idea what that argument might be—which brings me to the third thing that may have led Hofweber to think my view is incompatible with inexpressible properties and propositions.

(iii) Towards the end of §2.3 of *Things*, the section in which I introduce and explain the notion of a pleonastic proposition, I say that "there are three questions about something-from-nothing transformations that must be addressed" (67), the third of which is the unfortunately telescoped question: "What about inexpressible properties?" In answering this, as Hofweber notes, I say that:

there might be properties that are ineffable, or perhaps effable only in the languages of vastly more intelligent creatures, or of creatures with much different sensory abilities. My view here is that we can make sense of such properties just by virtue of our ability to make sense of there being a language—an enrichment of our own language or a completely different language—in which such properties are expressible. (71)

This passage appears to advert to the discussion on pp. 66–7 that immediately preceded my turning to "three questions about something-from-nothing transformations that must be addressed." That discussion concerned the thought experiment mentioned above, in which I contrasted the answer to the question "How could people with no concept of a volcano discover the volcanoes that exist in their world?"

with the question "How could people with no concept of a property discover the properties that exist in their world?" The contrasting answers labored the fact that, whereas it's possible to discover volcanoes and then acquire the concept of a volcano, it wasn't possible to discover properties and then acquire the concept of a property, and this because having the concept of a property, and thus the linguistic practices that manifest possession of the concept, is both necessary and sufficient for acquiring knowledge of the properties expressed by one's predicates. We don't need singular terms that refer to volcanoes in order to gain epistemic access to them, but we do need singular terms for properties in order to gain epistemic access to them. This is because it's the conceptual role by virtue of which a term expresses or refers to a property that fixes the individuation of that property well enough for us to express, refer to, and have knowledge of the property. This doesn't mean that properties don't exist with the individuating conditions they actually have in possible worlds in which there are no words to express them. It means merely that the only way to gain epistemic access to them in any possible world is to have expressions that signify them in that world. Properties are unlike volcanoes in that respect, and this is what makes apt David Armstrong's metaphor of properties as shadows of predicates.

The reader is right to be puzzled by the fact that the author of *Things* wrote that "we can make sense of ineffable properties just by virtue of our ability to make sense of there being a language... in which such properties are expressible" (71). It also puzzles me, since there is no reason I need to accept. The theory put forward in *Things* unproblematically entails that there may exist properties that are beyond our ken in the way that the property of a quark's having spin ½ is beyond the ken of language users whose IQ is no higher than 50. True, the theory implies that the individuating conditions of the properties our predicates express mirror, and are determined by, the underived conceptual roles of those predicates, and that consequently we can't gain epistemic access to those properties unless we have expressions with the right conceptual roles, but conditions for gaining epistemic access aren't the same as conditions for the existence of the accessed properties. So, I meant that in order to "make sense" of the *existence* of ineffable properties we need to suppose there could be a language in which such properties are expressible, then I was apparently confused about my own theory: ineffable properties aren't even a *prima facie* problem for my theory, and no special suppositions are needed to know that they are possible. If, however, I meant merely that in order to make sense of our having epistemic access to properties that are now ineffable there must be expressions for those properties whose conceptual roles individuate those properties for us, then the passage quoted from *Things* is both poorly stated and puzzling with respect to its implicature that ineffable properties pose some sort of apparent threat to the doctrine of pleonastic properties or propositions.

15.4 Propositional Identity: Response to Ian Rumfitt

Ian Rumfitt, like Thomas Hofweber, questions my reasons for abandoning the "Priorean" view of *Remnants* for the more ontologically committed view of *Things*,[24] but the problem he finds is different from any of the ones Hofweber raised. In the course of explaining my change of view in *Things* I remarked that *The Things We*

Mean was "more of a sequel to *Remnants of Meaning* than an apostasy of it."[25] One of the things I was alluding to was the fact that what the author of *Remnants* called the pleonastic sense of 'proposition' made it possible for him to say about propositions, with one exception, whatever the author of *Things* could say about them. For example, both authors could say 'The proposition that $17^0 = 1$ is true,' 'Betty believes every proposition Harold asserted,' and even 'The expression "that snow is white" refers to the proposition that snow is white.' The one exception was that the author of *Remnants* said that propositions didn't exist while the author *Things* saw no good reason not to say that they did exist. What came to disturb me, I then said, was that I couldn't see that the verbal disagreement between the two authors about 'exists' was sustained by a debate on any substantial issue.

Rumfitt sees things differently:

> Unlike Schiffer, I do discern a substantial issue which separates the parties here: namely, whether our way of ascribing beliefs is disciplined enough to sustain judgements of identity and distinctness about their contents. Objectual quantification is quantification over objects, and the mark of objects is that it makes sense to ask whether object a is identical with object b. So we shall be able to quantify objectually over propositions only if it makes sense to ask whether the proposition that P is identical with the proposition that Q. Such questions will make sense only if we have some idea how to answer them in favourable cases.... Schiffer's theory of pleonastic propositions does not by itself give us the resources to make sense of the question of propositional identity.[26]

Frege wrote that "if we are to use a symbol a to signify an object, we must have a criterion for deciding in all cases whether b is the same as a, even if it is not always in our power to apply this criterion."[27] Rumfitt concurs, so it's his view that for me to make sense of the question of propositional identity I must be able to provide a *criterion of identity* for them. The criterion of identity that Frege found for cardinal numbers was the "abstraction principle" that George Boolos was to call Hume's principle,[28] the principle that the number that belongs to the concept F = the number that belongs to the concept G iff the things falling under F are in one–one correspondence with the things falling under G. Frege nowhere claimed that every criterion of identity must be an abstraction principle, but Rumfitt evidently assumes that if there is a criterion of identity for pleonastic propositions, then, for some function f that maps its arguments onto pleonastic propositions and some equivalence relation R that is intrinsically specifiable without mention of pleonastic propositions, the criterion of identity will be the abstraction principle $\forall x \forall y(((f(x) = f(y)) \Leftrightarrow Rxy)$. I take it, then, that the reason Rumfitt claims that my theory of pleonastic propositions does not by itself give us the resources to make sense of the question of propositional identity is that nothing in my theory provides the resources for constructing an abstraction principle that could do for pleonastic propositions what Frege thought Hume's principle did for cardinal numbers.

Rumfitt is certainly correct in inferring from the fact that nothing I say in *Things* provides the resources for an abstraction principle that on my view no reasons need to be offered to justify that claim. But his further claim that my failure to provide those resources deprives me of the right to quantify over pleonastic propositions is also based on claims that he evidently also regards as self-evident, since he makes no attempt to justify them. These are the claims (i) that one is justified in quantifying over pleonastic propositions only if one has a way of knowing, at least in favorable cases, that pleonastic proposition P = pleonastic proposition Q, (ii) that to have such a way of knowing requires having a criterion of identity for pleonastic propositions, and (iii) that such a criterion of identity must be an abstraction principle like Hume's principle. None of (i)–(iii) is self-evident, but (iii) seems especially to demand justification, for there are sortal concepts for which we don't have abstraction principles but which may *seem* to be accompanied by criteria of identity for the things falling under them. For example, it's apt to seem that dog a = dog b just in case for every space s and time t, a occupies s at t iff b occupies s at t, but that isn't an abstraction principle, and I find it difficult to see how there could be an abstraction principle for dogs. But I don't want to say that pleonastic propositions enjoy a criterion of identity that isn't an abstraction principle. I maintain that my entitlement to quantify over pleonastic propositions requires neither a criterion of identity for them nor a way of knowing (in the sense intended by Rumfitt) that pleonastic proposition P = pleonastic proposition Q. In fact, I maintain that it's not even possible for us ever to know (in the sense intended by Rumfitt) that pleonastic proposition P = pleonastic proposition Q, but I also maintain that this isn't cause for concern, for, as we are about to see, we believe in the existence of things of many kinds K for which we have no way of knowing whether a K thing a = a K thing b.

It goes without saying that words and concepts may be vague; it's a matter of controversy, however, whether objects and properties that exist outside of language and thought may be vague, or whether they must be absolutely precise. If ϕ is a precise property, then ϕ admits of no borderline instances: the universe divides without remainder between the things that have ϕ and the things that don't have ϕ. A vague property, on the other hand, would be a property that isn't precise, and thus does admit of borderline instances—and even of borderline borderline instances, borderline borderline borderline instances, and so on.[29] A precise particular would be one that has precise conditions of individuation, and thus, if it exists in space and time, precise temporal, and spatial boundaries. If a precise particular x exists in space for a finite amount of time, then there are times t and t' such that x determinately comes into existence at t and determinately goes out of existence at t', and for every time t at which x exists there is a precise region of space s such that x is determinately entirely in s at t and every part of s at t is determinately occupied by some part of x, and for no t–s pair can it be indeterminate—or indeterminate whether it's indeterminate, or indeterminate whether it's indeterminate whether it's indeterminate, or . . . —whether that is so. If a particular isn't precise, then it's vague; that is to say, it doesn't enjoy precise conditions of individuation. Moreover, if x is a vague particular that exists in space and time, then not only will there be *some* time t and precise region of space s such that it's indeterminate at t both that x is entirely in s and that every part of s is occupied by some part of x; it will also be the case that for *no t* and s will it be determinately the case both that x is entirely in s and that every part of s is occupied by some part of x.[30]

It's my sense that the majority of philosophers who work on vagueness think there can be no vagueness outside of language and thought, and that, therefore, all objects and properties existing outside of language and thought are absolutely precise.

Suppose that is so. Suppose, too, that you believe that there is one and only one cat—your cat Meow Tse-tung—on the mat before you. As David Lewis pointed out,[31] your belief can't be right on the supposition that every physical object must have precise conditions of individuation, for on that supposition there will be many trillions of cats on many trillions of mats before each of the many trillions of persons with equal claim to be you, and each of those many trillions of cats will have equal claim to the name 'Meow Tse-tung.' While you know that cats exist and that many generalizations that quantify objectually over them are true, you are utterly incapable of knowing, even in the most favorable of cases, whether cat a = cat b. How could you? Your very limited powers of perceptual discrimination make it impossible for you to identify any cat, and thus impossible for you to *re*-identify any cat.

The same goes for the properties with which you think you are acquainted. Virtually every predicate in your idiolect is vague. That needn't be incompatible with the assumption that every property is precise. If you're an epistemic theorist of vagueness you will claim that each token of a vague predicate expresses a precise property and that the predicate's being vague consists in its being impossible for anyone to know which precise property in an infinitely dense crowd of nearly identical precise properties is the precise property your vague predicate token happens to express, where the explanation of your ineluctable ignorance is of a kind definitive of vagueness. But you won't be able to identify the precise property your predicate token expresses otherwise than as its being the property your predicate token expresses. Nor can you have any way of knowing whether the precise property expressed by one token of a vague predicate is identical to the precise property expressed by another token of the predicate, even if it was you who produced both tokens. The epistemic theory of vagueness is implausible if for no other reason than that it's implausible that there are facts about language use or mental states or anything else that would make it the case that, for some precise property ϕ, when you uttered 'She's somewhat neurotic' the token of 'somewhat neurotic' you uttered expressed ϕ.[32] A more sensible position to take on the supposition that all properties are precise is that no property is determinately *the* property expressed by a vague predicate token. Rather, for any token of a vague predicate there will be myriad precise properties each of which is such that it's indeterminate whether it's the property the predicate expresses, or myriad properties each of which is such that it's indeterminate whether it's indeterminate whether it's the property the predicate expresses, or.... But going this route on the semantics of vague predicates won't make it any less impossible for one to have an identifying thought about any precise property.

So much for precise objects and properties. Now suppose that vague language talks about vague objects and properties. Let's start with vague predicates and the vague properties they would be used to ascribe if there are vague properties. Suppose that in a conversation about American authors, Jane has occasion to remark, 'J. D. Salinger was reclusive.' The token of 'reclusive'—call it τ_r—Jane uttered is vague. In the discussion of precise properties we noticed that, even if all properties are precise, it's implausible that any precise property is definitely the one expressed by τ_r. If, however, there are vague properties, then it's not implausible that some vague property is definitely the one τ_r expressed. We can see this in the following way. Every theorist of vagueness is free to recognize that the vagueness of 'reclusive', like that of every vague predicate, consists in the fact that its tokens have *penumbras*, where the penumbra of a vague predicate token is the range of things to which its application is anything other than unqualifiedly true or unqualifiedly false. So, if something is a borderline case of a thing to which the token applies, then it's in its penumbra. (Likewise if something is a borderline borderline case of a thing to which the token applies, or a borderline borderline borderline case of a thing to which it applies, or...) A penumbra is like a sponge that soaks up every drop of indeterminacy that comes its way. If there are vague properties, then they, too, have penumbras, where the penumbra of a vague property ϕ is the range of things for which it's anything other than unqualifiedly correct or unqualifiedly incorrect that they have ϕ. If there are vague properties, then whatever the penumbra of τ_r is, there is a vague property ϕ_r that has the same penumbra, and the semantic status of the token of 'J. D. Salinger was reclusive'—whether it's true, or false, or borderline true/false, etc.—will be exactly the same as that of the proposition that J. D. Salinger had ϕ_r. It must therefore be that ϕ_r is the property expressed by τ_r. But if it's implausible that there are conditions pertaining to language use (or whatever) that determine some *precise* property to be *the* property expressed by τ_r, won't it be equally implausible that there are conditions pertaining to language use (or whatever) that determine some vague property to be *the* property expressed by τ_r? No, not if one has the right view of how ϕ_r gets to be the property expressed by τ_r. The wrong view would be that there are conditions that first select ϕ_r as the property expressed by τ_r and that predicate tokens simply inherit their penumbras from those of the properties they express. The right view is that τ_r is first determined to have the penumbra it has by whatever conditions determine the penumbra of a vague predicate token, and then ϕ_r is determined to be the property expressed by τ_r by the fact that τ_r has the penumbra it has together with the general truth that the property expressed by a token of a vague predicate is the property whose penumbra matches the token's penumbra.

There are two important facts about the penumbras of vague predicate tokens that will explain why we can't re-identify or even identify the vague properties they express. The first is that we neither know nor need to know what are the penumbras of the vague predicate tokens we utter. Recall Jane's utterance of 'J. D. Salinger was reclusive.' Virtually every predicate is vague, and therefore virtually every sentence is vague. Careful speakers try not to utter a sentence if they aren't confident that in doing so they would be making a statement that was definitely true. Jane, an intelligent and well-educated non-philosopher, is a careful speaker, and when she applied 'reclusive' to Salinger she knew that the predicate was definitely true of him. She didn't have to consider what would have to be true of Salinger in order for him to be in τ_r's penumbra, and we shouldn't expect her to know. In fact, no one knows what would have to be true of Salinger in order for him to be in τ_r's penumbra. If one did know what would have to be true of Salinger in order for him to be in τ_r's penumbra, then there would be a condition C such that one knew *that Salinger would have been in τ_r's penumbra iff it had been the case that C(Salinger)*. The trouble is, no one knows what determines a predicate token's penumbra. So, while, if there are vague properties, we would know that the property expressed by a given vague predicate token was whatever property has a matching penumbra, we aren't now able to know what that property is.

The second important fact about the penumbras of vague predicate tokens is that tokens of a vague predicate may, and typically will, have somewhat different penumbras (that is why I have spoken throughout not of the penumbra of a vague predicate but of the penumbras of a predicate's tokens). For example, in a discussion about what men Mary might like, it's suggested that she might like to meet Mike and someone protests, 'No, Mike's bald, and Mary's attracted only to men with luxuriant heads of hair.' That utterance, in those circumstances, may very well count as true, notwithstanding that Mike's scalp resembles a billiard ball only because he shaves his scalp. In another context, however, in which the discussion is about whether baldness runs in Mike's family, someone may say, 'Mike's not bald; he just shaves his head,' and in that context that utterance would also count as true. And there might easily be contexts in which an utterance of 'Mike's bald' counts as neither definitely true nor definitely false. Whether a thing is deemed a borderline instance of a vague predicate token will to some large extend depend on whether the interlocutors in the context in which the token is produced would count it as such. That will depend not just on the nature of the conversation in which the token was produced but on the idiosyncrasies of the speaker's and other interlocutors' verbal dispositions, personalities, moods, and the difficulty of categorizing cases when one enters the grey zone of a term's application. The shiftiness to which I'm alluding is well illustrated in the fact that if the same subject is made to go through a sorites series twice, each time judging, for each member of the series, whether or not the vague predicate in question applies to it, her judgments in the two trials are most likely to reveal differing judgments as regards what she takes to be the predicate's borderline applications, and her judgments on neither trial will be any less correct than her judgments on the other. This has a surprising consequence that bears on the re-identification of the properties expressed by tokens of a vague predicate. For suppose that the day after Jane's utterance Al says to Betty, 'Jane said that J. D. Salinger was reclusive.' A theorist who accepts that that-clauses refer to propositions is likely to hold that Al's saying report is true only if the proposition to which his utterance of 'that J. D. Salinger was reclusive' refers is identical to the proposition expressed by Jane's utterance of 'J. D. Salinger was reclusive.' But given the penumbral shift ubiquitous among tokens of a vague predicate, it's a good bet that the tokens of 'reclusive' uttered by Jane and Al will have somewhat different penumbras, and therefore will express somewhat different properties, and if that is so, then the proposition to which Al's that-clause refers won't be identical to the one expressed by Jane's utterance. (It's not immediately clear what to make of how this affects the truth assessment of propositions or saying reports—should we say that saying reports are rarely true, or that the mooted identity isn't required for truth of the saying report, or that the semantic status of a proposition is somehow relative to "contexts of assessment"?)

What was just said about the semantics of vague predicates on the assumption that there are vague properties will pretty much also apply, *mutatis mutandis*, to certain vague singular referring expressions. This is illustrated in the following example. Harry and Sally are walking in Paris when Harry says to Sally, 'Gertrude Stein used to live in this neighborhood.' The epistemic theorist of vagueness would say that the token of 'this neighborhood' Harry uttered—call it τ_n—uniquely refers to a precisely delimited area of Paris. The supervaluationist would say that there are myriad precisely delimited overlapping areas of Paris none of which is definitely the referent of τ_n but myriad of which are each such that it's indefinite whether it is its referent, or indefinite whether it's indefinite whether it is its referent, or... If, however, there are vague things, then one will be constrained to say that τ_n uniquely refers to a vague area whose penumbra matches τ_n's penumbra, where x is in τ_n's penumbra just in case it's anything other than unqualifiedly correct or unqualifiedly incorrect that x is in the area to which τ_n refers, and x is in a vague area a's penumbra just in case it's anything other than unqualifiedly correct or unqualifiedly incorrect that x is in a. But because we can't know what exactly τ_n's penumbra is, we also can't know which vague area is the one to which τ_n refers. Thus, whether areas are precise or vague, we are unable to know whether area a = area b. This, however, doesn't preclude objectual quantification over areas, as when one says 'There are fewer low-income neighborhoods in Manhattan than there used to be.'

If there are vague objects, then dogs are among them in that for no dog δ are there times t and t' such that δ definitely came into existence at t and definitely went out of existence at t', and for no time t and space s will it definitely be the case at t both that δ is definitely entirely in s and that every part of s is occupied by a part of δ. Nevertheless, if dogs have vague temporal and spatial boundaries, then we are in favorable cases able to know that dog a = dog b, and we do have a criterion of identity for dogs—viz. that dog a = dog b iff for every time t and space s, a occupies all of s at t iff b occupies all of s at t. But, it's important to notice, we have such a criterion of identity for dogs not just *if* dogs have vague temporal and spatial boundaries, but also *only if* they have them. For, as we noticed above, if dogs must have precise spatial boundaries, then we shall have to say that there are trillions of overlapping dogs where we thought there was only one and that two dogs may occupy the same space at the same time. Then we will have no way of identifying any particular dog, and therefore no way of knowing whether dog a = dog b.

Returning to propositions, we know that they fare worse than dogs as regards our ability to make sense of questions of identity. This is true no matter what theory of propositions is correct, for we can't know whether proposition P = proposition Q unless we can know that the properties or relations they ascribe are the same and that, I have argued, we can't know. Vagueness is even more of a nuisance for pleonastic and Fregean propositions, because on those accounts propositions are individuated in part by the ways one must think of the objects and properties the propositions are about in order to entertain those propositions, and those ways are a further source of vagueness that prevents making sense of questions of propositional identity.

So, to sum up, my response to Rumfitt is this. He points out that my theory of pleonastic propositions does not by itself give us the resources to make sense of the question of propositional identity and he takes that to be a problem with the theory because he thinks objectual quantification over propositions isn't possible unless we are able to make sense of the question of propositional identity. He also evidently claims that to make sense of that question one must have a criterion of identity for propositions and that that criterion must be an abstraction principle for propositions that does for propositions what Frege thought Hume's principle did for whole numbers. I acknowledge that we don't have an abstraction principle or any other criterion of identity for pleonastic propositions and even concede that we aren't able to make sense of the question of identity for them. My disagreement with Rumfitt is that I don't take any of that to show we aren't entitled to quantify objectually over pleonastic propositions, for, as regards the ability to make sense of questions of identity, there are things in the same boat as pleonastic propositions over which we clearly are entitled to quantify objectually.

15.5 Pleonastic Propositions in Moral Discourse: Response to Smith

15.5.1

One aim of Chapter 6 of *Things*, "Moral Realism and Indeterminacy," was to show how the theory of pleonastic propositions and properties—*the Theory*, for short—offered a solution to the meta-ethical puzzle generated by the motivated but incompatible claims cognitivism and non-cognitivism make about moral discourse. The incompatibility arises over the claim that there are moral propositions, cognitivism saying "yes," non-cognitivism "no." What elevates the incompatibility into a puzzle is that both -isms are armed with *prima facie* plausible arguments. I called one of the arguments for non-cognitivism *the Argument from Internalism*—*the Argument*, for short—and offered the following as one way of stating it:

1. Necessarily, one who accepts the judgment that she morally ought not to X has some conation against her Xing.
2. If there are moral propositions, then for a person to *accept* that she morally ought not to X is for her to *believe* the proposition that she morally ought not to X is true.
3. But such a belief is consistent with a person's not having any conation against her Xing.
4. ∴ There are no moral propositions. (240)

Now the Theory, which I had explained and for which I had tried to provide some motivation in the 237 pages leading up to Chapter 6, entails that there are moral propositions in exactly the same truth-evaluable sense of 'proposition' that applies to every other proposition in the ranges of the believing and stating relations. But I didn't begin Chapter 6 *assuming* that the Theory was correct and that therefore the Argument had to be unsound. Rather, I presented the Argument as a challenge to the Theory, in the following way. Since the Theory asserts that there are moral propositions and the Argument concludes that there are no moral propositions, the proponent of the Theory is as motivated as any cognitivist to show that, and where, the Argument goes wrong. But of course it's possible that the explanation of how the Argument goes wrong, should there be such an explanation, entails a version of cognitivism that is incompatible with the Theory, thereby providing a refutation of the Theory at the same time that it undermines the Argument. So at the least the Argument challenges the Theory to account for where the Argument goes wrong in a way that is consistent with the Theory. Yet there is a more interesting challenge with which the Argument intrigues those who would like to stay proponents of the Theory—namely, to explain how the Argument goes wrong *in a way that relies essentially on the Theory*. That challenge quickly became more specific when six pages into the chapter (on p. 243) I announced that I would target premise (3) of the Argument, the premise whose implicit Humean import is that it's impossible for there to be a proposition doxastically believing which is conation-entailing (I'll henceforth refer to premise (3) of the Argument as *Hume's Meta-ethical Principle*). My challenge then became to show how, given that there are moral propositions (and that they are propositions in just the way that every object of belief is a proposition), Hume's Meta-ethical Principle may be false, and, furthermore, to show this in a way that is uniquely made available by the Theory. The setup for the challenge is given in §6.2, "The Problem of Moral Judgements," but I didn't try to rise to it until §6.4, "Two Explanatory Debts: The Peculiar Nature of Moral Concepts." Before giving a restatement of §6.4's response to the challenge, I'll first make explicit the features of pleonastic properties and propositions on which the response relies.

It's a feature of the meaning of the sentence

(a) Eating animals is a source of protein

that a felicitous assertive utterance of it requires the speaker to believe that eating animals is a source of protein. Only a very blinkered non-cognitivist would deny that there is also *a* sense of 'believe' in which it's a feature of the meaning of the sentence

(b) Eating animals is wrong[33]

that a felicitous assertive utterance of it requires the speaker to believe that eating animals is wrong. An issue that divides cognitivists and non-cognitivists is whether the sense of 'believe' in a true utterance of, say,

(c) Jane believes that eating animals is a source of protein

is the same as the sense of 'believe' in a true utterance of, say,

(d) Jane believes that eating animals is wrong.

Now the non-cognitivist holds that (d) entails that, all else being equal, Jane desires that no one eats animals, and no one disputes that (c) has no comparable entailment. Does that difference suffice to show that 'believes' doesn't have the same meaning in (c) and (d), that its meaning in (d), but not in (c), is conation-entailing? No, it doesn't. It may be that the conative difference between (c) and (d) is owed not to 'believe' having a meaning feature in (d) that it doesn't have in (c), but rather to a crucial difference between the properties expressed by the predicates 'source of protein' and 'wrong'—namely, that, while believing an action to have the former property is *per se* conatively neutral, believing it to have the latter property isn't, as deploying the concept of that property in one's information processing requires one who believes that anything has that property to be negatively disposed towards anything's having it. But can the actuality of that possibility be made cogent in light of Hume's claim that no truth-evaluable proposition—or "matter of fact," as he called them—can be such that believing it entails having a certain conative attitude and of Mackie's supporting "argument from queerness"? The pleonastic conception of properties as "shadows of predicates"[34] offers to show how it may be made cogent.

Suppose we think in a neural system of mental representation M, the "brain's language of synaptic interconnections and neural spikes,"[35] which for all that presently matters may be taken to be a neural version of English. Let Jane be a normal thinker in M. For any proposition p, Jane believes p just in case for some σ, σ means p in M and σ is tokened in Jane's "belief box." Likewise, *mutatis mutandis*, for desiring p and for any other propositional-attitude relations that must be taken as primitive. An X box is defined in terms of the functional role definitive of a state's being an X state. Thus, for example if sentences σ and σ' are tokened in Jane's belief box, then, all else being equal, the sentence $\ulcorner \sigma\ \&\ \sigma' \urcorner$ will also be tokened there, and vice versa; if $\ulcorner \sigma \rightarrow \sigma' \urcorner$ and σ are tokened in Jane's belief box, then, all else being equal, σ' is also tokened there; if σ is tokened in Jane's desire box and $\ulcorner \sigma$ only if $\sigma' \urcorner$ is tokened in her belief box, then, all else being equal, σ' is also tokened in her desire box; and so on.

In addition to the functional roles that make states beliefs, desires, intentions, hopes, etc., there are functional roles that are possessed by the expressions of M, and, like other writers, I'll call these *conceptual roles*. The conceptual role of a syntactically complex expression is jointly determined by the conceptual role of its syntactical form and the conceptual roles of its constituent expressions. Conceptual roles augment the functional roles of the propositional-attitude states realized by expressions that have those conceptual roles. For example, if we know that a state is a belief, then we know that it has the functional role definitive of being a belief; if we know that it's a belief realized by the sentence σ—i.e. if we know it's the state of σ's being tokened in the belief box—then we know that the state has at least a functional role that is jointly determined by the functional role definitive of being a belief and σ's conceptual role. Conceptual roles are individuated by the ways expressions having them affect the functional roles of the propositional-attitude states containing those expressions. For example, the conceptual role of 'sibling' is such that, if 'I have a sibling' is tokened in Jane's belief box, then the sentence 'I am a sibling' is also tokened there, and the conceptual role of 'pain' is such that, if 'I'm in pain' is tokened in Jane's belief box, then, all else being equal, the sentence was caused to be tokened there by Jane's being in pain and the sentence 'I will cease to be in pain' is tokened in her desire box.

Since conceptual roles are merely functional roles of a certain kind, and since functional roles are simply properties that describe causal or transitional relations in a topic-neutral way, mentalese expressions will have numerous conceptual roles. But philosophers who use these terms of art often speak of *the* conceptual role of a mentalese expression. What they are really talking about is a mentalese expression's *maximal underived* conceptual role. Roughly speaking, a conceptual role c is an *underived* conceptual role of x's mentalese expression ε just in case ε would have c in x's mentalese regardless of whatever propositional-attitude states x happened to be in. For example, a plausible candidate for being an underived conceptual role of mentalese '&' might entail that if $\ulcorner \sigma\ \&\ \sigma' \urcorner$ is tokened in one's belief box, then, all else being equal, σ and σ' are also tokened there. A conceptual role c is the *maximal* underived conceptual role of x's mentalese expression ε just in case c is the conjunction of all the underived conceptual roles ε has in x's mentalese.[36] It is not unreasonable to suppose that a mentalese expression's maximal underived conceptual role wholly or partially determines its meaning,[37] and I'll touch on this again presently. The extreme vagueness of the word 'concept' is what enables philosophers to use it in quite diverse ways, but for a philosopher who identifies "concepts" with conceptual roles, the maximal underived conceptual role of a mentalese expression is the concept it expresses.

A conceptual-role hypothesis that no theorist should find objectionable is that there may be syntactical predicates (expressions that count as predicates by syntactical criteria) ϕ, ψ that have coordinated conceptual roles according to which certain sentences containing ϕ can be tokened in states that realize beliefs only if certain sentences containing ψ are tokened in states that realize desires or other affective states. This was already illustrated with the word 'pain', as this provides an instance of the generalization in which the same predicate is a witness both to 'ϕ' and to 'ψ'. This conceptual-role hypothesis, on its own, entails nothing about the meanings of ϕ and ψ, but it's at this point that the Theory kicks in: two features of the pleonastic conception of properties conjoin with the conceptual-role hypothesis to explain how predicates may have cognitive meaning *and* be conation-entailing in a sense relevant to the Argument.

The first feature is that, for any syntactical predicate ϕ and singular term α, the inference

α is ϕ
So, α has the property of being ϕ

is valid and the occurrence of 'the property of being ϕ' in its conclusion refers to the property of being ϕ.[38] This entails both that an inference such as

Hitler was evil
So, Hitler had the property of being evil

is valid and that it requires nothing more for its validity from 'evil' than that it be classed as a predicate by syntactical criteria. It's because of this feature that I called inferences like

Fido is a dog.
So, Fido has the property of being dog.

something-from-nothing transformations. That would be an egregiously inappropriate label if my view was that one was warranted in making a something-from-nothing inference from a sentence of the form 'α is F' to 'α has the property of being F' only if one had some independent warrant for believing that 'F' expressed the property of being F. As I pointed out in *Things* pp. 77–9 (and as Hofweber mentions in Chapter 2 of this volume), in this respect an essential feature of something-from-nothing transformations is shared with what the doctrine of "syntactic priority" ascribes to numerals, namely, that they count as referring to numbers just by virtue (nearly enough) of having the *syntactical* role of singular terms.[39]

The second feature of the pleonastic conception of properties needed to explain how a predicate can both have cognitive meaning and be conation-entailing is that not only do predicates express properties by virtue of having conceptual roles that make them count syntactically as predicates, but the properties they express have individuating contours that mirror the contours of the predicates' maximal underived conceptual roles. One example of this is that, if there are mentalese predicates ϕ, ψ whose maximal underived conceptual roles entail that, for any singular term α, ⌜α is ϕ⌝ is tokened in one's belief box only if ⌜α is ψ⌝ is also tokened there, then whatever property is expressed by ϕ entails whatever property is expressed by ψ. A second example reveals the sense in which a predicate may be conation-entailing: if there are mentalese predicates ϕ, ψ whose maximal underived conceptual roles entail that, for any singular term α, ⌜α is ϕ⌝ is tokened in one's *belief* box only if ⌜α is ψ⌝ is tokened in one's *desire* box, then that secures that the properties expressed by ϕ and ψ are such that one can't believe that a thing has the first property without desiring it to have the second property. A corollary of these two features is that, if a predicate ϕ is conation-entailing in the way just explained, then there can't be a predicate ϕ' such that both (i) ϕ' isn't conation-entailing and (ii) ⌜α is ϕ⌝ can be tokened in the belief box only if ⌜α is ϕ'⌝ is also tokened there. This would explain why no moral fact can be entailed by a non-evaluative fact if moral facts are conation-entailing. At the same time, nothing precludes a conation-entailing predicate ϕ from having a maximal underived conceptual role that requires ⌜α is ϕ⌝ not to be tokened in one's belief box unless there is some non-conation-entailing predicate or other ω such that ⌜Being ω entails being ϕ⌝ and ⌜α is ω⌝ are also tokened there. That wouldn't make either ⌜Being ω entails being ϕ⌝ or ⌜α is ω⌝ *true*, but it would secure that whenever one believed a thing to have a conation-entailing property, one also believed that the thing had that property by virtue of having a certain non-conation-entailing property. The stage is now set for me to explain what I was up to in §6.4, where I try to show how the Theory allows for conation-entailing truth-evaluable moral propositions.

Some writers on evaluative concepts recognize what they take to be a distinction between *thick* and *thin* evaluative concepts. Examples of thick evaluative concepts are *brave, cowardly, honest*, and *trustworthy*. Evidently, an evaluative concept v is thick if central to its individuation is a non-evaluative concept n such that v applies to a thing only if n does, as, for example, *trustworthy* applies to a person only if (roughly speaking) she tries always to keep her word. Abusive epithets are thick evaluative concepts (assuming they are evaluative concepts). An evaluative concept v is thin if it isn't thick. It's controversial whether there are any thin moral concepts, but in §6.4 I in effect conceded to the non-cognitivist for the sake of argument that *wrong, ought, right*, and others like them were thin, so that I could show how the cognitivism made available by the Theory could withstand such a large concession. But even a thin moral concept can be applied to a thing only on the basis of the thing's falling under some non-evaluative concept or other. In other words, for each of two people with mastery of our concept of moral wrongness there must be a non-evaluative property N such that each accepts, at least implicitly, the principle that acts having N are wrong; it's just that the concept of moral wrongness leaves open what non-evaluative property N might be, and nothing requires it to be the same for any two people with mastery of the concept. So, I wanted to show how a subject—call him Bob—could have in his mentalese a predicate 'wrong*' (called W in Chapter 6) whose maximal underived conceptual role is such that if 'That action is wrong*' is tokened in Bob's belief box, then there is some predicate or other η that expresses some non-evaluative property or other N such that 'That action is wrong*' is tokened in Bob's belief box only if (i) 'That action is η' is tokened in his belief box, (ii) 'η actions are wrong*' is tokened in his belief box, and (iii) 'No one does anything that is η' is tokened in his desire box. The cartoon character Bob I described in §6.4 was my attempt to describe such a character. A feature of 'wrong*' that I wanted to emphasize was that, while 'wrong*' judgments require 'wrong*' to be applied on the basis of *some* non-evaluative property, no particular such property is required to play that role, and therefore 'wrong*' could have the same meaning in the mentalese of two people even though their 'wrong*' judgments were based on different evaluative principles. The character Carla in §6.4 was intended to illustrate that possibility. I wanted 'wrong*' to mirror the fact that moral terms might have the same meaning in the idiolects of two people even though they accepted quite different ultimate moral principles, and thus applied 'wrong*' on the basis of quite different non-normative facts. The conjunction of the description of Bob and the Theory entails that in his idiolect 'wrong*' expresses what he would call the property of being wrong*. Bob is a caricature of a person who accepts the moral principle that N actions are wrong, and this by virtue of his not wanting anyone to do anything that is N and his believing that a given action is wrong only on the basis of believing that it's N. I made clear that the true story about 'wrong' would have to be more complicated and nuanced than the cartoon predicate 'wrong*', but all that I was trying to show was how, given the Theory, moral sentences such as 'Eating animals is wrong' can have cognitive meaning and be conation-entailing.

15.5.2

I turn now to Smith's spirited and helpful commentary. Some of his objections are based on misunderstandings of what I wrote, although I suspect that my tendency to write too densely may be responsible for some or all of those misunderstandings.

a. Smith says that the first part of the resolution I offer in Chapter 6 of the puzzle created by the Janus-faced nature of moral concepts is "an argument in favour of cognitivism based on the theory of pleonastic propositions" (96), which argument he says is given in the long passage he quotes from pp. 241–2. But I offer no argument for cognitivism in Chapter 6 based on the theory of pleonastic propositions. As I said above, when I get to Chapter 6 I take it to be *obvious* that the pleonastic conception of propositions and properties—i.e. the Theory—entails cognitivism. My concern was to add support to the Theory and the cognitivism it entailed by showing that it could resolve what should appear as a threat to it—namely, the Argument from Internalism. Smith represents the long quotation as ending in the sentence 'The doctrine of pleonastic propositions clearly entails cognitivism.' But that sentence isn't the conclusion of an argument contained in the lines that precede it. Those lines not only don't contain any argument for the claim that the Theory entails cognitivism, they don't contain any argument for anything. All those lines do is spell out what is required in order for cognitivism to be true, and those criteria hardly entail cognitivism. In fact, the sentence 'The doctrine of pleonastic propositions clearly entails cognitivism' doesn't occur on its own, but as part of the longer sentence:

The doctrine of pleonastic propositions clearly entails cognitivism, but even without that doctrine's being presupposed, the case for cognitivism is apt to seem compelling. (242)

Then the eighteen lines of the paragraph that follow that sentence lay out the case for cognitivism that is independent of the Theory and that is "apt to seem compelling" (it wasn't presented as *being* compelling). The sentence fragment that ends the quotation doesn't conclude any argument but is merely stating what is supposed to be an obvious consequence of the theory, essentially just another way of saying that it's an obvious consequence of the Theory that moral sentences express moral propositions. Smith calls my claim that "the doctrine of pleonastic propositions clearly entails cognitivism" *Schiffer's Conclusion*. He should have called it *What Schiffer Presupposed Based on His Prior Elaboration of the Doctrine of Pleonastic Propositions*.

b. After stating the Argument, I say that premiss (3) "derives its plausibility from the cogency of a familiar Humean worry [viz. that believing any proposition is consistent with one's feeling any way at all about the proposition's being true, and therefore for no proposition can believing it be conation-entailing]," and then I go on to announce that premise (3) is the one I aimed to challenge. Smith reports these set-up maneuvers by saying that, "though he doesn't explain why, Schiffer plainly doesn't share Hume's worry, so he rejects (3). The non-cognitivist's crucial argument therefore fails. So, at any rate, Schiffer concludes" (98). But as Smith seems to recognize later in his paper (p. 102), this ignores the chapter's structure. I don't dismiss Hume's worry; on the contrary, the chapter culminates in §6.4's attempt to show how, given the pleonastic conception of propositions and properties, moral beliefs can be both doxastic beliefs and conation-entailing. In that sense, I certainly do try to show how by my lights premise (3) of the Argument from Internalism, Hume's Meta-ethical Principle, fails.

c. Smith writes that

Schiffer's discussion of the Argument from Internalism is revealing in the light of Schiffer's Conclusion.... For... his own discussion of the Argument from Internalism suggests that we should reject Schiffer's Conclusion. This is because, according to that discussion, the theory of pleonastic propositions is itself *neutral* on the issue of cognitivism versus non-cognitivism. (98)

Why does Smith take me to have misunderstood my own theory in supposing it to entail cognitivism when in fact it's entirely compatible with non-cognitivism? Well, he quotes me as saying that "the nature of propositions, as pleonastic entities, is fully determined by the hypostatizing practices that are constitutive of the concept of a proposition together with those necessary a priori truths that are applicable to things of any kind." He recognizes that by "those necessary a priori truths that are applicable to things of any kind" I had in mind principles like the indiscernibility of identicals, but, reading me *au pied de la lettre*, he says that if Hume's Meta-ethical Principle is correct, then it's a necessary a priori truth applicable to all propositions, and therefore something that should partially determine the nature of pleonastic propositions. This is puzzling. If propositions are non-pleonastic propositions, then that would be a necessary a priori truth applicable to all propositions. Should I then be committed to a version of pleonastic propositions on which they are non-pleonastic propositions? I think Smith's real point isn't perverse, and may perhaps be put thus:

> The doctrine of pleonastic properties and propositions is stipulatively defined in terms of the claim that inferences of the form
>
> α is F
> So, α has <u>the property of being F</u>
>
> and of the form
>
> α is F
> So, <u>that α is F</u> is true
>
> are "something-from-nothing" inferences, which means that they are conceptually valid inferences in whose conclusions the underlined phrases refer to properties, as in the first form, or to propositions, as in the second. Inferences obtained from the forms by replacing the dummy letter 'F' with 'wrong' are therefore something-from-nothing inferences *if* the doctrine of pleonastic properties and propositions is correct. But if Hume's Meta-ethical Principle is correct, then they wouldn't be, for then they would either not be valid or the phrases 'the property of being wrong' and 'that α is wrong' in their conclusions wouldn't refer, respectively, to properties and propositions. Therefore, in order to determine whether
>
> Eating animals is wrong
> So, it's true that eating animals is wrong
>
> is a something-from-nothing transformation, one would first have to settle whether 'Eating animals is wrong' is semantically on a par with 'Eating animals is a source of protein', and thus expresses the proposition that eating animals is wrong, or whether its meaning is compatible with non-cognitivism, in which case in uttering 'Eating animals is wrong' a speaker wouldn't be expressing his belief in the proposition that eating animals is wrong, there being no such proposition in which to express one's belief, but would rather be expressing whatever affective attitude towards eating animals would constitute judging eating animals to be wrong.

The objection, however, is misdirected. It does indeed follow from the Theory that the displayed inferences are valid something-from-nothing inferences only if 'said'/'believes' in 'Jane said/believes that eating animals is wrong' means what it does in 'Jane said/believes that eating animals is a source of protein,' but it *also* follows from the Theory that that is *not* something one needs first to determine in order to determine whether inferences of the forms

α is wrong
So, α has the property of being wrong

α is wrong
So, that α is wrong is true

are valid something-from-nothing inferences. For, as explained above, the Theory entails that those inferences are valid something-from-nothing inferences *just by virtue of* 'wrong' being classed as a predicate merely by *syntactical* criteria (thereby securing that the premises of inferences of the displayed types are classed as indicative sentences by syntactical criteria). Once it's secured that there is a property of being wrong in exactly the same sense that there is a property of being a source of protein and that there is a proposition that eating animals is wrong in exactly the same sense that there is a proposition that eating animals is a source of protein, it *follows* that 'said'/'believes' has the same meaning both in 'Jane said/believes that eating animals is a source of protein' and in 'Jane said/ believes that eating animals is wrong'. Needless to say, the Theory is polemical in having these entailments, but my present point is that one merely begs the question against the Theory to claim that, because the Theory entails that 'says' and 'believes' are univocal in evaluative and non-evaluative utterances, one must determine whether that univocality obtains *before* being entitled to claim that the premisss of the alleged something-from-nothing transformations entail their conclusions, or that the ostensible references to properties or propositions really are references to those things.

d. Smith also takes himself to be warranted on independent grounds in accepting Hume's Meta-ethical Principle. His reason for accepting it is evidently that:[40]

> Loss of the want means that the agent is no longer in a state with the functional role of a want.... Loss of the belief, by contrast, like loss of any belief, means that she is no longer in a state with the functional role of a belief.... But these two states of mind—being in a state with the functional role of that belief but not in a state with the functional role of that want—look to be quite independent of each other. Someone could be in the one but not the other, or be in both, or be in neither. (101)

Here Smith goes from talking about the functional roles for being a *belief* and for being a *want* to claiming that, for *any propositions p, q*, the functional role constitutive of being a *belief whose content is p* neither entails nor is entailed by the functional role constitutive of being a *want whose content is q*. Well, it's true that the functional role constitutive of a state's being a *belief* neither entails nor is entailed by the functional role constitutive of a state's being a *want*. But, for any p, the functional role constitutive of a state's being a *belief that p* will entail, but won't be entailed by, the functional role for merely being a belief, and nothing whatever precludes that larger functional role from being such that in order to be in a state that has that functional role one must be in another state with a quite different functional role. For example, the functional role for being a belief doesn't entail the functional role for being a belief that one is a sibling, but that latter functional role is arguably such that being in a state that has it necessitates being in a different state that has the functional role for being a belief that one has a sibling. In the same way, nothing precludes the functional role for being *a belief that it would be wrong for one to ϕ* from entailing the functional role for being a want not to ϕ (more plausibly, a want not to ϕ *ceteris paribus*), just as the functional role for being *a belief that one is in pain* arguably entails the functional role for being a desire not to endure that pain (*ceteris paribus*).

e. Recall the characterization above of the concept *wrong** I stipulated for the character Bob at the beginning of §6.4. The point of the example was to stipulate for 'wrong*' a conceptual role that made clear how a state in which 'That action is wrong*' was tokened could have a functional role that both made it a belief and mandated that, for some non-normative predicate η, a tokening of 'That action is wrong*' in Bob's belief box had to co-occur (a) with a tokening in the belief box of ⌜That action is η⌝ and ⌜η actions are wrong*⌝ and (b) with a tokening in the desire box of ⌜No one does anything that is η⌝. Smith wonders if my characterization of 'wrong*' required Bob to believe that he desired that no one do anything that has M, where M is the property expressed by η. I hope my restatement above made clear that the correct interpretation of 'wrong*' reads me in the second way Smith proposes, according to which "conative attitudes enter into an account of the *possession* conditions of moral concepts, not their *application* conditions" (104).

f. Smith claims that there is a problem for my claims about what the "wrong*" example shows even when I'm read as forging the connection between doxastic and conative attitudes not through the application conditions of a concept, but through its possession conditions. He claims that what I'm offering

... is a hybrid theory according to which an agent's judgement that α [is wrong*] is the expression of both a belief—the belief that α has N—and also the expression of his wants concerning N. This view is compatible with internalism alright: Bob's believing that α has N and his wanting what he wants about N entails that he has those wants concerning N. But it is compatible with internalism in virtue of the fact that one element in the hybrid theory is simply equivalent to non-cognitivism. The cognitivist element in the hybrid theory is irrelevant to the explanation of compatibility. The explanation derives entirely from the non-cognitivist element. (105)

Not so. What I am offering to demonstrate via the conceptual role I stipulate for 'wrong*' is something that Smith claims is impossible—namely, that a state may have a functional role that *both* makes the state a belief *and* requires one also to be in a distinct state that has a functional role that make that state a desire. There is, as Smith says, nothing about Bob's belief that α has N which requires him to desire that N actions not be performed; that desire and that belief are distinct states, either of which can occur without the other. But that misses my point, which was to show how it could be that it's impossible for Bob to believe that an action is wrong* without desiring that no one perform any action that has the non-normative property that, by Bob's lights, makes that action wrong*.

g. In Chapter 6 I offered a couple of arguments to show that no substantive moral propositions can be determinately true or determinately false (the proposition *that one morally ought not to do what it's morally wrong to do* is an example of a non-substantive moral proposition). One argument assumed that if there were determinately true moral propositions, then there would be determinately true moral principles—general propositions like *One ought not to Φ* (e.g. *one ought not to kill anyone just for her money*), where substituends for 'Φ' express non-normative properties of actions—and that at least some of those principles would be knowable. Then the argument tried to show that no such principles would be knowable. A second argument assumed the account of indeterminacy advanced in *Things*. That account, as Smith points out, turns on a distinction between two kinds of partial beliefs, *standard* partial belief (*s*-belief) and *vagueness-related* partial belief (*v*-belief), and held that a proposition was neither determinately true nor determinately false if an ideally situated doxastically rational agent could simultaneously *v*-believe the proposition and its negation to positive degrees that summed to 1. Now recall that Bob's concept *wrong** precludes him from believing that an action is wrong* other than on the basis of some non-normative property which *he* takes to be sufficient for an action's being wrong*, but that this non-normative property could be any non-normative property, provided it held a certain position in Bob's system of desires. A general proposition *that it would be wrong* to perform any action that has M*, where *M* is a non-normative property, would be a moral principle, and the fact that the concept *wrong** needn't be linked with any particular non-normative property was intended to capture the non-cognitivist's insight that two doxastically rational people, each with perfect command of moral concepts and knowledge of all relevant non-normative facts, may have incompatible moral principles, thus explaining why a disagreement that comes down to a disagreement in moral principles—what Charles Stevenson called a "disagreement in attitude"[41]—would be rationally irresolvable. It was to reflect this feature that I had Bob apply *wrong** on the basis of non-natural property N^* but had Carla apply *wrong** on the basis of the different non-natural property M. The account carried with it an error-theoretic component, because although in order for a person to believe that an action was wrong* there must be a non-natural property which she thinks is sufficient for the action's being wrong*, that non-natural property won't actually be a sufficient condition for an action's being wrong*. For example, Bob holds that N^* actions are wrong*, but since the maximal underived conceptual role for 'wrong*', which is the same in Bob's idiolect and in Carla's, doesn't require 'wrong*' to be applied on the basis of N^* or any other particular non-normative property, there is nothing in the maximal underived conceptual role of 'wrong*' to make any non-natural property entail being wrong*. In other words, while the maximal underived conceptual role of 'wrong*' permits Bob to hold the principle that an action is wrong* just in case it has N^* and permits Carla to hold the incompatible principle that an action is wrong* just in case it has M, there is nothing in their use of 'wrong*' to make either principle determinately true or determinately false. This is why I concluded my description of Bob's and Carla's use of 'wrong*' with the interjection "Given the conditions governing the role of 'wrong*', it is patently absurd to suppose that either Bob or Carla has the determinately true belief in their dispute about whether being N^* entails being wrong*'" (257).

All this brings me to Smith's final objection. Suppose Bob wants not to live in a world in which N^* actions are performed, and (at least partly) because of that Bob holds that it's a necessary truth that an action is wrong* if it's N. Then, Smith argues:

> With [the foregoing supposition] in place, it may well be determinately true that N^* entails [being wrong*]. N^* is, after all, by hypothesis a non-normative feature of those acts that are performed in the possible worlds in which Bob *actually* wants not to live. It may therefore be determinately true that some act has that feature, and, if it is, then it is determinately true that

every possible world in which people perform acts that are N* is a possible world in which he, Bob, actually wants not to live. Bob's claim that N* entails [being wrong*] may therefore itself be determinately true. The mere fact that Carla's contrary claim may also be determinately true is neither here nor there. It presents us with no more of a puzzle than the fact that 'I want that p' may be determinately true when said under ideal epistemic conditions by Bob and determinately false when said under such conditions by Carla. (108)

Here Smith misunderstands me. The misunderstanding here is to suppose that it follows from my characterization of 'wrong*' that if it's determinately true *that an action has N* and *Bob holds the moral principle that being N* is sufficient for being wrong**, then Bob's claim *that N* is sufficient for being wrong** is true. That it doesn't entail that should be no more puzzling than the non-cognitivist's claim that the fact it's determinately true *that an action has N and you hold the moral principle that being N is sufficient for being wrong* doesn't imply the truth of your claim *that being N is sufficient for being wrong*.

Notes

1. We're told that a sortal term isn't "well-formed" if it's co-application conditions lead to contradiction (this volume: p. 51, n. 7).
2. Thomasson (2009: 4).
3. I wrote about the "pleonastic sense" of 'property' and 'proposition' before I came to believe in the existence of pleonastic entities (see e.g. Schiffer 1987). My change of mind was first displayed in print in my (1990). I also explained the notion of a pleonastic entity in several other publications before *Things*; see e.g. (1994) and (1996), (2000), and (2001).
4. Thomasson (2009: 5).
5. Thomasson (2009: 12).
6. Thomasson (this volume: 39).
7. Schiffer (2003: 53).
8. As I explained the notion, a theory T^+ conservatively extends a theory T just in case every theorem of T^+ that is expressible in T is also a theorem of T.
9. Thomasson (this volume: 42).
10. 'If "table" is true of x, then x is a table' and 'If "wife" is true of x, then x is female' are question-begging "application conditions."
11. Goodman (1955: 39).
12. The prodding occurred in numerous conversations we had in spring 1988 and in Johnston (1988).
13. Schiffer (2006: 235).
14. See also my response to Ostertag (Chapter 16, this volume).
15. See Schiffer (2010).
16. See for example Schiffer (1992).
17. This use of 'pleonastic' is not my own technical use of that term, so although Hofweber uses 'pleonastic' for nonreferential use of singular terms he wishes to invoked, in order to avoid confusion I'll use 'expletive'.
18. Schiffer (1987: 289).
19. See Hofweber (2006a).
20. In (2006a) Hofweber defines a *completely alien proposition* as a proposition that is "inexpressible by any speaker in any language in any context" (205) and asks whether we should believe there are such propositions. He says that the answer will depend on what

we are doing when we talk about and quantify over propositions, and that there can't be completely alien propositions if his theory is correct, for on his theory quantification over propositions isn't objectual quantification over a domain of propositions, there being no propositions to stock that domain, but is rather a generalization over possible substitution instances in one's language, and that secures that there can't propositions that are inexpressible in any language by any speaker in any context. This response, however, strikes me as somewhat question-begging. For our acquaintance with creatures—even humans—who are wholly incapable of entertaining quantum mechanics or the Banach-Tarski theorem seems to make it very easy for us to conceive of there being intelligent beings who are to us as we are to chimps or dogs. That intuition is independent of any theory one might hold about the existence of propositions or the semantics of language that is ostensibly about propositions, and therefore constitutes evidence against any theory which holds that completely alien propositions are impossible.

21. Schiffer (2003: 62). My distinction between two models of the name-named relation in (2010) was intended to put the point about individuation in a better and clearer way.
22. I had much of the doctrine of pleonastic objects worked out before I read Crispin Wright's *Frege's Conception of Numbers As Objects*.
23. There is some further elaboration of this in my response to Ostertag (Chapter 16, this volume).
24. The title of Rumfitt's essay, "Objects of Thought," is an *homage* to Arthur Prior's posthumously published monograph, *Objects of Thought* (1971), and Rumfitt calls my *Remnants* approach 'Priorean' because the approach "was first systematically expounded" in Prior's book. I agree that it was remiss of me not to discuss Prior's important work. I think the main reason I didn't was that it was unclear to me what positive view Prior had about the semantics of belief sentences. He clearly denies that that-clauses in belief sentences refer to anything, and he says he agrees with Quine (1960: 216) that 'Tom believes that Cicero denounced Catiline' should no longer be viewed as of the form '*Fab*' with a = Tom and b = the referent of 'that Cicero denounced Catiline', but rather as of the form '*Fa*' with a = Tom and 'F' a composite absolute general term (1971: 20). But nowhere, to my knowledge, does Prior advance any view about the complex predicate's semantic determination, about the semantic properties the words in 'believes that Cicero denounced Catiline' must have in order for the predicate to be true of a person just in case she believes that Cicero denounced Catiline.
25. Schiffer (2003: 9).
26. Rumfitt (this volume: 74).
27. Frege (1960: 73).
28. Boolos (1998: II Frege Studies).
29. This shouldn't be taken to mean that it's open for it to be the case that, say, while x definitely definitely definitely has φ it doesn't definitely definitely definitely definitely have φ.
30. This characterization is incorrect if the epistemic theory of vagueness as a certain kind of ignorance is correct, but I'm assuming that it isn't correct.
31. Lewis (1999a).
32. See e.g. Schiffer (2003: Chapter 5).
33. 'Wrong' throughout is short for 'morally wrong'.
34. David Armstrong (1989) coined the metaphor of properties as shadows of predicates to describe a theory of properties he rejected.
35. Lewis (1983: 346).
36. Just as mentalese expressions have numerous conceptual roles, so propositional-attitude states have numerous functional roles, and when philosophers speak of *the* functional role of a state, what they are really speaking about is the state's maximal underived functional

role. I need the notion of an expression's maximal underived conceptual role in what follows, but I have no need further to mention the notion of a state's maximal underived functional role.
37. An expression's maximal underived conceptual role determines the expression's meaning just in case its having that conceptual role is metaphysically sufficient for its having that meaning, and for partial determination replace 'sufficient' with 'necessary'.
38. I leave open whether this needs qualification in light of the Grelling or other semantic paradoxes.
39. Wright (1983).
40. I've changed Smith's example of a person's believing that she ought to ϕ to her believing that it would be wrong for her to ϕ.
41. Stevenson (1944).

Bibliography

Armstrong, D. (1989). *Universals: An Opinionated Introduction*. Boulder: Westview.
Boolos, G. (1998). *Logic, Logic, and Logic*. Cambridge: Harvard University Press.
Frege, G. (1960). *The Foundations of Arithmetic*, J.L. Austin, trans. New York: Harper and Brothers.
Goodman, N. (1955). *Fact, Fiction, and Forecast*. Cambridge: Harvard University Press.
Hofweber, T. (2006a). "Inexpressible Properties and Propositions." *Oxford Studies in Metaphysics* 2: 155–206.
Hofweber, T. (2006b). "Schiffer's New Theory of Propositions." *Philosophy and Phenomenological Research* 73: 211–17.
Johnston, M. (1988). "The End of the Theory of Meaning." *Mind & Language* 3: 28–42.
Lewis, D. (1983). "New Work for a Theory of Universals." *Australasian Journal of Philosophy* 61: 343–77. In Lewis (1999b).
Lewis, D. (1999a). "Many, but Almost One." In Lewis (1999b).
Lewis, D. (1999b). *Papers in Metaphysics and Epistemology*. New York: Cambridge University Press.
Prior, A. (1971). *Objects of Thought*. Oxford: Oxford University Press.
Quine, W. (1960). *Word and Object*. Cambridge: MIT Press.
Schiffer, S. (1987). *Remnants of Meaning*. Cambridge: MIT Press.
Schiffer, S. (1990). "Meaning and Value." *The Journal of Philosophy* 87: 602–14.
Schiffer, (1992). "Belief Ascription." *Journal of Philosophy* 89: 499–521.
Schiffer, S. (1994). "A Paradox of Meaning." *Noûs* 28: 279–324.
Schiffer, S. (1996). "Language-Created Language-Independent Entities." *Philosophical Topics* 24: 149–67.
Schiffer, S. (2000). "Pleonastic Fregeanism and Empty Names." In *Empty Names, Fiction and the Puzzles of Non-Existence*, edited by A. Everett and T. Hofweber, Stanford: CSLI.
Schiffer, S. (2001). "Meanings." In *Essays on Meaning & Truth: Investigations in Philosophical Semantics*, edited by J. Campbell, M. O'Rourke & D. Shier, New York: Seven Bridges Press.
Schiffer, S. (2003). *The Things We Mean*. Oxford: Oxford University Press.
Schiffer, S. (2006). "Reply to Hofweber." *Philosophy and Phenomenological Research* 73: 233–6.
Schiffer, S. (2010). "Vague Properties." In *Cuts and Clouds: Essays on the Nature and Logic of Vagueness*, edited by R. Dietz and S. Moruzzi, Oxford: Oxford University Press.
Stevenson, C. L. (1944). *Ethics and Language*. New Haven: Yale University Press.
Thomasson, A. (2009). "The Easy Approach to Ontology." *Axiomathes* 19: 1–15.
Wright, C. (1983). *Frege's Conception of Numbers As Objects*. Aberdeen: Aberdeen University Press.

16

De Re Belief Reports
Response to Gary Ostertag

The face-value theory of belief reports of the form '*A* believes that *S*' holds that an instance of that form is true just in case the referent of the '*A*' term stands in the relation expressed by 'believes' to the proposition to which the 'that *S*' term refers. The theory enjoys a *prima facie* motivation but can't be accepted before it's completed by an account of the nature of the propositions we believe and to which that-clauses refer. It can't be successfully completed by any of the best-known theories of propositions—Russellian propositions, Fregean propositions, or propositions as functions from possible worlds into truth-values—but, I argued in *Things*, it can be successfully completed by pleonastic propositions. The account of belief reports advanced in *Things* conjoins the face-value theory with the hypothesis that pleonastic propositions are the things we believe and the referents of that-clauses. Ostertag raises two problems that question "whether the theory of pleonastic propositions is a viable completion of the face-value theory."[1] I'll call the first problem *the parity-of-reasoning meaning-intention problem* and the second *the de re problem*. At the least, the problems Ostertag raises require me to clarify the account of belief reports offered in *Things*.

16.1 The Parity-Of-Reasoning Meaning-Intention Problem

This problem challenges me to explain why my pleonastic-proposition completion of the face-value theory is a better account of belief reports than the hidden-indexical theory of belief reports. More specifically, the implication is that if the version of the hidden-indexical theory I defined in "Belief Ascription"[2] suffers from what I there called the *meaning-intention problem*, then the pleonastic theory suffers from an analogous reference-intention problem, so that, conversely, if my theory doesn't have a reference-intention problem, then the hidden-indexical theorist doesn't have a meaning-intention problem. I will try to make clear the differences between my account and HIT that make my account innocent of anything like the meaning-intention problem that infects HIT.

I never accepted HIT. I proposed it as the best account of the logical form of belief sentences compatible with a natural language's having a compositional truth theory, but then I argued that the problems I raised for the theory were serious enough to challenge the compositionality hypothesis (which challenge, incidentally, didn't

DE RE BELIEF REPORTS: RESPONSE TO GARY OSTERTAG   427

disturb me, because I thought that natural languages neither had nor needed compositional truth theories).³ Here is how I defined HIT in "Belief Ascription":

As applied to the paradigmatic example

Ralph believes that Fido is a dog

the hidden-indexical theory says that the logical form of an utterance of this sentence may be represented as

($\exists m$) (Φ^*m & B(Ralph, <Fido, doghood>, m))

where Φ^* is an implicitly referred to and contextually determined type of mode of presentation. By a type of mode of presentation I mean merely a property of modes of presentation; Φ^*, for example, might be that property that a propositional mode of presentation has when and only when it requires thinking of Fido as being the dog who appears in the morning and requires thinking of doghood as a property shared by such-and-such similar-looking creatures. The reference to a type of mode of presentation is implicit in that, although the sentence requires the speaker to be referring to a type of mode of presentation whenever the sentence is uttered, there is no word in 'Ralph believes that Fido is a dog' which refers to that type (whence the 'hidden' in 'hidden-indexical theory'). The reference to the type of mode of presentation is "contextually determined" in that different types may be referred to on different occasions of utterance (whence the 'indexical' in 'hidden-indexical theory').⁴

The *meaning*-intention problem raised against HIT in "Belief Ascription" can also be put as a *reference*-intention problem, and putting it as a reference-intention problem will make salient the problem Ostertag thinks parity of reasoning makes for me. HIT's reference-intention problem may be put in the following two-part way.

a. HIT entails that for every token of the sentence

1. Ralph believes that Fido is a dog

(which has a truth-value—henceforth to go without saying) there is a type of mode of presentation Φ such that the token is true iff Ralph believes <Fido, doghood> under a mode of presentation of type Φ. Suppose Φ^* is the mode-of-presentation implicated in the truth condition of a particular token of (1). Then *something* must make it the case that Φ^* is the mode-of-presentation type implicated in the token's truth condition, and that "something" must be compatible with the accommodation of belief sentences in a compositional truth theory, for HIT was devised to be a theory consistent with such accommodation. The accommodation of (1) in a compositional truth theory requires there to be a finitely statable rule for determining the mode-of-presentation type that enters into the truth condition of an arbitrary token of (1). But there is simply no chance of such a rule being provided unless it tells us that Φ is the mode-of-presentation type that enters into the truth condition of a token of (1) only if the speaker refers to Φ in uttering that token. This should be clear to theorists who have considered how singular terms such as 'she', 'it', 'that', 'this', 'that boy', etc. might be accommodated in a compositional truth theory. The need becomes obvious when, for example, one asks how a compositional truth theory for English could complete the formula

For every token τ of 'she' and every x, x is the referent of τ iff $x = \ldots$

One pretty quickly realizes that the only completion in the offing would be something like

For every token τ of 'she' and every x, x is the referent of τ iff x = the female to whom the speaker referred with τ.

Closer to home, the need to invoke speaker-reference is also clearly manifested in the case of sentences for which a hidden-indexical semantics is found to be plausible even by theorists who don't have a horse in the race. 'It's raining' is such a sentence. It's plausible that (nearly enough) its meaning dictates that a token of the sentence is such that, for some location l, the token is true iff it's raining at l. If 'It's raining' is to be accommodated in a compositional truth theory, the theory must provide a rule for determining the location on which the truth of a token of the sentence depends. Since that location needn't be the location occupied by the speaker (an utterance of 'It's raining' by a speaker in New York might be true only if it's raining in London)—not to mention the fact that there is no such thing as *the* location occupied by the speaker—it ought to seem clear that accommodation in a compositional truth theory entails that a location enters into the truth condition of a token of 'It's raining' only if it's the location to which the speaker refers in uttering the token. If that seems right to you, then it ought also seem right to you that, given HIT, the accommodation of belief reports in a compositional truth theory would entail that a mode-of-presentation type Φ entered into the truth condition of a token of (1) only if the speaker referred to Φ in uttering that token.

b. Now speaker-reference is an intentional action, and in order for a speaker S to refer to x in uttering σ, S must utter σ with appropriate x-directed intentions. I speak of S's uttering σ *with appropriate x-directed intentions* rather than of S's uttering σ *intending to refer to x* because of the intimate connection between speaker-reference and speaker-meaning. For the Gricean, speaker-reference can be defined in terms of speaker-meaning,[5] and one very common way for a speaker to refer to a thing is by meaning a proposition that is about that thing. That is how a reference-intention problem can become a meaning-intention problem, and how a meaning-intention problem can become a reference-intention problem. HIT appears to have a meaning-intention problem because in producing an unembedded utterance of 'A believes that S' there seems not to be a mode-of-presentation type Φ such that the speaker utters 'A believes that S' with intentions that would suffice for her meaning *that A believes that S under a mode of presentation of type* Φ. And HIT appears to have a reference-intention problem because the speaker also seems not to have any other intentions that would suffice for referring to Φ.

As Ostertag says, there are ways one might try to challenge my intention-denying claims. My own view is that all the challenges of which I'm aware are extremely weak, much weaker than the compelling reasons for thinking the speaker wouldn't have the reference-to-Φ-entailing intentions HIT requires her to have. But never mind all that for now, for my concern here is to explain why, even if HIT has a meaning- or reference-intention problem, the account of belief reports offered in *Things* doesn't.

It may appear that if HIT has a reference-intention problem, then so does my account of belief reports. For on my account, while a token of the that-clause in

(1) ('Ralph believes that Fido is a dog') will refer to a Fido- and doghood-dependent proposition, each such proposition will impose constraints on how one must think of Fido or doghood in order to entertain that proposition, and if two tokens of the that-clause refer to two different propositions, the difference between them will consist in their imposing different requirements on what it takes to entertain them. For example, in one utterance of (1) the that-clause will refer to a proposition that requires thinking of Fido as the strange-looking creature Ralph is trying to feed dog biscuits, while the that-clause produced in a different utterance of (1) will refer to a proposition that requires thinking of Fido as a certain family's newly acquired pet. But on my account *something* must determine the proposition to which a that-clause in a belief report refers, *something* must make it the case that the token of a that-clause produced in one utterance of (1) refers to one proposition while the token produced in another utterance of the sentence refers to a different proposition. What is that "something"? If a proposition p is the referent of a that-clause token only if the speaker refers to p in uttering that token, then my account certainly has a reference-intention problem if HIT does. If, however, the factors that determine p to be the referent of the that-clause token don't require the speaker to refer p, then why shouldn't there be factors available to HIT for determining the reference to a mode-of-presentation type that don't require the speaker to refer to that mode-of-presentation type?

The answer runs as follows. On my account, the proposition to which a that-clause token refers is determined by factors that don't require the speaker to refer to that proposition, but the sort of factors that determine the referent of a that-clause token on my account aren't available to HIT to be what determines the reference to a mode-of-presentation type which that theory requires. That is because the reference-determining factors operative on my account aren't compatible with the accommodation of belief reports in a compositional truth theory and HIT is required to be compatible with a compositional truth theory. In other words, the reason HIT must hold that a mode-of-presentation type Φ enters into the truth condition of a token of a belief sentence only if the speaker refers to Φ in uttering that token is that that is HIT's only hope for reference determination compatible with a compositional truth theory's entailing for each sentence of the form 'A believes that S' the kind of theorem it needs to provide to tell us what must be the case in order for a token of the sentence to be true. Yet it's because of the implausibility of its only hope that it has a reference-intention problem (and, thereby in the way indicated above, a meaning-intention problem as well). Had my account needed to comport with a compositional truth theory, it, too, would have been forced, *faute de mieux*, to say that a that-clause token refers to a particular proposition only if the speaker referred to that proposition in her utterance of the token, and then my account would have had—which fortunately it doesn't have—its own reference-intention problem.

On p. 72 of *Things* I announce "that, in certain crucial respects, *the relation between that-clauses and the propositions to which they refer is importantly different from the usual relation between singular terms and their referents*," and for the next fourteen pages I elaborate on what those crucial differences are. The elaboration is intended to explain how the reference of the that-clause in a belief report is determined, and why its being determined in that way precludes belief reports from being accommodated in a compositional truth theory. But rather than rehearse what I say in those pages, I will try a different tack. My view is that belief reports of the form 'A believes that S' can't be accommodated in a compositional truth theory because of the way the that-clauses in them get their reference. If I'm right about belief reports, then nothing prevents there being syntactically simple singular terms which also get their references in a way that prevents sentences containing those singular terms from being accommodated in a compositional truth theory. Because that-clauses are complex entities that introduce issues that don't arise for syntactically simple singular terms, the explanation of why that-clauses can't be accommodated in a compositional truth theory is more complicated than the explanation of why the syntactically simple singular terms can't be so accommodated, even though essentially the same kind of explanation applies in both cases. Consequently, I propose to try to clarify my explanation of why belief reports can't be accommodated in a compositional truth theory by first offering an explanation of why sentences containing a certain syntactically simple name can't be accommodated in one and then pointing out how I intended the same sort of explanation to explain what it is about that-clauses which prevents the accommodation of belief reports. The syntactically simple name in question is 'Midtown', used as a name of a part of Manhattan. I will sketch a semantic hypothesis about 'Midtown' but will make no attempt to argue for its truth. This is because my sketch is presented merely to illustrate the kind of explanation offered in *Things* to show what it is about belief reports that precludes their accommodation in a compositional truth theory.

Carol and Frank are two intelligent and rational Manhattanites neither of whom knows anything about the philosophical problems of vagueness. Carol has just informed Frank that a mutual friend, Bob, is visiting Manhattan. Frank asks if Carol knows where Bob is staying, and Carol replies,

1. He's staying in Midtown.

'Midtown', so used, is a name, but it isn't the name of a precisely defined area of Manhattan. If you are in Times Square you are definitely in Midtown, and if from there you were to travel in a straight line in any direction you would eventually definitely not be in Midtown; but at no point would you have crossed an invisible line on one side of which you were definitely in Midtown and on the other side of which you were definitely not in Midtown. What, then, can be said about the reference of the token of 'Midtown' Carol uttered? Some theorists of vagueness would say that words and concepts are the only things that can be vague; vagueness, they would say, is wholly a feature of language and thought, and nothing in the extra-linguistic or extra-mental world can be vague. Let's call the token of 'Midtown' Carol uttered M_t. These theorists might say that, although no precise area is determinately the referent of M_t, myriad precise areas are each such that it's indeterminate whether it's the referent of M_t, or indeterminate whether it's indeterminate whether it's the referent of M_t, or indeterminate whether it's indeterminate whether it's indeterminate whether..., and so on. On the alternative view I will describe, M_t refers to a vague area; more specifically, M_t refers to that vague area whose *penumbral profile* matches its *penumbral profile*.

The penumbral profiles of tokens of 'Midtown' may shift somewhat from one token to the next. For example, an utterance of 'Jane works in Midtown' is apt to count as true if Jane works in a law firm located at 59th Street and Park Avenue, but an utterance of 'Jane lives in Midtown' may count as false or as neither definitely true nor definitely false if Jane lives in an elegant apartment building at that address.[6] Two tokens of 'Midtown' have the same penumbral profile just in case, for any location λ, if λ is in, or not in, the extension of one token, then it's in, or not in, the extension of the other; if it's indeterminate whether λ is in the extension of one token, then it's indeterminate whether it's in the extension of the other; if it's indeterminate whether it's indeterminate whether λ is in the extension of one token, then it's indeterminate whether it's indeterminate whether λ is in the extension of the other; and so on. Vague areas are areas that lack determinate boundaries, which means that certain locations will be such that it's indeterminate whether they are in the area, or indeterminate whether it's indeterminate whether they are in the area, or..., and it's thus that we can speak of vague areas as having penumbral profiles. We may say that vague area α = vague area α' just in case α and α' have the same penumbral profile, and that α and α' have the same penumbral profile just in case, for every location λ, if λ is in, or not in, α/α', then it's in, or not in, α'/α; if it's indeterminate whether λ is in α/α', then it's indeterminate whether it's in α'/α; if it's indeterminate whether it's indeterminate whether λ is in α/α', then it's indeterminate whether it's indeterminate whether λ is in α'/α; and so on.

Each token of 'Midtown', I'm assuming, has as its referent that vague area whose penumbral profile matches the token's. That follows trivially from the definitions of 'penumbral profile' and the assumption that tokens of 'Midtown' refer to vague areas (I leave the proof of this to the reader). Since the penumbral profiles of tokens of 'Midtown' may shift somewhat from one token to the next, it follows that different tokens of the name may have somewhat different vague areas as their referents. Suppose vague area α^* is the referent of M_t, the token of 'Midtown' Carol produced in her utterance of (1) ('He's staying in Midtown'). What makes it the case that M_t refers to α^*? That isn't answered by knowing that M_t and α^* have matching penumbral profiles, because nothing that was so far said rules out the possibility that something first makes it the case that M_t refers to α^* and then M_t *ipso facto* acquires a penumbral profile matching α^*'s. In fact, if one thinks of the reference of tokens of 'Midtown' on analogy with the way context-sensitive singular terms typically get their reference—in the way, for example, a person or animal x is made the referent of a token τ of 'she' by virtue of being the female to whom the speaker referred with τ—then one is apt to suppose there is a formula for determining the referent of any token τ of 'Midtown' such that once a vague area α is determined by that formula to be the referent of τ, then τ thereby simply acquires a penumbral profile that matches α's. And if one thought there was such a formula, then it would also be reasonable to assume that the formula entailed that a token of 'Midtown' referred to a vague area only if the speaker intended to refer to that area with that token, in which case part of what would have made α^* the referent of M_t was that Carol intended to refer to α^* with M_t. That, however, is a thought that can be quickly scotched, for Carol will neither know, nor will she need to know, that M_t refers to α^*. Carol knows that her utterance of (1) is unimpugnably definitely true because she knows that Bob is staying at the Bryant

Park Hotel at 40 West 40th Street, an address that must be in any precisification of 'Midtown.' But now suppose, having just uttered (1), Carol is asked what would count as a borderline case of a location that was in Midtown. Chances are, never having had reason to consider such a question, she will have little idea what to say, and if she does venture an answer it will have no special authority. This shows that α^* isn't made the referent of M_t even partly by virtue of Carol's having uttered M_t with the intention of referring to α^*. Nor can there be any formula of the kind just considered for determining the referent of a token of 'Midtown', a formula that would provide a criterion for determining α^* to be the referent of M_t independently of any assumption about M_t's penumbral profile. For M_t doesn't inherit its penumbral profile from α^*, the vague area to which it refers, and this because what makes α^* the referent of M_t *just is* the fact that it's that vague area whose penumbral profile matches M_t's.

Thus, whatever determines M_t's penumbral profile *eo ipso* determines its reference. So what does determine M_t's penumbral profile? How, for example, might we find out where the location 22nd Street and Lexington Avenue is in M_t's penumbral profile? To ask that is to ask what the truth status of Carol's utterance would have been had Bob been staying at that address. Such counterfactual questions rarely have determinate answers. But suppose the circumstances of her utterance were as close as possible to those that actually obtained, except that Carol's belief that Bob was staying at 40 W. 40th Street was mistaken, as he was really staying in a hotel at 22nd Street and Lexington Avenue, that that became known during the course of her conversation with Frank, at which time the question of the truth status of Carol's utterance—true, false, borderline true/false, borderline borderline true/false, etc.—was raised. Then I suspect that the utterance would be true if Carol and Frank accepted it as true, false if they accepted it as false, and neither determinately true nor determinately not true if it was indeterminate whether they accepted in as true, and so on. And I further suspect that how they would judge the truth status of the utterance would depend on an indeterminate congeries of factors such as the nature of their conversations, the dispositions to use 'Midtown' that each brought to the conversation, and even their moods of the moment.

Suppose all that is true. Then, I submit, no sentence containing 'Midtown', *qua* name of a part of Manhattan, can be accommodated in a compositional truth theory for any idiolect that contained the name. In order for a sentence to be accommodated in a compositional truth theory, the theory must make it possible *first* to determine the semantic values of the token's semantically relevant constituents and *then* on that basis to compute the truth status of the sentence token they compose. In order for that to be possible for sentences containing 'Midtown' (used as a name for a part of Manhattan), the accommodating truth theory would have to contain a base clause for 'Midtown' that provided a formula for determining the referent of an arbitrary token of the name which didn't require prior knowledge of the penumbral profile of the sentence token in which the token of the name occurs, and that is what is precluded on the sketch I have provided: on that sketch the referent of a token of 'Midtown' is determined by the token's penumbral profile, and that penumbral profile is determined by abstraction from the penumbral profile of the sentence token in which the token of 'Midtown' occurs.

The account offered in *Things* of how that-clauses get their references, and of why their getting their references in that way precludes their accommodation in a compositional truth theory, is very similar to the account of 'Midtown' I just sketched. Consider the sentence

2. Ralph believes that George Eliot was a man.

A token of (2) is true just in case Ralph believes the proposition to which its contained token of (2)'s that-clause refers. Different tokens of the that-clause may refer to somewhat different propositions, so two tokens of (2) uttered at the same time may have different truth statuses. If we ignore the vagueness of 'man' we may say that the proposition to which a token of the that-clause in a token of (2) refers is always an Eliot-dependent proposition that has the same modal profile as, but isn't identical to, the singular proposition <George Eliot, the property of having been a man>. It isn't identical to the singular proposition because in order for Ralph (or anyone else) to believe the proposition to which the that-clause token refers he must think of Eliot in certain not altogether determinate ways. For example, an utterance of (2) is likely to be true if Ralph believes Eliot to have been a man when thinking of her as the famous nineteenth century English novelist named 'George Eliot' who was the author of *Middlemarch*, *Silas Marner*, and other novels; and it's likely to be false if Ralph believes Eliot to have been a man but doesn't think of Eliot in any of the ways just mentioned. But there is always a fair amount of indeterminacy as to how Ralph must think of Eliot in order to count as believing the proposition to which the that-clause token in a token of (2) refers. Because of this indeterminacy, 'that George Eliot was a man' is a vague singular term, and thus its tokens have penumbral profiles. And because the proposition to which a token of the that-clause in a token of (2) refers is individuated in part by how one must think of Eliot in order to believe the proposition, that proposition will have somewhat indeterminate conditions of individuation, and will in that way be vague, and thus have a penumbral profile which must match that of the that-clause token that refers to it. The parallel with 'Midtown' continues: what *makes it the case* that a vaguely individuated proposition is the referent of a that-clause token (at least in a propositional-attitude report) is simply that its penumbral profile matches the token's; and what determines the token's penumbral profile is whatever somewhat indeterminate congeries of factors determines the penumbral profile of the sentence token in which the that-clause token occurs, for there is no way to determine the that-clause's penumbral profile other than by abstraction from the penumbral profile of the sentence token. That is what precluded sentences containing 'Midtown' from being accommodated in a compositional truth theory, and it's what precludes belief reports of the form '*A* believes that *S*' from being accommodated in one. I expand on these quite condensed points in a work that is in progress (Schiffer, forthcoming), but I *hope* I have said enough to throw some light on the pages in *Things* that quite understandably led Ostertag to wonder why the hidden-indexical theory, but not my account of belief reports, has a reference-intention problem.

16.2 The *De Re* Problem

Half-way down p. 84 of *Things* I announced that "my claim that that-clauses refer to fine-grained but unstructured propositions requires me to be very clear about referential occurrences of singular terms in that-clauses," and for the next two pages I expatiate on this in a way that falls somewhat short of being "very clear." I began that discussion by supposing that Harold points to Superman, who is wearing his monogrammed caped spandex outfit, and says

1. Lois believes that he flies,

and I continued:

Along with common sense, I count [Harold's utterance of (1)] true. I also want to say that the occurrence of 'he' in (1) refers to Superman—*in this sense*: first, *Harold* clearly counts as referring to Superman by his utterance of 'he' in our pre-theoretic sense of speaker reference; secondly, 'he' occurs there as a rigid designator of Superman, in that the proposition to which (1)'s that-clause refers is true in an arbitrary possible world just in case Superman flies in that world; and thirdly, that proposition is also [a Superman-dependent proposition], in that the proposition wouldn't have existed had Superman not existed and is therefore partly individuated with respect to Superman. I do *not*, however, claim that the occurrence of 'he' in (1) refers to Superman in any sense that allows us to say that it follows from the truth of (1) that Superman has the property expressed by the "open sentence"

2. Lois believes that x flies

.... [For] my view is that (2) is not an open sentence [in the sense of 'open sentence' familiar from predicate logic], since it expresses no property, and this because the occurrence of 'he' in (1) does more than refer to Superman in the sense in which I allow; it also plays its contextual role in determining the proposition to which (1)'s that-clause refers, even though the referent of the that-clause isn't compositionally determined by its structure and the referents of its parts.... We can have different substitution instances of (2)—e.g.
Lois believes that Superman flies
and
Lois believes that Clark Kent flies
—such that the two substitution instances have different truth-values, even though the singular terms replacing 'x' refer to the same thing, in the sense of reference I have explained.[7]

So far so good. But then I recognize an apparent threat to what I just said, which is that from Harold's utterance of (1) ('Lois believes that he flies') we may infer

3. There is someone such that Lois believes that he flies.

This is a threat because it appears to be an example of quantification into a that-clause, one that could be represented in logical notation as

4. $\exists x(\text{Believes}(\text{Ralph}, \text{that } x \text{ flies}))$,

which would be true only if something had the property expressed by the genuine open sentence 'Believes(Ralph, that x flies)'. What I said in response to this threat was (nearly enough) that we don't explain the truth of (3) by saying that someone has the property expressed by the ostensibly quantified open sentence in (4), 'Believes(Ralph, that x flies)', for there is no such open sentence and not only can't (4) be true, it's not even well formed, since the occurrence of 'x' in it can't be that of a variable bound by the initial quantifier.[8] Instead, we explain the truth of (3) in terms of Lois's believing, for some x, an x-dependent proposition that is true iff x flies.

Perhaps it would have been clearer what view I was trying to articulate had I gone on to explain that I intended to be mimicking Russell's move when he in effect suggested that the sentence

The duchess of Hoboken is bald

is a *masquerader* in that it doesn't have the logical form it appears to have. Its surface syntactical form suggests its logical form is represented by

Bald(the duchess of Hoboken),

a formula that is true just in case the referent of the singular term 'the duchess of Hoboken' has the property expressed by the open formula

Bald(x),

false just in case the referent doesn't have that property, whereas its actual logical form is represented by the generalization

$\exists x$ (!Duchess of Hoboken(x) & Bald(x))

Similarly, I intended to be suggesting that (3) ('There is someone such that Lois believes that he flies') is also a masquerader in that it, too, doesn't have the logical form it appears to have. Its surface syntactical form suggests its logical form is represented by

$\exists x$(Believes(Ralph, that x flies)),

which would be true only if

Believes(Ralph, that x flies)

did, contrary to all that I've said, express a property whose possession by Superman was necessary and sufficient for the truth of 'Lois believes that Superman flies', whereas its actual logical form is represented by

$\exists x,p(p$ is an x-dependent proposition that is true iff x flies & Lois believes p).

This position—the one I was aiming to articulate—has two notable consequences. First, while

Lois believes that Superman flies

∴ There is someone such that Lois believes that he flies

is valid in that there is no possible world in which its premise, but not its conclusion, is true, it's not *logically* valid. It's not logically valid because the inference isn't licensed by Existential Generalization or any other logical rule of inference. Nevertheless, like the inference 'Jones is a bachelor; therefore, Jones is unmarried', it's valid because it's necessarily equivalent to the following inference (wherein 'S^*' stands for the proposition to which 'that Superman flies' refers), which is logically valid:

> Believes(Lois, S^*)
> S^* is a Superman-dependent proposition that is true iff Superman flies.
> ∴ $\exists x, p(p$ is an x-dependent proposition that is true iff x flies & Lois believes p)

Second, the inference

> Superman is someone such that Lois believes that he flies
> ∴ Lois believes that Superman flies

is not in any sense valid, for it's equivalent to the inference

> $\exists p(p$ is a Superman-dependent proposition that is true iff Superman flies & Believes(Lois, p))
> S^* is a Superman-dependent proposition that is true iff Superman flies
> ∴ Believes(Lois, S^*)

whose invalidity is on all fours with that of

> Mary loves a Russian
> Vladimir is a Russian
> ∴ Mary loves Vladimir

"A slight awkwardness remains," I announced in *Things* after explaining why there was no conflict between my account of Harold's utterance of (1) ('Lois believes that he flies') and the sense in which it entails (3) ('There is someone such that Lois believes that he flies'). That "slight awkwardness" was that my position may appear to imply a contradiction. For given the way in which (1) entails (3), it must also be that

> 5. Lois doesn't believe that Clark Kent flies

Entails

> 6. There is someone such that Lois doesn't believe that he flies,

and when we put that together with the fact that Superman happens to be the person who verifies both (3) and (6), we get the *apparent* contradiction

> 7. Superman (aka Clark Kent) is someone such that Lois does and does not believe that he flies.

I then explained, what I hope should now be clear, that the appearance of contradiction is spurious, given that (7), on my view of its semantics, is on its relevant reading equivalent to

> $\exists p, q(p$ & q are both Superman-dependent propositions that are true iff Superman flies & Believes(Lois, p) & ¬Believes(Lois, q)).

I say "on its relevant reading" because, as Ostertag rightly observes, I should also allow for a reading of (6) on which it means the same as

$\exists x \forall p((p$ is an x-dependent proposition that is true iff x flies) $\rightarrow \neg$(Believes (Lois, p))).

I turn now to Ostertag's commentary on the two pages in question, the sections in his essay called "Pleonastic Propositions and *De Re* Belief Reports" and "Disbelief and Disagreement." There he makes two critical comments, only the second of which is intended to be an objection to my theory.

The first critical comment concerns my saying (in effect) that from the pair of sentences

    8. There is someone, namely Superman, such that Lois believes that he flies.

    9. There is someone, namely Superman, such that Lois doesn't believe that he flies

we can infer the *apparent* contradiction

    10. There is someone, namely Superman, such that Lois does and does not believe that he flies.

Ostertag claims that if on my account (10) really is a consequence of (8) and (9), then "this would certainly be a mark against the analysis."[9] But, he continues, it's unclear why I think (10) is a consequence of (8) and (9), since on my account (8) and (9) (on its relevant reading) are truth-conditionally equivalent, respectively, to the mutually consistent sentences

    11. For some Superman-dependent proposition p that is true iff Superman flies, Lois believes p

and

    12. For some Superman-dependent proposition p that is true iff Superman flies, Lois doesn't believe p.

I may be missing Ostertag's point, but I don't see how I could be mistaken in saying that (10) may be inferred from (8) and (9). After all, how could two sentences fail to entail their conjunction? Nor do I see why it "would certainly be a mark against [my] analysis" if from the sentences (8) and (9) we may infer the sentence (10), for, as I explained just above, (10) isn't the contradiction it appears to be, and this precisely because, given the reading on which (9) is true, (10) is equivalent to the conjunction of the mutually consistent sentences (11) and (12).

Ostertag's second critical comment is intended to be an objection to the way my account handles reports of disbelief such as 'Lois does not believe that Clark Kent flies.' I fear, however, that this objection never gets a foothold, for its based on a misrepresentation of my theory. My theory is that *every* that-clause in an utterance (that has a truth-value) of a sentence of the form '*A* believes that *S*' or '*A* doesn't believe that *S*' refers to a proposition. So it's also my view that the proposition to which the that-clause in an utterance of

    13. Lois believes that Superman flies

refers is a Superman-dependent proposition that is true iff Superman flies (as is the proposition to which the that-clause in an utterance of (5) ('Lois doesn't believe that

Clark Kent flies') refers; it's just that it's most likely that they refer to different but truth-conditionally equivalent Superman-dependent propositions). Ostertag misrepresents me when he says that "on Schiffer's view (13) is true just in case Lois believes a [Superman]-dependent proposition that's true iff Superman flies."[10] That is *not* my view, and nowhere in *Things* do I say anything that entails or even suggests that it is my view. On my view, as I've already said, the that-clause in an utterance of (13) refers to a *particular* Superman-dependent proposition that is true iff Superman flies. Let S^* be the Superman-dependent proposition to which the that-clause in an utterance of the sentence refers, and suppose the utterance is true. Then the fact that Lois believes S^* entails that Lois believes *some* Superman-dependent proposition that is true iff Superman flies; but of course the fact that Lois believes *some* such proposition doesn't entail that she believes S^*. Similarly, there is no "scope" or other ambiguity in an utterance of 'Lois doesn't believe that Clark Kent flies': the that-clause in the utterance refers to a particular Clark Kent (aka Superman)-dependent proposition, and the utterance is true just in case Lois doesn't believe that proposition. Ostertag's essay makes clear that he is aware that I take the that-clauses in utterances of the sentences in question to refer to Superman-dependent propositions. Does he take me to hold *both* that (i) the that-clause in an utterance of (13) refers to a *particular* Superman-dependent proposition that is true iff Superman flies—in which case the utterance is true just in case Lois believes *that* proposition—*and* that (ii) the utterance is true just in case Lois believes *some* Superman-dependent proposition that is true iff Superman flies? To attribute confusion of that magnitude should require textual evidence; yet the only citation given in support of (ii) is to p. 85 of *Things*, and nowhere on that page do I say anything that entails or even suggest that there is any sense in which

Lois believes some Superman-dependent proposition that is true iff Superman flies

entails

Lois believes that Superman flies.

I would like to think that if I were tempted to say that the first sentence entailed the second, then I would have seen that it also entails 'Lois believes that Clark Kent flies', and as Ostertag himself makes clear, I very explicitly recognize that utterances of 'Lois believes that Superman flies' and of 'Lois believes that Clark Kent flies' might very easily have different truth-values.

It's not clear to me what led Ostertag to say that "on Schiffer's view (13) is true just in case Lois believes a [Superman]-dependent proposition that's true iff Superman flies." It seems to be related to his effort to understand how I could claim that Harold's utterance of (1) ('Lois believes that he flies'), made while pointing to the guy in the monogrammed caped spandex outfit, "is Superman-involving and at the same time deny that it expresses a property *of* Superman."[11] Perhaps there is a problem here that I should see. If so, I don't see what it is. Harold's utterance of (1) is Superman-involving in that the that-clause in it refers to a proposition that is Superman-dependent and true iff Superman flies. It's clear that Superman must have certain properties in order for Harold's utterance to be true, but the utterance doesn't "express" a property of him in that the proposition expressed by the utterance (which of course is different from the proposition to which its that-clause refers) isn't also expressed by a sentence in which there is a referentially transparent occurrence of a singular term whose referent is Superman. In Quine's famous example 'Giorgione was so-called because of his size',[12] the occurrence of 'Giorgione' isn't referentially transparent because replacing 'Giorgione' in that true sentence with a co-referential singular term results in a false sentence. At the same time, the sentence expresses a property of Giorgione because it's equivalent to 'Giorgione was called "Giorgione" because of his size,' which does contain a referentially transparent occurrence of the name. On my view, however, there is no sentence that both expresses the same proposition as that expressed in Harold's utterance of (1) and in which a singular term that refers to Superman has a referentially transparent occurrence. That is a consequence of the view that the referents of that-clauses are not a function of the referents (or extensions) of the terms in the that-clauses that refer to them. I won't be amazed if that view turns out to be indefensible, but I don't see that it's indefensible just because it recognizes sentences that express object-dependent propositions but don't express (in the sense of 'express' intended by Ostertag) properties of the objects that help to individuate the propositions and enter into their truth conditions. In any case, the theory Ostertag shows to have a problem handling reports of disbelief isn't mine.

Notes

1. This volume: 112.
2. I proposed a somewhat different account of the hidden-indexical theory in Schiffer (1977). There I pointed out that different utterances of a sentence that could be used to make a *de re* belief report, such as the sentence 'Ortcutt is believed by Ralph to be a spy', could have different truth-values, and to explain this I proposed that such sentences contain "an implicit indexical component requiring reference to a mode of presentation or a type of mode of presentation." In this response 'hidden-indexical theory' shall refer to the version presented in Schiffer (1992).
3. See Schiffer (1987).
4. Schiffer (1992: 503). I've changed the numbering of the displayed sentences.
5. See Neale's contribution to this volume (Chapter 12) and my response to it (Chapter 21).
6. This sort of penumbral shift is a feature of every vague expression; for example, a man who shaves his scalp but would otherwise have a full head of hair may count as bald in one context, as not bald in another, and as borderline bald in a third.
7. Schiffer (2003: 84–5). The numbering of examples has been changed to conform to the style of the present text.
8. Although I emphasized (in the pages in question) that 'Lois believes that x flies' doesn't express a property whose possession by Superman is necessary and sufficient for the truth of 'Lois believes that Superman flies'—or for that matter any other property—instead of giving my account of 'There is someone such that Lois believes that he flies' by writing 'There is someone such that Lois believes that he flies iff $\exists x$(Lois believes an object-dependent proposition that's true iff x flies)' ['object' should have been 'x'], I inexplicably wrote (on p. 85) '$\exists x$(Lois believes that x flies) iff $\exists x$(Lois believes an object-dependent proposition that's true iff x flies)', as though the left-hand side could without further ado be used merely as shorthand for 'There is someone such that Lois believes that he flies'.

9. Ostertag *ibid.* (120).
10. Ostertag (this volume: 121); I've replaced Ostertag's numbering with my own.
11. Ostertag (this volume: 120).
12. Quine (1953: 139).

Bibliography

Ostertag, G. (2016). "Propositional Platitudes." (Chapter 5, this volume).
Quine, W. V. O. (1953). "Reference and Modality." In *From a Logical Point of View*. Cambridge: Harvard University Press.
Schiffer, S. (1977). "Naming and Knowing." *Midwest Studies in Philosophy* II: 28–41.
Schiffer, S. (1987). *Remnants of Meaning*. Cambridge: MIT Press.
Schiffer, S. (1992). "Belief Ascription." *The Journal of Philosophy* 99: 499–521.
Schiffer, S. (2003). *The Things We Mean*. Oxford: Oxford University Press.
Schiffer, S. (unpublished). "An Effect of Vagueness on Meaning."

17
The Relativity Feature
Response to Ray Buchanan

I'm grateful to Ray Buchanan for resurrecting the issues discussed in "What Reference Has to Tell Us about Meaning," unquestionably my most deeply buried publication. That paper was intended further to develop the pleonastic conception of propositions sketched in *Things* via an elaboration and defense of the following claims:

1. There is reason to suppose that the things we believe and say, and the referents of that-clauses in belief and saying reports, include propositions that have what I called *the relativity feature*, that being a feature a proposition has provided it's an x-dependent proposition the entertainment of which requires different people, or the same person at different times or places, to think of x in different ways.
2. No proposition of any of the most familiar kinds can have the relativity feature.
3. Various ways considered of trying to explain away the case for the relativity feature, including the no-semantic-content view suggested by John McDowell (McDowell 1984), Richard Heck (Heck 2002), and others, all confront serious problems.
4. Pleonastic propositions may have the relativity feature, and if, as I argued in *Things*, they are the contents of propositional speech acts, then myriad of those contents will have the relativity feature.

Buchanan says nothing about (4); he accepts (2); and while he agrees with (1) that there is *some* reason to think we believe and say propositions that have the relativity feature, he denies that we believe or say propositions that have that feature. The aim of his essay is to provide a version of the no-semantic-content theory that explains away the appearance of the relativity feature, thereby removing the no-semantic-content theory from the reach of my objections.

A literal utterance of an unembedded truth-evaluable sentence has a "semantic content" just in case there is a proposition p such that the speaker means p in making her utterance and her utterance is literal by virtue of her meaning p. In the event, p is the semantic content of her utterance. Fregean propositions are structured entities containing modes of presentation of the objects and properties the propositions are about. Let a *neo*-Fregean proposition be a Fregean proposition whose modes of presentation are *object*-dependent modes of presentation, where for present purposes that is any mode of presentation that is a mode of presentation of the same thing in every possible world in which it's a mode of presentation of anything. Every neo-Fregean proposition determines a Russellian proposition with which it has the same possible-worlds truth conditions. For example, if $<m_f, m_d>$ is a neo-Fregean proposition expressed by an utterance of 'Fido is a dog,' then its modal profile is determined by the Russellian proposition <Fido, doghood>. On the neo-Fregean conception of propositions, the difference between the neo-Fregean proposition <m_f, m_d> and the Russellian proposition <Fido, doghood> is truth-conditionally idle, and for any modes of presentation m, m', <m, m'> and <m_f, m_d> will have identical modal profiles if m is a Fido-dependent mode of presentation and m' is a doghood-dependent mode of presentation. The no-semantic-content theory Buchanan defends claims that, while neo-Fregean propositions are the contents of beliefs, no propositions of any kind are the contents of propositional speech acts or the semantic contents of utterances or the referents of that-clauses in belief or speech-act reports. The theory invites various questions. For example, the inference

Jill believes and told Jack that she won't fetch a pail of water.
So, there is something—namely, that she won't fetch a pail of water—that Jill both believes and told Jack.

seems to be formally valid, but the no-semantic-content theorist must evidently say that it's patently invalid, for, she must say, although its premise may be true, it's impossible for its conclusion to be true (according to the theory, if Jill *believes* something, that something is a proposition, but if she *told* Jack something, that something can't be a proposition; so nothing can be something that she *both* believes *and* told Jack). What struck me about the articles in which McDowell and Heck proposed the no-semantic-content view was that neither of them went on to consider the ramifications of their proposal for the semantics of propositional-attitude and speech-act *reports*. I think that if they had they would have anticipated the point of the two (rhetorical) questions I pressed on them in my article:

- Does the that-clause in 'I believe that I'm old enough to vote' refer to the proposition that I'm old enough to vote? It would seem that it must, given that believing is a relation to propositions. For if believing is a relation to propositions, then there must surely be some canonical way of specifying what proposition a person believes, and it's precisely that-clauses which provide our canonical way of specifying what believers believe.
- If the that-clause in 'I believe that I'm old enough to vote' refers to the proposition that I'm old enough to vote, then how could parity-of-reasoning considerations fail to require saying the same about the that-clause in 'I said that I'm old enough to vote'? And how could the valid inference

    Fiona said that I'm deranged.
    I believe what Fiona said.
    So, I believe that I'm deranged.

    be valid if the that-clause in its conclusion, but not the one in its first premise, refers to the proposition that I'm deranged?

Buchanan, of course, does deny that the that-clause in 'I believe that I'm old enough to vote' refers to the proposition that I'm old enough to vote. This suggests to me that I should have expanded on the first of the two just displayed questions. I hope the following expansion of it makes my point clearer.

Regrettably, English lacks a verb that expresses the two-place relation expressed by the open sentence '*x* purchased but never wears *y*,' so let me hereby add to the English lexicon the regular transitive verb 'to wruzle' with the stipulation that '*x* wruzles *y*' is to be true of a pair <*a*, *b*> iff *a* purchased but never wears *b*. What must I next do to secure meanings for the myriad substitution instances of '*x* wruzles *y*'? The answer of course is *nothing*. I've already done enough to secure those meanings, for the semantics enjoyed by English prior to my thoughtful addition needs only to be told the meaning of the added verb in order assign a meaning to each of the infinitely many sentences in which the verb now occurs. In particular, we should notice that, for *any* singular denoting expressions α, β, ⌈α wruzles β⌉ will have *a* reading on which the sentence is true just in case, for some *a*, *b*, α denotes *a*, β denotes *b*, and '*x* wruzles *y*' is true of <*a*, *b*>. Enough has also been done to determine a secondary reading for the substitution instances in question, one that corresponds to the reading 'I bought that shirt yesterday' has when Jack, pointing to the shirt Jill is wearing, utters the sentence in order to tell Jill that yesterday he bought a shirt of the same contextually relevant type as Jill's. Apropos of this second reading, it's also relevant to notice that there can be no escaping the fact that the semantics of English gives the sentence 'I wruzle that type of shirt' a reading on which an utterance of it would be true only if the speaker actually purchased the shirt-type to which she referred in uttering the sentence, however unlikely it is that anyone would intend that meaning when she uttered the sentence. Now, the no-semantic-content theory I attributed to McDowell and Heck (i) holds that 'believes' denotes a dyadic relation between believers and neo-Fregean propositions[1] but (ii) says nothing about the semantic status of the that-clause in instances of the sentence matrix

(B) *A* believes that *S*.

Yet if a theorist concedes that believing, the relation denoted by the open sentence

(B') *x* believes *y*,

is a relation between believers and things believed, then there is pressure on that theorist also to hold that a true substitution instance of (B) will be true because the that-clause in the sentence refers to something that the subject of the sentence believes. This is so for a few reasons:

a. The theorist is committed to there being myriad propositions that are believed, and therefore committed to there being myriad pairs of persons and propositions that satisfy the open sentence (B'). One should certainly *expect* speakers to have available to them ways of referring to the things they believe, that is to say, singular referring expressions that are substituends for '*y*' in true instances of (B'). Now, we can't point to propositions, and very few propositions are as lucky as logicism in having been given a name; but we do have that-clauses to put in the place held by '*y*' in (B') when we want to tell someone one of the things we believe. But suppose that the that-clauses in true substitution instances of (B) don't refer to things the subjects of those sentences believe. Then shouldn't we be very surprised to learn that, despite the fact that we're fortunate enough to have the single word 'believes' to express the relation that obtains between us and what we believe, and despite the incalculable importance of what we believe in determining all that we do, we don't have readily available to us *any* useful way of referring to the things we believe, any way, that is, of referring to a proposition a person believes in a way that enables us to know what she believes, the content of her belief?

b. Evidently, the sentence 'That $e = mc^2$ is Al's theory' is true just in case the proposition denoted by 'that $e = mc^2$' is Al's theory and the sentence 'That eating fish makes one smart is false' (more colloquially, 'It's false that eating fish makes one smart') is true just in case the proposition denoted by 'that eating fish makes one smart' is false. We noticed just above that if in a substitution instance of 'x wruzles y', $|\alpha$ wruzles $\beta|$, α denotes a and β denotes b, then $|\alpha$ wruzles $\beta|$ must have a reading on which it's true just in case $<a, b>$ satisfies the open sentence 'x wruzles y', and the generalization of that observation entails that if the that-clause in an instance of (B) denotes *anything* z, then the sentence has a reading on which it's true just in case the subject of the sentence believes z. Since we know that that-clauses can denote propositions, we should expect that, say, 'Ray believes that $9^0 = 1$' has a reading on which it's true just in case Ray believes the proposition denoted by 'that $9^0 = 1$'.

c. Like the words 'the late tenor' in 'the late tenor Pavarotti,' the words 'the proposition' in 'the proposition that mathematics reduces to logic' occur pleonastically: they add nothing to determine the reference of the larger expression in which they occur; that is to say, the reference of 'the late tenor Pavarotti' is determined by and is the same as the reference of 'Pavarotti,' and the reference of 'the proposition that mathematics reduces to logic' is determined by and is the same as the reference of 'that mathematics reduces to logic' (the sentence 'Jill believes the proposition that mathematics reduces to logic' is a pleonastic variant of 'Jill believes that mathematics reduces to logic'). But if 'the proposition that mathematics reduces to logic' refers to anything, how could it refer to anything but a proposition? How, for example, could 'The proposition that mathematics reduces to logic isn't a proposition' possibly be used to say something true?

d. 'Logicism' is a singular term that refers to something one may believe, and thus 'Jill believes logicism' may be true on its reading whose truth requires <Jill, logicism> to satisfy (B'). Logicism = the proposition that mathematics reduces to logic; so 'Jill believes the proposition that mathematics reduces to logic' must be capable of being true on its reading whose truth requires <Jill, logicism (i.e. the proposition that mathematics reduces to logic)> to satisfy (B'). From this we may also conclude that the validity of the inference

    (i) Jill believes the proposition that mathematics reduces to logic.

        The proposition that mathematics reduces to logic = logicism.

        So, Jill believes logicism.

is explained by its being of the form

    (ii) $R(a, b)$
         $b = c$
        $\therefore R(a, c)$

Yet we know that the sentence 'Jill believes the proposition that mathematics reduces to logic' is a pleonastic equivalent of the sentence 'Jill believes that mathematics reduces to logic,' and that therefore the inference (i) is a pleonastic equivalent of the inference

> (iii) Jill believes that mathematics reduces to logic.
> That mathematics reduces to logic = logicism.
> So, Jill believes logicism.

We may therefore conclude that the that-clause in (iii) is a singular term that refers to the proposition that mathematics reduces to logic and that (iii)'s validity is explained by its being of the form (ii).

There is a manifest appeal to the hypothesis that (a) 'believes' in '*A* believes that *S*' denotes the dyadic relation expressed by the open sentence '*x* believes *y*'; (b) 'says' in '*A* says that *S*' denotes the dyadic relation expressed by the open sentence '*x* says *y*'; (c) the first relation holds between believers and the propositions they believe, while the second holds between speakers and the propositions they say; and (d) that an instance of '*A* believes that *S*' is true only if its that-clause refers to a proposition the subject of the report believes, while an instance of '*A* says that *S*' is true only if its that-clause refers to a proposition the subject of the report says. At the same time, the hypothesis must confront the fact that that-clauses can't be required to refer to Fregean propositions, Russellian propositions, or sets of possible worlds, the three dominant and most familiar options. At this point the engaged theorist must either seek some fourth kind of proposition to be the propositions in the ranges of the belief and saying relations, or else reject one of the assumptions (a)–(d). In *Things* I took the first route and advanced my conception of pleonastic propositions as an account of the nature of the propositions we believe and assert, and in the paper Buchanan addresses, I try to increase the plausibility of that account by showing that pleonastic propositions also have the relativity feature, a feature propositions must evidently have if (a)–(d) are true. Buchanan, we know, favors a different approach. He accepts that believing is a relation between believers and the propositions they believe and that those propositions are neo-Fregean propositions; but he also accepts that that-clauses in belief reports refer not to *propositions*, but to proposition-*types*, and he denies that saying is a relation between speakers and propositions of any kind. His way of attempting to put all that into a single consistent and plausible package goes as follows.

The no-semantic-content theory Buchanan shares with McDowell, Heck, and others holds that, while believing is a relation to neo-Fregean propositions, saying isn't a relation to propositions of any kind, but it offers no account either of the semantic role of that-clauses in belief or saying reports or of what saying is. Buchanan commendably aims to fill both lacunae. He says that that-clauses in both kinds of reports refer to contextually determined neo-Fregean proposition-*types* and that saying is a relation to those proposition-types. This may seem puzzling, given that he also holds that believing is a relation to neo-Fregean *propositions*, not to neo-Fregean proposition-*types*; but the puzzle is removed by the account he offers of the logical forms of the two kinds of reports. Thus, consider this pair of reports:

1a. Jack believes that Robert Galbraith is a woman.

2a. Jack says that Robert Galbraith is a woman.

Buchanan's view is that, notwithstanding that (1a) and (2a) have the same surface structure and that 'that Robert Galbraith is a woman' in an utterance of either sentence refers to a contextually determined neo-Fregean proposition-type, the logical forms of the two sentences are quite different. That of (1a) may be represented as

1b. $\exists p(\Psi p \,\&\, B(j, p))$,

where 'p' ranges over neo-Fregean propositions and Ψ is a contextually determined proposition-type to which the that-clause in an utterance of (1a) refers. In other words, while 'believes' in (1a) denotes the dyadic belief relation that holds between believers and the neo-Fregean propositions they believe, the that-clause in (1a) refers not to a neo-Fregean proposition Jack believes if (1a) is true, but rather to a neo-Fregean proposition-*type*, and (1a) reports that Jack believes some proposition or other of that type. The logical form of (2a), however, is quite different. For some contextually determined proposition-type Ψ to which the that-clause in the utterance of (2a) refers, (2a)'s logical form is to be represented as

2b. $S(j, \Psi)$.

In other words, 'says' in (2a) denotes the dyadic saying relation that holds not between speakers and propositions they say, but between speakers and the neo-Fregean proposition-*types* they say. But what is it to say, not a proposition, but a *type* of proposition? Buchanan's answer (at least to a first approximation) is that:

For any neo-Fregean proposition type-Ψ and sentence σ, S said Ψ in uttering σ just in case (1) for some *Russellian* proposition p, a neo-Fregean proposition is of type Ψ only if it determines p as giving its possible-worlds truth conditions & (2) for some H, S uttered σ intending it to be mutual knowledge between S and H that S uttered σ intending H to accept *some* proposition of type Ψ, any Ψ proposition as good as any other.

This account of the saying relation is intended to capture the McDowell-Heck idea that successful communication doesn't require speaker and hearer to associate the same thought with the speaker's utterance, but merely thoughts that "stand, and are mutually known to stand, in a suitable relation of correspondence."[2] The "suitable relation of correspondence" allows the speaker and hearer to have different thoughts, but requires there to be a Russellian proposition to which both thoughts are necessarily equivalent.

Buchanan's clever proposal is worthy of further exploration, but if the proposal is to survive, that exploration will have to find good answers to the following two already touched-on worries.

    i. 'Logicism' isn't the name of any proposition-*type*; it's the name of the *proposition* that mathematics reduces to logic. I don't see how Buchanan can plausibly deny that 'logicism' in

3. Jill believes logicism

refers to the proposition that mathematics reduces to logic. But if he accepts that, then he should accept that 'the proposition that mathematics reduces to logic' in

4. Jill believes the proposition that mathematics reduces to logic

also refers to the proposition that mathematics reduces to logic. But, as already remarked, (4) is simply a pleonastic equivalent of

5. Jill believes that mathematics reduces to logic,

which evidently means that the that-clause in (5) has the same semantic status as the description in (4), and is therefore co-referential with it. But Buchanan's theory, Fregeanism$_E$, precludes his accepting that the that-clause in (5) refers to any proposition.

ii. At the end of his essay Buchanan recognizes the following issue for his theory. Certain inferences involving 'believes' and 'says' appear to be valid and are valid if what I called *the face-value theory*[3] is true, but "one might reasonably wonder whether the Fregean$_E$ can capture the apparent validity of such arguments," and he concludes that "addressing the question of how, if at all, the Fregean$_E$ can account for the validity of such arguments... must... wait for another occasion" (144). I find that conclusion puzzling, because it's quite clear that the Fregean$_E$ *can't* account for the validity in question, for on his theory those arguments are definitely *in*valid. This is readily seen by considering the following two inferences, which are simpler than, but make the same point as, the two Buchanan considers:

(6) Jill said that mathematics reduces to logic and Jack believes that mathematics reduces to logic.
∴ There is something that Jill said and Jack believes—to wit, that mathematics reduces to logic.

(7) Ralph believes that Milan is the capital of Italy.
That Milan is the capital of Italy is false.
∴ Ralph believes something false

(6) and (7) certainly appear to be valid, and on the face-value theory they are valid. On Buchanan's theory, however, both inferences are invalid. The Fregean$_E$ must pronounce (6) invalid because on his theory the inference has, for some contextually determined proposition-type Ψ, the form

$\exists p(\Psi p\ \&\ B(\text{Jack}, p))\ \&\ S(\text{Jack}, \Psi)$
∴ $\exists x((B(\text{Jack}, x))\ \&\ S(\text{Jack}, x))$

And the Fregean$_E$ must pronounce (7) invalid because on his theory the inference has, for some contextually determined proposition-type Ψ, either the form

$\exists p(\Psi p\ \&\ B(\text{Ralph}, p))$
$\exists p(\Psi p\ \&\ Fp)$
∴ $\exists p(Fp\ \&\ B(\text{Ralph}, p))$

or else the form

$\exists p(\Psi p\ \&\ B(\text{Ralph}, p))$
$F(\text{the proposition that Milan is the capital of Italy})$
∴ $\exists p(Fp\ \&\ B(\text{Ralph}, p))$

So I don't see how Buchanan can suggest that, for all we yet know, the Fregean$_E$ can account for the validity of inferences such as (6) and (7). The only avenue of exploration open to Buchanan is finding a way for him to explain away the apparent validity of those inferences.

* * *

The semantics and metaphysics of propositional attitudes and speech acts pose extremely difficult philosophical and linguistic questions, and we need to consider as many possible answers to those questions as ingenuity can muster. Ray Buchanan is to be commended for putting an interesting new candidate on the table. The fact that his offering confronts serious problems merely puts it in the same boat as what was already on the table.

Notes

1. In saying the relation is dyadic I'm ignoring syntax-induced reference to a time, and thus ignoring the fact that 'believes' would have to denote a triadic relation among believers, Fregean propositions, and times.
2. McDowell (1984: 222).
3. The face-value theory holds that a propositional-attitude statement of the form 'α Vs that S' is true just in case its subject stands in the dyadic relation expressed by the verb to the proposition to which the that-clause refers.

Bibliography

Heck, R. (2002). "Do Demonstratives Have Senses?" *Philosophers' Imprint* 2.
McDowell, J. (1984). "*De Re* Senses." *Philosophical Quarterly* 34: 283–94.
Schiffer, S. (2005). "What Reference Has to Tell Us about Meaning," in *Conteúdo e Cognição. Anais da série de seminaries de Filosofia Analítica 2003–4*, edited by J. Branquinho, Lisbon: University of Lisbon Press.

18

De Re Subtleties
Response to Nathan Salmon

18.1

Recall that Ralph believes that 'George Eliot' and 'Mary Ann Evans' are names of two different people, whereas Jane knows that they are names of the same person, and that Salmon allows that (1) and (2) are true.

1. Ralph rationally both believes that George Eliot was a man and disbelieves that Mary Ann Evans was a man.[1]
2. Jane rationally both believes that Ralph believes that George Eliot was a man and disbelieves that Ralph believes that Mary Ann Evans was a man.

Since George Eliot = Mary Ann Evans, it follows on Salmon's semantics for belief reports that (1) and (2) are equivalent, respectively, to

3. Ralph rationally believes and disbelieves that George Eliot was a man
4. Jane rationally believes and disbelieves that Ralph believes that George Eliot was a man.

How is it possible for Ralph and Jane rationally to believe the contradictory propositions they believe?

Salmon gives one answer that applies to both (3) and (4), and another that applies only to (3). The answer that applies to both (3) and (4) is this. First, for *any* proposition *p*, one can rationally believe and disbelieve *p* if, but only if, there are modes of presentation *m* and *m'* of *p* which one takes to be modes of presentation of two different propositions such that one rationally believes *p* under *m* and rationally disbelieves *p* under *m'*. Second, *the proposition expressed by 'George Eliot was a man'* and *the proposition expressed by 'Mary Ann Evans was a man'* are modes of presentation of the proposition *that George Eliot was a man* which Ralph takes to be modes of presentation of two different propositions such that Ralph rationally believes that proposition under *m* but rationally disbelieves it under *m'*. And third, *the proposition expressed by 'Ralph believes that George Eliot was a man'* and *the proposition expressed by 'Ralph believes that Mary Ann Evans was a man'* are modes of presentation of the proposition *that Ralph believes that George Eliot was a man* which Jane takes to be modes of presentation of two different propositions such that she rationally believes that proposition under *m* but rationally disbelieves it under *m'*.

To understand the answer that applies only to Ralph, we should begin by noticing that on Salmon's semantics for propositional-attitude sentences, (3) and (4) are equivalent, respectively, to

$\exists x(x$ = George Eliot & Ralph rationally believes and disbelieves that x was a man)
$\exists x(x$ = George Eliot & Jane rationally believes and disbelieves that Ralph believes that x was a man),

which may be restated in truth-conditionally equivalent symbol-free English in various ways, such as

George Eliot is such that Ralph rationally believes and disbelieves that she was a man.

Ralph rationally believes and disbelieves of George Eliot that she was a man.

George Eliot is such that Jane rationally believes and disbelieves that Ralph believes that she, Eliot, was a man.

Jane rationally believes and disbelieves of George Eliot that Ralph believes that she was a man.

Now one might suppose that if x is such that y rationally believes and disbelieves a proposition about x, then there must be modes of presentation m and m' of x which y takes to be modes of presentation of two different things such that y believes that proposition when thinking of x under m but rationally disbelieves it when thinking of x under m'.[2] Of course, if that is so, then (2) is a counterexample to Salmon's theory, for (2) is true but there aren't modes of presentation of George Eliot which Jane takes to be modes of presentation of two different people. It's therefore not surprising that Salmon should want to argue that it's only in *certain* cases that rationally believing and disbelieving a proposition about a thing requires having modes of presentation of it which one takes to be modes of presentation of two different things, and that the proposition about George Eliot that Jane rationally believes and disbelieves isn't among the cases subject to that requirement. The proposition about George Eliot that Ralph rationally believes and disbelieves is, however, subject to the requirement, Salmon claims. That is to say, according to Salmon, (3) ('Ralph rationally believes and disbelieves that George Eliot was a man') can be true only if there are modes of presentation of George Eliot m and m' which Ralph takes to be of two different people such that Ralph believes *that George Eliot was a man* when thinking of her under m but disbelieves *that she was a man* when thinking of her under m', but it's *not* the case that (4) ('Jane rationally believes and disbelieves that Ralph believes that George Eliot was a man') can be true only if there are modes of presentation of George Eliot m and m' which Jane takes to be of two different people such that she believes *that Ralph believes that George Eliot was a man* when thinking of Eliot under m but disbelieves that proposition when thinking of Eliot under m'. Whence the explanation of how Ralph can rationally believe the contradictory propositions about George Eliot that he believes for which no comparable explanation is either required or available for how Jane can rationally believe the contradictory propositions about George Eliot that she believes.

What is supposed to explain this asymmetry between (3) and (4)? Let's simplify our discussion a little by stipulating that one's rationally believing and disbelieving a proposition p_x (a proposition p in which x occurs) requires *mode-of-presentation confusion about x* when in order for one rationally to believe and disbelieve p_x there must be modes of presentation m and m' of x which one takes to be of two different things and which are such that one believes p_x when thinking of x under m but disbelieves p_x when thinking of x under m'. Then the generalization of our question about (3) and (4) is: *What is the difference between a proposition p_x that requires mode-of-presentation confusion about x in order for one rationally to believe and disbelieve it and one that doesn't require mode-of-presentation confusion about x in order for one rationally to believe and disbelieve it?*

Salmon's answer is that rationally believing and disbelieving p_x requires mode-of-presentation confusion about x when, and only when, for some property ψ, $p_x = \langle x, \psi \rangle$. Then the asymmetry between Ralph and Jane is explained by (what for Salmon is) the fact that the proposition Ralph believes and disbelieves is <George Eliot, the property of having been a man>, but that the proposition Jane believes and disbelieves is <<Ralph, <George Eliot, the property of having been a man>>, the belief relation>. Salmon arrives at this answer by finding important differences between sentences of the form

5. α believes of β that ϕ_{it}

and those of the form

6. α believes β to be such that ϕ_{it}

These differences are:

(a) Whereas 'believes' in (5) evidently expresses the two-place belief *de dicto* relation, B^2 (that relation that relates believers to the propositions they believe), and is equivalent to

7. $\exists x(x = \beta \ \& \ B^2(\alpha, \text{the proposition that } \phi_x))$,

'believes' in (6) expresses a three-place relation, B^3, and is equivalent to

8. $B^3(\alpha, \beta, \text{the property of being a thing such that } \phi_{it})$.[3]

(b) Whereas every instance of

α rationally believes and disbelieves β to be such that ϕ_{it}

requires mode-of-presentation confusion about β,[4] that isn't so for every instance of

α rationally believes and disbelieves of β that ϕ_{it}.

(c) One can infer (6) ('α believes β to be such that ϕ_{it}') from

α believes that ϕ_β

when, and only when, the proposition that ϕ_β = the proposition that β is such that ϕ_{it} = <β, the property of being such that ϕ_{it}>. In other words, every instance of (9) is necessarily true:

9. $B^3(\alpha, \beta, \text{the property of being such that } \phi_{it})$ iff $B^2(\alpha, \langle \beta, \text{the property of being such that } \phi_{it} \rangle)$

Salmon says nothing in support of the left-to-right direction of (9), but in support of the right-to-left direction of (9) he says two things. In his present essay he says that "if someone x believes the singular proposition expressed by 'It' + VP under the assignment of a particular value y to the variable 'it,' then the proposition believed—that y is F—has the simple structure, $<y, F>$, so that x indeed believes y to be F" (p. 151). But in "Illogical Belief" (Salmon 1989) he in effect commits himself to saying that 'α believes β to be such that ϕ_{it}' "virtually follows" from 'α believes that β is such that ϕ_{it},' although I don't understand what work the "virtually" qualification is doing here. After all, it's clear that the inference

B^2(Jane, <M.A.E., the property of being an x such that Ralph doesn't believe that x was a man>)

∴ B^3(Jane, M.A.E., the property of being an x such that Ralph doesn't believe that x was a man)

isn't *logically* valid. At the same time, it's clear that Salmon thinks that the premise conceptually entails the conclusion in the way that, say,

Ralph rationally believes and disbelieves that George Eliot was a man

conceptually entails

There are modes of presentation m and m' of George Eliot which Ralph takes to be modes of presentation of two different people such that Ralph believes *that George Eliot was a man* when thinking of Eliot under m but not when thinking of her under m'

But then, given that the entailment is merely "conceptual," one would like to know why Salmon is so confident that every instance of

α rationally believes and disbelieves that ϕ^β

doesn't conceptually entail its corresponding instance of

There are modes of presentation m and m' of β which α takes to be modes of presentation of two different things such that a believes that ϕ when thinking of β under m but not when thinking of β under m',

assuming, of course, that α isn't mode-of-presentation challenged about one of the other components of the proposition that ϕ^β.

Salmon also claims to garner support for his position from two further things. The first is the following dialogue he imagines between Socrates and Jane:

s: "Does Ralph believe that Mary Ann Evans was a man?"
j: "No, he doesn't."
s: "Does Ralph believe that George Eliot was a man?"
j: "Yes."
s: "What about Mary Ann Evans, then? Does Ralph also believe *she* was a man?"
j: "Ralph doesn't believe that *Mary Ann Evans* was a man. But you're now asking about Mary Ann Evans herself. Mary Ann Evans and George Eliot

are the same person, don't you know? And Ralph does indeed believe that she was a man."

S: "Very well. Is Mary Ann Evans someone Ralph also *doesn't* believe was a man?"

J: "Of course not; that would be logically impossible...."

The second thing Salmon offers in support of his position is a fuller explanation (i.e. fuller than the explanation mentioned on p. 449 above) of how Jane is able to believe both *that Ralph believes that George Eliot was a man* and *that Ralph doesn't believe that Mary Ann was a man*. He says that in believing those two propositions Jane has revealed herself to be a "closet neo-Fregean," and that prompts him, in the following way, to acquit Jane of irrationality in believing the contradiction that Ralph believes and doesn't believe that George Eliot was a man: (i) Jane mistakenly believes that 'Ralph believes that George Eliot was a man' and 'Ralph believes that Mary Ann Evans was a man' mean different propositions—perhaps (since she is a neo-Fregean) the propositions, respectively, *that Ralph believes that the author of Middlemarch was a man* and *that Ralph believes that the nineteenth-century unmarried woman who lived openly with the married critic George Henry Lewes was a man*, and (ii) she believes the singular proposition *that Ralph believes that Eliot was a man* when thinking of that proposition under the mode of presentation *the proposition expressed by 'Ralph believes that George Eliot was a man'* but disbelieves it when thinking of it under the mode of presentation *the proposition expressed by 'Ralph believes that Mary Ann Evans was a man.'*

18.2

I admire the ingenuity of Salmon's attempt to show that Jane isn't a counterexample to his theory, but I am not yet convinced he has succeeded, and this for the following reasons.

1. According to Salmon, α *rationally believes and disbelieves that* ϕ_β requires mode-of-presentation confusion about β *only if* the proposition that ϕ_β = the proposition that β is such that ϕ_{it} = <β, the property of being such that ϕ_{it}>. Now, I forgot to mention that

Jane believes *that Ralph believes that Mary Ann Evans wasn't a man*, but doesn't believe *that Mary Ann Evans was such that Ralph believes that she, Evans, wasn't a man*,

despite the fact that, in addition to being a highly educated native speaker of English, she is also an extremely brilliant logician. But can the following sentence also be true without insult to Jane's rationality or brilliance as a logician?

Jane believes *that if George Henry Lewes lived with Mary Ann Evans, then he was separated from Agnes Jervis*, but doesn't believe *that Mary Ann Evans i such that, if George Henry Lewes lived with her, then he was separated from Agnes Jervis*.

I submit that the answer is clearly no, and that therefore, *pace* Salmon, Jane can believe *that if George Henry Lewes lived with Mary Ann Evans, then he was separated from Agnes Jervis* but *not* believe *that if George Henry Lewes lived with George Eliot, then he was separated from Agnes Jervis* only if Jane has modes of presentation of George Eliot which she takes to be modes of presentation of two different people, which, of course, we know she doesn't have. Yet the proposition *that if George Henry Lewes lived with Mary Ann Evans, then he was separated from Agnes Jervis* isn't a singular proposition whose first member is Mary Ann Evans but is rather the complex proposition <<<<Lewes, Evans>, the having lived with relation>, <<Lewes, Jervis>, the having been separated from relation>>, the if-then relation>. This suggests that the displayed sentence is a counterexample to Salmon's claim that α rationally believes and disbelieves that ϕ_β requires mode-of-presentation confusion about β *only if* the proposition that ϕ_β = the proposition that β is such that ϕ_{it} = <β, the property of being such that ϕ_{it}>. It also suggests that the reason mode-of-presentation confusion about Eliot isn't required for Jane rationally to believe both *that Ralph believes that George Eliot was a man* and *that Ralph doesn't believe that Mary Ann Evans was a man* isn't that the proposition she rationally believes and disbelieves isn't, for some property ψ, the proposition <George Eliot, ψ>, but rather that the proposition *that Ralph believes that George Eliot was a man* $\neq$ the proposition *that Ralph believes that Mary Ann Evans was a man*, and that Jane appreciates that it's only *Ralph* who needs to have modes of presentation of George Eliot that he takes to be of two different people.

2. In Schiffer (2006) I argue (i) that while

10. Jane rationally believes both that Ralph believes that George Eliot was a man and that he doesn't believe that Mary Ann Evan was a man,

is true, it doesn't require mode-of-presentation confusion about George Eliot, but (ii) that the truth of (10) would require mode-of-presentation confusion about George Eliot *if Salmon's theory were correct*. Since Salmon agrees that the truth of (10) doesn't require mode-of-presentation confusion about George Eliot, what he needs to show is that that is consistent with his account of the meaning of (10), and we know that he does offer an argument to show that. At the same time, on Salmon's theory the proposition *that Ralph believes that George Eliot was a man* = the proposition *that Ralph believes that Mary Ann Evans was a man*, and it's incumbent upon him to explain how Jane can rationally believe and disbelieve the same proposition about George Eliot. He offers an explanation, but I find it problematic: I don't see how it's compatible with the truth of (10). To see this, let's start by noticing a striking difference between Ralph's belief and disbelief and Jane's: Ralph can rationally believe both *that George Eliot was a man* and *that Mary Ann Evans wasn't a man* even if he accepts Salmon's direct-reference semantics, but Jane can't rationally believe both *that Ralph believes that George Eliot was a man* and *that Ralph doesn't believe that Mary Ann Evans was a man* if she accepts Salmon's semantics. Accepting Salmon's theory, Ralph accepts that 'George Eliot was a man' means <George Eliot, the property of having been a man> and that 'Mary Ann Evans was a man' means <Mary Ann Evans, the property of having been a man>. What he doesn't accept is that both sentences mean the same proposition. If, however, Jane accepted Salmon's theory, then she would know that 'Ralph believes that George

Eliot was a man' and 'Ralph believes that Mary Ann Evans was a man' mean the same proposition, in which case (10) could be true only if she knowingly believed and disbelieved one and the same proposition, and that's ruled out by the stipulation that she is rational.

Salmon, of course, is well aware of this, and that is why he says that (10) reveals Jane to be a neo-Fregean, and why he attempts to explain the truth of (10) in the following way:

Being a neo-Fregean, Jane takes the sentence 'Ralph believes that George Eliot was a man' to mean, say, the proposition *that Ralph believes that the author of Middlemarch was a man*, and she takes the sentence 'Ralph believes that Mary Ann Evans was a man' to mean, say, the proposition *that Ralph believes that the nineteenth-century unmarried woman who lived openly with the married critic George Henry Lewes was a man*. Consequently, Jane believes <<Ralph, <George Eliot, the property of having been a man>>, the belief relation> when thinking of that proposition as the proposition expressed by 'Ralph believes that George Eliot was a man' but disbelieves it when thinking of it as the proposition expressed by 'Ralph believes that Mary Ann Evans was a man'.

So, when Jane utters 'Ralph believes that George Eliot was a man, but he doesn't believe that Mary Ann Evans was a man' she is expressing her belief *that Ralph believes that the author of Middlemarch was a man, but he doesn't believe that the nineteenth-century unmarried woman who lived openly with the married critic George Henry Lewes was a man*. How, then, can her utterance show that she believes <<Ralph, <George Eliot, the property of having been a man>>, the belief relation> under the mode of presentation *the proposition expressed by 'Ralph believes that George Eliot was a man'* but disbelieves it under the mode of presentation *the proposition expressed by 'Ralph believes that Mary Ann Evans was a man'*? To see this, suppose a contemporary Mrs Malaprop utters the sentence 'The *Times* delivery person is too erotic' because she thinks that sentence expresses the proposition *that the Times delivery person is too erratic*. That would hardly show that she believes *that the Times delivery person is too erotic* under *any* mode of presentation. She doesn't believe that proposition when thinking of it as the proposition expressed by 'The *Times* delivery person is too erotic,' for she doesn't think that that sentence means *that the Times delivery person is too erotic*. She thinks it means *that Times delivery person is too erratic*. How, then, can Jane count as believing the singular proposition that the sentence 'Ralph doesn't believe that Mary Ann Evans was a man' means if Salmon's theory is correct when she believes that the proposition expressed by that sentence is the proposition *that Ralph doesn't believe that the nineteenth-century unmarried woman who lived openly with the married critic George Henry Lewes was a man*? But might not Salmon protest that, surely, Jane, a highly educated native speaker of English, knows *that 'Ralph doesn't believe that Mary Ann Evans was a man' means that Ralph doesn't believe that Mary Ann Evans was a man*? *Of course* she knows that—*but not if Salmon's semantics for belief sentences is correct*. If his theory is correct, then we should say that, just as Mrs Malaprop knows that the *sentence* '"The *Times* delivery person is too erotic" means that the *Times* delivery person is too erotic' is true but doesn't know the truth that it expresses, so all we can say about Jane, *if Salmon's theory is correct*, is that, while she knows that the *sentence*

'"Ralph doesn't believe that Mary Ann Evans was a man" means that Ralph doesn't believe that Mary Ann Evans was a man' is true, she doesn't know the truth that it expresses. To be sure, as I said, it's preposterous that she doesn't know that truth, but that is why Jane presents a counterexample to Salmon's theory.

3. I am puzzled by features of the dialogue between Jane and Socrates that Salmon offers to support his account of Jane's beliefs. Recall Salmon's explanation of why Jane's belief and disbelief about George Eliot doesn't require mode-of-presentation confusion about George Eliot: Jane would need modes of presentation of George Eliot which she, Jane, took to be of two different people, if one could infer from her believing both *that Ralph believes that George Eliot was a man* and *that Ralph doesn't believe that Mary Ann Evans was a man* that she also believed both *that George Eliot is such that Ralph believes that she was a man* and *that Mary Ann Evans is such that Ralph doesn't believe that she was a man*, but, Salmon argued, one could rationally believe *that Ralph believes that George Eliot was a man* without also believing *that George Eliot is such that Ralph believes that she was a man*. Given that, I'm puzzled by the transitions made in the following part of Jane's conversation with Socrates:

 s: "Does Ralph believe that George Eliot was a man?"
 j: "Yes."
 s: "What about Mary Ann Evans, then? Does Ralph also believe *she* was a man?"
 j: "Ralph doesn't believe that *Mary Ann Evans* was a man. But you're now asking about Mary Ann Evans herself. Mary Ann Evans and George Eliot are the same person, don't you know? And Ralph does indeed believe that she was a man."

First, I can't make sense of this unless Jane's believing *that Ralph believes that George Eliot was a man* implies her believing *that George Eliot is believed by Ralph to have been a man*. But that implication is precluded by Salmon's explanation of why Jane's believing and disbelieving the same proposition about George Eliot does not require mode-of-presentation confusion about Eliot. So why is Jane agreeing that George Eliot is such that Ralph does indeed believe that she was a man? Second, if Salmon can help himself to the displayed exchange, why couldn't the conversation have taken the following slightly different course?

 s: "Does Ralph believe that Mary Ann Evans wasn't a man?"
 j: "Yes."
 s: "What about George Eliot, then? Does Ralph also believe *she* wasn't a man?"
 j: "Ralph doesn't believe that *George Eliot* wasn't a man. But you're now asking about George Eliot herself. George Eliot and Mary Ann Evans are the same person, don't you know? And Ralph does indeed believe that she wasn't a man."

But of course Salmon can't allow that the two conversations are equally good, for then Jane would believe George Eliot to be such that Ralph believes and disbelieves that she was a man, and for that Jane would need modes of presentation of George

Eliot which she took to be of two different people. Third—and back to the exchange as stipulated by Salmon—since the logician Jane thinks that Socrates is asking whether Ralph believes *that the author of Middlemarch was a man*, she is apt to agree with David Kaplan and many other philosophers that it's not sufficient for x to believe *de re* of y that it's G that, for some F, y is uniquely F & x believes *de dicto* that the F is G, and that for x to have any *de re* belief about y x must stand in a certain relation of "rapport" to y. Given that, Jane wouldn't be so quick to accept 'George Eliot is such that Ralph believes that she was a man' just on the basis of her believing that Ralph—whom she knows never to have read anything by George Eliot—believes that the author of *Middlemarch* was a man.

Notes

1. To disbelieve a proposition is to believe its negation.
2. ... or else—a qualification I shall follow Salmon in ignoring—when x is rationally believed and disbelieved by y to be F, it may be that that is explained by there being modes of presentation m and m' of the property of being F which y takes to be modes of presentation of two different properties such that x is believed by y to be F when y is thinking of the property of being F under m but disbelieved by y to be F when y is thinking of that property under m'.
3. My "evidently" qualification is because, although Salmon is explicit about the representation of (6) (see p. 451), he's not explicit about the representation of (5). I infer that he would represent (5) as (7) because if 'believes' in (5) expressed a three-place relation, it's third term would have to be the property expressed by the open sentence 'ϕ_x', and that would evidently make (5) equivalent to (6)—unless, which I think is highly unlikely, Salmon were to hold that there were *two* three-place belief relations, B'^3 and B^3, such that, while (5) was of the form $B'^3(\alpha, \beta,$ *the property of being a thing such that* $\phi_{it})$, (6) was of the form $B^3(\alpha, \beta,$ *the property of being a thing such that* $\phi_{it})$.
4. More strictly correct, "requires mode-of-presentation confusion about the referent of the substituend for 'β'."

Bibliography

Salmon, N. (1989). "Illogical Belief." In J. Tomberlin, ed., *Philosophical Perspectives, 3: Philosophy of Mind and Action Theory* (Atascadero, Ca.: Ridgeview, 1989), pp. 243–85; reprinted in *Content, Cognition, and Communication: Philosophical Papers II* (Oxford: Oxford University Press, 2007).

19

Vagueness and Indeterminacy
Responses to Dorothy Edgington, Hartry Field, and Crispin Wright

19.1 Introduction

Most theorists of vagueness take a positive stand on the truth-values of borderline propositions:[1] epistemicists accept the semantic principle of bivalence and claim that borderline propositions, like all other propositions, are true or else false; supervaluationists accept excluded middle but reject bivalence and thus accept truth-value gaps, propositions that are neither true nor false; degree-of-truth and other many-value theorists hold that borderline propositions enjoy a positive truth-value somewhere between absolute truth and absolute falsity. I began Chapter 5 of *The Things We Mean* by arguing against each of those options, and in arguing against gap and many-value theories I endorsed Crispin Wright's objection that

> it is quite unsatisfactory in general to represent *in*determinacy as...any kind of middle situation, contrasting with both the poles (truth and falsity)...since one cannot thereby do justice to the absolutely basic datum that in general borderline cases come across as hard cases: as cases where we are baffled to choose between conflicting verdicts about which polar verdict applies, rather than as cases which we recognize as enjoying a status inconsistent with both. (2001: 69–70)

That set the stage for my own *psychological* theory of vagueness, a theory that is logically neutral on the kind of truth-value borderline propositions do, or don't, have and that aspires to understand vagueness in terms of the ambivalent state of mind that is characteristic of one who takes a proposition to be borderline. That ambivalent state of mind was elaborated in terms of an alleged distinction between two kinds of partial belief: *standard partial belief* (SPB), which under idealization is normatively governed by the axioms of classical probability theory when the s-believed propositions (i.e. propositions that are the objects of SPBs) are taken to be determinately true or determinately false, and *vagueness-related partial belief* (VPB), which even under idealization is never normatively governed by the axioms of probability theory. I claimed VPB to be the operative attitude when one takes a proposition to be borderline. My characterization of VPB was divided into two parts. In the first part I inventoried the important differences between s-believing and v-believing a proposition, and this gave what I regarded as the intuitive core of the SPB/VPB distinction. In the second part I made a stab at specifying the laws that normatively govern the formation of complex VPBs and the interactions of VPBs and SPBs. I admitted to being more confident of the first part than of the second part. The primary problem in explicating vagueness is to say in what being a borderline case consists, and I offered an account of what it is to be a borderline instance of a property in terms of VPB. This account spawned an account of what it is for a proposition to be indeterminate, whether or not its indeterminacy derives from vagueness. Armed with that account of indeterminacy, I then argued that the trouble-making propositions in classically valid sorites inferences are indeterminate, and that, given the truth-values of the other steps in those inferences, it is therefore indeterminate whether those inferences are valid in the sense of validity at play in classical logic.

Dorothy Edgington, Hartry Field, and Crispin Wright together challenge most of what I thought I had to say about vagueness. I would have enjoyed reading their commentaries much more if they had been about someone else's theory of vagueness.

19.2 Complex VPBs and the Interaction of VPBs and SPBs

Suppose

- that you believe to degree 0.5 both that your keys are in your office and that your keys aren't in your office;
- that you also believe to degree 0.5 that the Atlantic City Flounders will win the Superbowl, that the Flounders won't win the Superbowl, that it will rain tonight, and that it won't rain tonight;
- that you take the following propositions to be probabilistically independent: that your keys are in your office, that the Flounders will win the Superbowl, and that it will rain; and
- that you're both rational and have the conceptual resources to form likelihood beliefs.

Then quite likely your beliefs are SPBs and thus:

- you take the proposition that your keys are in your office to be either determinately true or else determinately false, in a sense of 'taking' that is compatible with your not having the conceptual resources explicitly to judge that the proposition is determinately true/false;
- you are *uncertain* whether or not your keys are in your office, but you're not *ambivalent* about whether or not to judge that your keys are in your office;
- you take yourself not to be in the best epistemic position to judge whether or not your keys are in your office;
- you think that there is a fifty–fifty chance that your keys are in your office; and
- you s-believe to degree 0.125 [that your keys are in your office & the Flounders will win the Superbowl & it will rain tonight].[2]

Now, when you take a proposition to be borderline, you're apt to have some inclination to say it's true and some inclination to say it's not true. Let's suppose these inclinations manifest propositional attitudes called VPBs. Then suppose:

- that you v-believe to degree 0.5 both that Harry is bald and that he's not bald;
- that you also v-believe to degree 0.5 that Harry is tall, that he's not tall, that he's thin, and that he's not thin;
- that you take the following propositions to be probabilistically independent: that Harry is bald, that he is tall, and that he is thin; and
- that you're both rational and have the conceptual resources to form likelihood beliefs.

Then quite likely:

- you take Harry to be borderline bald, and thus take the proposition that he is bald to be neither determinately true nor determinately false, in a sense of 'taking' that is compatible with your not having the conceptual resources explicitly to judge that Harry is borderline bald, or that the proposition that he's bald isn't determinately true/false;
- you are *ambivalent* about whether or not to judge that Harry is bald, but you're not *uncertain* whether or not he's bald;
- you don't think you could be in a better epistemic position for judging whether or not Harry is bald;
- you don't think that there is a fifty–fifty chance that Harry is bald (a non-philosopher would be completely flummoxed by the question "What's the probability that Harry is bald?"); and
- you v-believe to degree 0.5 that Harry is bald, tall, and thin (you certainly aren't confident to degree 0.875 that the conjunction is false!).

The foregoing is a snapshot of one sort of manifestation of what I regarded as the intuitive core of the SPB/VPB distinction. Yet even if it's completely solid, it leaves open how the formation of complex VPBs and the interaction of VPBs and SPBs are normatively governed, and in *Things* I made the following proposals. Concerning the formation of complex VPBs, I bracketed consideration of the conditional and proposed that VPBs about negations, conjunctions, and disjunctions are normatively governed, respectively, by the Łukasiewicz rules

$VPB(\neg p) = 1 - VPB(p)$
$VPB(p \& q) = Min[VPB(p), VPB(q)]$
$VPB(p \vee q) = Max[VPB(p), VPB(q)]$

(the rules for the universal and existential quantifiers were to be based on those for conjunction and disjunction in the familiar way). Concerning the interaction of VPBs and SPBs, I proposed that its normative governance went by the rule

$SPB(p) + SPB(\neg p) + VPB(p) + VPB(\neg p) = 1.$

At least three things contributed to my lack of confidence in these two proposals.

First, while the displayed rules were the best I could think of on the assumption that there were neat rules governing complex VPBs and the interaction of VPBs and SPBs, I wasn't entirely confident that there were neat rules (I'll return to this in section 19.2, below); I knew that the proposed rules hadn't been adequately tested; and I knew that I hadn't provided a deep motivation for them. The motivation they did enjoy was that they cohered with what I said in the "intuitive core" about v-believing conjunctions of borderline propositions, and that I hadn't been able to think of better rules.

Second, all other things being equal, I would have preferred saying that SPB(p/¬p) was *undefined* when VPB(p) + VPB(¬p) = 1, rather than that SPB(p) = SPB(¬p) = 0, as required by the displayed sum-to-1 rule. I went with the rule because I didn't see any other way of getting the math to come out in a coherent way. What bothered me was that there seemed to be a tension in saying that, e.g., VPB(p) = 0.5 when SPB(p) = 0. I said above that s-believing both p and ¬p to degree 0.5 went with believing that there was a fifty–fifty chance of p's being true. Shouldn't s-believing p to degree 0 go with believing that there was no chance of p's being true? Yet v-believing p to degree 0.5 was supposed to represent an inclination of degree 0.5 to judge p to be true. Shouldn't one who thought that there was no chance of p's being true have no inclination to judge p to be true? The best response to these worries is that we are here dealing with technical notions that must be understood functionally in terms of the laws that implicitly define those notions. But how good a response is that?

Third, I was ambivalent about the way the Łukasiewicz rules flouted the intuitions some have about those analytic connections Kit Fine (1975) had called "penumbral connections." Suppose Mary is a borderline widow because her husband is borderline alive. Then my Łukasiewicz rules mandate v-believing *that Mary is a widow & her husband is alive* to a positive degree, whereas some philosophers have the intuition that one should simply believe that the conjunction is false. Likewise as regards the conjunction *that Al is bald & Bob isn't bald* when both men are borderline bald but Bob is balder than Al. And likewise about the most egregious case, v-believing an explicit contradiction. If you v-believe to degree 0.5 both that Harry is bald and that he isn't bald, then conformity to my Łukasiewicz rules requires you to v-believe to degree 0.5 that Harry is and isn't bald. In discussing a degree theoretic account of vagueness that would give a positive degree of truth to such contradictions, Timothy Williamson (1994) rhetorically asks, "How can an explicit contradiction be true to any degree other than 0?" (136). One who shares Williamson's incredulity will have the same reaction to my version of the Łukasiewiczian commitment. Still, there are those of us whose intuitions aren't so adamant. Remarking on Fine's claim that it's obviously false to say of a color shade that it's both red and pink when it's on the red/pink borderline, Kenton Machina (1976) confessed to "being completely insensitive to that intuition of a penumbral connection" (177). I schooled myself to share Machina's arguably tin ear, and in *Things* I addressed the problem penumbral connections presented for my commitment in the most forceful form the problem takes for me, v-believing an explicit contradiction to a positive degree:

Perhaps the most salient feature of VPB is the intuitiveness of the claim that Sally would v-believe to degree .5 that Tom is bald and thin when she v-believes each conjunct to degree .5.... This is captured by [the Łukasiewicz rule for VPB(p & q)]. What will give one pause is that it follows that Sally will also v-believe to degree .5 that Tom is bald and not bald when she v-believes each conjunct to degree .5. But is this really unacceptable?.... [T]he truth-theoretic Łukasiewiczian [rule for (p & q)] isn't unmotivated, and there is something degree-of-truthish about v-believing a proposition, for if one v-believes that Harry is bald to a degree greater than one v-believes that Tom is bald, then one s-believes that Harry is balder than Tom.... The truth-theoretic version of [&] isn't unmotivated because if, as it were, God were to assure you that it was a *fact* that *both* the proposition that Tom was bald *and* the proposition that he wasn't bald were true to degree .5, then how could you rationally think that the conjunction of those two propositions was itself true to a degree other than .5? (218)

That is where things stood on the most tentative part of the VPB/SPB distinction when my book was published. Subsequently, however, John MacFarlane (2006 and 2010) pointed out the following problem. The Łukasiewicz rules plus the "basic law"

$$SPB(p) + SPB(\neg p) + VPB(p) + VPB(\neg p) = 1$$

underdetermine the rules for computing rational SPB and VPB degrees to (p & q) and $\neg$(p & q) given assignments to p, q, $\neg$p, and $\neg$q, and MacFarlane revealed that there are examples in which SPB(p & q) + SPB($\neg$(p & q)) + VPB(p & q) + VPB($\neg$(p & q)) < 1 when the computation is made using principles to which I appealed in working through various examples. He concludes with a good point to which I'll presently return: "The basic problem should be evident: the norms governing SPBs and VPBs are fundamentally different, so they are not going to march in the kind of lockstep that would be needed to keep them summing to 1" (2010: 446).

So that was how things stood with me on complex VPBs and the interaction of VPBs and SPBs before encountering the doubts on those issues of Edgington, Field, and Wright. What do they add or subtract?

Field remarks that my "assumption that there are neat compositional laws governing 'vagueness-related degrees of belief' appears under-motivated if the only role of such 'degrees of belief' is to characterize our conflicting inclinations in cases where our standard degrees of belief in a sentence and its negation add to less than 1" (182). This is an important point, and I'm inclined to agree with it. I say something more about it later.

Edgington and Wright return to the issue of penumbral connections.[3] Edgington is confident of the judgments she would make:

Let v(Tom is tall) = 0.5, v(Tom is not tall) = 0.5, and let Harry be also borderline tall, but slightly less tall than Tom: let v(Harry is tall) = 0.4. Tom is taller than Harry. I have *no inclination at all* to believe that Harry is tall and Tom is not. I am not at all ambivalent or in a quandary about that: it is something I confidently judge to be definitely wrong. Yet by the Min-rule for conjunction, v(Harry is tall and Tom is not tall) = 0.4: not to be rejected out of hand. (159)

Wright, more ambitious, speaks for others and says that my Łukasiewicz-style matrices both "mispredict the level of partial belief which normal thinkers will repose in conjunctions of vague but incompatible conjuncts" (207) and predict "variations in the V-credibility of conjunctions of the form, Fk and ~Fk', k and k' adjacent in a sorites series, which are surely not empirically confirmed—one would expect a uniformly low valuation, irrespective of the place in the series of k" (207). Suppose Jane v-believes to degree 0.5 that Tom is tall and to degree 0.498 that Dick, whom she knows to be 1/8th inch shorter than Tom, is tall. Then Wright's point, applied to these examples, is that my commitment to the rule

VPB(p & q) = Min[VPB(p), VPB(q)]

predicts that Jane will v-believe

Tom is and isn't tall

to degree 0.5 and will v-believe

Tom is tall but Dick isn't tall

to degree 0.498, whereas the much better bet is that she will simply deny both propositions.

My guess is that Jane is liable to be flummoxed by the contradiction in ways that make it difficult to predict how she will react to it, but that it is plausible that she would simply deny the second conjunction. What is less clear is how serious an objection this makes. I endorsed the Łukasiewicz-style matrices not as generalizations about how people react to conjunctions of borderline propositions, but as generalizations about how they should react to them. An ordinary person's quandary state of ambivalence when confronted with borderline-bald Harry strikes me as a spontaneous reaction, untainted by conceptual noise, such as clumsy theorizing. Not so a reaction to a penumbrally challenged conjunction, or to a statement that only one of two people is tall when they are virtually indistinguishable in height. Think of the gambler's fallacy; think of Kahneman and Tversky's fascinating experiments. After all, Jane might take her denial of the contradiction to imply an instance of excluded middle, which she might also be unwilling to accept, and we already knew to be forewarned about intuitive reactions to soritical pairs, since the "tolerance" intuitions they tap are of a piece with what makes sorites premises appear plausible.

Apropos of this last point, Edgington and Wright also take me to task for mispredicting our response to a sorites proposition such as that there isn't a height such that a man of that height is tall but a man 1/8th of an inch shorter isn't tall. The Łukasiewicz rules I accept together with relevant logical equivalences I also accept commit me to saying that one should v-believe that proposition to a degree very close to 0.5. But what makes that proposition induce sorites paradoxes is that it's apt to strike us as *true*. Again, however, I don't see the objection. My Łukasiewiczian commitments don't *predict* anyone's response to sorites premises. They merely engender commitments about the degrees to which one *should* v-believe them (except that I would predict that if (i) Tom and Dick are standing shoulder-to-shoulder before a normal adult in conditions that are ideal for her discerning their respective heights, (ii) she v-believes Tom to be tall to some positive degree, and (iii) Dick is discernibly 1/8th inch shorter than Tom, then she will v-believe that Dick is tall to very nearly the same degree that she v-believes that Tom is tall). *Every* theorist (except perhaps certain nihilists) must hold that we are tempted to believe such propositions to incorrect degrees. A different point, one made by both Edgington and Wright, is that I fail to explain why we're tempted to these misbegotten beliefs. Maybe that is so, but neither addresses the explanation I offer in §5.8, which sees these vagaries as an ineliminable glitch constitutive of our vague concepts in a way that explains why the sorites paradox enjoys no "happy-face" solution.[4]

Finally (for this section), Edgington raises the following problem concerning my endorsement of the rule $SPB(p) + SPB(\neg p) + VPB(p) + VPB(\neg p) = 1$. I give an example in *Things* in which the hairs on Tom Cruise's scalp are being plucked one by one and after each plucking Sally has to say whether Tom is bald. When the plucking begins and for many pluckings right after that, Sally will confidently judge that Tom isn't bald. But now consider the point at which her confidence is ever-so-slightly diminished. Edgington says that at that point Sally "is undecided between a strong s-belief that [Tom] is definitely not bald, and a strong v-belief pulling in the direction of not bald" (163), and she charges that that is inconsistent with the proffered rule for combining VPBs and SPBs.

Sally is in the midst of a forced-march sorites, and her position in that march on which Edgington focuses is one I describe in *Things* as the area in which we enter the tricky realm of higher-order vagueness. The problem Edgington raises for me is reminiscent of a problem that arises for proponents of many-valued treatments of vagueness. Consider a theorist who claims that there are three, and only three, truth-values, 1, 0, and ½. If Harry is definitely bald, then this theorist says that the proposition that Harry is bald has value 1; if Harry is definitely not bald, then he says that the proposition has value 0; and if Harry is borderline bald, then the theorist says that the proposition has value ½. But there is an unclarity in the theorist's claim which becomes salient when we suppose that Harry is on the borderline between being definitely bald and borderline bald. Does the theorist's claim that 1, 0, and ½ are the only truth-values mean that every proposition has one of those values? If so, then the theorist will find himself in the unenviable position of having to be an epistemic theorist of higher-order vagueness; he will have to say that the proposition that Harry is bald either has value 1 or value ½, but we can't know which. That position is unenviable because one wonders why the theorist doesn't simply dispense with his third value, ½, and go epistemicist all the way down. Clearly, what the theorist needs to hold is that it's indeterminate what truth-value the proposition that Harry is bald has, where in this case that means that both the proposition *that the proposition that Harry is bald has value 1* and the proposition *that the proposition that Harry is bald has value ½* have value ½. Somewhat analogously, my stance on higher-order vagueness can't imply that every considered proposition is s-believed or v-believed to some definite degree. Rather, it will typically be indeterminate what the degree is, and it will sometimes be indeterminate whether a person s- or v-believes a proposition. But higher-order indeterminacy is indeterminacy, and on a psychological account it must be handled in the same way as first-order indeterminacy. In other words, by the account in *Things*, Harry's being on the borderline between being definitely bald and borderline bald means that one should v-believe to positive degrees that sum to 1 both the proposition that one should, and the proposition that one shouldn't, v-believe both that Harry is bald and that he isn't bald to positive degrees that sum to 1. Nothing so far yields an inconsistency with the rule $SPB(p) + SPB(\neg p) + VPB(p) + VPB(\neg p) = 1$. What now of Edgington's claim that Sally "is undecided between a strong s-belief that [Tom] is definitely not bald, and a strong v-belief pulling in the direction of not bald"? (p. 163). By the lights of my psychological theory of vagueness, that either means that it's indeterminate whether Sally s- or v-believes that Tom is bald, or it means that she is in a psychological state that is neither an SPB or a VPB. I believe I'm constrained to opt for the first disjunct, but either way I don't see any inconsistency with the rule in question.

19.3 VPB and the Explication of Vagueness and Indeterminacy

Pretend that I had given a faultless characterization of VPB and of the distinction between it and SPB. One could still find fault with the way I tried to use VPB to explicate vagueness and indeterminacy. In fact, quite apart from any questions about whether the account I sought to convey is correct, I'm dissatisfied with the way I packaged that account in *Things*. I can better get to the heart of the criticisms of Edgington, Field, and Wright if I begin with a rough characterization of what I *should* have said in *Things*, before touching on what I actually did say there.[5] My initial focus in the book, as it will be here, was on what it is for a thing to be a borderline instance of a property, i.e. a borderline case of a thing which has the property, but in sketching that account I shall also speak of being a borderline instance of a concept, where that is being a borderline case of a thing to which the concept applies.

What I should have offered in my book was a certain precisification of the following two-part idea, which I'll call *SHS* (for 'should have said'), where a "property-concept" is that concept of a property ϕ expressed by a predicate that refers to ϕ:

(SHS-1) For any property-concept Φ and thing x, x is a borderline instance of Φ iff there is some condition C such that:

1. x satisfies C, and
2. possessing Φ metaphysically entails being primitively disposed to v-believe to positive degrees that sum to 1 that a thing is Φ and that it's not Φ when one is certain that the thing satisfies C.

Let's call condition C *a penumbral condition of the concept* Φ. Then we also have:

(SHS-2) For any property ϕ and thing x, x is a borderline instance of ϕ iff there is some condition C such that:

(a) x satisfies C, and
(b) C is a penumbral condition of every property-concept of ϕ.

The intended precisification of SHS would include—but, alas, wouldn't be exhausted by—the following points.

i. My use of 'concept' is stipulative. Helping myself to the heuristic that each of us processes information in a language-like neural system of mental representation, I assume that every mentalese expression has a functional property—what is often called a *conceptual role*—which determines, or at least partly determines, the expression's meaning. I take concepts to be individuated by those conceptual roles which figure into the determination of the meaning of any expression which has that conceptual role; to *have* a particular concept is for there to be an expression in one's mentalese which has a conceptual role which individuates that concept.

ii. Restated, the second part of SHS says that x is a borderline-instance of the property φ just in case x is a borderline instance of every property-concept of φ. The strategy is to explain being a borderline instance of a concept in terms of conceptual roles, and then to explain being a borderline instance of a property in terms of the prior account. I doubt that this would make sense independently of (what I call) my pleonastic conception of properties. This is an attempt to spell out the truth in David Armstrong's (1989) metaphor that properties are shadows of predicates, and a key tenet of the attempt is that the property expressed by a mentalese predicate is at least partly individuated by features of the predicate's conceptual role. In this way, it's an essential feature of the property expressed by a particular use of 'bald' that one who apprehends it will be primitively disposed to v-believe that someone like Harry has that property.

iii. Considerable care is needed in determining what might be a true substitution instance of 'x is a borderline instance of φ.' For example, the sentence type 'Harry is a borderline instance of the property of being a bald man' can't, qua sentence *type*, be a true substitution instance. This is because of the way the penumbras of vague terms dilate or constrict from one context of utterance to another, depending on the communicative interests of the speaker and her hearer. If we're debating whether we should fix Harry up with Sally, someone who knows that Sally prefers men with luxuriant heads of hair might say, 'No, Harry's bald,' and count as speaking truly. In a context in which we're casting for a Yul Brynner look-alike, an utterance of 'Harry isn't bald' might be true. In other contexts an utterance of 'Harry is borderline bald' would be true. If the penumbras of 'bald' can fluctuate in such ways, then there can be no such thing as *the* property expressed by 'bald,' even when applied to a normal guy like Harry.

iv. Here's something I hope will make salient the intuitive idea underlying SHS. For each vague contingent property (i.e. a vague property it's metaphysically possible for something both to have and not to have) φ, there is the further vague contingent property, *the property of being a borderline instance of* φ. Also associated with φ will be a range of properties such that having any property in that range metaphysically entails being borderline φ (of course this isn't a precisely delimited range: for some properties it will be indeterminate whether or not having them entails being borderline φ, or indeterminate whether or not it's indeterminate whether or not having them entails being borderline φ, and so on, conceivably, up the ladder of higher-order vagueness). For example, what makes Harry borderline bald is the fact that he has a certain visible configuration of hairs on his scalp; and what makes Jane's sensation a borderline pain is its precise phenomenal quality, whether or not anyone has a word or other neat expression in her public language for that quality. So a property φ's *penumbral properties*—the properties whose possession make a thing a borderline instance of φ—typically don't have anything to do with VPBs.[6] But *what accounts for their being penumbral properties* does have to do with VPBs. Let β be the neural correlate of that use of 'bald' in Jane's idiolect whose application to Harry is borderline. The conceptual role of β will induce Jane to s-believe with certainty the proposition expressed by 'so-and-so is β' when she perceives the hair situation on so-and-so's scalp to fall within a certain range of hair situations S. The fact that β has a conceptual role with that feature is what primarily explains β's meaning a property that a man definitely has when the hair situation on his scalp falls within S. There is another range of hair-on-scalp situations, S^-, such that β's conceptual role induces Jane to s-believe with certainty the proposition expressed by 'so-and-so isn't β' when she perceives the hair situation on so-and-so's scalp to be within S^-. The fact that β has a conceptual role with that feature is what primarily explains β's meaning a property that a man definitely does not have when the hair situation on his scalp falls within S-. In between S and S^- there is a third range of hair-on-scalp situations, $S^{/-}$,[7] such that (perhaps defeasibly) when Jane perceives that the hair situation on so-and-so's scalp is within $S^{/-}$, the conceptual role of β precludes her from s-believing to any positive degree the propositions expressed by 'so-and-so is β' and 'so-and-so isn't β' and instead induces her to v-believe both propositions to positive degrees that sum to 1. The fact that β has a conceptual role with this feature is what primarily makes the hair situations within $S^{/-}$ penumbral properties of the property its conceptual role determines, or partly determines, β to mean in Jane's mentalese, the property expressed by one use of 'bald' in her public language idiolect. The fact that VPB enters into the conceptual role in the way just indicated is what makes β and the baldness property it expresses vague, and belongs to the explanation of what makes someone a borderline instance of that property.

SHS is a better statement of the account I wanted to endorse in *Things*. The version I actually gave—call it *OV* for *original version*—was that

x is a borderline instance of φ iff someone could have a φ-concept-driven VPB* that x is φ,[8]

where:

- A *VPB** is a VPB formed under ideal epistemic conditions, where this primarily means justified confidence about the supervenience base for the vague property that enters into the v-believed proposition.
- To say that someone could v*-believe that x is φ is to say that there is some possible world similar in relevant respects to the actual world in which someone v*-believes that x is φ, where the "relevant respects" are defined by the supervenience base for having φ (e.g. as regards being rich, the monetary worth of a person's assets).
- And a VPB* that x is φ is "*φ-concept-driven* when one is in ideal circumstances for judging x to be φ and one's concept of being φ precludes one from s-believing to any positive degree either that x is φ or that x is not φ and determines one to v-believe [that x is φ and that x is not φ to positive degrees that sum to 1]" (*Things*, 212).

Given what I intended OV *to convey*, as revealed by the role of the supervenience base for the vague property in my gloss of "ideal epistemic conditions," the problem with it from the perspective of its alleged improvement SHS has to do more with its expression than its content. OV misleadingly reads as though being a borderline instance of φ directly supervenes on the ability of someone to v*-believe that a thing is φ, whereas what SHS makes explicit is that there are two distinct parts to the story. First, for some typically non-psychological condition C—φ's penumbral condition—*what makes x a borderline instance of φ* is simply that x satisfies C (e.g. the hair situation on Harry's scalp falls within a certain range). Second, *what makes C φ's penumbral condition* is that the canonical concept of φ—roughly, the concept expressed by the relevant use of 'φ'—is related to v-believing that x is φ in the way spelled out in the first part of SHS. This way of presenting the view makes better sense of Crispin's Wright's acute observation that "borderline cases are cases where a competent judge may be put in quandary despite conditions obtaining which are optimal for judgement in clear cases" (2003: 487).

I'm also in need of an SHS version of my original version of a proposition's being indeterminate, which was that

p is indeterminate iff someone could v*-believe p.

This revision would also have two parts, counterparts of the two parts of SHS. The second part would give a (typically) non-psychological condition whose satisfaction by a proposition p metaphysically entailed that p was indeterminate, while the first part would give an account in terms of a concept, or of concepts, involved in the entertainment of p, which uses v-believing p to explain how satisfaction of that condition made p indeterminate. It may not be so easy to state a univocal first part, since the conceptual roots of indeterminacy aren't the same for every kind of indeterminacy. I won't here say anything more about how the *Things* version of my account of indeterminacy should have been stated.

I turn now to the objections Edgington, Field, and Wright have to my account of borderlineness, primarily in so far as their objections can be directed at SHS and aren't based on their worries about VPB per se.

Edgington offers three objections to the original versions of my accounts of borderlineness (OV) and indeterminacy (call it OV^{in}). One of them is a variation on Fitch's paradox of knowability. Suppose x is borderline red and that no one ever v-believes that x is red. Then the conjunction

(Q) x is red and no one ever v-believes that x is red

is borderline, hence indeterminate, and thus OV^{in} entails that someone could v-believe (Q). "But no rational and minimally self-aware person could have a VPB that: x is red and no one has a VPB that x is red" (161). This tricky example does seem to me to be a counterexample to OV^{in}. But note that it's not a counterexample to OV or, more importantly, to SHS, and it wouldn't be a counterexample to a revision of OV^{in} that mirrored the SHS revision of OV.

Her second objection is that it's epistemically possible that there is a property φ and a thing x such that (1) x is a borderline instance of φ and (2) φ is metaphysically inaccessible to humans in such a way that it's metaphysically impossible for any human to entertain the proposition that x is φ. Edgington's objection is well taken: for all we know there are such properties; and if for all we know there are such properties, then for all we know OV is false. But I don't think it's an objection to my SHS revision of OV. For it's consistent with SHS that there are concepts we can't have: the concepts in question are concepts of mind-independent properties; concepts are individuated by concept-constituting conceptual roles; and our functional architecture may make it impossible for our neural systems of mental representation to realize those conceptual roles. This needs elaboration; the elaboration would make clear why, though our concepts are of mind-independent properties, it's necessary and sufficient for our being able to have knowledge of those properties that we have the concepts that individuate them. I'd like to think that the desired elaboration may be found in Schiffer (2010).

Edgington's third objection is this:

> Schiffer defines vagueness in terms of an ideal epistemic agent with v*-beliefs, and such an agent, it seems to me, has transcended any initial bafflement [or ambivalence].... I can't see such an all-knowing perfectly rational person as ambivalent; and that notion doesn't seem to do any work. She just knows she is right to judge that Tom is a borderline case (to whatever degree) of baldness. (161)

In other words, a sophistical rational person can know that Tom is borderline bald even though she experiences no inclination to judge that he is bald or that he isn't bald, and so can't be said to v-believe that Tom is bald or that he isn't bald to any positive degrees. Did my book give the impression that taking a man to be borderline bald was like the felt internal conflict of one who craves a piece of cake while also struggling not to fall off his Atkins wagon? V-believing to degree 0.5 both that Tom is bald and that he isn't bald had better be possible without experiencing any bafflement or felt ambivalence concerning Tom's baldness. The question is about the propositional attitude the sophisticate should have towards the propositions that Tom is bald and that Tom isn't bald. If Edgington's own account is right, the sophisticate should believe that each of those propositions has a "degree of verity" of 0.5. Very well, that tells us what propositional attitude she should have to the proposition *that the proposition that Tom is bald has degree of verity 0.5*, but—unable to resist the *tu quoque*—what should be her attitude towards the propositions that Tom is bald and that Tom isn't bald? Field, as we're about to see, can say that she should believe both to degree 0, but Edgington can't agree with that. Evidently, she must say that the sophisticate must *in some sense* believe each of those propositions to 0.5, but, I should hope, not in a sense that entails believing that there is a 50 percent chance that Tom is bald. I acknowledge that I didn't give a complete functional characterization of VPB, but if it's a genuine species of propositional attitude, then one must be able to v-believe a proposition to a positive degree without being in a state of bafflement because one recognizes that an essential feature of a concept involved in the proposition speaks simultaneously in favor of applying and of withholding the concept.[9]

Even with this clarification about the relation between VPB and "ambivalence," Crispin Wright would still offer two counterexamples to the idea that possession of a vague concept entails a disposition to v-believe borderline propositions. We need consider only one of his examples to get his point. Tim, who is intended to be confused with Tim Williamson, has the same stock of vague concepts as the rest of us but "has persuaded himself, by a variety of more or less philosophically questionable moves, of the correctness of the classical epistemicist conception of vagueness" (193), and therefore would s-believe, rather than v-believe, that borderline Harry is bald to degree 0.5, and would s-believe to the meager degree 0.125 that Harry is bald, thin, and intelligent, when he takes those three conjuncts to be probabilistically independent and, taking them each to be borderline, s-believes each to degree 0.5.

I don't doubt that Tim is possible, but I question whether he's a counterexample. Earlier I quoted Wright himself as saying that "borderline cases are cases where a competent judge may be put in quandary despite conditions obtaining which are optimal for judgement in clear cases." I should think that '*may* be put in quandary' is vague enough to protect Wright from being forced to recognize Tim as a counter-example to his, Wright's, quandary account of vagueness, and I should hope that the vagueness of 'entails a *disposition* to v-believe borderline propositions' offers similar protection. Presently, however, I will try to say something with less of my tongue in my cheek.

Hartry Field also offers a couple of trouble-making characters, both directed at OV^{in} and both intended to show that v^*-believing a proposition isn't sufficient for its being indeterminate. The first guy takes Dick Cheney to be borderline wealthy "on the ground that [Cheney] has quite a bit less than Bill Gates" (184), and thus v^*-believes that Cheney is wealthy, notwithstanding that by any reasonable measure Dick Cheney is determinately very wealthy. Field says that I can't reply that the guy's VPB can't be a VPB^*, a VPB formed under ideal conditions, because "that response presupposes that the notion of indeterminacy is available independently of the ideality constraints on degrees of belief, which doesn't fit with Schiffer's proposal of using ideality of degrees of belief in explicating determinateness" (184). That's too fast. The concept *I* attach to 'wealthy' is such that anyone apprised of Cheney's wealth would have to be egregiously irrational in ways that have nothing to do with indeterminacy in order to take Cheney to be borderline wealthy, and if the guy is rational by the concept *he* attaches to 'wealthy', his eccentric conceptual behavior makes no trouble for me.

Field's second character is "an extraordinarily rational Dummett-like anti-realist who believes that contingent claims about the past are all indeterminate" (184), and thus v^*-believes that Napoleon was less than six feet tall, even though, in fact, it's determinately the case that Napoleon was less than six feet tall. But being an extraordinarily rational Dummett-like anti-realist doesn't entail being an extraordinarily rational person, and it's pretty hard to imagine how any plausible explanation of how the guy came to accept anti-realism about the past wouldn't reveal him to have transgressed some rule of ideal epistemic behavior that has nothing to do with indeterminacy. Perhaps, however, all Field really needs to make his point is the not unreasonable claim that for all we know there might be a proposition that had a determinate truth-value even though an ideal epistemic agent in the best epistemic position to assess the proposition would be rationally constrained to take the proposition to be indeterminate. I won't try to debate that because I don't see how this sort of case can arise for SHS, the account of being a borderline case that better fits what I was groping for in *Things*, and I haven't yet worked out the details of how that account is to be mirrored by the revised account of indeterminacy generally. No one who took x to be borderline φ—and thus v-believed both that x was φ and that x wasn't φ to positive degrees that summed to 1—on the basis of some theory she was, or wasn't, justified in accepting could provide a problem for SHS, since, on that account, the only thing that could make x borderline φ would be x's satisfying some (typically non-psychological) condition C such that a possession condition for φ was being primitively disposed to v-believe both that x was φ and that x wasn't φ to positive degrees that sum to 1 when one was certain that x satisfied C.

Field's two guys challenge the sufficiency of my account of indeterminacy; he also presents what he takes to be a counterexample to its necessity: something might be borderline round in conditions that make human life impossible, and thus impossible for someone to v*-believe that it's round. I think this example simply misses its target. In *Things* I said that

x is a borderline case of being F only if someone could v*-believe that x is F,

and then I explained how I intended 'could' to be understood:

To say that someone could v*-believe that x is F is to say that there is *some* possible world similar in relevant respects to the actual world in which someone v*-believes that x is F. In many cases, the relevant respects are defined by the supervenience base for being F—e.g. the hair situation on Tom's scalp. (208)

The supervenience base for being round consists of relevant geometrical properties. If x is borderline round by virtue of definitely having geometrical properties Γ, then it's required, by the just-displayed condition, that there is some possible world in which x has Γ and someone v*-believes that x is round. None of this is challenged by Field's example.

Finally, Field questions whether there is any need either for VPBs or for attempting a psychological reduction of indeterminacy:

In my view, Schiffer's attempt to explicate indeterminacy in terms of the psychology of ideal agents is overkill: the point that rational standard degrees of belief can depart from the laws of classical probability, in ways that allow for the standard degrees of belief in *p or not p* to also be less than 1, is enough to illuminate the nature of vagueness without any such explication. (184)

On my account of "rational standard degrees of belief"—SPBs—and on Field's, s-believing both p and ¬p to degrees that sum to less than 1 is a measure of the extent to which one takes p and ¬p to be indeterminate. S-believing both p and ¬p to degree 0 implies that one takes p and ¬p to be determinately indeterminate, and in the event one should s-believe (p ∨ ¬p) also to degree 0. For me, but not for Field, that correlation with indeterminacy is owed to the fact that, when SPB(p) + SPB(¬p) = 0, VPB(p) + VPB(¬p) = 1, since one's v-believing p and ¬p to positive degrees that sum to 1 is what directly means that one takes p and ¬p to be indeterminate. Field's first reasonable question is whether VPB is carrying any share of the load, especially since s-believing (p ∨ ¬p) to degree 0 "seems enough by itself to undermine the sense that we are committed to belief in a fact about which we are ignorant" (182). Field's second reasonable question is why, once unburdened of VPB, we need explicitly to define indeterminacy in terms of partial belief, since allowing that one may appropriately s-believe (p ∨ ¬p) to a degree less than 1 is all by itself "enough to illuminate the nature of vagueness."

I'll start with the second reasonable question. First a relatively small point: since vagueness-induced indeterminacy is but one kind of indeterminacy, it's simply false that we do enough to "illuminate" the nature of *vagueness* simply by recognizing that one may rationally believe instances of excluded middle to degrees less than 1. More to the present point, however, is that I doubt that the recognition even does enough to "illuminate" the nature of indeterminacy. For assume that there is just one relevant notion of partial belief and that taking p to be indeterminate is to be equated with believing both p and ¬p to degree 0. There is then the question of *what explains the appropriateness of those beliefs*, and one possible answer is that p's being indeterminate = p's being neither true nor false, and 0 is the degree to which one should believe p and ¬p when one knows that p is indeterminate. So one doesn't avoid a third-possibility account of vagueness—which Field and I are both motivated to avoid—just by requiring the rational agent to believe both p and ¬p to degree 0 when she takes p to be indeterminate. Whether taking p to be indeterminate consists in v-believing both p and ¬p to positive degrees that sum to 1 or consists merely in believing both propositions to degree 0, we need to explain why they are the appropriate attitudes to have, and one possible explanation for either proposal is that the privileged attitude doesn't *constitute* p's being indeterminate but merely *tracks* it: somehow it's a necessary truth that the privileged attitudes are the appropriate attitudes to have when one knows that p has the entirely non-psychological property of being indeterminate, and the best way of making sense of that possibility would be if the tracked property of p's being indeterminate entailed that p was neither unqualifiedly true nor unqualifiedly false. Whence the thought that it's important to show that being indeterminate is somehow *conceptually dependent* on the kind of propositional attitude one should have towards p when one takes p to be indeterminate. That is the point of an account such as SHS, and the point is independent of whether the best construal of taking x to be borderline F involves v-believing that x is F and that x is not F to positive degrees that sum to 1 or simply believing to degree 0 both that x is F and that x isn't F. I certainly don't want to insist that an explicit reduction like SHS is mandatory in order to display the right conceptual connection between a proposition's being borderline and the right attitude to have to it, but it's no doubt the clearest way, if you can get it (or even approximate it in some relevant way).

This returns us to Field's first reasonable question. The motivation for an account of x's being a borderline instance of ϕ that reveals the conceptual priority of the characteristic mental state of taking x to be borderline doesn't obviously favor a view which takes that mental state to consist in v-believing that x is ϕ and that x isn't ϕ to positive degrees that sum to 1 over one that takes it to consist merely in s-believing both those propositions to degree 0. Four reasons are more or less explicit in *Things* for preferring the first option. First, on the second, Field-preferred, view, the mental state appropriate to taking x to be borderline ϕ is believing to degree 0 that x is ϕ, the same degree to which one should believe a proposition one knows to be determinately false. Intuitively, however, one's attitude towards a proposition one takes to be teetering on the true/false borderline shouldn't be the same as one's attitude towards a proposition one takes to be definitely false. Second, if one takes both Tom and Dick to be borderline tall while knowing that Dick is taller than Tom, then, intuitively, one should in some sense be more inclined to accept that Dick is tall than that Tom is tall, but on the Field-preferred view one should believe both propositions to degree 0. Third, there do seem to be VPBs and v-believing that x is ɸ does seem to be characteristic of taking x to be borderline ɸ. And fourth—though this is much vaguer than the three preceding reasons—it seemed easier to give a non-third-possibility explanation of the inappropriateness of s-believing that x is ɸ to a positive degree, when x is borderline ɸ, when we could say that the SPB was precluded by the dominant VPB. In any case, the force of those reasons depends on our being able to take VPB to be a propositional attitude in good standing, and I return to this thought in the final section of this response.

19.4 VPB, Validity, and Logic

According to one very familiar concept of validity, validity is necessary truth preservation. In other words, an argument is valid just in case it's metaphysically impossible for its conclusion not to be true when its premises are. Let's call this concept *classical validity—c-validity*, for short—since classical logic is supposed to be the theory of *formal* c-validity, i.e. the theory of those argument forms every substitution instance of which is c-valid. C-validity is also the default notion of validity used by philosophers outside of formal logic. When 'valid' is used by a philosopher in a non-technical context, it is nearly always used to express c-validity when the concern is deductive validity. My main point about validity in Chapter 5 of *Things* was that it is indeterminate whether sorites arguments are c-valid, notwithstanding that classical logic deems them to be c-valid. For consider these two sorites inferences, which I'll refer to as S1 and S2, respectively:

A person with $50,000,000 is rich.
For any n, if a person with $n is rich, then so is a person with $n − 1¢.
∴ A person with only 37¢ is rich.

A person with $50,000,000 is rich.
A person with only 37¢ isn't rich.
∴ There is an n such that a person with $n is rich but a person with $n − 1¢ isn't rich.

On the account of vagueness offered in *Things*, the trouble-making steps in both S1 and S2—the sorites premise in S1, the conclusion in S2—are indeterminate. Since S1's other premise is true and its conclusion isn't true, it's indeterminate whether S1 has true premises and a conclusion that isn't true, and therefore indeterminate whether it's c-valid. Since S2 has true premises and an indeterminate conclusion, it's indeterminate whether it's c-valid as well.

In a sense, the saliency of c-validity in my book's discussion of the sorites was unnecessary. The reason sorites inferences present paradoxes is that they present us with propositions that are apt to seem plausible when considered on their own, without reflection on the trouble they might get us into, but which also seem to be such that they can't all be true together. The point I was primarily concerned to advance in *Things* was that it's indeterminate whether the propositions in question can all be true together. For example, the trouble-making appearances presented by the just-displayed sorites inference S1 are (1) that its first premise is true, (2) that its second premise is true, (3) that its conclusion is false, and (4) that appearances (1)–(3) are mutually incompatible. What I suggested was that (1) and (3) were definitely true, but that it was indeterminate whether (2) was true, and therefore, evidently, also indeterminate whether (4) is true. One can agree with that while taking any one of a number views about the proper conception of validity. After all, Field's own theory commits him to holding that it's indeterminate whether the paradox-inducing propositions can all be true together.

In any case, two of the five sections of Field's paper are critical discussions of what I say about validity in connection with vagueness. What, exactly, are Field's objections, and how good are they?

(a) Since Schiffer takes the premises of [S2] to be true..., but doesn't take the conclusion to be true..., it would seem natural for him to conclude that [S2] isn't really valid, despite the fact that classical logic says it is.... But Schiffer insists that the proper conclusion is *not* that [S2] is invalid.... He says, rather, that the question of whether the argument is valid is itself indeterminate: the argument is neither determinately valid nor determinately invalid. (176)

This is puzzling, since, as Field himself notes in his next sentence, what I actually say isn't that it's indeterminate whether S2 is valid; what I actually say is that it's indeterminate whether S2 is *c*-valid. Field makes clear that for him the "proper conclusion" should be that S2 is invalid. Does he mean to disagree with my claim that it's indeterminate whether S2 is *c*-valid? On the contrary; he must agree with me that it's indeterminate whether S2 is c-valid. For S2's conclusion is indeterminate on Field's own theory of vagueness, and he knows that its premises are true. (Similarly, he must agree with me that it's indeterminate whether S1 is c-valid, since he, too, holds that its sorites premise is indeterminate, and he knows that its first premise is true and its conclusion is false.) So what exactly is his quarrel with me about validity?

(b) Since Field must agree with me that it's indeterminate whether S2 is c-valid, but thinks that the proper thing to say is that S2 is invalid, he must think that that is the best thing to say about S2 *given the purposes for which we want a notion of validity*; and he must think that this is an issue that divides us. Now, one way we have of acquiring knowledge is by *inferring* propositions from other propositions we already know, and from this point of view we would want a logic, and an attendant notion of validity, whose goal was to tell us which inferences were knowledge preserving. A notion of validity which preserved *determinate* truth would do this: you would, roughly speaking, come to know a proposition you hadn't known if you correctly inferred it from propositions you already knew (provided your inferring the proposition didn't destroy your knowledge of those other propositions). On this notion of validity, S1 would be deemed valid, S2 invalid, just as, in fact, Field recommends. But if that is what Field intends (and it evidently is, given his claim that validity should be taken as "a primitive notion that governs our inferential or epistemic practices" (185)), I don't see what he takes the *disagreement* between us to be, since I was already pretty explicit on this score. His accusation that I think "that any notion on which [S2] is determinately invalid is a merely technical notion lacking philosophical interest" (176) is false, and I thought—evidently wrongly—that I had made myself clear on this. I said that if we construed classical logic as a theory of c-validity, then the correct thing to say about it was that it was indeterminate whether it was correct, and that, so construed, so-called "alternative" logics shouldn't be taken to be incompatible with classical logic. Then I added:

Of course, there is one important sense in which the non-classical fuzzy logic would fill a logical need created by the indeterminacy of classical logic. Since, as we've seen, classical logic can take us from determinately true premisses to an indeterminate conclusion, we do have a need to know what inference rules will preserve determinate truth, and the Łukasiewiczian continuum-valued logic, or some not too dissimilar to non-classical logic, may do that. (230)

That may also stand as my (not wholly satisfactory) response to Wright's remark that I have "yet to provide [my] own account of the shape a logic should assume to remedy [classical logic's] defect [of not being knowledge-preserving]" (207).[10]

(c) Field charges that I was wrong to claim that it's indeterminate whether S2 is c-invalid, since, by his lights, it's determinately c-invalid:

[E]ven if we stick to Schiffer's preferred sense of 'valid'—necessary truth preservation—it is not at all clear that [S2] isn't determinately invalid. For what sort of necessity is involved here? Not "metaphysical necessity," whatever exactly that is: for the inference from 'There is water in the sink' to 'There is H$_2$O in the sink' preserves truth by metaphysical necessity, but is not valid. The notion of necessity that is involved, rather, is *logical* necessity. And it could certainly be argued that the fact that [the premises of S2] are determinately true and [its conclusion] isn't is enough to show that *logic* doesn't require that if [the premises of S2] are true, then so is [its conclusion], so that it's enough to show that *it is not logically necessary that* the inference preserves truth. (177)

I must confess that I wasn't aware that 'Logic' was the proper name of a discipline according to which it couldn't be indeterminate whether it's logically necessary that an inference preserves truth if it were indeterminate whether it's formally necessary that the conclusion of the inference is true if its premises are. And actually I did intend to mean metaphysical necessity by my use of 'necessity'. I recognized three notions: *c-validity*; *formal c-validity*; and *logical c-validity*. An argument is *c-valid* just in case it's metaphysically necessary that, if its premises are true, then so is its conclusion. If it's metaphysically necessary *that Mary has a spouse if she is a spouse*, then this would explain the sense in which many philosophers would count the inference 'Mary is a spouse; so, she has a spouse' as valid.[11] If it's metaphysically necessary that there is H$_2$O in the sink if there is water in the sink, then, while that might well be regarded as an unwelcome consequence of the stipulated definition of c-validity, that would show that the inference 'Water is in the sink; so, there is H$_2$O in the sink' was also c-valid. An argument is *formally* c-valid just in case it's a substitution instance of a form every substitution instance of which is c-valid. And an inference is *logically* c-valid just in case it's formally c-valid and derivable in an intended system of formal logic. Anyway, I don't see what all the fuss is about. Who cares how we do or don't use 'valid'? What is important is that there are numerous relations that a given proposition p might bear to a given set of propositions Γ—whether p is metaphysically entailed by Γ; whether p must be determinately true if the members of Γ are; whether p must have some designated value other than truth or determinate truth if some or all the members of Γ have it—and all these relations are worth studying in the mathematical way definitive of what we call logic.

(d) In *Things* I was explicit that the conditional in my renditions of sorites inferences was the material conditional. Field says it follows from the account of indeterminacy offered in the book that no inference would be determinately c-valid, not even 'p, therefore p', since 'p or not p' is on my view indeterminate when p is indeterminate, and he implies that he views this "as having an intolerably high cost." Two comments. First, 'Determinately p, therefore determinately p' is c-valid: there is no possible world in which p is determinately true and 'not p' isn't. But how can it be indeterminate whether 'p, therefore p' is c-valid? How could it be indeterminate whether there is a possible world in which the premise, p, is true but the conclusion, p, isn't? Well, if p is indeterminate, then so is 'not p', and the view I advanced did have the arguably counterintuitive consequence that when p and 'not p' are indeterminate, so is 'p and not p'. To say that the contradiction is "indeterminate" isn't to say that it has some *chance* of being true; there is no chance that the contradiction is determinately true or any closer to truth than being indeterminate. I tried to remove some of the feeling that it was preposterous to say that a contradiction isn't determinately false with the remark that there is something degree-of-truthish about v-believing a proposition to degree 0.5, and observing that the Łukasiewiczian truth-theoretic version of VPB(p & q) = Min[VPB(p), VPB(q)]—viz. T(p & q) = Min[T(p), T(q)]—isn't unmotivated "because if, as it were, God were to assure you that it was a *fact* that *both* the proposition that Tom was bald *and* the proposition that he wasn't bald were true to degree 0.5, then how could you rationally think that the conjunction of those two propositions was itself true to a degree other than 0.5?"[12] Second, Field's implying that this consequence of my view has an "intolerably high cost" is somewhat puzzling, since he, too, is committed to saying that no inference is determinately c-valid when the conditional is read as material implication. No doubt he meant that a notion of validity according to which no inference was determinately valid wouldn't be much of a guide when we try to expand our knowledge by making inferences; but with that I wouldn't disagree. In any case, although I should have seen that my view had that consequence when I wrote *Things*, I evidently didn't. If I had, it wouldn't have changed my views on indeterminacy, but I would have emphasized the questionable *utility* of c-validity, and I wouldn't have given the truth conditions I gave for conditionals, for as Edgington and Field both point out, a consequence of the account I gave of them in Chapter 7 is that there are no determinately true conditionals if there are no determinately c-valid arguments.

19.5 Verdict Exclusion

Is it metaphysically possible for a proposition to be both borderline and known? I say no, and thereby commit myself to the thesis Wright calls Verdict Exclusion (VE). I do so for three reasons. First, my intuition is that if p is known, then p is definitely true: if Henry *knows* that his socks are brown, then his socks are definitely brown, and thus not borderline brown. Second, when one confidently takes a proposition to be borderline, one seems to know that nothing could conceivably be forthcoming to show that p was true or that it was false; that all relevant considerations are already in. And third, taking a proposition to be borderline—such that the appropriate attitude to have to the proposition is to v-believe it and its negation to positive degrees that sum to 1—is evidently incompatible with s-believing it in a way that could sustain knowledge. Wright is familiar with these reasons, but nevertheless demurs; "we should," he says, "be agnostic about the possibility of knowledgeable verdicts in borderline cases" (194). He offers two positive reasons for this agnosticism, and he has replies to the reasons others, including myself, have offered for accepting VE.

Wright's first positive reason is that the "entitlement intuition" embodied in our practice regarding borderline cases is in tension with VE, and that resolving the tension in VE's favor would require an implausible error theory. The "entitlement intuition" is the intuition that a "judgment"—possibly hesitant and qualified—that x is F or that x isn't F isn't precluded from being epistemically entitled by x's being borderline F. The tension with VE is induced by the fact that if VE were true, then these judgments about borderline cases wouldn't be the products of successful feats of cognition; they would instead "amount to no more than a kind of cognitive incontinence" (195), and knowledge of this would make it impossible for us coherently to have the entitlement intuition. Wright doesn't say why the error theory thus foisted on the proponent of VE would be difficult to maintain, but I'm confident that he is right about this, if the tension he claims to find really is there.

My doubt is whether the tension really is there. There are two kinds of case to consider. The first is when the qualified "judgment" that x is, or that x isn't, F is made by one who takes x to be borderline F. Wright himself alludes to the following sort of example. Jane is going along a soritical row of color samples, running from definite red to definite orange, having to say of each sample whether or not it's red. She confidently pronounces the first few samples to be red, but as she moves down the line, her inclination to describe the sample before her as red becomes weaker and weaker until, somewhere near the orange end, it becomes non-existent. Now let's revisit Jane at the mid-point, where, we may suppose, her inclination to describe the sample before her as red is matched by an equally strong inclination to say that it's not red but orange—she is inclined, so to say, to degree 0.5 both to describe the sample as red and to describe it as not red. Jane's qualified "judgment" that the sample is red would be the propositional attitude that induces her 0.5 degree inclination to describe the sample as red. It's my view that this propositional attitude is not at all in tension with VE. It would be if it were Jane's s-believing to degree 0.5 that the sample was red, and was thus accompanied by her believing that there was a fifty-fifty chance that the sample was red—but I have argued that the propositional attitude isn't such an SPB. Wright seems to agree with me about this, so it's not clear to me why he thinks there is for this kind of case a tension with VE.

The second kind of case is the belief that one may have that x is F when x is borderline F but where one doesn't take x to be borderline F, even though conditions are optimal for judging whether or not x is F. Because of the way the penumbras of vague predicates dilate or constrict from one context of utterance to another, it's difficult to describe clear examples in which someone in optimal circumstances is justified in believing a statement which is in fact borderline, but perhaps the following example will give the right flavor. Michael has no visible hair on his scalp. But that is because he shaves his scalp; if he didn't he would have a luxuriant head of hair. Is Michael bald? Suppose that, as regards the use of 'bald' in the idiolects of educated people whose first language is English, the question has no determinate answer. Among people whose use of 'bald' is as good as anyone else's, some would say that Michael is bald, some would say that he isn't bald, and some, reflecting on the divergent uses of 'bald', would say that it's indeterminate whether Michael may correctly be said to be bald. Now consider Al, who would say that shaving your scalp can't make you bald. Given his concept of a bald man, into whose penumbra Michael doesn't fall, he thinks a true thought when, upon learning that Michael would have a luxuriant head of hair but for the fact that he shaves his scalp, he says to himself, "So, Michael isn't bald." But in so far as he thinks a true thought, Al also knows the true proposition he thinks—the proposition *he* expresses in *his* context of utterance. Since Al knows that proposition, he does nothing to support Wright's agnosticism about VE—nor, of course, does he threaten it; his example, as so far described, is irrelevant to the issue. To get a relevant example, we need to have Al offer a verdict on a statement that is borderline. So suppose that Betty's concept of a bald man counts a man who shaves his scalp as bald, and suppose the question arises between Al and Betty whether Michael is bald. Although there is a sense in which Al and Betty have different concepts of baldness, the very pliant criteria by which we individuate propositions permit their context of utterance to be one in which, notwithstanding their conceptual difference, there is a single question at issue, the question, as it may be described, whether Michael is bald. Suppose that the conversation between Al and Betty then proceeds as follows. Betty straightway blurts out that Michael is bald, Al that he isn't. Conversation ensues, in which it becomes clear that, owing to the vagaries of 'bald' in their shared English dialect, neither uses 'bald' incorrectly. It then seems to me that, in so far as they are debating a univocal question, that question has no determinately correct answer, and therefore neither of them is epistemically entitled to insist that he or she knows its answer. I conclude that, properly understood, the "entitlement intuition" is not at odds with VE.

Wright's second positive reason for agnosticism about VE is that it's incompatible with a view he calls Evidential Constraint (EC), and which he thinks we aren't in a position to disbelieve. EC holds that the conditional forms

If Fx, then it's feasible to know that Fx

If ¬Fx, then it's feasible to know that ¬Fx

will result in forms whose substitution instances are true when 'F' is replaced by the sort of predicates apt to enter into sorites paradoxes—'red', 'bald', 'wealthy', etc. VE's incompatibility with EC is clear; for if VE were true, it wouldn't be feasible to know that x is F when x was borderline F, and thus conjunction with the EC conditionals would entail the contradiction (¬Fx & ¬¬Fx). Wright doesn't claim to believe EC; he merely insists that we are in no position to deny it. VE implies that "colors, baldness, heaps and so on can all be undetectable, even under unimprovable conditions of observation" (196), but it's his intuition that we don't know anything of the sort. I, on the other hand, don't share his intuition, especially when we redescribe the implication he finds unpalatable as the claim that, if, for example, a thing is borderline red, then, no matter how good the conditions are for judging color, we can't know that it's red (or that it's not red).

Wright brackets a discussion of whether v-believing a proposition and its negation to positive degrees that sum to 1 is incompatible with knowing the proposition or its negation, but replies to the other two reasons I mentioned above for accepting VE, and also to EC-threatening arguments of Rosenkranz and Williamson. I'm sympathetic to his replies to Rosenkranz and Williamson. His response to my conceivability argument for VE raises many interesting questions, but their depth precludes further discussion here. I will, however, say something further about the intuitive basis for thinking that if someone knows that x is F, then x isn't borderline F. The point is simple. Suppose you took a wall to be borderline red, but on better inspection resolved that it was red. You would certainly then not continue to claim that it was borderline red. This seems to me to show that our concept of being borderline makes it conceptually incoherent to claim that something was both borderline F and known by someone to be F. If something is taken to be borderline F, there may well be the possibility that it may really be known to be F (or not to be F), but that is precisely to envisage the possibility of its not really being borderline. My claim isn't that confident judgments of borderlineness are infallible; but that 'borderline F' and 'known to be F/not F' are descriptions that can't be true of a thing at one and the same time. At one point in his discussion of VE Wright seems willing to go along with this: "If someone prefers to understand 'borderline case' in such a way that the knowledge that something is a borderline case ought to inhibit any verdict, then a way of expressing the entitlement intuition is that there are no clear—definite—borderline cases in a typical sorites series" (195). This strikes me as a significant concession, the conceptual incompatibility of being borderline F and known to be F/not F. It reduces the issue to a question about the epistemological status of a posteriori judgments of being borderline. I feel confident that, where my own concepts are concerned, I can sometimes believe, regarding one of them, that a certain thing is a borderline instance of it. I see no reason to think my belief can't be justified. It may also be true. Nothing Gettier-like need be in the offing. Why wouldn't that count as my knowing that the thing was a borderline instance of my concept, and thus of the property that concept was a concept of?

19.6 Is VPB a Kind of Belief?

Although neither Edgington nor Field nor Wright directly take on the issue, Field and Wright make it clear that they are less than persuaded that VPB is appropriately classed as a kind of partial *belief*. Field, I already noted, also remarks that my assumption that there are neat compositional laws governing VPB "appears undermotivated if the only role of such 'degrees of belief' is to characterize our conflicting inclinations in cases where our standard degrees of belief in a sentence and its negation add to less than 1" (182). The *raison d'être* of beliefs—SPBs—is to provide us with information about the world so that we may survive in it. What *raison d'être* do VPBs enjoy? In *Things* I tentatively suggested that VPBs behaved "*as if* they were SPBs about the degree to which their propositional contents were true" (232), but I'm embarrassed to confess that I gave the thought so little elaboration that it's extremely difficult to know what I meant by it.

What I think I meant was this. Suppose that propositions have Łukasiewiczian degrees of truth, and suppose p is true to degree 0.5. What would then be the appropriate belief-like attitude to have towards p? If one's conceptual repertoire contained an explicit Łukasiewiczian notion of truth, then—perhaps—one should simply believe that p is true to degree 0.5. But it's reasonable to suppose that if propositions have such degrees of truth, then this would be reflected in the appropriate propositional attitudes even of agents who lacked an explicit degree-theoretic notion of truth—or even lacked an explicit notion of truth altogether. My thought was that these appropriate attitudes would be VPBs, and that the ideally placed rational agent would v-believe p (and thus not p, too) to degree 0.5.

There are various questions one might have for this proposal, not the least of which would be that, if it's correct, it might be hard to see what work the qualification "as if" was doing, hard to see, therefore, why its correctness wouldn't imply the correctness of the Łukasiewiczian degree-theoretic account of vagueness. Another is that the proposal seems to get the phenomenology of VPB wrong. The warring factions in the ambivalence one is liable to feel when confronted with a borderline proposition are, on the one hand, an inclination to judge the proposition to be *absolutely true* versus, on the other hand, an inclination to judge it to be *absolutely false*. Why should something that is tantamount to recognizing that the proposition is both true and false to degree 0.5 induce an inclination to think that it has either of those other, quite distinct, truth-values?

In (2010) I suggested that, perhaps, VPBs aren't proper propositional attitudes but just conceptual noise, a *sui generis* kind of ambivalence caused by certain features of borderline cases.[13] That wouldn't per se show that vagueness isn't explicable in terms of them, but it should seem preposterous to suppose that the possession condition for a vague concept requires conceptual noise in the face of certain objective features of borderline cases. At the same time, I continue to be persuaded that the correct account of vagueness—assuming, what I actually think is doubtful, that there can be *any* theory that definitely has that exalted status—won't entail either that borderline propositions are, or are not, absolutely true or absolutely false. So by my lights we continue to need a psychological account of vagueness. The problem of vagueness goes on.

Notes

1. I'm helping myself to the assumption that propositional attitudes and propositional speech acts are relations to propositions and that propositions can be vague. Neither assumption is accepted by every theorist of vagueness. For example, one kind of theorist would claim that what makes an utterance vague is that it's indeterminate which of myriad precise propositions it expresses. However, in the present context these assumptions are intended merely to simplify the exposition, and theorists who disagree with either assumption should have no trouble restating what I say in a way that avoids those assumptions.

2. Field complains that "what Schiffer calls *standard partial belief* (SPB) is *initially* explained as the kind of partial belief that under suitable idealization of logical omniscience can be identified with subjective probability" (179). He finds this very misleading because my official view is that it can't be identified with subjective probability, since I allow that SPB (p) + SPB(¬p) should be 0 when VPB(p) + VPB(¬p) = 1. But I didn't initially explain SPB in the way he alleges. What I actually said was that "SPB is the kind of partial belief which—subject to a qualification that I'll ignore until I get to it in 5.7—can under suitable idealization be identified with *subjective probability*" (*Things*, p. 199). Section 5.7 is where I take up the interaction of SPBs and VPBs. Since my primary concern was to introduce the new kind of partial belief, VPB, against the foil of SPB, I was concerned to make clear that the original core notion of SPB was the notion of partial belief with which every philosopher was already very familiar.
3. Edgington also gives a counterexample (165) like the one I give in my displayed response to MacFarlane, and on this there need—now—be no disagreement between us.
4. I elaborate on the distinction between happy- and unhappy-face solutions to classical philosophical paradox in my response to Paul Horwich, this volume, Chapter 11.
5. What I should have said in my book is one thing; what I should say today is another.
6. Thus I fully accept, but find no objection in, Edgington's remark that "a competent judgement that something is borderline red... is as much a response to how things are as is a competent judgement that something is red" (162).
7. Given higher-order vagueness, the three hair-situation ranges S^-, S^+, and $S^{-/+}$ can't exhaust the possible hair-situations on a man's scalp.
8. I've changed some of the book's notation to that used in this paper.
9. I think I may have clarified my view of "quandary" in (2010).
10. In (forthcoming), I argue against Wright's attempt to use intuitionist logic to repair the defect.
11. As I point out in (d) below in the text, on my account of indeterminacy it's indeterminate whether the material conditional 'Mary is a spouse → Mary has a spouse' is metaphysically necessary, since 'Mary isn't a spouse or she has a spouse' is indeterminate if it's indeterminate whether Mary is a spouse.
12. (2003: 2180).
13. This is further explored in Schiffer (2010).

Bibliography

Armstrong, D. (1989). *Universals: An Opinionated Introduction*. Boulder: Westview Press.
Fine, K. (1975). "Vagueness, Truth and Logic." *Synthese* 30: 265–300.
Machina, K. (1976). "Truth, Belief and Vagueness." *Journal of Philosophical Logic* 5: 47–78.
MacFarlane, J. (2006). "The Things We (Sorta Kinda) Believe." *Philosophy and Phenomenological Research* 73: 218–24.
MacFarlane, J. (2010). "Fuzzy Epistemicism." In *Cuts and Clouds: Essays on the Nature and Logic of Vagueness*, edited by R. Dietz and S. Moruzzi, Oxford: Oxford University Press.
Schiffer, S. (2010). "Vague Properties." In *Cuts and Clouds: Essays on the Nature and Logic of Vagueness*, edited by R. Dietz and S. Moruzzi, Oxford: Oxford University Press.
Schiffer, S. (forthcoming). "Quandary and Intuitionism: Crispin Wright on Vagueness." In *Logic, Language and Mathematics: Essays for Crispin Wright: Volume II*, edited by A. Miller, Oxford: Oxford University Press.
Williamson, T. (1994). *Vagueness*. London: Routledge.
Wright, C. (2001). "On Being in a Quandary: Relativism, Vagueness, Logical Revisionism." *Mind* 110: 45–98.

20
A Source of Paradox
Response to Paul Horwich

On the first page of his book *Paradoxes*, Mark Sainsbury defines a paradox as "an apparently unacceptable conclusion derived by apparently acceptable reasoning from apparently acceptable premises" (1). This definition doesn't pass muster as an analysis of the notion of a paradox exemplified in Sainsbury's book. If it were adequate, then every counterexample to what had seemed to be an apparently acceptable claim, such as Gettier's counterexample to the analysis of knowledge as justified true belief, would constitute a paradox, and for most philosophers the inference

A man 2 meters in height is tall.

For any number n, if a man n meters in height is tall, then so is a man $n - 0.001$ meters in height.

∴ A man 1 meter in height is tall.

would not constitute a paradox, since its second premise would not appear acceptable to them. Yet I doubt that I just said anything that would have surprised Sainsbury when he wrote the "definition." The "definition" isn't surrounded by the usual signs of a serious effort to analyze a philosophically important concept: there are no attempts to state necessary and sufficient conditions followed by considerations that force revisions followed by further attempts followed by further revisions followed by a final attempt followed by explanations of why none of the remaining counterexamples are really counterexamples. Sainsbury's book isn't about defining 'paradox,' and it's not clear why that should be thought to be of much interest; his book is about understanding and coming to terms with certain philosophically important paradoxes, such as the sorties, the liar, and Newcombe's paradox, and that enterprise doesn't at any stage require the provision of necessary and sufficient conditions for something's being a "philosophical paradox." The "definition" of a paradox that occurs on the book's first page is intended merely to present a quick and easy initial sense of what the book is about. The same sort of thing may be said of my throwaway line that an inference like the above-displayed sorites inference "presents a paradox because it tempts us to say three things that are mutually inconsistent: its first premise is true; its second premise is true; and its conclusion is false,"[1] or that "a philosophical paradox is a set of apparently mutually incompatible propositions each one of which enjoys some significant degree of plausibility when viewed on its own."[2] My concern wasn't to define 'paradox' but to come to terms with particular paradoxes that have set much of philosophy's agenda for the past 2400 or so years.

Philosophical paradoxes may be represented as sets of classically inconsistent propositions. The following three sets of propositions, for example, represent three famous paradoxes, namely, Cartesian skepticism (C), the problem of free will (F), and Grelling's "heterological" paradox (G), respectively:

(C1) I know that I have hands.

(C2) If (C1), then I know that I'm not a handless brain-in-a-vat being caused to have just the experiences I'm having.

(C3) I don't know that I'm not a handless brain-in-a-vat being caused to have just the experiences I'm having.

(F1) We sometimes act of our own free will.

(F2) Everything we do or think or want is caused by events of which we are ignorant and over which we had no control.

(F3) (F1) and (F2) are incompatible.

The predicate 'word,' being a word, is true of itself; the predicate 'dog,' not being a dog, isn't true of itself. Let's now introduce the predicate 'heterological' with the stipulation that a predicate is *heterological* iff it's not true of itself. Then we have the following paradox set whose sole member is:

(G3) 'Heterological' is or isn't heterological.

A *happy-face solution* to a paradox is a solution to a paradox which shows that the paradox isn't engendered by any "glitch" (or "bug")[3] in the concepts implicated in the paradox, and that therefore nothing about those concepts needs to be fixed or revised in order for us to be free of the paradox; we will be free of it once we recognize the *mistake* that led us into it. The concepts that are crucially involved in a paradox that has a happy-face solution may apply to everything (e.g. the concept of being self-identical) or to nothing (e.g. the concept of a round square), but they are typically ones that definitely apply to some things and definitely don't apply to other things, while also having a penumbra, a region of logical space in which their application is something less than unqualifiedly definite. Familiar attempts to provide happy-face solutions, such as compatibilist solutions to the problem of free will, aim to identify which member of the paradox set is definitely false, while recognizing that such an identification will be convincing only when accompanied by a good account of the mistake that kept us from recognizing that the proposition was false. In principle, however, a happy-face solution might try to show (i) that one or more of the propositions in the paradox set involve penumbral applications of key concepts in a way that makes it something less than unqualifiedly definite which member (or members) of the paradox set is false or (ii) that the set of classically inconsistent propositions isn't, or isn't definitely, the set of mutually incompatible propositions it might appear to be.[4] The Barber is a paradox that paradigmatically enjoys a happy-face solution. Before we realized its concealed inconsistency, we saw nothing wrong with the supposition that a village might contain a barber who shaves everyone in the village who doesn't shave her- or himself; but when we see the entailed contradiction, we rightly conclude that it's impossible for there to be such a barber. John Pollock, writing about the liar, said that a solution to it "must consist of an explanation of the meaning of 'true' and a demonstration that, given that analysis of 'true' the Liar sentence is not paradoxical."[5] Many other philosophers also give the impression that they suppose that a solution to a paradox must be a happy-face solution.

An *unhappy-face solution* to a paradox aims to resolve the paradox by locating its source in a glitch in one (or more) of the concepts responsible for the paradox and, once the glitch is identified, raises the further question of what to do about it. Charles Chihara, another philosopher who suspects that hardly any of the classical philosophical paradoxes have happy-face solutions, divides unhappy-face solutions into two parts. Picking up on Tarski's remark that "the appearance of an antinomy is ... a symptom of a disease,"[6] Chihara sees paradoxes (that require unhappy-face solutions) as raising two problems. The *diagnostic problem* is the problem of saying *what disease* the paradox is a symptom of; that is to say, it's "the problem of pinpointing that which is deceiving us and, if possible, explaining how and why the deception was produced...."[7] Using my own metaphor, I would say that the diagnostic problem is the problem of locating and explaining the conceptual glitch that engenders the paradox. The *preventative problem* is that of "devising languages or logical systems which capture certain essential or useful features of the relevant ... concepts, but within which the paradox cannot arise."[8] This is tendentious if it's intended to apply to every philosophical paradox that doesn't have a happy-face solution. I would call the second problem that needs to be addressed in an unhappy-face solution the *curative problem* and say that it's the problem of what to do about the glitchy concept that leads to paradox: Does the glitch prevent the concept from doing the work we want it to do? If not, is there a revision of, or replacement for, the concept that would do the job?

What I mean by a concept's having a glitch is that the underived, or protoconceptual role that individuates the concept and determines its content (insofar as anything determines its content) disposes one to make inconsistent judgments, and there is nothing in the concept itself to resolve that conflict. When we realize that there is this glitch in the concept's proto-conceptual role, we don't take it to determine an impossible content, but rather feel stymied by it. Realizing that the concept is defective in the way revealed by the glitch needn't prevent us from using the concept in cases, if there are any, unaffected by the glitch: even Tarski would have told you 'The earth is flat' is false. But the fact that the semantic paradoxes don't admit of a happy-face solution does show that the semantic concepts that engender those paradoxes are unfit for the important job we'd like the notion to play in formal metalogical theories. That is why the most important work on the semantic paradoxes is focused on finding an adequate replacement, of which there may be more than one. In the case of other unhappy-face paradoxes, such as the skeptical and free will paradoxes, the paradox-causing glitches infect all uses of the concepts. However, unlike the case of truth, it's not clear what talk of conceptual revision would even mean in these areas, given that philosophy books and journals are not widely read by the population at large. But let me not get into that now.[9]

What is there to be said for the hypothesis that certain philosophical paradoxes admit only of unhappy-face solutions? Well, for one thing, it explains the weak spot in known attempts to achieve happy-face solutions to those paradoxes. Philosophers in search of a happy-face solution to a given paradox have little difficulty coming up with what they take to be the odd-guy-out. For example, as regards the above displayed skeptical paradox, Sextus Empiricus and David Hume might reject (C1); Fred Dretske and Bob Nozick would reject (C2); many philosophers would reject (C3), although it might be hard to find three of them who reject it for the same reason; and contextualists reject (C1) in "high-standard" contexts and (C3) in "low-standard" contexts. As regards the paradox of free will, "hard determinists" reject (F1); "libertarians" reject (F2); and "compatibilists" reject (F3). Where these attempts saliently come up short is in their apparent inability to explain—or worse, their not even trying to explain—how it is that their now-exposed masquerader came by its excellent disguise in the first place. Consider, for example, attempts to solve the skeptical paradox by claiming that we do know that we're not brains-in-vats etc. If we know it, then how do we know it? The brain-in-the-vat skeptical hypothesis is a contingent hypothesis that, if true, explains why we have the experiences we have. So it's hard to see how we could have empirical evidence for its truth, nor does it seem the sort of proposition that we can know *a priori*. There may well be a sense in which we're "entitled" to accept that we're not brains-in-vats without having any reason to suppose that it's *true*, but what can that sort of entitlement do to show that we *know* that the proposition that we're not brains-in-vats is *true*? If, however, these paradoxes don't have happy-face solutions, then the designated odd-guy-out can't be unmasked in a way compatible with a happy-face solution. But can't we know that, say, (F3) is false without being able to explain why it seems plausible to so many people? After all, you may know that Harrisburg is the capital of Pennsylvania even though you can't explain why Clem believes that it's Pittsburgh. True enough, but that has nothing to do with the epistemic position of one for whom the problem of free will is a *paradox*. Anyone who has ever taught the problem of free will in a first philosophy course knows how easy it is to get students to feel the intuitive force of Bertrand Russell's quip that, while we may be able to do as we please, we can't please as we please,[10] and given that intuition the problem is this: The claim that acts are free when caused in the normal way by normal propositional attitudes and the claim that acts are not free if they are caused by events of which we were ignorant and over which we had no control, are, if true, conceptual truths, and the primary "evidence" for them is our inclination to accept them, our introspective knowledge of how we would judge hypothetical cases. Insofar as we're disinclined to suppose the concept is incoherent, we take our inclination to accept the one claim to be evidence against the other. Therefore, it's imperative that a satisfactory happy-face solution to the problem of free will not merely remind us of what we already know to be the intuitive case for the propositions in the paradox set with which a theorist's chosen odd-guy-out is in conflict, but must also explain away what by the theorist's lights is the spurious intuition that the designated proposition is true. An advantage, therefore, of the unhappy-face hypothesis is that it explains the conflicting intuitions that engender a paradox.

So, the proposal that a given paradox has an unhappy-face solution holds that the paradox is engendered by a glitch in one or more of the concepts essentially involved in the paradox. Horwich evidently doubts that any of the well-known philosophical paradoxes have unhappy-face solutions, and he has his own proposal for what engenders such paradoxes. Let's first look at his objections to the glitch proposal before examining his positive proposal.

The considerations Horwich brings to bear as reservations about the glitch theory are, together with my responses to those reservations, as follows:

i. Horwich says that my proposal is that "*every* classical philosophical paradox is caused by a concept... that is defective, in that its possession conditions incline us (in certain circumstances) towards incompatible beliefs,"[11] and he then goes on to give six examples of what he says are classical philosophical paradoxes that have happy-face solutions. These are Hempel's Ravens, Negative Existentials, Agrippan Skepticism, Normativity, Zeno, and Free Will.

Response. My proposal wasn't that *every* classical philosophical paradox has an unhappy-face solution; what I actually wrote was that "*few* of the classical philosophical paradoxes have happy-face solutions."[12] Besides, the notion of a *paradox* is pretty vague, the notion of a *classical* paradox even vaguer. In any event, the only ones of Horwich's six examples I would say are classical philosophical paradoxes that don't have happy-face solutions are Normativity and Free Will. *Cartesian* skepticism is a genuine paradox, and it doesn't in my view have a happy-face solution, but it isn't on Horwich's list, and I don't consider *Agrippan* skepticism, which is on his list, to be a paradox, since there are numerous propositions—e.g. *that I'm now having visual experiences* or *that if 3 is a number, then 3 is a number*—we evidently know even though we don't know them on the basis of knowing other propositions. Nor do I think many today consider Negative Existentials to be much of a *paradox*. Hempel's Ravens, however, is genuinely a paradox and does seem to have a Bayesian happy-face solution.

ii. Horwich's first reservation derives from his claim that he can give complete happy-face solutions to several classical philosophical paradoxes, where a "complete" such solution not only identifies which of the paradox-generating assumptions isn't the definite truth it might appear to be, but also explains how it came by its spurious appearance. His second reservation is that, since none of those unmaskings involves "conceptual revision,"

even if... Schiffer were right that one cannot undermine the apparent plausibility of any of the premises of a classical paradox [by showing that philosophers make a certain mistake in the deployment of perfectly OK concepts], we would have to demur from his particular explanation of this inability: namely, that our acceptance of the conflicting premises is tied to the deployment of certain operative concepts. (218–19)

Response. Two points. (a) The reason it's important that a solution to a paradox explain why the assumption identified by the theorist as the culprit seemed plausible is that unless that can be done we can't be confident that the culprit is what the theorist says it is. Sure, one can often know that a person's belief is definitely false without having a clue as to why she holds it: we might have such conclusive reason to think that the proposition is false that we know it can't be defeated by learning why so-and-so mistakenly believes it. But in the most powerful paradoxes our disposition to believe a proposition in the paradox set is based on one's intuition that it's true, but one's disposition to disbelieve it is likewise based on an intuition that the proposition can't be true, so we have a situation in which we have counterbalancing evidence for and against a proposition, and therefore can't have warrant to believe or disbelieve the proposition before one has discredited the opposite intuition. (b) The mere fact that one is in a position to believe that a paradox-generating proposition is false doesn't show that conceptual revision isn't called for. For example, as Horwich notes, Quine said that the principle that every instance of the schema

'F' is true of x iff x is F

"simply reflects what we mean in saying that adjectives are true of things,"[13] but given his commitment to classical logic and the fact that the classically inconsistent Grelling sentence

'Not true of itself' is true of itself iff it's not true of itself

is an instance of the schema, Quine was warranted in claiming not only that the principle articulating the meaning of 'true of' defined no coherent concept, and so must be false, but also that therefore a revised notion of truth was needed for the metalogical work for which logicians believe a notion of truth is needed.[14]

iii. Horwich's third reservation is that it's false that "if a concept is 'glitchy'... then no particular one of these commitments can be... identified as the false one which ought to be given up" (219).

Response. I completely agree—it's obvious that, for example, neither the "heterological" sentence (G) nor the sorites premise in a sorites inference of the kind displayed above can be definitely true—but to what that I say is it an objection?

iv. Many classical philosophical problems—the mind/body problem, the problem of knowledge, the problem of induction, the problem of free will, the sorites problem, etc.—derive from paradoxes. A striking thing about these paradoxes is that we are still trying to solve them, and in most cases have been trying to solve them for more than two thousand years. It's commonly assumed that two closely related things are required in order to solve a paradox. First, a solution must identify the odd-guy-out: it must show that the propositions comprising the paradox aren't really mutually incompatible, that they can all be true together, or else it must show which member of the set isn't true. Second, it must give a correct explanation of how the identified masquerader came by its spurious plausibility. These two requirements are closely related in that it would be impossible to know how a claim came by its spurious plausibility without knowing that the claim wasn't true, and it's hard to see how an argument could show that, say, a particular proposition in a paradox set was false without also explaining why that false proposition appeared to be true. To seek such a solution is to seek a happy-face solution. What explains the fact that after all this time there is no happy-face solution that any one of these paradoxes is widely recognized to have? Theorists have no trouble selecting this, that, or the other element of a paradox as being the odd-guy-out, but, I suggested, the difficulty in each case is in locating the mistake that led us to view a straightforwardly incorrect proposition as plausible. My suggestion was that philosophers haven't found the kind of solutions they seek because the problems for which they seek those solutions don't have them; they have instead unhappy-face solutions. That suggestion is the target of Horwich's final reservation. He raises two objections. The first is that, as he has already pointed out, the fact that paradoxes are engendered by conceptual glitches in the way I suggested "is in fact perfectly consistent with a determinate identification of which of the clashing commitments is the irrational one, the one to be abandoned or altered" (220). His second objection is that even if classical philosophical paradoxes have only unhappy-face solutions, that would not explain

> the inability of us philosophers to lay certain paradoxes permanently to rest. What it would lead us to expect, rather, is the existence of widespread agreement on the general need for unhappy-face solutions.... What we actually observe is that different philosophers endorse different approaches, debates are frequent and searching, yet consensus fails to emerge. And Schiffer's theory leaves us in the dark as to why that should be so. (220)

Response. I agree with the point made in the first objection but don't take it to be an objection, since my point is that there aren't successful happy-face solutions because philosophers don't succeed in explaining away the plausibility of what they take to be the mistaken step that engenders paradox. Virtually everyone who works on the sorites knows that the culprit is the assumption that if, for some designated sorites prone F, something is F, then so is something that is minutely and indiscernibly less F, but that hardly resolves the sorites. The second objection is one whose point I take, and it's a point that has troubled me for some time. Suppose the idea that, say, Free Will had no happy-face solution was one that became as well known and as much discussed as compatibilist happy-face solutions. It's an extremely safe bet that that wouldn't result in Free Will's being crossed off the list of unsolved philosophical problems in the way Fermat's conjecture has been crossed off the list of unsolved mathematical problems; the result would merely be that philosophers had merely increased the number of possible resolutions they disagree about. That would evidently show that the quest for happy-face solutions couldn't be the sole explanation for why philosophers continue to struggle with classical problems.

So much for Horwich's objections to the glitch theory of philosophical paradoxes. He also makes his own, Wittgenstein-inspired, positive proposal about the source of these paradoxes. The *over-generalization* approach, which is what he calls his proposal, claims that philosophical paradox issues from a certain kind of *fallacious reasoning*—namely, that (a) "by extrapolating irresponsibly from paradigm cases in which a term is deployed we ... wrongly persuade ourselves of some overly general principle about its proper application" (220) when (b) upon being made aware of the conflict between the overly general principle and the way we actually use the term in question we "refuse to let go of [the over-generalization] despite the mass of counter-evidence" (220) and (c) the reason we both accept these false over-generalizations and refuse to give them up, "despite the mass of counter-evidence" (220), is that "we tend to have a *scientistic* attitude towards philosophy: we search for simple theories, we expect them to hold, we hope thereby for discoveries that are interesting—even dramatically counterintuitive—and we feel that such results must be obtainable in principle if our subject is to be worthwhile" (220-1). Furthermore, "[T]he real reason certain paradoxes have remained philosophical problems for hundreds of years, even though some philosophers may have clearly stated their correct happy-face solutions, and thus the reason that the sort of progress displayed in physics and biology is seldom encountered in philosophy... is, ironically, the yearning for philosophy to resemble a science in delivering simple theories.... For such ambitions... are typically both the initial source of a paradox and the cause of our inability to agree on the right way out of it" (222).

Let's look at how Horwich applies his over-generalization view to two paradoxes that I believe don't have happy-face solutions, Normativity and Free Will. The paradox of Normativity is that, on the one hand, it seems to be the case both that there are moral facts and that, necessarily, awareness of those facts is intrinsically motivating, while, on the other hand, those two features seem incompatible. If it's an objective *fact* that eating animals is wrong, then why can't one's feeling about that fact be anything at all? Horwich's happy-face application of his over-generalization view is this:

> The main flaw here... is that... we have been guilty of over-generalization. No doubt *most* facts [are not intrinsically motivating].... But, if—as is indeed plausible—our conviction that torture is wrong *is* intrinsically motivating, then the extrapolation to *normative* facts is clearly a mistake.... After all: a normative fact is simply a true normative proposition. So if we believe... that torture is wrong, we can trivially infer the truth of the proposition that torture is wrong; and we thereby commit ourselves to the fact at issue [i.e. we commit ourselves to the existence of intrinsically motivating normative facts]. (217)

Moreover, Horwich is further committed to saying, the reason philosophers have a hard time seeing that their mistake here is inferring that no facts are intrinsically motivating because *most* aren't is that they are burdened with a "scientific attitude" towards philosophy.

I don't think Horwich has sketched a satisfactory happy-face solution. I don't even see how he has given the explanation his theory demands. The third sentence in the displayed quotation really needs to be:

> But if (a) it's a fact that torture is wrong (in the same sense of 'fact' that it's a fact that Hilda believes that torture is wrong) and (b) believing that torture is wrong is intrinsically motivating, then the extrapolation to normative facts is a mistake.

True enough, but how does that either address the worry that (a) and (b) are incompatible or show that belief in the incompatibility has anything to do with extrapolation or a scientific attitude? Philosophers don't worry about the compatibility of (a) and (b) because they are prone to over-generalization or have a scientific attitude. How would that explain how easy it is to get philosophy tyros to see the problem? What respectable philosopher who worries about the compatibility of (a) and (b) would try to justify her worry by saying that no non-moral facts were intrinsically motivating? Philosophers worry about the compatibility at least partly because they can't see what coherent story can be told about the information-processing by which one might come to know that torture has the property, where that processing was available only to those who feel a certain way about torture. Or suppose that two people of equal intelligence and imagination are agreed on all relevant non-normative facts but have different conative attitudes about euthanasia, which leads the one with the positive attitude to believe that euthanasia is morally justified whenever certain conditions are met and the one with the negative attitude to believe that euthanasia is always wrong. How would anyone know which of the two, if either, was right? If one person is right, how could she know that she is right? What theory of knowledge acquisition might be brought to bear to show that one person, but not the other, knows? In any case, the explanation of the paradox that is really implied by what Horwich says doesn't rely on either over-generalization or a scientistic attitude. It relies more on his minimalist theory of truth and of propositions, and thus of facts, and I doubt that those who don't yet accept those minimalist theories are being hampered by over-generalization or a scientistic attitude. Besides, it seems to me that, even given Horwich's minimalist conceptions, the most that he can explain is why it's no barrier to believing the proposition that torture is wrong that having that belief necessitates also having a negative attitude towards torture, but that doesn't imply that there is a determinate fact of the matter as to whether or not torture is wrong.

Free Will is a paradox in part because many have trouble seeing how an action can be done of one's own free will if one's doing it was caused by events that occurred before one was born, of which one is ignorant, and over which one had no control. And as anyone who has taught the problem of free will in an introductory course knows, it takes about ten minutes to get beginning students to see the problem. So perceiving a problem in supposing free will and determinism to be compatible evidently has nothing to do with over-generalization or a scientistic attitude. What, then, is the happy-face solution of this paradox implied by the over-generalization view? Horwich says that

> our normal naïve attitude is, very roughly speaking, to regard an act as un-free only when its causes bypass any deliberation or decision by the agent. Thus we do *not* intuitively think... that no externally-caused action can be voluntary. Rather, we think (roughly) that if a decision results from a normal process of deliberation and leads, in the normal way, to the act decided upon, that that act is free—and it doesn't matter if the deliberative process was itself somehow caused by external events. (218)

This strikes me as ignoring the problem rather than solving it. The 'thus' that begins the second of the displayed sentences is inappropriate. Horwich is right that we are inclined to judge an act free when caused by normal beliefs and intentions, but the reason Free Will is a *paradox* is that when determinism is spelled out for a person she then finds it difficult to think that an action caused by normal beliefs and intentions is free if those states supervene on physical states that were caused by other physical states of which one is ignorant and over which one has no control. Horwich seems to be denying rather than explaining the intuition of incompatibility, the intuition well expressed by Bertrand Russell when he wrote:

> If when a man writes a poem or commits a murder, the bodily movements involved in his act result solely from physical causes, it would seem absurd to put up a statue to him in the one case and to hang him in the other.[15]

If there is a happy-face compatibilist solution to the problem of free will, then it ought to be possible to identify the *mistake* from which this specious incompatibilist view arises, the mistake that leads this theorist to respond to compatibilism with another of

Russell's quips—one already cited—that of course we can do as we please, but we can't please as we please. Horwich does nothing to explain away this intuition, let alone show that it results from over-generalization or the scientistic attitude of philosophers.

To sum up, I agree with Horwich that the glitch theorist should be worried about the fact that taking his view seriously wouldn't shorten the lives of philosophical paradoxes, but would merely result in adding one more position on the paradoxes for philosophers to disagree about. At the same time, I don't see that the over-generalization approach has yet been developed in a way that shows it to be promising.

Notes

1. (1996: 317).
2. (2003: 68). Charles Chihara (1979: n. 24) reminds us that Tarski quickly followed his definition of a true sentence as "one which says that the state of affairs is so and so, and the state of affairs is indeed so and so" with the comment: "From the point of view of formal correctness, clarity, and freedom from ambiguity of expressions occurring in it, the above formulation obviously leaves much to be desired. Nevertheless, its intuitive meaning and general intention seem to be quite clear and intelligible" (1956: 155).
3. My use of 'glitch' is an extension of the notion of a software glitch or bug, where that is a flaw in a computer program that prevents the program from working as it's supposed to work.
4. A set of propositions is classically inconsistent if a contradiction may be derived from them in classical logic; propositions are mutually incompatible if it's impossible for them to be true together.
5. Pollock (1970: 79), quoted by Chihara (1979: 608), with whom I share the view that most classical philosophical paradoxes have unhappy-face solutions.
6. Tarski (1969: 66).
7. Chihara (1979: 590).
8. Chihara (1979: 591).
9. See Schiffer (1996), (2004).
10. In fact, while Russell makes a closely related point (Russell 1910: 38–9), the attribution is spurious.
11. Horwich (this volume: 216); my emphasis.
12. Schiffer (2003: 197); emphasis added.
13. Quine (1966: 7).
14. See also Chihara's discussion of his Seclib example in (1979).
15. (1957: 32).

Bibliography

Chihara, C. (1979). "The Semantic Paradoxes: A Diagnostic Investigation." *The Philosophical Review* 88: 590–618.
Pollock, J. (1970). "The Truth about Truth: A Reply to Brian Skyrms." In *The Paradox of the Liar*, edited by R. Martin, New Haven: Yale University Press.
Quine, W. (1966). "The Ways of Paradox." In *The Ways of Paradox and Other Essays*, New York: Random House.
Russell, B. (1957). *Why I am Not a Christian*. London: Routledge.

Sainsbury, M. (1987). *Paradoxes*. Cambridge: Cambridge University Press.
Schiffer, S. (1996). "Contextualist Solutions to Scepticism." *Proceedings of the Aristotelian Society* 96: 317–33.
Schiffer, S. (2003). *The Things We Mean*. Oxford: Clarendon Press.
Schiffer, S. (2004). "Skepticism and the Vagaries of Justified Belief." *Philosophical Studies* 119: 161–84.
Tarski, A. (1956). "The Concept of Truth in Formalized Languages." In *Logic, Semantics, Metamathematics*, Oxford: Clarendon Press.
Tarski, A. (1969). "Truth and Proof." *Scientific American* 220: 66.

21

Gricean Semantics and Reference
Responses to Anita Avramides, Stephen Neale, and Kent Bach

21.1 Introduction

The three essays in this section—by Anita Avramides, Stephen Neale, and Kent Bach—are interrelated in that the essays by Avramides and Neale are concerned, albeit in different ways, with the viability of Gricean semantics, while Bach's essay raises issues about definite descriptions that are close to the issues about "aphonic" singular terms raised by Neale.

Avramides distinguishes between Grice's program of providing necessarily true biconditionals that correlate semantic notions on their left-hand sides with propositional-attitude notions on their right-hand sides, and the program I called *intention-based semantics* (IBS), which was concerned not merely to *define* the semantic in terms of the psychological, as per the Gricean program, but also to *reduce* the semantic to the psychological, an important distinction for one who, like Avramides, would like to combine Gricean analyses of meaning with the Davidsonian view that propositional-attitude notions and meaning notions are interlocking notions neither of which can be explicated independently of the other.[1] Avramides claims that I threw the baby out with the bathwater when in *Remnants of Meaning* I rejected Gricean semantics along with IBS; that is to say, she claims that the objections I raised in *Remnants* against IBS weren't also objections to Gricean semantics, and that, consequently, while I had good reasons to reject IBS, I mistakenly took those reasons also to be reasons to reject the Gricean program, which they weren't. I take issue with that claim in my response to Avramides, and spell out the argument in *Remnants* that I thought, and continue to think, is devastating to the Gricean's attempt to define notions of meaning in terms of propositional-attitude notions.

In "The Basis of Reference" (1978) and "Indexicals and the Theory of Reference" (1981) I tried to show how the various notions of speaker- and expression-reference could be defined in terms of the Gricean's definitions of speaker- and expression-meaning. Neale is sympathetic to those aspirations but worries about how "aphonic" referring expressions, such as the linguist's PRO, can be kept from frustrating them. I try to indicate the Gricean's best strategy for accommodating aphonic singular terms, but I have combined my response to Neale with my response to Avramides because my discussion of the issues about aphonics raised by Neale concludes with the claim that if the argument I rehearsed in responding to Avramides is sound, we have no reason to care how aphonics might best be brought under the Gricean umbrella, for the argument shows that the umbrella can't be opened in the first place.

The issues about aphonics raised by Neale are of direct relevance to questions about the plausibility of Russell's theory of definite descriptions. For most defenders of Russell's theory claim that the best way for the theory to accommodate "incomplete" descriptions like the one in 'The cat is sleeping' is to see sentences of the form 'The F is G' as expressing the propositional form $[the_x: Fx\ at\ t_u\ \&\ \Delta_x\ at\ t_u]Gx\ at\ t_u$, where '$t_u$' indicates a tense-mandated slot for the time of utterance and 'Δ_x' indicates a slot for a property, which may in the limit be the null property, that was implicitly expressed in the utterance of 'The F is G', and was thus an unarticulated constituent of the asserted proposition relative to the surface form of 'The F is G', and intended by the speaker to conjoin with the property of being F to yield a complex property that was instantiated by just one thing. This analysis raises for these Russellians the question whether expressions of the form 'the F' have an unpronounced indexical whose referents would be the values of the unarticulated property constituent in the propositions asserted in literal utterances of sentences of the form 'The F is G'. In "Descriptions, Indexicals, and Belief Reports: Some Dilemmas (But Not the Ones You Expect)" (1995) and "Russell's Theory of Definite Descriptions" (2005) I argued (in effect) that no unarticulated-constituent version of Russell's theory of descriptions could be correct, and that the semantic content of a literal utterance of 'The F is G' when 'the F' is used referentially is a nondescriptive x-dependent proposition, where x is the F thing to which the speaker refers with her utterance of 'the F'. Bach's preferred way of being a Russellian, however, is not the unarticulated-constituent way I discussed in my two articles. On his version, the proposition expressed by every sentence of the form 'The F is G' is the propositional form $[the_x: Fx\ at\ t_u]Gx\ at\ t_u$, which implies that an utterance of 'The cat is sleeping' is true only if at the time of the utterance the universe contains one and only one cat, thus forcing Bach also to hold that what a speaker means in uttering a sentence of the form 'The F is G' is hardly ever the proposition that is the semantic content of her utterance. Bach's essay is concerned to show that, while I may have raised good objections to the versions of Russell's theory I discussed in my articles, those objections don't apply to his version, thus leaving his theory as the version of the theory of descriptions that best undermines the motivation for claiming that the meaning of definite descriptions gives them a use as genuinely referential singular terms. In my response to Bach I suggest that some of the objections I raise to the versions of Russell's theory I discussed also apply to his theory, and that, in any case, there are good objections to his theory that don't apply to unarticulated-constituent versions of the theory of descriptions.

21.2 Is Gricean Semantics Defensible? Response to Anita Avramides and Stephen Neale

Let *Gricean semantics* be a commitment to these two claims:

1. A certain notion of speaker-meaning is definable, without reference to any public-language semantic notions, in terms of acting with certain audience-directed intentions.[2]

2. All other public-language semantic notions are definable, without reference to any public-language semantic notions, in terms that include those that define speaker-meaning.

The particular notion of definability appealed to in these conditions has it that to define a notion is to specify *a priori* metaphysically necessary and sufficient conditions for its application. When a philosopher defines what it is to be F by writing an open sentence of the form 'Fx iff C_1x & ... & C_nx' what she really means is that the universal closure of that formula is a metaphysically necessary truth. A definition in this sense doesn't *logically* entail that the notion it's defining *reduces* to the notions specified in its definiens, for it's *logically* consistent with the truth of a definition, in the stipulated sense, that notions appealed to on its right-hand side can't themselves be defined, or otherwise explicated, other than in terms of the notion they are serving to define.

Let *intention-based semantics* (IBS) be Gricean semantics plus (a) the claim that Gricean definitions *reduce* all questions about linguistic representation to questions about mental representation, in a sense of 'reduce' that precludes explaining mental representation—i.e. propositional attitudes—even partly in terms of any public-language semantic notions, together with (b) the claim that a principle motivation for pursuing the Gricean program is that it's mandated by the best strategy for reducing all intentional notions to physical or functional notions. The view encapsulated in (b) is that propositional-attitude tokens and types must be reducible to physical or functional tokens and types in order to account for their causal-explanatory roles, and that the best strategy for reducing the semantic and the psychological to the physical/functional is first to reduce the semantic to the psychological, and that the best strategy for reducing the semantic to the psychological is via Gricean semantics. For all that presently matters, we may understand reduction for the IBS theorist to require identifying target properties and relations with those specified in their Gricean analyses.[3]

Anita Avramides rejects both parts of IBS, but she evidently accepts both parts of Gricean semantics. Her essay aims to defend Gricean semantics from objections I made to it in *Remnants of Meaning*. Stephen Neale wonders whether Gricean semantics can be saved, as he hopes it can be, from a feature of linguistic theory that he takes to threaten a Gricean accommodation of expression-reference. I'll begin with Neale but will interrupt my response to him to respond to Avramides, as my response to her will provide me with what I need to complete my response to Neale.

21.2.1 Neale: Are aphonic terms consistent with Gricean semantics?

Neale's essay presents a marvelously clear and comprehensive exposition of Gricean semantics, and, from the perspective of that program, an exhaustive account of implicit reference. As a Gricean, he endorses the attempt to explain speaker-reference in terms of speaker-meaning, and expression-reference in terms of speaker-reference, but his study of implicit reference has revealed to him that a certain view he accepts is in tension with his acceptance of Gricean semantics.

Since the publication of Chomsky's *Lectures on Government and Binding* in 1981, mainstream linguistic theory has recognized that sentences may contain "*null constituents* (also known as *empty categories*)—i.e. constituents which have grammatical and semantic features but lack phonetic features (and so are 'silent' or 'inaudible')."[4] 'Aphonic' is Neale's word for terms that are null constituents of the sentences in which they occur. Neale sees that certain claims about the need for aphonics—especially the need for them in sentences whose utterances are paradigms of implicit reference—are based on views for which no one has yet provided good reasons to accept, but, at the same time, he has no compelling arguments against those views and, more importantly, he believes that there are sentences whose logical forms do contain aphonic referring terms. What Neale has come to appreciate, as we'll now see, is that his acceptance of aphonic referring terms is in tension with his acceptance of Gricean semantics.

Neale understands that a Gricean account of reference must recognize (*inter alia*) three reference relations:

(A) S refers to x in (the course of) uttering u.
(B) In uttering u, S refers to x with the ith occurrence of e in u.
(C) The ith occurrence of e in u refers to x relative to S's utterance of u.

The problem Neale understands aphonics to create for Gricean semantics is that, on the one hand, aphonics must be counted among the witnesses to 'e' in (C), but that, on the other hand, it's difficult to see how aphonics can satisfy the defining conditions of (C), given the way the Gricean appears to be constrained to define (C) in terms of (B) and (B) in terms of (A). This may be spelled out in the following way.

For the Gricean, (A) is the fundamental notion of reference in that all other notions of reference are to be directly or indirectly defined in terms of it, while it itself is defined in terms of the Gricean's account of speaker-meaning. In (1981) I took the core case of (A) to be what I called primary, or first-order, speaker-reference (reference$_p$) and defined it as:

S refers$_p$ to x in uttering u iff in uttering u, S performs an act of speaker-meaning whose propositional content is an x-dependent proposition,

where an *x-dependent proposition* is a proposition that wouldn't exist if x didn't exist and is individuated partly in terms of x. In order to avoid the daunting but unavoidable complexity of a full-on Gricean semantics, Neale harmlessly (for his purposes) pretends that all referring-in is primary referring-in, and that an x-dependent proposition is a singular proposition of which x is a constituent. Now, suppose Jane utters

1. He is Canadian, but he is Australian,

indicating Tom with her first utterance of 'he', Dick with her second. Then Jane would have referred both to Tom and to Dick *in* uttering (1), and she would have referred to Tom *with* the first occurrence of 'he' in (1) and to Dick with the second. It is to secure her audience's recognition of the things to which she is referring *in* uttering a sentence that a speaker refers to those things *with* terms that occur in the sentence, and in (1981) I gave what was tantamount to the following first approximation to a definition of (B) (relative to the pretense that all referring-in is primary referring-in):

In uttering u, S refers to x with the ith occurrence of e in u iff for some audience A and relation R, in uttering u S intended it to be mutual knowledge between S and A

that R holds among the ith occurrence of e in u, S's utterance of u and x, and, primarily on the basis of this, that S is referring to x in uttering u.[5]

Although the *raison d'être* of reference-with is to enable the speaker's audience to identify the thing, or one of the things, about which she means something, it isn't a necessary condition of S's referring to x *in* uttering u that she also refer to x *with* some part of u. For suppose that the adulterous lovers Hansel and Gretel agree on the following simple signal: if either places a blue light in his or her bedroom window, he or she will mean thereby that his or her spouse is away. If Gretel now places a blue light in her bedroom window, then in doing so she means that her husband, Fritz, is away, and therefore refers to Fritz *in* placing the light in the window, but there is no part of that simple signal *with which* she referred to him. In (1981) I said cases of implicit reference were also examples of referring-in unaided by referring-with, as when in uttering

2. It's raining

Sid meant that it was raining in Paris, and therefore referred to Paris in uttering (2). But aphonics hadn't yet been conceived when I wrote that paper and, consequently, I assumed that if in uttering a sentence σ S referred to something with an expression that occurred in σ, then that expression was *uttered* in the course of uttering σ. Had I known about aphonic terms when I wrote (1981)—and especially if I had anticipated the view Neale calls *truth-conditional semantics*, and with it the need to claim that in the sentence that is phonologically realized as (2) there lurks an aphonic term whose referent relative to Sid's utterance of (2) was Paris—then I would have said that

S *implicitly* refers to x in uttering u iff S refers to x at least once in uttering u without referring to x with his *utterance* of some proper part of u,

thereby leaving it open whether in uttering (2) Sid referred to Paris with some *un*uttered—i.e. aphonic—term in (2).

It is of the essence of Gricean semantics that the semantic properties of linguistic expressions are to be explained in terms of the Gricean's account of speaker-meaning. The explanation may, however, be indirect, and in the case of the referential properties of expressions the idea is that expression-reference is first to be explained in terms of speaker-reference, and then speaker-reference in terms of speaker-meaning. More specifically, the idea as regards (C) is that:

The ith occurrence of e in u refers to x relative to S's utterance of u iff in uttering u, S refers to x with the ith occurrence of e in u.[6]

So the problem aphonics pose for the Gricean should now be clear:

I. It follows from the Gricean's definitions of (C) and (B) that

The ith occurrence of e in u refers to x relative to S's utterance of u iff for some audience A and relation R, in uttering u S intended it to be mutual knowledge between S and A that R holds among the ith occurrence of e in u, S's utterance of u and x, and, primarily on the basis of this, that S is referring to x in uttering u.

II. But ordinary speakers are unaware of the existence of aphonics, and it's therefore difficult to see how they could have the intention the Gricean requires them to have.

Recall Sid's utterance of (2), whose semantic content was the proposition *that it was raining in Paris*, and suppose, as some would have it, that (2) contains the aphonic location pronoun α, so that, using bold font to represent aphonic expressions, we could at a certain stage of syntactic analysis represent (2) as

3. It's raining **in α**.

It would then follow that the occurrence of **α** in (2) referred to Paris relative to Sid's utterance of (2). But how could there have been a relation R such that Sid, who is completely ignorant of the fact that (3) represents the logical form of (2), have uttered (2) intending it to be mutual knowledge between him and his audience that R holds among the occurrence of **α** in (2), Sid's utterance of (2) and Paris, and, primarily on the basis of that, also mutual knowledge between them that Sid referred to Paris in uttering (2)? Neale says he is galvanized in part by "Chomskyan talk of tacit knowledge of language, and more general talk of tacit beliefs, desires, and intentions (including Loar's (1976a) suggestion that both S's communicative intentions and A's recognition of them might be partly unconscious),"[7] to take seriously the idea that, for some relation R, an ordinary guy like Sid might—in a sense of 'tacit' "that would need to be elucidated"[8]—*tacitly* intend it to be mutual *tacit* knowledge that R holds among the occurrence of **α** in (2), Sid's utterance of (2) and Paris, and, primarily on the basis of that mutual *tacit* knowledge, mutual *non*-tacit knowledge between them that Sid referred to Paris in uttering (2). It seems quite clear to me, however, that no appeal to "tacit mental" states can help the Gricean with the problem aphonics pose for him. Let me explain.

Neale mentions both Chomsky's and Loar's talk of tacit mental states, but they definitely can't be "tacit" mental states in Loar's sense.[9] Actually, Loar doesn't use the word 'tacit' but speaks rather of *implicit* beliefs and intentions. Of course, the fact that he uses 'implicit' rather than 'tacit' is irrelevant; what matters is what he means in speaking of implicit intentions or other propositional attitudes. To see what he means, consider your belief two minutes ago that you weren't then nude, or your belief this morning that the sidewalks were wet because it rained during the night, or your desire not to be hit by a speeding car which explained your stepping back to the curb when you saw a speeding car headed your way, or your expectation, when engrossed in philosophical conversation, that when I hear you say to me 'Please pass the salt' I will pass you the salt because you requested me to pass you the salt. These are the sorts of propositional attitudes apt to be "implicit" in the sense Loar intended: one has these propositional attitudes without being consciously aware that one has them, but it typically wouldn't require much effort for one to become consciously aware of them, although sometimes, when they are part of a complex explanation of one's behavior, one may have to be patiently brought to see that one has them, as someone might have to be brought to see that her intention in uttering 'It's snowing in Tucson' was that her hearer would take her to be confident that she knows that it's snowing in Tucson and to have that as the evidence on which he comes to believe that it's snowing in Tucson. Loar was calling attention to the nature of these propositional attitudes in order to defend Gricean accounts of speaker-meaning from the charge that they lacked psychological reality owing to the complexity of the propositional attitudes they required speakers to have. These "implicit" beliefs and intentions are beliefs and intentions in the most straightforward, vernacular sense of 'belief' and 'intention', and back in the day Griceans always supposed it to go without needing to be said that the intentions Griceans hypothesized were nearly always "implicit" in Loar's sense. It's obvious that in that sense of 'implicit knowledge' no ordinary speaker implicitly knows that 'It's raining' includes an aphonic location pronoun.

An altogether very different sense of 'tacit knowledge' (aka 'subdoxastic/subpersonal belief')[10] is the kind of state that Chomsky would regard as justifying the claim that each speaker knows the correct grammar of her I-language. Chomsky spoke of "knowledge" of language because he wanted to emphasize that he wasn't concerned with a version of knowledge-how, or any similar dispositional notion of the sort acceptable to behaviorists. But all he meant by saying that the language user has knowledge of her language was that the grammar that defines the language was subpersonally represented. It doesn't follow from this that the state in which it's represented is a state of propositional knowledge in any sense remotely like what we ordinarily take to be a knowledge state. As Ray Jackendoff remarked, the sense in which a three-year-old child "knows" that 'every' is a Determiner in English is the same sense as that in which the child "knows that the fifth note of *Happy Birthday* is a perfect fourth above the first note... even though she knows no music theory and wouldn't have the slightest idea what a 'perfect fourth' is."[11] Subpersonal representational states are knowledge-like only in the sense that they need to represent truths if they are to function properly in our information processing. They are not available to consciousness, and they are not inferentially integrated with ordinary propositional attitudes in the way those propositional attitudes are with one another, so that, for example, if one intends to perform a certain act only if such-and-such is the case and one believes that such-and-such is the case, then, all else being equal, one will at least try to perform that act; but if one intends to perform a certain act only if such-and-such is the case and one is in a subpersonal state that represents such-and-such as being the case, then that will have no effect on whether or not one performs the act. Chomskyan "tacit" knowledge and subdoxastic/subpersonal "beliefs" and "intentions" are not knowledge, beliefs or intentions on any reading of those terms a Gricean can recognize: for a Gricean to claim that 'intends' in his definition of speaker-meaning or speaker-reference should be read as subsuming "tacit" intentions would be like a linguistics professor giving everyone in her syntax course an A because there is good reason to suppose her students have tacit knowledge of the principles of syntax her course was about.

The "tacit mental" state account of how aphonics secure their reference is extremely implausible quite independently of whether or not holding the account would require a theorist to relinquish any claim to being a Gricean. For to hold the account would be to hold an account of aphonic reference that was hostage to an empirical speculation about language processing for which there was not the slightest bit of evidence. If it's reasonable to take the tacit-state line on what determines the reference of aphonics, then it's just as reasonable to take any other line wherein aphonic reference is secured by subpersonal information processing of a kind we have no reason to believe occurs. If there is any way for a Gricean to recognize that (2) might contain an aphonic location pronoun α, his only hope is to find a view that doesn't require the speaker to refer to a location *with* the occurrence of α in (2). In other words, he must recognize that, if there are aphonic referring expressions, they constitute counterexamples to his above-displayed definition of (C) in terms of (B) and thus require him to seek another way of defining (C) that is compatible with the essential tenets of Gricean semantics. Whether or not this can be done is a question I will later touch on.

There is also a challenging question to be confronted by any theorist who recognizes aphonic referring expressions, whether or not she is a Gricean. For suppose that the LF representation of (2) ('It's raining') is (3) (⌜It's raining in α⌝). Then it's reasonable to assume that the occurrence of α in (2) refers to location l relative to S's utterance of (2) just in case in uttering (2) S meant *that it was raining in l* (since S refers to location l in uttering (2) iff in uttering (2) S means *that it's raining in l*). It's also reasonable to assume—in fact, it would be incredible not to assume—that the presence of α in (2) plays *some* essential role in enabling S to refer to the location to which he refers in uttering (2). Indeed, a constraint that should be satisfied by *any* account of expression-reference is:

> Expression-reference constraint (ERC)
>
> If an occurrence of τ in a sentence σ refers to x relative to S's utterance of σ in part because S referred to x in uttering σ, then that occurrence of τ in σ should be implicated in the explanation of how S was able to refer to x in uttering σ.

Phonic referring expressions—i.e. referring expressions that are uttered whenever a sentence containing one is uttered—have no trouble satisfying ERC, for if an occurrence of phonic τ in σ refers to x relative to S's utterance of σ, then that is because S referred to x *with* that occurrence of τ in σ. But that can't be true of aphonic referring expressions. How, then, can *aphonic* referring expressions satisfy ERC? How, for example, would the occurrence of the aphonic location pronoun in (2) enter into the explanation of how a speaker was able to refer to a particular location in uttering (2)? The only answer I can think of consists in the elaboration of two claims, which I shall state as regards their application to Sid's unembedded utterance of (2) *on the assumption that its logical form contains the aphonic phrase* ⌜in α⌝.

> A. *That Sid was able to refer to Paris in uttering (2) is explained in part by the meaning of (2).* Elaboration: For any S, p, and x, S means p in uttering x only if for some feature ϕ and audience A, S utters x intending A to recognize that x has ϕ and to infer in part therefrom that S uttered x with those intentions constitutive of S's meaning p in uttering x. When x is a sentence of a language shared by S and A, the operative feature ϕ will be x's having the meaning it has in that language. For Sid to refer to Paris in uttering (2) is just for him to mean *that it's raining in Paris* in producing that utterance. To know the meaning of (2) is to know that in a literal and unembedded utterance of (2) there is a location l such that in uttering (2) the speaker means *that it's raining in l*. Sid intends his audience, A, to infer from the fact that [he uttered (2) and (2) has

the meaning it has] that for some location *l* he means in uttering (2) *that it's raining in l*; and then he intends other facts that are mutual knowledge between Sid and his audience to enable her to infer that *l* = Paris. That is how the meaning of (2) is implicated in explaining how Sid was able to refer to Paris in uttering (2).

B. *The meaning of (2) is determined by the semantical import of its syntactic structure and the meanings of its constituent morphemes, including those that are aphonic, and it's the presence of the aphonic phrase ⌜in α⌝ that brings with it the requirement that in a literal and unembedded utterance of (2) there is a location to which the speaker refers in uttering (2).* Elaboration: Speakers know that the meaning of (2) requires one who produces a literal and unembedded utterance of it to mean, for some location *l*, that it's raining in *l*, and that alone accounts for the role (2)'s meaning plays in enabling Sid to refer to Paris in uttering (2). It doesn't matter what determines (2) to have that meaning, and neither Sid nor his audience needs to know what determines that meaning. At the same time, given the assumption that (3) represents the logical form of (2), the occurrence of the aphonic phrase ⌜**in α**⌝ in (2) plays its essential role in determining the meaning of (2). Had Sid uttered 'It's raining there' to mean that it was raining in Paris, then there would be a different explanation of how Sid was able to refer to Paris in uttering that sentence, and that explanation would entail Sid's referring to Paris *with* his utterance of 'there', and hence would require Sid to know not just the meaning of that sentence but the meaning of 'there' as well.

So that, I submit, is how ERC would be satisfied if (2) is as (3) represents it to be. The question now is whether that explanation is consistent with Gricean semantics. My response to Avramides will position me to answer that question.

21.2.2 *Avramides: Can Gricean intentions abide?*

In *Remnants of Meaning* I rejected the reductionist aspirations of IBS, but I also rejected Gricean semantics. Avramides worries whether I might not have thrown out the Gricean baby with the IBS bathwater. More specifically, she says that I took a wrong turning when I elaborated Grice's work in the context of IBS:

> To reject Griceanism because one rejects IBS is to overlook the fact that IBS always had *two* components [viz. Griceanism and the IBS increment]. What linked the two components in Schiffer's mind was always reductionism. And it is reductionism that Schiffer has grown wary of.[12]

Here I must protest. I didn't reject Griceanism in *Remnants* because I rejected reductionism. I rejected Griceanism for reasons that were entirely independent of anything added by IBS. One reason was that I came to doubt whether one could define speaker-meaning wholly in terms of non-semantic propositional attitudes, but what I took to be the strongest objection in 1987 (and continue to think is the strongest objection) is one I stated in Chapter 9 of *Remnants*. It is essential to Gricean semantics that one be able to use its definition of speaker-meaning to give an account of expression-meaning (Gricean semantics would hardly be of much interest if it merely offered an account of speaker-meaning with no indication of how that account might need to figure into an account of expression-meaning), but in the chapter to which I just referred I argued that, *even if the Gricean could define speaker-meaning in terms of acting with non-semantic intentions, that account of speaker-meaning would not be of any use in defining expression-meaning.* The argument for this may be elaborated in the following way.

In his 1957 article "Meaning," Grice distinguished a central sense of 'meaning' applicable to speakers, as in

> In uttering 'Il pleut', Pierre meant that it was raining in Paris,

from the sense of 'meaning' applicable to sounds and marks, as in

> 'La neige est blanche' means in French that snow is white,

and he proposed the following account of speaker-meaning (wherein 'to utter x' is stipulated to mean the same as 'to do or produce something x'):

> S meant something in uttering x iff, for some person A and response r, S uttered x intending
>
> (i) to produce r in A;
> (ii) A to recognize S's intention (i);
> (iii) A's recognition of S's intention (i) to function as at least part of A's reason for A's response r.

(Grice offered no formula for specifying what S meant, but he did imply that when, for some proposition p, S intends A to believe p, then S meant p.)

At the end of his short article, Grice very briefly touches on expression-meaning. He offers two equivalences without any elaboration. The first is that:

> 'x meant something' is (roughly) equivalent to 'Somebody meant something [in uttering] x'.

For example, if Gretel rolls her eyes to communicate to Hansel that the speaker is a pretentious bore, then, by the definition, Gretel's eye rolling meant something. The second generalization is that:

> 'x means (timeless) that so-and-so' might as a first shot be equated with some statement or disjunction of statements about what "people" (vague) intend (with qualifications about "recognition") to effect by x.

A careful reader should be puzzled by what Grice says about expression-meaning. First, the equivalence offered for 'x meant something' seems not to be an analysis of any obvious pre-theoretic notion, but is more in the nature of a stipulation whose theoretical purpose hasn't been revealed. Second, there is no mention of word meaning. And third, the second equivalence, which is intended to cover indicative sentence meaning, appears to ignore the fact that every natural language has infinitely many sentences that will never be, or even could be, uttered. So why is Grice's article so famous and thought by many to be of such great importance? Does the importance of Grice's article reside wholly in his suggested account of speaker-meaning, never mind any relevance that account might have for an account of expression-meaning?

I don't think so. Those who perceive Grice's article to be important do so because they take themselves to discern in his account of speaker-meaning an *invisible hand* that guides them from the intentions that define speaker-meaning to an account of expression-meaning in terms of those intentions. In order to make that invisible-hand strategy visible, we need first to make explicit something that is implicit in Grice's 1957 account of speaker-meaning, and then we need to tweak it in one further respect. Suppose that Ann utters 'It's raining' with the intention of informing Ben, by means of his recognition of her intention to inform him, that it's raining in Boston. How will Ann expect Ben to know that she uttered 'It's raining' intending to inform him that it was raining in Boston? What Grice had in mind was that, for some feature ϕ, Ann intended what she uttered to have ϕ, intended Ben to recognize that it has ϕ, and intended the fact that it has ϕ to be taken by Ben to be a premise in an abductive inference—an "inference to the best explanation"—to the conclusion that Ann uttered 'It's raining' intending to inform him that it's raining in Boston. This is captured in the following refinement of Grice's definition:

S meant something in uttering x iff for some feature ϕ, person A and response r, S uttered x intending

(i) x to have ϕ;
(ii) A to recognize that x has ϕ;
(iii) A's recognition that x has ϕ to function as at least part of A's reason for believing that S uttered x intending:
(iv) to produce r in A;
(v) A's recognition of S's intention to produce r in A to function as at least part of A's reason for A's response r.

When these conditions are realized, numerous features of x will satisfy (i). For example, when Ann uttered 'It's raining' she expected Ben to recognize that 'It's raining' was an English sentence and expected that recognition to be crucial to his inferring that Ann uttered the sentence intending to inform him that it was raining in Boston. What the invisible-hand strategy isolates is that feature of x which is, loosely put, the *maximal* feature the speaker intends to be evidentially relevant irrespective of facts about the circumstances of utterance. Let's call this feature of x its *inference-base feature*—its *IB-feature*, for short.

The foregoing revision of Grice's account of speaker-meaning requires a further tweak before it's suitably set up to generate the Gricean strategy for explaining expression-meaning in terms of the conditions that define speaker-meaning. The further revision is initially mandated by the fact that Grice's original definition of speaker-meaning fails to provide a set of jointly sufficient conditions for speaker-meaning, and fails in a way that can't be repaired by adding more n^{th}-order intentions that $(n-1)^{th}$-order intentions be recognized. Griceans may dispute the best way of achieving a sufficient condition, but I believe that some version of the revision I suggested in *Meaning* provides the best and clearest way of showing how speaker-meaning is supposed to combine with general principles of rational action to yield an account of expression-meaning. What I suggested was that to achieve a sufficient condition we needed what I called *mutual knowledge*, a notion very close to

David Lewis's notion of *common knowledge*, though the two accounts were arrived at independently. There are better and worse ways to understand mutual knowledge, and I might not have opted for the best way in my book. The essential job mutual knowledge needs to perform is to capture the sense in which acts of communication require the defining features of speaker-meaning to be "out in the open" between speaker and hearer. In *Meaning* I offered a set of finite conditions for generating mutual knowledge, and I now think that I would have done best simply to have identified mutual knowledge with a version of those base conditions. In any case, for present purposes I'll continue to use 'mutual knowledge' and its cognates as dummy expressions for whatever turns out to be the best accommodation of the requisite out-in-the-openness. It should, however, be noted that in whatever way we choose to understand the notion of mutual (or common) knowledge, the notion must encompass every condition that is necessary for speaker-meaning, from which it follows that if a necessary condition for S's meaning p in uttering x is that S utter x intending S and her audience, A, mutually to know that S uttered x with such-and-such intentions, then it's also a necessary condition for S's meaning p in uttering x that S utter x intending S and A mutually to know that S uttered x intending S and A mutually to know that S uttered x with such-and-such intentions. What is needed is a way of capturing this that avoids a vicious regress, and I'm not confident that can be done. The following revision of Grice's definition doesn't quite achieve a set of conditions that can confidently be taken to be jointly sufficient for speaker-meaning, but they would, I think, be entailed by conditions that could confidently be taken to be sufficient, if such conditions are obtainable:

> [SM] S meant p in uttering x iff for some ϕ and A, S uttered x intending it to be mutual knowledge between S and A that x has ϕ and, at least partly on that basis, mutual knowledge that S uttered x intending A to believe p and intending their mutual knowledge that S uttered x intending A to believe p to be at least part of A's reason for believing p.

The definition of imperatival meaning—S's meaning that so-and-so is to do such-and-such—is *mutatis mutandis* the same. Grice's definition can stand further improvement, but we're now well enough positioned to see how Gricean speaker-meaning implies a strategy for defining expression-meaning in terms of it.

The Gricean takes *meaning properties* to be optimal IB-features, and it's not difficult to see why that should be if sentence meanings are such that to produce an unembedded utterance of a sentence in conformity with its meaning requires the speaker to mean a proposition of a certain specific form, as, for example, the meaning of 'It's raining' requires one who produces an unembedded utterance of it to mean, for some location l, *that it's raining in l*, if her utterance is to conform to the sentence's meaning. The Gricean invisible-hand strategy for explaining expression-meaning in terms of the Gricean's account of speaker-meaning then runs, to a rough approximation, as follows:

- First, the account of speaker-meaning is combined with a well-known means-end principle of rational behavior to get the result that when a normal communicator utters something x to communicate p to her hearer, there is some feature

of x, ϕ, such that she takes ϕ to be an IB-feature that is optimal in the circumstances for enabling her hearer to infer that she, the speaker, uttered x with... intentions, where they are the intentions that, by the Gricean's lights, are constitutive of communicating p.
- Second, the account of speaker-meaning is combined with further principles of rational action to show that in any normal population of communicators there will come to be an utterance type Ω such that, for some propositional form Ψ, Ω has *the property of being such that it's mutual (or common) knowledge in the population that there is in the population a practice, or practices, conformity to which requires a speaker who produces an unembedded utterance of Ω to utter Ω with... intentions,* where, for some proposition p of form Ψ, those intentions are constitutive of her meaning p.
- What sustains those practices is that those properties constitute optimal IB-features, and the optimality of meaning properties as IB-features is explained by *identifying them with the non-semantically specifiable optimal IB-features generated by the Gricean invisible hand.* In other words, the meaning of 'It's raining' is an optimal IB-feature in a population P because having that meaning just is the property of being an utterance type Ω such that it's mutual (or common) knowledge in P that there is in P a practice, or practices, conformity to which requires a speaker who produces an unembedded utterance of u to utter u with... intentions, where, for some location l, those intentions are constitutive of meaning *that it's raining in l.*

The Gricean takes his invisible-hand strategy to be most clearly and paradigmatically exhibited in his account of simple signals,[13] and a little thought experiment will show how that is supposed to work. There is a weekly seminar regularly attended by the same people. Their practice is to raise their hands if they want to be called on, but they have no simple way of indicating that what they want to contribute is a follow-up question. During one session, a visitor from the University of Latvia, Zuzka, raises her hand during a lively discussion and moves her index finger rapidly up and down. It's clear to all that Zuzka intends to communicate something by this gesture, but at first no one can figure out what it is. After several minutes it somehow transpires that in Latvian universities that sort of finger movement means that one has a follow-up question. Now suppose that during another exchange the following week one of the attendees, Harvey, raises his hand and moves his index finger rapidly up and down. In this case, everyone in the class will know straightway that Harvey means that he has a follow-up question. What explains this dramatic difference? Why was it that no one knew what Zuzka meant in moving her finger in way Ω, whereas one week later the very same people effortlessly and immediately knew that in moving his finger in way Ω Harvey meant that he had a follow up question? The answer, of course, is that at the time Zuzka performed the finger movement it had no feature that was an effective IB-feature in the seminar for meaning that one had a follow-up question, but after that the movement had a few features it didn't previously have, and these features separately and together constituted quite an effective IB-feature for meaning that one had a follow-up question. One of these features was that of being mutually known to be such that it was performed by Zuzka in her attempt to communicate to the seminar that she had a follow-up question; another was that of being mutually known to be the standard way in Latvian universities to communicate *that one had a follow-up question* (Q, for short). Since it benefited the seminar to have a simple way to indicate that one had a follow-up question, now that no one doubts what one would mean by moving one's index finger in way Ω, it's apt to catch on, so that it soon becomes mutual knowledge in the seminar that there is a practice of meaning Q by moving one's index finger in way Ω, and that mutual knowledge makes the gesture an optimal IB-feature as regards meaning Q in the seminar.

You may recognize that we have entered the territory of the kind of self-perpetuating regularities that David Lewis showed to be conventions, and at this point it seems correct to say that the gesture means Q in the seminar. In order to explain this, the Gricean is apt to offer the following, or something very much like it, as his account of simple-signal meaning:

[SIMP] For any γ and propositional form Ψ, γ is a simple signal which means Ψ in P iff (a) it's mutual knowledge in P that there is a practice in P of uttering γ when, for some proposition q of form Ψ, the speaker means q in uttering γ, and (b) in such acts the speaker intends her hearer to know what she meant at least partly on the basis of it's being mutual knowledge in P that that practice obtains in P.[14]

Of course, we can't hope to account for the meanings of natural language sentences in a similar way, since a sentence has its meaning even if no one has ever uttered it. How, then, might the Gricean invisible-hand strategy apply to natural languages? The Gricean expects that if σ means Ψ in the language L of a population P then, while there needn't be any practice of uttering σ, there will prevail in P a set of practices pertaining to L such that one utters σ in conformity with those practices only if in uttering σ one means a proposition of form Ψ. The question is, what might those practices be?

The Gricean's first thought might be that what is needed is a set of practices each of which pertains to a morpheme or primitive structure of L (e.g. a practice of uttering 'red' when, or only when, ...), but this route would entail incredible complexity, and couldn't be achieved at least until we could specify the syntax of L. The only feasible hope for the Gricean is to adopt an ingenious strategy proposed by David Lewis.[15] This strategy needn't be incompatible with the Gricean's impracticably complex and ambitious first thought, but it avoids both the complexity and the over-ambition. Pursuing this strategy, one begins by defining a language as an abstract pairing of expressions ε and meanings μ. If L assigns μ to ε, then we may say that ε means* μ in L, where '*' signifies that

ε means* μ in L iff L assigns μ to ε (i.e. $L(\varepsilon) = \mu$)

is merely a stipulative definition, not something made true by the way anyone *uses* ε. The notion of meaning that is the philosopher's target is a use-dependent notion, and that is the notion of an expression ε's meaning μ in a population P. Here the Gricean will say that

ε means μ in population P iff $\exists L[(\varepsilon$ means* μ in L) & (L is a public language of P)]

The hard part is then to define the *public-language relation*, that relation that must hold between a population of communicators and a language in order for the language to be used by the population as a public language of communication. Here the Gricean might proceed as follows. First, he will stipulate that

There is a *practice in P of meaning in L* =$_{df}$ often when a member of *P* means something, she utters a sentence of *L* and what she means in uttering that sentence fits its meaning* in *L*.[16]

Then he is apt to propose, as a first shot, that:

[PLR]   *L* is a public language of *P* iff for any sentence σ of *L* and member *S* of *P*, if *S* means something in uttering σ and her audience, *A*, is a member of *P*, then, for some Ψ, *S* intends σ's IB-feature to be that it's mutual knowledge between *S* and *A* both that (i) σ means* Ψ in *L* and (ii) there is a practice in *P* of meaning in *L*.

Now I can try to state more clearly the two objections I gave in Chapter 9 of *Remnants* to show that, and why, the Gricean strategy for defining expression-meaning in terms of the Gricean's definition of speaker-meaning can't succeed.

Although the first objection applies to Gricean accounts of any kind of expression-meaning, to demonstrate it we need only consider a Gricean account of simple-signal meaning, the theorist's showcase example of how his invisible-hand strategy is supposed to work, and for this we may take SIMP as representative, in that what will be found objectionable about it is unavoidably a feature of Gricean accounts of any kind of expression-meaning. Actually, we can make things a little simpler by considering not SIMP in its full generality, which quantifies over every kind of act of speaker-meaning, but only as restricted to the very simple case in which a certain hand gesture, *g*, is a simple signal which means *that the gesturer's spouse is away* in the population consisting of the adulterous lovers Hansel and Gretel:

[SIMP$_g$]   *g* is a simple signal which means *that one's spouse is away* among Hansel and Gretel iff (a) it's mutual knowledge between Hansel and Gretel that there is a practice among them to "utter" *g* in order to mean *that one's spouse is away*, and that (b) in such acts the utterer intends the other to know what the former meant at least partly on the basis of its being mutual knowledge between them that there is a practice among them to utter *g* in order to mean *that one's spouse is away*.

The problem with SIMP$_g$ is this. In principle, there are three relevant readings of SIMP$_g$, but the only one that satisfies the Gricean's program of defining expression-meaning in terms that include those that define speaker-meaning is a reading no one can reasonably take to be true. For suppose a theorist's program is to define *A* in terms of *X* and *Y* and then to define *B* partly in terms of *A with the result that she has thereby indirectly defined B partly in terms of X and Y*. She is not guaranteed to have satisfied the goal of her program if her definition

$B =_{def} \ldots A \ldots$

is true. Her goal will be satisfied only if '*A*' in the definition occurs there with its ordinary sense and reference, so that '*A*' refers to *A* and may therefore be replaced *salva veritate* in the definition with its definiens '...*X*...*Y*...'. Yet such substitutivity needn't hold in all contexts. For example, it needn't hold in certain intentional contexts created by occurrences that specify propositional-attitudes contents. If you define 'leprosy' as a disease characterized by conditions $C_1, \ldots, C_7$, and you then define 'leprophobe' as someone who fears that she has leprosy, then you haven't thereby defined 'leprophobe' as someone who fears that she has the disease characterized by conditions $C_1, \ldots, C_7$. For

Zelda fears that she has leprosy

may be true while

Zelda fears that she has the disease characterized by conditions $C_1, \ldots, C_7$

is false. Should that be so, then we can see that the notion of a leprophobe wasn't defined in terms of *leprosy*—i.e. the disease characterized by conditions $C_1, \ldots, C_7$—but was rather defined in terms of a certain *concept* of leprosy. Now, on the reading of SIMP$_g$ that may strike one as plausible, it's not a reading on which 'speaker-meaning' in the definiens refers to *speaker-meaning*; it is instead a reading on which it refers to a primitive *concept* of speaker-meaning. In order for SIMP$_g$ to be part of a program that shows expression-meaning to be definable wholly in terms of non-semantic propositional attitudes, 'speaker-meaning' in the definiens of SIMP$_g$ would have to refer not to a concept of speaker-meaning, but to speaker-meaning itself, in which case SIMP$_g$ would be equivalent to its Gricean expansion:

[ESIMP$_g$] g is a simple signal which means *that one's spouse is away* among Hansel and Gretel iff (a) it's mutual knowledge between Hansel and Gretel that there is a practice among them for g to be what one of them, S, utters when for some x and ϕ S utters x intending it to be mutual knowledge between S and the other one of them, A, that x has ϕ and, at least partly on that basis, mutual knowledge that S uttered x intending A to believe that S's spouse was away and intending their mutual knowledge that S uttered x intending A to believe that S's spouse was away to be at least part of A's reason for believing that S's spouse was away, and (b) in such acts S intends ϕ to be the property of being such that it's mutual knowledge between Hansel and Gretel that there is a practice among them for g to be what one of them, S', utters when for some x' and ϕ' S' utters x' intending it to be mutual knowledge between S' and the other one of them, A', that x' has ϕ' and, at least partly on that basis, mutual knowledge that S' uttered x' intending A' to believe that S''s spouse was away and intending their mutual knowledge that S' uttered x' intending A' to believe that S''s spouse was away to be at least part of A''s reason for believing that S''s spouse was away.

I dare say that whatever plausibility SIMP$_g$ seemed to enjoy is far outweighed by the implausibility that ESIMP$_g$ manifestly suffers. For on the reading of SIMP$_g$ that comes across to us as most plausible, the ostensible references to speaker-meaning in the definiens aren't references to *speaker-meaning* but rather to a primitive *concept* of speaker-meaning.

So long as we read the that-clauses in SIMP and PLR as having a straightforwardly *de dicto* reading, then even if those two definitions constitute a correct account of expression-meaning, and even if SM, the Gricean's account of speaker-meaning, is correct, the Gricean will not have succeeded in doing what his program requires him to do, viz. define expression-meaning partly in terms of the propositional-attitude notions that define speaker-meaning. On that *de dicto* reading neither SIMP nor PLR make any direct contact with the Gricean's account of speaker-meaning. If those accounts are true, their truth is determined by properties of a certain commonsense *concept* of speaker-meaning, *not* by properties of the Gricean's *definition* of speaker-meaning, and for this reason such accounts can't be the result of the invisible-hand strategy for defining expression-meaning in terms of the Gricean's definition of speaker-meaning.

The straightforwardly *de dicto* reading of SIMP and PLR just discussed is, I believe, our instinctive reading of those definitions when they strike us as having even a small degree of plausibility, but there is another way of reading those definitions that permits their talk of speaker-meaning to be replaced *salva veritate* by the conditions that define speaker-meaning but doesn't founder on the psychological implausibility that makes ESIMP$_g$ seem preposterous. We might understand talk of speaker-meaning in the Gricean's definitions of expression-meaning as having a *de re*, rather than a *de dicto*, occurrence. On the most helpful version of this suggestion, we might have the following. First, let M be that relation which obtains among x, S, A, and p when A is S's audience and in uttering x S means p. Then, if we pretend that the set-theoretic idioms merely abbreviate ordinary language idioms that could be used to specify what ordinary people know, the suggestion would be that:

g is a simple signal which means *that one's spouse is away* among Hansel and Gretel iff (a) Hansel and Gretel mutually know *of M* that there is a practice among them for g to be what one of them, S, utters when A is the other one of them and for some x <x, S, A, and the proposition *that S's spouse is away*> instantiates M, and (b) when <g, S, A, and the proposition *that S's spouse is away*> instantiates M, S intends S and A mutually to know *of M* that <g, S, A, and the proposition *that S's spouse is away*> instantiates M largely on the basis of their mutually knowing M to be such that there is a practice among them for g to be what one of them, S', utters when A' is the other one of them and for some x' <x', S', A', the proposition *that S's spouse is away*> instantiates M.

In this *de re* version of ESIMP$_g$ 'M' occurs in a wholly extensional position outside the scope of any propositional-attitude operator and is therefore replaceable *salva veritate* by the Gricean's defining conditions for M (provided, of course, that the Gricean's definition is correct). Nevertheless, even if this *de re* version of ESIMP$_g$ is more psychologically plausible than its *de dicto* version (which it's not clear that it is), it still wouldn't help the Gricean. This is because the *de re* version would still share the feature of the *de dicto* version that would make the *de dicto* version unacceptable to the Gricean even if it weren't psychologically implausible: the account of simple-signal meaning would still be wholly isolated from the Gricean's *account* of speaker-meaning, would still be isolated from the Gricean's invisible-hand strategy for defining expression-meaning in terms of speaker-meaning. For nothing about the *de re* version of ESIMP$_g$ requires the speaker-meaning relation M to be definable in Gricean terms; its plausibility would be independent of whether or not M was definable, let alone definable in Gricean terms. If the seriousness of this charge isn't yet clear, imagine a theorist, Rice, whose program is simply to obtain definitions of speaker-meaning and expression-meaning in non-semantic terms, but without regard to whether either definition requires the other definition, or whether there is any motivated connection between the two accounts. It's very doubtful that Rice would, or should, be taken seriously.

That was the first objection I gave in Chapter 9 of *Remnants* to a Gricean account of expression-meaning, and it should be obvious that it applies, *mutatis mutandis*, to PLR, the Gricean's account of public-language meaning. The second objection from that chapter applies only to Gricean accounts of the public-language relation, such as PLR. The problem is this. On its *de dicto* reading, PLR requires ordinary people to know facts of the form σ *means** μ *in L*, which, given the stipulative definition of 'means*', means that PLR requires ordinary people to know facts of the form $L(\sigma) = \mu$. Let's assume that there is a workaround of the fact that on its *de dicto* reading PLR requires ordinary speakers to know some set theory. The real problem is that, in whatever vocabulary the definition is recast, its *de dicto* reading requires ordinary speakers to know a finite specification of the infinite function L. Such knowledge, however, would be tantamount to knowing a finitely specifiable meaning theory of L (i.e. a finitely specifiable theory whose theorems correlate each sentence of L with its meaning in L), where by 'knowledge' I mean *knowledge* and not merely Chomskyan internal representation. Yet no "expert" or anyone else has such knowledge. If there is a plausible version of PLR, it must be one that merely requires ordinary people to have *de re* knowledge of their language, i.e. it must be a version of PLR in which the variable 'L' has only extensional occurrences. The trouble is that the *de re* version runs into a problem I mentioned to Lewis in 1968, when *Convention* was about to go to press, and which Lewis subsequently dubbed the *meaning-without-use problem*.[17] For suppose L is Dave's language, and consider the finite subset of L, L_u, whose domain consists of all the sentences that might actually be uttered by anyone. L_u will be a subset of infinitely many languages that are distinct from L. For example, if English is Dave's language, then there will be a language English$^+$ that is the same as English but has 'dog' and 'cat' exchange meanings in every sentence containing more than 60,000 words. If, therefore, L is the only language Dave uses, then he must have a way of thinking of L that distinguishes it from the infinitely many other languages that overlap L with respect to L_u. That way of thinking of L can't be, say, "the language I use," for the enterprise is to say what makes a language the language one uses. It's difficult to see what such a way of thinking of L might be that didn't require knowing the correct syntax and semantics for L.

Lewis gave up on trying to use his notion of convention to define the public-language relation. He said that the unused languages that overlapped L with respect to L_u all had "bent" grammars, as opposed to the "straight" grammars that linguists and philosophers suppose the languages we use to have, and his final proposal was the incomplete proposal that language use somehow or other determines the meanings of the sentences that might be used, and that the language that was used was then distinguished from the other languages we don't use but which overlap the used language with respect to the sentences that might be uttered by the fact that it had the straightest grammar compatible with the use-determined meanings. A problem with Lewis's proposal is that it rules out something that seems entirely possible—namely, that a group might deliberately construct and decide to use a language with a bent grammar, or we might discover—doubtless to our great surprise but possible nevertheless—that the internally represented grammar implicated in our language processing was a bent grammar.[18] A more plausible variant of Lewis's proposal would say that L was the subpersonally represented language implicated in the language processing by which the members of a population come to know what speakers mean in uttering sentences of the population's language.[19] But, again, even if speaker-meaning enjoys a Gricean definition, that way of capturing the public-language relation would fail to make a relevant connection with the specifics of the Gricean's definition. As far as the account of linguistic meaning was concerned, all that would matter was that a connection was made with acts of speaker-meaning: nothing about the account would require a Gricean account of speaker-meaning. For all that expression-meaning cared about, speaker-meaning could be a primitive, indefinable notion, or a notion that enjoyed an entirely unGricean analysis. Of course, it's *conceivable* that we should have a correct Gricean account of speaker-meaning *and* an account of expression-meaning that reduced that notion to physicalistically kosher terms, but not the terms used in the analysis of speaker-meaning, and perhaps that would satisfy erstwhile IBS reductionists like Jerry Fodor. But however implausible Gricean accounts of speaker-meaning now seem, they would seem considerably more implausible if they promised no leverage on explaining expression-meaning. No philosopher would be attracted to a program that proposed an account of speaker-meaning and then an account of expression-meaning that made no contact with its account of speaker-meaning. Expression-meaning has always been the key notion in the philosophy of language, and what drew me and others to the Gricean program lo those many years was what we took to be its insight that expression-meaning needed to be understood in terms of an intention-based account of speaker-meaning. Break that link and you break the appeal the program had for me, as well as for Paul Grice. Anyway, the foregoing objections to Gricean semantics don't depend on IBS's claim to *reduce* the semantic to the psychological, but only on its claim to define expression-meaning in terms of its account of speaker-meaning. They are my reasons for thinking that Gricean intentions can't abide.

21.2.3 Back to Neale and the problem aphonics pose for Gricean semantics

I have two brief comments. The first is that if the objections I've raised against Gricean accounts of expression-meaning are correct, then we have no reason to *care* whether aphonic referring expressions can be accommodated in a Gricean semantics. My second comment is that, *strictly speaking*, a Gricean account of expression-meaning can absorb subsentential expressions that are inaccessible to ordinary speakers. For what is essential to the Gricean's program is that in normal communication knowing what a speaker meant in uttering a sentence σ requires knowing that σ has Θ, where Θ is the non-semantically specifiable property that constitutes σ's having the meaning it has, and taking the fact that σ has Θ as *evidence* of what the speaker meant in uttering σ. It's not, however, obvious that even the most reductive of Gricean theories requires that the hearer come to know that σ has Θ by way of knowing the meaning-constituting properties of the structures and morphemes that compose σ. It's even compatible with a Gricean reductive analysis of expression-meaning that one doesn't in any way *infer* what a sentence means on the basis of one's knowing what its parts and structures mean. At the same time, it does seem to be essential to Gricean semantics that speaker-reference be definable in terms of speaker-meaning, and that expression-reference be definable in terms of an expression's meaning playing a role in enabling knowledge of speaker-reference by enabling knowledge of what the sentence containing the expression-means. But, as I pointed out in (I), an expression's meaning can play that role without a hearer's *inferring* the sentence's meaning on the basis of knowing how the sentence's meaning is compositionally determined. The way sketched in (I) of how that might be achieved could serve the Gricean if all the other parts of his program were in place. What I have tried to show is in doubt is his ability to get those parts in place.

21.3 Meaning, Reference, Descriptions: Response to Kent Bach

21.3.1 Formulating the question

A language is an abstract object that may or may not be used by anyone. For the purposes of this response I shall join Kent Bach in assuming that there are such things as sentence meanings. Philosophers who make that assumption do well to follow David Lewis in stipulating a language to be any function that maps sequences of marks or sounds (or whatever) onto sets of things eligible to be sentence meanings. If L is a language and $L(\sigma) = \mu$, we shall say that μ is the meaning of σ in L.[20] The stipulation immediately raises two questions: What are sentence meanings? What relation must obtain between a population P and a language L in order for L to be the (or a) public language of P—that is to say, in order for the expressions of L to mean in P what they mean in L?

To know the meaning a sentence has in a population is arguably to know two things: the kind of speech act a member of that population must perform in a literal and unembedded utterance of the sentence, and the kind of propositional content that speech act must have. If that is right, then at a certain level of theorizing we may represent sentence meanings as ordered pairs of the form $<A, \Phi>$, where A is a kind of speech act and Φ a propositional form. For example, letting '⊢' stand for *meaning-that* and '?' for *asking-whether*, we might represent the meanings of 'She is asleep' and 'Is she asleep?' as, respectively:

<⊢, the propositional form x_f is asleep at t_u>

<?, the propositional form x_f is asleep at t_u>,

where 'x_f' indicates that a value must identify the female to whom the speaker referred with his utterance of 'she', and 't_u' that a value must identify the time of utterance.

It is evidently more of a challenge to specify the relation—call it the *public-language relation*—that must obtain between a language and a population in order for the former to be the latter's public language. Still, there are some things we seem able to say. For example, we should expect there to be the following two constraints on the public-language relation, and thus on the use-dependent meaning relation that relates expressions to their meanings:

(A) If σ means $\langle A, \Phi \rangle$ in P—i.e. if for some L σ means $\langle A, \Phi \rangle$ in L and L is P's public language—then σ is a *conventional device* in P for performing speech acts of kind A with propositional contents of form Φ, and, in consequence, when a member of P produces an unembedded token of a sentence whose meaning in P is $\langle A, \Phi \rangle$, she is, *ceteris paribus*, thereby performing an act of kind A with a propositional content of form Φ. Of course, *cetera* won't always be *paria*: if you ask Betty whether Lester is thin and she responds, 'Well, he does have to walk around in the shower to get wet,' you won't take her to mean thereby that Lester has to walk around in the shower to get wet. When theorizing about what expressions of a certain kind mean, it's important to keep in mind the sort of facts that determine meaning.

(B) Suppose σ means $\langle \vdash, \Phi \rangle$ in P. Then S's unembedded utterance of σ in P is *literal* just in case, for some proposition q, S meant q in uttering σ and q is of form Φ. For example, if in uttering 'She's asleep' I meant that Jane was asleep at that time, then my utterance was literal because 'She's asleep' means $\langle \vdash, x_f$ is asleep at $t_u \rangle$, my speech act was an act of meaning-that, and the proposition I meant was of the form x_f is asleep at t_u. Now, it is virtually always the case that, for *any* proposition q, if as a result of perceiving S's utterance of σ H knows that in uttering σ S meant q, then, *regardless of whether or not S's utterance was literal*, the fact that σ means what it does in their shared language will play an indispensable role in the information processing that takes H from her perception of S's utterance of σ to her knowing that in uttering σ S meant q. For I take it to be obvious that it's virtually always the case that whenever a hearer knows what a speaker meant in uttering a sentence as a result of perceiving the speaker's utterance (and not, say, as the result of being told what the speaker meant), then the fact that the hearer understands the sentence uttered will be part of the explanation of how she was able to know what the speaker meant. Clearly, the fact that my hearer knows the meaning of 'She's asleep' plays an ineliminable role in explaining how he knew that I meant that Jane was asleep, but the point also holds when one knows the speaker is speaking nonliterally—say, ironically or metaphorically. If you didn't know what 'He has to walk around in the shower to get wet' meant, then you could hardly know that in uttering it Betty meant that Lester was very thin. The reason for the "virtually" qualification is merely to recognize that in certain circumstances one can hear the utterance of a sentence and know what someone meant in uttering it other than on the basis of understanding the sentence, as one might be able to infer what the speaker meant just from the fact that he said anything, or that he said what he did in a certain tone of voice, or in Japanese. But of course these cases are the exception.

Relative to the framework just provided, a Russellian theory of sentences of the form 'The F is G' holds that the version of English we speak is one in which *the* meaning of 'The F is G' includes a propositional form expressible as a completion of the schema

<⊢, [the$_x$: Fx at t$_u$ ...] Gx at t$_u$>,

where Russellians may dispute among themselves about what, if anything, should replace '...' (thus a limiting case of a Russellian theory would be Bach's view that 'The F is G' expresses the propositional form [the$_x$: Fx at t$_u$] Gx at t$_u$). Now, referential uses of definite descriptions are ubiquitous, and it's easy to see the threat they pose to Russellian theories.[21] Sally and Herb are dining at *Chez Tomaine* when Sally notices that Warren Buffett is dining at the next table. Not sure if Herb knows who Buffett is, Sally directs Herb's attention to the table next to theirs and whispers, 'The guy wearing a maroon shirt is a billionaire,' thereby referring to Buffett and telling Herb that he, Buffett, is a billionaire. An utterance like this appears threatening to the Russellian because it appears to be as literal a use of the uttered sentence as a use of 'It's windy' to assert that it's windy in Kansas City, and the asserted proposition seems not to be descriptive, but rather to be a referent-dependent proposition whose truth or falsity turns entirely on whether or not the indicated man is a billionaire. Every Russellian must deny that it's the case both that (i) the utterance of the sentence was literal and (ii) the only proposition meant was nondescriptive. The challenge to every Russellian is to account for referential cases in a way that is both defensible and incompatible with the conjunction of (i) and (ii).

21.3.2 Bach's Russellian response to the referentialist threat

In "Russell's Theory of Definite Descriptions" I discussed, and rejected, two Russellian attempts to meet the referentialist challenge. I took it as a datum that in a literal utterance of, say, 'The cat is on the mat,' the speaker could mean something that fit the sentence's meaning, and that therefore the sentence's meaning didn't require the literal speaker to mean a proposition that entailed that the universe contained exactly one cat and exactly one mat. Consequently, both the versions of Russell's theory I considered held that the propositional form expressed by 'The F is G' is

[the$_x$: Fx at t$_u$ & Δ_x at t$_u$]Gx at t$_u$,

where 'Δ_x' indicates a slot for a property, which may in the limit be the null property (as e.g. in an utterance of 'The second wife of Henry the VIII of England was beheaded'), that (i) was implicitly expressed in the utterance of 'The F is G,' and thus an unarticulated constituent of the asserted proposition relative to the surface form of 'The F is G,' and (ii) was intended by the speaker to conjoin with the property of being F to yield a complex property that was instantiated by just one thing.[22] The two attempts differ on how they attempt to accommodate the facts about referentialist utterances that aren't in dispute. "Standard" Russellianism derives from Stephen Neale's *Descriptions* and I take it to be the version accepted by most contemporary Russellians; it concedes that Sally's utterance of 'The guy wearing a maroon shirt is a billionaire' was literal *and* that she was primarily concerned to communicate a nondescriptive, referent-dependent proposition. The standard Russellian can accept that conjunction because he further holds that, in addition to meaning the singular proposition <Buffett, the property of being a billionaire>, Sally *also* meant, and said, a descriptive, non-referent-dependent proposition, and that the singular proposition was conversationally implicated by her saying the descriptive proposition. Standard

Russellianism is implausible because it's implausible that Sally meant anything other than the referent-dependent proposition whose communication to Herb was the purpose of her utterance. Bach agrees with this objection to standard Russellianism.[23]

The second version of Russellianism I considered was also due to Neale, who in some recent publications has rejected the version of Russellianism he argued for in *Descriptions* and offered a revised version designed to accommodate the fact that the only proposition typically meant in a referential utterance of 'The F is G' is the referent-dependent proposition the communication of which was the whole point of the utterance.[24] Neale continued to hold that 'The F is G' expressed the propositional form [the_x: Fx at t_u & Δ_x at t_u]Gx at t_u, but that is where agreement with his former self ended. The newer version implies that there is only one proposition that Sally means in uttering 'The guy wearing a maroon shirt is a billionaire,' and that that proposition is both of the form expressed by the sentence and referent-dependent. The one proposition that is supposed to be at once meant, descriptive, and referent-dependent is the proposition *that the guy wearing a maroon shirt who is Buffett is a billionaire*.[25] Since that proposition is of the form expressed by the sentence Sally uttered, her utterance is literal. I raised a few problems for Neale's most recent version of Russell's theory; presently I'll discuss the application of two of those problems to Bach's version of Russell's theory.

One of Bach's central concerns in his paper is to argue that his own version of Russell's theory is immune to the objections I raised against the two I considered in "Russell's Theory of Definite Descriptions"—viz. standard Russellianism and Neale's recent emendation of it. Bach's theory, as he now presents it, includes the following claims:

B1. The propositional form expressed by 'The F is G' is [the_x: Fx at t_u] Gx at t_u. So, for example, the form expressed by the sentence type 'The dog is barking' is

[the_x: dog(x) at t_u] barking(x) at t_u,

which entails that a literal utterance of 'The dog is barking' would be true if, but only if, at the time of the utterance there existed one and only one dog in the universe, and that dog was barking. Bach of course acknowledges that hardly any utterances of 'The F is G', whether attributive or referential, are literal, thus bringing to mind the quip that one person's *modus ponens* is another's *modus tollens*.

B2. What makes an utterance of 'The F is G' *referential* is that the speaker means a proposition of the form

[the_x: Fx at t_u & (x = a)] Gx at t_u

Bach is therefore in complete agreement with Neale about what proposition the speaker means when descriptions are used referentially. The difference between them concerns the propositional form expressed by 'The F is G' and the relation to it of the proposition they agree is what speakers mean in referential utterances of the sentence. According to Neale's 2004 theory, but not according to Bach's theory, the proposition a speaker means in a referential utterance of 'The F is G' is of the form expressed by that sentence, and therefore—for Neale, but not for Bach—referential uses are literal uses of the sentence.[26]

B3. The only thing a speaker could mean in a *literal* utterance of 'The *F* is *G*' at *t* is *that the one and only thing that is F at t is G at t*. Consequently, Bach sensibly holds that when speakers use descriptions they virtually never *mean* the proposition a literal utterance of the uttered sentence would require them to mean. He does, however, maintain that speakers *say* those propositions and that those propositions are the sentence's "semantic content" relative to the context of utterance. I assume Bach's use of 'saying-that' and 'semantic content' is doing theoretical work for him. I'm not sure what that work is, but it is probably to be located in developments of the next two tenets of his theory.

B4. The proposition meant in a referential utterance of 'The *F* is *G*'—viz. *that the F that is α is G*—is not a *conversational implicature* of what the speaker said, but is rather (what Bach calls) an *impliciture* of what the speaker said in uttering 'The *F* is *G*'. Implicitures, according to Bach, are either "completions" or "expansions" of the uttered sentence's semantic content, depending respectively on whether the sentence's semantic content is a mere propositional "radical" or a complete proposition. For example, when in uttering 'Phil is late' the speaker means that Phil is late for dinner, the proposition *that Phil is late for dinner* is an impliciture that is a "completion" of the "propositional radical" that is the semantic content of the speaker's utterance of 'Phil is late'; but when in uttering 'The baby is asleep' the speaker means *that the baby who is α is asleep*, that proposition is an impliciture that is an "expansion" of the complete proposition that is the semantic content of the sentence uttered.

B5. Because Referential uses of 'The *F* is *G*' aren't *literal* uses of the sentence, they also aren't *conventional* uses of it; but they are *standardized* uses of the sentence.

What is standardization? A form of words is standardized for a certain use if this use, though regularized, goes beyond literal meaning and yet can be explained without special conventions. In each case, there is a certain core of linguistic meaning attributable on compositional grounds but a common use that cannot be explained in terms of linguistic meaning alone. The familiarity of the form of words, together with a familiar inference route from their literal meaning to what the speaker could plausibly be taken to mean in using them, streamlines the process of identifying what the speaker is conveying. The inference is compressed by precedent. But were there no such precedent, in which case a more elaborate inference would be required, there would still be enough contextual information available to the hearer for figuring out what is being conveyed.[27]

One of Bach's illustrations of standardization is of a professor saying to his class, 'Everyone must attend class' and meaning thereby that everyone *taking the course* must attend class. For here, Bach says, "what is meant is something the speaker could have figured out, *in Gricean fashion*."[28] That example is of an "expansion" impliciture. Another of his illustrations involves a "completion" impliciture: when a speaker utters 'I'm ready' and means thereby that she is ready to leave the house, what she means is a "completion" of the "propositional radical" expressed by 'I'm ready'.[29]

21.3.3 Problems for Bach

The point of Bach's paper is to show that his version of Russell's theory is immune to the objections I leveled against the two versions I considered in (2005), to wit, standard Russellianism and Neale's emendation of it. I think that Bach's claim is false; but even if it were true there would remain good reasons for rejecting his theory.

I'm puzzled by Bach's claim that his version of Russell's theory escapes the problems of the two I considered. For most of the problems I raised for Neale's newest version of Russell's theory are problems for Neale's claim that the proposition the *speaker* means in a referential utterance of 'The *F* is *G*' is a proposition of the form [*the*$_x$: *Fx* at t_u & (x = α) *at* t_u] *G*(*x*) at t_u, and on this Bach is in complete agreement with Neale. Let me mention two of those problems.

The truth-conditions problem. Recall Sally's saying to Herb, 'The guy wearing a maroon shirt is a billionaire,' thereby referring to Buffett and ascribing to him the property of being a billionaire. Intuitively, or so it seems to me, the proposition Sally meant is true in an arbitrary possible world just in case Buffet is a billionaire in that world. He doesn't also have to be wearing a maroon shirt in that world. But the general proposition *that the man wearing a maroon shirt who is Buffet is a billionaire* evidently does require Buffet to be wearing a maroon shirt in every possible world in which the proposition is true. If Neale were to claim that what Sally really meant was *that the man wearing a maroon shirt in ω who is Buffet is a billionaire*, where ω is the world in which her utterance occurred, his proposal would run into a problem pointed out by Scott Soames.[30] Since a person who didn't believe, but might have believed, the proposition Sally meant would believe it in worlds other than ω, he wouldn't have the kind of contact with ω that would enable him to believe an ω-dependent proposition, which is what the proposition Sally meant would be if rigidified to the world of her, Sally's, utterance. Even worse, when in the counterfactual world the person reported 'I believe what Sally communicated, namely, that the man wearing a maroon shirt who is Buffett is a billionaire,' the theory would have him referring not to ω, but to the counterfactual world in which his utterance occurred.

Since Bach's view is identical to Neale's as regards the proposition the speaker means in a referential utterance, the truth-conditions problem is as much of a problem for him as it is for Neale. But Bach doesn't even mention this problem, let alone respond to it. How, then, can he claim that his version of Russell's theory is immune to the problems I raised for Neale's version?

The determination problem. An utterance of 'the *F*' is referential with respect to *x* just in case the speaker means an *x*-dependent proposition as a result of using 'the *F*' to refer to *x*. The determination problem for Neale is that nothing in his theory entails that on the assumption that her utterance was both literal and referential with respect to Buffett, the proposition Sally meant was *that the man wearing a maroon shirt who is Buffett is a billionaire* ('μ', for short). If all we are given is that Sally's utterance was literal, then we can't predict that she meant μ as opposed, say, to the proposition *that the man wearing a maroon shirt at the table next to theirs is a billionaire*, and when we add that her utterance was also referential, then we can't predict that she meant μ as opposed, say, to the proposition that *the man wearing a maroon shirt at the table next to theirs who is Buffett is a billionaire*. So what entitles Neale to claim that in a referential utterance of 'The *F* is *G*' the speaker means *that the F that is α is G*?

The determination problem is exacerbated for Bach, since for him referential uses of descriptions aren't literal uses of them, thereby depriving him of a constraint that Neale enjoys. Consequently, the problem for Bach is to tell how his theory implies that, if her utterance was referential, then the proposition Sally meant was μ, as opposed, say, to the proposition *that Buffett is a billionaire* or the proposition *that the man wearing a maroon shirt at the table next to theirs who is Buffett is a billionaire*? Bach doesn't address the question of why on his account Sally should mean μ rather than the singular proposition *that Buffett is a billionaire*, but he does offer an explanation of why she would mean μ rather than, say, the proposition *that the man wearing a maroon shirt at the table next to theirs who is Buffett is a billionaire*:

> [U]nder the circumstances no embellishment of the description ['the man wearing a maroon shirt'] is needed to enable the hearer to figure out who the speaker is talking about. If more were needed, presumably the speaker would have included it. So the hearer can reasonably take the description at face value, assuming that the [man] that comes to mind can only be the one the speaker has in mind.[31] (375)

But this response seems insensitive to the distinction between what a speaker aims to communicate and what words she needs to utter in order to communicate it. When you ask me whether Marlon Brando is dead or alive, and I say 'Dead', what I mean is that Marlon Brando is dead, but it was enough to *say* 'Dead' to mean that proposition. Similarly, when the detective arrives at the murder scene and on the basis of the mutilated state of the corpse says 'The murderer must be insane,' his use of 'the murderer' is attributive and what he means is e.g. *that the murderer of that guy must be insane*, but given the mutual knowledge that obtained between him and his hearers, all the detective needed to utter to mean that proposition was 'The murderer must be insane.' Bach doesn't say how Sally's utterance of 'the man wearing a maroon shirt' is intended to "bring Buffett to mind," but I would think that it brings him to mind because in the context uttering it brings to mind the property of *being the man wearing a maroon shirt at the table next to theirs*, which is really what Herb uses to identify the person to whom Sally referred with her utterance of 'the man wearing a maroon shirt.' One might therefore have expected Bach to say that, as between μ and the proposition *that the man wearing a maroon shirt at the table next to theirs who is Buffett is a billionaire*, it's the latter that Sally meant, and the mutual knowledge that obtained between her and her nephew made it possible for her to mean that proposition just by uttering 'The man wearing a maroon shirt is a billionaire.'

So I don't see that Bach's version of Russell's theory, ingenious as it is, is immune to the problems I raised in (2005) for Neale's latest version.

I have been supposing, as Bach supposes, that a sentence's having meaning consists in its standing in the meaning relation to some thing that is its meaning. What should therefore be of paramount concern to the theorist of meaning isn't *what a sentence means*—the thing that is its meaning—but rather its *meaning property*, the composite property, for some <A, Φ>, of meaning <A, Φ> in population P. That composite property has two components, a *meaning*, <A, Φ>, and *the meaning relation*: that relation a sentence must bear to thing and a population if it's to mean that thing in that population. Speculation about what members of a class of expressions mean should be constrained by what it's reasonable to suppose about what determines expressions to mean what they do; constrained, that is to say, by the nature of the meaning relation. In trying to figure out what sentences of the form 'The *F* is *G*' mean, we must take the meaning relation into account.

On the conception of the meaning relation rehearsed above (512–13),

σ means <A, Φ> in population P iff there is a language L such that (i) σ means <A, Φ> in L and (ii) L is the (or a) public language of P.

Since meaning in a language is a use-independent logical fact, the task of explaining how use determines meaning reduces to the task of saying in what the public-language relation consists. The debate between Bach's and other versions of Russell's theory is a debate about which language we speak. Let's assume for the sake of argument (i) that some version of Russell's theory of descriptions is correct and (ii) that Bach and Neale are correct in claiming that the proposition the *speaker* means in a referential utterance of 'The F is G' is a proposition of the form $[the_x: Fx\ at\ t_u\ \&\ (x = \alpha)\ at\ t_u]\ Gx\ at\ t_u$. Further, let E^b be that Lewisian language in which 'The F is G' means $<\vdash, [the_x: Fx\ at\ t_u]\ Gx\ at\ t_u>$ (i.e. E^b('The F is G') = $<\vdash, [the_x: Fx\ at\ t_u]\ Gx\ at\ t_u>$) but is otherwise as much like English as it can be, and let E^n be that Lewisian language in which 'The F is G' means $<\vdash, [the_x: Fx\ at\ t_u\ \&\ \Delta_x\ at\ t_u] Gx\ at\ t_u>$ but is otherwise as much like English as it can be. And let's add to assumptions (i) and (ii) the further assumption (iii) that our language is one of E^b or E^n. Then the question of moment becomes: Given assumptions (i)-(iii), is our language E^b, or is it E^n?

At the beginning of this response to Bach's essay, I suggested that the public-language relation should be subject to the following two constraints:

(A) Communication is the *raison d'être* of public languages, and the *raison d'être* of public language sentences is as vehicles of communication. It's no accident that what a speaker means in uttering a sentence typically fits the meaning of that sentence. What explains this conformity of speaker-meaning to sentence meaning is that sentences of a public language are *conventional devices* for performing acts of speaker-meaning that fit the meanings of the sentences speakers utter. In other words, if σ means <A, Φ> in P—i.e. if for some L σ means <A, Φ> in L and L is P's public language—then σ is a *conventional device* in P for performing speech acts of kind A with propositional contents of form Φ, and, in consequence, there is a defeasible assumption that when a member of P produces an unembedded token σ, she is thereby performing an act of kind A with a propositional content of form Φ.

(B) It is virtually always the case that, for *any* proposition q, if as a result of perceiving S's utterance of σ H knows that in uttering σ S meant q, then, *regardless of whether or not S's utterance was literal*, the fact that σ means what it does in their shared language will play an indispensable role in the information processing that takes H from her perception of S's utterance of σ to her knowledge that in uttering σ S meant q.[32] Recognition of this fact about the relation between sentence meaning and speaker-meaning is of course a cornerstone of Grice's theory of implicature.

Bach's version of Russell's theory fares worse with respect to constraints (A) and (B) than Neale's version. As I remarked in my initial discussion of the defeasible assumption described in (A) (on p. 513), there will of course be many utterances for which the assumption is defeated. For example, the last thing you would conclude from an utterance of 'Life's but a walking shadow, a poor player, that struts and frets his hour upon the stage, and then is heard no more' is that the speaker meant that life was a certain sort of actor. But what I think we should not expect is for a language to contain *an entire syntactical category of much used expressions*—in this case expressions of the form 'the F'—such that when speakers utter sentences containing those expressions they hardly ever mean something that conforms to the uttered sentence's meaning. Given assumptions (i)–(iii), speakers of E^n do speak literally in uttering 'The F is G,' and are therefore using it as a conventional device for meaning a proposition that fits the sentence's meaning. Not so for speakers of E^b. This difference between the two languages implies an important difference in how hearers process utterances of 'The F is G' in the two languages, and this segues to constraint (B).

The relevance of constraint (B) to the outcome of E^b vs. E^n is that we understand the relation between sentence meaning and speaker-meaning if we speak E^n: for then knowing what a speaker means in a typical utterance of a description-containing sentence is a matter of information that takes a hearer from her recognition that the speaker uttered a sentence with a certain meaning to a conclusion about which among the propositions that fit the uttered sentence's meaning the speaker is most likely to have meant. To be sure, there is a great deal we don't know about this familiar kind of information processing, but we know it's information processing that constitutes the normal case, and is therefore processing we know we *have* to understand. But what sort of information processing would take a hearer from her representation of the meaning of 'The F is G' to the belief, for some x, that the proposition which the speaker meant (and which didn't conform to the sentence's meaning) was *that the F that is x is G*?

A possible answer that would show how constraint (B) was satisfied will occur to those familiar with Grice's theory of conversational implicature. Grice's *stipulated* understanding of 'saying' was that *S says p* in uttering σ just in case in uttering σ *S means p*, and *p* fits the meaning of σ. (A corollary of this notion of *saying* is that an unembedded utterance of a sentence is *literal*—and the speaker speaks *literally* in producing the utterance—just in case she says something by her utterance.) And Grice's *stipulated* understanding of 'conversational implicature' was that *S conversationally implicates p* in uttering σ iff in uttering σ *S means p* and *p* doesn't conform to the meaning of σ (there is supposed to be a sense in which a proposition that is *conventionally* implicated in the utterance of a sentence does conform to that sentence's meaning). Grice's substantive theory of conversational implicature wasn't his stipulative definition of 'conversational implicature'. It was a theory of how things that are conversational implicatures by that definition are generated and understood. One pattern of generation made familiar by Grice is where the speaker says one thing and in so doing implicates something else, as when someone says that there is a gas station two blocks away and thereby implicates that the gas station is open for business. Another pattern made familiar by him was when one is correctly taken to mean a certain proposition that one isn't saying because it's obvious that one can't be saying anything—say, because the only thing one could be saying in the context was already known to be obviously true or obviously false. Hyperbole is a good example of this. A speaker utters 'Hilda is the worst friend in the world' and the hearer correctly takes him to mean that Hilda is a pretty bad friend, and this partly as a result of knowing that the speaker can't have meant that Hilda was the worst friend in the world, because it's completely obvious that Hilda isn't nearly as bad as, for example, friends who swindle their friends. Consider now the sort of run-of-the-mill description-containing sentence that people often utter, such as 'The baby is sleeping.' On the version of Russell's theory that Bach accepts, the only thing that could be meant in a literal utterance of that sentence is a proposition that is true only if at the time of the utterance there was just one baby in the universe and it was sleeping. This suggests that Bach might have in mind the following sketch of how Hilda might hear her husband, Sam, utter 'The baby is sleeping' and correctly interpret him as meaning thereby what Bach would say she would mean, namely, *that the baby who is α is sleeping*, where α is the relevant baby, perhaps Sam and Hilda's very own:

Even if Sam expected Hilda immediately to know what he meant, he nevertheless (no doubt tacitly) intended the proposition he meant to be one that Hilda could work out by reasoning roughly as follows: "In uttering 'The baby is asleep' Sam can't have meant *that the only baby in existence is sleeping*, which is what he would have meant had he been speaking literally, for it's mutually obvious to Sam and me that, as there are very many babies, that proposition is obviously false. Yet it's clear that he intends to communicate something, so he must mean something that is somehow relevantly related to the proposition he would have meant had he been speaking literally. Well, given what we mutually know in this context, it's most probable that our baby, Clyde, is such that what Sam means is *that the baby who is Clyde is sleeping*.

This is not a plausible account of how speakers mean what they do when they use descriptions referentially. It seems intuitively clear that in no sense does the information processing that takes a hearer from her perception of an utterance of 'The baby is sleeping' to her belief about what the speaker meant rely on the belief that the speaker can't have been speaking literally because there is more than one baby in the universe; nor does it seem at all plausible that such a belief would be implicated in any ordinary speaker's attempt explicitly to work out what the speaker meant. Fortunately, Bach agrees that that isn't how one comes to know what a speaker meant when she uses a definite description referentially: "the Russellian is not committed to the claim that because Russell's theory entails that a sentence containing an incomplete definite description in subject position is false, the hearer must (at least tacitly) take this into account and, in effect, treat the speaker's utterance as a quality implicature" (383, fn. 28). To be sure, but constraint (B) on the meaning relation requires the fact that the uttered sentence means what it does to be somehow implicated in the information processing that is supposed to take the hearer from her perception of the speaker's referential utterance of 'The baby is sleeping' to the conclusion that Bach would have her reach, to wit, *that the baby who is α is sleeping*, where α is the baby to which the speaker referred. What is that way? Bach says that "the incompleteness of the description by itself triggers any needed search for some individuating condition or some particular individual that must be identified for figuring out what the speaker means" (373). To be sure again, but that doesn't tell us how the hearer is supposed to use her understanding of the sentence uttered in figuring out what the speaker meant. Bach's real answer, I believe, is the point of tenet B4 of his theory, his claim that the proposition meant in a referential utterance of 'The F is G'—viz. *that the F that is α is G*—is not a *conversational implicature* of what the speaker said, but is rather what he calls an *expansion impliciture* of what the speaker said in uttering 'The F is G,' and this because the proposition *that [the$_x$: Fx at t_u & (x = α) at t_u] G(x) at t_u>* is an "expansion" of the proposition *that [the$_x$: Fx at t_u] Gx at t_u>*.[33]

Of course, what is given by just B4 can't explain how Bach's theory satisfies constraint (B), and in fact it's not clear how the introduction of this new terminology is supposed to help with anything. As Grice stipulatively used 'conversational implicature' (see above p. 520), Bach's implicitures are merely a subclass of conversational implicatures. From Grice's perspective, it's as though for some so-far unrevealed reason Bach had introduced the term 'squealiciture' to stand for implicatures delivered in a squeaky voice. The fact that Bach's implicitures are merely conversational implicatures (in Grice's stipulated sense) that bear a certain relation to the meaning of the uttered sentence tells us nothing to suggest that there isn't a unified non-disjunctive account of how all conversational implicatures are generated and understood. I think that Bach is sensitive to this point, and that tenet B5 of his theory, wherein he distinguishes between "conventional" and "standardized" uses of expressions, is intended to address it. That is, he might say that it's because referential uses of descriptions are *standardized* uses that they don't generate those implicatures that Bach calls expansion implicatures by way of causing the hearer to infer what the speaker meant from the fact that it's mutually obvious to speaker and hearer that no literal utterance of the sentence would be true. Unfortunately, no such achievement is pulled off by the explanation Bach gives of standardization, which, it may be recalled, is this:

> What is standardization? A form of words is standardized for a certain use if this use, though regularized, goes beyond literal meaning and yet can be explained without special conventions. In each case, there is a certain core of linguistic meaning attributable on compositional grounds but a common use that cannot be explained in terms of linguistic meaning alone. The familiarity of the form of words, together with a familiar inference route from their literal meaning to what the speaker could plausibly be taken to mean in using them, streamlines the process of identifying what the speaker is conveying. The inference is compressed by precedent. But were there no such precedent, in which case a more elaborate inference would be required, there would still be enough contextual information available to the hearer for figuring out what is being conveyed.[34]

Yet this gloss of standardization applies to all those paradigm conversational implicatures that Grice called generalized conversational implicatures, as when in almost any ordinary conversational context an utterance of 'I broke a finger' would implicate that the finger the speaker broke was one of his own. And of course Grice allows that a hearer may "intuitively grasp" an implicature, which is why he requires only that the implicature be "capable of being worked out."[35] The *question* for Bach is the kind of inference required in order to work it out. The *problem* for Bach is fourfold: (1) his theory entails that in nearly *every* utterance of 'The F is G,' whether referential *or* attributive, the proposition the speaker means is a conversational implicature (in Grice's stipulated sense); (2) the speaker can't be saying anything that isn't mutually known to be egregiously false; (3) the Gricean implicature-generation story (i) and (ii) are apt to suggest intuitively strikes us—and Bach—as very implausible; but (4) Bach offers no alternative account of how the meaning of the 'The F is G' is involved in the information processing that takes a hearer from her perception of the sentence's utterance to a conclusion about what the speaker meant in uttering the sentence—or, in other words, offers no alternative account of how the fact that the uttered sentence means what it does figures essentially in the inference that would be required if one were to work out what the speaker implicated in making his utterance. All this explains why it seems clear to me that, given the (admittedly unpalatable) assumption that we speak either E^b or E^n, it's E^n that we speak.

One final comment. I suspect that Bach's holding his "minimalist" version of Russell's theory is based at least partly on a false belief. That false belief is that (1) if L is a population's public language, then it enjoys a compositional meaning theory, where a *compositional meaning theory for L* is a finitely statable theory whose theorems assign to each of the infinitely many sentences of L its meaning in L, and (2) a compositional meaning theory for L precludes any sentence of L from expressing a propositional form whose instances have constituents that are unarticulated (in John Perry's sense[36]) with respect to "phonic" components of the sentence (i.e. it can't recognize semantic contents with constituents that are values only of aphonic components of a sentence's LF or are unarticulated with respect to all of the sentence's syntactic forms). If (1) and (2) were true, then 'The F is G' couldn't mean $<\vdash, [the_x: Fx$ at t_u & Δ_x at $t_u]Gx$ at $t_u>$, and 'Is it raining?' couldn't mean $<?, $ *it's raining in place* π *at* $t_u>$. Yet I'm not aware of any argument that supports this claim about compositionality, and in any case, the claim is false. There may be reasons for thinking natural languages can't have true finitely statable meaning theories, but allowing for unarticulated constituents isn't one of them. Sentence meanings are constraints on what can be said in uttering the sentences whose meanings they are, and so are word and structure meanings: since they determine the constraint imposed by sentences containing them, they too impose constraints. Why shouldn't the base axiom for 'to rain' conspire with the base axioms for relevant syntactical forms to assign to 'Is it raining?' the meaning $<?, $ *it's raining in place* π *at* $t_u>$?

So I am not yet persuaded that Bach's version of Russell's theory does anything to increase the probability that some version of Russell's theory of descriptions gives the correct semantics of definite descriptions.

Notes

1. Avramides (1989).
2. *Public-language* semantic notions pertain either to notions of semantic speech acts (roughly, speech acts that entail speaker-meaning) or to notions of the semantic properties that linguistic expressions or other things (e.g. smoke signals and traffic lights) have by virtue of the way they, or their components, are used in communication. Examples of semantic properties that aren't public-language semantic properties are the truth-values of propositions, the contents of perceptions and propositional attitudes (at least according to certain views), and the various model-theoretic constructions used to define logical truth.
3. Neale's essay isn't concerned with the reductionist aspirations of IBS, but at one point he makes the parenthetical remark that I appear "to have been happy with a functionalist account of psychological states and *expressed no interest in providing a naturalistic account*" (my emphasis). I find this puzzling, since it went without saying among functionalists in the seventies that if psychological states were functional states, those functional states were *realized by physical states,* and that an account of psychological

states that identified them with functional states realized by physical states was a naturalistic account of those states *par excellence*—that is to say, an account of those states that indisputably revealed their place in the natural order.
4. Radford (2004: 108).
5. This is arguably at best a first approximation in view of the fact that S might refer to x more than once in uttering u. It might have been better to have said something along the lines of:

> In uttering u, S refers to x *with* the ith occurrence of e in u iff for some ρ, ρ is a reference that S makes to x in uttering u, and for some audience A and relation R, in uttering u S intended it to be mutual knowledge between S and A that R holds among the ith occurrence of e in u, S's utterance of u and x, and, primarily on the basis of this, that S is making reference ρ to x in uttering u.

But see Neale's discussion of the difficulty in counting acts of referring-in (245–46).
6. Note that according to this definition a token of 'the man drinking a martini' may refer to a man who is drinking water in a martini glass. Consequently, a theorist might want to introduce a notion of *semantic reference* to co-exist with the displayed definition of (C). If we think of the meaning of a referring expression as a partial function that maps the expression and its occurrences in uttered sentences onto the referents of the expression relative to those occurrences, then we might say (to a quite rough approximation):

> The ith occurrence of e in u *semantically* refers to x relative to S's utterance of u iff In uttering u, S refers to x with the ith occurrence of e in u and the meaning function for e maps the ith occurrence of e in u onto x, relative to S's utterance of u.

7. The quotation is from the version of Neale's chapter to which this response was written, and the wording that occurs in Neale's chapter on p. 320, which I didn't see until my responses were in page proofs, is slightly different.
8. Neale, *ibid*.
9. Chomsky e.g. (1986); Loar (1976a).
10. For 'subdoxastic belief', see Stich (1978); for 'subpersonal belief', see Dennett (1969).
11. Jackendoff (2002: 70).
12. This volume, p. 346.
13. γ is *simple signal* in population P just in case, for some sentence-size meaning μ, γ means μ in P, but there are no constituents of γ such that the meaning of γ is a function of the meanings of those constituents.
14. Talk of γ's meaning Ψ may be regarded as shorthand for something that admits of various possible precisifications, one such being that γ means that function f such that, for any utterance γ_u of γ, $f(\gamma_u) = q$ iff (i) q is of form Ψ and (ii) q is the proposition the speaker meant in producing γ_u; nothing otherwise.
15. Lewis (1983).
16. If σ means propositional form Ψ, then a proposition q "fits" Ψ iff q is of form Ψ.
17. Lewis (1992).
18. Lewis (1992); Schiffer (2006).
19. Brian Loar gave an account of the public-language relation along these lines in Loar (1976b).
20. Lewis (1983).
21. Referential uses of "definite descriptions" pose the same problem for Russellians whether or not the descriptions are "complete" or "incomplete." Contrary to what Bach says, I nowhere supposed that only "incomplete" definite descriptions could be used referentially. Who could think that 'the man in the purple and green striped suit' could be used referentially only if two or more men were wearing purple and green striped suits?
22. Bach seems not to have understood what I said was the meaning the Russellian theories in question ascribed to 'The F is G.' He charges that I don't explain how a speaker's uttering 'The F is G' and meaning thereby, for some H, *that the F-&-H is G* "should count as

speaking literally, as if one had uttered ['The F-&-H is G'] rather than the unembellished 'The F is G'" (369). But I did explain this in the publications he discusses: (a) An unembedded utterance of a sentence σ is *literal* iff for some kind of speech act A and propositional form Φ, (i) σ means <A, Φ> and (ii) in uttering σ the speaker performed an act of kind A whose propositional content was of form Φ; (b) bracketing tense-induced temporal reference, the Russellian theories in question hold that 'The F is G' means <⊢, the propositional form [*the$_x$*: Fx & Δ_x]Gx >; and therefore (c) For any H, the proposition *that the F-&-H is G* is an instance of the propositional form [*the$_x$*: Fx & Δ_x]Gx. Bach also objects that I don't explain why "just because speakers of ['The F is G'] are likely to mean different things in different contexts, [the Russellians in question hold that the sentence type 'The F is G'] lacks a context-independent truth-value" (370). But again, the Russellians in question don't hold that 'The F is G' lacks a context-independent truth-value "just because speakers mean different things in uttering it," but because the propositional form expressed by the sentence—viz. [*the$_x$*: Fx & Δ_x]Gx—doesn't determine any context-independent proposition. In other words, speakers mean different things in uttering 'The F is G' for the same reason speakers mean different things in uttering 'It's raining': because the meanings of those sentences allow them to, and would be useless if they didn't.

23. Bach says that my main objection to standard Russellianism is what he calls my "*no-determinate-H* objection," and he states what he takes that objection to be as follows: "When the speaker uses an incomplete description referentially, there is no determinate completer of the description's nominal that fills out what the speaker says or means. So the speaker does not say or mean any descriptive proposition, not even indeterminately" (p. 368). First, the inference, an obvious non sequitur, is not one I made. Second, while in Schiffer (1995) I argued that the best version of standard Russellianism would say that in uttering 'The F is G' it was typically indeterminate which proposition of the form *the thing that is F-&-H is G* the speaker meant, I never said (or thought) that that was an *objection* to the theory. At the same time, I do hold that in a typical referential utterance of 'The F is G,' there is no descriptive proposition the speaker even indeterminately means.
24. Neale (2004). My consideration of this version of Russell's theory shows that it's false that "Schiffer maintains that Russell's theory requires [that a literal speaker in a referential utterance of 'The F is G' must mean a descriptive proposition in addition to any object-dependent proposition she also means]" (364). (Incidentally, in his contribution to this volume Neale implies that he no longer thinks that referential uses of definite descriptions can be accommodated in any version of Russell's theory of descriptions.)
25. Here 'Buffett' occurs in the that-clause as directly referring to Buffett.
26. Actually, Bach isn't consistent in what he says is the proposition meant in a referential utterance of 'The F is G' and sometimes writes as though what is meant is simply the singular proposition that α is G: "the route the speaker takes in forming his intention to convey the object-dependent proposition that the referent *a* is G by uttering 'The F is G' is not via the descriptive proposition expressed by 'The F is G'. And the hearer's inferential route from hearing 'The F is G' to thinking that the speaker means the object-dependent proposition that *a* is G is not via this descriptive proposition. Rather, the hearer figures out that the speaker is using 'the F' to refer to *a* and then infers that he means that *a* is G" (376).
27. Bach (1998).
28. *Ibid*. (my emphasis).
29. *Ibid*.
30. Soames (1998).
31. (375). Here and in the paragraph to follow I substitute my Sally example for the structurally identical example Bach uses.

32. Recall that S's unembedded utterance of a sentence σ is *literal* just in case for some L, A, and $\varPhi$, σ means $<A, \varPhi>$ in L and L is the (or a) public language of the population of speakers to which S belongs.
33. Calling the one proposition an "expansion" of the other strikes me as an unfortunate choice of words. How does the proposition *that the one and only baby in the universe who is α is sleeping* "expand" the proposition *that the one and only baby in the universe is sleeping* when the "expansion" doesn't imply the proposition it "expands"? I can see how the proposition *that the one and only baby in the universe is **soundly** sleeping* might be said to expand the proposition *that the one and only baby in the universe is sleeping*, but not how a proposition whose truth doesn't require there to be only one baby in existence expands one whose truth does require that.
34. Bach (1998).
35. Grice (1989: 31).
36. Perry (1986).

Bibliography

Avramides, A. (1989). *Meaning and Mind: An Examination of a Gricean Account of Language*. Cambridge: MIT Press.

Bach, K. (1998). "Standardization Revisited." In *Pragmatics: Critical Assessment*, edited by Asa Kasher, London: Routledge. <http://online.sfsu.edu/kbach/standard.html> (references are to the online version).

Chomsky, N. (1981). *Lectures on Government and Binding*. Dordrecht: Foris.

Chomsky, N. (1986). *Knowledge of Language: Its Nature, Origin, and Use*. Westport, CT: Praeger.

Dennett, D. (1969). *Content and Consciousness*. London: Routledge and Kegan Paul.

Grice, H. P. (1957). "Meaning." *Philosophical Review* 66: 377–88. Reprinted in Grice (1989).

Grice, P. (1989). *Studies in the Way of Words*. Cambridge: Harvard University Press.

Jackendoff, R. (2002). *Foundations of Language: Brain, Meaning, Grammar, Evolution*. Oxford: Oxford University Press.

Lewis, D. (1969). *Convention: A Philosophical Study*. Cambridge: Harvard University Press.

Lewis, D. (1983). "Languages and Language." In *Philosophical Papers I*. New York: Oxford University Press.

Lewis, D. (1992). "Meaning without Use: Reply to Hawthorne." *Australasian Journal of Philosophy* 70: 106–10.

Loar, B. (1976a). The Semantics of Singular Terms. *Philosophical Studies* 30 (6): 353–77.

Loar, B. (1976b). "Two Theories of Meaning." In G. Evans and J. McDowell (eds.) *Truth and Meaning: Essays in Semantics*. Oxford: Oxford University Press.

Neale, S. (1990). *Descriptions*. Cambridge: MIT Press.

Neale, S. (2004). "This, That, and the Other." In *Descriptions: Semantic and Pragmatic Perspectives*, edited by A. Bezuidenhout and M. Reimer, Oxford: Oxford University Press.

Perry, J. (1986). "Thought without Representation." *Proceedings of the Aristotelian Society Supplementary* 60: 263–83.

Radford, A. (2004). *Minimalist Syntax: Exploring the Structure of English*. Cambridge: Cambridge University Press.

Schiffer, S. (1972). *Meaning*. Oxford: Oxford University Press.

Schiffer, S. (1978). "The Basis of Reference." *Erkenntnis* 13: 171–206.

Schiffer, S. (1981). "Indexicals and the Theory of Reference." *Synthese* 49: 43–100.

Schiffer, S. (1987). *Remnants of Meaning*. Cambridge: MIT Press.

Schiffer, S. (1995). "Descriptions, Indexicals, and Belief Reports: Some Dilemmas (But Not the Ones You Expect)." *Mind* 104: 107–31.

Schiffer, S. (2005). "Russell's Theory of Definite Descriptions." *Mind* 114: 1135–83.

Schiffer, S. (2006). "Two Perspectives on Knowledge of Language." *Philosophical Issues* 16: 275–87.

Soames, S. (1998). "The Modal Argument: Wide Scope and Rigidified Descriptions." *Noûs* 32: 1–22.

Stich, S. (1978). "Belief and Subdoxastic States." *Philosophy of Science* 45: 499–518.

Bibliography of Stephen Schiffer's Writings

Books

1. 1972. *Meaning*. Oxford: Clarendon Press. Reissued in paperback with a new Introduction, 1988. Chapter IV reprinted in S. Nuccetelli & G. Seay, eds., *Philosophy of Language: The Central Topics* (Lanham, Maryland: Rowman & Littlefield, 2008).
2. 1987. *Remnants of Meaning*. Cambridge: Bradford Books/MIT Press. Preface reprinted in *Mind & Language* 3 (1988) (special issue on *Remnants of Meaning*). Estonian translation of Chapter 1 in J. Kangilaski et al., eds., *Meaning, Truth and Method* (Tartu: Tartu University Press, 1999). Reprint of chapter 5 in P. Ludlow, ed., *Readings in the Philosophy of Language*. (Cambridge: MIT Press, 1997).
3. 2003. *The Things We Mean*. Oxford: Clarendon Press 2003.

Books Edited

4. 1988. *Cognition and Representation* (with Susan Steele). Boulder: Westview.

Articles

5. 1965. "On Saying and Being." *Analysis* 25 (1): 94–8.
6. 1976. "Descartes on His Essence." *Philosophical Review* 85: 21–43. Reprinted in V. Chappell, ed., *Essays on Early Modern Philosophy: From Descartes and Hobbes to Newton and Leibniz, Vol. I* (New York: Garland, 1992) and in V. Chappell, ed., *Descartes's Meditations: Critical Essays* (Lanham, Maryland: Rowman and Littlefield, 1997).
7. 1976. "A Paradox of Desire." *American Philosophical Quarterly* 13: 195–203.
8. 1977. "Naming and Knowing." *Midwest Studies in Philosophy, Vol. II: Studies in the Philosophy of Language*: 28–41. Reprinted in P. A. French, T. E. Uehling, Jr., and H. D. Wettstein, eds., *Contemporary Perspectives in the Philosophy of Language* (Minneapolis: University of Minnesota Press, 1979).
9. 1978. "The Basis of Reference." *Erkenntnis* 13: 171–206.
10. 1981. "Truth and the Theory of Content." In H. Parret and J. Bouveresse (eds.), *Meaning and Understanding*. Berlin: Walter de Gruyter.
11. 1981. "Indexicals and the Theory of Reference." *Synthese* 49: 43–100.
12. 1982. "Intention-Based Semantics." *Notre Dame Journal of Formal Logic* 23: 119–56.
13. 1985. "Meaning and Thought." In A. Kasher and S. Lappin, eds., *New Trends in Philosophy*, Hebrew (translated by Dorit Bar-On) and English editions. Tel Aviv: Yachdav and Highland Park, NJ: Humanities Press.
14. 1985. "Compositional Semantics and Language Understanding." In R. Grandy and R. Warner, eds., *Philosophical Grounds of Rationality: Intentions, Categories, Ends*. Oxford: Oxford University Press. Reprinted in F. Récanati, ed., *Communication et Cognition* (Paris: CNRS, 1985).
15. 1986. "Kripkenstein Meets the Remnants of Meaning." *Philosophical Studies* 49: 147–62.
16. 1986. "The Real Trouble with Propositions." In R. Bogdan, ed., *Belief: Form, Content and Function*. Oxford: Clarendon Press. Russian translation in V. Tselischev, ed., *Logic, Cognitive and Computer Research* (Novosibirsk: Novosibirsk University Press, 1991).
17. 1986-7. "Intentionality and the Language of Thought." *Proceedings of the Aristotelian Society* 87: 35–55.

18. 1986. "Functionalism and Belief." In M. Brand and R. Harnish, eds., *Problems in the Representation of Knowledge and Belief*. Tucson: University of Arizona Press.
19. 1986. "Stalnaker's Problem of Intentionality." *Pacific Philosophical Quarterly* 67: 87–97.
20. 1986. "Peacocke on Explanation in Psychology." *Mind & Language* 1: 362–71.
21. 1987. "Extensionalist Semantics and Sententialist Theories of Belief." In E. LePore, ed., *New Directions in Semantics*. London: Academic Press.
22. 1987. "The 'Fido'-Fido Theory of Belief." *Philosophical Perspectives* 1: 455–80.
23. 1988. *Précis* of *Remnants of Meaning* and responses to articles on the book by Norbert Hornstein, Mark Johnston, and Barbara Partee. *Mind & Language* 3: 53–63. (Special issue on *Remnants of Meaning*.)
24. 1988. "Introduction" (with Susan Steele), in S. Schiffer and S. Steele, eds., *Cognition and Representation*. Boulder: Westview.
25. 1990. "Physicalism." *Philosophical Perspectives* 3: 153–85.
26. 1990. "The Mode-of-Presentation Problem." In C. Anderson and J. Owen, eds., *Propositional Attitudes: the Role of Content in Logic, Language, and Mind*. Stanford: CSLI. Reprinted in C. Peacocke, ed., *Understanding and Sense* (Aldershot: Dartmouth Publishing Co., 1993).
27. 1990. "Fodor's Character." In E. Villanueva, ed., *Information, Semantics and Epistemology*. Cambridge, MA: Blackwell.
28. 1990. "The Relational Theory of Belief: A Reply to Mark Richard." *Pacific Philosophical Quarterly* 71: 240–5.
29. 1990. "Meaning and Value." *Journal of Philosophy* 87: 602–14. Reprinted in R. Shafer-Landau, ed., *Metaethics: Critical Concepts in Philosophy* (New York: Routledge, 2008).
30. 1991. "Ceteris Paribus Laws." *Mind* 100: 1–17.
31. 1991. "Does Mentalese Have a Compositional Semantics?" In B. Loewer and G. Rey, eds., *Meaning in Mind: Essays on the Work of Jerry Fodor*. Oxford: Blackwell.
32. 1992. "Boghossian on Externalism and Inference." In E. Villanueva,ed., *Information, Semantics and Epistemology*. Oxford: Blackwell.
33. 1992. "Belief Ascription." *Journal of Philosophy* 89: 499–5.
34. 1993. "Compositional Supervenience Theories and Compositional Meaning Theories." *Analysis* 53: 24–9.
35. 1993. "Belief Ascription and a Paradox of Meaning." *Philosophical Issues* 3: 89–121.
36. 1993. "Actual-Language Relations." *Philosophical Perspectives* 7: 231–58.
37. 1993. "Yes: A Reply to Brian Loar's 'Can We Confirm Supervenient Properties?'" *Philosophical Issues* 4: 93–100.
38. 1994. "Meanings and Their Nature." *From the Logical Point of View* 2: 12–26.
39. 1994. "A Paradox of Meaning." *Noûs* 28: 279–324.
40. 1994. "Thought and Language." In S. Guttenplan, ed., *A Companion to Philosophy of Mind*. Oxford: Blackwell.
41. 1994. "The Language-of-Thought Relation and Its Implications." *Philosophical Studies* 76: 263–86 and *Philosophical Issues* 5: 155–75.
42. 1994. "Reply to Yagisawa." *Philosophical Studies* 76: 297–300.
43. 1995. "Descriptions, Indexicals, and Belief Reports: Some Dilemmas (But Not the Ones You Expect)." *Mind* 104: 107–31. Reprinted in W. Kunne, A. Newen, and M. Anduschus, eds., *Direct Reference, Indexicality and Propositional Attitudes* (Stanford: CSLI, 1997) and G. Ostertag, ed., *Definite Descriptions: A Reader* (Cambridge: MIT Press, 1998). Slovakian translation in R. Cedzo and M. Zouhar, eds., in *Philosophy of Language*, Bratislava, Slovakia: Kalligram, 2005).
44. 1995. "Reply to Ray." *Noûs* 29: 397–401.
45. 1995/96. "Contextualist Solutions to Scepticism." *Proceedings of the Aristotelian Society* 96: 317–33.

46. 1996. "The Hidden-Indexical Theory's Logical-Form Problem: A Rejoinder." *Analysis* 56: 92–7.
47. 1996. "Language-Created Language-Independent Entities." *Philosophical Topics* 24: 149–67.
48. 1997. "Williamson on Our Ignorance in Borderline Cases." *Philosophy and Phenomenological Research* 62: 937–43.
49. 1998. "Doubts about Implicit Conceptions." *Philosophical Issues* 9: 89–91.
50. 1998. "Two Issues of Vagueness." *The Monist* 88: 193–214.
51. 1999. "The Epistemic Theory of Vagueness." *Philosophical Perspectives* 13: 481–503.
52. 1999. "Meanings and Concepts." In K. Korta, E. Sosa, X. Arrazola, eds., *Cognition, Agency and Rationality*. Dordrecht: Springer. Slightly shortened version reprinted in *Lingua e Stile* 33 (1998): 399–411.
53. 1999. "Propositional Attitudes in Direct-Reference Semantics." In K. M. Jaszczolt, ed., *Pragmatics of Propositional Attitude Reports*. Oxford: Elsevier Sciences. French translation published as "Les Attitudes Propositionnelles dans la Sémantique de la Référence Directe," in R. Vallée (ed.), *Langage et Çontexte: La Sémantique des Expressions Indexicales* (Paris: Cahiers du Crea, 1999).
54. 2000. "Pleonastic Fregeanism and Empty Names." In A. Everett and T. Hofweber, eds., *Empty Names, Fiction and the Puzzles of Non-Existence*. Stanford: CSLI.
55. 2000. "Pleonastic Fregeanism. In A. Kanamori, ed., *The Proceedings of the Twentieth World Congress of Philosophy, Vol. 6, Analytical Philosophy and Logic*. Bowling Green: Philosophical Documentation Center.
56. 2000. "Vagueness and Partial Belief." *Philosophical Issues* 10: 220–57.
57. 2000. "Replies to Commentators on 'Vagueness and Partial Belief'." *Philosophical Issues* 10: 321–43.
58. 2001. "Meanings" and "Forward." In J. Campbell, M. O'Rourke & D. Shier, eds., *Essays on Meaning & Truth*. New York: Seven Bridges Press.
59. 2001. "Communication." In N. J. Smelser and P. B. Baltes, eds., *The International Encyclopedia of the Social and Behavioral Sciences*. Oxford: Elsevier Science.
60. 2001. "A Little Help from Your Friends?" *Legal Theory* 7: 421–32.
61. 2001. "The Ontological Status of Fictional Entities." *Yearbook for Philosophical Hermeneutics* 1: 188–96.
62. 2002. "Amazing Knowledge." *Journal of Philosophy* 109: 200–2.
63. 2002. "The Things We Believe." In C. Moulines and K. Niebergall, eds., *Argument et Analyse*. Paderborn: Mentis.
64. 2003. "Moral Realism and Indeterminacy." *Philosophical Issues* 12: 286–304.
65. 2003. "Knowledge of Meaning." In A. Barber, ed., *Epistemology of Language*. Oxford: Oxford University Press.
66. 2003. "That-Clauses and the Semantics of Belief Reports." *Facta Philosophica* 5: 163–82.
67. 2004. "Skepticism and the Vagaries of Justified Belief." *Philosophical Studies* 119: 161–84.
68. 2005. "Pleonastic Propositions." In J. Beall and B. Armour-Garb, eds., *Deflationary Theories of Truth*. Chicago: Open Court.
69. 2005. "Russell's Theory of Definite Descriptions." *Mind* 114: 1135–83 (special issue edited by Stephen Neale celebrating the centenary of Russell's "On Denoting").
70. 2005. "Paradox and the A Priori." In T. Gendler and J. Hawthorne, eds., *Oxford Studies in Epistemology* I. Oxford: Clarendon Press. Reprinted in R. Dottori, ed., *Reason and Reasonableness* (Münster: Lit Verlag, 2005).
71. 2005. "What Reference Has to Tell Us about Meaning." In J. Branquinho, ed., *Conteúdo e Cognição: Actas do Seminário de Filosofia Analítica 2003–4*. Lisbon: University of Lisbon Press.
72. 2006. "A Problem for a Direct-Reference Theory of Belief Reports." *Noûs* 40: 361–8.

73. 2006. "*Facing Facts'* Consequences." *ProtoSociology: An International Journal of Interdisciplinary Research* 23: 50–66.
74. 2006. "Propositional Content." In E. Lepore and B. Smith, eds., *Oxford Handbook of Philosophy of Language*. Oxford: Oxford University Press.
75. 2006. "Vagueness." In M. Devitt and R. Hanley, eds., *The Blackwell Guide to Philosophy of Language*. Malden, MA: Blackwell.
76. 2006. "Two Perspectives on Knowledge of Language." *Philosophical Issues* 16: 275–87.
77. 2006. Symposium on *The Things We Mean* (précis of *The Things We Mean* together with replies to articles by Thomas Hofweber, John MacFarlane, and Crispin Wright). *Philosophy and Phenomenological Research* 73: 208–43.
78. 2007. "Interest-Relative Invariantism." *Philosophy and Phenomenological Research* 75: 188–95.
79. 2009. "Evidence = Knowledge: Williamson's Solution to Skepticism." in P. Greenough and D. Pritchard, eds., *Williamson on Knowledge*. Oxford: Oxford University Press.
80. 2010. "Vague Properties." In R. Dietz and S. Moruzzi, eds., *Cuts and Clouds: Essays on the Nature and Logic of Vagueness*. Oxford: Oxford University Press.
81. 2012. "Propositions, What Are They Good For?" In R. Schantz, ed., *Prospects for Meaning*. Berlin: de Gruyter.
82. 2013. "Meaning in Speech and in Thought." *Philosophical Quarterly* 63: 141–59.
83. 2015. "Meaning and Formal Semantics in Generative Grammar." *Erkenntnis* 80: 61–87.
84. 2016. "Cognitive Propositions." *Philosophical Studies* 173: 2551–63.
85. Forthcoming. "Quandary and Intuitionism: Crispin Wright on Vagueness." In A. Miller, ed., *Logic, Language and Mathematics: Essays for Crispin Wright Volume II*. Oxford: Oxford University Press.
86. Forthcoming. "Intention and Convention in the Theory of Meaning." In B. Hale, A. Miller and C. Wright, eds., *Blackwell Companion to the Philosophy of Language*. Oxford: Blackwell.
87. Forthcoming. "Deflationist Theories of Truth, Meaning and Content." In B. Hale, A. Miller and C. Wright, eds., *Blackwell Companion to the Philosophy of Language*. Oxford: Blackwell.
88. Forthcoming. "Philosophical and Jurisprudential Issues of Vagueness." In G. Keil and R. Poscher, eds., *Vagueness in Law*. Oxford: Oxford University Press.
89. Forthcoming. "Amie Thomasson's Easy Approach to Ontology," *Philosophy and Phenomenological Research* (special issue on Amie Thomasson's *Ontology Made Easy*).

Reviews

90. 1977. Critical Notice of Charles Travis, *Saying and Understanding: A Generative Theory of Illocutions*. *Canadian Journal of Philosophy* 7: 637–50.
91. 1988. Gareth Evans, *The Varieties of Reference*, *Journal of Philosophy* 85: 33–42.
92. 1992. Review Essay: *How to Build a Person: A Prolegomenon*, by John Pollock. *Philosophy and Phenomenological Research* 52: 713–24.
93. 1996. Review Essay: *Direct Reference: From Language to Thought*, by Francois Recanati. *Linguistics and Philosophy* 19: 91–102.
94. 1996. Marian David, *Correspondence and Disquotation: An Essay on the Nature of Truth*, *International Studies in Philosophy* 28: 112–13.
95. 1998. Review of Jerry Fodor, *Concepts: Where Cognitive Science Went Wrong*. *The Times Literary Supplement*, June 26, 1998.
96. 2000. "Horwich on Meaning: Critical Study of Paul Horwich's *Meaning*." *Philosophical Quarterly* 50: 527–36.

Index

actual-language relations 5–9, 506–9
Agrippa, H. C. 217, 225, 486
analyticity 36, 52
  see also conceptual truth
Anscombe, G. E. M. 325
aphonic reference 28, 236–7, 260, 281–5, 295, 306, 314–15, 321–2, 336, 499–300
argument from queerness 414
Armstrong, D. M. 242, 266, 405
Audi, R. 331
Avramides, A. 28–9, 30, 493–5, 501–11

Bach, K. 29–30, 145, 275, 325, 330, 331, 332, 493–4, 512–23, 524–5, 526
Bad Company Objection 48, 52
Banach-Tarski Theorem 402, 424
belief reports see face-value theory, direct reference theory, hidden-indexical theory, neo-Fregeanism
Benacerraf, P. 397
Bennett, J. 4
Bennett, K. 52
Bertolet, R. 327, 332
Bezuidenhout, A. 380
Blackburn, S. 147, 225
Boolos, G. 406, 424
borderline case see vagueness, borderline case of
Bratman, M. 331
Braun, D. 145, 155, 335
Brentano, F. 2, 355
Brentano's Problem 2, 355
Brogaard, B. 170
Bromberger, S. 328, 330
Buchanan, R. 30, 126, 127, 271, 381, 382, 441–8
Burge, T. 93

Cameron, R. 35, 50
Cappelen, H. 325
Carlson, G. 147
Carnap, R. 34, 51, 65
Carruthers, P. 34, 51, 65
Carston, R. 291, 334
Castañeda, H. N. 336
character 13, 291, 294–306, 335, 336
character* 13, 130, 132, 138, 374, 377, 383
Chierchia, C. 147, 336
Chihara, C. 484, 491
Chomsky, N. 248, 320, 321, 331, 400, 495, 498–9, 510, 524

Churchland, P. 350
Clark, B. 370
cognitive tension 211–12, 218, 220
cognitivism 17–18, 24, 95–110, 388, 412–25
Collins, J. 336
common knowledge see mutual knowledge
compositionality
  compositional meaning theory 15, 20, 30, 31, 55, 59–60, 68, 90, 112, 231–3, 246–7, 250–1, 290, 295–6, 305–6, 308–10, 322, 335, 336, 344–6, 357, 382, 398, 512, 516, 522–3
  compositional supervenience theory 9, 31
  compositional truth theory 400, 426–30, 432–3
  of that-clauses 51, 55, 59–60, 68, 114, 126, 141, 400, 432–3
conceptual analysis 2–4, 14, 28–9, 256, 326, 347–52, 389
conceptual entailment 167, 393, 452
  see also conceptual truth
conceptual revision 26, 165–6, 214, 216, 218, 484, 486–7
conceptual role 26, 103, 108, 134, 145, 158, 166, 214, 347, 356, 362, 405, 414–17, 421–2, 424, 425, 465–7, 469, 484
  see also functional role
conceptual truth 15, 28, 34, 36, 38–50, 51, 52, 76, 390, 399, 485
conditionals 24, 63, 166–70, 171, 178–9, 188, 476
contextualism 19, 125–6, 313, 336, 485
convention 5–6, 257, 262, 270, 275, 279, 343, 506, 510, 513, 519–20
conventional implicature 324, 334
conversational implicature 123, 229–30, 237–8, 240, 250, 258, 259, 267, 271, 274, 285, 291–2, 309, 322, 324, 327, 330, 331, 334, 364, 365, 368, 370, 373, 379, 383, 516, 519–23
  see also indeterminacy
Crimmins, M. 319

Dale, R. 30, 31, 71, 127
Davidson, D. 331, 346–8, 359, 360, 493
Davies, M. 146
de re belief 19, 21–2, 113, 118–22, 124, 128–47, 149–55, 426–40, 449–57
de se attitudes 128–47
definite descriptions
  ambiguity of see referential-attributive distinction

definite descriptions (*cont.*)
  Russell's Theory of 29–30, 126, 290–3, 334, 364–84, 494, 514–23, 525
  see also incompleteness
Dennett, D. 524
Devitt, M. 325, 330, 331
direct reference theory 18–19, 20–2, 91, 133–4, 149–55, 324, 381, 449–57
Donnellan, K. 245, 276–8, 283, 292, 366
Donnellan's distinction *see* referential-attributive distinction
Dorr, C. 188, 395
Dretske, F. 323, 485
Dummett, M. A. E. 78, 93, 155, 184, 188, 470

easy ontology 14–15, 34–53, 389–95
Edgington, D. 22–4, 458–65, 468–76, 479, 481
Eklund, M. 52
epistemicism *see* vagueness, epistemic theories of
equipollence 17, 82–92
Evans, G. 145, 146, 297, 305, 316
expression meaning 3–9, 11, 30, 231, 232, 250, 254, 256, 257, 274, 278, 279, 294, 331, 493, 501–11
expression reference 233–5, 244, 256, 258, 266, 281, 286, 306, 323, 327, 495, 497, 500, 512

face-value theory 12, 17–18, 75–8, 80, 92, 111–27, 129, 131, 132, 136, 140, 144–5, 426–40, 447, 448
Fara, D. G. 146
Favia, A. 30
fictional entities 15, 34, 36, 51, 61, 76, 389, 392
Field, H. 361, 397, 399, 462, 465, 468–76
Fine, K. 31, 35, 50, 88, 93, 461
Fitch's Paradox 161, 170, 468
Fodor, J. A. 13, 30, 31, 330, 331, 345–6, 350–2, 355, 357–8, 359, 362, 511
Forbes, G. 122, 124, 126, 142, 146
four-dimensionalism 329
free enrichment 19, 28, 125, 309, 365, 371, 375, 379
Frege, G. 19, 61, 62, 67, 73–93, 125, 133, 145, 146, 153, 266, 310, 316, 380, 388, 397, 403–4, 406, 412, 424
Frege's Constraint 21, 134, 149, 152
functional role 10, 31, 101, 109, 134, 192, 414, 420–1, 424
  see also conceptual role
functionalism 10–11, 31, 255, 353, 361, 414, 523

Geach, P. T. 234, 323
Gibbard, A. 225
Godfrey-Smith, P. 323
Goldbach's Conjecture 202
Goodman, N. 397, 423

Grandy, R. 360, 361
Grice, H. P. 2, 4, 29, 30, 52, 229–31, 238, 245, 255–9, 265, 267, 276, 278, 290–4, 307, 324, 325, 326, 327, 330, 331, 332, 334, 336, 343, 346, 347–52, 356, 359, 360, 361, 368, 369, 382, 502–3, 511, 520, 522, 526
grounding 30, 50

Hale, B. 34, 35, 37, 40, 48, 50, 51, 52, 62, 71
happy-face solution *see* paradox
Harman, G. 277, 331
Harnish, R. 325, 330, 381
Harris, D. 30
Hawthorne, J. 31, 328, 330, 331–2
Heck, R. G. 20, 137, 145, 441, 442–3, 445–6
Heim, I. 324
Hempel, C. G. 216, 225, 486
hidden-indexical theories 18–19, 29, 112–15, 118, 124, 125, 127, 311, 320, 426–33, 439
Higginbotham, J. 336
higher-order vagueness 464, 466, 481
Hodes, H. 93
Hofweber, T. 15–16, 41, 50, 52, 387, 388, 396–405, 415, 423
Horn, L. 330
Horwich, P. 25–6, 180, 357, 362, 481, 483–92
Hume, D. 98, 100, 388, 485
Hume's Principle 36–7, 51, 388, 406

I-language 499
implicit reference 28, 109, 113, 124, 229, 230, 233, 236–50, 256, 259, 260, 266, 267, 271, 281, 284, 285–97, 306, 308–21, 324, 325, 332, 335, 336, 427, 495–503
  see also aphonic reference
Impliciture (Bach) 516, 521–2
incompleteness 29–30, 229, 290, 292–4, 312, 313, 317–18, 323, 364–84, 494, 521, 524, 525
indeterminacy
  belief reports and 114, 117, 433
  conversational implicature and 237, 271, 317–18, 381, 388
  incomplete definite descriptions and 381
  moral predicates and 105–9, 388, 412, 421
  vagueness and 156–71, 176–9, 205–6, 409, 458–81
inferential role 16, 39, 63–5, 388, 396
Intention-Based Semantics (IBS) 3–8, 29, 229, 256, 265, 268, 278–9, 316, 333, 343–63, 493, 495, 511, 523
internalism 18, 98, 99, 102–5, 388, 412, 417–18, 421
  see also non-cognitivism
interpretation 253–5, 262, 265–6, 270–5, 282–4, 292, 298, 299, 306, 331
intuition 248, 361, 370, 371, 424

Jackendoff, R. 499, 524
Jackson, F. 31, 109
Johnston, M. 30, 43, 357–9, 362, 398, 423

Kahneman, D. 463
Kaplan, D. 13, 122, 124, 126, 132, 151, 154–5, 266, 283–4, 294–5, 300–1, 305, 311, 326, 327, 329, 330, 334–5, 382, 457
King, J. 71, 126, 330, 335
knowledge of meaning 13–14, 31, 499
Kratzer, A. 324
Kripke, S. 3, 31, 234, 241, 283, 285, 323, 334, 367, 381

language of thought 8, 9, 11, 30, 134, 145, 252, 414–17, 424, 465–7
 see also mentalese
LePore, E. 328, 330, 331
Levinson, S. 330
Lewis, D. K. 5, 9, 31, 165, 169, 171, 361, 408, 506, 510, 512
LF ("logical form") 247, 310–11, 377, 500, 523
liar paradox 171, 189, 214, 222, 226, 227, 483–4
Lillo-Martin, D. 328
Linnebo, O. 52
Linsky, L. 234, 283, 323
Loar, B. 30, 325, 330, 343, 349, 353, 359, 361, 498–9, 524
logical form problem 19, 114
logical form see face-value theory, logical form problem, LF
Ludlow, P. 240
Łukasiewicz rules 157, 159, 163, 168, 170, 205–6, 209, 460–3, 476, 480

MacFarlane, J. 170, 462
Mackie, J. L. 225, 414
Marshall, O. 30
Mates, B. 154
Maudlin, T. 188
McCracken, M. 52
McDowell, J. 19, 109, 136–7, 145, 146, 441–3, 445–6, 448
McGee, V. 162
McLaughlin, B. 162
meaning-intention problem 19, 27, 113–14, 117–18, 124, 309–21, 332, 426–33
meaning-without-use problem 9, 510
mentalese 145, 252, 414–17, 424, 465–7
 see also language of thought
metaontology 34, 35, 51
metaphysical nihilist 387, 395
Millianism see direct reference theory
Millikan, R. 30, 323
Min-Max rules see Łukasiewicz rules
mindreading 253–4, 321, 325

mode of presentation 21–2, 112–14, 311–20, 336, 398, 427–9, 439, 441–2, 449–57
Moltmann, F. 71
Montague, R. 69
Moore, G. E. 348, 360
Moore, J. G. 93
mutual knowledge 5–8, 19, 27–8, 30, 87, 89, 123, 136, 138, 257, 279–80, 332, 343, 446, 496–8, 501, 503–8, 518, 524

Nagel, T. 161
naturalism 1, 3, 4, 30, 45, 255, 343–7, 352–7, 523–4
Neale, S. 26–8, 117, 145, 146, 364, 367, 380–1, 383, 493–501, 511–12, 515, 517, 519, 524, 525
neo-Fregeanism
 in the philosophy of language 124, 136–7, 140, 152–3, 441–6, 453, 455
 in the philosophy of mathematics 34, 35–7, 40, 48, 51, 61–2, 73–93
Nicolle, S. 370
no-theory theory of meaning 11, 346–7, 357–9
non-cognitivism 96, 98–9, 105, 418–19, 421
non-literality 364, 371, 379, 382
Nozick, R. 485

object-dependent proposition 118–23, 126–35, 234, 241, 258, 259, 326–7, 364–8, 371–4, 376, 379, 380, 383, 402, 439, 441, 525
Olber's Paradox 212
Oppy, G. 109
ordinary objects 34, 35, 38, 49, 387, 394–5
Ostertag, G. 18–19, 52, 71, 109, 147, 155, 227, 271, 381, 423, 424, 426–40

paradox 25–6, 46, 51, 93, 165–6, 169, 171, 211–28, 425, 482–91 see also Fitch's Paradox and Sorites
partial belief see standard partial belief
Pautz, A. 126
Pears, D. 73
penumbral shift 410, 439
Perry, J. 238, 305, 319–20, 336, 526
Pettit, P. 31
philosophical analysis see conceptual analysis, conceptual truth
physicalism 3, 9–11, 29, 354–6, 361, 362, 397, 511
pleonastic propositions see propositions, pleonastic
Pollock, J. 146, 183, 491
pragmatic enrichment see free enrichment
Prior, A. N. 73, 75, 93, 424
proposition radical 45, 516
propositional anaphora 118

propositional attitude reports *see* face-value theory, direct reference theory, hidden-indexial theory, neo-Fregeanism
propositional guises 149–55 *see also* mode of presentation
propositions
  inexpressible 16, 58–66, 401, 403–4
  pleonastic 3, 12, 14, 15–20, 23–4, 34, 56, 67, 74, 77, 95–102, 109, 112–27, 167, 345, 387–8, 396–425, 426, 437, 441, 445
  Russellian 18–19, 126, 131, 149–55, 266, 288, 289, 335, 449–57
  unstructured 45, 114–15, 126, 434
public-language meaning *see* expression meaning
Pupa, F. 30
Putnam, H. 48, 90

Quandary 25, 156, 159–60, 191, 197, 201–4, 207, 209, 462–3, 468, 470, 481
Quine, W. V. 34, 35, 52, 118, 213, 215, 224, 225, 323, 355, 361, 397, 424, 487

Ramsey, F. P. 169, 226
Recanati, F. 125, 141–2, 143, 146, 291, 308, 324, 334, 336, 380
reductionism 1, 3–4, 9–11, 29, 343–6, 350–9, 360, 362, 398, 495, 501, 511, 523
referential-attributive distinction 312–18, 325, 327, 332–3, 334, 336, 364–83, 514, 518, 522
relativity feature 19–20, 128–48, 441–8
Renfrew, C. 331
Richard, M. 330
rigid designation 234, 247–9, 285–7, 306, 334, 434
Rumfitt, I. 16–17, 170, 388, 405–12, 424
Russell, B. 18, 29–30, 126, 145, 146, 310, 364–84, 490, 491
Russellian propositions *see* propositions, Russellian

Sainsbury, M. 482
Salerno, J. 170
Salmon, N. 20–2, 125, 127, 132, 155, 326, 330, 335, 449–57
Sandler, W. 328
Saul, J. 127, 330
Schaffer, J. 35, 50
Scientism 26, 220, 222–3, 488–91
Searle, J. 30, 316, 324, 326, 350–1, 361
Sellars, W. 30
semantic externalism 268, 273
sentential dualism 354–5
sententialism 11, 345
Sextus Empiricus 485

Sider, T. 48–50, 52, 394, 395
Skyrms, B. 31, 323
Smith, M. 17–18, 388, 412–25
Soames, S. 132, 336, 376, 381, 517, 525
something-from-nothing transformations 12, 17, 36, 45, 50, 56, 59, 61, 64, 66, 76–8, 115, 169, 387, 390–5, 403–4, 415, 419–20
Sorensen, R. 170
Sorites 22, 24, 156, 164–6, 173, 176–7, 185–6, 190–1, 195–7, 200, 204–7, 208, 209, 225, 226, 410, 459, 462–4, 473–6, 482, 487–8
speaker meaning 1–6, 11, 28–9, 30, 146, 230, 231–4, 237, 249–50, 254–9, 267–70, 274–83, 290, 316, 318, 325, 326, 330, 331, 337, 368, 428, 494–9, 501–12, 519–20, 523
speaker reference 26, 230, 234–7, 244, 248, 256–8, 280–2, 286–7, 292, 298, 306, 323, 325, 327, 428, 495–9, 512
speech acts 13, 30, 96–7, 324, 335, 512–13, 519, 523, 525
Sperber, D. 238, 257, 267, 271, 291, 316–17, 325, 331, 334
Stalnaker, R. 30, 330
standard partial belief (SPB) 23, 105, 157, 160, 163–4, 179–81, 183, 192, 422, 458, 460–5, 471, 481
standardization 516, 522
Stanley, J. 125, 309, 335, 336, 337
Stevenson, C. 422, 425
Stich, S. 524
Stine, G. C. 327, 332
Strawson, P. 30, 52, 229, 234, 239, 257, 290, 323, 325, 326, 330, 351, 360, 380
subdoxastic belief 254, 499, 524
substitutional quantification 15, 55, 57–8, 64–5, 93, 388, 396, 401–2
supervaluationism *see* vagueness, supervaluationist theories of
syntactic priority thesis, 61–2, 403–4, 415
Szabó, Z. 309, 315

tacit knowledge 320, 349, 498–9
Tarski, A., 165, 402, 424, 484, 491
Taschek, W. 90–1
that-clauses 11–12, 15, 16–17, 18, 20, 51, 54–71, 73, 77, 78, 80, 111–27, 128–32, 139–44, 145, 146, 152–3, 387–8, 398–400, 403–4, 410, 424, 426, 428–30, 433–4, 437–9, 441–7, 448, 508, 525
  see also substitutional quantification
Third Possibility View (Wright) 156, 158, 162, 184, 191, 194–5, 197, 200, 472–3
Thomasson, A. 14–15, 387, 389–95, 423
Tversky, A. 463
Twomey, R. 30

unarticulated constituent 116, 125, 290, 319, 494, 514, 523
unhappy-face solution *see* paradox
utterance meaning *see* speaker meaning

vagueness
  belief and *see* vagueness-related partial belief
  borderline cases of 23–5, 105–6, 156–62, 172–9, 183, 188, 190–210, 225, 409, 432, 458–9, 465, 468–71, 477–80
  epistemic theories of 23, 172–6
  supervaluationist theories of 172–6, 177, 186–8, 411, 458
  validity and 24, 163–6, 171, 173, 175–9, 184–7, 188, 189, 206–7, 459, 473–6
  see also indeterminacy, penumbral shift
vagueness-related partial belief (VPB) 23–4, 105–6, 157–60, 170, 179–84, 188, 191–4, 202–6, 207, 208, 209, 210, 422, 458–8
  see also standard partial belief

Van Inwagen, P. 38, 48
verdict exclusion 25, 191, 194–6

Walker, R. 330
Warner 360, 361
Whitaker, M. 30
Wiggins, D. 263
Williamson, T. 52, 162, 172, 187, 209, 350, 461, 470, 479
Wilson, D. 238, 257, 267, 271, 291, 316–17, 325, 331, 334
Wisdom, J. 348, 360
Wittgenstein, L. 30, 211, 213–15, 221, 223–4, 323, 325, 358, 488
words 239, 245, 260–2, 328, 329
Wright, C. W. 23, 25, 34, 35, 37, 40, 48, 51, 52, 62, 71, 156, 158, 162, 403, 425, 458–9, 462–3, 465, 469–70, 476–9

Yablo, S. 50, 51, 52